Continuity and Change
in China's
Rural Development

Continuity and Change in China's Rural Development

Collective and Reform Eras in Perspective

Louis Putterman

New York   Oxford
OXFORD UNIVERSITY PRESS
1993

Oxford University Press

Oxford   New York   Toronto
Delhi   Bombay   Calcutta   Madras   Karachi
Kuala Lumpur   Singapore   Hong Kong   Tokyo
Melbourne   Auckland

and associated companied in
Berlin   Ibadan

Library of Congress Cataloging-in-Publication Data
Putterman, Louis G.
Continuity and change in China's rural development : collective
and reform eras in perspective / by Louis Putterman.
p. cm.   Includes bibliographical references and index.
ISBN 0-19-507872-1
1. Rural development—China.   I. Title.
HN740.Z9C668   1993
307.1′412′0951—dc20   92-18541

Permission to draw on portions of the following articles, granted
by Sage Publications, is gratefully acknowledged: "Group Farming and Work Incentives in Collective-Era China," *Modern
China,* October 1988; and "Entering the Post-Collective Era in
North China: Dahe Township," *Modern China,* July, 1989.

Permission to draw on portions of the following articles, granted
by Academic Press, is gratefully acknowledged: "Pre- and Post-
Reform Income Distribution in a Chinese Commune: The Case of
Dahe Township in Hebei Province," with Bingyuang Hsiung, in
Journal of Comparative Economics, September 1989; and "Effort,
Productivity and Incentives in a 1970s Chinese People's Com-
mune," *Journal of Comparative Economics,* March 1990.

Permission to draw on portions of the following article, granted
by the American Economic Association, is gratefully acknowledged:
"Does Poor Supervisability Undermine Teamwork? Evidence from
an Unexpected Source," *American Economic Review,* September
1991.

For Serena and Mark

Acknowledgments

This book is the product of a number of years of research both by the author and by several students and collaborators. First thanks go to the latter, who have allowed me to draw on their work or on work done jointly with me for this book. In particular, Chapter 6 is the result of joint research with John P. Burkett, Chapter 8 that of joint research with Woosung Park, Chapter 9 reports on joint research with Martin Gaynor, and Chapter 10 on joint research with Bingyuang Hsiung. Chapter 7 draws heavily on the Brown University doctoral thesis of Si Joong Kim. Thanks are also due to Calla Wiemer and to Justin Yifu Lin for permitting me to discuss their unpublished papers in Chapters 4 and 7, to Wiemer for providing me with a copy of her programs, and to Kim and Wiemer for supplying answers to several queries about their respective analyses.

I am indebted to an embarrassingly large number of Brown University undergraduate and graduate students who contributed to this work as research assistants and econometric programmers. These include Alyssa Koo and Fannie Tseng for Chapters 1 and 2, Bingyuang Hsiung and Yin Fum Lum for Chapter 3, Si Joong Kim for Chapters 3 and 11, Jun Il Kim and Hong Soo Kim for Chapter 5, Song Huan Oh for Chapter 6, Ajit Ranade for Chapters 2 and 6, Kyung-Sup Chang for Chapter 9, Amit Dar for Chapters 4 and 9, and Hsiung, Kim, and Dar for sequentially serving as general purpose number crunchers whose computations are scattered throughout the text. I also gratefully acknowledge the support of departmental staff, and in particular Mrs. Marion Wathey, who typed the entire manuscript in "LaTex."

A number of organizations that made this work possible through their financial and logistical support, or by their cooperation, must be mentioned. The Committee on Scholarly Communication with the People's Republic of China, jointly sponsored by the American Council of Learned Societies, the National Academy of Sciences, and the Social Science Research Council, supported my first visit to China in 1983 and my visit to Dahe Township in 1986. The Mellon Foundation supported an A.C.L.S.-S.S.R.C. Fellowship that facilitated my study of Chinese institutions in 1983–1984. The Ford Foundation funded the preparation of the Dahe data sets for analysis and dissemination. The Wang Institute for Chinese Studies supported me with a fellowship that permitted time off from teaching in 1986–1987. And the National Science Foundation through two grants, SES-8520380 and SES-8721382, supported portions of the data collection in 1986, a brief visit to China in 1990, the collaboration of Martin Gaynor, and most of the research assistance mentioned above. On the Chinese side, my thanks go to members of the Hebei Academy of Social Sciences, the Hebei Province Government, and officials of Huailu County and Dahe Township who facilitated my research there in 1986, and to individuals and institutions too numerous to mention who provided interviews and other forms of cooperation during visits in 1983, 1986, 1989, and 1990.

The list of scholars to whom I have incurred debts along the way is also too long to reproduce here, but a few deserve special mention. Nicholas Lardy, Keith Griffin, and Dwight Perkins nurtured my early interest in China and facilitated my research in numerous ways. My colleagues at Harvard's Fairbank Center for East Asian Research—especially Kathleen Hartford, Jean Oi, Terry Sicular, and David Zweig— have provided a sounding board and a source of much input to my evolving views of rural China. For help in initial identification of the Dahe Commune data I am indebted to Lee Travers, Peter Calkins, and Robert Dernberger, and for his cooperative responses to numerous inquiries, to Steven Butler. Allison Ansell, William Byrd, Elizabeth Croll, Frederick Crook, Keith Griffin, Roger Hay, Nancy Hearst, Justin Yifu Lin, Bruce Stone, Shwu-Eng Webb, and David Zweig were helpful in making available other relevant data and research materials, while Loren Brandt, Joel Guttman, Barry Naughton, Carl Riskin, Scott Rozelle, and Terry Sicular provided comments on portions of the research. Participants in an informal Fairbank Center study group on rural China, including Gao Xiaomeng, Luo Xiaopeng, Lu Mai, Kathy Hartford, and Jean Oi, also commented thoughtfully on drafts of two chapters. For invaluable feedback on econometric and related questions, I thank Zvi Griliches for Chapter 5, Robert Moffitt for Chapters 5 and 8, Mark Pitt for Chapters 7 and 9, and Harl Ryder for Chapter 10. Finally, for helpful discussions of theoretical issues that are taken up repeatedly but especially in Chapter 5 and in the appendix to Chapter 7, I wish to thank John Bonin and Gil Skillman.

After laboring for a number of years on a project of this sort, it would be a source of great satisfaction to feel that the result might stand as a model of what can be done in the field of applied research. While I hope that some merit will indeed be found in this product, I have a number of regrets about things that might have been improved upon. This applies especially to the collection of the data sets at Dahe Township. Although many parameters of the data collection exercise were outside of my control, there are nonetheless things that I might do differently were I designing the surveys today with the hindsight afforded me as I complete the manuscript. To all who have assisted me, I offer apologies that I cannot show you a more perfect result. Let the reader know that I alone take responsibility for the flaws that will be found here.

I will keep my list of personal debts much shorter. Whereas my morale was always bolstered by family members and friends, and while the love and joy brought by my daughters Laura and Serena did their part to sustain the effort, the brunt of the sacrifices entailed in the preparation of this book and in the research leading up to it fell upon my wife, Vivian. To her goes my most sincere expression of appreciation.

Providence, Rhode Island   L. P.
July, 1992

Contents

Continuity and Change
in China's
Rural Development

Introduction

The vast and populous land of China often seems to be like the proverbial elephant touched by the hands of many blind men but fully comprehended by none. In the 1970s, a China largely closed to the outside world was seen by some members of the international development community as a model of equitable development. Others, however, saw it as falling behind culturally similar neighbors, and therein found confirmation of the costs of centralized resource allocation and of nonparticipation in world markets.

The transformed China of the 1980s became a symbol of the tide of market-oriented policies and ideology that swept across the world in that decade. The breathtaking speed and apparent successes of China's economic reforms, especially in the rural sphere, provided inspiration to believers in the power of entrepreneurship and of the pursuit of self-interest. Thus, the Nobel laureate economist Milton Friedman (1990) could write

> Talk about "the enormous costs of moving to a free-market economy" is much too gloomy. There is no reason why total output cannot start expanding rapidly almost immediately after the totalitarian restrictions of people's activities are removed. That certainly was the case in the agricultural sector of China after the major reforms of the late 1970s (p. 36).

Friedman's optimism was not shared by all, and his statement would probably have puzzled many East Europeans a year after the collapse of their Communist regimes. Nonetheless, China's economic growth spurt of the 1980s served as a sobering cause for reassessment by many admirers of its pre-reform brand of socialism.

While both China and the world had changed during the 1980s, changes in perception frequently outstripped those of reality. Just as China in the late 1960s and 1970s was never quite the utopia of other-directed peasants depicted by Maoist propaganda, so it had also not really become a mecca of free market forces in the post-Mao 1980s. Whatever one thinks of its political system, China did make great strides in the provision of basic necessities to its population between 1949 and 1978. The inefficiencies of its central planning and its modest showing in comparison with a few exceptional neighbors did not prevent China from laying an industrial foundation during that period that compares favorably to the achievements of other poor nations. While the successes scored by economic reform in the first post-Mao decade were great, they were also not unaccompanied by problems, including threats to China's basic needs achievements and resilience of many undesirable elements of the old politico-economic regime.

This book is about change and continuity in China's rural economy in the collective era of the 1960s and 1970s, and in the post-collective era of the 1980s. Among the changes, three types stand out. The first of these are changes in the institutions or organizational structure of the rural economy at the micro level, epitomized by the replacement of farming by collective teams with farming by households. The second are changes in the economic policies that define the environment facing rural economic agents, illustrated by the expanding scope of free markets for the sale of rural products after 1978, by the increase in state prices for farm products in 1979, and by the partial elimination of two-tier state pricing of those products in 1985. The third and last type are changes in economic structure, occasioned largely by the relaxation of controls over resource allocation, but facilitated also both by the higher incomes made possible by more favorable crop prices, and by the greater efficiency in crop production resulting from micro-organizational change. Among these structural changes are the increasing share of *crop* income due to nongrain products, the increasing share of *agricultural* income due to noncrop production (such as animal husbandry), the increasing share of *rural* income due to nonfarm production (such as construction and manufacturing), and the reallocations of labor force and other inputs accompanying these changes in output structure. Changes in the three dimensions of institutions, policies, and economic structure helped to bring about both rising productivity of China's agricultural resources and a roughly two-and-one-third-fold increase in average real rural incomes between 1978 and 1986.

Dramatic as were the changes in the Chinese rural economy between the Maoist era of collectivism and centralized resource allocation and the post-Mao era of more household-based production organization and market activity, there remained important continuities spanning the two periods. At the level of micro-organization, the independence of households in the farm production process remained significantly circumscribed. Administrative interventions to influence cropping patterns remained important as the 1980s ended. In more developed regions of China, while households now bore responsibility for carrying out more labor-intensive farm tasks once handled by collective teams, plowing, planting, irrigation, and management of other aspects of crop production by village-level entities was common. In addition, the most dynamic sector of the rapidly growing rural economy of the 1980s was rural industry, which continued to be dominated by local "collective" enterprises: the township- and village-owned units that, from an organizational standpoint and in most cases with a change of name only, succeeded the commune and brigade industries of the Mao era. With respect to marketization, state procurement of staple crops at submarket prices, and state rationing of inputs such as fertilizer and credit, continued to play important roles. For many peasants, sales and purchases involving state and local government partners remained more important than those on free markets, and even the latter markets were often subject to intervention by government.

Turning to the bigger picture of the place of the rural economy in China's overall social and economic system, what stands out is that while constraints on temporary movement of labor among localities and from countryside to cities had been loosened, the gap between rural and urban incomes and entitlements remained large, and most farmers remained tied to their land and to their status as peasants thanks to the persistence of the residence permit system and the denial of a range of public benefits to those holding agricultural classification. As will be seen in the chapters that follow, the state's resolve to improve the terms of trade between agriculture and industry in favor of peasants, which bears much responsibility for increased farm incomes and production between 1979 and 1984, had definite limits. The fundamental pattern of state predation on the farm sector to finance the industrialization program and the benefits provided to urban, especially state sector, workers, remained substantially unchanged. The prime manifestation of this conflict was that a significant part of the cultivation of grain, cotton, and oil-bearing crops that occupied roughly 88% of China's sown area and accounted for about 76% of gross crop output even under the state-depressed prices that prevailed for many transactions, was the result of state interventions rather than a response to economic opportunities.[1]

China had already achieved much in the sphere of rural development before the advent of the Deng Xiaoping leadership in late 1978. Through increased application of labor, fertilizer, irrigation, and improved seed varieties, the country managed to expand food output to feed a one generation population jump that, in the years between 1949 and 1978, produced an increment to population equal to the entire population of Western Europe at the end of that period. In a significant minority of regions, the groundwork for rural industrialization and the mechanization of some farm tasks had been firmly laid. Overt landlessness, appropriation of large shares of farm output by landowners, the economic power conferred by concentrated control of land and credit, and the class polarization characterizing the rural areas of other poor developing countries were largely absent. Improvements in health care and promotion of a much-needed transition to lower rates of natural increase also compared favorably with many rural areas of the Third World. Yet, the quality of peasant diets was no better in 1978 than in the 1950s, and improvements in access to consumer goods such as bicycles and radios had been slow. Against the background of a 2–3% annual growth rate of peasant living standards during the 1960s and

---

[1]Figures are for 1987. This is not to suggest that China would switch wholesale from these crops if the rural economy were organized along market principles; however, discussion of this and of related points must be deferred for the time being.

1970s, the doubling of their incomes between 1978 and 1984 stands out as a most impressive accomplishment. So, too, does the simultaneous increase in per capita grain consumption and in production of virtually every other farm product, as well as the shift in output structure whereby the share of rural gross output value attributable to crop production fell to 48% by 1987.

Scope and Plan of this Book

Although it might seem an easy matter to dismiss the rural institutions of China's Maoist era as an aberration having little intrinsic interest, there are a number of reasons why they are worthy of further investigation. Because China was substantially closed to outside observers, and because its own social science community was inactive or barred from meaningful research during most of the collective era, the arrangements that successfully (if not plentifully) fed a quarter of the world's population for a quarter of this century remain poorly understood. Among the various social arrangements available for scientific investigation in the modern world, China's commune system would appear to be one of the more interesting laboratories for testing propositions about human behavior and the implications of institutional design. From a more contemporary standpoint, an understanding of the causes and an evaluation of the achievements of China's rural reforms can hardly be complete without some depth of understanding of the starting point of those changes. A substantial portion of this book is accordingly devoted to the study of the production and distribution system of China's collective-era communes. The approach of this study is to marry institutional knowledge to applied microeconomic theory, and to test the latter by means of econometric analysis of detailed Chinese data.

While analysis of the inner workings of the commune system that preceded the reforms occupies a major part of the book, at least equal space is devoted to studying the economic arrangements that succeeded that system and the nature of the transition from one to the other. Although the analysis is highly microanalytic in nature, many of its findings point to important conclusions for an understanding of China's political-economy at the macro level. As foreshadowed above, continuity of extractive state policies, and of the fundamental conflict between agriculture and the structural objectives of the Chinese state, will emerge as our most pervasive theme. By focusing on a local case study, we will find that while ideological restrictions may have played a unique part in preventing China's collective institutions from achieving their full potential, the elimination of those restrictions has not been accompanied by the overcoming of the more fundamental distortive effects of state control over agriculture in the service of industry. While Lardy (1983) and other authors have made clear that these interventions were carried to irrational extremes in the 1970s, the effects of the remaining distortions on China's post-collective rural economy are perhaps less widely appreciated. Those effects include inefficient factor allocation among rural activities, general underinvestment in agriculture, conflicts between the state and local governments over the pace of investment in nonagricultural projects, and the related competition for scarce resources that has helped to fuel inflation and to complicate the mixed plan-cum-market industrial system of post-Mao China.

While much has been written about the progress and problems just reviewed, our own approach, and the particular contribution of the present work, will be to document the changes and continuities in the transition to China's reform era rural economy by focusing on detailed local data, which are analyzed by descriptive methods and by econometric testing of relevant theoretical models. Simultaneously, an attempt will be made to address the limitations of the method of local study by placing the case material in proper context, and by comparing it to results obtained by analysis of more aggregated data. Finally, we will attempt to draw broad conclusions that may differ in detail or emphasis from those of other scholars. Insofar as our conclusions may rest heavily on our local data set and may be subject to unreliability due to deficiencies in that data, we will not presume that our inferences about China are always definitive; our hope is simply that we may usefully contribute to a picture that will continue to emerge through ongoing study and debate. The structure of the book is as follows.

Chapter 1 reviews the history of rural development in post-revolutionary mainland China with an emphasis on micro-organization, but also with considerable attention to state policy, China's underlying political economy, and economic outcomes. Chapter 2 surveys the major regions of China, focusing on the question of regional variation and on laying a foundation for understanding the representativeness of the case study site. Analysis of our local case material begins with Chapter 3, which provides a descriptive overview of the economy of the site in question, Hebei province's Dahe[2] Township, in both the collective and post-collective periods. Economic growth, structural change, and institutional reform are all featured here.

Econometric analysis begins with Chapter 4, which looks at changes in the productivity of agricultural and sideline activities at Dahe in the 1970s and early 1980s, and provides evidence that Dahe's production teams and households were prevented from allocating their labor and other resources to higher-return nonfarm activities to the degree that would have been dictated by the pursuit of maximum private and collective economic advantage. Attempts to decompose output growth into that attributable to increasing applications of specific inputs and that due to increasing productivity of inputs are also presented in that chapter, although identifying the share of productivity growth attributable to specific reform measures is deferred to a later one. Chapter 5 takes a detailed look at the operation of the incentive systems within collective production teams at Dahe in the 1970s, and Chapter 6 considers the question of individual labor supply to the teams in the same

---

[2]A hint on the pronunciation of this recurring proper noun might be helpful to the reader. The first syllable rhymes with the first syllable of "mama"; the "e" in the second syllable sounds like "oo" in "good." The "h" may be pronounced with a slight rasp.

period. Chapter 7 returns to the question of productivity change and focuses on attempts to measure the impact of the adoption of household farming.

In Chapters 8 and 9, our attention is focused on the reform-era economy in two different ways. Chapter 8 studies resource allocation at the household level, again pointing to the existence of pressures to produce crops for self-consumption and for the state. The simulation model developed in that chapter is also used to investigate (counterfactually) the possibilities for meeting state crop output goals through price-incentive methods, and the effects of operating a land market in Dahe township. Chapter 9 considers the influence on farm productivity of the method of land division among households.

While the focus of Chapters 4 through 9 is on productivity, incentive, and resource allocation issues, Chapter 10 surveys the evidence on the impact of the reforms on income distribution, and the nature of income distribution under both the collective and post-collective systems. Chapter 11 summarizes the findings from the Dahe case studies, discusses their broader implications, and concludes with some observations about the prospects for further reform and economic growth in China.

1

China's Rural Economy under Two Regimes

Background

When the Communist Party came to power in the Chinese mainland in 1949, a nation of 1/2 billion people (this number was to grow to 1.1 billion by 1990) became one of the most dynamic laboratories of social change in recorded history. During its first decade in power, the C.C.P. reorganized virtually the whole of China's agricultural and industrial system along the lines laid down by the Communist Party rulers of the Soviet Union two decades earlier. Further changes came beginning in 1958. First, China lurched dramatically in the direction of more radical policies (the "Great Leap Forward"). Then, it retrenched in the face of economic calamity, then veered off into another dozen years under radical leftist policies (the "Cultural Revolution Decade"). Finally, as Communist China prepared to enter its fourth decade, a momentous Party plenum at the end of 1978 marked the beginning of a transition to a more "pragmatic," mixed economy variant of Soviet-type socialism. In 40 years, therefore, China traveled the vast distances from its post-War starting point as an economically underdeveloped semi-capitalist society, first to orthodox Stalinism, then to radical Maoism, and finally to a reformist model having much in common with the New Economic Policy regime of Lenin's mid-1920s Soviet Union.

The 85% of China's population who dwelt in rural areas felt the impact of these changes as much as, and possibly more than, any other segment of Chinese society, for these four decades saw their transformation from tenants to small peasants, from small peasants to members of people's communes and collective farm production teams, then back again to household cultivators and entrepreneurs. Before the revolution, 30% of China's farmers were tenants, rents averaged 50% of output, and 73% of farm households had one or fewer hectares of land to farm.[1] Disease was rampant in the countryside, and life expectancy at birth for rural dwellers was 20–25 years.[2] In the first years after the ascent of the Chinese Communist Party to power, landlords and rich peasants were expropriated of roughly 46.7 million hectares of

---

[1]See Riskin (1987).
[2]Perkins and Yusuf (1984, p. 133).

cultivated land, which was redistributed to about 300 million poor peasants.[3] Rents were abolished, and agricultural taxes to the state were set at relatively low levels, amounting to roughly 12% of the average value of farm output, including roughly the same share of total grain produced, in 1952.[4]

The years following the completion of China's land reform witnessed a process of cooperative formation and collectivization that was at first gradual and relatively voluntaristic, then increasingly rapid and coercive, with output's continuing recovery from the devastation of decades of turmoil and war apparently undisturbed or even enhanced by institutional change. These years also saw the first steps in the construction of a government monopoly on crop procurement and the fixing of crop prices and delivery quotas in the service of the government's industrialization program.

By the end of 1957, virtually all Chinese farmers were members of village-sized Soviet-style collective farms known as Advanced Producers' Cooperatives. Private property in land, draft animals, and other equipment had been abolished, and peasants' incomes depended upon the outcome of their cooperatives' production activities and their own shares of the total labor supplied to them, plus supplementary earnings from private vegetable gardening and animal husbandry. Then, buoyed by the country's success in averting a crisis of the sort precipitated by the Soviet collectivization of agriculture a quarter century earlier, Mao threw the weight of his support behind an original adventure in collective gigantism and social engineering, creation of the peoples' communes which contained an average of 5,000 households (22,000 persons). With the replacement of the advanced cooperatives by the communes as units of accounting and work organization, Mao and his comrades snatched defeat from the jaws of victory. Within a year, China's agriculture experienced a more precipitous collapse than had the Soviet Union's in the 1930s. Within 3 years, as many as 30 million more Chinese (mostly rural) than expected by demographic trends had died of starvation and of health problems aggravated by hunger.[5] China's agricultural crisis went beyond that of the Soviet Union in another respect. That country had been able to increase agricultural procurements even as total output fell, so that agricultural crisis had little observable impact on industrial growth. Partly because of the country's smaller cushion of farm surplus, however, retrenchment in China meant a sharp reduction of industrial investment and growth.[6] Growth resumed in 1962, but it took until 1965 for China's grain production to approach its 1957 level, until 1978 for the same indicator to reachieve its 1957 level

---

[3]Cheng (1982, p. 66).

[4]Lardy (1983, pp. 103, 104, 149).

[5]See Piazza (1983), Ashton, et al. (1984), and Riskin (1990).

[6]While agricultural output in the Soviet Union in 1928 amounted to about 480 kg of grain per member of the overall population, that in China in 1957 was only about 256 kg of grain per capita. The differences reflect long-term differences in population densities and levels of economic development, more than the short-term effects of policies pursued by the two governments. For a detailed analysis, see Tang (1984, pp. 38–51).

in per capita terms, and as long or longer for poultry, fish, vegetable oil, and other products to regain and surpass their 1957 per capita production levels. Industrial output also declined between 1960 and 1962, recovering its 1960 peak level again only in 1966.

Land reform, the cooperative movement, collectivization, formation of the communes, and the resulting collapse of agriculture are historically important and fascinating episodes in the annals of institutional change in China, but they are not the immediate subjects of this book; it concentrates instead on the periods that followed— especially, the collective farming era of the 1970s, and the reform era of the 1980s. One reason for this focus is that the data with which to study the workings of the economic and social institutions of rural China in the 1950s and 1960s, especially at the micro level, have been limited. Aggregate statistics on some series are available for the 1950s, but China's statistical system collapsed along with its economy during the Great Leap Forward (G.L.F.), and data that were compiled for the end of the 1950s are tainted by exaggeration. By contrast, the end of the 1970s saw two parallel developments that made possible a new dimension of quantitative scholarship on China's rural economy. First, China's official statistical system was rebuilt, and current data on a wide variety of variables began to be published by a number of national and province level organizations. Second, the reopening of China's universities and research institutions and the country's "open door" policies with respect to international economic and cultural relations meant that more local-level data began to be gathered in surveys by both Chinese and foreign researchers. One such set of surveys, initiated by an American researcher in a rural township in Hebei Province, made possible investigations of both the collective farming years of the 1970s and the transition to household farming in the early 1980s which constitute the bulk of the analysis reported in this book.

China in the Collective Era: Agricultural Intensification and the Three-Tier System

Initially, the poor harvest of 1959 went unnoticed by China's leaders, and in the high-pressure, campaign-like atmosphere of that year, the center received false reports of bumper crops. With such reports in hand and determined to push ahead with its industrialization program, the government extracted larger amounts of grain than ever from the countryside, exacerbating the food shortage and the resulting hunger.[7] When the enormity of the crisis began to be perceived, however, many areas quietly retreated from the effective control of farm production and distribution by the communes, giving more autonomy to small teams and households. A household contract farming system is reported to have been practiced throughout Anhui Province from 1959 to 1961, and households had probably been restored to their

---

[7]Bernstein (1984).

position as production units in numerous other localities by the end of the "3 bad years."[8] More "pragmatically" oriented leaders within the C.C.P., who had all along opposed collectivization until the day when China would be able to support a more mechanized agriculture, looked not unfavorably upon this return to household-based farming.

While the influence of these leaders had grown in direct proportion to the failure of the G.L.F., Mao Zedong and his allies managed to forge a compromise solution that was to preserve collective farming in China for nearly two more decades. Their compromise was a multitiered organizational structure, in which small production teams took on the task of immediate farm management and disbursed payments based on labor contribution and need. Above the teams, larger production brigades and the communes (now considerably smaller than their original scales) undertook tasks of supervision, and of nonfarm production, capital construction, and service provision—tasks to which larger scales were viewed as appropriate. Below the teams, the households themselves, in a sense a fourth tier, were permitted to maintain small vegetable gardens and to engage in some animal husbandry and handicraft production, typically earning between a quarter and a third of their total incomes in these ways. The compromise was codified in a document known as the Sixty Articles, which was published in September of 1962. It was initially implemented in a relatively liberal period, in which restrictions on private activities and rural markets were comparatively mild, in which farmers were offered relatively attractive state prices and above-quota bonuses, and in which team leaders were encouraged to use piece rates and other material incentives and to minimize egalitarianism in distribution. However, the basic organizational structure elaborated in these Articles was to remain in place during the more radical period that followed, and to survive to as late as 1983 in much of rural China.

Population Growth and Technological Change

The story of Chinese agriculture in the 1960s and 1970s is not one of institution-building only. On the contrary, these decades saw dramatic changes in the resource base of the agricultural sector and in the types of technology applied to farming. In brief, massive growth of inputs and outputs occurred, marked by a sharp deterioration in the man-land ratio, the rapid spread of irrigation, the development and populariza-tion of improved seed varieties, and enormous increases in the application of chemical fertilizer. While large gains in grain yields were achieved, output of other crops stagnated. Also, growth in grain output was accompanied by a decline in output per workday, and total grain production failed to recover its late 1950s per capita levels. At the same time, China's indigenous development of green revolution

[8]Kojima (1988, p. 709).

technology, its construction and importation of substantial fertilizer production capacity, its improvement of gravity-based irrigation systems, and its installation of vast numbers of power-operated tubewells laid the groundwork for an impressive agricultural growth spurt—a burst of productivity that was to follow the raising of farm prices, relaxing of crop and marketing constraints, and improvement of production incentives through restoration of household farming in the early 1980s. Also, rural industrialization under commune and brigade auspices, in the more progressive and (usually) better located of China's communes, laid the foundation for one of the most dynamic sectors of Chinese industry in the reform era, the township and village enterprises which would grow to account for nearly 20% of national industrial output in 1989.[9]

China's population grew from 575 million in 1952 to 673 million in 1962 and 963 million in 1978, or at an annual rate of 1.6% during the first period and 2.3% in the second. Rural population accounted for almost 88% of the total in 1952, and for 81% in 1979, with reported agricultural labor force rising from 173 million at the beginning to 294 million at the end of the period, for an annual growth rate of 1.9%.[10] According to official statistics, cultivated area declined from 108 million hectares in 1952 to 103 million in 1962 and under 100 million in 1979. With the irrigated share of this land rising from 19% in 1952 to 30% in 1962 and to 45% in 1979, the typical hectare produced 1.5 crops a year in 1979 versus 1.3 in 1952, so sown area saw a modest increase from 141.3 million to 148.5 million hectares over the period. In addition, increasing irrigation was complemented by a near tripling of organic fertilizer use (from 729 million to 2,072 million tons) and a 165-fold increase in application of chemical fertilizer (from 318,000 to 52 million tons) between 1952 and 1979, an increase in labor days on the order of 250%,[11] and improvements in seeds and other aspects of technology. As a consequence, grain yields rose from 1,296 kg per sown hectare in 1952 to 2,527 kg/ha in 1978, reflecting a 1.9% growth rate for rice yields, a 3.5% growth rate for wheat yields, and a 2.8% growth rate for corn yields.[12] Total grain output thus rose from 161 million tons in 1952 to 305 million tons in 1978 and 332 million tons in 1979, causing output per person to rise from .28

[9]Rural private enterprises and joint urban-rural enterprises accounted for another 6.7% of industrial output in that year (State Statistical Bureau 1990).

[10]While we prefer to use 1978 as the endpoint of the Maoist era, because the post-Mao reforms began in 1979, some data are more readily available for the latter year. Fortunately, the difference is consequential primarily when looking at output and yield figures, only. Moreover, as will be seen below, 1979 marked reforms in prices and marketing, but Chinese agriculture remained overwhelmingly collective in that year.

[11]Taylor's (1988) estimates, based on those of Schran and Rawski, indicate a doubling of labor days per rural worker, if the midpoint of the 1975 range is used as a measure for 1979 labor days.

[12]Although some growth in yields occurred during the 1950s, this was erased by the Great Leap Forward, which left 1962 yields slightly below those of 1952. Thus, net growth can be thought of either as occurring or as being recouped and then furthered between 1962 and 1978, and growth rates in that shorter period are substantially higher: 4.4% for grain as a whole, and 3.4%, 6.3%, and 4.7% for rice, wheat, and corn, respectively.

tons in 1952 (or .24 tons in 1962) to .32 tons in 1978 and .34 tons in 1979. Combined with a change from being a small net exporter to being a net importer of about 7.1 million tons of grain in 1978 and 10.2 million tons in 1979,[13] this permitted China's per capita grain consumption to rise from 198 kg in 1952 to 207 kg in 1979, a modest 4.5% increase over the period as a whole.[14]

As mentioned above, output of many nongrain products failed to rise in step with grain production, and for several of these, output fell in per capita terms. Cotton production fell from 1.3 million tons in 1952 to 0.8 million in 1962 and rose only to 2.2 million tons in 1978, leaving per capita output roughly constant. Production of oilseed crops such as peanuts, rapeseed, and sesame fell from 4.2 million tons in 1952 to 2 million tons in 1962, then rose to 5.2 million tons in 1978, for a net decline of nearly 26% in per capita output. Total soybean production stood at only 7.5 million tons in 1979, down even in absolute terms from 9.5 million in 1952. This meant that China's population had to make due with less cooking oil and soy products at the end of the third decade under socialism than at the start of the first. Not all farm products showed level or declining output trends, however. While population grew by a factor of 67% between 1952 and 1978, the combined output of pork, mutton, and beef rose by 153%, that of sugarcane and sugarbeets by 214%, that of fruits by 169%, and that of fish and other aquatic products by 158%.[15] Moreover, since net growth of most of these products was negative between 1952 and 1962, due to the Great Leap, growth rates for 1962 to 1978, when Chinese agriculture was organized under the three-tier collective system, were quite high, ranging from 5.7% for meat to 13.9% for sugarbeets. Even crops the output of which just kept pace with or grew more slowly than population during 1952–1978 as a whole registered relatively high growth rates between 1962 and 1978, including 4.3% a year for grain, 6.9% for cotton, and 6.2% for oilseeds.[16]

Chinese yields of rice, wheat, and corn in 1979 equaled or exceeded world and Asian averages, although they fell below average yields for the United States, South Korea, and Japan.[17] The Chinese diet at the end of the 1970s was a spartan one, with cereals accounting for fully 79% of calories and 67% of protein consumed, while animal products accounted for less than 8% of calories and 15% of protein. However, per capita daily availability of calories and protein exceeded both then current F.A.O. requirements, and the achievements of other low income countries such as India, Pakistan, Bangladesh, Sri Lanka, and Nepal.[18]

---

[13]World Bank (1983a, Vol. II, pp. 421 and 425).

[14]The growth rate of output plus imports exceeds that of consumption in part because of increases in indirect consumption, as feed.

[15]The final figure is based on the terminal year 1979.

[16]All rates in absolute rather than per capita terms.

[17]Perkins and Yusuf (1984, Table 3-7, p. 38).

[18]World Bank (1983a, Volume III, Tables 2.5 and 2.6). Estimated protein availability was the same in China and Pakistan to the nearest full gram. Cereals refers to the international definition, which excludes pulses and tubers, and not the Chinese definition, which includes them.

Assessment

The 1960s and 1970s saw China struggle with the Herculean task of feeding the world's largest and (in absolute terms[19] most rapidly growing population within the context of a collectivized institutional regime founded on relatively small operational units. This struggle was waged with both assistance and interference from a state bent on rapid industrialization and thus continuing to exploit agriculture by demanding deliveries of output at relatively unremunerative prices, but conceding the need to provide farmers with an increasing supply of modern inputs, especially chemical fertilizer. It succeeded in the sense that as of 1978, 963 million people, over 300 million of whom represented a net addition since 1961, were being fed slightly better (on average) than at the beginning of this period, and not much worse than at the economic high point of the late 1950s. This success was reflected in the fact that life expectancy in China, which had risen from 32 to 57 years between 1949 and 1957, resumed its increase following the demographic catastrophe of 1959–1961, to reach 65 years in 1978, a phenomenal achievement when compared with the 51 year life expectancy of Indians, the 52 year life expectancy of Indonesians, the 49 year life expectancy of Pakistanis, or the 47 year life expectancy of Bangladeshis in the same year.[20] That achievement resulted partly from the combination of public attention to health care and the low-cost, prevention-centered approach followed, but probably to a still greater degree from the comparatively equal distribution of the country's food supplies.[21] The commune system played a major role both in the delivery of health care, and in the distribution of basic foodstuffs to the population, none of whom, despite their massive pressure on a meager base of land, suffered the landlessness and associated deprivation faced by tens of millions of rural dwellers in China's otherwise similar populous Asian neighbors.

But in other respects, China failed. As descendants of a people with the world's longest record of unbroken civilization and statehood, Chinese tended to compare their country not with the poorest of the developing world, but with the most developed countries in the world, and with more rapidly developing neighbors such as Japan, Hong Kong, and South Korea. A larger population of longer-living but still poor Chinese produced little satisfaction; the minimal caloric requirement in a diet dominated by grain might keep the body alive, but failed to satisfy the spirit. The

---

[19]That is, in terms of the absolute annual increments to population, although not the population growth rate as a percentage of existing population.

[20]World Bank (1983b).

[21]Greater absolute per capita supplies could also have played a role in the better health outcomes for China as compared with India and Bangladesh, but not as compared with Pakistan and Indonesia. Per capita calories available in China in 1977 were roughly 2,262, compared to 2,281 in Pakistan, 2,272 in Indonesia, 2,021 in India, and 1,812 in Bangladesh. (World Bank, 1983b, Table 2.6, p. 33. We derive our 1977 estimate for China by multiplying the Bank's 1979 estimate, 2,441 calories, by the ratio of 1977 to 1979 grain consumption, according to Chinese statistics. Those statistics show vegetable oil, pork, beef, mutton, poultry, and eggs available increasing by similar or greater margins between 1977 and 1979.) Note, however, that per capita food availability differed across regions within China, as shown by Walker (1984 and 1989).

revolution that succeeded in liberating China from feudalism and imperial incursions had restored the integrity of the nation-state, but despite impressive achievements in laying the basis for an industrial economy, the mass of China's farmers remained peasants sinking ever deeper into the back-breaking drudgery of an agriculture dependent on increasing applications of human muscle-power. Making these perceptions vivid to millions of China's urban elites was one of the most important consequences of their banishment to the countryside during the last decade of Maoism. That vividness was rendered the more poignant when, upon their return to the cities, the same individuals were suddenly allowed to glimpse the still sharper contrast with the late 20th century world to which China had opened itself upon the end of Maoist rule. Rural people, too, experienced rising aspirations as television sets became common in much of the countryside and images of developed countries were revealed to them.

More narrowly, China's rural development policies in the 1960s and 1970s failed in the sense that the costs of achieving the key target of those policies, raising grain output, had been too high. Those costs included, as we have seen, lessened per capita consumption of such basics as cooking oil and soy products, and for urban consumers, limited variety and poor quality of fruits, vegetables, and other nonstaples. It included, too, the massive, and sometimes wasteful, inputs of human labor, in winter capital construction campaigns and sometimes economically irrational drives to raise the level of multicropping, under the direction of leaders and cadres who often appeared to view the pains of others' labor as being of no account at all. And it included the costs of local grain self-sufficiency, which deprived grain-basket areas of their markets, forced producers of higher-value crops to divert land away from their traditional specialties, and imposed ecological harm on many of China's forests and grazing lands. The country's very success in feeding an ever-larger population could be seen as a hollow victory because, rather than being able to feed a larger share of the nation, agriculture had taken on a greater character of self-sufficiency, with the proportion of grain output leaving the countryside[22] actually falling from 17% in 1952 to 14% in 1978. Beyond this, the country's economic performance in these decades was unsatisfactory in the more global sense that emphasis on heavy industry and capital goods, and the gap between a capital-intensive industry and a labor-intensive agriculture, left improvements in consumption standards small, and differences in living standards between urban and rural dwellers, and between residents of different rural regions, large. Peasants were deprived of the freedom to grow more profitable or palatable crops, faced restrictions on private gardening and small husbandry activities and on the ability to trade in rural markets, and were forced to participate in the collective system with its long and regimented work hours and small and nondiscriminating remuneration. To many of them, liberation from the landlords of the past may

---

[22]That is, state-procured grain not resold to the agricultural population as a proportion of total grain harvested. State Statistical Bureau (1988, p. 627).

now have appeared to be only a delivery into the bondage of a new serfdom to the vast administrative edifice stretching from Beijing to the production team. This judgment, if not already sealed by the disaster which began the 1960s, may have been more and more the consensus of China's peasants as the extremes of Cultural Revolution ideology failed to bear material fruit in ordinary villages, and as the leftist propaganda machine was exposed to ridicule by the transparency of political machinations at the pinnacle of power.[23]

Causes: Micro-, Meso-, and Macroeconomic

China's long record of policy changes and the resulting changes in economic outcomes are of immense value to observers who wish to sort out the causes of particular outcomes in specific periods. The dramatic reforms in China's rural policies and institutions between late 1978 and the end of 1983, and their impact on the rural economy, are especially helpful for the light they shed on the weaknesses, as well as the strengths, of the rural system of the previous decades. The experiment is imperfect, to be sure, in that too many changes occurred at more or less the same time, making identification of the impacts of individual reforms more difficult. Nonetheless, the analytical problems here have attracted substantial attention from scholars in recent years, and some progress—including (it is hoped) findings to be presented in later chapters of this book—has been made. The aim in the present section is primarily to frame the question and to lay out in broad terms some of the more relevant factors to be considered.

A reasonable way to organize an examination of the causes of failure and success in Chinese rural development in the Mao era is to begin by distinguishing between micro-organizational factors, and macro- and mesoeconomic policy factors. The first term refers to the organization of production at farm or workshop level, while the second refers to state policies concerning investment, prices, output planning, and market controls. At the level of micro-organization, we consider the collective nature of farm production, the payment and distribution systems employed, the internal organization of communes, brigades, and teams, and the scope of the household economy including private plots. "Mesoeconomic" is a more recently coined term referring to price and marketing policies and institutions. Here, we are concerned with China's state monopoly over crop procurement and supply of manufactured inputs, along with state controls over rural free markets, and the prices that prevailed in each of these spheres. We can also include here direct state controls over crop

---

[23]The last remark has particular reference to the Lin Biao affair, as discussed by Chan et al. (1984; see below). Of course, attitudes can be expected to have varied depending upon the pre-1949 living standard of the individual peasant, and the success of the commune and collective unit to which he or she belonged. Members of what were prior to 1949 the poorest households may have remained grateful for land reform, and some members of the richest 20% of teams, concentrated in the suburban communes near large, especially coastal cities, may have judged the system rather favorably.

planning. By "macroeconomic," we refer more to national economic strategy and its implications for various economic sectors than to the behavior of national aggregates like GNP, to which the term points in discussions of market economies. The macro level factors of central concern for us are state policies on investment in agriculture versus industry, the priority given to heavy versus light industry, and the role of the rural sector in the country's overall economic development strategy. Our discussion moves from macro- and mesoeconomic to microeconomic and organizational factors.

The Macro- and Mesoeconomic Setting

The key macroeconomic issue, with direct manifestation in the pricing relations of the mesoeconomic environment of China's agriculture, is the question of intersectoral resource transfers. Although the topic is fraught with conceptual problems, there is agreement among leading analysts that China's agriculture has provided a significant share of the funds for the government's industrialization program. For the 1950s, Perkins and Yusuf (1984) estimate that the state derived about Y 3 billion per year from agricultural tax, equal to roughly 12% of gross crop value.[24] They also estimate that the state earned about Y 5 billion annually in profits on the sale of consumer and producer goods to farmers, and that the tax implicit in compulsory sales at below market prices was in the neighborhood of Y 2–3 billion a year. Against this, they calculate the total value of state expenditures in rural areas including meteorology services, rural relief, and education and medical services as Y 3–4 billion per year. They argue that the implicit tax in procurements should be viewed as an income transfer from peasants to urban workers, rather than the state, but that the remaining Y 4–5 billion net transfer from peasants to the state accounted for about 16% of total state funds for industrial investment, national defense, and general administration. The phenomenon of dual peasant underwriting of both urban living standards and the state industrialization program, found by Perkins and Yusuf, will be seen to be an abiding theme in China's recent political economy.

Despite the disaster of 1959–1961, the state monopoly on crop purchasing was never suspended, although more freedom to sell some crops in rural free markets existed in the early 1960s and to a lesser extent again in the early 1970s. While crop prices were raised by an average of 28% against an increase in input prices averaging only 5%, in 1961, further improvements in the terms of trade were more gradual and

---

[24]The symbol Y before a number denotes units of Chinese currency, or *yuan*. Sample average official exchange rates are:

1953–1971	ca. 2.5 *yuan* per U.S. dollar
1973	1.99 *yuan* per dollar
1980	1.50 *yuan* per dollar
1983	1.98 *yuan* per dollar
1985	2.94 *yuan* per dollar
1987–1989	3.72 *yuan* per dollar

(International Monetary Fund: *International Financial Statistics*)

minor. In his 1983 analysis, Lardy argues that the state continued to extract surplus resources from agriculture throughout the 1960s and 1970s in the form of state agricultural tax, the gap between free market and procurement prices, and profits on sales of manufactured inputs. In the same period, the state directly invested only about Y 2 billion a year in agriculture, or less than 12% of public capital construction funds.[25] In an article published in 1987, a research team of the Development Institute of the Research Center on Rural Development of the State Council of China concluded that the state appropriated over Y 600 billion from peasants for urban development and industrialization between 1957 and 1987 "by suppressing the prices of agricultural products and inflating the prices of industrial products."[26] This would mean that while agriculture was the recipient of an average of 10–12% of public capital construction investment over most of that period,[27] it provided about 22% of China's savings and capital accumulation, which amounted to about Y 2,788 billion according to official statistics.[28]

Perhaps an equally large burden borne by China's farm population during the 1960s and 1970s is one that had no beneficiaries at all. This is the local grain self-sufficiency policy, rationalized by the desire to sustain a resistance effort in any region cut off from other parts of the country by a Soviet attack, but perhaps also reflecting a general Maoist antipathy to commerce. The costs of this policy in the decades of the three-tier commune have been effectively elaborated in an influential book by Lardy (1983). Although that author documents gains from the policy's relaxation at the beginning of the reform era, the observation that grain self-sufficiency and other barriers to specialization have survived de facto and at least to some degree into the post-Mao era, will be an important and recurring theme of this book.

Micro-organizational Factors and the Performance of the Collective System

While the impacts of meso- and macroeconomic policies will be given considerable attention, the central focus of this book is on the micro-organizational aspects of the Chinese rural economy both before and after the 1978 reforms. This micro dimension pertains to the most local and small-scale institutions, yet the analysis of those institutions is never entirely separated from their broader social and political context.

[25]In the 3 years preceding the Cultural Revolution, the figure was closer to 18%. See Stone (1988, pp. 784–5).
[26]Development Institute (1987). The World Bank's 1990 country study of China gives a similar figures: "Between 1955 and 1985, manipulating the rural-urban terms of trade allowed the state to transfer an estimated Y 600–800 billion to other sectors" (World Bank, 1990).
[27]Stone (1988, p. 784).
[28]State Statistical Bureau (1988, p. 50). As noted in Chapter 11, the *net* transfer of resources from agriculture to nonagriculture remains an analytically complex and theoretically ambiguous issue that this book does not attempt to resolve.

When discussing micro-organization in the collective period, in fact, we propose a distinction between *intrinsic* characteristics of a system of collective ownership, production, and distribution, and *extrinsic* characteristics resulting from specific government policies, ideological and political interventions, and either the broader political climate of Mao's China, or the influence of Chinese peasant world views and cultural norms upon the operation of Maoist institutions. By distinguishing between these two sets of characteristics, some problems and strengths of China's collective system can be identified as endemic to any system with similar institutional features, while others will be found to result from political or social forces determining the ways in which that system operated in the specific context of China.

The key micro-organizational issues of an intrinsic nature are the plusses and minuses of farm management on a scale typically involving two or three dozen households, as opposed to the individual household farms prevailing both before and after the collective era in China, and in labor intensive sericulture throughout Asia and the Third World. Any technological and risk-sharing benefits to be had from farm amalgamation must be set off against the difficulties of providing adequate work incentives in a team setting. The absence of either ownership or usufruct rights in land on the parts of individuals or households—with the exception of the small private plots—might also be listed. To be sure, separating the intrinsic factors from those specific to the political and social context here is possible, at best, only at a high level of abstraction; for example, the internal organizational and motivational problems of group farming were in practice much influenced by the top-down imposition of the system, the subtle forms of political terror used to unnerve would-be challengers, and the imbeddedness of team decision making in a larger bureaucratic structure controlled by the Party and state and charged with implementing the state's extractive program. Nonetheless, useful observations about these issues are possible. First, while there may have been some potential gains to be had from larger-scale farm units and management—for example, reduction of land lost to field boundaries, the possibility of rationalizing the construction and utilization of some irrigation systems, the introduction of machine plowing in some localities, and the easier dissemination of new technologies and hastened introduction of improved seeds[29]—these gains appear to have been offset by reduced farmer work incentives which seem to have been weakened when looked at either from the standpoint of raw effort or from that of the intelligent and appropriate exercise of discretion. Moreover, physical economies of scale at the cultivation stage are thought by many students of agricultural development economics to be limited if present at all. Large-scale farm management may have led to otherwise avoidable errors, for example those of inappropriate technological innovation, or mistakes made through team and brigade leaders' ignorance of highly local variations in physical conditions (slope, soil moisture,

---

[29]For an example of the argument that collective farming can improve peasant productivity and well-being, see Freyhold (1979, Ch. 2).

disease, and pest infestation, etc.) that might have been known to the farmer of a much smaller family plot. Even the sometimes alleged "conservatism" of peasants, which proponents of collectivization have argued could be overcome through collective introduction of new technologies, may in fact amount to prudent avoidance of risks that the small production team was in no position to insure against, but had the power to arbitrarily force members to bear. As for the risk-sharing aspect of group farming (Carter, 1987), such insurance is in principle possible without actual pooling of land, a practice that may carry significant moral hazard costs if work is not costlessly observable.

The question of work incentives raises fascinating problems for assessing the operation of China's collective system and for comparing it with the "decollectivized" successor regime. While logically treacherous and perhaps not fully resolved, these issues have yielded to interesting analyses that are conceptually linked to the progress made by economists on a number of related topics in recent years. The essential problem is how to elicit effort when there may exist a disjunction between effort and individual reward due to the team character of production and the difficulty of distinguishing the contributions of more and of less diligent and/or capable workers. Whereas the farm operated by an individual owner or a (fixed-rent) tenant solves this problem by causing the supplier of effort to appropriate the full increment of output that results from it, eliciting effort in the face of its imperfect observability is probably the quintessential problem of the production team, whether it be the team of a Mao-era collective farm, a voluntary and democratic workers' cooperative, or the workshop of a labor-hiring family business or of a large, shareholder owned corporation. Although certain purely theoretical solutions have been proposed,[30] real-world approaches usually involve some combination of enforcement of observable criteria (work hours), attempts to monitor imperfectly observable effort on the job, use of rewards and sanctions (such as bonuses, promotions, fines, and terminations) linked to these observations of individual performance, and simple sharing of team net earnings—or what may be called "collective material incentives."[31] Insofar as there is an observable individual output, on the other hand, the problem can be addressed by employing piece rates, although these are subject to numerous dangers, including debasement of quality (which results from the fact that that which is observable is but an imperfect proxy for the end result which is desired).

---

[30]The effort problem has appeared solvable in theory either by (a) severely penalizing all team members if output falls short of that expected when all provide optimal effort (in this case it is not necessary to threaten that shirkers will be discovered and punished, since punishment falls on shirkers and diligent workers alike), or (b) having all members commit themselves to optimal effort provided that they observe the associated output, and to severely suboptimal effort after any period in which suboptimal output is observed. In the latter case, a result identical to that in case (a) is obtained in a repeated game context without requirement of a boss or manager. For (a), see Holmström (1982); for (b), see MacLeod (1988), and its formal antecedent in Friedman (1977).

[31]Riskin (1974). The idea here is no different from the profit-sharing observed in medical and legal partnerships and, increasingly, in Western corporate settings. On the latter, see the surveys of recent literature collected in Blinder (1990).

It is doubtful that any feasible form of team production can succeed in getting all members to work fully as hard as they would were they self-employed and facing the same objective opportunities to trade effort for income.[32] Where such self-employment is a viable alternative, therefore, it will tend to exhibit more productive outcomes than does team work. More precisely, where there are no technological gains to be had from working in groups, individual or household enterprises can be expected to prevail. Where such gains are to be had, the question is whether they are large enough to compensate for the probable incentive losses of team production. Clearly the answer would be in the affirmative for much modern manufacturing activity, but very likely it would not be for most agricultural production, especially where resource availability dictates use of labor-intensive methods.

While cultural background, attitudes toward the organization and activity, and other factors may interact with organizational form in determining the results achieved, it seems likely that some methods of organizing team production will be more successful than others. In market economies in which people are free to form or join a variety of alternative types of organization, most work is performed under an employment relationship in which workers accept the authority of the employer over the details of their work assignment, can be fired for malfeasance (or when market or other circumstances make them redundant), are compensated mostly in the form of predetermined wages, and may also be motivated by the prospect of promotion if they are perceived to be good or loyal workers.[33] In China's collective-era agricultural production teams, membership was mandatory, came automatically with residence, and could not be terminated. Mobility was sharply restricted, payment was based partly on household size and partly on points awarded for work days completed, and leadership of the team was chosen by the members subject to approval by higher levels. Team membership and the market employment relationship thus differed in that the former lacked voluntarism, was more explicitly egalitarian in its payment rules, and was less unambiguously hierarchical with respect to management at the level of the production unit. Since the employment relationship has survived the test of market competition while the Chinese team system was politically imposed and later dismantled with considerable popular support, there is reason to question whether the team system was based on an efficient organizational design.

Much of the economic literature on the problem of incentives in the Chinese teams and other similar institutions has focused on the egalitarianism of their payment systems. In Chapter 5 of this book, this question will be explored in some detail. For

---

[32]Possible exceptions are cases in which the social dynamics of the team, perhaps interacting with the perceived desirability of such an outcome, lead workers to value the work activity, to compete with one another for social recognition as dedicated workers, or to otherwise be motivated without a link between effort and personal returns. The pre-eminent modern example is the Israeli kibbutz, on which see Barkai (1977, 1987), Morawetz (1983), and, for a theoretical discussion, Putterman (1983a). Reasons why such dynamics could not be sustained in China's rural teams are addressed below.

[33]For introductions and references to the literature on incentives and internal organization in capitalist firms, see Williamson, et al. (1975), Nalbantian (1987), and Lazear (1991).

now, it can be noted that the issue is one with respect to which the intrinsic/extrinsic dichotomy proposed above may be particularly relevant. In brief, egalitarianism of payment in the teams can be attributed, broadly speaking, to three types of factors, of rather different origin, although conceivably interacting with one another. On the intrinsic side are problems with observing quantitative and qualitative differences in labor input leading to the awarding of roughly equal numbers of work-points to both diligent and negligent, capable and incompetent team members. These problems have been attributed, variously, to the special character of agricultural production, which is spatially dispersed and lacking in measurable intermediate products, and to the nature of collective production, for which it is argued that the inability of any one individual to capture the benefits from more efficient operation left none with sufficient incentives to undertake the monitoring task with full earnestness.[34] On the extrinsic side were the political demand that grain and other necessities be rationed to members on a per capita basis, and various guidelines with respect to the differentiation of work-points, which reached the extremes, in the Cultural Revolution decade, of forbidding the use of piece rates, and of pressing for adoption of the Dazhai system in which team members reached agreement on how many points each was to receive for a standard workday after exhausting self- and mutual-evaluation meetings. One may also list among extrinsic factors the influence of peasant community social dynamics (or in particular, the Chinese variant thereof) upon the implementation of the institutions and policies imposed on the rural villages. These types of factors, rather than the political intentions of China's leaders or the intrinsic character of the institutions, may help to explain why, for example, the Dazhai system degenerated into a process for assigning workers pro forma ratings, with narrow differentials based primarily upon age and sex.

Nonmaterial Incentives[35]

The last paragraph can be summarized by saying that while teams may have been too egalitarian in their payment practices to encourage diligent work, this may have been a result of the norms and dynamics of social life in a Chinese village, of the overt political interventions of the Communist Party, of the inherent unobservability of differences in diligence, or of a combination of all three factors. Of course, this discussion of incentives, and most others in this book, betrays the economist's typical assumption that material rewards are necessary to motivate effort, or in other words, that work is a source of disutility which must be compensated by the payment of money or other goods. Maoism, on the other hand, emphasized that aspect of Marxist thought according to which human motivation is neither unitary nor immutable but is

---

[34]Alchian and Demsetz (1972), Bradley and Clark (1971), Nolan (1988). See also the related discussion in the Appendix of Chapter 7 of this book.
[35]This section draws on material in Putterman (1988c).

instead the product of specific social conditions. The attitudes of antipathy to labor and of willingness to perform it only as a *quid pro quo* for material reward, which characterize a capitalist economy, need not, on this view, prevail under a socialist system in transition to communism. Team members might rather have been induced to contribute their efforts in production through appeal to their desire to help build the new society, it could be asserted.

We may briefly consider the function and effectiveness of nonmaterial incentives in Chinese collective agriculture, beginning with the question, Why were such incentives given so much weight? Among the explanations which might be offered, one of the most important (albeit cynical, perhaps) would seem to be that they functioned as a substitute for material incentives in the exchange relationship between peasants and the state. To the extent that they worked, they were infinitely cheaper than paying the peasants in real resources. The state's commitment to guaranteeing a basic level of subsistence to all peasants could also have come into the picture here. The greater the degree of egalitarianism in the intra-community income distribution, the less total income would have to remain in rural communities in order to guarantee the subsistence of the poorest, but the more necessary it was, then, to supplement material with nonmaterial rewards. Finally, nonmaterial motivation, like egalitarianism, was favored in its own right, as something to be strengthened in the transition to a communist society. The timing of this transition to full communism was a major bone of contention between Mao and those leaders who saw transition to the prior Marxian stage of *socialism* as requiring a lengthy period of time during which economic construction should take precedence over other concerns.

How effective were nonmaterial incentives in China? In spite of the implicit assumption of the need for material incentives in most of this book, I do not suppose that nonmaterial incentives were of no efficacy whatsoever, or even that they were never adequate to the tasks assigned them in China. The important question, in my view, is one of the sustainability and self-sufficiency of such motivation. Consider the account of the experience of a village in Guangdong by Chan et al. (1984). These writers (p. 92) refer to the Dazhai workpoint system, introduced there in 1966, as a "method . . . relying on peer group pressure to get people to work as hard as they could and to cooperate as closely as possible with other members of the work unit." According to the authors, the method was initially effective.

> [D]uring the height of the Mao study campaign, the villagers' spirit of collective concern and their willingness to engage in mutual scrutiny . . . ran strong, and the Dazhai system was effective in prodding them all forward. More rice shoots survived transplanting; people stayed out after dark to finish their chores; harvests were cut more efficiently and more quickly [p. 93].

Over time, however, the system ceased to work well.

> [T]he Dazhai system depended upon a high morale among the peasants. But . . . the peasants [no] longer put any great faith in Mao's teachings that

human spirit and correct attitudes could conjure up economic miracles . . . [D]iscouraged by the collective sector's performance and prospects, the peasants were plowing more of their energies into private economic endeavors [p. 248].

What went wrong at Chen Village? The proximate cause mentioned before the last quotation was a reduction in collective earnings due to misguided investment plans and bad weather. Two other sources of lowered morale can be inferred from other parts of the narrative. They are shifting political campaigns and struggles that were exhaustingly played out at the village level, and inconsistencies at the national level, especially regarding the rise and fall from political grace of Mao's lieutenant, Lin Biao, which strained belief in the infallibility of the "Helmsman."

Generalizing from this, it appears that Chen village provides evidence that what Benjamin Ward (1967) once described as a mobilizational economic system, that is, one based upon appeals to duty and social pressure rather than individualistic responses to perceived opportunities for benefit, is possible at least in the short run. The question is whether such mobilization can be maintained for long without the appearance of policy errors, contradictions, or factional clashes that, as was the case in the Chen Village account, eventually undermine the ability of leaders to mobilize. Economic theory suggests that planning errors will tend to be made because it is difficult for the center to gather and process the necessary technical information on which to base campaigns to raise production levels. More important, perhaps, is that while errors will be made in any system, they are likely to affect more people when decisions are taken centrally. For both this and other reasons, an economic system based on dispersed material incentives may be more resistant to shocks and errors than is one based on mass appeal to public duty, in which public confidence might be shaken irreparably by a major shock or an accumulation of even modest disappointments. Finally, history suggests that social systems based on high levels of mobilization rarely last for as long as a generation, or beyond the lifetime of the founding charismatic leader. The reason may lie not only in errors and contradictions of the types already mentioned, but also in the possibility that it is the nature of human beings to prefer less intensive and psychologically less intrusive methods of being roused to work. Perhaps also the social energy required to maintain mobilization eventually sags; mobilization falls prey to the force of entropy, and people go back to working simply to feed themselves and to meet obligations arising in their immediate social networks.

Stalinism, Maoism, and the Rural Sector

From 1949 until 1978, China's overall economic strategy adhered to the standard Soviet or Stalinist pattern in many key respects. Transforming a substantially agrarian economy into an industrial one was the foremost goal; the transformation was to be achieved through administrative resource allocation largely without reference to market forces; success was to be measured in terms of output of basic industrial products such as steel; and priority was assigned to the producer goods industries. The overriding of market forces was particularly apparent in the lack of consideration given to national and regional comparative advantage, and in the capital intensity and bias toward massive plants in industry. Within this strategy, agriculture's role was to supply food and raw materials to industry; to do this at low prices while purchasing industrial products at high prices, thus helping to underwrite industrial growth; and to supply the industrial sector with additional labor, insofar as required. Since independent peasants do not tend to sell substantial surpluses to the market at administratively depressed prices, this strategy, and the role of agriculture within it, implied that the relationship of the state to the rural population would be antagonistic in some respects, and would require some coercion. Collectivization of agriculture fit into the strategy as a tool to facilitate this coercion by making it easier for the state to intervene in planting and labor deployment decisions through its control over the main units of farm production, and by helping it to enforce the involuntary delivery of produce.

These roles of collectivization require further clarification, for they leave open at least two quite different ways of construing the rationale for collectivization. The first interpretation is that collectivization facilitated state intervention in the rural economy not by acting as a means of *control,* but simply by aiding in administrative rationalization—e.g., the lowering of information costs. For example, it is in principle more efficient for the state to enforce its procurement quotas by checking up on quota fulfillment with a few hundred thousand collective farms or communes, within which a well-developed local administration would oversee participation by individual farm households, than for the state to deal individually with tens or hundreds of millions of separate household farms. The potentially greater efficiency with which new technology and inputs could be transferred to the farm sector given a group farming structure likewise fits in this rubric. What brings about rationalization, according to this interpretation, is simply the reduction of the number of units with which the state must deal; the state shrugs off the costs of transmitting information to lower levels, presumably forcing the collective units to bear them using their own resources.

The alternative, and in the author's view more plausible, interpretation is that the advantage of collectivizing agriculture lay primarily in the political domain—that is, in facilitating the projection of state power into the countryside, and the neutralization of potential opposition. Preventing the formation either of independent peasant movements or of economically based rural elites that might challenge the state's extractive policies were indeed quite effectively accomplished by eliminating individual rights in land and organizing farm households into entities that could be effectively controlled by the government and Party. By contrast, the advantages of an administrative efficiency type may be entirely imaginary, since in the absence of an underlying opposition of interest between peasants and the state, the lower level administrative bodies that were needed to facilitate crop collection or input dissemination could have been brought into being independently of whether farming was a household or a group activity. Unless there were genuine economies of scale to be found in group farming, the control rationale would thus appear to offer a better explanation of the role assigned to collectivization in the Stalinist strategy. Indeed, even if some such economies could be reaped under ideal conditions, in the context of antagonistic state-peasant relations and state intervention in the setting of collective policies and choice of collective leaders, those economies were likely to have been overwhelmed by negative disincentive and morale effects.

Finally, it should be noted that the political control advantages of collectivization dovetailed with a politico-ideological desire to achieve a social transformation of the peasantry. In agrarian societies, the independent, landholding peasant producers represented a *petit bourgeousie* unlikely to share the class interests of industrial workers as understood by Marxism; they were therefore frequently viewed by Marxists as a possible social base for a restoration of capitalism. Internally, peasant society was itself stratified, and even after a degree of equalization was achieved by land reform, differentiation by landholding, wealth, and level of reliance upon wage labor—as employer or employee—persisted and by some accounts grew.[36] If building socialism meant the replacement of existing patterns of class differentiation with a universal working class, this rural social structure had to be changed. Although turning all peasants into workers in state farms would be the most direct way of universalizing proletarian status, such a step was judged too drastic and risky for the state to undertake. Like the replacement of peasant farming by state farms, collectivization leveled rural society locally and replaced private farms with institutions of ostensibly socialistic character, easily controlled by the authorities. Unlike state farms, however, collectives caused the peasants, rather than the state, to bear agricultural risk.[37,38]

These remarks may apply to the classical Stalinist strategy implemented in the Soviet Union after 1928, but should they not be modified to take account of the differences in China's initial conditions, the choices taken by its Communist leadership, and the unique aspects of Mao Zedong's philosophy and leadership? After all, Mao's ascendance to supremacy in the Chinese Communist Party and his leadership of that Party into power in the Chinese mainland had turned upon his ability to appeal to the interests of peasants. Perceiving China's "peasant-based" revolution to be fundamentally different from the Soviet one, some observers have accepted Chinese claims that the state accorded priority to agriculture and to peasant concerns.

---

[36]See Chao (1970, p. 42).

[37]In a state farm, the peasant-worker receives a guaranteed wage, so crop fluctuations result in changing state revenues. A collective farm is expected to fulfill its state sales quotas over a wide range of crop realizations, so fluctuations affect the value of work-points but not the state's share.

[38]To be sure, the vision of social transformation went along with a genuine belief that more socially advanced forms (from the standpoint of the Marxian stage theory of history) are also technologically more progressive. The Communists' strategy for converting surplus labor into physical capital in the form of terraced fields and irrigation works, which has often been compared to the ideas of the economist Ragnar Nurkse, should also be mentioned. The advantages of the commune-style organization for mobilizing such labor while avoiding the inflationary side-effects of public works programs in other countries, are discussed by Putterman (1992a). Nurkse's views appear in Nurkse (1957); for a related discussion, see Bruton (1965).

But China's differences from the Soviet Union in these respects are easily exaggerated. Few dispute that the peasant political base of the revolution meant that the C.C.P. was better prepared than its Soviet counterpart to mobilize peasants for land reform and to capture the benefits of that program in the form of political good will. That good will, combined with grass roots organizing ability and a basic understanding of the material and organizational requirements of agricultural recovery, may have permitted local C.C.P. cadres to play a positive role in promoting the revival of Chinese agriculture in the framework of a more equal but more fragmented ownership structure during 1952–1956. Partly by continued appeal to the gift of land and the modest level of overt agricultural tax, partly by wielding the potent threat that discontent would be treated as a sign of bad class orientation, party cadres were also able to mitigate the negative economic incentive and political morale effects of the price scissors which the state turned against the peasants beginning in the 1950s, and to organize the formation of cooperatives with only limited resistance and disruption of production.

However, the basic elements of involuntary extraction of farm produce and use of the resulting surpluses to support industrialization did not differ in the Chinese and Soviet cases.[39] Mindful of the Soviet catastrophe of the early 1930s and with better channels of communication to the rural populace, China's leaders managed a step-by-step transition to collective farming through early 1956 without triggering massive resistance, large-scale slaughtering of livestock, or a general decline in output. Yet, once it became apparent that voluntarily formed lower-stage cooperatives (in which both labor and property contributions were compensated) would not readily attract most peasants, that these cooperatives displayed serious internal problems due to conflicts between the interests of property and of labor contributors, and that to press forward to the formation of "higher stage" socialist cooperatives (in which remuneration was based solely on labor) could be done only against the wishes of larger landowners and owners of draft animals and other property, Mao and supporters, over the objection of more moderate leaders, pushed through a forced collectivization on a speed and scale that made the Soviet precedent look almost glacial by comparison. Perhaps the majority of peasants stood to benefit from the acquisition of the land and property of richer neighbors without compensation by the collectives, and this may explain the lack of immediate opposition by them. The ensuing political isolation of the better-off minority of peasants rendered any opposition which that group might mount suicidal. Although the data might be questioned, the existing record suggests that production, far from falling into crisis,

---

[39]As Zweig writes: "Although China's revolution was a rural one, the policies of the Chinese Communist Party since 1949 have not been as favorable to China's farmers as one might have expected from a band of peasant revoluntionaries. . . . [T]he basic principle underlying agricultural policy has been urban industrialization at the expense of the countryside." (1990, p. 19) See, however, the argument of Oi (1989), about the distinctive normative aspects of the state-peasant relationship in China, and the central position of the concept of "surplus."

kept rising in the face of the collectivization of most Chinese villages in a single season. Be this as it may, by the end of the Great Leap Forward, much if not most of the confidence that the poor majority of peasants may have placed in the Communist Party leadership is likely to have evaporated. But under the Sixty Articles, as was the case for all intents and purposes from the formation of the higher stage cooperatives in 1956, peasants had no right to leave their collective units.[40]

The early 1960s saw the adjustment of economic strategy and the proclaimed shift in economic priorities on which the claim that China's policies were pro-peasant and pro-agriculture was thenceforth to be based. Agriculture was to be given relatively more attention, farm prices were improved, and the state invested heavily in the provision of new material inputs to agriculture, especially fertilizer. As Anthony Tang (1984) convincingly argues, however, the apparent shift from milking agriculture to support industry, to using industry in the service of agriculture, did not amount to a change of priorities in fact. Just as the Soviet Union of the 1930s found itself investing in tractor production with hopes of shoring up its agricultural sector after the massive loss of animal traction in its collectivization campaign, so China too was forced by agriculture's 1959–1961 crisis, and by the immediate and pronounced effect on the country's ability to carry out its industrialization program, to invest resources in the sector so that it might resume its role as a net contributor to industry.[41] And even if the proclaimed reordering of priorities in the early 1960s was genuine in some respects, the familiar pattern of assigning a passive and exploited role to agriculture resurfaced with great clarity following the resurgence of Mao's power from the middle of that decade.[42]

Agriculture's exploitation during periods of Maoist ascendance in China was to be seen in the extreme rates of investment in national income. According to official statistics, the share of accumulation exceeded 30% in 1958–1960, 1966, and 1970–1980 and reached as high as 43.8% in 1959 and 36.5% in 1978.[43] According to the same sources, agriculture's share of this investment averaged less than 11% for the period 1953–1978,[44] while, according to Lardy, the state earned profits not only by extracting cheap farm produce from the countryside, but also by selling manufactured inputs, sometimes involuntarily from the purchasers' standpoint, at prices

[40]In a recent attempt to explain why farm productivity rose through 1957 or 1958, yet failed to fully recover under the team system which operated between 1962 and the late 1970s, Lin (1990) contends that peasants perceived themselves as being able to withdraw from the collective farms with their previous landholdings until formation of the communes in 1958. However, this claim is inconsistent with a large body of Western scholarship, including Walker (1966), Nolan (1976), Shue (1980), and Selden (1982).

[41]According to Tang, China differed from the Soviet Union in that weak agricultural performance more immediately hurt industrial growth there, whereas with its higher per capita farm output, the Soviet economy could force most effects of poor harvests to be absorbed by the farm population without affecting state purchase levels and hence without severely impacting upon industrial growth.

[42]The notion that "pragmatists" Liu Shaoqi and Deng Xiaoping were significantly more pro-agriculture than was Mao also seems largely belied by the record of the Deng regime from late 1978, as will be seen below.

[43]China Statistical Yearbook (1988, p. 50).

[44]Reported in Dernberger (1989, Table 10).

providing high profit margins. Beyond this, Lardy shows (as mentioned earlier) that Mao's insistence on local self-sufficiency in grain imposed high costs on much of the countryside. Finally, the fact that China unlike the Soviet Union found itself unable to absorb any significant number of rural migrants in industrial employment, and therefore stemmed the flow of migration by erecting administrative barriers, permitted a large income gap between city and countryside to persist with little hope of exit for the disadvantaged rural dwellers. Indeed, mobility even within the countryside was extremely difficult, so that birth in a poor locality meant more or less permanent confinement to it.

Of course, the imposition of these grim realities upon China's peasantry can be understood without inconsistency as having been conceived by China's leaders not as exploitation but as sacrifice required to build a prosperous and classless future society. Sacrifices demanded of rural dwellers were perhaps little greater, *relative to* their prerevolutionary status, than were those expected of the urban population, including cadres. In this connection, it may be suggested that while the differences between Soviet and Chinese agricultural policies were not great at the level of practice, there were a host of differences at the level of ideology, style of implementation, and articulated objectives. In particular, Maoism gave far greater emphasis to the "subjective" purpose of collectivization, which was not merely to create a classless society, but to serve as midwife to the birth of a "new socialist man." This thrust of Maoism complemented, and was in turn complemented by, a greater emphasis on egalitarianism and on the struggle against individualism, materialism, and bureaucracy. All of this required far stronger, and one is led to believe sometimes more successful, efforts to indoctrinate peasants. Finally, Mao's vision included bows in the direction of classical Marxian (and utopian) notions of the elimination of differences between city and countryside, and between mental and manual labor— notions that contributed to efforts to support rural industrialization, both during the Great Leap Forward (of "backyard furnace" infamy) and the Cultural Revolution (when the sector thrived in at least a significant minority of localities). The sending down of educated urbanites to the countryside also fit under this heading, although more direct motives were provided both by China's urban job creation problems and by Mao's political struggles with intellectuals.

A fair evaluation also requires one to recall that by no means were all of the realities of Chinese rural development under the Maoist model grim ones. On the contrary, one has only to compare again Chinese statistics on hunger, disease, and mortality with those of other poor developing countries, such as India, Indonesia, or Bangladesh, to see why China's 1970s claims about offering a superior model of rural development commanded serious attention from foreign observers. Even if Communist beliefs in the superiority of collective farming as such represented at best self-delusion and at worst deliberate deception of the rural population with the goal of imposing the forms of political control that have been referred to in this section, it could nonetheless be argued that the three-tier commune system contributed in quite positive ways to the provision of basic health care and education, to the popularization of better sanitation practices, to greater food-security for those who would likely have been poor and landless peasants in a nonsocialist society at a similar level of development, and to the utilization of off-season labor for farm capital construction and nonfarm activities. From an ethical standpoint, the relevant question is whether these gains, especially by the poor, were worth the sacrifice (assuming there was one) in terms of the rate of economic growth, the lower living standard of those peasants who would otherwise have been better off, and the loss of freedom for peasants in general. From a positive as well as an ethical standpoint, one may also ask how much greater the gains might have been, and how much smaller the sacrifice, in a less extractive national policy setting. No definitive answers can be given to this last question, since rather than simply changing the environment within which the collective farm system of the Mao era operated, the reforms that began in the late-1970s also changed many of its institutional premises.

Post-Mao Reform

Although Mao's most powerful leftist followers were arrested and eliminated from the political scene within weeks of his death, his chosen successor, Hua Guofang, perpetuated the Dazhai model of collectivism and moral incentives. The number of villages practicing brigade as opposed to team level accounting, a policy favored by the leftists as a step toward full socialism and communism, may in fact have risen more rapidly during 1976–1978 than in any previous period since 1962.[45] However, following the political rehabilitation of Deng Xiaoping and his decisive capture of political power in late 1978, these policies began to be reversed. Whereas Hua, in line with his import-intensive technological approach to China' economic problems, had hoped to speed both modernization and socialization by rapid mechanization of agriculture, Deng realized the financial and manpower constraints on China's absorption of new technology. Like Mao in the 1950s, he turned to organizational change as the key to boosting agricultural performance. This time, though, the change amounted to a reversal of course that the Chairman would hardly have countenanced.

To say that the Deng leadership chose organizational change as its main strategy for speeding rural development does not mean that Deng had in mind starving agriculture of material resources. The government was to continue its emphasis on increasing supplies of fertilizer; moreover, it declared its intention to markedly raise agriculture's share of state investment outlays. What was new about Deng's policy, however, was its plan to alter institutions and prices so as to provide more individual material incentives to China's farmers.

In some respects, the changes introduced by Deng in late 1978 were quite similar

----

[45]Zweig (1985).

to those promoted by Liu Shaoqi and Deng in the early 1960s: more attractive state agricultural prices and bonuses for overfulfillment of quotas, greater allowance for private plots and sideline production and for the operation of rural free markets, and more emphasis on individual material incentives within the context of team production. With Mao now dead and respectfully entombed beside Tiananmen Square,[46] however, the compromise approach of the Sixty Articles was no longer binding. While micro-organizational change after 1978 thus began with a shift toward smaller work groups and closer links between output and pay, approaches also favored in the early 1960s, the reforms soon progressed to the wholesale liquidation of group production modes, and to the restoration of households to their former status as China's nearly universal units of farm production.

The precise timing and other details of these reforms have been recorded elsewhere[47] and will be only briefly summarized here. Reform began with adjustment of state procurement prices. In 1979, the base procurement prices for grains were raised an average of roughly 21%, while the premium for sales in excess of base quotas was raised from 30% above to 50% above the base price, or to an average of 39.5% above the previous premium price.[48] Quota (above-quota) prices for cotton, soybeans, peanuts, rapeseed, sugar cane, sugar beets, tobacco, and live hogs also rose by an average of 16.2% (41.5%).[49] With quota obligations reduced in some poorer areas, and with their levels staying relatively constant in absolute terms while output and sales rose, average payments for sales to the state continued to rise through 1984 even for crops such as grain for which there were no further changes in the price structure. Other crops, including soybeans and cotton, enjoyed further price increases in 1980 and 1981.

Simultaneously, the farm sector benefited from other measures. The lifting of many restrictions on sales in rural free markets, permission for peasants to sell surplus output in nearby cities, and elimination of procurement quotas on many nonstaple crops raised the profitability especially of nonstaple crops and animal husbandry, and meant that the state itself had to offer farmers something close to the higher market prices in order to obtain nonquota and above-quota products.[50] Whereas peasant

---

[46]In the 1960s, Mao had complained of being "treated like an ancestor" after the debacle of the Great Leap. This time, his former comrades could assure themselves that the Chairman would not complain at such treatment, and his remaining supporters proved unable to use his name to effectively block change.

[47]See, *inter alia,* Travers (1984), Nolan (1983, 1988), and the special issue of *China Quarterly,* December 1988, especially Ash.

[48]These figures are based upon unweighted averaging of prices for indica and japonica rice, wheat, and corn, China's most important grain crops, assuming the indica and japonica prices to be identical in 1978. For the data used in these calculations, see Sicular (1988a, Tables 2 and 3).

[49]Calculated from Table 4 in Sicular (1991). The figure for the increase in the quota price is obtained using an unweighted average over the prices of nine commodities, which are cotton in north and south China (counted separately) plus the other seven mentioned in the text. The figure for the increase in the above-quota price is obtained with an unweighted average over the prices of six commodities, which are those mentioned above minus sugar cane, sugar beets, and live hogs.

[50]Note, however, that many "above-quota" sales were actually covered by quotas of their own, which were more or less mandatory. Most sales in excess of these amounts took-place at so-called "discussion" or "negotiated" prices, close to those in the free market.

households had experienced restrictions on the scope of private activities in earlier years, these began rapidly to evaporate now, and free markets came alive in both countryside and cities, paying an especially rich dividend to the government in the form of a bounty of fresh produce for an urban populace that for too long had been provided with only small allowances of meat and stale cabbage to accompany their grain rations. Increased consumer goods production by the industrial sector in turn led to greater availability of those goods in the countryside, which stimulated peasants' appetites for cash. Pressure on teams to plant multiple crops of grain and to desist from the planting of more profitable crops were also eased somewhat, leading to reductions of the grain sown area by 0.9% in 1979, 1.9% in 1980, and 1.0% in 1981. This permitted increases of 6.6%, 46.8%, 12.2%, and 4.4% in areas planted to cotton, oil seeds, sugar cane and beets, and vegetables, among other crops.[51]

With respect to farm organization, change initially focused on the raising of limits on the area which could be allocated to private plots from around 7% to 15% of cultivated area,[52] and on attempts to improve individuals' work incentives by switching from time to piece or task rates where possible, restoring teams as production units where brigades had assumed that function, and promoting smaller teams and workgroups whose material rewards could be tied to group results. Experiments with contracting farm responsibility to individual households, which were to sweep the country in 1982 and 1983, were originally limited to a few areas such as parts of Anhui province (a leader in the aborted shift to household contracting in the early 1960s), and were not formally sanctioned by the government in Beijing.

Viewed against the backdrop of slow agricultural growth in the previous two decades, the initial results of these reforms were spectacular. Despite reduced area, grain output rose by 9% in 1979. Although output slipped slightly in 1980 and 1981, output per capita stood at .325 tons in the latter year, nearly 8% above the 1957 level of .302 tons. The increase implied a nearly 12% increase in output per sown hectare between 1978 and 1981.[53] Output of other crops and of animal husbandry products rose by even larger margins. For example, cotton output rose by 36.8%, combined output of oil seeds rose by 90.9%, and output of sugar cane and sugar beets rose by 51.3%, while land devoted to these crops grew less than proportionately thanks to a 28% increase in cotton yields, a 27% increase in oil seed yields, and 79% and 40% increases in sugar beet and sugar cane yields, respectively. Moreover, output of rural industry and of services such as transportation and commerce increased still more rapidly. While the gross value of crop output as a whole rose by 43% in terms of 1970 constant prices, animal husbandry output rose by 86%,[54] and the output value of

[51]Based on Tables 3, 6, and 13 in Walker (1988), and Table 7 in Coady et al. (1990).
[52]Kojima (1988, pp. 707 and 711). The same article is a good source on the organizational reforms in Chinese agriculture as a whole.
[53]The yield figure for the latter year was already attained in 1979, followed by a drop in 1980 and recovery in 1981. Hence, the gains here are arguably attributable in their entirety to the parts of the reform package introduced in 1979, which emphasized price, marketing, and crop-planning but entailed movement away from collective farming in a few localities only.
[54]Field (1988, Table A.2).

commune and brigade enterprises rose by 51%, including a 50% increase in industrial output and a 102% increase in the output of commune and brigade construction enterprises.[55] The average income of China's peasants rose more rapidly still, benefiting not only from higher output but also from at least a short-term improvement in the terms of trade between agriculture and industry. Per capita peasant income in current prices rose by 67% during 1978–1981, while a constant price estimate for the same period puts the real increase at 38%, for a rate of 11.4% per year.[56]

Returning to organization, the production responsibility systems evolved to full household farming and residual claimancy by the end of 1983 by routes too varied and—taking the long view—unimportant to deserve detailed discussion here.[57] The main outlines of the transition can be seen in two dimensions: that of distribution and residual claimancy, and that of the size of the contracting group. With respect to the first dimension, the contract form evolved from one of production by the team with distribution to the household or individuals based on indicators of work input and need, to one of production by subgroups within the team, with distribution based upon the actual output achieved. In this respect, preliminary or intermediate forms involved the awarding of additional work-points, units of product, or cash for production in excess of internally established targets, while the final, more radical form involved retention of the whole product by the producing subgroup, after payment of a fixed amount to the team—which means abandonment of the team's role as a basic unit of distribution, as well as that as a unit of production. With respect to the second dimension, the size and character of the subgroups in question, these at first consisted of several households or workers, but then evolved to be the households as such—a form scrupulously avoided when the transition began.

Lumping together as intermediate forms all those in which the team retained its primary distributive role and/or in which contractees were units other than households, it can be recorded that by the end of 1981, approximately 37% of the production teams in China had adopted intermediate forms of responsibility system, 38% had adopted full household contracting (Chinese: *baogan daohu*), and the remainder continued to operate under the old system.[58] The share of teams practicing each system was not equally distributed among regions, however. Poorer regions were allowed or even encouraged to adopt more radical forms of responsibility system long before more advanced ones, and this is reflected by the fact that in 1981, the adoption rate for intermediate forms and *baogan daohu* combined was negligible

[55]State Statistical Bureau (1988, p. 258).

[56]The current income estimate is from the State Statistical Bureau large-scale annual rural income sample surveys, reported in Kueh (1978, Table 2), and Travers (1984, Table 1). The constant income estimate is from Travers, Table 3, and includes adjustments which if applied to the estimated growth rate of current income would reduce that estimate from 67% to 53%.

[57]But see Hartford (1985), Watson (1983), Griffin (1984), and Tsou et al. (1982).

[58]Kueh (1985, p. 125). It might be noted that even where teams continued to formally operate as production and primary distribution units, so that "decollectivization" could not yet be said to have begun, households might be given responsibility for some operations, as we will see in Chapter 3 in the case of the system called *jiti gengzhong fenhu guanli* practiced in some Dahe township brigades as early as 1976.

in Beijing, Heilongjiang, and Shanghai, below 10% in Tianjin, Liaoning, Jilin, and Jiangsu, but above 50% in Fujian, Henan, and Guangxi and above 80% in Anhui, Guizhou, and Gansu.[59]

While perhaps secretly approved by pro-reform leaders such as Deng, early trials of the intermediate and advanced responsibility systems were either explicitly disapproved by the leadership as a collectivity, or were agreed to with seeming reluctance. In 1982, however, the movement rapidly gathered speed and legitimacy. That year began with the C.C.P. Central Committee's Document No. 1 declaring agricultural contracting to households (both *baochan* and *baogan daohu*) to be consistent with socialism, and it ended with the share of teams practicing intermediate and radical responsibility systems reaching about 22% and 70%, respectively, for China as a whole.[60] Even teams in Jiangsu province, with one of the largest concentrations of economically advanced communes, reached 38% adoption by the end of 1982. The year of consolidation was 1983, with the adoption rate for *baogan daohu* reaching at least 94% nationally by December, at which point another 5% were reportedly practicing some other form of household contracting system.[61] Rather than lagging behind changes taking place in the provinces, the central government now appeared to be leading the way, and there were reported to be cases of local resistance to reform being overcome by pressures from above.[62]

Spurred by still-rising average procurement prices, by high market and state "discussion" prices (the latter being prices at which the government purchased grain from farmers beyond quota obligations), by increased input supplies at relatively fixed prices, and by the organizational reforms just discussed, strong agricultural growth continued through 1984. Total grain production grew by 9% in both 1982 and 1983, and by 5% in 1984, despite a further drop of about 0.6% in the area sown to grain. Moreover, the proportion of grain output that was sold rather than consumed or otherwise retained by the producers had risen from 20% in 1978 to 24% in 1981 and continued to rise, reaching 35% in 1984. (Minus resales in the countryside, the numbers become 14%, 15%, and 23%, respectively.) Thus, the self-sufficient orientation of Chinese farming began to give way to a more commercial stance. Production of other crops also rose. By 1984, cotton output had soared by 111% over its 1981 level, with sown area increasing by 34% and yields by 58%. Despite a 5% drop in sown area, output of oilseed crops rose by 16.7% in the same period, with a 23% improvement in yields. Sugar cane and sugar beet output rose by a total of 33%, with a 25% increase in sown area and with 13% and 1% increases in yields, respectively. With rising crop output being sold at higher prices, added to rapid increases in income from other sources, rural household incomes continued their rapid growth from Y 223 per capita in 1981 to Y 355 per capita in 1984. Deflating by

[59]Based on the data provided by Justin Lin which are used in the studies by Lin that are reviewed in Chapter 7.
   [60]Kueh (1985, p. 125).
   [61]Kueh (1985).
   [62]Unger (1985).

China's general retail price index, this gives a growth rate of 14.3% per annum for that 3-year period, contributing to a 14.5% rate for 1978–1984 as a whole.[63]

The Extent and Causes of Productivity Growth

An important question raised by the reforms of 1979–1983, and by the strong response of Chinese agriculture to them, concerns the degree to which the transition from team to household farming, and the more direct incentives thought to face farmers in the latter units, is responsible for the results attained. The interpretation frequently offered by the foreign press and by Chinese and Western economists is that since growth rates accelerated dramatically in 1979 after more than 20 years of collective agriculture, decollectivization, or the restoration of "private production incentives," must bear primary responsibility. One problem with this approach is that it neglects the fact that inputs as well as outputs rose in the post-Mao period. A change in policies or institutions can be said to have acted as a source of growth in its own right only if it caused output to grow more rapidly than would be implied by the growth of inputs, or if that change was itself responsible for the discovery or drawing forth of previously untapped inputs.

With respect to crop production, Stone (1988), who surveys developments in agricultural technology in the post-Mao period, argues that "yield growth for staple crops . . . was already accelerating prior to 1978 (p. 818)." He attributes this growth to the spread of improved plant varieties, improved water control, and growth in supplies of chemical fertilizers. The first two factors he argues, were continuations of Mao-era trends, while the last was due to production from large-scale synthetic fertilizer complexes, expansion and improvement of smaller fertilizer plants, and rapid growth of imports. According to official statistics, total chemical fertilizer consumption, which grew by 55.3% annually between 1962 and 1968, then slowed to a growth rate of 1.9% per year between 1968 and 1979, accelerated its growth to a rate of 9.9% per year between 1979 and 1984.[64] As Stone points out, however, the capital construction investments for the large plants that produced much of the new output "were entirely undertaken during the Maoist period"—indeed, there was a "lapse in . . . investment from the later part of the 1970s (p. 820)" which was "accentuated in the early 1980s" (p. 810)—while growth of the small plant sector was also "a highly identifiable development of [that period] (p. 820)." This leaves only import growth as the result of post-Mao decisions.[65] By the early 1980s, imports accounted

---

[63]The rate for 1979–1984 works out to 14.0%. The Y 355 figure for 1984 translates into Y 334 in constant prices of 1981, using the same deflator.

[64]State Statistical Bureau (1988, p. 197); this source indicates that the figures are calculated "on the basis of 100% effectiveness."

[65]In fact, roughly the same quantity of fertilizer was imported in 1980 as in 1970, but its share of total supply was far larger in the earlier year. The "post-Mao development" was not the initiation of imports as such, but the decision to allow new growth in the level of imports after stagnation and mild decline in the mid-1970s.

for only about 7% of total fertilizer use by weight, and their contribution to the increased supply of fertilizer was of the same order of magnitude.[66]

Other modern farm inputs also showed healthy growth, although in some cases it is difficult to know what share of an input's supply was used for crop production. Between 1978 and 1988, the total horsepower of agricultural machinery is reported to have increased at an annual rate of 8.8%, the number of large and medium-size tractors by 7.4% per year, the number of small and "walking" tractors by 15.7% per year, the number of combine harvesters by 11.2% per year, and the number of "trucks for agricultural use" by 29.6% per year.[67] The generating capacity of small rural hydropower stations reportedly increased by 5.5% annually between 1979 and 1984, while total rural electricity consumption grew at 10.4% per year in the same period.[68] On the other hand, the total cultivated area fell from 99.5 million ha in 1979 to 96.9 million ha in 1984, according to these statistics, so that the rate of decline accelerated from 0.22% per year during 1962–1979 to 0.54% per year during 1979–1984. The irrigated area, and the percentage of the latter that was irrigated by power-operated equipment, stayed essentially unchanged,[69] while the number of tubewells and the combined wattage of motors for agricultural drainage and irrigation rose at annual rates of 2.5% and 3.1%, respectively, between 1978 and 1984, and the multiple cropping index declined from 151.0 in 1978 to 146.4 in 1983. The number of workers in the agricultural sector, defined as farming, animal husbandry, fishery, forestry, and farm sidelines, is reported to have grown by 31.5 million between 1978 and 1984, or at an annual rate of 1.8%, compared with a 2.6% growth rate for the number of rural workers as a whole. The growth rate for workers in the crop sector per se was almost certainly slower, and perhaps even negative, with available figures indicating an absolute decline between 1983 and 1985.[70]

With some inputs growing rapidly, others slowly, and still others declining, a determination of whether output grew more rapidly than inputs in the aggregate requires one to have a scheme for weighting the different inputs. The standard method is the use of output elasticities taken from production function estimates. This addresses one problem, but leaves others unresolved. For example, qualitative information on inputs (e.g., labor time and intensity, nutrient content of fertilizer, effectively irrigated area, adoption of improved seeds) is generally imprecise or unavailable in accessible forms. Production relationships estimated at highly aggregated levels, such as provinces, and for aggregated output concepts, such as the gross

---

[66]Stone (1990), writes: "Rapid growth in staple crop production during the late 1970s and 1980s has been primarily a process of cashing in on the fruits of investments in technical change undertaken since the 1950s, by relieving the final constraint to their full realization—insufficient availability of soil nitrogen. With the rapid removal of this final obstacle . . . yield growth, calculated in terms of national averages, accelerated to high and unsustainable rates, and then inevitably slowed down."

[67]State Statistical Bureau (1988, p. 189).

[68]State Statistical Bureau (1988, p. 197).

[69]A detailed discussion is provided by Stone, who finds that much of the decline apparent in published statistics is due to the correction of earlier overstatements.

[70]Taylor (1988, p. 755).

value of crop output, raise interpretive problems given the likely heterogeneity of technical relations within and across units, as well as the absence of prices reflective of underlying scarcities.

In addition to the need to account for both input and output growth, another problem with assuming that the post-1978 rural growth spurt resulted from farm decollectivization is that both the policies of the 1960s and 1970s, and the reforms beginning in late 1978 came in "bundles," including directives on the form of farm production organization and (in the case of collectives) internal distribution rules, and decisions on prices, cropping plans, and marketing restrictions. This "bundling" feature makes it difficult to know which part of each package—assuming the packages to be at least potentially decomposable—should be held responsible for which results.

While it will never be possible to resolve these problems in a fully satisfactory way, the sequencing and the geographic variation of policy change in the reform period do permit some exploratory exercises to be performed. The most sophisticated of these exercises involve the estimation of production functions and/or of technical efficiency parameters, using available information on both outputs and inputs. Efforts to disentangle the effects of different parts of the post-1978 reform package on Chinese agriculture are discussed at length in Chapter 7.

Other Consequences of Reform

Aside from the immediate rise in farm and nonfarm production in the rural areas, the rural economic reforms had numerous other consequences, intended and unintended. Although the number of large and small tractors in use continued to rise, as just mentioned, the tractor-plowed area fell from 42.2 million ha in 1979 to 34.9 million in 1984, a trend widely believed to have resulted from the reduced ease of tractor use in the smaller household as opposed to team-run farm plots. (The demand for the tractors is largely explained by their use in providing nonagricultural transport services, such as transportation of building materials.) The constancy of the irrigated area and of the share of that area irrigated using power equipment were also seen as indicating or at least coinciding with a weakening of the mechanisms for mobilizing labor and financial resources for rural capital construction and maintenance work, which had been a much-remarked strength of the commune system. Concerns were voiced that the agricultural boom of 1978–1984 would be short-lived as the farm capital built up over previous decades began to be run down through neglect and nonreplacement. With respect to the role of the state, the intended increase in agriculture's share of state investment funds, to which the government had committed itself in 1978, failed to materialize. With agriculture responding so smartly to policy changes, including the higher prices which were paid to farmers without being passed on to urban consumers, the government appeared to decide that its limited funds were more badly needed elsewhere, and state agricultural investment fell from an average of Y 4.9 billion in 1976–1980 to only Y 3.7 billion in 1984, or from 10.5% to 5% of overall state investment in agriculture and industry.

There was, to be sure, the hope that China's increasingly prosperous farmers would raise their individual levels of savings and investment to make up the shortfall. But aside from the problem that individual investment would not compensate for collective and public investments in larger projects, due to their public goods nature, private farm investment proved disappointing for two reasons. First, a large proportion of farmers' new savings went not into productive assets but into home construction, which enjoyed a boom on a scale probably unparalleled in all human history in terms of total square feet of housing.[71] Second, with relative returns substantially higher in animal husbandry and in such nonagricultural pursuits as construction and transportation, much of the private investment in productive assets that did take place did not go to farming. A related concern here was that farmers would skimp on investments in the land they farmed, including applications of organic fertilizer having long-term effects on soil fertility, because of uncertainty of tenure rights.

In its initial phases, the household production responsibility system often entailed giving households responsibility for working a specific plot of land for a portion of the production cycle only. As more radical forms were adopted, household obligations and use rights extended first to a full year, then to 3 or 4 years, and then, in the center's Document No. 1 of 1984, to a 15-year period. Longer periods were permitted for control of privately reclaimed wasteland, and use rights could be passed on to children within the period of their effective duration. This evolution from shorter to longer duration of use rights was an explicit response to concern about incentives to invest in and maintain land given a system of individual use and collective ownership, but the idea that full private ownership rights should be granted to the operators also began to be discussed. At the same time, there were debates about the proper system for assigning land to households, and concerns were aired about the scale of farm operations and the excessive scattering of plots seemingly required to reduce household risk in the absence of the automatic pooling of the collective system.[72]

Questions also began to be raised about the social impacts of decollectivization. The commune system had played a role in providing basic health services and education in the countryside. In some villages in which collective organization had been relatively weak, the abandonment of collective farming meant the disappearance of collectively provided services, including health clinics. Where these services had been of poor quality anyway, and where private incomes rose sufficiently to allow villagers to purchase substitutes from private practitioners, this may have

---

[71]See Lardy (1986).

[72]According to one estimate, each household farmed an average of over nine parcels in the mid-1980s. Land tenure issues are discussed at greater length in Chapter 9.

caused no harm. Where collective services had been strong and were maintained, there may also have been gains in terms of either improved services or the added choice of private alternatives. In some areas, however, services seem to have declined, and reports surfaced of reversals in long-term trends of decline in mortality rates.[73] With regard to education, the major change was that the opportunity cost of keeping children in school rose with the lifting of restrictions on a wide range of private income-earning activities, as a result of which school enrollments were reported to have dropped in many rural areas.[74] In more economically advanced areas, on the other hand, the returns to education rose more rapidly than the opportunity costs, in the reform period, causing an increase in the demand for education which could be better funded there out of local resources.

A much debated aspect of the impact of China's rural reforms was its effect on population. The one type of growth that the country's leaders wanted least, as the country moved into the 1980s, was growth in population, which was seen as undercutting the effects of output growth on the standard of living, and even as posing a threat to China's ability to ever achieve developed economic status.[75] The same leadership which put the country on the path of economic liberalization after 1978 thus also embarked on the strictest population control program in history, the one-child family policy under which couples were to be penalized for and in some cases simply prevented from having more than one child. The family size targeted by this policy was far less closely approached in rural than in urban areas, and an often asked question was whether the economic liberalization program was not in some respects in conflict with China's population goals. The liberalization had, as just noted in the discussion of education, raised the immediate economic value of children to their parents. The cost of raising a child had also gone up with the elimination of rations based on household size and the refusal to adjust land allotments with the addition of extra children; but with higher incomes, families would be better able to

---

[73] A useful recent review is provided by Hussain and Stern (1990). These authors note that "[o]n the eve of the rural reforms in 1979," China's "much admired rural health insurance system" covered "about 85% of the rural population," although coverage varied between richer and poorer areas. "[B]y 1985, the cooperative health insurance survived in a mere 5% of villages or brigades (p. 17)." They also cite both official and reconstructed figures showing a mild rise in China's crude death rate and infant mortality rate beginning 1978 or 1979, and declining numbers of part-time rural health care workers and rural hospitals and hospital beds. However, they conclude that over two-thirds of the increase in the crude death rate can be explained by the aging of China's population (p. 24), and that "[a]ny attribution of rising age-specific mortality rates to the reforms would have to await more careful research (p. 25)."

[74] Following Davis (1989, pp. 582 and 587), Selden (1992) reports that "primary school enrollments dropped from 151 million in 1975 to 128 million in 1987; junior high school enrollments dropped from 50 million to 42 million, and high school enrollments from 18 to 8 million. The decline was almost entirely a rural phenomenon."

[75] The latter view was based on calculations by Chinese demographers concerning the optimal ratio of population to fixed resources. As the one-child family policy intensified, these experts put forward the notion that the optimal population was 650–700 million, and they projected that persistent application of the policy would cause the country's population to peak at around 1,200 million in the early part of the 21st century and to then decline toward the desired 700 million, which would be achieved in 2080 (after which reproduction at replacement rates could be resumed). See *Beijing Review*, April 13, 1981.

afford these costs. While, under the reforms, women were more drawn into remunerative activity and stood to lose more from the time lost in childbearing and child-care, such losses may have been rather minimal, for many jobs pursued by rural women allowed considerable flexibility in work schedule, and most extended families had members who could take on child-care responsibilities with little or no cost in foregone earnings.

A consideration raised by some observers was that the loss of collective social security previously accorded by the communes and their subunits may have raised the demand for children as a form of old-age insurance. This hypothesis may be based on largely false premises, however. Because most communes had been able to offer so little in the way of old-age support, and because the need for such support carried so great a stigma to the recipient, this factor may not have been of much if any consequence. Another question is whether the economic independence which households gained from the reforms had seriously reduced rural cadres' abilities to implement the Party's population policies through appropriate rewards and penalties. There may be some basis for this concern, but by in large, the tools still at the disposal of rural cadres in implementing the one-child family policy were numerous, including the right to allocate land, to assign procurement targets and contracts, to contract out resources such as orchards and fishponds, to distribute subsidized inputs and access to credit, and so forth. Indeed, the question reveals naïveté regarding the degree to which cadre power and presence had declined in rural China following economic reform, although a caution here is that there appears to have been significant variation among localities.[76]

Even though from a narrow standpoint the Party and government did have fairly powerful tools of enforcement at their command, by the mid-1980s they appear to have softened their stance on the fertility issue, for all intents and purposes accepting something resembling a two-child norm in the countryside. Only part of the explanation for this retreat seems likely to lie in the international outcry at tales of forced late-term abortions, rising female infanticides, and the like. Probably more important was that fierce resistance to the stricter form of the policy by peasants raised its costs to unacceptable levels in the Party's eyes. The main connection between economic liberalization and the softening of the one-child family policy may not have been that the liberalization made the policy unenforceable with the available tools, but rather that China's leaders did not have the stomach to see the good will created in the countryside by their economic policies being totally negated by the anger of tens of millions of son-less farmers.

A final social policy issue meriting brief discussion here (but to which we will devote the entirety of Chapter 10) is the subject of changes in income distribution and inequality. As is well known, China's reform leaders took what appears to outsiders

---

[76]Accounts emphasizing the continuing power of rural cadres include Oi (1986a, 1990), Crook (1990), and Christiansen (1992).

as a surprising step for a Communist Party, adopting the slogan "Fight Egalitarianism" as a rallying cry of reform. In Chapter 10 we will examine a body of local evidence indicating that equality of incomes among households, production teams, and villages was in fact lessened by the reforms, a principal cause being occupational variation across households and increasing variation in the returns to those occupations. As Chapter 2 will show, on the other hand, equality of living standards across rural areas, such as provinces and counties, was never particularly great in China, and indications are that inequality has increased at these levels also. The reasons include the large differences in opportunities for economic diversification and structural change among regions. Villages and townships near cities and on major transportation routes advanced at a faster pace than more remote villages and townships, due to the opportunities to engage in transport, construction, and commerce with rural and urban customers, to enter industrial subcontracts with urban enterprises, and to obtain information about new marketing opportunities in their regions and even overseas.

Entire regions such as the Yangze and the Pearl River deltas benefited from the advantages of existing industrial infrastructure, abundance of technical skills, and dense local markets, or from the proximity of foreign investors and international trading centers. While basically acceptable to China's leaders as part of a process of economic development that they hoped would gradually spread to other parts of the country, the disparities had some undesired consequences, including substantial interregional migration of temporary labor, and urban resentment of rich "suburban" entrepreneurs. A final, contrasting point deserving of some emphasis is that within localities, the ideology of egalitarianism showed strong staying power, and egalitarian constraints appeared operative with respect to a wide array of policies including the distribution of scarce village and township enterprise jobs, distribution of land use rights and inputs, and the strong-arming applied to successful local entrepreneurs to bring them to underwrite construction of schools, clinics, and other social services.

The "Second-Stage" Reform

The events of the second half of China's first reform decade are not only of interest in their own right, but also help to shed light on the character of the gains achieved during the first 6 years. In 1985, following a bumper harvest, record state outlays to purchase above-quota grain, and strains on state grain storage and transportation capabilities, the government radically changed its grain purchasing policies to guarantee purchase of only a fixed amount of crop at a unified price representing a weighted average of earlier above- and below-quota prices.[77] This step fundamentally changed the incentives facing farmers, since it not only reduced the price on the last unit sold to the government, but also caused the true marginal price of grain to

---

[77]This followed similar changes with respect to the purchase of oilseed crops in 1983 and cotton in 1984. See Sicular (1991).

become the more unpredictable market price, which in 1984 had just equaled the state above-quota price on average, and even fell below that price in some localities and seasons. While reformers expressed the hope that the change would facilitate the full commercialization of agriculture, which they proclaimed to be the task of the "second stage" of rural reform, the results were (predictably, in fact) a step away from, not toward, commercialization of trade in the most important food grains.[78] Grain cultivated area, production, and marketing dropped sharply in 1985, many peasants evaded contract sales obligations, and in early 1986, the government had to admit that grain contracts were not strictly voluntary commercial arrangements but were obligations—which means that they were little else than procurement quotas under a new name.[79] Whereas early in 1985, the previous year's surfeit of output kept market prices for grain below the new state contract price and some local units lobbied for the right to sell more grain to the government,[80] by the end of the year, the substantially reduced output (reflecting peasant expectations of continuing low prices) was causing market prices to shoot upward once again. The gap between them and state contract prices was to continue growing, for the most part, through 1989.

Despite upward revisions of contract prices by an average of about 5.2% in 1986, 2.5% in 1987, and 1.3% in 1988,[81] and despite reductions in contract purchases and substitution for these of "negotiated price" purchases at an average of 24% above contract prices,[82] grain production stagnated, returning to its 1984 absolute level again only in 1989, by which time the intervening rise in population meant that further growth would have been needed to match the previous level in per capita terms. Whereas in 1984 one could compare a grain output growth rate of nearly 5% per annum with the 2.5% rate for 1952–1978 and reach glowing conclusions about China's agricultural reforms, the longer-term rate for 1978–1988 was only 2.6%, little different from that for the pre-reform era.

[78]Some objectives of the second stage reform were, however, achieved with respect to other crops, such as vegetables, fruits, and some of the more minor grains. See Sicular (1991).

[79]This reality seems ultimately to have led to a reverse change of terms, from *liangshi hutong dinggou* (contract grain purchase) in 1985 to *guojia dinggou* (state quota purchase) toward the end of 1990.

[80]Oi (1986b).

[81]These calculations use unweighted averages of the prices of indica rice, japonica rice, wheat, corn, and soybeans, as reported by Sicular (1988b, Tables 2 and 3). The 1987 and 1988 soybeans prices, not reported there, are assumed equal to 1986 prices. Where multiple prices for a single grain are reported, the simple average is used.

[82]Webb (1991) uses the following data to calculate producer and consumer price subsidy equivalents: (a) the ratio of negotiated to contract price averaged 1.25 in 1985, 1.29 in 1986, 1.16 in 1987, and 1.27 in 1988; (b) contract grain procurement fell from 59.61 million metric tons in 1985 to 50 million metric tons (trade grade) in 1988; (c) the share of negotiated price procurements in total procurements (including contract and negotiated price purchases and agricultural tax paid in kind) rose from 24.8% in 1985 to 47.2% in 1988. (Background data transmitted in personal communication.) Whereas the volume of contract purchases in 1985 was close to the average of total quota and above-quota price purchases in 1982 and 1983, these purchases came to fulfill less and less of the state's purchasing objectives, and the ratio of "negotiated" to "contract" price purchases crept upward after 1985 much as had the ratio of "above-quota" to "quota" price purchases earlier in the 1980s. One may reasonably wonder whether at least some "negotiated" price purchases were no more voluntary than had been many "above-quota" purchases, for which sales quotas had in fact existed before 1985.

It would be a mistake, to be sure, to equate grain with crop production more broadly. Many crops continued to do well after 1984. Oil-bearing crops, including peanuts, rapeseed, and sesame, exceeded their record 1984 output level by over 32% in 1985, and although unable to repeat that performance, nonetheless averaged nearly 21% above the 1984 level during the half decade from 1985 to 1989. Similarly, sugar cane production exceeded its 1984 record by over 30% in 1985, and by an average of 25% during 1985–1989 as a whole. Silkworm cocoons, tea, tobacco, and fruit production all grew more or less steadily through 1989, registering gains of 37%, 29%, 56%, and 86%, respectively, in 1989 as compared with 1984. Among the major crops only cotton, next to grain the most important target of state procurement, did poorly in the second half of the 1980s. After exceeding the record output of 1983 by 35% in 1984, it dropped below the 1983 level in 1985 and failed to recover that level in the remainder of the decade. Cotton output averaged slightly less in the second than in the first half of the 1980s.

Justifiably or not, however, the decline of grain production triggered a sense of agricultural crisis in Beijing. And the inability or unwillingness of China's leaders to respond to the problem by further movement toward the use of price signals stood as testimony both to the incompleteness of the agricultural reforms, and to the apparent *uncompletability* of those reforms in the deadlocked political atmosphere of the period. Grain production was finally raised decisively in 1989 not primarily by market incentives but rather by administrative methods, and the costs in terms of production of other crops, and in spill-overs on other rural sectors, were high. The 3.4% increase in 1989 over 1988 grain output was accompanied by a 6% decline in production of sugar crops, a 2% reduction in the output of tea, a 2% reduction in oil-bearing crops, and an almost 9% reduction in the output of cotton, although output of silk cocoons, fruits, and tobacco continued to grow. Rural industrial output recorded its lowest growth rate in years, 23% compared with the 46% of 1988 and 38% of 1987,[83] partly in connection with a broad austerity and credit restriction policy meant to cool down the accelerating price inflation of the previous year. The latter policy was implemented with increased harshness and with added bias against rural industry—which was felt to be competing for resources with both state industry and agriculture—after the crushing of the "Democracy Movement" in June of 1989.

Input growth trends after 1984 reflect lagging state investment and sagging farmer incentives, but also administrative efforts to respond to perceived agricultural problems. Those efforts were strengthened by the re-emergence of local government authority in areas where it had seemed to fade with the process of decollectivization. The rate of increase of chemical fertilizer use slowed from the nearly 10% level recorded in 1979–1984 (and nearly 12% for 1978–1984) to 5.3% during 1984–1988, reflecting both a decline in imports and the lack of domestic investment earlier in the decade, which was noted above. But Stone (1988) reports that the lack of investment

---

[83]Deflated by the overall retail price index, the growth rate works out to 5% in 1989 versus 27% in 1988 and 31% in 1987.

in new fertilizer plants "began to change after the poor harvest in 1985" (p. 812). Horsepower of agricultural machinery grew at 8.4% and small and "walking" tractors at 17.1% annually between 1984 and 1987, although the number of large and medium-sized tractors grew by only 1% and the number of combine harvesters declined. The declining trend in tractor-plowed area was reversed after 1983, with the growth rate for 1983–1987 recorded at 3.4% a year, so that about 40% of China's cultivated land was reported plowed by tractor in 1987. Although the irrigated area and the proportion irrigated with power failed to rise, the rate of contraction of the cultivated area declined from 0.54% a year in 1979–1984 to 0.39% a year in 1984–1988. During the same period, the wattage of motors for agricultural drainage and irrigation rose by 2.7% per year, the reported sown area rose slightly, and the multiple cropping index rose from 1.48 to 1.51. Stepped up agricultural investment both by central and local governments was a major theme of policy pronouncements as the end of the decade approached.

As in the first part of the decade, agricultural growth continued to be vastly outpaced by the growth of other sectors of the rural economy in the late 1980s. While crop output value, in current prices, rose by 67% between 1984 and 1989, forestry output rose by 76%, animal husbandry by 207%, fishery by 310%, and sidelines by 130%, so that the crop production share of what Chinese statistics refer to as "agriculture" declined from 68.3% in 1984 to 56.2% in 1989. Crop production's share of total rural output value dropped still more, from 43.4% in 1984 to 25.3% in 1989, as rural industry, construction, transportation, and commerce scored gains of 407%, 148%, 289%, and 231%, respectively, over their 1984 output levels (in current prices), to jointly account for nearly 55% of rural output value in 1989. Although for the most part such structural change should be viewed as a healthy sign of economic growth, and although the successful growth of nonagricultural activities in parts of China's countryside are causes for optimism about those regions' economic prospects, there is reason to fear that the outflow of resources from crop production was greater than what economists would view as socially optimal. Resource movement away from agriculture can be expected to have been exaggerated by the distorted price structure facing rural producers and by the asymmetrical use of administrative tools in some but not other sectors of the rural economy.

Sectoral Conflicts as Barriers to Reform

The failure of the second stage or second half-decade of China's agricultural reforms can hardly be seen as the result of simple policy "errors." Rather, it reflected deep problems in the structure of the economy.[84] The reform program begun in 1978 had to run up against definite limits so long as these fundamental problems remained

---

[84]These points are further discussed in Chapter 11 and in Putterman (1992b). See also the articles in the Symposium on Institutional Boundaries, Structural Change and Economic Reform in China in the January and April 1992 issues of *Modern China*, edited by the author.

unaddressed. The decision to end unlimited state grain purchases at the relatively attractive above-quota prices of 1984 was a direct consequence of the inability of the government to bear the rising subsidies required by the coupling of high producer prices with low-priced sales of rationed grain to urban residents. As such, it was a reflection of a structure of state-peasant and urban-rural relationships that had become deeply ingrained in the Chinese political-economic system since the 1950s, and that failed to be overturned by a reform process that had evolved so boldly in other respects. State reliance on low-priced staples to keep down urban wage costs and to maintain high state industry profits and capital accumulation rates could simply not be foresworn without abandoning either the implicit wage contract with the urban population or the drive for industrialization under state auspices. Against this background, the liberalization of agricultural decision-making contained a built-in limitation: that the state could only afford to increase prices for procured staples by a modest increment, while the increasing returns on nonstaple crops and noncrop production activities, resulting from the relaxation of controls on the rural economy, made the level of increases necessary for eliciting desired grain supplies grow ever larger.

As the gap between state and market prices for grain opened wider in the late 1970s, more and more special economic inducements, such as the tying of fertilizer and other manufactured input supplies to grain deliveries, and more and more administrative pressures, including direct interventions to determine cropping patterns in localities where a large shift from staples was privately rational at prevailing prices but unacceptable to local authorities, were needed to assure that state purchase plans were fulfilled. Because peasant resistance to selling their staple produce to the government was directly proportional to the size of the market/contract price gap, governments at various levels also resorted to attempts to control the market itself. Sometimes these attempts took the form of forbidding private trading in grain until an area's state purchase targets had been fulfilled; at other times they involved tight limits on the amounts of grain that could be privately transported across jurisdictions.[85] One result was that the free market for grain tended to remain thin and underdeveloped, a fact that must have contributed to the persistence of self-sufficiency oriented behavior by most peasant households.

The results to be expected from such a situation according to simple economic analysis are straightforward. The conflict between state purchasing objectives and free markets, leading to underdevelopment of those markets, can be expected to have retarded progress toward further commercialization and specialization in China's agriculture. Allocation of labor and other inputs among staple and nonstaple crops, and between agriculture and nonagricultural pursuits, would be expected to be

---

[85]Both forms of intervention are mentioned by Sicular (1991), who writes that "[i]n a nationwide survey of over 10,000 farm households, 12% of the households reported that in 1987 after meeting contracts, local government departments did not permit free purchases and sales of grain" (p. 22).

skewed away from more optimal patterns, with market forces contributing to the neglect of staples in particular and of agriculture in general due to their artificially lowered returns, even as administrative forces fought to counter these tendencies. Where local authorities tried to secure staple crop production levels by intervening in planting decisions, inefficient factor mixes—too land-using in staples production, too intensive in nonland factors in production of other crops—could be expected to prevail.[86] While presently available data make it impossible to demonstrate the fulfillment of *all* of these expectations, some of them are clearly reflected in the findings of the chapters that follow.

How, then, are China's agricultural reforms to be understood in terms of the more macro- (and political-) economic frameworks employed above? In brief, we may state that while China took the unorthodox step of ending collectivization and made quite a bit of headway with respect to permitting markets to operate and to influence rural factor allocation, the late 1980s still saw the country clinging to the traditional pattern of taxation of agriculture in support of industry and the urban workforce. Moreover, while acreage and total output targets were officially dropped, administrative interventions and measures to secure physical quantities of staple crops remained widespread, and the habit of attempting to influence outcomes through direct controls rather than price incentives was not broken. The loosening of the means of control over peasant behavior, being unaccompanied by a rectification of price relations that could have made such control dispensable, betrayed the continuing vacillation of the country's leaders. With fundamental objectives unchanged but tools of control weakened, it is no wonder that in the late 1980s, some officials remembered the days of the collectives with a distinct wistfulness.

Concluding Remarks

This chapter has attempted to lay out the long-term institutional perspective within which the microanalytical investigations that occupy most of this book can be situated. A central theme of our discussion has been that of the intertwining of change and of continuity in Chinese rural development. While the transition from collective to household-based forms of farm organization that occurred between 1978 and 1984 was a dramatic one, there remained some major points of continuity in the Chinese approach to rural development.

In both the 1980s and the decades that preceded it, China demonstrated a capacity to feed its enormous population on the basis of limited land resources by increasing applications of complementary inputs. One essential difference, however, is that the collective-era solution entailed pushing the absorption of *labor* by

---

[86]Note that local governments themselves tended to respond to distorted incentives by evading higher government directives to moderate nonagricultural investments and to channel more resources into agriculture. For a discussion in the context of the retrenchment policies of 1989, see Oi (1990).

agriculture to a counterproductive extreme of added work days and constraints on diversification, despite mammouth disguised unemployment. The 1980s showed that it was possible to make do with relatively fewer farm laborers and fewer farm labor days. Similarly, where previous decades saw dramatic growth in irrigation facilities and equipment and in the practice of multiple cropping, growth was less dramatic in some of these dimensions and nonexistent in others, in the 1980s. These curtailments of growth for selected inputs may be seen as dividends of the reforms, which permitted the more efficient utilization of the water and manpower resources that were already in place. However, the other basic elements of the agricultural productivity (or "green") revolution that permitted China's food self-sufficiency achievements in earlier decades—namely, continued development and dissemination of improved seed varieties, and increasing supplies of fertilizer—remained a major part of the output growth story in the 1980s.

With respect to the welfare achievements of the Chinese rural system of the pre-reform period, it would appear that many were preserved, although some were weakened. While land was distributed to individual households in the early 1980s, it continued to be viewed as collective property, and the principles of distribution were egalitarian. On the other hand, basic health services once provided by collective entities sometimes failed to be replaced by either public or private alternatives in poorer localities, contributing to a decline or even to a reversal in the long-term downward trends in rural mortality. School enrollments declined and birth rates rose as families faced new opportunities to employ their children in remunerative activities. Income inequality, which was very low locally, widened, and regional differences, already significant, widened further.

Whatever the drawbacks of China's rural reforms, it must be remembered that they were associated with a dramatic increase in average rural incomes, a fact that outweighs distributional concerns in the minds of most observers, including many who place great weight on poverty alleviation. The average real per capita income of agricultural households in 1988 was roughly one and one-third times higher than what it had been 10 years earlier.[87] Rural reform also benefited urban residents by improving the quality of their diets, supplying an array of nonfood goods and services, and providing markets for the products of many urban enterprises. Overall, the per capita calorie consumption of the average Chinese citizen rose from 2,262 in 1977 to 2,632 in 1988, increasing the gap with the other low income countries

---

[87]*China Statistical Yearbook 1990*, p. 299, shows average agricultural household income rising from Y 133.57 in 1978 to Y 544.94 in 1988. Deflating by the overall retail price index, which was 135.9 in 1978 and 234.6 in 1988 (1950 = 100), gives an increase of 136%. Note that almost all of the improvement appears to have taken place by 1985, which explains why the same estimate was given in the Introduction for the period 1978–86. It may also be noted that use of the retail price index for purposes of inflation adjustment may lead to some overstatement of the change in real income, both because the index itself may be biased downward, and because some of the increase in farm income is attributable to the higher valuation of self-consumed produce. In view of the second factor and given the market imperfections prevalent in China, a weighted average of the retail price and farm and sideline purchasing price indices (the second of which rises more rapidly than the first) may be more appropriate. See Chapter 3.

mentioned earlier in the chapter.[88] While some of those countries scored gains with respect to life expectancy, compared with a more or less unchanged picture for China, a significant gap in China's favor remained here as well.[89]

Although the reforms began with an improvement in the terms of trade facing rural producers, this aspect of the program proved to be less than fully sustainable in the long term. Instead, change in the institutions of farm production, and greater diversity in the forms of productive organization and in the channels of trade in other sectors, stand out as hallmarks of the rural reforms. Surely the transition from team to household farming was the most important single institutional change. But the combined impacts of the much greater freedom of farm households to engage in nonfarm activities, and the diversity of organizational forms and ownership arrangements permitted in those spheres, are of at least equal significance. These changes were associated with increasing labor productivity, and with a marked reallocation of labor from agriculture to industry and services. Structural change was accompanied by institutional continuities, as well as changes. The commune and brigade industries, in particular, lived on as township and village enterprises, and the corresponding levels of economic and political organization remained powerful and economically important.

Perhaps, the most important theme to emerge is that of the degree of continuity in the structural position of agriculture in the economy. A somewhat surprising result of our discussion, and a major theme of this book, is that the extractive approach to agriculture, and the concommitant opposition of interests between the government and rural producers, did not end with the decollectivization of agriculture, the freeing up of rural labor, and the partial marketization of the rural economy. Those changes posed new problems to the old and persistent pattern of state extraction, but in the short run at least they neither led to, nor were accompanied by, a transcending of that pattern. Decollectivization complicated the problem of enforcing compulsory sales obligations. The growth of commercially oriented activities fed by rural labor mobility on the one hand filled gaps in the old publically controlled economy, but on the other generated competition with state industry for scarce resources. And newly created free markets in key agricultural products could not be left entirely free, as became evident whenever their existence threatened the state's ability to implement its own planned purchasing programs.

Some of these themes will be found to intersect with the microanalytic investigations featured in Chapters 4 through 10. The connections will be drawn

[88]The 1977 figure is as estimated above. 1988 figures from the *World Development Report 1991* (p. 258) include Bangladesh, India, and Pakistan at 1,925, 2,104 and 2,200 calories, respectively, little changed from the figures given earlier. Only Indonesia, at 2,670 calories, showed an improvement rivaling China's.
[89]The *World Development Report 1991* puts life expectancy at birth in China at 70 years, equal to the *World Development Report 1980* estimate for 1978 although above the *World Tables* (World Bank, 1983b) estimate cited earlier. The 1991 Report's estimates for Bangladesh, India, Indonesia and Pakistan in 1988 are 51, 59, 61, and 55 years, respectively.

together, and the larger picture will be reconsidered in light of those investigations, in Chapter 11, which concludes the book. In the next two chapters we build a bridge to our micro studies by moving first from the discussion of China in general to the recognition of its regional and local diversity, and then by drawing a portrait of our micro research site in the setting thus established.

2

Regional Variation
in the Rural Economy

Anyone studying economic performance and change in a country as vast and internally heterogeneous as China faces a dilemma, for statements made about China in the aggregate or on average may be accurate for almost no part of China in particular, while statements which apply to specific regions and localities may apply little or not at all to others. A case in point is the observation that in 1987, agriculture's share of total rural output value for the first time dipped below 50%, and that rural industry accounted for 35% of that output value.[1] This statement could lead to a misimpression even at the aggregate level: because the ratio of input costs to gross output value is higher for industry than for agriculture and because some agricultural output prices were artificially depressed relative to those of industry, the share of industry in gross output value exaggerates its contribution to net social output or value added. Industry's shares of total rural employment and of rural household income were also substantially less than its gross output share. But unless treated with caution, the statement could be even more misleading from the standpoint of regional variation. This is because, even using such large units as China's 29 provinces, autonomous regions, and directly administered municipalities[2] one finds that in the year indicated, fully 55.3% of China's rural industrial output value was generated by just four provinces and one municipality[3] containing 29.6% of the country's total

---

[1] Here and elsewhere in this chapter, "agriculture" includes animal husbandry, forestry, fishery, and sidelines, unless otherwise indicated. Aside from agriculture and industry, total rural output value also includes construction, transportation, and commerce.

[2] The basic level of administration below the central government consists of 21 provinces, the autonomous regions of Inner Mongolia (Nei Menggu), Tibet (Xizang), Xinjiang, Ningxia, and Guangxi, and the three province-level or directly administered municipalities (including surrounding rural counties) of Beijing, Shanghai, and Tianjin. In 1988 the island of Hainan was separated from Guangdong province to become China's 22nd province and 30th province-level entity. Since virtually all of our data predate Hainan's separation from Guangdong, we do not treat Hainan as a province in its own right. Technically, the island of Taiwan, considered part of China by both the R.O.C. government based there and the P.R.C. government in Beijing, is also a province, but consideration of its rural development experience will fall outside the scope of this book. For convenience, the term "province" will sometimes be used to refer to any entity having provincial administrative status, including autonomous regions like Tibet, and the directly administered municipalities of Beijing, Shanghai, and Tianjin.

[3] These were Hebei, Shandong, Jiangsu, Liaoning, and Shanghai.

agricultural population,[4] and that the share of industry in gross rural output value was less than 35% in 20 of 29 provinces, and below 20% in 11 of these.[5] Moreover, in a sample of one in ten of China's rural counties, selected at random,[6] only 20% of counties show nonagricultural output value (which is more comprehensive than industrial output value) occupying more than 50% of total social output, and agriculture accounted for 60% or more of total social output value in fully 68% of the counties. A good indication of the degree to which national statistics are skewed by a small minority of more developed counties is the fact that in "the average county" the share of total output coming from agriculture is 66% (here, the shares are averaged giving each county equal weight), whereas agriculture's share is only 49.6% for the nation as such (a result which can be obtained by averaging the shares with each county's figure weighted by its share of national output).

The issue of regional variation is important to a study such as the present one, which analyzes the performance of the rural economy and the effects of institutional and policy change primarily at the micro levels of individuals, households, production teams, and villages. Research at such fine levels of disaggregation is clearly necessary to understand the nuances of household labor supply and local income differentiation, or to analyze relationships (functions) on a scale such that interpretation is not complicated by differences in climate, soil types, and techniques. However, given heterogeneity of localities, no local research site can adequately represent all of China, or even all of a given province or county. Pointing out the dangers of generalization from different local experiences, for example, Jean Oi has recently (1990) noted that the seeming contradiction between Victor Nee and Su Sijin's (1990) finding that rural townships and villages were rapidly selling off collective assets to local private entrepreneurs, and Oi's own findings that township and village governments were becoming stronger and more dominant actors in the rural industrial field, probably result from the fact that Nee conducted research in the southern province of Fujian, while her own work was done in the northern provinces of Shandong and Liaoning. Similarly important differences might emerge even between two localities in the same province.

In appreciation of such dangers, the present chapter will be devoted to studying the question of regional and local variation, and to laying the groundwork for establishing the representativeness and limitations of this book's primary case, Dahe

[4]The latter are defined as individuals or members of households having agricultural household registration *(hukou)* status. Many such individuals may be engaged in nonagricultural work, but they are distinguished from households with nonagricultural registration by the fact that they are not entitled to purchase grain from the state, and they typically have access to land with which to produce their own subsistence requirements.

[5]State Statistical Bureau (1988, p. 179).

[6]Data on these counties are taken from China County-Level Economic Statistical Abstract (hereafter State Statistical Bureau, 1989). The sampling procedure was to select one of every 10 counties, including nonprovincially administered municipalities (that is, the smaller municipalities, designated *shi* in Chinese), with replacement of randomly drawn counties until approximately the same proportion of municipalities versus nonmunicipalities had been drawn within each province.

Township in the northern province of Hebei. The rest of the chapter discusses variation among China's major regions and economic differentiation at the levels of regions, subregions, and provinces. Toward the end of the chapter, emphasis is given to north China and Hebei province, to the differences between it and other regions of the densely populated eastern portion of China's territory, and to differentiation at county level within Hebei. Chapter 3 provides a detailed portrait of Dahe Township, and there, further attention will be devoted to placing it properly within its regional context.

China's Major Regions and Provinces

The territory controlled by the People's Republic of China since 1949 (which is much the same as that claimed by the predecessor Nationalist government and the area ruled by the Qing emperors in the 18th and 19th centuries) covers a land mass of 9,552,998 square kilometers. In size, therefore, China closely resembles the United States, is about two-fifths as large as the Soviet Union, and is nearly three times as large as the next most populous nation, India. In lattitude, China stretches from the 53rd parallel north at its northernmost point in Heilongjiang province to the 18th parallel north at the southernmost point on Hainan island,[7] while in longitude, it reaches from the 73rd meridian east at its westernmost point, in Xinjiang, to the 135th meridian east at its northeastern tip, again in Heilongjiang. In the east, China borders on the Yellow, East China, and South China Seas of the Pacific Ocean, while on the northeast, north, west, and southwest it is landlocked, bordering on North Korea, the Soviet Union, Mongolia,[8] Afghanistan, Pakistan, India, Nepal, Bhutan, Burma, Laos, Vietnam, and the city-colonies of Hong Kong and Macao. Most of China's population, and most of the 92% of that population who are of the Han nationality, reside in the eastern portion of the country, where the rural economy has traditionally been dominated by crop cultivation. Only a relatively small proportion of the population, including such non-Han groups as the Mongolian, Uygur, and Tibetan peoples, live in western portions of the country which are more sparsely populated and in which the economy has traditionally been dominated by animal husbandry. Thus, the provinces (autonomous regions) of Inner Mongolia, Gansu, Ningxia, Xinjiang, Xizang (Tibet), and Qinghai account for almost 55% of China's land mass, but contained only about 8.5% of its population in 1988.[9] Given the large historical, demographic, cultural, and economic differences between China's eastern and western regions, it may be appropriate at the outset to devote more of our attention to the central and eastern regions, to which our local data can be compared most directly; but differences with the western areas will also be highlighted in what follows.

[7]China also claims a number of small islands extending as far south as the 4th northerly parallel.
[8]To be distinguished from Inner Mongolia or Nei Menggu, a province of China.
[9]Alternatively, if a line is drawn from Huma on the northern border of Heilongjiang province and Siberia, to the border of Yunnan province and Burma at the Salween River, bisecting China into two parts, the eastern portion contains roughly 36% of China's territory but 94% of its population (Ma, 1987, p. 4).

There are any number of ways of dividing China into regions for purposes of studying regional variation. Use of the 29 provinces (or province-level entities) is often convenient—for many purposes, it is more or less necessitated—because of availability of data. But these units may be unnecessarily small for purposes of assessing broader regional differences, and they are imperfectly correlated with agro-climatic zones as well as with industrial and transportation corridors, each of which often cut across provincial boundaries. In distinguishing regions, we want simultaneously to give weight to differences in topography, soil type, and climate, on the one hand, and to those of level of economic development and relation to transport routes and other manmade geographic features, on the other. (Differences of ethnicity and dialect, or of mineral resources, might be important for other purposes, but will not be emphasized here.) The compromise adopted in this chapter involves 1) use of provincial boundaries, to take advantage of data availability, and 2) the partly arbitrary division of China into regions with varying degrees of coarseness. A coarser division consists of six regions, which are the coast (Liaoning, Hebei, Beijing, Tianjin, Shandong, Jiangsu, Shanghai, Zhejiang, Fujian, and Guangdong), the central region (Shanxi, Shaanxi, Henan, Hubei, Anhui, Hunan, and Jiangxi) the northeast (Heilongjiang, Jilin, and sometimes Liaoning), the northwest (Xinjiang, Gansu, Ningxia, and Inner Mongolia), the Qingzang region (Qinghai and Tibet), and the southwest (Sichuan, Yunnan, Guizhou, and Guangxi). In a finer division, we divide the coast into north (Hebei, Beijing, Tianjin, Liaoning, and Shandong), central (Jiangsu, Shanghai, and Zhejiang), and south (Fujian and Guangdong) subregions, and we divide the central region into a south central subregion (Hunan, Hubei, Jiangxi, and Anhui) and a north central subregion (Henan, Shaanxi, and Shanxi).[10] We will also note that given the peculiar geography of Hebei, this province or parts of it might also have been placed in the north central group, while Liaoning belongs both to the coast and to the northeast. The six regions and five subregions are outlined on Figure 2.1. Selected data for the regions and subregions and their relations to national totals are shown in Tables 2.1–2.4.

The Coastal Region

With few exceptions, the most developed industrial and commercial centers of China are located in the coastal and northeastern provinces. Although China was not

---

[10]Among possible alternatives to this division, see the three region system adopted by some Chinese sources, and the six region division used by the United States Department of Agriculture. The former, illustrated by an article in *Beijing Review* (Vol. 29, No. 49, [Dec. 8, 1986], pp. 21–24), has an eastern area overlapping our "coast" with the addition of Guangxi, a central region that excludes Shaanxi and adds Inner Mongolia, Heilongjiang and Jilin to our own central region, and a western region that includes everything else. The USDA classification, as shown in CPE Agriculture Report (1990 [Jan./Feb.]), adds Qinghai and Shaanxi to the northwest, Tibet to the southwest, Guangxi to the south coast, and Shanxi and Henan to Hebei, Shandong, Beijing, and Tianjin but not Liaoning in an area called "north." Unlike our own, the USDA system is based on cropping patterns, only. Economic development considerations led us to group Guangxi with the southwestern provinces, despite the fact that it also has a significant coastline.

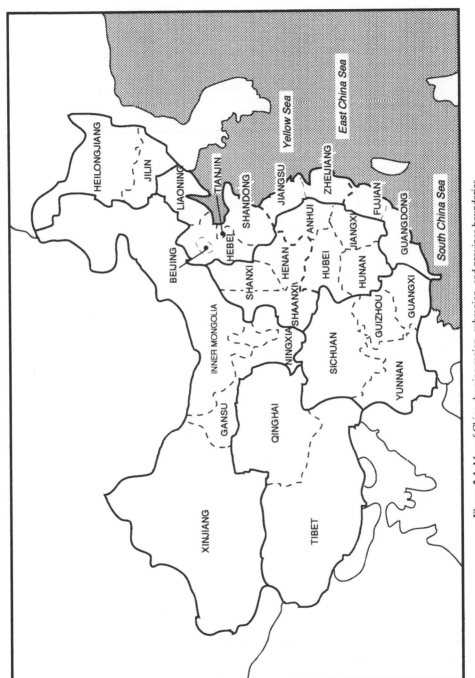

Figure 2.1 Map of China showing region, subregion, and province boundaries.

Table 2.1. Selected Region and Subregion Shares of National Totals

	Population	Cult. Area	GVAO	GVIO	Rural GVIO	TVE Output	% Output Agric.[a]	Cult. Land ha/pers[a]
Coast	0.37	0.30	0.45	0.60	0.71	0.64	0.79	0.80
North coast	0.18	0.19	0.18	0.26	0.26	0.25	0.77	1.04
Central coast	0.11	0.07	0.14	0.25	0.37	0.29	0.63	0.64
South coast	0.09	0.04	0.12	0.10	0.09	0.10	1.19	0.51
Central	0.31	0.29	0.29	0.21	0.19	0.32	1.27	0.93
North central	0.13	0.15	0.10	0.08	0.09	0.09	1.18	1.16
South central	0.18	0.14	0.19	0.13	0.10	0.13	1.33	0.77
Northeast	0.04	0.13	0.05	0.06	0.03	0.04	0.84	2.51
Northwest	0.06	0.13	0.06	0.03	0.01	0.02	1.43	2.29
Qing-zang	0.01	0.01	0.01	0.00	0.00	0.00	1.75	1.40
Southwest	0.20	0.14	0.15	0.09	0.06	0.08	1.45	0.73

[a]Ratio of region or subregion average to national average.

Figures in columns 5 and 6 are for 1987. All others are for 1988.

traditionally a maritime nation, modern industry spread to China under the influence of the Japanese in Manchuria (present day Liaoning, Jilin, and Heilongjiang provinces) and of the Europeans in other coastal enclaves including Hong Kong, Shanghai, and Tianjin. Climatically and topologically, the region varies considerably. In the north, where winter wheat and summer corn crops are the norm, daily high temperatures average in the mid- to upper-20°s C (upper-70°s F) in summer and a few degrees below 0° C (around 32° F) in winter, with an average of about 200 to 250 frost-free days. In the central portion, where rice is the dominant grain with a

Table 2.2. Area, Population, and Density by Region and Subregion

	Area in km^2	Population ('000s)	Rural Share of Pop.[a]	Population Density	Cultivated Area/Total Area	Cultivated Area per Person
Country	*9552998*	*1,080,730*	*0.79*	*110.00*	*0.10*	*0.09*
Coast	1069098	403,110	0.77	382.29	0.27	0.07
North coast	525457	193,430	0.76	373.01	0.34	0.09
Central coast	210741	117,150	0.77	563.25	0.31	0.06
South coast	332900	92,530	0.79	282.40	0.13	0.04
Central	1232500	335,460	0.83	276.23	0.23	0.08
North central	528900	137,750	0.84	264.40	0.27	0.10
South central	703600	197,710	0.82	285.12	0.19	0.07
Northeast	641600	57,700	0.59	91.01	0.20	0.22
Northwest	3284800	60,410	0.74	18.57	0.04	0.20
Qing-zang	1948400	6,360	0.75	3.32	0.00	0.12
Southwest	1376600	210,840	0.86	155.35	0.10	0.06

[a]Agricultural residents as share of total population.

Figures in Columns 2 and 3 are for 1987. All others are for 1988.

Table 2.3. Level of Development and Economic Structure by Region and Subregion

	National Income per Capita[a]	Output per Capita[a]	GVAO/ Output	GVIO/ Output	Income per Capita of Agricultural Households	Industry's Share of Rural GVO	Share of Agricultural Household Income from the Collective Sector	Agriculture's Share of Rural Labor	Industry's Share of TVE Output	TV[b] Share of TVE Output
Country	*878.49*	*2197.65*	*0.24*	*0.60*	*544.94*	*0.41*	*0.09*	*0.79*	*0.69*	*0.68*
Coast	1220.38	3338.73	0.19	0.65	730.95	0.54	0.16	0.69	0.77	0.76
North coast	1123.05	2943.79	0.19	0.65	634.97	0.50	0.15	0.73	0.70	0.67
Central coast	1511.87	4569.06	0.15	0.70	887.46	0.65	0.23	0.60	0.87	0.88
South coast	1054.81	2608.69	0.29	0.51	733.43	0.35	0.06	0.74	0.63	0.65
Central	693.53	1591.92	0.31	0.55	461.54	0.31	0.05	0.82	0.71	—
North central	641.55	1465.62	0.29	0.56	409.32	0.37	0.05	0.81	0.70	—
South central	729.74	1679.96	0.32	0.54	497.94	0.27	0.05	0.84	0.71	0.60
Northeast	1075.49	2454.03	0.20	0.64	583.45	0.25	0.05	0.86	0.54	0.50
Northwest	704.34	1580.45	0.35	0.49	441.04	0.11	0.02	0.86	0.43	0.52
Qing-zang	699.21	1179.57	0.43	0.36	453.96	0.07	0.01	0.90	0.39	0.53
Southwest	549.05	1192.92	0.35	0.50	433.12	0.21	0.03	0.89	0.54	0.55

[a]"National income" refers to net material product, or gross output value minus value of materials consumed in production. "Output" refers to "total product of society" or gross material product.

[b]Township- and village-owned enterprises.

Figures in columns 1, 4, 8, 9, and 10 are for 1987. All others are for 1988.

Table 2.4. Agricultural Characteristics by Region and Subregion

	Irrigated Share of Cult. Area	Multiple Cropping Index	Diesel Irrig. Share of Cult. Area	Tractor Plowed Share of Cult. Area	Agr. Mach. per Hectare (watts)	Tractor Power per Hectare (watts)	GVAO per Capita	Grain Output per Capita (kg)	Grain Share of Crop Output[a]	Crop Share of GVAO	Husbandry Share of GVAO
Country	*0.46*	*151.34*	*0.10*	*0.43*	*2776.27*	*858.22*	*535.08*	*0.36*	*0.55*	*0.56*	*0.27*
Coast	0.61	162.72	0.18	0.59	4,409.18	1,125.63	641.74	0.35	0.46	0.54	0.26
North coast	0.53	137.82	0.19	0.63	4,139.08	1,001.05	548.88	0.34	0.47	0.60	0.25
Central coast	0.80	201.00	0.26	0.69	5,194.15	1,447.43	702.30	0.42	0.53	0.51	0.28
South coast	0.65	207.97	0.04	0.28	4,313.38	1,145.29	758.88	0.28	0.36	0.46	0.23
Central	0.52	176.38	0.12	0.39	2,749.49	850.62	492.99	0.38	0.61	0.58	0.27
North central	0.40	145.68	0.08	0.50	2,512.30	889.26	420.80	0.32	0.53	0.64	0.22
South central	0.65	208.55	0.17	0.27	2,998.02	810.14	543.32	0.43	0.65	0.55	0.29
Northeast	0.12	95.96	0.02	0.54	1,296.83	728.98	501.16	0.57	0.73	0.71	0.20
Northwest	0.40	97.72	0.02	0.37	1,505.92	749.68	549.48	0.34	0.48	0.59	0.31
Qing-zang	0.36	91.66	0.01	0.22	1,859.82	1088.06	495.36	0.24	0.58	0.38	0.49
Southwest	0.42	180.11	0.01	0.12	1,978.29	515.43	422.59	0.30	0.61	0.53	0.33

All figures are for 1988.

[a]Using weighted average state and market gain price to value grain as measured by the aggregate grain output series.

secondary role for wheat, daily high temperatures average 28° C (82° F) in summer and 3° C (37° F) in winter, and the growing seasons extends through most of the year. In the south, where rice accounts for fully 88% of the annual grain crop, daily high temperatures average 29° C (84° F) in summer and 13° C (55° F) in winter, and the growing season is year round.[11]

The North Coast

In addition to wheat and corn, the north coastal subregion, in which we include Beijing, Hebei, Liaoning, Shandong, and Tianjin, is also a major producer of cotton and peanuts. This subregion includes the north China and Liaohe plains, as well as mountainous and hilly areas in western Hebei, western and eastern Liaoning, and the Shandong peninsula. Slightly over one-third of the land surface was under cultivation in the late 1980s, as shown in Table 2.2. Rainfall averages about 500 mm a year in Hebei, 635 mm in Beijing, and 725 mm in Liaoning's Shenyang. Fifty-three percent of the cultivated land is irrigated, mostly by power-driven tubewells. In the late 1980s, the subregion produced 27% of China's wheat crop and 35% of its corn, or 17% of grain as a whole (by weight). It also produced 43% of the nation's cotton, 47% of its peanuts, and 19% of its soybeans. The region was comparatively well supplied with fruits and vegetables, producing 35% of the nation's total fruit output and exceeding national per capita output of vegetables and melons by 42% and of fruits by 69%.[12]

The subregion includes China's second, third, and fourth largest industrial centers. These are Beijing (1987 population 6.7 million, 1987 gross value of industrial output [GVIO] Y 32.8 billion), Tianjin (population 5.5 million, GVIO Y 30.8 billion), and Shenyang (population 4.4 million, GVIO Y 18.0 billion).[13] It also includes another 18 cities with over 1 million residents, of which six had over Y 5 billion industrial output value.[14] The three provinces and two municipalities included in the subregion as we define it included about 18% of China's population and cultivated area in 1988, but they accounted for nearly 26% of the nation's industrial output, causing the subregion's per capita output to be 34% higher than the national average. Both the suburban townships and the rural counties surrounding these cities contain large concentrations of rural industry, much of it village and township owned. In 1987, the north coastal subregion accounted for 25.6% of the country's rural

[11]Data on climate are based on information contained in *The New Encyclopaedia Britannica,* 1987.
[12]Data on crop output patterns are averages for the 3 years 1986, 1987, and 1988, from various issues of Statistical Yearbook of China.
[13]Urban data are from State Statistical Bureau (1990b). The 1987 GVIO is given in 1980 constant prices.
[14]These are Dalian (2.3 million, Y 10.8 billion), Anshan (1.3 million, Y 7.9 billion), and Fushun (1.3 million, Y 6.8 billion) in Liaoning, Shijiazhuang (1.2 million, Y 6.8 billion) in Hebei, and Jinan (2.1 billion, Y 7.8 billion), Qingdao (1.3 million, Y 9.4 billion), and Zibo (2.4 million, Y 6.7 billion) in Shandong.

industrial output, and for 24.4% of the output of China's township- and village-owned industrial enterprises. In 1987, the average share of nonagricultural output in total gross output value in randomly selected rural counties of the subregion was 47%, versus the national sample average of 34%.[15] The percentage of the population registered as agricultural, in the subregion, was 76%, versus 79% nationally. About 73% of the rural labor force were reportedly engaged in agriculture, versus 79% nationally, in 1987. The share of rural industrial output produced by township and village enterprises in 1987 was 63.6%, slightly below the national average of 66.7%.

The Central Coast

The central coastal subregion, which consists of Jiangsu, Shanghai, and Zhejiang, is China's richest agricultural and industrial area. Except for southern Zhejiang, the land is flat, and much of it is crisscrossed by a dense network of rivers, lakes, and canals. With 563 persons per square kilometer in 1988, the subregion's population density was the highest in China—over five times the national average—and its land/man ratio of .056 cultivated hectares per capita was lower than all other regions and subregions except the south coast. That the land/man ratio is not worse still is explained by the fact that the region's flat topography and river-fed irrigation network permit the central coast to enjoy by far the highest share of irrigated land in total cultivated area among the subregions and regions, roughly 80% in 1988, and one of the highest multiple cropping indexes, 2.01 in the same year. Together with excellent soils and climate, this helped the central coast to achieve an agricultural output value per rural resident over 30% above the national average. With just under 11% of China's population, and 7% of its cultivated land, the region produced 18% of the country's rice, 12% of its wheat, 14% of its cotton, 23% of its rapeseed, 17% of its jute, 25% of its tea, and nearly half of its silkworm cocoons, and a total of 14% of China's gross agricultural output value (including animal husbandry, fisheries, forestry, and sidelines).

The central coastal region constitutes China's most formidable center of both urban and rural industry. Shanghai alone, with an urban population of 7.2 million, produced Y 68.5 billion worth of industrial goods in 1987, followed by Jiangsu's Nanjing (2.4 million, Y 12.9 billion) and Zhejiang's Hangzhou (1.3 million, Y 9.4 billion) and Ningbo (1.0 million, Y 5.5 billion). The region also contained another ten cities of over 1 million people, and several smaller cities serving as major centers of industrial and/or commercial activity, such as Jiangsu's Wuxi, Suzhou, and Changzhou, the mutual proximity of which rendered this zone of southern Jiangsu and Shanghai China's nearest equivalent of a "megalopolis." The 11% of China's population living in the subregion as a whole accounted for over 25% of the country's gross industrial output value in 1988. The subregion had more than twice the national

---

[15]These figures are computed by averaging over counties, with each assigned equal weight. The counties belong to the random pool discussed in note 6 above.

average per capita output, and accounted for over 37% of the nation's rural industrial output and nearly 43% of the industrial output of township- and village-run enterprises.

The level of development of the subregion's rural areas was far above the national average, as measured by structural and other indicators. In 1987, the average share of nonagricultural sectors in total gross output value in randomly selected rural countics of the subregion was 62%, nearly twice the national sample average of 34%, and 13% above the next most developed region or subregion as measured by this criterion. The rural employment structure showed a corresponding deviation from the national average, with only 60% of rural labor reportedly devoted to agriculture, which is far below the 79% average for all China or even the roughly 73% shares reported for the northern and southern coastal subregions (which show the next lowest shares). Not only was industry's share of total social output value the highest of any of our regions or subregions, at 70.4% in 1987, but the rural or TVE[16] share of its industrial output was exceptionally high: rural industry constituted 34.7% of overall industrial output value (about 44% in both Jiangsu and Zhejiang but only 13.5% in Shanghai) versus 23.8% nationally. While township- and village-owned enterprises were particularly strong in southern Jiangsu and northern Zhejiang (the areas closest to the Changjiang River and Shanghai), some other areas, notably southern Zhejiang's Wenzhou municipality, were noted for their small-scale private enterprises. Overall, however, the former pattern was dominant, so that the township- and village-run enterprise shares of TVE output as a whole and of TVE industrial output in particular were 88% and 90%, respectively, in 1987, far above the corresponding figures for other regions and subregions and the national averages of 68% and 77%.

The Southern Coast

The southern coastal subregion, consisting of the provinces of Guangdong and Fujian, accounts for about 3.5% of China's land area and 8.6% of its 1988 population. Although above the national average, the subregion's population density, at 175 per square kilometer, is below those of the other coastal and central subregions, the basic reason being the hilly topography which causes a comparatively small share of the land surface to be cultivated. Cultivated area per capita was lower than any other region or subregions, standing at only .044 hectares in 1988. At the same time, the subregion is second only to the central coast in the share of cultivated land which is irrigated, 65.5%, and in 1988 it led all regions and subregions with a multiple cropping index of 2.08. In addition to producing 13% of China's rice, the area produced 12% of its peanuts, 46% of its sugar cane, 15% of its tea, and 19% of its fruit

---

[16]That is, township and village enterprises, including both those run by township and village governments, and other rural private enterprises and partnerships. Note the difference between TVE and township- and village-*run* enterprises, which is a subcategory.

in the late 1980s, and its per capita agricultural output value stood at nearly 42% above the national average. That the south coast's 8.6% of China's population produced only 6.4% of its grain in the late 1980s made the subregion a chronic grain importer, a phenomenon of some significance given China's limited internal trade and the centrality of grain in the nation's food supply.

Proximity of Fujian to Taiwan (an integral part of the province during imperial times) has helped to lure an increasing flow of foreign capital in recent years, while proximity of Guangdong to Hong Kong, the New Territories of which share a land border with it, has had an even more pronounced impact on that province's economy. Despite these factors, the subregion's economic development is concentrated in local pockets, such as Guangdong's Pearl River Delta, and, taken as a whole, it still lags far behind the central coast in overall industrialization and prosperity. The subregion's share of national industrial output, 9.5% in 1988, was only a little larger than its share of population, and agriculture still accounted for over 29% of combined agricultural and industrial output value, compared with only 15% in the central coast. Per capita output in 1988 stood below the other two coastal subregions, although still 19% above the national average and above the two central subregions and the other four regions.[17]

Guangdong industry is dominated by Guangzhou (also known as Canton, population 3.4 million, GVIO Y 17.5 billion), China's fifth ranking city by industrial output. None of the three remaining Guangdong cities with over 1 million people figure in even the top thirty cities by this measure, nor does Fujian's Fuzhou, with a population of 1.2 million. Guangzhou itself accounted for only about 15% of the subregion's industrial output value. Thus, much of that output must have originated in small towns and rural counties, such as those in Guangdong's well-known Pearl River Delta that enjoy close links both to Guangzhou and to Hong Kong.[18] Nonetheless, the rural share of industrial output in 1987 stood at only 24.8%, far below the 44% figures of Zhejiang and Jiangsu and just slightly above the 23.8% average for the nation. Similarly, the agricultural share of the rural labor force was reported to be 73.7%, closer to the national average of 79% than to the central coast's 60.5%. In terms of the composition of rural nonagricultural activities, industry accounted for only 63% of TVE output, versus 70% in the north coast and 87% in the central coast. The township- and village-run enterprise shares of TVE total output and industrial output, respectively, were also correspondingly lower, at 65% and 72% (in each case slightly below the national average). Although even these numbers may

[17]The 1988 per capita output of Guangdong excluding Hainan, at Y 3,024, was below that of Zhejiang (Y 3,414) and Jiangsu (Y 4,118) provinces, although far above that of north China's Hebei (Y 1,623), on which we will focus later in the chapter. The central coast's per capital output was a little higher than that of the northeast.

[18]For an interesting discussion of the recent development of this region which emphasizes those links, see Vogel (1989).

exaggerate the importance of township- and village-run enterprises,[19] the statistics such as they are do bear out the widespread perception that the role of private enterprise in rural industrialization has been greater than the national average and far greater than in the other two coastal subregions.[20]

Overall, the ten provinces and directly administered municipalities of the coastal region, covering only 11% of China's land mass, contained 37.3% of its total population in 1988; 77.3% of that population was classified as nonagricultural, compared to China's average of 79.2%. 1987 per capita net material product averaged Y 1,223, per capita gross output was Y 3,145, and the share of combined industrial and agricultural output value from agriculture was 15.9%, compared with averages of Y 878, Y 2,127, and 20.3%, respectively for China as a whole. In 1988, the region accounted for over 60% of China's industrial output. Within the rural sector, agriculture in 1987 accounted for only 46.3% of combined output value in the coastal region, versus 58.7% nationally, and the region accounted for 71.5% of the nation's rural industrial output, 76% of its output from township- and village-run industries, and 64% of the nation's rural enterprise (TVE) output as a whole. From an agricultural standpoint, the region contained nearly 30% of China's cultivated area and 39.3% of its irrigated area, and it produced nearly 45% of the country's agricultural output by value despite a land/man ratio roughly 20% below the national average. Grain output was 36.5% of the nation's total in 1988, for a per capita output of 0.35 kg, just below the national average of 0.36. On the other hand, grain's share of total crop output value averaged just 46%, versus the national average of 55%.[21] The region's overall multiple cropping index of 1.63 and its irrigated share of cultivated land, 61.0%, contrasted with 1.51 and 46% figures for China as a whole.

The Central Region

The central region as designated here consists of a second and third tier of provinces in terms of distance from the coast, still largely in the eastern third of China and in the overwhelmingly Han portion of the country sometimes referred to as "China proper." Directly to the west of the coastal provinces of Hebei, Shandong, Jiangsu, Zhejiang, and Fujian are the "second tier" provinces of Shanxi, Henan, Anhui, and Jiangxi. To

[19]It is widely alleged that many effectively private enterprises are registered as belonging to township and village governments, for the sake of the political benefits of such registration. We cannot, however, speak with any confidence about the relative incidence of such deceptive practices among regions.

[20]For some supporting evidence based on the comparison of counties in the different regions and subregions, see Byrd and Lin, (1990).

[21]In this chapter, grain's share of crop output value is calculated using an average grain price of Y 454.5 in 1988, which is slightly higher than the average contract price based on Sicular (1988b), as calculated by the methodology described in Table 1 of Putterman (1992b). Both grain value and total crop value would be increased if market prices for grain were either substituted for or given greater weight in this average price, and this would cause an upward shift in the grain share figures. Note, however, that the proportion of grain sold in the market was probably under 20% of total grain sales and under 6% of total grain production.

the west of these, in turn, lie Shaanxi, Hubei, and Hunan. As a whole, the region contains 31% of China's population, 12.9% of its land mass, and 29% of its cultivated area. Its population density is a little less than half that of the coast, but well over twice that of China as a whole, while its cultivated area per capita is a little below the national average.

The level of economic development of the central region lags behind that in the coastal region and the all-China average (which is strongly influenced by that region), as shown by a higher share of agricultural population, a smaller industrial output share, and lower values of both income and gross output value per capita. Thus, 83.2% of the population was classified as agricultural in 1987 (versus 77.3% in the coastal region and 79.2% nationally), 1987 industrial output accounted for 54.7% of combined industrial and agricultural output value (versus 64.9% on the coast and 60.1% nationally), 1987 national income (net material product) per capita was Y 693.5 (versus Y 1,220 in the coastal region and Y 878.5 nationally), and total social output value per capita averaged Y 1,595.4 (versus Y 3,145.9 in the coastal region and Y 2,127.4 for the nation). All of the provinces in the region except one had 1987 per capita national incomes of between Y 600 and Y 700, lower than any coastal province. (The exception, Hubei, had a per capita income of Y 907, which is considerably above the levels of the two poorest coastal provinces, Hebei and Fujian, and a little behind that of another coastal province, Shandong.) The region's average per capita income trailed not only the national average of Y 878, but also that of all other regions except the southwest—although it was not far behind the northwest and Qingzang. Other comparisons are shown in Table 2.3.

The per capita value of agricultural output in 1988 (as usual in this chapter—following Chinese statistical practice—including forestry, fishery, and animal husbandry) was Y 493, versus the coastal region's Y 642 and the national average of Y 535. The region produced 28.6% of the nation's agricultural output value and 33% of its grain in 1988. Per capita grain production was 0.38 kg, a little above the national average of 0.36; 52.4% of its land was irrigated (below the coastal region's 61% but above the national average of 46%), and the multiple cropping index averaged 1.76, above both the coast's 1.63 and the national average of 1.51. Industry accounted for 30.7% of rural output value, far behind the 53.7% figure of the coast but ahead of the shares in the remaining four regions. In step with this finding, 82.5% of the rural labor force was reportedly engaged in agriculture in 1987, above the coast's roughly 69%, but below the figures for the other regions.

The North Central Subregion

This chapter subdivides the central region into subregions not according to proximity to the coast, but by division into northern and southern groupings. The four more southerly members (Hubei, Anhui, Hunan, and Jiangxi), which lie along the course of the Changjiang River, will be treated as a south central subregion, while the three more northerly members (Shanxi, Shaanxi, and Henan), which lie along the path of the Huanghe (Yellow) River, are treated as a north central subregion. Forty-one percent of the region's population, 43% of its land mass, and 51% of its cultivated land are found in the northern subregion, the remainder to the south.

Climatically, the north central subregion experiences similar temperature ranges to the north coast, but with more variation due to varying elevations, and without the moderating influences of the sea. Average rainfall varies from less than 250 mm a year in northwest Shanxi to up to 1,000 mm per year in the southern mountains of Shaanxi, which form part of the Changjiang rather than the Huanghe watershed. Most areas experience winter frost for 100 days or longer. Topographically, the north central subregion is dominated by the Loess Plateau of the Huanghe River and of its tributary, the Weihe, and by mountainous areas in the west of Henan, the north, east, and west of Shanxi, and the south of Shaanxi. Although some of the lands watered by it formed the historical cradle of Chinese civilization, the Huanghe is infamous for frequently flooding the adjacent plains which in many areas lie at lower elevations than the river, and for carrying much of the area's topsoil to the sea. Only 40% of the subregion's cultivated land is irrigated, and the multiple cropping index was only 1.46 in 1988. An average of 50% of the land was reported to have been plowed by tractor in that year, above the national average of 43% but below the coast's 59%. Yields of wheat and corn, the two major grains, were 9% and 28% below national averages, respectively, in the late 1980s. By cultivating 16% more land per capita than the national average, the region's inhabitants managed to produce almost precisely their per capita share of national grain output, as well as similar shares of oilseeds (including peanuts), hempcrops, and fruit. They also produced almost 17% of the nation's cotton and jute, and 21% of its tobacco, with grain's share of crop output value, at 53%, lying just below the national average. Animal husbandry accounted for less than 13% of GVAO, below the national average of 17.5%.

Whereas industrial output accounted for 65% of total social product in the coastal region, it comprised 56% in the north central subregion in 1987, and the subregion contributed only 8% of the nation's industrial output despite its nearly 13% population share. Xi'an (Shaanxi), Taiyuan (Shanxi), and Zhengzhou (Henan) are the largest cities in the north central subregion, with populations of 2.6, 2.0, and 1.6 million, respectively, giving them national ranks of 10th, 17th, and 19th in size. Xi'an's industrial output value of Y 8.4 billion and Taiyuan's of Y 6.8 billion made them China's 16th and 21st industrial cities, while the industrial output of Zhengzhou fell a little below Y 5 billion. Only two other north central cities, Shanxi's Datong and Henan's Luoyang, surpassed 1 million in population.

The proportion of industrial output produced in rural areas in 1987 was 24.6%, similar to the national average and to the proportions displayed by the north and south subregions of the coast. However, industry's share of rural gross output value was only 30%, below the coast's 45% and the nation's 35% average, and 81% of the rural labor force was engaged in agriculture, slightly above the national average. At 46% of the total, output of township- and village-run enterprises was a relatively small share of total rural enterprise output, compared with 68% nationally and 76% in the coast. The subregion thus offered a counterexample to the pattern observed in the central coastal subregion.

The South Central Subregion

Climate and topography within the south central subregion are also varied. Northern Anhui is part of the north China plain and enjoys only 200–230 frost-free days; in contrast, Jiangxi enjoys a growing season of up to 11 months, and January lows in the southern part of that province and of Hunan average above freezing. January temperatures range from average highs of around 0° C (32° F) in Anhui to average lows of around 4° C (39° F) in southern Jiangxi. The Changjiang River meanders through southern Hubei, forms part of the Hubei-Jiangxi boundary, then runs through southern Anhui, on its way to Jiangsu and the sea. Apart from the Changjiang River Valley, that of the Ganjiang in Jiangxi, and the Huai River Basin in northern Anhui, the land is mostly hilly in the east and mountainous in the west. As in the central coast, rice dominates but wheat is also an important grain crop in Hubei and especially in Anhui, while rice accounts for about 95% of the total grain crop in Hunan and Jiangxi. With 18.3% of China's population, the subregion produced 22% of its grain crops, including 39% of its rice, 18% of its cotton, 19% of its oilseeds, 39% of its hempcrops, and 34% of its tea in the later 1980s, and its share of the nation's 1988 GVAO was 18.6%.

As in its northern counterpart, industry is relatively underdeveloped in the south central subregion, which produced only 12.5% of China's industrial output in 1988. Even this showing, like a number of other statistics for the subregion as we have defined it, gives a somewhat exaggerated impression of the region's industrialization, due to the strong influence of Hubei and especially of the Wuhan area. Formed by the merger of three formerly separate cities, Wuhan holds the impressive ranks of fifth largest in population (3.6 million) and sixth largest in gross industrial output value (Y 16.6 billion) in the nation, and thus stands as one of the few exceptions to the coastal location of China's main industrial centers. On the other hand, while Hubei boasts another five cities (Suizhou, Xiaogan, Xiantao, Macheng, and Tianmen) of over 1 million people and Anhui (Huainan, Haozhou) and Jiangxi (Nanchang, Pingxiang) each have two such cities, none of these ranks in China's top twenty by population and the one with the largest industrial output, Hubei's Tianmen, ranked only thirty-fifth nationally. The share of the population registered as agricultural in the subregion was 82.4% in 1987, versus 79.3% nationally. In 1987, the average share of nonagricultural sectors in total gross output value in randomly selected rural counties located in the south central subregion was 41%, above the national sample average of 34%, but far below the central coast's 62% share. The share of rural industrial output produced by township- and village-run enterprises in 1988 was 55%.

The Northeast Region

In China, the three provinces of Liaoning, Jilin, and Heilongjiang are known collectively as the northeast; except for some changes in its border with Inner Mongolia, the same region was known in the past as Manchuria. Lying entirely to the north of China's Great Wall, it was sparsely populated by people of Manchu nationality and joined the mainstream of Chinese history when its rulers vanquished China's decaying Ming Dynasty to establish their own Qing Dynasty in 1644. It remained largely closed to Han Chinese settlement for over two more centuries, but ultimately Han immigration combined with Manchu integration in Chinese society to largely erase the ethnic distinction. (In the 1990 census, 9.8 million Chinese gave their nationality as Manchu, but the combined non-Han shares of the populations of Liaoning, Jilin, and Heilongjiang were only 15.6, 10.2, and 5.7%, respectively.) Substantial Japanese involvement in the region's economy began around 1905, and led to full-fledged colonization in 1931. By the time of Japan's invasion of China proper in 1937, the region had become one of the most industrialized in the country. Today, it is by far the most urbanized, boasting a number of large cities and having rural areas which are comparatively sparsely populated by Chinese standards. Reflecting this high level of urbanization and industrialization, the region's per capita income is ahead of all other regions except the coast.

Since it is rightly speaking a coastal province and, unlike Guangxi, fits the coastal profile with its comparatively high level of development, the southernmost northeastern province, Liaoning, has been treated above as part of the coastal region and the north coastal subregion. Except where indicated, therefore, this section will define the northeast region as consisting only of the two more sparsely populated and landlocked provinces of Jilin and Heilongjiang. Accounting for under 7% of China's land surface, this region contained only 5.3% of its population and 4.0% of its agricultural population in 1987. Overall population density in the region was 91.0 in 1988, less than one-tenth that of the central coast and less than one-fifth that of the coast as a whole, although not much below the all-China average of 110. Only 59.4% of the region's population, a figure strikingly below the national average and that of any other region (but essentially unchanged if Liaoning is included), was classified as agricultural in 1987.

The topography of the northeast is marked by the large northeast plain running from north to south in the western sections, and by several small mountain ranges in the east. For the most part, the region lies in a temperate zone, with an average annual precipitation of between 500 and 700 mm. In the north, there are only 80–120 frost-free days annually; the January mean temperature is as low as $-27°$ C $(-17°$ F), and summer temperatures average around $23°$ C($73°$ F). Southern parts suffer somewhat shorter and less cold winters, with January temperatures averaging $-17°$ C $(2°$ F), and somewhat warmer summers. The northeast's overall land/man ratio in 1988 was 0.219 hectares per person, reaching its all-China high of 0.255 hectares in Heilongjiang.

With a short growing season, irrigation covering less than 12% of the area cultivated, and a multiple cropping index standing at only 0.96, the region's per capita gross agricultural output value fell below the national average. But with a disproportionately large share of crop production devoted to grain—73% of crop output value in 1988, versus an average of 55% nationally—the region's 5.3% of China's population produced over 8% of China's grain in the late 1980s, including 24% of its corn and 41% of its soybeans. Grain output per sown hectare averaged 3.9 tons, a little below the national and a little above the coastal averages, while per capita grain output, at 0.57 kg in 1988, was the highest of any Chinese region, and the northeast's advantage in this respect is still more pronounced when only the agricultural population is used as a denominator. In addition to grain, the region also produced 16% of China's hemp crops, 52% of its sugar beets, and 7% of its tobacco.

A relatively unique feature of northeastern agriculture is that due to low population densities and large expanses of flat land, some large-scale mechanized farming is carried out along lines reminiscent of the north American plains. The tractor plowed area and number of large tractors per agricultural resident, at 54% of the cultivated area and 0.39 per rural dweller, were well above all China averages of 43% and 0.10 per rural dweller in 1988 and 1987, respectively, and led all other regions and subregions. The phenomenon is also reflected in the data for the randomly chosen rural counties, in which agricultural horsepower per person in 1987 stood at 1,173 in the northeast, above the national average of 418 and the coast's 359. The region had already achieved the highest levels of agricultural mechanization in China during the collective farming era, and although it would take us beyond the scope of this study, it would be of interest to study in some depth how the advantages and disadvantages of the switch to household responsibility differed here from other regions. The significant continuing use of machine plowing here, as elsewhere in eastern China, suggests that ways have been found to combine large-scale plowing and harvesting under village auspices with the carrying out of other farm operations by individual households.[22]

The region contains four cities of over 1 million inhabitants. Harbin, in Heilongjiang, is the largest. Its 1987 population of 2.7 million and gross industrial output value of Y 9.7 billion placed it at the eighth and tenth ranks in China, by these measures. The other large cities are Jilin's Changchun (population 2.0 million, GVIO

---

[22]Note that nationally, the tractor-plowed area dropped from 42 million ha in 1979 to under 34 million ha in 1983, then gradually recovered to 41 million ha in 1988. This suggests that it took time for some localities that had used machinery in their collective operations to learn how to integrate mechanical plowing with household responsibility. An alternative interpretation is that economically rational levels of tractor use under household farming were initially lower than levels attained in the collective period, and that higher levels became justified later in the 1980s due to the rising opportunity cost of labor and the increasing size of the capital stock in many localities. However, the levels of tractor use observed in the late 1980s may also reflect the pricing distortions discussed in Chapter 1. That is, with grain prices in particular too low to entice enough able-bodied labor into the fields, local officials in the more developed rural areas may well have turned to mechanization as a way of meeting their political responsibility to maintain and boost staple crop production.

Y 7.4 billion) and Jilin City (1.2 million, Y 5.8 billion) and Heilongjiang's Qiqihar (1.3 million, Y 3.7 billion).

The rural areas accounted for only 9.5% of the region's industrial output (versus the all China average of 23.8%), and industry accounted for only 25.3% of overall rural output value, versus the national average of 41.2%. These figures suggest that the northeast had a sharper division between urban and rural areas than the coast. (Liaoning, with 51.7% of rural output from industry, fits better into the coastal pattern, and is in fact slightly ahead of the north coast subregion average, in which it has been included.) The simple (unweighted) mean of the nonagricultural share of gross output value for 1987 in randomly selected rural counties of the region was only 30%, versus the national sample average of 34% and the coastal average of 49%. The shares of overall TVE output and of TVE industrial output produced by township- and village-run enterprises in 1987 were 50% and 65%, indicating a surprisingly small role for the latter enterprises when compared with the much higher figures of 76% and 82%, respectively, for the coast, or even the 68% and 77% figures for the nation as a whole. A relatively large proportion of the rural labor force, or 86.2%, were still employed in agriculture as of 1987.

Per capita net material product averaged Y 1,075 in 1987, putting the region close to the north and south (though below the central) coastal subregions, and significantly above the rest of the country, in terms of this development indicator. Income per capita of agricultural households was reported to be Y 583 in 1988, leading all other regions except the coast.

The Northwest Region

The region consisting of Inner Mongolia, Ningxia, Gansu, and Xinjiang covers a vast territory of 3.28 million square kilometers, which accounts for 34.4% of China's territory. However, only 5.6% of China's people live here. Topographically, the region consists of mountains approaching 2,000 meters above sea level in Inner Mongolia and ranging from 3,000 to more than 5,000 meters in Xinjiang, surrounding arid and semi-arid basins, with an average elevation of 500 to 1,000 meters in Inner Mongolia and 1,000 to 1,500 meters in Xinjiang. In 1988, only 4% of this territory was cultivated, compared with 27% in the coastal and 23% in the central regions. The area of land cultivated had in fact fallen by 6.9%, or 903,000 ha, since 1979, partly in response to the government's reversal of the policy of promoting grain self-sufficiency throughout China, including traditional animal husbandry areas. Recent years have been marked by official concern with soil erosion, desertification, and other issues impacting on the region's ecology.

The histories of the various parts of this region differ. Although the ancient silk road trading route that linked China to the Mediterranean passed through Gansu and Xinjiang, much of the region was traditionally populated by non-Han ethnic groups who were incorporated into China relatively late in its over 3,000 year history.

Reflecting this, three of the four province-level entities constituting the region are formally "autonomous regions": Inner Mongolia, historically populated by the people whose 13th century rulers controlled the only empire ever to span both China in the east and portions of the European continent in the west, and among whom a form of Tibetan Buddhism is prevalent; Ningxia, historically populated by the Hui nationality, a Chinese-speaking Moslem group; and Xinjiang, historically populated by the Uygur nationality, another Moslem group with roots in the area of present-day Turkey. By 1987, the three autonomous regions had populations that were roughly 81%, 67%, and 38% Han Chinese, respectively.

The second largest cultivated area per capita following the northeast, or 2.3 hectares, only partly offsets the fact that the region's climate and soils do not support as intensive an agriculture as that of China's coastal and central regions. Forty percent of the cultivated area is irrigated, similar to the north central region and well above the northeast's 12%. Notwithstanding this fact, the multiple cropping index in 1988 stood at only 0.98, barely above its value in the latter region. The main explanation is once again the fact that with a short frost-free period, lasting only some 80–150 days a year, only one crop can be grown. January average temperatures are $-15°$ C (5° F) in Xinjiang's Urumqi and only slightly higher in Hohhot, Inner Mongolia. July temperatures average 27° C (80° F) or less. In addition, annual rainfall is small and unevenly distributed, ranging from 200–300 mm in the northwest to 400–500 mm in the southeast, and the annual evaporation exceeds this rainfall, resulting in a very dry climate. Nearly all of China's deserts are found here.

While yields per sown hectare averaged only 58% of the national average, the large cultivated area allowed per capita grain output in the late 1980s to slightly exceed the national average. The principal grains grown are wheat followed by corn, with the region producing nearly 10% of the nation's wheat and about 7% of its corn in these years. Grain accounted for only 48% of crop output value, compared with a national average of 55%. Other major crops are oilseeds, of which the region produced 9% of the national total, and sugar beets, of which it produced 39%. The share of combined agricultural output value occupied by animal products approached 31% in Inner Mongolia and averaged 24% in the region as a whole, exceeding the national average of less than 18% and the levels of all other regions except Qingzang.

The average level of economic development in the region is comparatively low. The region's net material product per capita level of Y 704 in 1987 fell significantly behind the coast and northeast but slightly ahead of the central region and Qingzang, and significantly ahead of the southwest. Structural measures tell a similar story. For example, about 35% of the region's output value in 1988 was from agriculture in the broad sense (including animal husbandry and other related activities), a ratio surpassed only by Qingzang's 43%, equal to that of the southwest, and above the 31% of the central region and the 20% and 19% figures for the northeast and coast. This is despite the fact that only 74% of the region's population are reported to be agricultural, less than the country's 79% average. The region had only three cities of more than 1 million people (Inner Mongolia's Bautou, Gansu's Lanzhou, and Xinjiang's Urumqi) none of which figured among the top 25 Chinese industrial cities, and its share of national industrial output value, at 3.5% in 1988, was significantly below its population share (5.6%).

In rural areas, fully 89% of 1987 gross output value continued to be from agriculture, the highest such figure except for Qingzang's 93%. Correspondingly, 86% of the rural labor force were reported to be employed in agriculture, compared with 82% in the central and 69% in the coastal region. Only 7% of the region's industrial output came from rural areas. In a region as poor and underdeveloped as the northwest, we might expect rural collective institutions to be comparatively weak. This is borne out in that township- and village-run enterprises were statistically less prevalent than the national average, accounting for 52% versus 68% of total TVE output, and for 68% versus 77% of TVE industry output. Township- and village-run enterprise output nonetheless accounts for a substantial majority of the output of offically recognized rural enterprises in the region, and the difference between the output share of these enterprises in the northwest and that in other regions, with the exception of the central coast subregion, could be viewed as relatively minor.

The Qingzang Plateau

A large plateau with mountains 4,000–6,000 meters above sea level and terraces at elevations of 3,000–5,000 meters, the area consisting of the Tibetan Autonomous Region (Xizang) and the province of Qinghai is largely inhospitable to crop cultivation. Apart from its lake basins and valleys, the plateau is mainly grassland. Average January temperatures are −8° C (18° F) in Qinghai's Xining and −2° C (28° F) in Lhasa, Tibet; average July temperatures are 17° C (63° F) in Xining and 15° C (59° F) in Lhasa. Rainfall varies dramatically with elevation, averaging 450 mm a year in Tibet but only 100 mm a year in Qinghai.

With its harsh climate and rugged terrain, the region has the lowest cultivated share of total area, only 0.4% in 1988. Of the latter, only 36% was irrigated, only 22% was plowed by tractor, and the multiple cropping index was the lowest of all regions, at 0.92. The region's per capita grain production stood at only two-thirds of the national average, and it exceeded its per capita share of national output only for wheat, rapeseed, and tobacco, among major crops. On the other hand, the animal product share of agricultural output stood in the late 1980s at 51% in the region, far exceeding the nation's 18% and the next closest region, the northwest where the share was 24%. This compensating factor allowed the region's share of national GVAO (which includes animal husbandry) to fall only slightly short of its population share.

The region is the least industrialized in China, with 42.6% of total 1988 output value being agricultural (compared to the national average of 24.35%); in rural areas, the agricultural share is 93%. It also suffers from the lowest average per capita output (Y 1180 in 1988) of the six major regions as grouped here, although its reported per capita net material product (Y 699 in 1987) was comparable to that of the central and northwest regions and well above that of the southeast. It occupies 20.4% of China's territory but accounted for only 0.59% of the country's population in 1988. In 1990, Tibet's population was 96% Tibetan and 4% Han Chinese, while Qinghai was about 42% Tibetan and Mongolian, 58% Han Chinese.

Of the region's 6.4 million people, about 25% held nonagricultural registration in 1987. Qinghai's Xining, the largest city in the region, had only 623,000 inhabitants and ranked 116th nationally in industrial output value in 1987. For the region as a whole, industrial output per capita stood at just half the national average. In rural areas, industry accounted for only 7% of gross output value, and fully 90% of the rural labor force was reportedly employed in agriculture, suggesting the smallest degree of rural industrialization among China's regions. The shares of overall TVE output and TVE industrial output produced by township and village enterprises in 1988 were 69% and 53%, respectively, placing Qingzang at roughly the median rank among our six regions in development of rural private as opposed to collective enterprises.

The Southwest Region

A little larger than the central region in total area, ranking third, behind the central and coastal regions, in population share, but by far the poorest region in terms of per capita income, the southwest region consists of China's most populous province, Sichuan (1988 population 105.8 million), and three provinces of more typical size, Guizhou, Yunnan, and Guangxi. In 1988, the region accounted for 19.5% of China's population and for 14.4% of its land area. In that year, it reported a per capita net material product of only Y 549. Population density, at 155 persons per square kilometer, was below the coast's 382 and the central region's 276 but above the northeast's 91, the northwest's 19, and Qingzang's 3. The average density fell in the range of 167–182 persons per square kilometer in Sichuan, Guizhou, and Guangxi, but at a smaller 88 persons per square kilometer in Yunnan. The region includes portions of the Tibetan plateau in the north and west of Sichuan and Yunnan, steep mountain slopes, hills, and gorges in central portions of Yunnan, Guizhou, and Guangxi, and some fertile river valleys in the east, including the four tributaries of the Yangze that give Sichuan its name and that helped bring portions of that province into the mainstream of Chinese culture at an early date. Climate is similarly varied, with July average temperatures ranging from the 27° to 32° C (80° to 90° F) range in Guangxi and southeastern Sichuan, to the 22° to 24° C (71° to 76° F) range in Yunnan and Guizhou, to only 20° C (68° F) in western Sichuan. January average temperatures vary correspondingly from the mild 12° to 16° C (54° to 60° F) range in parts of Guangxi and eastern Sichuan to −8° C (18° F) in the Western part of that province. Annual rainfall averages around 900–1700 mm in Guangxi, 800–1,300 mm in Guizhou, 1,200–1,450 mm in Yunnan, and slightly over 1,000 mm in Sichuan.

In 1988, the region's population farmed only 0.063 hectares per person, a land-man ratio below that of any of our other regions, although above that of two of the subregions: the central coast (with 0.056 hectares) and the southern coast (with 0.044 hectares). Unlike the latter subregions, however, only 42% of the cultivated area was irrigated, and only 9% was irrigated with power equipment. The multiple cropping index in 1988 stood at 1.80, not far behind the central and south coast and south central subregions (which stood at 2.01, 2.08, and 2.09, respectively). However, crop output value per rural resident was only Y 227 in 1987, versus Y 397 in the central coast and Y 340 in both the south coast and south central subregion, and Y 331 for China as a whole.

The southwest produces somewhat less than its per capita share of China's grain crop. It produced 16% of China's grain in 1986–1988, but held 19.5% of the country's population. Rice is the most important grain crop, accounting for 58% of the region's total grain output and for 22% of the nation's total rice crop, while the region also produced 25% of the national output of tubers. Crop diversification as indicated by the grain share of overall crop output value was behind the coastal and national averages, at 61% versus 46% and 55% respectively, in 1988. The southwest's grain share was lower than that of the central and northeastern regions, however. Important nongrain crops are rapeseed and jute, of which the region produced 30% and 16%, respectively, of China's late 1980s output, sugar cane, of which it produced 40%, and tobacco, silk, and tea, of which it produced 31%, 29%, and 24%, respectively. The animal husbandry share of the net output of inclusively defined agriculture was nearly 22%, about four points above the national average and above all other regions except for the northwest and Qingzang.

In 1987, the region contained nine cities of over 1 million inhabitants, of which five were located in Sichuan, including China's seventh and ninth largest cities by population, Chongqing and Chengdu. The former ranked eighth nationally by industrial output value, which stood at Y 10.8 billion, while the latter's Y 8.4 billion GVIO placed it fifteenth in the nation. Of the remaining seven cities, only Yunnan's Kunming produced more than Y 5 billion worth of industrial products, placing it at number 29 among industrial producers.

Like the northwest and Qingzang regions, the relative poverty of the southwest region is correlated with a relatively backward economic structure. For the region as a whole, including urban areas, industry accounted for only 50% of the gross value of output, versus 60% nationally. In rural areas, agriculture (broadly defined) accounted for about 79% of rural gross output value in 1987, versus 21% from industry, far below the national average of 41.3%; 86.4% of 1987 population held agricultural registration, and 89% of the rural labor force was reported to be employed in agriculture. Within the rural enterprise sector, 54% of 1987 output value was from industry (versus 69% nationally), while 46% was from construction, transportation, commerce, and services. The share of TVE output due to township and village enterprises was also relatively low, at 55% for the region versus 68% for China, and at only 42% in Guangxi and 36% in Guizhou. The region accounted for only 6% of the nation's rural industrial output, and for only 6% of the output of township- and village-owned industries, a disproportionate share of which were in Sichuan.

Comparative Summary

Table 2.1 summarizes some key regional figures in relation to national totals and averages, while Tables 2.2–2.4 summarize selected regional data in raw form. In Table 2.1, we see that two regions, the coast and central regions, dominated the country in population shares, with over 30% of the total in each case, while a third region, the southwest, held an intermediate position, with 20%, and the remaining three each held 6% or less of China's population. Agricultural output (GVAO) was more unevenly distributed, with fully 45% generated in the coastal region and only 27% from the northeast, northwest, Qingzang, and southwest combined. The same skewness is evident but considerably more pronounced for industrial output, of which 60% is produced by the coastal region, with only 18% deriving from outside of the coast and center. The pattern is slightly more skewed still for output of rural enterprises (TVEs), and considerably more so for rural *industrial* output, of which the coast accounted for a full 71%, the coast and center together for 90%.

From Table 2.2, we see that population density was negatively correlated with the agricultural share of population and the cultivated area per capita, and positively correlated with the proportion of surface area cultivated. Agricultural population share varies in a relatively narrow range from 74% in the northwest to 86% in the southwest, with the northeast an outlier at 59%. Population density has a much larger variance, as does the cultivated share of surface area, which ranged from 34% in the north coast to below 1% in Qingzang.

With respect to cultivated area per capita, a fact of particular interest is that, contrary to naïve expectations, that variable is negatively rather than positively correlated with both the overall level of economic development (see, for example, GVIO/Output in Table 2.3), and agricultural output per capita (see Table 2.4). In other words, it appears that rather than indicating a handicap, a high man-land ratio appears to signify, in a comparative sense, that an area has relatively fertile land or high agricultural development potential, perhaps partially built up by increasingly intense cultivation practices themselves. Intensive agricultural activity has gone hand-in-hand with more rapid economic development and structural change.

Levels of economic development and indicators of economic structure are shown in Table 2.3. Net material product (national income) per capita differs by a factor of nearly three to one between the central coast, China's richest area, and the southwest, its poorest. Variation of output per capita is even more pronounced. Economic structure, as indicated by the shares of agriculture and industry, respectively, in the total product of society, shows a decided correlation with both measures, with the agriculture (GVAO) share lowest in the central coast, at 15%, and highest in Qingzang, at 43%, while the industrial (GVIO) share reaches 70% in the former and is only 36% in the latter. Industry's share of *rural* output value is highly correlated with its share of regional output as a whole, but the differences among regions and subregions are more pronounced, with the share ranging from 65% in the central coast (for many of whose villages the term "rural" has become a misnomer) to only 7% in Qingzang and 11% in the northwest. Income per capita of agricultural households, which shows less variation, is nonetheless highly correlated with this industry share indicator. Agriculture's share of the rural labor force remains greater than its share of output in most cases, reflecting the lesser labor-intensity of industry, but it shows a nearly perfect negative correlation with industry's share of rural output, ranging from a low of 60% in the central coast to a high of 90% in Qingzang. The pattern is also reflected in the share of rural enterprise (TVE) output occupied by industry, which varies from a high of 87% in the central coast to a low of 39% in Qingzang. The importance of township- and village- (TV) owned enterprises in the rural enterprise total, by output value, also follows a similar pattern, being highest in the coast and especially the central coast, although showing less variation in the remainder of the country, where it falls in the 50–60% range. The much lower share of agricultural household income coming from the collective sector is in turn correlated with the TV enterprise share.

The pattern is largely repeated also within agriculture. The irrigated proportion of cultivated area varies positively with the level of development, although the northeast is a significant exception. The multiple cropping index is also correlated with level of development, although an important correction is required to account for the lower values in more northerly and colder regions. There are clear correlations between the tractor-plowed share of cultivated area, agricultural machinery per hectare, tractor power per hectare, and the level of development. The tractor-plowed share is as high as 69% in the central coast and as low as 12% in the southwest, with the low figures there and in the south coast also reflecting the hilly terrains, the greater difficulty of plowing wet rice fields, and the lesser strength of collective organization. Grain's share of crop output value, and the crop output and animal husbandry shares of general GVAO, do not show very clear patterns, and would thus appear to be governed by more idiosyncratic factors.

Hebei Province

Most of the data to be analyzed in subsequent chapters comes from a single township, Dahe, in Hebei province. In order to better establish the relative economic standing of Dahe, this section will take a closer look at that province. While it will turn out to be a simple matter to establish that Dahe township was well above the Hebei average and closer to overall coastal averages by most development indicators during the period under study, there is an additional reason for examining Hebei in some detail. It is that the province offers an excellent example for the study of local variation at subprovince level, complementing the provincial and regional contrasts above. Indeed, it serves rather well as a microcosm of the country as a whole in terms of differing levels of economic development, illustrating the influences of topography and of proximity to urban centers and transportation corridors.

With almost 58 million people in 1987, Hebei accounted for 5.4% of China's population and for 2.1% of its land mass. Like the coastal provinces in general, Hebei is thus more heavily populated than the national average, but its 299 persons per square kilometer in 1986 was far below the coastal region's average of 578 persons and closer to the central region's 271 persons per square kilometer. Like a number of other Chinese provinces, Hebei's size and population would place it among moderately large nations if it were a country in its own right. In land area and late 1980s population, the province was comparable to the United Kingdom and to what was then the Federal Republic of Germany.

Hebei, as indicated by the Chinese characters that form the province's name, lies to the north of the Yellow River. It has an expanse of 650 km from west to east and 750 km from north to south. Although its northern climate assures that Hebei agriculture differs in significant ways from the agricultures of China's more southerly provinces, Hebei's overall economy and its internal diversity resemble China's as a whole. Hebei is a coastal province—indeed, China's Great Wall rises from the sea at Shanghaiguan in Hebei—but its Bohai Gulf coastline, interrupted by that of Tianjin, is equalled by its land-bound eastern border with Shangdong, and in the north and west it extends far inland to Inner Mongolia and Shanxi, giving much of the province a noncoastal character. Hebei's 1987 per capita national income (net material product) of Y 785 was the lowest of all coastal provinces, substantially below the coastal average of Y 1,220, and even below the national average of Y 878. Four *noncoastal* provinces—Hubei, Heilongjiang, Jilin, and Xinjiang—surpassed Hebei in per capita income that year. Measured by this indicator, its level of development, like its population density, was closer to the average for the central region (with per capita income Y 694) than to that of the coast. Hebei's per capita income was greater than that of 15 province-level entities but less than that of the remaining 13, placing it almost exactly at the median rank among the 29 units. The same relationships hold between the income per capita of Hebei's agricultural households and the per capita household incomes of peasants in other provinces.

A further indicator of the province's relatively low level of development is that in 1988, agriculture's share of combined agricultural and industrial output in the province was 27%, exceeding the other coastal provinces except Fujian, and standing close to the figures for central China's Hubei and Shaanxi provinces. Hebei's per capita social output of Y 1808 in 1987 was also below both its region's and the nation's averages for this indicator, although above those for the central region's provinces except Hubei.

To be sure, Hebei's relative backwardness can be viewed as an artifact of the carving out of two large, economically more advanced areas to which it has a certain geographic claim—that is, the directly administered municipalities of Beijing and Tianjin. Merging those highly industrialized zones with Hebei would mean a reconstructed province with roughly the same per capita income as that of the north coastal subregion as a whole. Recognition of this fact underscores the importance of local variability; but there is no lack of such variability within Hebei minus these two "province-municipalities," either.

While industry's share in output stood below that of coastal neighbors, more of Hebei's industrial output (32%) originated in rural areas in 1987 than was true of any other coastal province except Zhejiang and Jiangsu.[23] Partly, this may be a function of the fact, again related to the carving away of Beijing and Tianjin, that only 14.2% of Hebei's population was considered nonagricultural in 1987, versus 19.7% nationally. Curiously, however, the township- and village-run enterprise share of this rural industrial output was only 57%, far less than their share of rural industrial output in other coastal provinces and one of the lowest in China as a whole.

At .113 ha per person, Hebei's cultivated area per capita in 1988 was above the national average (.087), a characteristic it held in common with the northeast and with many interior provinces. Fifty-five percent of this land was irrigated, most of it being by power-driven tubewells. During the 3-year period 1986–1988, Hebei produced about 9% of the nation's wheat and corn, 4% of its soybeans, and .5% of its rice, for a total of 5% of China's grain, putting per capita grain production roughly 16% below the national average. Despite this, grain's share of crop output value was close to the average. The province's most important agricultural contribution was as a producer of cotton, of which it grew slightly over three times the national average in per capita terms, to account for over 14% of the total crop.

As suggested above, Hebei's claim to representativeness is based upon both its overall "averageness" in terms of income and level of economic development, and on the high degree of internal heterogeneity which permits it to serve as a microcosm of China as a whole. This heterogeneity is manifested at many levels. At the local level, an example is provided by Huailu County, in which Dahe is situated. Here, the richest town or township level unit in 1985 was Tongye Zhen (town), with average per capita income (among 7,000 households) estimated at Y 708. Within this "town," however, there was a poor mountain village, Qiaomengou, whose 85 households had average per capita incomes of only Y 270.

The most comprehensive subprovince data available are those at county level.[24] For 1985, these data show a mean per capita income, over the 31 rural counties for which an estimate is given, of Y 378, with a standard deviation of Y 106, a minimum of Y 208, and a maximum of Y 548. Eight of the counties reported incomes falling in

---

[23]The figure for Shandong was only half a percentage point below that for Hebei.

[24]Data discussed in this section are from Hebei Economic Statistical Yearbook, 1986, 1987, and 1988. In contrast with our use of a random selection of county data for all China, above, data for all 132 of Hebei's rural counties *(xian)* are considered here when available. County-level units officially designated *shi* (city, municipality) are not analyzed, although those units also contain some agricultural households.

the Y 200 to Y 300 range, 10 fell in the Y 300 to Y 400 range, and 13 reported average incomes above Y 400.[25] These same 31 plus an additional 96, or 96% of the counties, provided data on per capita income in 1987. The average in this case was Y 445, the standard deviation Y 144. A further breakdown illuminates the variation of income levels among the counties in 1987. Seventeen percent of the counties had average incomes below Y 300, 24% had average incomes of Y 300 to Y 400, 23% had average incomes between Y 400 and Y 500, 19% had average incomes in the Y 500 to Y 600 range, 13% had average incomes between Y 600 and Y 700, and the remaining 4% had average incomes above Y 700. Huailu county's per capita income in 1987 is listed by the same source as Y 680.

Although only counties officially counted as *rural* are considered, the levels of "rurality" and industrialization appeared to vary significantly as well. In 1985, the nonagricultural share of population averaged 5.6%, with a standard deviation of .02 and a range from 0.1% to 16.1%. The share of gross output value due to industry averaged 31%, with a standard deviation of .08 and a range from 10% to 61%. In that year, Huailu County's reported share of gross output value generated by industry stood just at the average of 31%.[26]

Agricultural conditions also appear to vary significantly among Hebei's rural counties. While 58% of all Hebei counties produced between 0.2 and 0.4 tons of grain per capita and another 28% of the counties produced between 0.4 and 0.6 tons in 1987, ten counties, or 7.6%, produced less than 0.2 tons, and two counties, or 1.5%, produced more than 1 ton per capita. The proportion of grain sold to the government likewise varied, with 31 counties selling less than 10% of the grain they produced, 59 selling 10–20% of their grain, 24 selling 20–30%, 10 selling 30–40%, the remaining 4 on which data are available selling more than 40%, and the average over 128 counties being 17%. A regression with share of grain output sold to the state as dependent variable and cultivated area per capita as explanatory variable explains 54% of the variance in the sales ratio, with the positive coefficient on area per capita significant at the .01% level.[27] Interestingly, per capita grain output, unlike the share of grain output marketed to the state, shows a significant *negative* correlation with cultivated area per person. When per capita grain output takes the place of the dependent variable in the regression just mentioned, the coefficient on area per capita is negative and significant at the .1% level, although the adjusted R^2 is only .12.[28]

[25]Huailu County is not among the 31 counties providing data. In 1985, per capita income in Dahe Township is estimated to have averaged Y 590.

[26]These calculations are based on data shown on pp. 602–13 of the 1986 Yearbook. That Huailu County's industrial output share was so close to the median as well as to the mean of the distribution raises some doubt abouts data quality, since one would have expected a result rather above the average.

[27]If sown area per capita is used as the explanatory variable, it is equally significant, but the adjusted R^2 falls to .36.

[28]The negative correlation between area farmed and grain output per capita at county level resembles the finding that provinces with larger cultivated areas per capita had lower levels of agricultural productivity, a finding that we interpreted as reflecting a link between population density, on the one hand, and land quality and intensity of cultivation, on the other.

Ninety-two of 129 reporting counties had average cultivated areas per capita of 0.007–0.013 ha (0.1 to 0.2 *mu*), and another 30 fell in the 0–0.007 ha (0 to 0.1 *mu*) range. On the other hand, the proportion of cultivated land that was irrigated, which averaged 59% over all counties, had a standard deviation of .32, indicating substantial variation, and the multiple cropping index, which averaged 1.38, had a standard deviation of .58. Chemical fertilizer per 1,000 ha, which averaged 2,762 tons, had a standard deviation of 1,667 tons. As a result of these factors and perhaps also differences in underlying soil quality, yields also varied appreciably among counties. With an average of 70% of total cultivated area being used for grain (standard deviation 0.13), average grain output per grain cultivated hectare averaged 47.4 tons per hectare, with a standard deviation of 23.7 tons.

Conclusions

As we probe the regional, provincial, and county level statistics of China, what emerges is, not surprisingly, a picture of great diversity. Perhaps the most important lesson to be drawn from this is that the distribution among localities of the signs of structural change and economic development is a highly skewed one. That is, the average level of economic development, as measured by, say, income per capita or the nonagricultural share of total gross output value, is below the national mean in the great majority of localities, because the mean is pulled up by a small number of advanced areas.[29] Figure 2.2 ((a) and (b)) illustrates this by plotting the percentage of counties in the all-China random sample used a number of times in this chapter, against nonagricultural shares of gross rural social product, grouped by deciles, for 1985 and 1987. As elsewhere in this chapter, agriculture has the broad Chinese statistical definition which includes animal husbandry, forestry, fishery, and household sidelines, while nonagriculture consists of industry, construction, transportation, and commerce and food services. In 1987, the median nonagricultural share, below (above) which 50% of the county values lie, is 33.1%, which lies substantially below the mean value for China nationally, 50.4%. The modal decile band, which is the 30–40% range, includes the median share.[30]

This has important implications when assessing the degree of representativeness of any county or township which may be chosen for closer study. Insofar as economic development and structural change are among the central stories of China's rural transformation since 1949, and especially in the 1970s and 1980s, national data give a somewhat misleading impression of the state of progress of *typical* localities. One may go beyond this to say that the whole concept of *rural industrialization* that is such a prominent part of China's economic story in recent decades has to some degree been

[29]In his own survey of regional variation, Walker (1989) goes so far as to say that "by 1986 the diversification of the rural economy had not significantly affected most of China" (p. 450) and that "modernization and rural development had barely touched more than a few areas" (p. 466).

[30]The median share for 1985 is .265, which also lies inside the modal percentile band for that year.

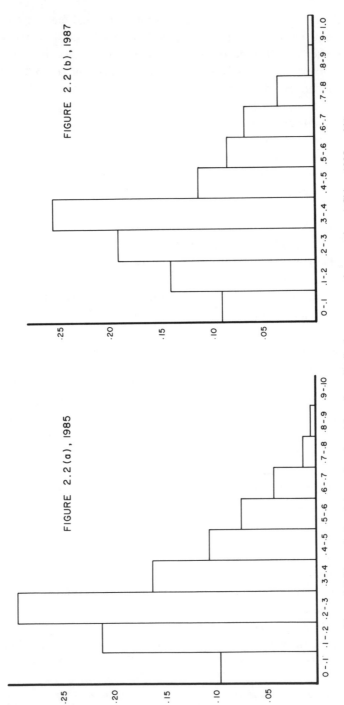

Figure 2.2 Nonagricultural share of rural social product: distribution among random counties, a) China, 1985, and b) China, 1987.

misnamed, for the great bulk of rural industry is to be found clustered near cities and in the developmental pockets that dot eastern China and that are far more rare in the country's interior. It may get closer to the truth to describe what is happening as the expansion of existing cities and the growth of new city satellites through the gradual urbanization of their rural hinterlands, than to describe it as a broad diffusion of industrial activity to rural China as a whole, even if a process of the latter type is also going on to some smaller degree.

Aside from the tendency of statistical averages to convey misinformation when not analyzed with great caution, there is an important terminological source of misperception which is deeply rooted in China's peculiar political economy. This is the unique system of administrative nomenclature that retains the term "agricultural" for the populations of former people's communes on which the state is unwilling to confer the right to buy subsidized grain, and who accordingly continue to be required to self-provide their staples, either directly (by production) or indirectly (by purchase in the market). It is this peculiarity of the Chinese landscape that leaves urbanizing areas within the rural or at least agricultural domain long after farming has become a minor sideline for most residents.[31] This issue is close to the heart of the institutional segmentation that is a fundamental continuity in China's political economy, to which we will return in the final chapter of this book.

[31]Complicating matters, however, is a change in the official Chinese definition of "urban," in 1984, which caused the agricultural populations of many rural towns to be counted as urban, and brought about a jump in the number of "urban residents" from 242 to 331 million in a single year. Since the time of that change, the exaggerated definition of "urban" has coexisted with the understated definition of "nonagricultural" in Chinese statistical publications.

3

Dahe Township[1]

Introduction

Dahe Township, formerly Dahe People's Commune, is located in the southwestern part of Hebei Province, 15 km west northwest of Shijiazhuang, a city of 1,128,000 people which is the provincial capital, and 10 km northeast of the seat of the county to which it belongs, Huailu.[2] In 1979–1980 and again in 1986, Dahe was the site of rural development studies by American scholars supported by the Committee on Scholarly Communications with the People's Republic of China (C.S.C.P.R.C.). The two studies yielded large sets of socioeconomic data tracking the development of the township on an annual basis from 1970 to 1985, at the production team level, and recording the economic status of the members of roughly 250 households in five of the production teams in 1979 and 1985, years reflecting very early and relatively mature stages, respectively, of China's rural economic reforms. Additional data on the brigade or village level and on township, village, and private nonfarm enterprises were also collected for the years 1980–1985, along with a register of agricultural contract terms for each of the township's roughly 5,800 households in 1985. Through the support of the Ford Foundation, these and related sets of data collected at Dahe were entered in computer files and published with an accompanying bilingual codebook in 1989.[3] The Dahe data sets represent one of the few available resources for quantitative micro-study of China's collective era rural economy, and possibly the only such resource permitting longitudinal analysis of the effects of decollectivization and other aspects of systemic and structural change in post-Mao rural China.[4]

---

[1]Portions of this chapter are adapted from Putterman (1989a) and Putterman (1988a).
[2]This is the local pronunciation. The standard Chinese reading is Huolu.
[3]Putterman (1989).
[4]Although the Dahe data sets are unusual if not unique in their longitudinal depth and cross-sectional variation, they are by no means without their problems for the purposes to which they will be used in this book. Missing values cut the size of the available team panel by half or more, for many of the analyses. The household survey follows only five teams, selected by less than perfectly random methods, and has information on 2 years (1979 and 1985) only. Serious deficiencies also include the lack of reliable data on capital allocation between crop and noncrop sectors, the absence of data on input allocation by crop, apparent inconsistencies between data collected in 1980 and those gathered in 1986, nondecomposability of private and contract-sector incomes after 1983, and other problems to be mentioned at relevant points in the text. Some of these problems may be attributed to the fact that uses to which the present author would put the data were not anticipated by Steven Butler, a political scientist, when he began the data collection in 1980. Others were not anticipated by the author himself (see my *mea culpa* in the acknowledgments).

This chapter introduces Dahe Township and its economy in the collective era, and discusses the nature of the rural economic reforms there. Most of the chapters that follow this one use data from Dahe Township to test hypotheses about the behavior of rural China's collective era economic institutions, the nature of the post-collective economy, and the effects of the transition from the one to the other. However, whereas the analysis of those chapters is for the most part based on micro-theoretical modeling and employs econometric methods for purposes of estimation and testing, the present chapter paints a broader portrait of Dahe using institutional information and data of a type that is amenable to interpretation using more straightforward descriptive methods.

Dahe Township is found to have been atypical of China as a whole in that the end of collective agricultural production at Dahe was associated with a standstill in previously vigorous growth in yields of the main grain crops, wheat and corn. We will argue, however, that this pattern is not unusual for an area that, by the late 1970s, had already achieved gains from improved agricultural practices (especially increased chemical fertilizer use) that were to spread to other localities somewhat later. We will argue, too, that grain production at Dahe had been pushed beyond the limits of economic rationality by 1979, and that the difficulty of sustaining it in the more liberalized economic environment of the early 1980s foreshadowed similar problems at a national level after 1984.

A second aspect of the reforms that is discussed is change in the structure of income sources and labor deployment. As expected, the share of agricultural income generated by nongrain crops and the share of total rural output value deriving from nonagricultural goods and services both rose under the reforms, as did the share of nonagricultural activities in both net earnings and employment. The relative position of the village and township enterprises in the overall pattern of economic growth will also be investigated, with the essential finding being that these enterprises remained important despite the growth of household and private enterprise activities.

The nature of the institutional and organizational changes that took place in Dahe's production sectors is the third major topic on which we will focus. First, we will look at the evolution of household farming and the demise of the production teams. Then the changing contractual forms of nonfarm enterprises will be examined.

Background to the Studies

As mentioned, Dahe Township is located in Huailu County, which lies just west of the city of Shijiazhuang, capital of Hebei province. The city ranks 27th in China by

---

Time constraints and the urgings of local accountants and research assistants also put limits on the degree of disaggregation that was judged feasible, and it is indeed doubtful that much more disaggregation or accuracy could have been achieved for most items in view of the inevitably retrospective nature of much of the data collection, and the types of records kept at Dahe. For more information on the collection and preparation of the data sets see Butler (1983), and "Introduction to the Dahe Commune/Township Data Sets and Codebook" in Putterman (1989).

population, and its total of roughly 1.2 million residents include 0.3 million holding agricultural household registrations. Located 283 km (175 miles) south southwest of Beijing, near the western edge of the north China plain, Shijiazhuang itself was a small village under the jurisdiction of Huailu County at the turn of the century. The intersection there of the rail line from Beijing to Hankou (now Wuhan), completed in 1902, with the line running from Zhengding to Taiyuan, built in 1907, laid the basis for the city, which received its present name only in 1947. In 1968, it became Hebei's provincial capital, replacing the older but now smaller city of Baoding, 131 km to its north. Shijiazhuang experienced rapid industrial growth after the founding of the People's Republic, becoming a center for the manufacture of textiles, chemicals, and machinery and electronics.

Huailu County, in which Dahe is situated, is one of three counties bordering directly on Shijiazhuang Municipality, and one of two brought under the administration of the municipality in the early 1980s. Roughly a quarter of the county (23%), lying on the eastern side (adjacent to Shijiazhuang), is flat land, while fully three-fifths (61%) of its 603 km^2 are classified as mountainous, leaving a central band covering 16% of the county's area that is classified as hilly. The county had a 1985 population of 302,250 living in 5 towns *(zhen)* and 16 townships *(xiang),* which are further divisible into 206 natural villages. Huailu came under Japanese occupation in 1937 and returned to Guomingdang control in 1945. It came under the control of the Communists in May, 1948, 17 months before the founding of the People's Republic.

One of the 21 townships and towns of Huailu County, Dahe Township is located entirely within the plain area in the northeast portion of the county. Although the township's name means "big river," only a canal bringing water to Shijiazhuang from a nearby reservoir and some small streams flow through its boundaries today. Dahe did not distinguish itself by early cooperative activity. According to older informants, its first elementary cooperatives containing 10 or so families were formed in 1954, and only in 1956 did all families become cooperative members with the formation of higher stage cooperatives, of which there was one in each of the 14 villages existing at that time within the present boundaries of the township. In 1958, Dahe village, which remained the township center through the 1980s, became the headquarters of a people's commune called *Gangtie* (steel) containing fully 37 villages. Ultimately, 23 of these were made part of three neighboring communes.

In 1961, Dahe People's Commune was established within the boundaries that persisted through the period of our research. It consisted of 14 villages or brigades, 2 of which were later subdivided to yield a total of 16. In the 1970s and early 1980s, these brigades contained roughly 100 production teams (the exact number varying over time between 94 and 104 as teams were at times split up, at other times joined together). In 1985, Dahe's 16 villages contained 5,818 rural households with a total of 22,980 rural residents. The villages varied in size, with Dahe, the largest, having 868 households, and with the smallest of the villages having only 133 households. The average size of the villages, excluding Dahe village, was 322 households.

The township covers 40.07 km^2 and has an officially recorded cultivated area of around 2,100 ha,[5] of which all are irrigated, primarily by wells outfitted with deisel or electric pumps. The cultivated area of about 0.10 ha (1.5 *mu*) per capita at Dahe in 1985 compares with about 0.12 ha (1.8 *mu*) per rural inhabitant nationally and 0.15 ha (2.2 *mu*) per capita in Hebei province.[6] With the exception of a portion of the southern flood plain of the Hutuo River, forming an area of lower elevation in the northeast corner of the township,[7] the land is more or less uniformly flat, a level plain transversed by tree-lined dirt roads and irrigation channels, here and there giving way to brick yards from which the topsoil has been removed for brick making. In the mid-1980s, the typical village at Dahe was surrounded by a band of vegetable gardens, and in some cases by an outer brick wall. Inside were rows of walled family compounds of northern Chinese style, some newer houses, workshops, shops, and an occasional factory, and village offices and schools. Two paved roads, a north-south road connecting Shijiazhuang with the reservoir located about 30 km north-northwest of the city, and an east-west road connecting the first road with sections of Dahe and neighboring communes and linking to a road to Huailu County Town, passed through the township. Another north-south road cut through its eastern edge.

Dahe in the Collective Production Era

Organizationally, Dahe's economy typified China's three-tier rural institutional structure of the 1960s and 1970s. Each household, with an average of 5.8 total members and 2.2 working members in 1975, belonged to a production team, averaging 44.2 households in the same year. The great majority of team members of working age spent the bulk of their work time, ranging from winter work days of 5–6 hours to peak season summer work days of as many as 14 hours, in agricultural or other activities organized by team leaders whose incomes derived from the same pool as that of other team members. Income from private plots, animal husbandry, and sideline activities is unlikely to have been above the average for rural China as a whole, making up in the neighborhood of one-quarter to one-third of household income.[8] As suggested by the fact that a portion of its teams' nominally "private"

---

[5]These figures are those of a statement by the head of the township in 1986, and closely match those given by Liu *et al.* (1990). The area indicated does not include reclaimed river bed land in the northeast section of the township, which according to Butler's "land use adjustment data" (see Putterman, 1989c) accounted for 131 ha in crops and 112 ha in orchards in 1980. (Liu *et al.* give substantially larger figures for river bed and orchards in 1988: 800 and 288 ha, respectively.)

[6]*Statistical Yearbook of China 1986* and JPRS, 1986.

[7]The river flows through Zhengding County, on which Huailu County and Dahe Township itself border. Some of the land brought into cultivation in the flood plain is unirrigated but most is watered with the help of streams and channels which flow through this somewhat marshy land.

[8]See, for example, Chinn (1978). No pre-1979 estimate exists for Dahe. A complicating factor is that according to interviews with former team and brigade leaders conducted in 1986, as much as one-quarter of workpoints awarded to team members were for deliveries to the team of manure from pigs raised and owned by the households. If we treat this portion of collective distribution as a return to private activity, the overall private income share could be rather larger than one-third. Conceptually, while the source of these

plots were actually collectively planted to grain by the teams, household activities generating incomes in cash or kind were if anything more restricted at Dahe than elsewhere.

Evaluated at the prices used in internal accounts, which appear to approximate state base procurement prices, an average of 26% of team disbursements to members took the form of cash, with the rest being in grain. Team members earned workpoints based on personal capability ratings and number of days worked,[9] and all disbursements were based on these points, the value of which varied by team and year depending upon team earnings net of taxes and costs, and on the amount of earnings retained for collective investment and other purposes.[10] However, an average of 74% of the distributed grain was allotted to households on the basis of sex- and age-adjusted population, with the nominal value of such allotments being debited against cash workpoint earnings.[11] A minority of team members worked in enterprises owned and run by their brigades or the commune, by other communes, or by the state (at county or province levels). In these cases, payments were sometimes made to the team which in turn compensated the members with workpoints, sometimes directly to the workers. A few Dahe residents were permanent state employees, examples being certain teachers, employees of the state supply and marketing cooperative, and workers in a county-run factory located within (or at least surrounded by[12]) the commune. Even if married to commune members, such individuals were not considered team or commune members, and had neither responsibilities to nor benefits provided by the commune and its subunits.[13]

Dahe's economy was predominantly agricultural and its agriculture was based upon grain and cotton during the 1960s and 1970s. Information provided by team level accountants indicates that as much as 92% of team revenue in 1970 was generated by crop production; the corresponding figure for 1980 was 70%. Of this crop output value, as much as 90% during the 1970s was attributable to grain crops

---

payments was team revenues, this can be seen simply as an input cost borne by the teams. However, households apparently fed their pigs with grain provided by the teams at the low internal accounting price, so the activity was partly subsidized by the teams.

[9]But see the previous note about payment for manure deliveries.

[10]In cases of extreme indigence and in the absence of family members capable of providing support, individuals and households may also have received payments out of team welfare funds, which averaged 0.7% of team earnings net of taxes and production costs, or around 0.9% of total distribution to team members.

[11]The implications of this practice for the work incentives of team members will be highlighted in Chapter 5.

[12]A technical school and the factory belonging to the county or higher levels were viewed by commune and village officials as lying outside of their territory even though they were entirely surrounded by it.

[13]This is a manifestation of the *hukou* or household registration system, described by Christiansen (1990). The remarkable hold of this system upon the local or at least official mindset was brought home to the author when the township office clerks who undertook the household survey in 1986 had to be explicitly instructed that state employees were to be counted as part of the rural households of which they were full time residents and members.

and cotton, with grain alone appearing to account for about 75% of the total.[14] An average of 85–95% of the teams' cultivated land as well as a portion of all "private plots" (as mentioned, this part was in fact farmed collectively) were sown to grain and cotton during the 1970s.

The request that led the Chinese Academy of Social Sciences and Hebei provincial authorities to select Dahe Commune in 1979 to be the site of research by an American post-doctoral fellow, Steven Butler, was for a commune in a Mandarin-speaking region that was not a model or suburban commune, that was of more or less average size and wealth, and that had experienced growth in the output of food grains over the previous ten years.[15] Data supplied to Butler at an all-commune level show that Dahe readily met his site selection requirement with respect to sustained yield improvements. Average grain yields per cultivated hectare, which allows for double cropping, rose from a low of around 2,250 kg in 1961 and 1962 to reach roughly 4,500 kg in 1965. During the remainder of the 1960s, possibly under Cultural Revolution influence, yields dropped slightly. Starting in 1970, one can turn for yield information to the data at team level, which give an average yield of 5,003 kg per ha in that year. As Table 3.1 shows, the average yield figure from this source rises steadily to reach 10,100 kg per ha in 1979. The typical grain plot was planted to wheat in winter (October seeding, June harvest) and corn in summer (May seeding between wheat rows, September harvest), with the computed multiple cropping index for grain fields being 1.89. Average yields for wheat rose from 1,904 kg per ha in 1970 to 6,335 kg per ha in 1978 before dropping slightly to 5,842 kg per ha in 1979. Average yields for corn were 3,199 kg per ha in 1970, reached a high of 4,883 kg per ha in 1974, and stood at 4,544 kg per ha in 1979. Dahe's yields of corn and wheat were far above national and provincial averages by the late-1970s: nationally, wheat yields averaged only 2,136 kg per ha and corn yields averaged only 2,984 kg per ha in 1979. Average yields for cotton at Dahe were unstable during the 1970s, with a high level of 600 kg per ha being achieved in 1970 and a low of 142 kg per ha recorded in 1976.

In spite of the great intensification of grain production in the 1960s and 1970s at Dahe, the percentage of their grain output marketed by the commune's production teams remained slightly less than the national average, with no rising trend over time. Average total grain sales to the state as a percentage of grain output began the decade at 19% in 1970 and ended at 18% in 1979, with variations to a low of 14% in 1971 and

---

[14]This is a rough calculation since no accounting value for grain output is given in the team data. We value quota sales at the average base procurement price for grain, and above-quota sales and all distributed and retained grain at the average above-quota price. This ignores peculiarities in the mix and qualities of grains produced at Dahe. Retained and distributed grain were most likely valued in internal accounts at the base procurement price, as suggested by the implicit valuation of grain distributed to team members (see Chapter 5). Hence, total crop output value had to be revalued for our calculations. If retained and consumed grain is instead valued at base procurement prices, as was probably done in internal accounts, the share of grain in crop output value would have averaged about 70%.

[15]Butler (1983, p. 101). The paper contains other details on the site selection and data-gathering process.

Table 3.1. Grain Yields and Output by Year, 1970–1985, Dahe

Year	Corn Yield[a]	Total Corn Output[b]	Wheat Yield[a]	Total Wheat output[b]	Grain Yield[a]	Total Grain Output[b]
1970	3,198.8	2,336.0	1,903.5	1,885.5	5,003.3	5,990
1971	3,506.3	2,802.0	2,048.3	1,909.5	5,518.5	6,390
1972	2,979.0	2,507.0	3,180.0	3,221.5	6,345.8	7,677
1973	2,898.8	2,296.5	3,135.0	3,397.0	6,369.0	7,152
1974	4,882.5	2,697.5	4,278.8	4,804.5	8,594.3	9,652
1975	4,332.0	2,370.0	4,830.0	5,463.0	8,973.8	9,964
1976	4,359.0	2,090.0	5,520.0	6,215.0	9,430.5	10,386
1977	4,076.3	2,518.0	5,571.8	6,118.0	9,329.3	10,114
1978	4,611.0	3,227.5	6,335.3	7,324.5	9,921.0	11,244
1979	4,543.5	3,860.5	5,841.8	6,649.0	10,100.3	11,452
1980	4,884.0	5,736.0	4,120.5	5,399.0	8,577.8	12,170
1981	4,743.0	5,599.0	5,180.3	6,679.5	9,537.0	13,297
1982	4,784.3	4,953.5	4,792.5	5,484.0	9,207.8	11,554
1983	4,662.8	5,337.5	5,244.8	6,234.0	9,554.3	12,473
1984	4,918.5	5,461.0	5,807.3	6,924.0	10,374.8	13,282
1985	5,076.8	5,702.5	5,039.3	5,981.0	9,645.8	12,333

[a]Average of kg per sown ha across reporting teams.

[b]Average yield times average sown area across reporting teams, times number of teams in commune/township.

Note: Data was not provided by three or more teams in 1970, 1971, 1972, 1980, and 1981, for all items, and in 1978 for items pertaining to corn. Total output figures may be biased if reporting teams were not representative (see [b]).

Source: Putterman (1989, Table 1), based on Dahe team accounts.

to a high of 23% in 1977. With absolute quota levels unchanged and total output rising, meaning rising absolute levels of sales, sales at quota price fell from 12% of grain output in 1970 to 6% in 1979, while those at above-quota prices rose from 7% of output in 1970 to 12% in 1979. With output steadily rising and the share of output marketed holding roughly constant, there was a significant upward trend in per capita distribution of grain to team members. Distributed grain averaged about 239 kg per capita in 1970, rose to 262 kg in 1975, and reached 345 kg in 1979 (see Table 3.2). Rising per capita grain availability at Dahe can be attributed in part to a low rate of population growth, averaging 0.52% per year during the 1970s, compared with a national average of around 1.7% for the rural areas.[16] However, the main cause is clearly the higher output per capita, which reached 635 kg in Dahe while it stood at only 420 kg for all of rural China in 1979. The commune's per capita distribution of grain grew from about 28% above the national per capita consumption level in 1970 to about 47% above the corresponding level for 1978.[17] Reported per capita consumption in the five teams surveyed at household level was 261.5 kg in 1979,

[16]World Bank (1983b, p. 86). For more on Dahe's demographics, see below.

[17]State Statistical Bureau (1988).

Table 3.2. Grain Output and Distribution, and Distributed Collective and Total Income per Capita by Year, 1970–1985, Dahe

Year	Grain Output Per Capita[a]	Distributed Grain Per Capita[a]	Distributed Collective Income Per Capita[b]	Total Per Capita Income[b]
1970	324 (.71)	239 (.71)	75.32 (.84)	n.a.
1971	345 (.84)	206 (.84)	73.67 (.84)	n.a.
1972	415 (.76)	233 (.76)	78.25 (.92)	n.a.
1973	389 (.98)	224 (.98)	77.96 (.99)	n.a.
1974	527 (1.0)	261 (.99)	84.40 (1.0)	n.a.
1975	530 (.99)	262 (.99)	81.06 (.99)	n.a.
1976	543 (1.0)	259 (1.0)	79.95 (1.0)	n.a.
1977	544 (.99)	259 (.99)	90.44 (.99)	n.a.
1978	612 (.98)	288 (.98)	106.77 (1.0)	n.a.
1979	635 (.99)	345 (.99)	128.64 (1.0)	n.a.
1980	603 (.80)	323 (.80)	172.82 (.95)	197.26 (.95)
1981	650 (.82)	327 (.82)	176.40 (.95)	198.49 (.95)
1982	586 (.75)	333 (.75)	180.91 (.98)	205.68 (.99)
1983	576 (.65)	443 (.65)	n.a.	386.14 (1.0)
1984	610 (.65)	408 (.65)	n.a.	507.32 (1.0)
1985	558 (.63)	368 (.63)	n.a.	589.86 (.99)

[a]Reported "private plot" grain output is added to reported grain output and grain distribution figures. Figures are in kilograms.

[b]Figures are in *yuan*.

n.a., No figures available, or concept not applicable.

Numbers in parentheses indicate the proportion of *total* teams that provided data on the item in question. Figures based on incomplete reporting may be biased if reporting teams were not representative.

Source: Putterman (1989a, Table 2), based on Dahe team accounts.

26% above average per capita grain consumption for China as a whole. This implies that about 24% of the total grain distributed to households was used for animal feed.[18]

Animal husbandry and orchards provided negligible or negative net earnings to the average team at Dahe in the 1970s, and there is no reported team income from fishponds, at least a few of which could be found in the township by the mid-1980s. However, team revenues from "sideline," transportation, and "other" enterprises rose from negligible to substantial levels during the 1970s, achieving a high of nearly 47% of team net income in 1978 before falling, in response to agricultural price increases, to 32% in 1979. A similar trend is reflected in the deployment of team labor. The number of workers in agriculture fell from about 83% of total team labor in 1970 to

[18]The possibility exists that the distributed grain figures for Dahe in the 1970s as reported in the text and Table 3.2 inflate the true figures by about 10%. A variable labeled "output of grain from private plots" has been added to "total grain distributed to members" to obtain the figures reported, on the belief that the first variable is not included in the second. Unfortunately, we are unable to establish that assumption with certainty. However, comparison of the column 2 numbers in Table 3.2 for the 1970s with those for 1980–1985, a period in which private plot grain output was zero, suggests that the assumption is accurate.

Table 3.3. Revenue and Labor Earnings by Organizational Level, Dahe Commune/ Township, Selected Years, 1970–1985

	1970	1973	1976	1979	1982	1985
Gross Revenue						
Commune/township	NA[c]	284	846	898.0	881	1,885
Percent	0	6.8	12.4	10.0	9.9	6.6
Brigade/village	231	441	1,599	2,308	3,416	8,608
Percent	7.5	10.5	23.4	25.7	38.4	30.3
Teams & households[a]	2,849	3,458	4,371	5,784	4,603	17,927
Percent	92.5	82.7	64.1	64.3	51.7	63.1
All levels, total	3,080	4,183	6,816	8,990	8,900	28,420
Net Revenue[b]						
Commune/township	NA	33	316	280	297	493
Percent	0	1.3	9.5	6.0	4.5	2.5
Brigade/village	116	265	763	1,044	2,130	4,706
Percent	5.4	10.7	23.0	22.4	32.6	24.5
Teams & households	2,037	2,173	2,245	3,344	4,103	14,011
Percent	94.6	87.9	67.5	71.6	62.8	72.9
All levels, total	2,153	2,471	3,324	4,668	6,530	19,210
Wages, Collective Distribution, and Self-Employment Income						
Commune/township	NA	NA	79	85	87	203
Percent	0	0	3.9	2.6	1.6	1.3
Brigade/village	22	130	268	465	535	1,867
Percent	1.4	7.5	13.2	14.2	9.8	11.9
Teams & households	1,527	1,609	1,678	2,733	4,834	13,569
Percent	98.6	92.5	82.9	83.2	88.6	86.8
All levels, total	1,549	1,739	2,025	3,283	5,456	15,639
Population, total (thousand)	20.3	20.6	21.0	21.2	21.7	22.7

[a]Data for teams and households are largely restricted to the team level before 1980. Beginning in 1981, and especially after 1983, they include information on the production of individual households and on partnership enterprises called new economic unions.

[b]Net revenue is gross revenue minus current nonlabor expenses and taxes.

[c]Figures not available. In this case, percentage breakdown is based on assumption that the missing figure is zero.

All figures (except population) in thousands of *yuan*.

Source: Putterman (1988a). Data for the 1980s are from township-provided summary tables. Data for the 1970s are from tables at brigade and commune levels, plus team accounts.

under 72% in 1979, while workers in "sideline" and "other" enterprises grew from 12% of the total in 1970 to over 20% in 1979.

Although agriculture retained its dominant position in the economy at team level, the combined output value of commune and brigade level enterprises (CBEs), which were mostly nonagricultural, was rising from approximately 8% of combined three-level (commune/brigade/team) output value in 1970[19] to 23% in 1974 and 36% in 1979 (see Table 3.3). In 1980, six enterprises at commune level employed a total of 290 workers (compared with a total of 9,283 workers in the production teams),

[19]No output data are available for the commune level in this year.

producing total output worth 850 thousand yuan, and generating net earnings, including payments to managers and workers, of 181 thousand yuan. The corresponding figures at brigade level were 23 enterprises (an average of 1.4 per brigade), 852 workers and managers, 2.62 million yuan gross output, and 1.89 million yuan profits and wages. The combined output value represented 41.6% of the output value of all three collective levels (teams, brigades, and commune); the combined wages represented about 11.5% of the combined distributed income of the three levels.[20] The commune-level enterprises consisted of a hydroelectric station, a repair and spare parts workshop, a phosphate fertilizer factory, a stone quarry, a tractor plowing station, and a farm. At the brigade level, five of the sixteen brigades had no enterprises at all, six had only one enterprise, and only one had more than three. The most common brigade-level enterprises were brick making (5 brigades), clothing (3 brigades), metal casting (2 brigades), electroplating (2 brigades), flour mills (2 brigades), and orchards (2 brigades). According to the township head, 24.9% of combined gross value of output (GVO) of the commune's three levels were from industry in 1980, with the remainder being from agriculture. However, using the narrower definition of agriculture that distinguishes it from the animal husbandry, forestry, fishery, sideline, and transportation branches, agriculture's share of three-level GVO was approximately 50% in 1980.

Despite the rising levels of per capita grain distribution already noted, during most of the 1970s the monetary value of the incomes earned by Dahe's families from their production teams was stagnant and below the maximum of around Y 80 achieved in the late 1950s (Butler, 1985).[21] As Table 3.2 shows, the average distributed collective income, computed from team level data, was approximately Y 75 in 1970. It rose to Y 84 in 1974, but was down again to some Y 80 in 1976. A noticeable upward trend began in 1977, when distributed income reached a little over Y 90. This rose again to nearly Y 107 in 1978 and to almost Y 129 in 1979. Although part of the increase would have been offset by higher prices,[22] and part reflects the higher valuation of grain distributed for household consumption, these numbers undoubtedly signal the beginning of an improvement in real living standards.[23]

---

[20]Note that incomes paid out by these three levels do not cover all income sources of Dahe commune residents. Left out are earnings from household sidelines and the wages of state and county enterprise workers.

[21]While the standard of living more broadly defined might be said to have risen, because of probable increases in life expectancy and in the availability of education (assuming Dahe to have been similar to the rest of China), residents interviewed in 1986 failed to raise such qualifications when asked to evaluate the trend in their living standard between the 1950s and 1985. Rather, they stated flatly that their living standard had not increased between the 1950s and 1978.

[22]The official general index of retail prices (Statistical Yearbook of China 1986) rose by less than 5% between 1976 and 1979. This is often held to be a conservative estimate from the standpoint of urban residents, but it may be reasonable for rural residents, who provided most of their own food, a major source of the price inflation facing urban consumers.

[23]A reasonable inflation adjustment puts distributed per capita collective income in 1979 at 117.44 instead of 128.64, still giving a 46.9% gain in real distributed collective income over this period. (Method: the average of 62.6% of income distributed in the form of grain, valued at Y 80.53, is revalued at its 1976 price equivalent of Y 71.52. The remaining Y 48.11 distributed in cash is revalued at its 1976 equivalent of Y 45.92, adjusting by the change in the general index of retail prices.)

Moreover, the gain in collective distributed income was almost certainly accompanied by increasing household-generated incomes, not shown in the team level data. Our one collective-era observation of incomes based on a household survey, which is for 1979 and for a slightly atypical sample of five teams, shows an average total income per capita of Y 288.39, of which Y 180.76 (62.7%) was distributed by the teams, Y 31.78 (11.0%) was from private plot output, Y 56.55 (19.6%) was from other household sidelines, and the remaining Y 19.30 (6.7%) was from wages paid by other units.[24] Since restrictions on the private sector were stringent at Dahe earlier in the decade, the private plot and sideline figures probably represent a substantially higher fraction of income than was derived from household sidelines in 1976 or earlier years.

The Reform Period

Between 1980 and 1985, Dahe People's Commune underwent economic reforms paralleling those in China as a whole and emerged as Dahe Township. By 1983, most agricultural production tasks were delegated to the individual households, which had rights to the residual output after paying various fixed obligations. Teams were disbanded and brigades were renamed villages. Both output and employment structures shifted, diversifying partially away from grain and cotton, in the case of crop production, and shifting away from agriculture and toward construction, transportation, and industry, in the case of the economy overall. There were also major institutional changes in the organization of nonfarm activities.

At Dahe as in China as a whole, a dramatic immediate result of the reforms was an increase in household incomes. In the previous section, we saw that per capita distributed income from the teams, which showed virtually no growth between 1970 and 1976, recorded a 17% annual growth rate between 1976 and 1979. As Table 3.2 shows, this category of income grew at a 12% rate between 1979 and 1982, thereafter ceasing to be relevant since teams no longer distributed income to their constituent households, which instead made contributions to the teams out of their own separate earnings. Total per capita (nominal) income, including that generated by farming plots contracted out by the teams or villages, as well as private plot, sideline, and wage earnings, rose at a 24.5% annual rate during 1980–1985, according to team and village estimates (Table 3.2). An alternative source of income data, the household survey, shows average per capita income of the 234 households providing complete data in 1979 to be Y 301.52, and that of the 238 households providing needed data in 1985 to be Y 778.45, giving an average annual growth rate of 17.1% over that 6-year period. Unlike most of the 1970s, when prices in China were quite stable, 1979 and

---

[24]Assuming that the same proportion of income came from noncollective sources in other Dahe teams, and using the data on collective distributed incomes from the team-level accounts, average per capita income for all of Dahe's households would have been Y 205 in 1979. The representativeness of the five teams covered in the household survey is discussed in Chapter 10.

the early 1980s saw annual retail and producer price increases averaging around 4% and 8%, respectively, so the post-1979 growth rates require some adjustment for inflation. Deflating all figures by the general index of retail prices (State Statistical Bureau, 1988, p. 692), the per capita income figures from team and village data imply a 21% real annual growth rate, while the figures from the household survey (in five teams only) imply a real growth rate of 13.6% per year. Applying the same price deflator to the series on agricultural household income per capita in *China Statistical Yearbook 1989,* p. 649, gives a 12.8% growth rate for rural household incomes in China as a whole during the 1979–1985. If instead income in the form of self-consumed produce is deflated to terms commensurate with the prices of 1979 using the general index of purchasing prices of farm and sideline products,[25] and if cash income is deflated by the general index of cost-of-living prices of staff and workers (State Statistical Bureau, 1988, p. 692), the average 1985 income from the household survey becomes Y 583.03 in terms of 1979 prices, giving a somewhat lower 11.6% annual growth rate based on the household data.[26] Applying the same deflator to the team and village figures lowers their implied real income growth rate to 19% per year. All of these rates of growth remain impressive compared to the stagnant incomes of the 1970s at Dahe.[27]

The degree to which *economic growth* accelerated at Dahe in 1979–1985 versus the 1970s may be somewhat overstated by income figures, because most growth during the collectivist 1970s was not converted into income gains for households. According to the team accounts, per capita gross output value[28] rose from an average of Y 92.28 in 1970 to Y 149.81 in 1979, and then to Y 578.04 in 1985. This gives nominal growth rates of 5.5% per year for the 1970s and 25.2% per year for 1979–1985, or real rates of 5.0% and 21.3%, deflating by the general index of retail prices. An alternative source which includes output generated by the brigade (village) and commune (township) as well as the team and later household levels, shows total gross output value rising from Y 3.1 million in 1970 to 9.0 million in 1979 and to 28.4

---

[25]Self-consumed produce should be valued at market prices in the Dahe data sets, although we cannot check the consistency of accounting practice. The purchasing price index might not deflate sufficiently, because it is based on prices paid by the state; however, the difference with market prices of the main crops was not large in 1985.

[26]There is a slight change in the sample due to exclusion of households providing insufficient data for the required disaggregation.

[27]It may be noticed that per capita income distributed by the teams rose more rapidly between 1976 and 1979 than between 1979 and 1982. This conclusion is strengthened using an adjustment by the general retail price index, which rose at a 1.6% rate during 1976–1979 versus a 3.4% rate during 1979–1982. The apparent inconsistency with the finding that incomes grew more rapidly in the early 1980s than in the 1970s may be explained in part by the fact that incomes from sources outside of the teams rose more rapidly than those from the teams during the early reform period (1979–1985). It seems more important to note, though, that radical decollectivization of agriculture did not occur at Dahe until 1983, that the 1976–1979 figures reflect both the sharp producer price increases of 1979 and the elimination of what appear to have been nondistribution constraints (see Chapter 10), and that the absolute increase in incomes was slightly higher in the second period but constituted a smaller percentage increase due to the then larger income base.

[28]That is, team revenue minus costs and taxes, divided by team population. It is "gross" in the sense that it is prior to the deduction of team accumulation and other nondistributed funds.

million in 1985 (Table 3.5), for nominal growth rates of 12.6% per year in the 1970s versus 21.1% during 1979–1985, or real rates of 12.1% and 17.2%, respectively, using the general retail price index, or of 9.2% and 15.8%, respectively, using the general purchasing price of farm and sideline products index. Thus, all sources indicate a speeding up of growth in the early reform period, but (especially in the last case) not necessarily a change *from stagnation to growth* as suggested by the data on household incomes.

Reform and Grain Production

One respect in which Dahe's performance was impressive in the 1970s but lackluster in the early 1980s was grain production. We have now seen how grain yields rose at Dahe people's commune during the 1970s. These trends were replaced by reversal and stagnation in the 1980s. As Table 3.1 shows, average wheat yields dropped sharply to 4,121 kg per ha in 1980, then recovered partially but failed to surpass 5,300 kg per ha in all but one of the remaining years covered, standing at 5,039 kg per ha in 1985. Average corn yields slightly exceeded their 1974 high, reaching 4,884 kg per ha in 1980, then remained roughly stable, with a low of 4,663 kg per ha in 1983 and a high of 5,077 kg per ha in 1985. Total grain output per cultivated hectare dropped to 8,578 kg in 1980, then climbed back above 9,500 kg in 1981, 1983, and 1985, with a slight dip in 1982 and a new high of 10,375 kg in 1984. Although the lack of data on some teams for earlier years reduces confidence in these computations, direct inference from the data available assuming that reporting teams are representative indicates that total grain output per cultivated hectare grew at 8.1% per annum between 1970 and 1979 but declined by 0.8% per annum between 1979 and 1985. Wheat yields grew by 13.3% per annum from 1970 to 1979 but declined by 2.4% per year between 1979 and 1985. Corn yields grew at 4.0% per annum between 1970 and 1979, but by only 1.9% per year between 1979 and 1985. Total grain output at team and household levels grew at a rate of 7.5% per year during 1970–1979 but at only a 1.2% annual rate during 1979–1985. Output per capita, which rose from 324 kg in 1970 to 635 kg in 1979, declined to 558 kg in 1985 (see Table 3.2).

A possible objection to using these trends as indicators of pre- and post-reform performance is that the choice of 1979 as a dividing line perhaps unfairly assigns gains associated with the price increases of 1979 to the pre-reform era. The Dahe data, however, indicate that the growth of grain output in 1979 was only slightly more rapid than the trend growth rate for the 1970s as a whole. Using 1980 as the start of the reform period at Dahe is justified, on the other hand, by the fact that team farming did not begin to be superseded by household-based farming at Dahe until that year (see below).

A more valid concern is that failures to maintain yield and output growth under the agricultural reforms at Dahe must be seen against a backdrop of extremely high yields already attained there in the 1970s, the absence of additional cultivable land,

and the gradual removal of land from cultivation for industrial use. Wheat yields of 5,500–6,500 kg per ha achieved at Dahe by the late 1970s must be compared with the national average of 2,939 kg per ha, or with the Hebei provincial average of 1,994 kg in 1982, a year in which Shanghai led China's provinces, regions, and directly administered municipalities in wheat yield at 4,190 kg per ha. Corn yields somewhat above 4,500–5,000 kg per ha at Dahe must be compared with the 1985 national average of 3,598 kg per ha, the 1982 Hebei average of 3,493 kg per ha, and the high yields of 6,050 kg per ha reported by Shanghai municipality and 4,828 kg per ha reported by Liaoning province in the same year. Furthermore, total grain output per cultivated hectare, which hit highs of 10,100 kg in 1979 and 10,375 kg in 1984 at Dahe, compare very favorably with yields in the highest grain-yield counties in north China, which were 9,378 kg for the highest-yield county in Hebei, 9,040 kg for the highest-yield county in Liaoning, and 9,430 kg for the highest-yield county in Shandong.[29] Under a given state of agricultural technology, further increases in yields may be physically difficult and economically unjustifiable because of increasing marginal costs. Indeed, Butler (1985) reports that fertilizer usage declined at Dahe in 1980 when teams and brigades were given greater autonomy to determine input levels, strongly suggesting that higher authorities had driven Dahe to raise yields by economically irrational methods during the 1970s.[30]

All the same, the discovery (see below) that adoption of household responsibility systems raised peasant incomes through diversification of crops, higher crop prices, and especially through diversification *out* of agriculture, and not by quantitative increases in crop production, must be seen as an important finding from the analysis of the Dahe data. For one thing, there is reason to suspect that Dahe's situation resembled that of other Chinese townships that achieved agricultural gains during the era of collective production. At the case study level, Huang (1990) reports comparable findings for a similarly advanced unit in southern Jiangsu province. There is also a suggestive finding from the statistics of localities throughout China, namely the data on randomly selected counties which was drawn on in the previous chapter. As an exercise, the counties were ranked by grain output per sown hectare in 1980. Then the 10% of counties (20 counties) with the lowest 1980 grain yields, the 10% with the highest 1980 grain yields, and the 10% with yields closest to the mean for 1980 were selected, and average grain yields and level of chemical fertilizer applied per hectare were computed for 1980 and 1987. The results show that grain yields grew by an average of 90% during 1980 to 1987 in the low yield counties, by an average of 31% in the medium yield counties, and by an average of only 14% in the

[29]Provincial and county yield data are from the China Agricultural Yearbook, 1983, reprinted in JPRS, 1986. National data are from State Statistical Bureau (1986).

[30]Butler's data on this point are cited by Lardy (1983: 235, note 15; see also p. 114) in support of the proposition that commandism by higher-level cadres led to excessive input use in some locations. Wiens (1985: 93, note 5) also concludes that farming intensity at Dahe was unusual for North China, arguing from this that Butler's belief that farming was unprofitable because of too low product prices and too high input costs should not be generalized from Dahe to other areas.

high yield counties, with the gap between originally high and originally low yield counties closing from 5.1 : 1 in 1980 to 3.4 : 1 in 1987. Similarly, fertilizer usage per hectare grew by an average of 102% in the low yield counties, by an average of 83% in the medium yield counties, and by an average of only 44% in the high yield counties, with the gap in average fertilizer application per hectare declining from 4.2 : 1 in 1980 to 3.0:1 in 1987. Such a correlation between yield improvements (and input intensification) and original yield (and input use) levels is consistent with the relative stagnation of grain production at Dahe in the early 1980s, although the high-yield counties in the sample do show some further gains, on average.[31]

In addition to its relevance to the experience of other agriculturally advanced localities during the same period, Dahe's experience in the early 1980s might be viewed as an early indicator of more general problems in Chinese agriculture, and especially grain production, in the second half of that decade. As we saw in Chapter 1, after the state's unification of purchase prices and removal of guarantees to buy grain in excess of contracts in 1985, the nation's grain production, which exceeded all expectations with the bumper harvest of 1984, stagnated and hence returned to the fore as a political and economic issue. Policy statements admitted that production at late 1980s prices was not economically attractive to farmers and that substantial new price increases were not affordable (see *Wall Street Journal*, 1988; *Beijing Review*, 1988). In a sense, therefore, Dahe's response to the reforms was a precursor of problems facing China as a whole in the mid- to late-1980s. Those problems surfaced earlier at Dahe because the relative attractiveness of grain production was already lower than average in the early 1980s, due to the fact that its advantageous location gave it greater than average access to lucrative nonagricultural and high value crop production opportunities.

At Dahe, the reforms led to the transfer of large amounts of labor and some quantities of other resources out of agriculture. Because Dahe's grain yields and input use were very high by national standards, it is not surprising that relaxation of central controls over the allocation of its productive resources led to a reallocation of those resources into more profitable activities. Some of that reallocation, however, was both unplanned by and unacceptable to local officials. As a response, the area devoted to grain cultivation at Dahe actually rose in the 1980s, strongly suggesting that authorities at the township and higher levels responded to the unplanned diversion of resources by asserting control over the resource over which they could most easily exercise authority: land use.[32] From an economic point of view, use of acreage constraints to secure grain output targets gives rise to an obvious inefficiency: Land

---

[31]Reduced input use and grain yields may have been occurring in some of the more advanced townships in these counties but could have been masked by the impact on aggregate county results of increasing input use and yields in other townships.

[32]Compare the evidence on village-level land use planning reported by Sicular (1991) (cited in Chapter 1). Rozelle (1991), likewise reports cadre control of crop choice in the late 1980s in a sample of Jiangsu Province villages.

devoted to grain because of planning constraints could have produced more crops of higher value in other uses, and the mix of land, labor, and other inputs in both grain and nongrain fields became distorted from economically optimal proportions. Similar efficiency losses are undoubtedly being registered in much of rural China today. Thus the data from Dahe provide evidence of what is perhaps the central problem of Chinese rural development today: that further progress toward market coordination of economic activity is impeded by an inability to complete the reform of the price structure with respect to staple crops shows.[33] A tentative conclusion might be that hog production was relatively unimportant at Dahe, and that the fertilizer motive for raising hogs may have been adversely affected by the unprofitability of many crop production activities and, more speculatively, by uncertainty over continuity of land use rights.

Changes in Economic Structure

Although the concept of economic reform focuses on changes in the mode of economic *organization,* changes in the *structure* of economic activity in rural China have been as pronounced as have those in economic institutions. Because economic structure—i.e., the allocation of labor and other resources, and the breakdown of output, by activity or product—is often an indicator of the level of economic development, the magnitude of these changes is arguably a measure of the success of China's rural economic policies. Rising shares of nongrain earnings in agriculture are typical of growing economies, because the income elasticity of demand for grains is lower than that for fruits, vegetables, animal products, and other farm products. Rising shares of nonagricultural activities in both output and employment also mark developing countries for the same reason. All of these trends are observed in rural China of the 1980s and illustrated by the data from Dahe Township.

Data on income at team level continued to be recorded through the end of 1985. With the adoption of *baogan daohu* in 1983, however, teams were forced to obtain most such data from surveys of their members, since most income no longer passed through team control before accruing to the households. The change of method caused some data on incomes from private plots and sidelines to enter into the team

---

[33] A reader of a previous version commented, quite appropriately, that even if the sale of grain is not profitable at existing prices, use of grain to feed hogs and livestock might be. Moreover, hog production is intimately tied to farming from the standpoint of fertilizer. Although both the Dahe surveys and their analysis to date might be faulted for relative inattention to this issue, it can be stated here that reported hog and poultry production rose little in the surveyed households between 1979 and 1985, and that the number of households indicating that they raised these animals declined. Although the team-level survey shows an increase in household incomes from animal husbandry, the sector's importance at Dahe was well below the average for rural China, as Table 3.4 shows. A tentative conclusion might be that hog production was relatively unimportant at Dahe, and that the fertilizer motive for raising hogs may have been adversely affected by the unprofitability of many crop production activities and, more speculatively, by uncertainty over continuity of land use rights.

accounts for the first time.[34] Despite confusion due to change in coverage,[35] it is possible to get a rough overall picture of structural change occurring at the team and household levels from these accounts. This picture can be supplemented by analysis of the data collected by the researchers at household level in five of the teams, data which have reference to the years 1979 and 1985.

The major trends of interest are the reduction of the labor force in agriculture, and the reduction of the share of income coming from crop production (excluding animal husbandry, orchards, and fishponds) in general, and from grain in particular. Crop production's share of gross income over all reporting teams rose from 72% in 1979 to 80% in 1980 and 81% in 1981, but thereafter fell to 69% in 1982, 66% in 1983, 59% in 1984, and 55% in 1985. With respect to income net of expenses, agriculture's share already had fallen to 53% in 1978, but it recovered to 69% in 1979 and 1980, and 70% in 1981, reflecting price increases and most likely also greater efficiency in input use, including the mentioned decline in outlays on fertilizer. The crop production share of net income records a sudden drop to 58% in 1982, however, and declines thereafter, falling to only 50% in 1985. Because most output at village and township levels is nonagricultural, the share of agricultural output in overall gross and net income is considerably smaller.[36] The share of total agricultural (crop) revenue at the team (later, household) level attributable to grain fell from 88% in 1979 to 50% in 1985, while the share of cotton in agricultural income (at those levels) fluctuated between 15% and 35% during that period.[37] The proportion of the labor force employed in crop production, according to team-level data, fluctuated between 71% and 73% from 1976 to 1982, then dropped to 66% in 1983 and 60% in 1985 (see Table 3.4).

The beneficiaries of crop production's *relative* decline were animal husbandry,

[34]The exception is grain produced on the private plots, which appears in the team accounts for the 1970s. As indicated above, however, this grain was actually produced and distributed collectively.

[35]In the 1986 survey, which at the team level pertained to the years 1980 through 1985, team accountants were asked for a breakdown of total incomes into three categories: those produced collectively, on contracted land, and under other contracts to the collective; those produced individually; and those produced by "new economic unions" (see below). But the data show what appear to be dramatic inconsistencies across brigades, suggesting a failure to agree on whether income earned on contracted plots—i.e., under *baogan daohu* for crop production—belonged properly in the collective or in the individual category. There were also indications of a lack of uniformity of practice with respect to inclusion of private plot output, and no satisfactory method could be found for establishing which practice was being followed by which teams and in which years. This confusion makes it impossible to estimate with great precision what fraction of the increase in output occurring in 1983–1985 should be attributed to real gains associated with *baogan daohu* and other reforms, and what portion reflects the change to a more inclusive statistical reporting system; that difficulty will be discussed further in Chapter 7.

[36]A figure of 27% would be derived on the basis of team accounts for household production and from a township summary sheet drawn up by the chief township clerical officer for village and township levels, assuming as before that crop output is a negligible part of the product of the latter. A more detailed source of data on village and township enterprises, the enterprises data set, is missing information on some enterprises. A third source, a verbal summary presented by the township head, is inconsistent with the summary sheet, and suggests the higher figure of 35% of gross output value from crop production. This source is used to compile Table 3.4.

[37]As above, these are rough calculations only. See note 14. A similar method was applied to the calculations for cotton.

Table 3.4. Share of GVO and Employment by Sector, 1980 and 1985, Dahe

| | Gross Value of Output, % | | | | | | Employment, % | | | |
| | Dahe, All Levels | | Dahe, Excluding Villages and Township[a] | | China, Rural[b] | | Dahe[c] | | China Rural | |
	1980	1985	1980	1985	1980	1985	1980	1985	1980	1985
Agriculture (Crop production)	47	35	80	55	49	36	71	60	83	67
Animal husbandry, forestry, fishery, sidelines	2	6	3	10	20	21	6	2	6	15
Transportation, commerce, construction	5	10	8	16	12	15	13	25	2	6
Industry	47	49	9	19	20	28	9	12	6	7

[a]Includes household, team, private,and partnership enterprises. Excludes production of state-owned units in township boundaries or incomes earned by Dahe residents in state employment.

[b]Coverage should match that of first Dahe columns. Excludes county and other state enterprises and incomes earned by rural residents employed by them.

[c]Excluding state employees except contract workers.

Sums of GVO shares may differ from 100% due to rounding. Sums of employment shares are below 100% due to exclusion of some job categories. For other technical notes, consult the text and footnotes.

Sources: Putterman (1989a, Table 3), based on Dahe data sets and Byrd and Lin (1990).

the net income share of which rose (at the household or team level) from 3% in 1980 to 11% in 1985; sideline enterprises, the share of which rose from 2% to 9% in the same period; transportation, which rose from 4% to 13%; and the catch-all category labeled "other," which rose from 21% to 27%. Team level labor force data (covering allocation by member households, although perhaps with questionable accuracy) indicate that the bulk of nonagricultural workers in 1985 could be found in sideline enterprises (12%) or in the "other" category (22%). The data for individuals from the household survey lists 302 farmers, 121 workers in village-run enterprises, 26 workers in township-run enterprises, 21 workers in "new economic unions" (see below), 30 contract workers in county enterprises, 24 construction workers, 36 transport workers, 16 restaurant and commercial workers, 64 household workers, and 87 "other" workers. This means that only 45.6% of those not listing "housework" as their principal occupation in the five surveyed teams reported those occupations to be agriculture, while 23% listed work in enterprises run by the township, villages, or groups of individuals. It is also interesting to note that 15.5% of the women in the workforce listed their principal occupation as housework.[38] Table 3.5 gives an

---

[38]Housework is not listed as an occupational category in the 1979 survey. It is possible that some of what respondents called housework was in fact animal husbandry, crop production, or sideline activity carried out in the family courtyard and nearby vegetable gardens, even though those activities were also offered as responses to this survey question.

Table 3.5. Characteristics of Labor Allocation by Individuals at Dahe, 1985

T^a	Cat^b	$No.^c$	m^d	f^e	Mean Age	Mean % of Worktime					s.d. of % of Worktime				
						c	s	w	t	h	c	s	w	t	h
1	c	84	51	33	35	90					20				
2	s	91	72	19	42		98					8			
3	w	75	59	16	34			94					13		
4	t	161	86	75	12				100					4	
5	h	60	8	52	57					91					23
6	c,s	63	58	5	36	33	67				19	19			
7	c,w	95	65	29	32	28		72			17		18		
8	c,t	26	15	11	17	19			82		13			13	
9	c,h	203	32	171	38	74				25	16				15
10	s,w	3	3	0	34		55	42				27	23		
11	s,t	1	0	1	15		10		90						
12	s,h	5	4	1	51		70			16		35			6
13	w,h	19	12	7	35			75		20			19		17
14	t,h	3	1	2	14				90	10				0	0
15	c,s,w	3	3	0	33	30	38	30			17	14	9		
16	c,s,h	9	0	9	38	61	21			18	15	12			6
17	c,w,h	15	1	14	34	31		54		16	20		25		9
18	c,t,h	1	1	0	17	10			90	10	0			0	0
19	$None^P$	403	182	220	28										

[a]Type of individual.
[b]Category; presents the activities in which each type of individual participates.
[c]Total number of people belonging to each type.
[d]Total number of males belonging to each type.
[e]Total number of females belonging to each type.
c Crop production; s sideline activity; w wage-earning activity; t student; h housework.
[P]Type 19 reported no activities.
Source: Park (1989, Table 2), based on Dahe data sets.

occupational breakdown of 1985 survey respondents, including those who listed two or three different uses of time. The table shows the number of persons in each occupation (or occupational mix) category, the number of males and females, their average age, the average share of time reported to be devoted to each activity, and the standard deviations of the shares.[39]

In addition to the shift away from crop production in general, changes in the composition of cultivated output toward an increasing share of nongrain crops should also be noted as an element of structural change at Dahe, paralleling a similar shift in rural China as a whole. In the 1970s, vegetable cultivation at Dahe appears to have been restricted to a portion of the private plots only, and was geared toward home consumption. By 1985, many families were using contracted collective plots to grow crops such as watermelons and medicinal herbs for sale in the markets of Shijiazhuang and elsewhere. According to the director of the township government, typical

[39]Respondents and enumerators were asked to treat 100 as 100% of a typical workday, allowing those who seemed to work more than a locally typical workday to report a sum greater than 100.

profits from a hectare of grain were Y 1,500, profits from cotton were up to Y 3,000 per ha, but those from vegetables, melons, or herbs could reach Y 15,000 per ha. The area devoted to high-value crops experienced growth but remained fairly limited, almost certainly because of the previously discussed administrative pressures to sustain grain and cotton production, although perhaps also because these crops are intensive in labor for which there were attractive alternative uses. Team level data show the percentage of the cultivated area devoted to watermelons growing from 0 in 1980 to 0.3% in 1982 and to 1.0% in 1985. The share of land devoted to peanuts jumped from 0.2% to 0.3% of cultivated area during 1980 to 1983, to 2.1% in 1985, while vegetables, showing an erratic trend, reached 7.6% of cultivated area in 1985, up from 5.2% in 1980.[40] Observation and interviews in 1986 suggested that most able-bodied young men not employed in transportation, construction, or factory work were engaged in raising high-value nongrain crops for sale in urban markets.

During the 1980s, five new commune or township enterprises were established at Dahe, bringing the total number of township enterprises to ten. Although we have survey data giving some detail for most individual enterprises, the more aggregated data of the township summary sheet permit the most comprehensive description of output, profit, wage, and employment trends. The GVO of township (commune) enterprises grew from Y 850,000, or 10% of three-level (commune, brigade, and team) gross output in 1980, to approximately Y 1.9 million, which constituted less than 7% of total township, village, and household (hereafter also referred to as three-level) GVO in 1985 (see Table 3.3). Village (brigade) enterprise-generated GVO rose from Y 2.6 million (31% of three-level output value) in 1980 to Y 8.6 million (30% of three-level GVO) in 1985. These 1985 figures put GVO of township and village industries at only a slightly higher percentage of the three-level total than the national average for townships, villages, and collectives, which was 33.2% (State Statistical Bureau, 1986: 183). The *net* income of township enterprises grew from Y 181,000 (3.4%) to Y 493,000 (2.5%), while that of village enterprises grew from Y 1.9 million (35.7%) to Y 4.7 million (24.5%) over the period (with figures in parentheses indicating percentage of three-level net income). The 1985 breakdown of net income by source at Dahe shows a somewhat smaller share from households and a larger share from township and village enterprises than the national average.

From 1980 to 1985, workers' earnings from township enterprises rose from Y 31,000 to Y 203,000, increasing as a share of earnings at all three levels from 0.7% to 1.3%. Earnings from village enterprises also both rose in absolute terms and increased their share, from Y 452,000 (10.8%) to Y 1.9 million (11.9%). The combined shares of peasants' personal incomes from the two collective levels are only slightly above the national figure of 11.9% from township, village, and collective enterprises. That township and village enterprises at Dahe had declining shares of gross and net output but rising shares of personal income generation is

---

[40]No data are available on these crops before 1980. Note that the respective shares of *sown area* may be lower, because the majority of Dahe's land grows two crops per year.

consistent with a finding of rapidly rising wages for their employees. Calculating from the summary sheet, from 1980 to 1985 the average annual earnings of township enterprise workers rose from Y 146 to Y 630, while that of village enterprise workers rose from Y 453 to Y 811, suggesting either upward pressure from improving alternative opportunities, worker influence on enterprise management or village and township governments, or a combination of both. As wages rose, the share of profits in net income declined, from 82% to 56% for township enterprises and from 75% to 55% for village enterprises, while the share of wages correspondingly rose, from 18% to 44% and from 25% to 45%, respectively, mirroring national trends.[41] Complementing the rise in average earnings, the number of workers and managers employed by township enterprises rose from 212 to 322, while those employed by village enterprises increased more rapidly, from 998 to 2,312 workers. This included an undetermined number of temporary workers from other parts of Hebei and China.[42] Despite the decline in profit as a share of net earnings, total value of assets rose from Y 810,000 to Y 2,276,000 for township enterprises and from Y 2,710,000 to Y 10,520,000 for village enterprises. Township enterprise profits over the 5-year period equaled 83% of the change in asset value, while village enterprise profits exceeded the addition to assets by 33.5%, so each level could have self-financed most if not all new growth.[43]

Our discussion of industry at Dahe in the 1980s is incomplete without considering a new enterprise type: "new economic unions" or partnership-owned enterprises (the ownership and related characteristics of which are discussed in the next section). According to the township summary sheets, GVO of partnerships or economic unions, which are not recognized by the data for 1980, reached Y 900,000 (3.2% of total GVO) in 1985. In the same year, their net income was Y 500,000, slightly more than that of township enterprises, and accounting for 2.6% of total township net income. A total of 110 households are listed as owners or partners in 36 enterprises, employing 257 workers, including partners and members of their families. The average annual earnings of workers of all types, including but not limited to partners, is given as Y 1,673, about twice the average earnings of workers in township and village enterprises.

Some data on enterprises of yet another type, those owned by individuals, are included in the enterprise survey and will be briefly discussed in the next section. Separate data for this category are not included in the township summary sheet, however, so consistent conclusions about their shares in GVO, net income, or wages

---

[41] As noted in Byrd and Lin (1990), rising wages and falling profit shares were typical during this period in rural China as a whole, and in the township and village enterprises of four counties studied by the joint Chinese-World Bank project on which they report.

[42] Village-owned brick factories were said to obtain almost all of their unskilled labor from places as far away as Henan and even Sichuan. The workers lived in dormitories and had no rights to settle in the village in which they worked.

[43] This observation abstracts from the specific time path of profits and investment. Unfortunately, we lack data on loans incurred by townships and village enterprises at Dahe.

cannot be derived. Note, however, that registered individual enterprises remained relatively rare in 1985, and that these are to be distinguished from household enterprises, which were ubiquitous and accounted for most of the activity in what was previously the team level and is referred to as the team and household level of the three-tier scheme used throughout this section and in Table 3.3.

Structural change at Dahe may be compared briefly with national averages. As shown by Table 3.4, the share of GVO due to agriculture in the narrow sense (i.e., crop cultivation) at Dahe was some 2% below the national rural average in 1980 (47% versus 49%) and, after both shares declined, was about 1% less than the new average in 1985 (35% versus 36%). The shares of forestry, livestock, fishery, and sidelines were far below the national average (2% versus 20%) in 1980 and, after some growth, still low compared to that average (6% versus 21%) in 1985. The shares of construction, transport, and commerce were likewise low (5% versus 12%) in 1980, but made up some of their gap with the national average (to reach 10% versus 15%) by 1985. The share of industry was far above the national average (47% versus 20%) in 1980 and remained high (49% versus 28%) in 1985.[44] Because almost all output of the village and township levels was in industry,[45] the shares of nonindustry are higher when these levels are excluded, as Table 3.4 also shows. But the share of industry in output even at the levels of households and private and partnership enterprises has been growing rapidly since 1980.

In an analysis of regional differences in the composition of rural industry output, Wang Tuoyu (1990) identifies a "machine building/building material" pattern as being characteristic of Hebei, Liaoning, and Guangdong provinces. Data on output of township, village, private, and partnership enterprises at Dahe can be grouped by product category, following Wang's classifications insofar as possible. The results indicate that 42% of the gross value of output from enterprises providing data in 1985 belongs to the materials industry, 29% to the metalworking industries, 3–5% each to the chemicals, food-processing, and garment-making industries, and 9% to enterprises providing no product information. It seems likely that the prominence of machine building in province-wide rural industry that is noted by Wang reflects suburban townships better than even well-located rural ones such as Dahe. The prominence of building materials, on the other hand, is consistent with the Hebei pattern, and with the patterns in fully 16 other provinces in which this is the leading sector of rural industry. But the relative importance of construction and other

[44]In these calculations, Dahe team reports of "other" income are treated as equivalent to construction and commerce, categories which are not listed in the team data sets. To avoid double-counting, income accruing to teams from brigade and commune sources is not counted in the team-level total. For consistency, the sum of the included income categories, rather than the supplied total that sometimes differs, is used as denominator. Output data for village and township levels are taken from the township summary sheet, and all output is assumed to fall in the "industry" category, which may introduce a small amount of bias in its favor. National data are from the State Statistical Bureau, as reported in Byrd and Lin (1990). Percentages may not add to 100 because of rounding.

[45]Moreover, as the previous note indicates, all village and township output are assumed to be in industry for purposes of the calculations reported above and in Table 3.4.

trades—often carried on by households and partnerships too small to appear in the enterprise data set—among the nonagricultural activities at Dahe is to be interpreted, according to Wang, as a sign of an "underdeveloped" rural industrial structure.

With respect to labor force, the share of workers employed in agriculture proper dropped from roughly 71% in 1980 to 60% in 1985, according to the Dahe team-level data, while nationally this share dropped from 83% in 1980 to 67% in 1985 (see Table 3.4). Forestry, livestock, sidelines, and fishery accounted for 6% of workers at Dahe and also 6% nationally in 1980, but for only 2% of workers at Dahe versus 15% nationally in 1985. Workers in construction, transport, and commerce accounted for 13% of the total in 1980 and 25% in 1985 at Dahe, versus 2% in 1980 and 6% in 1985 nationally. Workers in industry accounted for 9% in 1980 and 12% in 1985 at Dahe, versus 6% in 1980 and 7% in 1985 nationally.[46]

These findings can be summarized by stating that 1) Dahe's overall output structure was already far more oriented toward industry than was the average rural township in 1980; 2) industry's output share grew more slowly at Dahe than nationally, from 1980 to 1985; and 3) the latter result was due to the conjunction of strong gains by private enterprises with growth by village and township enterprises that was slower than Dahe's three-level average output growth rate. The common tendency for agriculture's share of employment to exceed and for industry's to fall far below their respective shares of output is observed in both the national and Dahe data. The employment share of industry thus diverges far less from the national average at Dahe than does that sector's output share. Rapid reductions in agricultural employment occurred both at Dahe and nationally, but whereas the noncrop farm activities (animal husbandry, etc.) and sidelines played the greatest part in absorbing released labor nationally, it was transportation, commerce, and construction that played this role at Dahe. The importance of the latter sectors reflected Dahe's proximity to an urban center and the construction boom there and in neighboring towns in the early to mid-1980s. That importance is in a sense understated by the partition of Table 3.4, because building materials are an important part of the output of industry at Dahe. Earnings of household-based enterprises in these sectors could also be systematically underreported in the Dahe accounts.

At the beginning of this section, it was suggested that the rising shares of commerce, construction, transportation, and industry in output and employment at Dahe and in China nationally may reflect the success of rural economic reform in

---

[46]As above, national data are for rural areas only. They are taken from the State Statistical Bureau, as cited in Byrd and Lin (1990). Labor data for Dahe are from the Dahe team accounts and treat all workers in township- and village-run enterprises as part of industry. The number of workers listed under "specialized households" and "new economic associations" was dropped in this calculation after it was found that the sum of workers in the categories provided by the data set more closely matched the separately indicated total number of workers in the absence of these categories, implying that they may have been counted twice: once under industry and once by type of enterprise. Parallel statistics for labor allocation in 1985 from household-level data of the five teams surveyed, based on a somewhat different occupational partition, are 46% in agriculture; 2% in forestry, livestock, sidelines, and fishery; 11% in construction, transportation, and commerce; and 30% in industry. Percentages add to less than 100 because of noninclusion of some categories, such as teachers and health workers.

fostering economic development. It is worth commenting here that the rise in nonagricultural activity in China, including Dahe, also illustrates an internationally *atypical* pattern of industrialization and economic diversification: that is, that this process took place without much change in the locus of economic activity (in other words, without much permanent rural-urban migration). The release of labor from agriculture in the China of the 1980s represents a watershed in the country's recent economic history, because change in the output structure over the three previous decades had occurred without major change in the allocation of the country's labor force. The transfer of labor from agriculture in the China of the 1980s was possibly the single most important result of rural economic reform. The relative rapidity of this process may be attributable to the existence of a backlog of reallocable labor built up over three decades of massive population growth and incipient rural industrialization. What limits to labor transfer were in force during the 1970s, and whether limits to such transfer remained in place in the early 1980s at Dahe, will be explored further in the next chapter.

A Note on Demographics

Earlier, it was pointed out that reported net population growth in the 1970s was only 0.5% per year at Dahe versus 1.7% for China as a whole. Our data for the 1979–1985 period indicate a 1.1% annual growth rate, above the 1970s figure and only slightly below the corresponding all China figure of 1.2%. Conceivably, the reforms at Dahe combined with the population momentum effect of a large cohort of women reaching child-bearing age could have triggered a rise in fertility, or increasing economic opportunities could have reduced outmigration or increased inmigration.[47] On the other hand, the difference between the rates reported for Dahe in the 1970s and in the early 1980s could result from statistical error, and it may be unwise to place much weight on the appearance of change.

To investigate whether fertility and mortality patterns at Dahe differed significantly from Chinese averages, and to consider the role of migration, we consider data provided in the household survey conducted in 1986. First, respondents indicated the number of household members who died between the 1980 and 1986 surveys. The total of such reported deaths was 43 out of a population of 1,154 in 1979,[48] which gives a crude death rate of roughly 6 per thousand per year, just slightly below the 6.8 per thousand average rate for Chinese counties during 1980–1985.[49] Second, respondents indicated the number of members of survey households (in 1986) born after 1979. These births totaled 144 in a 1985 population of 1,087, which gives a birth

---

[47]Note that the only immigrants likely to appear in the survey as regular residents are spouses of native Dahe residents. Temporary migrants such as those working in village brick factories will not have appeared since they had no team membership.

[48]This could give a slight undercount since deaths could have occurred subsequent to outmigration among some of the 277 sample members reported to have left these Dahe teams.

[49]State Statistical Bureau (1988, p. 76).

rate of roughly 22 per thousand per year, somewhat above the 19.9 per thousand average for Chinese counties in 1980–1985.[50] Thus, ignoring differences in migration rates, these Dahe teams would have experienced a higher rate of population growth than rural China as a whole.

Another source of both fertility and mortality data are responses to questions about the number of children ever born to adult women in the 1986 household survey, and the number of the latter surviving in 1986. Unfortunately, the responses here appear to be unreliable. According to the survey responses, the number of children ever born to women in their 20s (37% of whom appear to have been married[51]) in 1985 averaged 0.33, and the number born to women in their 30s, 40s, 50s, 60s, and 70s averaged 1.7, 3.0, 3.5, 3.0, and 2.0, respectively.[52] The child survival rate calculated from the survey figures is 97% for women in their 20s and 98%, 99.6%, 100%, 94%, and 95% for women in their 30s through 70s, respectively. These figures fail to reflect the downward trends in both fertility and mortality (of children in the case of the younger women, of children and or adults in the case of older ones) that would be expected for the China of recent decades. The coincidence of an implausibly small number of children reported born and an implausibly high proportion of children reported surviving, for the older cohorts of women, suggests strongly that children who had died or long since left the village were for some reason underreported.[53]

With respect to population movement, 277 out of the 1,154 individuals present in 1979 departed the survey teams by the end of 1985 for various reasons (including death), while 109 individuals moved into the teams from other localities, with 82 of the outmigrants and 74 of the inmigrants reporting marriage as a reason. The 101 person excess of births over deaths was thus exceeded by a 168 person excess of outmigrants over inmigrants, yielding a net loss of 67 persons in the population of the surveyed households. Since the five teams were in this respect not fully representative of the township as a whole, which reportedly gained rather than lost population, it is impossible to draw firm conclusions on the basis of the household survey.

Organizational Change

Agriculture

Like many other moderately prosperous communes, Dahe was fairly late in adopting agricultural responsibility systems of the more radical type in which households

---

[50]State Statistical Bureau (1988).

[51]Since no question on marital status per se was included in the survey, this is computed by counting all women reporting having given birth to one or more children, plus any other woman indicating that she was the spouse or parent or grandparent of the household head.

[52]The respective proportions ever married would appear (using the method described in the previous note) to be 86%, 100%, 98%, 87%, and 63%, and the numbers of children for women reporting one or more births are 1.3 (for those in their 20s), 2.0, 3.1, 4.1, 3.7, and 3.6.

[53]Note also that the method described in note 51 probably led to inaccurate imputations of the proportion of women ever married in note 52.

replaced the teams as basic units of farm production. In 1976, before the second purging of Deng Xiaoping, and again in 1978 and 1979, after his reemergence,[54] some of Dahe's production teams report having both increased their use of piece rates (instead of Dazhai-like time rates used earlier in the decade) and having given their households continuing responsibility for certain tasks on specific plots of land after field preparation and planting—a management technique referred to as *jiti gengzhong fen hu guanli* ("the collective plows and plants, [then] divides to the households to manage"). These practices, designed to increase work incentives, left the teams in place as the basic units of farm production. Team members thus continued to receive shares of output and revenue based on workpoints and household size after the usual deductions for expenses, taxes, accumulation, and other collective funds. Unlike later, more radical management reforms, the number of points to be earned on the responsibility fields was fixed in advance, rather than varying with the output achieved. The departure from the basic system that had dominated two decades was minor enough or occurred in few enough teams that it was not even noted by Butler, who states that "Dahe used the 'Dazhai' system of workpoint allocation right up until 1979" (1985, p. 104).[55]

With the 1980 wheat crop (that is, the crop planted in autumn of 1979), some teams at Dahe began introducing a somewhat more radical form of responsibility system in which households were not only asked to manage a crop on a certain piece of land, but also earned workpoint, cash, or in-kind bonuses according to the amount harvested in excess of a target level based on historic yields. As in the system of the 1960s and 1970s, the bulk of the crop still went to the team, and distribution of cash and grain to the households was still primarily determined by workpoints. Unlike the experiments of the late 1970s, however, households could now earn more for a larger harvest on their responsibility fields. The new systems were referred to under the name *lianchan jichou* ("linking reward to output"). They were initially introduced in only a minority of teams and were sometimes practiced for one or two major crops (for example, wheat, or wheat and corn) but not others (cotton, or cotton and corn) in a given team. In 1980, 37.5% of the teams used *lianchan jichou* for at least one of these crops; in 1981 66.4% used it, and in 1982, the number appears to have been 100.0%.[56] In Chapter 7, we will report on an econometric analysis of the team input and output data which suggests only a modest productivity gain, and only in the case of corn, for teams adopting the new system. Although the evidence also indicates a positive impact of the system on productivity in terms of combined gross crop output value (GVCO), the fact that roughly one-third, then two-thirds, then all teams adopted *lianchan jichou,* is consistent with the interpretation that decisions regarding

[54]Reference to these national political events was made by Dahe officials in response to questions about the timing of these reforms.

[55]The partial division of fields to individual management nonetheless strikes the present author as a major change insofar as it substantially addressed the issue of observability of individual work effort, a question that looms large in the theoretical debate over work incentives (see Chapter 5 and the appendix of Chapter 7).

[56]This item was left blank on the survey form of one team.

adoption of the new form were taken by higher levels, probably without excessive attention to local conditions and results.

The most radical form of responsibility system, *baogan daohu* ("contract work to the household") or simply *da baogan* ("the greater contracting"), was introduced in all of Dahe's teams (and, apparently, in all Huailu County teams) in a single stroke with the 1983 wheat crop. At Dahe, as elsewhere in China, *baogan daohu* entails the distribution of team lands to the households, which are given responsibility for paying their share of the state agricultural tax, for selling a quota of output to the state, and for meeting certain obligations to their team in cash, produce, or labor. The households receive the earnings on quota deliveries, and are free to sell any additional output to the state or market, or to retain it for their own consumption. In effect, the households become separate farm units using land leased to them by their team or village for a fixed "rent" consisting of state tax plus collective obligations plus the tax implicit in obligatory sales at quota or contract prices. Land farmed collectively during the 1960s and 1970s was allotted to team members in 1983 according to formulas that considered the number of persons in the household, the number of workers, and the households' requests for land. Land distributed according to household size was referred to as *kouliang di* ("grain ration land"), indicating that it was viewed as something to which the household was entitled as a means of meeting its grain consumption requirements.[57] The remaining distributed collective land was referred to simply as *chengbao di* ("contracted land"). Besides this, households continued to have rights to their private plots, without tax, quota, or collective obligations. In 1985, when at least 92% of the cultivated land in the township was distributed to households in one form or another,[58] the five teams surveyed at household level had about 11% of this land distributed in the form of "private plots," while 63% was distributed as "contracted land," and 26% as "grain ration land."[59] The effects of variation in the land allotment formula on farm productivity are examined in detail in Chapter 9.

With the adoption of *baogan dauhu,* collective agriculture proper ceased to

---

[57]The term *kouliang* has been used to denote the grain that teams distributed on a per capita basis under the collective system of the 1960s and 1970s.

[58]In 1980, a total of 171 ha, 109 of which were orchards, were cultivated by the brigades, representing about 8% of the cultivated area of Dahe People's Commune. Approximately the same figures appear to hold for 1985, although portions of both the orchards and the nonorchard plots were contracted to individual management at that time.

[59]During the data collection process, some confusion arose as to whether land in the last two categories constituted separate plots. Following institutional information conferred by the township statistical officer, the household data set for 1985 reports activity on each plot, treating "contract" and "grain ration" plots separately. However, members of the rural economy institute at the Hebei Academy of Social Sciences, who later conducted their own study of Dahe, asserted in the course of discussions with the author in 1990 that the distinction between the two types of land existed only as an accounting and land allocation device, and that the plots were not in fact separated or separately identifiable. This implies that the distinctions adhered to in the household survey responses were fabricated in response to an institutional misperception on the part of the researcher—a sobering illustration of the pitfalls of survey research. This misunderstanding would not, however, affect the validity of the data on the *proportions* of land allotted under each principle, either at household or at team levels.

exist. In particular, the problem of individual work incentives in a team disappeared because, as in other systems of fixed-rent tenancy, each household now stood to gain or lose 100% of the change in revenue attributable to working harder or smarter, or to not doing so, at the margin. However, the degree to which the farming system reverted to an individualistic process can easily be overstated.[60] Not only did households remain subject to constraints regarding what they would grow, as conveyed through state delivery obligations (or, since 1985, grain and cotton purchase "contracts")[61] but they also purchased inputs and received many agricultural services from agricultural service stations located in each village (that is, the former brigade), and this undoubtedly influenced the planning of their individual farm operations. For example, at Dahe, autumn plowing, planting of wheat by seed drill, mechanized threshing of that crop, and certain fertilizer applications were provided by the service stations on a common schedule, at fees varying with the ability and interest of each village in subsidizing its families' farm operations. Irrigation also required coordination, although this was apparently decentralized to the point that holders of individual fields simply negotiated with the collectively appointed operator of the well serving those fields, who released water to them in exchange for a small fee. Nor was Dahe particularly exceptional in these respects. A Ministry of Agriculture study reported that while only 2.4% of China's cultivated area continued to be farmed collectively in 1987, 85% of the irrigation, 80% of crop layout, and 76% of plowing was done by villages or other collective units in the eastern portion of China, with 50% of fertilizer and pesticides and 65% of diesel oil being collectively allocated in this region.[62] Beyond this, it appeared that officers of collective units continued to see themselves as responsible for promoting currently favored agricultural practices, and that households were unlikely to depart from their instructions regarding matters such as the spacing of the corn crop (which continued to be manually planted at the time of the author's visit).

Thus, the transition from the collective to the reform or "post-collective" era in rural China was marked by both change and continuity. One major change in the system of collective units following the introduction of *baogan daohu* was the disappearance of the production teams at the end of 1985. Although the brigades and the commune itself also ceased to exist in name, each of these levels was replaced, without change of jurisdiction, by village and township government units. On the other hand after adoption of *da baogan*, the production teams saw their functions disappear. Team leaders and accountants, at first assistants to the brigade or village leaders in the implementation of the new contracts, soon found that their services

[60]For earlier general discussions of these issues, see Khan and Lee (1983) and Putterman (1985a).

[61]These contracts appear to have been allocated to the households in exactly the same fashion as had the earlier quotas, rendering the change nominal from the peasants' viewpoints. See also the discussion in Chapters 1 and 12.

[62]See Sicular (1991, Table 2). It is consistent with these figures that there existed a great number of localities in which essentially all irrigation, crop planning, plowing, and input supply was managed by the collective.

were not needed as land allocation was worked out at village (brigade) level. The few viable team-level enterprises were contracted out to individual households or turned into partnerships. The number of team cadres was reduced by steps and, at the end of 1985, the larger villages created units (called *pianr*) composed of two or three former teams to help oversee village-supervised farm operations, while smaller villages abolished their teams without substituting any subunit. Former team cadres either turned to full-time farming or moved into any of a variety of nonagricultural activities growing in importance at Dahe, including management and accounting positions in village-run enterprises.

Nonagricultural Enterprises

By 1985, the organizational form of nonfarm enterprises at Dahe had changed nearly as much as had that of farming. For example, many township- and village-owned enterprises had been transformed by the adoption of contracting systems that, in essence, leased the enterprises to their managers in exchange for payment of fixed fees to the owning collective unit, with possible stipulations about investment and employment. According to the director of the Township Industry Station, which managed the township's relations with its ten enterprises, there were three varieties of contracts in 1986, which stipulated that after payment of costs and state taxes the remainder would be split either (type 1) 40% to the industry station, 40% to the enterprise, and 20% to its managers and workers, (type 2) a fixed amount paid to the industry station, and the remainder split 50% to the managers and workers, 30% to the enterprise, and 20% to the township, or (type 3) a fixed amount to the industry station, which undertook to finance the enterprise, and the remainder divided among the managers and workers. In the last case, the typical division of profits was said to follow the principle that the director could get up to three times as much profit as an ordinary worker. The example of which township leaders were proudest was that of the peddi-cab factory, which was said to have been transformed by its manager from a repair and scrap recasting factory employing ten workers and making losses, to a highly profitable enterprise employing sixty workers and having Y 300,000 worth of fixed assets. Its manager, a former enterprise staffer still holding local peasant registration, was said to have earned Y 70,000 in 1985, and to have set aside 70% of this to establish a home for the aged, which would be named in his honor.[63] The earnings of the director in this case appear to have exceeded the 3-to-1 guideline just mentioned.

Two species of enterprise new to China were the "partnership" and "individual" enterprises for which some statistics were given earlier. The Chinese term for the

---

[63]Unfortunately, these figures from the account of the township head are not fully corroborated by the enterprises data set. We do not known which source is more accurate. In any case, the report of a "voluntary" charitable donation by a rich villager is reminiscent of numerous accounts of cadre arm-twisting from other parts of China during the period.

former type was *xin jingji lianheti*, translated in the *Statistical Yearbook of China* as "new economic unions." Although the name and descriptions given by leaders at Dahe and in official Chinese sources initially suggests a new form of cooperative that is distinguished from the old collectives by its voluntary character, a look at the structure of the associated enterprises at Dahe suggests that a better match is with the Western concept of a business partnership. The partners of the association generally invest personal savings and money loaned by relatives and friends, which may be supplemented by funds obtained on loan from the local branch of the Agricultural Bank of China (ABC) and the local Rural Credit Cooperative (RCC) affiliated with it. Having used these funds to finance the construction of a factory or shop or the purchase of equipment (such as tools required by a construction team), the partners proceed to hire as many workers as they require at wages which they are free to determine. Some but not all partners also work in their enterprise as managers of one kind or another. After paying wages, other production costs, taxes, and loan payments, the investor-managers divide their profits (if any) among themselves, generally in proportion to the size of their investments. Profit-sharing with the hired workers is possible but not typical.

An example of such a partnership is a textile factory built outside of the residential area of Dahe Village in February 1986. The factory was owned and run by four partners, all men from Dahe Village, two of whom had been brigade leaders in the past. Each partner invested Y 20,000 in the factory, and together they borrowed an additional Y 100,000 from the credit cooperative. In addition to the four managers, the factory employed 38 workers. The factory owned 16 electrically powered looms and produced heavy cloth for collar linings, which was sold to the Shijiazhuang City Printing and Dying Mill. Workers were hired for Y 25 per month as apprentices, then after 3 months, received Y 0.035 per meter produced (with 100 meters said to be possible in a shift if power did not fail). The wage scale was said to be based on that of a township-owned enterprise that produced the same product by the same method. The workers were from Dahe and surrounding villages, although two were formerly technicians at a Shijiazhuang factory. The partners had to pay Y 1300 annually for the 0.17 ha of land on which the factory sat and Y 0.4 per square meter annually for use of the factory buildings which formerly housed a brigade-level animal husbandry enterprise.

It may be worth noting that the example just given of the partnership enterprise in which half of the partners were former cadres seemed not atypical. Although no systematic data on the backgrounds of owners and managers were collected, most of the partnership enterprises visited by the author involved former cadres.[64] It was difficult to avoid the impression that they had been encouraged to set up these

---

[64]Financial data were obtained for most enterprises in the township, but only a few enterprises were visited, the selection being made by township staff. Conceivably, that selection was biased toward enterprises run by persons in their own social network.

enterprises by current township and village leaders, who were anxious to display the township's progressive character (at a time when government policies had just shifted in favor of a more "mixed" economy) by promoting noncollective industries. Former cadres probably enjoyed an advantage in access to ABC and RCC funds, which, in practice, were rationed and applications for which required the support of local officials. On the other hand, the former cadres in question projected an image of managerial competence and energy, and the possibility that the same personal traits might explain their emergence as leaders of the collective sector in one era, and of the private sector in the succeeding regime, should not be overlooked.

As for "individual" or private enterprises, only a few that were considered substantial and permanent enough to be registered with the township, and that were required to pay taxes, are reported in the enterprises data set. The first two appear in 1983. Their number grew to eight in 1984 and to fifteen in 1985. These enterprise had an average of slightly more than two owner-managers in 1985, and only three of them reported hiring any employees, with the number hired averaging 6.33 in those cases. The average gross revenue of the individual enterprises was Y 43,000 in 1983 and Y 52,337 in 1984, but fell to Y 14,273 in 1985. Average net revenue was Y 7,193 in the latter year, from which the average reported profits paid to each manager-owner (11 enterprises) was Y 2,228 and the average tax was Y 666. The average current value of fixed assets among the enterprises was Y 13,780.

Many small private entrepreneurial activities were being carried on at Dahe outside of the formal, taxable enterprise sphere. Aside from widespread animal-husbandry activities, the most common of these were transport enterprises usually based upon ownership, by the household, of one or more tractors. These 12-horsepower four-wheel tractors were employed during most of the year moving bricks, which were produced by the village-owned brick kilns scattered throughout the township, to buyers in Shijiazhuang and elsewhere. According to team level data, the total number of tractors owned by teams or households rose from 8 in 1974 to 88 in 1978, 116 in 1982, 198 in 1983, and 393 in 1985, with the proportion of these owned by households rising from 1.9% in 1980 to 8.6% in 1982, 68.7% in 1983, and 97.7% in 1985. Assuming that no household owned more than 1, this meant that more than 1 in 15 households owned a tractor in 1985, compared with the national average of 1 tractor (of all size classes) per 21.6 households.

Twenty-four households in the five teams surveyed at the household level appear to have owned or shared ownership of a tractor.[65] Almost all of these households had only one member listing transportation as a principal occupation, to which an average

[65]This inference is based on the fact that one or more household members listed transportation as an occupation, the household had gross earnings of at least Y 3,000 from transportation, and the household reported at least Y 2,500 in capital assets. These indirect criteria were applied because no question about tractor ownership per se was included in the household survey. The number of households identified by these three criteria in each surveyed team is similar but not identical to the number of privately owned tractors in the same team as reported in the team level data set.

of 90% of their work time was reportedly devoted. Only one household indicated that a second member devoted part time to transport work, and the average share of total remunerative work time devoted to transport work by the households in question was 33%. The households reported hiring no outside labor. Their gross incomes from the transport enterprise alone averaged Y 5,708, and their net income from this activity averaged Y 3,292, slightly less than the average total household income *from all sources* in surveyed households as a group and about four times the average annual earnings of workers in village enterprises.[66] Readers already familiar with conditions in rural China will know that tractors are notorious for being employed, essentially in place of trucks, for everything *but* agricultural work. Even these readers may nonetheless be surprised (as was the author) to learn that the reported area cultivated per worker and per capita was actually smaller in tractor-owning than in non-tractor-owning households, according to the survey, and that agricultural income per capita and per worker is also smaller for the tractor owners. Some income reported under "transport" enterprise may have consisted of payments for tractor hire by other farmers, and some transport services probably entailed hauling manure to fields, hay to pigsties, crops to market, and so on. Interviewed tractor owners confirmed, however, that the bulk of tractor use was nonagricultural.

Periodic markets had long been held in Dahe Village, but activity was extremely limited during the late 1960s and the 1970s. Visits to these markets in the summer of 1986 showed a scene of vibrant commercial activity. The market stretched a distance of roughly one-half mile on each of two perpendicular streets, included dozens of stalls, and was crowded with hundreds of customers and at least three roving hawkers of ice sticks and candied apples. Cloth and clothing, ranging from bulk fabrics to manufactured clothing and shoes and on-the-spot tailoring stands, accounted for upward of one-half of the stalls, with small tools, pots, pans and buckets, and fruits, vegetables, beans, and spices occupying most of those remaining. The sellers included individual peasant households from Dahe and nearby townships, and representatives of collective or partnership enterprises from the same areas. Tax collectors circulated among the stalls collecting taxes from the vendors while the buying and selling proceeded noisily.

A Note on Investment

One of the most important questions that has been raised regarding the impact of the reforms upon Chinese agriculture concerns its effect on investment in productive assets and infrastructure (Lardy, 1986). The data from Dahe show that accumulation funds as a share of net income at team level varied from 7% to 23% during the 1970s,

---

[66]From the data, it appears that tractors were assessed by their owners at an average value of no more than about Y 5,000. If they could be kept operating for more than 2 years, the rate of return on the investment would therefore appear to be very respectable.

with values above 15% each year during 1974 through 1978. The corresponding ratio of accumulation to net income is never more than 10% after 1980 and falls below 3% in 1983, 1984, and 1985. The share of accumulation in net earnings of the brigades (villages) is available for 1980–1985 only, and hovers around 50% without trend. In absolute terms, accumulation per capita by production teams was around Y 9 in 1970, Y 31 in 1977, Y 26 in 1981, and Y 15 in 1985. Accumulation per capita by brigades (villages) rose from around Y 12 in 1980 to around Y 28 in 1985, thus surpassing accumulation by teams in the latter year.

Per capita assets owned by teams rose from Y 58 in 1970 to Y 168 in 1981, then fell to only Y 75 in 1985. However, productive assets owned by households and teams combined probably had a continually rising trend during the reform period. Teams may not have counted the value of assets held by households in their reports of total asset value in the 1980s, but the data which they provided on individual assets owned by households suggests that combined team and household asset value continued to rise from around Y 163 per capita in 1982 to Y 223 per capita in 1985.[67] Per capita assets owned by villages also shows a rising trend, from around Y 115 in 1980 to around Y 180 in 1985. Overall, then, investment in productive assets by villages and households appears to compensate for the decline in investment by teams. However, another concern raised by Lardy, that regarding investment in land improvements and maintenance, cannot be directly investigated with these data, which include no estimates of this type of investment. That question will be discussed further in Chapter 9.

Dahe in the late 1980s: A Postscript

The data collected at Dahe township in 1980 and 1986 reflect the township's experience during the final decade of the collective production era, and during the first half decade of China's agricultural and more general economic reforms. In Chapter 1, it was noted that in China as a whole the second half of the 1980s saw general stagnation in grain production, slower growth in the production of other crops, more rapid growth of rural industry and other nonagricultural activities, and the need for stepped up pressures by various bureaus and levels of government to implement state plans for contracted purchases of grain and other staple crops in the face of a widening gap between contract and market prices. In this chapter, it has been suggested that Dahe's abnormally high grain yields and favorable access to urban industry and markets caused its response to the *early* 1980s reforms to be a kind of

---

[67]The data provide physical quantities but not prices for the individual inputs. Approximate prices are obtained by regressing the total value of asset figure at team level on the quantities of component items for the years 1977–1981, in which most assets were still team owned. The resulting coefficients are then used to compute a total asset index for all years. (A similar procedure will be reported in Chapters 4 and 7.) The index matches the team asset variable well during 1970 to 1980 but continues to rise when that variable falls after 1981.

"leading indicator" of the late 1980s period for other parts of rural China. While detailed data on Dahe's own experience in the second half of the 1980s are unavailable, a general and tentative picture can be sketched on the basis of information obtained during a brief visit by the author to Shijiazhuang and Dahe township in August of 1990. Apart from oral reports and visual observations, that information includes the contents of a monograph on Dahe prepared by members of the Hebei Academy of Social Sciences' Rural Economy Institute and Dahe's Communist Party Secretary (Liu et al., 1990) and a report by the township's government and party offices (Communist Party Committee of Dahe Township and Dahe Township People's Government, 1990).

Shortly before the author's return visit to Dahe, an article appeared in *People's Daily (Renmin Ribao)* titled "The Big River Flows This Way—An Account of Dahe Township, Huailu County, Hebei Province." Dated May 22, 1990, the article cited Dahe as a model of production, and stated that in 1989, the township's total grain output was 17,398 tons, said to represent a 47.2% increase over 1985. The first question needing to be addressed in the brief follow-up visit was clearly, Had Dahe broken through to new records of grain productivity even as China as a whole was mired in a series of poor harvests (a reversal of the early 1980s situation in which Dahe's grain production was stagnant while China's was growing)? The answer turned out to be a clear "no." According to data provided by Liu et al. (1990), Dahe's grain output rose to a new high in 1986, fell slightly in 1987, then reached yet another high in 1988; the *People's Daily* figure for 1989 represented an 8% increase over that last figure. However, from the sown area and yield figures provided by Liu et al. (1990), it is easily calculated that 85% of the output growth between 1985 and 1988 was due to an increase in the *area sown to grain,* while only 15% was due to an increase in yields.[68] Most of the increase in area sown to grain came from a reduction in area sown to cotton, which after peaking at 681 ha in 1984, fell to only 142 ha in 1988. Thus, rather than representing an exception to the general Chinese pattern of the late 1980s, what we know of Dahe's record might be read as further confirmation of a pattern in which grain output was sustained ever less by increases in productivity and ever more by diversion of other resources to grain production, often more in response to administrative than to market signals.

According to rural development experts interviewed in Beijing, the shift away from cotton at Dahe was part of a pattern of relocation of cotton sown area from traditional to new sites within Hebei province. While township officials cited profitability reasons for this change, higher level administrative coordination may

[68]Without information on sown area in 1989, it cannot be known what portion of that year's growth was due to yield versus area change. During my brief visit to Dahe in 1990, I was told that corn yields had exceeded 6,000 kg per ha in 1988 and 1989, and were expected to be close to 6,750 kg in 1990. This would represent a sharp rise above the 4,000–5,000 kg range that characterized the entire 1974–1985 period (Table 3.1), and the officials with whom I spoke stated that a new seed variety had played a key role. Despite this change, overall grain output per hectare was less than 5% higher in 1988 than in 1985, and still substantially below the 1984 record, according to Liu et al. (1990).

also have played a part. The switching of cotton land back to grain, rather than to crops of higher value, is especially unlikely to be explained primarily by market forces. On the contrary, it is consistent with the early 1980s pattern of increasing the area devoted to grain despite the falling relative profitability of grain crops. With respect to households' own planting behaviors, it is impossible to establish precisely the roles played by administrative coordination—facilitated by village-level plowing and planting of grain fields—versus the influence of economic factors—such as the unwillingness of households to substitute grain purchased on the unstable and high-price market for either their household consumption requirements or their state sales obligations. An indication that market forces played a facilitating role, and that they had to be respected by local officials, is that the township and village factories making corn starch, alcohol, and flour from corn and wheat paid Dahe farmers at market prices for these products; for example, in 1989, they paid Y 0.76 per kg of corn, versus the state contract price of Y 0.34. This suggests that even if Dahe residents grew grain partly because township and village officials were anxious to please their counterparts in the county, municipal, and provincial governments, economic inducements were also used: the township and village governments had boosted grain production partly by providing a ready market for grain surpluses, and had "met their residents halfway" from the standpoint of marketing and pricing.

The book by Liu et al. (1990), the report, and information provided verbally by the township Party Secretary provide incomplete and inconsistent information about the growth of overall output value. According to the Secretary, the gross value of agricultural output, including animal husbandry, orchards, and fishponds, doubled between 1986 and 1989, reaching Y 22 million in the latter year; but the book gives a value of 38.5 million for 1988. The Secretary reported industrial gross output value of "over Y 80 million" in 1989, versus about Y 16 million in 1986; the book reports Y 84.6 million in 1988, but gives a total gross output value for that year of Y 114.5 million. Comparing the Secretary's figures for 1989 with the all level gross revenue figure for 1985 of Y 28.4 million given in Table 3.4, combined output value would have risen by nearly a factor of 4, or at a rate of 39% per year; using the book's combined figure for 1988, the growth rate would be 59% per year.[69] Even the second but especially the first of these figures is not inconceivable, since most output growth would have been in industry and services in which revenue has grown more rapidly than value added and the growth rate between 1982 and 1985, as computed from Table 3.3, was 47% per year. Moreover, these figures are in current price terms, and inflation ran higher in the late than in the early 1980s. According to the *People's Daily* article and the Secretary, per capita income in the township reached Y 1,115 in 1989, which implies a nominal growth rate of 16% a year using the 1986 figure of Y 715

[69]Here, I assume that by "over Y 80 million," the secretary means Y 84.5 million, a figure given for 1988 by the book. The growth rate to 1988 is based on the Y 114.5 million figure, not the even higher Y 123.1 million that would result from adding together the separately given figures for gross value of crop output and gross value of industrial output in 1988.

given by the newspaper article, and 17% a year using the 1985 figure of Y 590 given by Table 3.2. This indicates a slower rate of growth of real income than in 1980–1985, since the annual growth rate in current *yuan* was then over 24% (from Table 3.2), and inflation was higher in the later part of the decade. For example, deflating by the official overall retail price index,[70] real per capita income growth averaged 20.5% per year in 1980–1985 but only 4.9% per year in 1985–1989. On the other hand, growth at Dahe far outpaced that for rural incomes nationwide, which was barely over 1% a year between 1984 and 1988.

With respect to changes in economic structure, data provided by Liu et al. (1990, p. 68) suggest a continuation of earlier trends, although the categories used are partly incomparable to those in our data sets. Table 3.4 shows the share of the transportation, commerce, and construction industries in gross output value rising from 5% to 10% between 1980 and 1985. The book's figures exclude construction from this category, and give the share of the remaining industries, now including "services," as 7.2% in 1988. The book does not distinguish between crop production and the other agricultural subsectors (such as animal husbandry), but it lists their total share of GVO as 33.7% in 1988, in line with a continuing decline from 49% in 1980 and 41% in 1985. Industry's share appears to continue its increase, reaching 59.1% in the book's figures for 1988 versus 49% in 1985 according to Table 3.4 (although the first figure includes the value of construction whereas the second does not). On the employment side, the same trends hold, with the combined share of agriculture (including animal husbandry, etc.) falling from 77% in 1980 and 62% in 1985 (Table 3.4) to 54.1% in 1988, industry (including construction) rising to 30.6% in 1988 (without construction, it is 12% in 1985, by Table 3.4), and transportation, commerce and services standing at 15.2% in 1988. Those authors' data on gross output value by ownership form (p. 69) is somewhat less consistent with that given in Table 3.3 above. They report the township level's share to be 13.3% in 1988, up from Table 3.3's 6.6% in 1985, but down from their own 13.8% figure for 1984. Their village level figure for 1988 is 38.1%, similar to the figure for 1982 and above that for 1985 in Table 3.3.[71] They report private and partnership *(lianheti)* enterprises as producing 48.6% of output in 1988, versus the 63% share for 1985 given in Table 3.3. Their breakdown attributes 58% of the total to private enterprises and 42% to partnerships. It is not clear where household farming of contracted land fits in this calculation.

The moderating growth trend toward the end of the 1980s at Dahe could be interpreted as reflecting a "natural" moderation of the growth trend of a rapidly developing economy, but there are reasons to see it also as the reflection of two factors operating for China more generally. First, the agricultural growth rate slowed after

---

[70] State Statistical Bureau, 1990a.
[71] They report the much higher figure of 57.2% for village *and team* levels in 1984, but these levels are not combined in Table 3.3.

1984, with the most likely culprits being 1) the one-time nature of the gains from transition to the household responsibility system, and 2) the deterioration of the terms of trade facing agriculture following a period of relative improvement during 1979–1984. Second, the growth rate of the construction industry and of related industries such as building materials, transport and brickmaking was widely affected by state-ordered reduction of the number of new construction projects, especially beginning in 1988, and the growth rate of rural industry was slowed in 1989 and 1990 by the government's macroeconomic stabilization program, which reduced the availability of rural credit and attempted to increase the share of that credit going to agriculture. Since building-related activities were a major growth sector at Dahe in the early 1980s, one would have expected a significant impact of the changes in that area. As for the credit squeeze on industry, the Secretary stated that whereas the township's gross value of industrial output had roughly doubled in each of the years 1987 and 1988, its growth rate was only 30% in 1989 and was also expected to be comparatively slow in 1990.[72] He indicated that township and village enterprises had borrowed about Y 4 billion from local households and Y 3 billion from enterprises and other organizations in Shijiazhuang, and that money thus collected had saved twelve of the enterprises from bankruptcy.

Despite the moderation of its growth rate in the late 1980s, Dahe is certainly still to be described as a rapidly growing rural township with prospects for further rapid economic transformation and productivity growth in coming years. Proximity to Hebei's capital and principal industrial city, and the more favorable environment for economic interaction since the commencement of the reform process, continue to be the main factors at work. The former agricultural communes within the boundaries of Shijiazhuang proper, referred to as its "suburban district," have enjoyed rapid industrialization and de facto urbanization in recent years. Their development has been based on this same proximity, the relative flexibility afforded by the "rural collective" as opposed to state or large urban collective form of enterprise organization, and the many niches in the urban economy left unfilled by the state sector. The suburbs' roles as subcontractors to state enterprises and suppliers of vegetables to the city have increasingly shifted to villages in counties beyond the municipal border proper as the suburbs themselves become more urbanized and their residents command higher wages. Townships such as Dahe accordingly find themselves in a position to follow the suburbs in this gradual but steady process of development. As an indicator of things to come, Dahe township had designated a new township center, located adjacent to the main road between Dahe (the old center) and Jiacun villages. Symbolizing the central role of local party and state structures, one of the first projects to be completed was a new four-story township office building, more modern than

---

[72]It is hard to know what to make of the claim of a doubling of output, which is inconsistent with the GVIO data reported just above. Perhaps it refers to industry more narrowly defined. In any case, the statement comparing 1989 and 1990 with 1987 and 1988 probably has some qualitative validity.

any existing structure at Dahe, yet maintaining the traditional aspect of a walled compound, with police and judicial buildings in its front courtyard. Factories and a residential area, which the Secretary predicted would house about 10,000 people by the end of the decade, were set to follow. Plans were also underway for Dahe to be designated a town *(zhen)* rather than township *(xiang)*, and the construction and planning of the new center were to be assisted by provincial and municipal governments, with Dahe Town being viewed as a satellite town of Shijiazhuang. It thus appears possible that a visitor to Dahe in the year 2000 will find it well on its way to becoming an industrial suburb of Shijiazhuang, with limited resemblance to the rural people's commune that Steven Butler visited 20 years earlier.

Concluding Remarks

This book's in-depth analysis of China's collective and reform era rural economy and of the transition between the economic systems of those two eras relies heavily upon data gathered at a single site. Because no single locality provides a microcosm of rural China as a whole, this chapter and the one before it have provided an array of information that may help the reader to understand both the variation of conditions among China's many regions, and the basic conditions prevailing at Dahe Township in the period under discussion. A general summary of our findings might be that while Dahe was certainly not average, due to its proximity to a provincial capital and the intensity of cultivation that it achieved during the collective era, it was also not entirely atypical of portions of the coastal region of rural China. With respect to level of industrial development, per capita income, and economic structure, Dahe in the 1970s and 1980s was moderately, but only moderately, advanced. With regard to organizational and institutional dimensions, Dahe also appears to be reasonably representative, although the radicalism of its collective practice and the strength of its surviving collective entities were also above average during the 1970s and 1980s, respectively. Thus, while it is impossible to know just how far the findings of the analytical exercises that follow would generalize to other parts of China, it is reasonable to proceed on the assumption that even if they are not precisely the norm, it is also unlikely that they have no wider applicability.[73]

Dahe differed from such rural areas as Wuxi County, Jiangsu, in which township and village enterprises played a still more dominant role in economic development, and also from townships of the type found in much of the Pearl River Delta or Zhejiang's Wenzhou, in which private manufacturing enterprises or traders acquiring inputs from remote Chinese or foreign sources (in the former case aided by the proximity of Hong Kong), and attuned to the demands of far-flung markets, dominated. Most of its industrial enterprises focused on the production of parts and

---

[73]Note that qualitative relations among variables are more likely to be generalizable than are rates of growth or specific parameter magnitudes.

materials for nearby urban industry and construction, and on the manufacturing of crude textile and paper products that made use of local agricultural byproducts. Its villages added to their revenues by operating brick kilns and quarries, and its households, aside from basic crop production and employment in such enterprises, contributed to the local economy also by providing transport services, forming construction teams, marketing higher value crops, and engaging in small commercial activities with considerably more limited expansion of animal husbandry, forestry, and fishery sectors than was typical of rural China as a whole during the same period. This economy of relatively limited commercial horizons and generally low technology production is perhaps typical of the rural hinterland of a comparatively inward-looking Chinese industrial city, as compared with the more outward-oriented and technically dynamic rural areas near such high-growth coastal zones as Guangdong or southern Jiangsu.

Our preliminary examination of the data collected at Dahe suggests that the township's experience illustrates the strengths and weaknesses of both the collective and the reform-era institutional regimes in rural China. Dahe's success in boosting grain production in the 1960s and 1970s examplifies not only the technological achievements of China's home-grown "green revolution" of seeds, fertilizer, and irrigation—the generalization of which contributed to more widespread gains in the 1980s—but also the economic and social irrationality of that revolution's initial concentration on certain vanguard localities, and the concomitant constraints placed on crop diversification and income enhancement in such localities. Yet emphasis on relatively unprofitable grain production, in agriculture, did not entirely deter Dahe's teams from gradually shifting the structures of both employment and income generation toward more remunerative activities during the 1970s, and the commune and its brigades began to build a significant industrial base in that decade.

In 1979, a year that saw substantial producer price increases, wheat and corn output posted growth rates slightly higher than the already strong trends earlier in that decade. On the other hand, the liberalization of production decision making in the early 1980s led to a reduction of grain yields and output at Dahe. By 1984, previous yields were restored, and small increases in output were attained both through administratively guided maintenance and expansion of the acreage in grain, and through establishment of a system of agricultural service stations to support mechanized plowing, seeding, and fertilizer and chemical use. With respect to the form of farm production organization, the milder form of responsibility system introduced in 1980–1982, *lianchan jichou,* was apparently cumbersome to manage. Of the three crops studied individually, it appears to have improved performance with respect to corn only, although the observed productivity increase with respect to aggregate crop output value (GVCO) could also reflect release of labor from staple to nonstaple crops. The phased introduction of the system throughout the commune is accordingly consistent with the interpretation that the reform process was managed by higher levels, without much sensitivity to local results. *Baogan daohu,* the more radical responsibility system introduced at Dahe in 1983, appears to have facilitated the release of labor from agriculture while easing the administrative demands of agricultural management sufficiently to permit eventual elimination of the team level of organization. Although the marginal incentives of farm households became identical with those of fixed-rent tenant farmers under the new system, administrative controls such as assignment of grain and cotton sales "contracts," provision of many farm services by village-level stations, and likely interventions into the choice of crops grown, continued to bind household farms to a larger collective (or, more accurately, local administrative) structure.

Three key conclusions are 1) that enthusiasm for grain production lagged as grain prices leveled off and as the two- or three-tier price system, with its higher marginal price, was abolished in 1985; 2) that political authorities continued to press for grain production in localities, such as Dahe, in which other crops were far more profitable for farmers; and 3) that the grain market itself was thin enough so that virtually all rural households at Dahe continued to grow grain for their own subsistence needs, even when (as in 1984 and 1985) market prices were low. These findings are indicative of fundamental problems facing Chinese agriculture and, more broadly, China's economic reform, as the decade approached its conclusion. The flattening out of grain yields in the early 1980s at Dahe was a precursor of national trends that were to become apparent after the backlog of available technological improvements and inputs had (partly through expanded input supply) been more widely assimilated by Chinese farmers, after the initial impact of price and organizational reform had been spent, and after the land-improving investments of the collective era had failed to be either extended or fully maintained.

Finally, the industrial infrastructure of commune and brigade enterprises established at Dahe in the 1970s continued its growth under township and village auspices in the 1980s, but while they increased their share of the total returns to labor, the accelerated pace of growth of those enterprises was not enough to maintain their shares of total gross output and of net revenue in the midst of still more rapid private and household enterprise growth. Private partnerships, often sponsored by local officials and frequently producing products identical with those made by a township- or village-owned enterprise, grew rapidly to match the township's share of total output value. Household-based transport, commercial, and construction enterprise also rapidly increased their shares of output and, still more so, of employment. Upward pressure on wages reduced township- and village-enterprise profits, potentially threatening those enterprises' long-term growth prospects. Our postscript showed that industrial growth was in fact slower in the late 1980s, but perhaps as much because of the influence of national economic problems as because of the internal dynamics of the economy of Dahe Township.

4

Factor Allocation and Productivity Growth: Some Views from Team Level

Introduction

Until 1983, teams were the major units of crop production and carried on a significant share of small-scale food processing, transport, and other nonagricultural production and service activities at Dahe. The broadest and deepest of the data sets gathered at Dahe in 1980 and 1986 is that at team level, which attempts to account for all teams in the township on an annual basis for the 16-year period 1970 to 1985, including coverage of activities carried on by each team's constituent households after the 1983 "decollectivization" of agriculture. In all, information on 153 variables was gathered for the 1970s, and data on 222 variables was collected for 1980–1985, with 104 of these variables being collected for both periods. Although some of the desired information could not be provided retrospectively by the brigade (village) and team officials from whom it was requested, and although some of what was provided must be treated as being of questionable accuracy, this data set provides a basis for investigating many questions central to the study of rural development in general and of the development process specific to China in particular.

The present chapter has two principal concerns: factor allocation and productivity growth, issues of quite general concern to the study of rural development. The chapter that follows continues the analysis of the team level data but focuses on an issue special to the Chinese context: the nature of the incentive system in the collective period. (Chapter 6 further investigates the incentive system by analysis of the survey data on individuals.) The related question of the impact of household responsibility systems or decollectivization upon farm productivity is touched upon cursorily in the longitudinal analysis of the present chapter, but an in-depth study is reserved for Chapter 7. The final chapter to make extensive use of the team panel data, Chapter 9, will focus on the impact of alternative methods of land allotment, under the household responsibility system, on farm productivity.

Technical and Allocative Efficiency

An economy is said to be efficient in production when it produces as many units of each good as is technically feasible given the available inputs, the output level of every other good, and the state of technical knowledge. Although efficiency is not the only desideratum of an economy, it is hard to argue with the idea that more goods (by definition, desirables) are better than less, especially if the comparison is carried out assuming that all else (including effort, distributive equity, environmental quality, and nonmaterial aspects of well being) is otherwise unchanged.[1]

Economic growth (as opposed to development, which is a broader term involving also a variety of social dimensions[2]) occurs when there is an increase in a society's per capita output and consumption. Since the "output" of a society is always a set of heterogeneous goods and services, which are aggregated on a money basis using prices as weights, growth may take place either through increases in the *level* of production of some or all goods, unaccompanied by declines in the production of other goods, or by a change in the *composition* of production toward products of higher value to their consumers. Increases in the level of output may be achieved either by acquiring or discovering additional resources and more fully employing resources already known to exist—a process known as "extensive growth"—or by utilizing existing resources more effectively, either in the sense of better allocation of resources among activities, or in that of application of previously unattained "best practice" techniques, and elimination of organizational "X-inefficiency." An increase in the value of output due to a change in the *composition* of what is produced is an example of growth through improvement of resource allocation, as is growth in the *level* of output due to better allocation of factors among activities. In sum, then, the sources of growth are (a) increased inputs, (b) increased technical efficiency, and (c) improved allocative efficiency. Note that increases in effort from given workers brought about by improvements in incentive systems should be classified under (a), although under a rather common semantic convention, they are often counted under (b).[3]

Given possibility (a), it must be recognized that increases in economic efficiency are *not* prerequisites of economic growth: A society that perpetually suffers from use of inappropriate techniques, weak incentives, and allocate inefficiency can in principle achieve output growth by means of marshaling more and more resources. The type of economic system initiated under Stalin in the Soviet Union of 1928 and substantially copied by Mao's China beginning in the 1950s has sometimes been said to be marked by high growth without increasing efficiency, achieved through such a marshaling of resources. However, during the past quarter century a strong consensus

---

[1]A further discussion is given in Putterman (1990a).

[2]See Sen (1988), and references cited therein.

[3]If "X-inefficiency" (see Leibenstein, 1966, 1978) is due to undersupply of effort by individual workers and/or managers, the change is strictly speaking one in the level of inputs, and not in technical efficiency at all. This exemplifies a semantic problem that is often difficult to avoid under the present state of the art: Partly because effort is not easily measured or quantified, we often treat workers rather than efficiency units of effort as inputs, whereupon it becomes common to view output growth through increased effort as a case of improved efficiency, when this is not strictly speaking correct. A further complication is that increased effort could go along with a decline in welfare, if the higher output resulting from it does not suffice to compensate workers for the foregone leisure or added drudgery.

has emerged among economists in both socialist and capitalist countries, viz., that the prospects of such "extensive growth" are limited to an early stage of economic development or industrialization, and that it must be replaced by "intensive growth," or growth by means of higher technical efficiency, more concerted effort, and improved resource allocation, if economic development is to continue. This idea is frequently cited as the reason behind attempts to reform Soviet-type economies beginning in Eastern Europe and the Soviet Union in the 1960s and spreading to China and other centrally planned socialist economies in the late 1970s and 1980s.

In terms of the discussion just completed, China's relatively respectable economic growth between 1949 and 1978 might largely be attributed to "extensive growth," although some might also assign a prominent role to "statistical illusion" stemming from the inclusion in aggregate output of a considerable quantity of unneeded and socially undesired product in the form of low quality, technically regressive, or unneeded output, especially capital goods. In agriculture, output of grain increased by 86% between 1952 and 1978, while gross value of agricultural output (including animal husbandry, fisheries, forestry, and sidelines) rose by 110%; but this growth can be seen as extensive in nature, since the number of workers and of work days grew by 68% and 250%, respectively, irrigated hectares rose by 125%, and mechanical power and chemical fertilizer use rose from negligible levels to 117 billion watts and 10.9 million tons, respectively.[4] While exact conclusions depend upon detailed assumptions, including the choice of factor weights,[5] the "extensive growth" interpretation is supported by the findings of studies such as Tang (1984) and Wen (1989, cited by Lin, 1990) that total factor productivity in Chinese agriculture— that is, the ratio of gross output value to a weighted index of inputs—declined between 1952 and 1978. By 1978, the belief that the "extensive" growth phase had to end and that "intensive" growth was now needed, was gaining more adherents in China's policy circles. With labor transfer *out of* rather than into agriculture desirable for general economic development purposes, with land being taken out of cultivation at a rapid rate and with its replacement by development of new cultivated areas being a costly proposition, with large-scale mechanization being judged on economic criteria to be inconsistent with China's level of development, and with the nation's program to expand fertilizer production already receiving high priority, further increases in agricultural output to keep pace with population growth, provide industrial raw materials, hold down costly imports, and gradually improve the quality of the people's diets appeared to depend heavily on reversing the decline in per unit output and achieving significant increases in productivity.

[4]All data from *China Statistical Yearbook 1988*, pp. 35, 123, 189, 197, and 212, except for those on the increase in rural workdays. The latter combine the CSY estimate on rural workers with the estimate on average annual labor days given by Taylor (1988, Table 4). In our computation, the average of the estimate range given by Taylor for 1975 is used as the estimate for 1978.
[5]Chiacu (1992) shows that the weights used by Tang differ sharply from the output elasticities found in most available production function estimates, and that his conclusions are reversed when weights based on some of those estimates are used.

The question of the efficiency of Chinese agriculture must also be seen in relation to efficiency and growth of the economy as a whole. In developing economies, labor productivity is almost universally higher in industrial than in agricultural activities, and raising agricultural productivity and/or eliminating constraints on nonagricultural employment so as to allow movement of labor into nonfarm pursuits has been viewed as a central aspect of the process of growth. Whereas Maoist China restrained labor force movement from countryside to cities and shackled its rural workers with the burden of expanding grain output regardless of cost, post-Mao China began to see the possibilities of using far less labor to provide its staple foods, and of transferring the hands thereby freed to the production of other farm products, and to industrial and service activities (mostly still in the countryside, but also with substantial rural-urban movement at least of a temporary nature). Whether to allow agricultural land to be shifted to nonfarm uses, and whether to expend scarce resources on developing new farmland and producing more farm equipment, chemicals, and fertilizer were questions needing to be viewed in terms of opportunity costs not to agriculture alone, but to the economy as a whole. With respect to the rural sector, increased technical efficiency within agriculture and improved allocation of rural resources both among agricultural activities and between agriculture and nonagricultural activities were important sources of the economic growth that China's post-Mao reformers hoped to foster.

Growth, Productivity, and Structural Change at Dahe

There are a number of ways of examining the process of economic growth, productivity change, and changes in factor allocation and economic structure in Dahe commune/township's production teams. However, the possibilities presented by the available data are not endless, and some ideal approaches are in fact ruled out by data limitations.

Our basic approach to the study of growth and productivity change is the estimation of production functions, analysis of the resulting technical efficiency parameters, and application of growth accounting techniques. In terms of data availability, this approach can be used with least difficulty at the most aggregated level: that is, if the gross value of output from all activities of a team is taken as the dependent variable, and if all inputs are included as independent variables or regressors. A problem with this approach, however, is that it aggregates over a number of products that may have very different production processes. Problems are raised also by the fact that the prices used to aggregate products and inputs may not reflect relative scarcities. Moreover, some of the prices that prevailed are simply unknown to us because they are not given explicitly in the data. Production function estimation at team level suffers from an additional problem following decollectivization in the early 1980s: since teams are no longer units of production in that period, the estimates aggregate over different producers, the households.

Ideally, production functions should not be estimated by direct methods—that is, with output as the dependent variable and levels of factor inputs entering as regressors. Input levels may have been determined after decision makers had knowledge of conditions—such as weather—that affect productivity but are unobservable from our own vantage point. Input levels would then be correlated with the error terms of the regression equations. Standard responses to this problem include replacing the factor input variables with instruments, including their prices, and estimating profit or cost functions. We are unable to use such techniques because we lack adequate instruments, including detailed price data, and because estimation of profit or cost functions might be inappropriate for China in the periods studied, since those approaches assume profit-maximizing input choices. Indeed, the controlled nature of most of the relevant prices, and the administrative interventions in planting and other input use decisions, mean that prices, even if available, might make poor instruments for input levels. Also, planning, along with less formal interventions in the post-collective period, may mean that input usage was less affected by contemporaneous conditions than is usually the case, so that direct estimating methods are less objectionable. Use of cross-section and time-series dummy variables or similar techniques also helps to control for some of the unobservable factors causing correlation between input levels and error terms.

We will want to estimate separate production functions for differing sectors of Dahe's economy (such as crop production and sidelines, or grain and nongrain crops) both for reasons of greater technical homogeneity, and to aid in explicit consideration of intersectoral factor allocation issues. Once we move toward estimating such sectoral or product-specific production functions, however, additional problems arise due to incomplete disaggregation of the input data. Our data for labor in work days—units that may not be perfectly standardized across teams and years—are not disaggregated among activities, while the corresponding data on labor force allocation are disaggregated among crop production, sidelines, and some other activities, but not to specific crops within crop production. The same is true of current production expenditures, which are broken down by sector and for categories such as seeds and fertilizer within crop production, but not by crop. Only sown area of land is disaggregated to crops. Information on interteam variations in land quality is sketchy, though, and none is available on a crop-by-crop basis.

While we have disaggregated information on some capital goods, including farm equipment, this is not helpful in establishing how much capital was used in given sectors. As mentioned in Chapter 1, tractors, in particular, may have been employed as much or more in nonagricultural as in agricultural activities, but precise information on this intersectoral allocation issue is unavailable. Prices for individual capital goods are also lacking. Aside from the aggregation problem, the capital information is not ideal both because it is given as a stock while other inputs are reported as flows, and because methods of valuing capital goods are unclear and may have been inconsistent.[6] Finally, in the 1980s, team reports of gross capital asset value tend to show declining asset stocks while the numbers of assets in most categories rise, suggesting that the value series is biased downward by noninclusion of items transferred to household ownership, or acquired by households following decollectivization. A reasonable remedy, which we employ, is to substitute for the reported series an index projecting gross capital asset value from listed capital goods in the 1980s based on a regression estimate of the relationship between the components and the aggregate value series for the late 1970s.

A number of other problems result from missing data or strikingly implausible values. A missing value for any variable included in a model to be estimated dictates the exclusion of the case in question. With panel data, in which there is both cross-sectional (here: production team) and longitudinal (here: annual) variation, observations on a team for which data are missing for some years but not others may continue to be included in the sample. However, inclusion of such teams in random effects models (see Chapter 5) is technically demanding, so missing values in any year lead to dropping of the team for all years when we attempt estimates incorporating the assumptions on error structure defining such models.

Errors will unavoidably exist in our data series. These will have arisen at two stages. First, there may have been errors in the teams' own accounts, misunderstandings regarding the information requested, misreporting, and copying errors on the part of the accountants or other team or brigade officials supplying the data. Second, errors may have been made when copying the data onto coding sheets and entering it into computer files. A number of efforts were made to minimize these errors,[7] but with limited resources, many errors undoubtedly remain. We applied value range or other checks, when possible, to identify gross inconsistencies, and tried to scan each series used in our analysis for similar purposes. The discovery of apparent inconsistencies raises problems of its own, such as whether plausible values should be substituted or the case should simply be dropped. Which procedure was adopted in each situation will be mentioned where appropriate in this and subsequent chapters and appendices.

Two data-related problems of acute importance to the analysis of the team level data should be mentioned at the outset. The first is that even when the same terminology was employed, inconsistencies between data provided in 1980 (for

---

[6]According to Butler, "Teams did not depreciate assets, so an item generally appeared on the books at purchase price or construction cost until it was retired or sold. This obviously makes it difficult to interpret the figures for gross value of capital assets. There were also some teams that drastically revalued their assets downward when it became clear that they would in the future be required to depreciate assets and set aside money each year based on a percentage value of their existing assets." (Quoted in Putterman (1989c, p. 121).) Even without such problems, though, capital stock variables are notorious for showing weak statistical significance in agricultural production functions, and the fact that we obtain reasonable results at least some of the time is thus relatively reassuring.

[7]For some details, see Putterman (1989c, pp. 14–15).

1970–1979) and that provided in 1986 (for 1980–1985) appear to have arisen, perhaps due to changes in statistical methodology or personnel in the intervening period. The second is that when teams ceased to be the operators of farms and sideline enterprises, but instead passed those responsibilities on to their constituent house-holds, team level data changed from being a record of production activity at team level to an estimate of activity by households based on household surveys. In the transition, some household level activities previously unreported in the team accounts, e.g., cultivation of private plots, came to be included in team data. Since this change could be expected to cause an increase in reported total team output due to data coverage and independent of real production increases, an effort was made to distinguish between income sources in the 1980s data. Unfortunately, subsequent analysis has revealed this effort to have failed, either because the distinction was beyond the capacity of the local statistical system or because different accountants had different understandings of the concepts employed.[8] The upshot of both problems mentioned in this paragraph is that we are left with an additional element of guesswork in estimating the true effect of decollectivization on farm productivity at Dahe. While these difficulties should be borne in mind when reading the present chapter, they are even more important to the analysis of Chapter 7, where they will be brought to the reader's attention once again.

Wiemer's Two-Sector Estimates for the 1970s

An attempt to estimate changes in the productivity of resources in team level production at Dahe in the 1970s, and to study issues of intersectoral resource allocation, is carried out by Wiemer (1990a). Wiemer begins by selecting teams that provided complete data on the input and output variables to be used in the analysis for at least 6 of the 10 years 1970–1979. This yields a sample containing 44 of the 94 teams existing in 1979, accounting for about one-half of Dahe's population and cultivated area. She then estimates production functions for agricultural (crop production) and sideline products, which together cover all team revenue-generating activities except for forestry, animal husbandry, and fisheries, which (as seen in the previous chapter) were of little importance during this period. Given the absence of data indicating how teams' capital stocks were assigned to the two sectors, a model in which these assignments can be imputed from the available data is needed. The model estimated is

$$ln(Y_c) = a_0 + a_t t + a_L ln(L_c) + a_e ln(E_c) + a_m M$$
$$+ a_k ln[K(\phi_1 D_1 + \ldots + \phi_N D_N)] + \epsilon_c \tag{4.1}$$

[8]See data set 1, variables 156–158. While "income produced under unified and contracted management" was meant to capture agricultural output on land contracted to households but not private plots, the frequency of unexpectedly small values in the responses indicates that many accountants took a much narrower view of this category.

$$ln(Y_s) = \beta_0 + \beta_t t + \beta_L ln(L_s) + \beta_e ln(E_s)$$
$$+ \beta_k ln[K\{(1 - \phi_1)D_1 + \ldots + (1 - \phi \& s'N.)D_N\}] + \epsilon_s \tag{4.2}$$

where Y indicates output in value terms, subscript c stands for crop production and s for sidelines; t indicates the year; L, E, M, and K are the factor inputs labor force (in person days),[9] current expenditures (in *yuan*), land (in *mu*),[10] and gross value of capital assets; D_1 to D_N are dummy variables identifying the N teams; α, β, and ϕ coefficients are parameters to be estimated, with both the α's and the β's restricted to sum to unity, and the ϵ's are stochastic error terms assumed to be independent and identically distributed. (4.1) and (4.2) are thus Cobb-Douglas production functions with constant returns to scale imposed by assumption and with a time variable added to capture the trend in productivity change over time. The only unusual feature is the presence of the ϕ terms, which are central to the strategy to overcome the lack of explicit disaggregation of the capital stock variable, just referred to. In particular, the equations embody the assumption that each team, say j, allocated a constant fraction ϕ_j of its capital stock to crop production in all years in which it appears in the sample, with the remaining $(1 - \phi_j)$ of its capital stock being used in sidelines. Values of ϕ can differ among teams, and are determined endogenously by simultaneous estimation of the two equations using nonlinear least square. While teams can differ in their intersectoral capital allocations, the dummy variables D_j enter only in interaction with the ϕ's; therefore, teams are assumed to face an identical technology, and no differences in total productivity—such as might be attributable to the presence of unmeasured factors—can be accommodated by the specification.[11] Time effects are also forced to appear in trend form only, leaving open the possibility that year-specific effects of weather, pests, production plans, and prices will spuriously affect α_t and β_t (or even other coefficients, if time and input levels are correlated). (4.1) and (4.2) are estimated simultaneously using a nonlinear least squares procedure.

Table 4.1 shows the mean values of variables in the included sample, and Table 4.2 reproduces Wiemer's estimation results. The standard errors indicate that each of the independently estimated elasticities α and β is statistically significant at the 1% level, except that on capital in crop production, which is significant at 10%.[12] The estimated elasticities are intuitively reasonable in that in crop production, the contribution of land dominates, followed by that of labor, while in sidelines, capital

---

[9]As mentioned above, sectorally disaggregated data refer to number of workers only. To convert to days, Wiemer assumes the average number of work days per worker to be common across activities. The reported work days variable is itself in accounting units, not natural ones, as indicated by the fact that its value typically exceeds 365.

[10]1 *mu* = .0667 ha.

[11]That is, any such differences as may actually have existed may affect the estimates of the ϕ's and other parameters in unintended ways that may be impossible to identify. Inclusion of an additional vector of free-standing team dummy variables could address this problem but would cut sharply into the remaining degrees of freedom, especially in cases where only a few observations are available on each team.

[12]The constant returns restriction reduces the number of meaningful standard errors in each equation by 1.

Table 4.1A. Means of Sample Variables, Dahe Teams: Wiemer's Subsample[a]

	1970	1979	1985
Crop output[b]	27,115	40,296	91,663
Agr. labor[c]	63.7	78.2	69.5
Land[d]	21.9	21.9	20.6
Agr. inputs[b]	8,157	16,857	21,399
Agr. capital[e]	6,515	19,570	56,924
Sdln. output[b]	3,834	12,618	
Sdln. labor[c]	16.9	35.2	
Sdln. inputs[b]	1,097	2,116	
Sdln. capital[e]	3,030	9,124	

Table 4.1B. Means of Sample Variables, Dahe Teams: Author's Subsample[f]

	1970	1979	1985	1970–1979	1980–1985
Crop output[b]	29,193	40,445	91,392	31,856	64,350
	(9,901)	(13,422)	(26,158)		
Agr. labor[c]	88.2	78.6	70.3	81	79
	(60.5)	(34.3)	(22.2)		
Land[d]	23.5	22.0	20.6	22.4	20.8
	(7.5)	(6.7)	(5.4)		
Agr. inputs[b]	8,603	17,012	21,253	14,443	19,421
	(4,363)	(5,953)	(7,839)		
Agr. capital[g]	5,478	14,191	27,785	10,896	20,658
	(3,760)	(8,130)	(15,250)		
Noncrop output[b]	2,809	15,471	97,977	12,967	42,405
	(4,014)	(7,970)	(74,431)		
Noncrop labor[c]	19.3	30.0	49.6	24	34
	(8.3)	(9.0)	(19.6)		
Noncrop inputs[b]	1,154	6,861	26,220	4,704	7,428
	(1,903)	(4,921)	(38,771)		
Noncrop capital[g]	1,616	5,169	10,597	3,828	7,583
	(1,785)	(3,065)	(4,138)		

[a]1979 and 1985 figures for agriculture are as shown in Wiemer (1990a, Table 3). Corresponding figures for sidelines are author's computations for Wiemer's sample. The 1970 averages are calculated by applying reported inputs and output growth rates to 1979 reported averages.

[b]In *yuan.*

[c]Number of workers.

[d]Cultivated area in hectares.

[e]In *yuan.* Allocation of capital between sectors is by econometric imputation as discussed in the text.

[f]Numbers in parentheses are standard deviations.

[g]In *yuan.* Applies Wiemer's capital allocation coefficients to divide capital between sectors.

Table 4.2. Production Function Estimates by Wiemer

Variable	1970–1979		1983–1985	
	Coefficient	(t statistic)	Coefficient	(t statistic)
Crop Sector				
Constant	2.86	(19.067)	3.29	(6.826)
Labor	0.233	(6.853)	0.179	(2.712)[a]
Land[b]	0.631	(16.179)	0.316	(3.224)
Capital	0.044	(1.630)	0.347	(3.305)
Current inputs	0.092	na[c]	0.158	(1.816)
Time trend	0.024	(4.800)	0.089	(2.781)
n = 305	R^2 : 0.79		R^2 : 0.77	
Sideline Sector				
Constant	0.725	(2.705)		
Labor	0.355	(4.931)		
Capital	0.435	(6.042)		
Current inputs	0.210	na[c]		
Time trend	0.039	(3.000)		
n = 305	R^2 : 0.68			

The 1970–1979 estimates are simultaneous for the two sectors using nonlinear least squares. Team dummy variables are interacted with capital allocation parameters but do not enter the estimation separately.
[a]This t statistic differs from that indicated in Wiemer's paper due to a correction transmitted in personal communication.
[b]Cultivated area in *mu*. 1 *mu* = .0667 ha.
[c]The constant returns to scale constraint reduces by 1 the number of standard errors estimated per equation under the simultaneous-equations nonlinear least-squares procedure.
Source: Wiemer (1990a, Table 1).

has the largest elasticity, followed by labor and current inputs. The 44 estimates of φ imply that an average of 69% of the capital stock was used for crop production, and 31% for sidelines, still exceeding the sideline share of output value (which stood at 24% in the sample teams in 1979).[13] The equations are also estimated without restricting the elasticities to sum to unity, and an F test supports the maintained hypothesis of constant returns to scale at the 5% level.

With the previously mentioned *caveat* that they may partly reflect year-to-year changes in weather, plans, and pricing relationships, and are sensitive to selection of starting and final year, the coefficients on the time variable provide a measure of the rate of growth of factor productivity. Decomposition of observed output growth into the shares due to the growth of each factor input and to the time trend, or technological change, is complicated by the fact that Wiemer's sample exhibits varying degrees of completeness in different years. For example, only 8 of the teams in the sample

[13]The estimates, which were unconstrained, range from .27 to .96, with a standard deviation of .19. Twenty-four (55%) of the estimated values lie between .5 and .8, with an additional 14 (32%) falling between .8 and .96. Thirty-five of the 44 parameter estimates are statistically significant at the 10% level, 27 at the 1% level.

Table 4.3. Growth Accounting with Wiemer's Production Function Estimates for Dahe Teams, 1970–1979

Factor or Variable	Growth Rate, %[a]	Elasticity	Contributed Growth Rate, %	Share of Total Growth Rate
a. Crop Sector				
Labor	2.3	.233	0.54	.12
Land	0	.631	0.00	0
Capital	13.0	.044	0.57	.13
Current inputs	8.4	.092	0.77	.17
Trend	2.4		2.4	.53
Output	4.5			
Unexplained				.05
b. Sideline Sector				
Labor	10.24	.355	3.64	.26
Capital	13.03	.435	5.67	.40
Current inputs	7.57	.210	1.59	.11
Trend	3.9		3.9	.28
Output	14.15			
Unexplained				−.05

[a]From regression estimate, as reported by Wiemer, for the crop sector, and as computed by the author, for the sideline sector.

provided data on all included variables in 1970, while 42 did so in 1979. Estimates of the growth rates of the inputs and output based on the averages of the variables in those years are therefore biased, and a growth decomposition undertaken on their basis "overexplains" the total growth thus estimated by 33%. Wiemer, however, reports growth rates of crop sector output and inputs calculated by regressing the log of each variable on a time index and the set of 44 team dummies. The same procedure was used by the author to calculate corresponding growth rates for the sideline sector. These rates are used to carry out the growth decomposition analysis shown in Table 4.3.

In the 44 sample teams, Wiemer reports that crop output value grew at an average rate of 4.5% per year.[14] Her estimate for α_t, which is significant at the 1% level, indicates that the productivity of combined factor inputs, or total factor productivity (TFP), was rising at a rate of 2.4% per year in crop production, explaining a little over one-half of this output growth. The remaining 2.1% growth rate would then be explained by the 2.3% growth rate of farm labor use, the 8.4% growth rate of current input use, and the (imputed) 13% growth rate of farm capital,[15]

[14]Although some of the difference with the 7.5% growth rate for grain output implied by Table 3.1 could be due to differences in the sample, the main explanation is almost certainly that grain output did indeed increase more rapidly than crop output value as a whole. This is reflected in the fact that, using the method reported in note 14 of Chapter 3, the share of crop output value due to grain rose from around 59% in 1970 to about 88% in 1979.

[15]This is equal to the known 13% growth rate for the combined capital stock, since the φ's are assumed constant over time.

all of which she reports to have been added to an essentially unchanging cultivated area. In Table 4.3.a, the input growth rates, reported in column 1, are multiplied by the estimated elasticities of Table 4.2, reprinted in column 2, to obtain the output growth rates implied by them. As recorded in the final column, the analysis suggests that 12% of output growth could be attributed to growth in labor input, 13% to growth in capital stock, 17% to growth in current inputs, and 53% to the trend rate of growth of factor productivity, leaving a 5% residual attributable to imprecisions of various types including that related to changing sample composition.

In the sideline sector, Wiemer reports output value to have grown at an average rate of 14.2% during 1970–1979 in the sample teams. The estimate for β_t, which is also significant at the 1% level, indicates that TFP was rising at a rate of 3.9% per year in this sector, thereby explaining only a little more than one-quarter of this output growth. Input and output growth rates calculated by Wiemer's log regression method are shown in the first column of Table 4.3.b. Multiplied by the estimated factor elasticities, the estimated 10.2% annual growth in sideline labor force accounts for a 3.6% growth rate in output, the 13.0% annual growth in capital stock adds another 5.7% to output growth, and the 7.6% annual growth in current input use adds 1.6% to the outut growth rate. Combined input growth thus accounts for 77% of output growth, while the time trend accounts for 28%, thus "overexplaining" output growth by the same margin (5%) as it is "underexplained" in the crop sector.

Due to the incompleteness of pricing data for Dahe's teams, Wiemer does not try to distinguish between changes in real output and current inputs, and changes in their value due to price changes. While price changes were not very large in the China of the 1970s, the estimated productivity growth rates in the two sectors are also not very large, so a correction for value changes could significantly alter the conclusions about factor productivity growth. A crude exercise along these lines involves deflating the crop output series by the general index of purchasing prices of farm and sideline products, deflating the current input series by the general index of retail prices of industrial products in rural areas, and deflating the sideline output series by an unweighted average of the two indices. The first index rose at an annual rate of 3.48% between 1970 and 1979, the second declined at a rate of 0.20%, and the mixed index rose at a rate of 1.77%. For each sector, the product of the second index and the estimated elasticity of output with respect to current inputs can be subtracted from the appropriate index for output value to obtain a deflator for factor productivity growth.[16] For crop production, this deflator is $3.48 - (.092)(-0.20) = 3.50\%$, which would turn the 2.4% TFP growth rate estimated by Wiemer into a 1.10% rate

---

[16]Since inflation affects the current input series by causing input growth to be exaggerated, the greater was input price inflation, the greater was true factor productivity growth. The converse applies if input prices were falling. For example, with input prices declining during the 1970s at a rate of 0.20% per year, then the level of current input use was growing at 8.6% per year, rather than the 8.4% shown in Table 4.3. The contributed growth rate due to current inputs should thus be raised in column 3 of the table by an extra $(0.2\%) \times (.092) = 0.018$, while the output growth attributable to changing total factor productivity should be reduced by the same amount.

Table 4.4. Value of Marginal Product Estimates by Wiemer

	Labor (Y/worker)[a]		Land (Y/hectare)[b]	Capital (Y/Y1)		Current Inputs (Y/Y1)	
	Crop	Noncrop		Crop	Noncrop	Crop	Noncrop
1970	87.50	133.37	637.2	0.164	0.979	0.370	1.076
1971	97.76	186.12	665.7	0.177	0.926	0.300	0.913
1972	84.30	307.33	782.6	0.137	0.546	0.219	1.436
1973	93.50	366.47	796.1	0.166	0.865	0.216	0.563
1974	90.85	334.55	877.1	0.106	0.764	0.209	1.084
1975	94.17	318.47	913.0	0.093	0.728	0.193	1.530
1976	88.96	343.72	926.5	0.084	0.713	0.190	1.319
1977	93.78	390.49	970.0	0.080	0.795	0.193	1.150
1978	102.63	407.64	1030.0	0.081	0.823	0.175	1.450
1979	109.11	418.72	1055.5	0.080	0.851	0.201	1.769
1983	157		1093.0	0.536		0.589	
1984	205		1215.9	0.505		0.702	
1985	234		1389.8	0.553		0.671	

[a]Units converted for 1970s from Y/labor day.
[b]Units converted from Y/mu.
Source: Wiemer (1990a, Tables 2 and 3).

of *decline* in total factor productivity. For sidelines, the deflator is 1.77 − (.210)(−.20) = 1.81%, which would reduce the 3.9% TFP growth rate estimated by Wiemer to a smaller but still positive rate of 2.1%. Deflating the reported output growth rate by the output value index gives a real crop output growth rate of 1.02%, of which −108% would be due to the TFP decline and +208% to input growth. The same procedure gives 12.43% real output growth in sidelines, of which 16.8% would be attributed to TFP growth, the remainder to increases in the inputs.

Intersectoral Factor Allocation

A particularly interesting aspect of Wiemer's findings from the Dahe team data concerns the existence of systematic divergences between the value marginal products of inputs in crop production versus sidelines. Table 4.4 shows the average values of the marginal products of labor, land, current expenditures, and capital goods for each year of the 1970s at Dahe, as implied by Wiemer's estimates and the raw data on inputs and outputs. The estimated VMP of labor in crop production is relatively stable over time, and lies in the range of Y .22 to Y .27 per "work day," or Y 88–109 per average worker per year. Compared to the *average* product per worker net of production costs and taxes, which was Y 268 per year, and the average payment to each team laborer, which was Y 216,[17] this value of marginal product is low,

[17]Calculations based on the teams analyzed in Chapter 5.

consistent with the expectations of theories to be discussed in the next chapter. The VMP of labor in sidelines is more unstable, with indications of a long-term rising trend including a temporary, mid-decade decline. Nevertheless, labor's VMP is always higher in sidelines than in crop production, with the difference ranging from 52% to 316% and averaging 237%, or a ratio of 3.4 to 1.

Qualitatively identical gaps between marginal products in crop production and sidelines appear also for current inputs and capital. The VMP of current inputs shows an almost uniform declining trend in crop production and a less consistent rising trend in sidelines, with a gap ranging from 160% to 790% and averaging 442%, giving a ratio of 5.4 to 1. There is a similar declining trend for the VMP of capital in crop production, but no distinct trend for the VMP of capital in sidelines. In this case, where it will be recalled that the allocation itself is that imputed via the estimation process, the VMP gap ranges from 299% to 960% and averages 584%, or a 6.8 to 1 ratio. Since land is used only in crop production, no marginal productivity gap is to be seen in the present intersectoral comparison. The estimated marginal product has a plausible value and shows a smooth rising trend, consistent with the increasing application of labor, current inputs, and capital goods to the fixed cultivated area.

Maximizing the returns on scarce inputs requires that the marginal productivity of any given resource be equalized across activities, failing which there are output gains to be had by transferring resources from low productivity to high productivity uses. The marginal product gap for Dahe teams in the 1970s thus suggests that teams were not pursuing a maximum income objective, or were seeking maximum income only subject to certain constraints. It is not difficult to find such constraints based on our institutional knowledge of the Chinese rural economy. In the first instance, teams were obligated to produce grain, cotton, and small quantities of other crops, for sale to the government at sub-competitive prices. In principle, the quota obligations could be treated as a fixed portion of each team's production plan, leaving resource use in excess of quotas to be determined by profitability, and thereby restoring the expectation that factors should have common marginal product values across uses. However, the Dahe data lumps quota and other crop production in the same aggregate production and output value figures. It is accordingly possible that marginal products in unconstrained activities were equalized across the crop production and noncrop production sectors, whereas what Table 4.4 shows are *average* marginal products in crop production, the values of which are lowered by inclusion of the quota-meeting portion of factor use.

If administrative controls over crop production were sufficiently wide-ranging in the 1970s, on the other hand, the distinction between intra- and infra-marginal production may be irrelevant. The magnitude of the gap between marginal products in the two sectors, and the relatively small share of output sold to the state (see Chapter 3), are consistent with the idea that team leaders (and the brigade and commune leaders who guided many of their decisions) sought not only to meet state quota obligations, but also to satisfy member households' consumption requirements for grain, vegetables, cooking oil, and other farm products, even in disregard of the ostensibly lower returns on factor inputs entailed by this objective. There was probably a good economic reason for such behavior, namely that many of the products in question could be purchased on the market (if they were available at all) only at a much higher cost than is reflected in the state purchasing prices at which most output was probably valued in the team accounts. In this sense, which corresponds more to private than to social resource calculations, the marginal productivity gap between sectors is overstated by the data, since at the expected private purchase prices (i.e., the relevant opportunity costs) of the products involved, VMPs in crop production may in fact have been quite close to those in sidelines. At the same time, such strictly economic reasoning at team level was buttressed by administrative pressures to achieve local self-sufficiency in basic farm products, and the high cost and/or unreliability of provisioning through the market as opposed to self-production probably reflected administrative interventions in favor of local self-sufficiency— intervention that kept down the volume of products for which marketing was permissible, while restricting marketing of other products (e.g., grain) to state channels. At the level of social as opposed to private resource calculations, the productivity gaps observed by Wiemer would remain real ones, providing further confirmation of the costs of imposed production plans and related administrative interventions found in the more microanalytic exercise of Sicular (1986).[18]

Even if the above explanations of the seeming misallocation of factor inputs between crop production and sidelines by Dahe teams is accepted, there remains the question of why the marginal product gaps differed among inputs. With value-added maximization subject to a binding output constraint in the crop sector, marginal products should be lower in crop production than in sidelines, but (as is shown formally for the household model of Chapter 9) optimization requires that the ratio of marginal products across sectors be the same for all inputs. Yet Wiemer's results show the average marginal product gap varying from 3.4 : 1 for labor to 5.4 : 1 for current inputs and 6.8 : 1 for capital, with still larger gaps for some individual years. While it is possible that these differences in the ratios of estimated marginal products are largely due to measurement error or unreliable assignment of capital, the observed pattern of interfactoral differences in these ratios appears consistent with certain institutional and behavioral factors. Current inputs were in reality heterogeneous, and many of them were probably available only through administrative channels, which favored the allocation of scarce chemical fertilizers, seeds, and other farm inputs to high yield-growth townships, like Dahe, for which we have already noted evidence of economically excessive input use in the 1970s (see Chapter 3). With respect to capital goods, teams were pressured to retain large fractions of their net revenues for

---

[18]In that study, alternative returns on individual plots planted to different crops are entered into a linear programming model, and the foregone returns due to the administratively imposed production plan for 1979 are calculated by linear programming methods. The study thus uses more detailed plot level and pricing information than is available from the Dahe surveys; however, its findings are intra- rather than intersectoral in the terminology of this section.

purposes of capital accumulation, and the state made capital goods for crop production more available to rural units than alternative types of assets, and may even have mandated certain purchases (as with current inputs) and proscribed others. With farm capital thus artificially cheapened, very low rates of return on farm capital, and a correspondingly large gap with the rates of return on nonfarm capital goods, present no mystery.[19]

Extending the Analysis into the Reform Period

Wiemer attempts to extend her analysis into the reform period, but finds the team level data from Dahe seriously incomplete for some years of the 1980–1985 period in crop production, and for all years of that period in sidelines. She accordingly estimates a team-level crop production function for 1983–1985, in which each team's capital stock is assumed to be fully used in crop production. She then separately estimates an enterprise-level production function for village- and township-owned enterprises in the years 1980–1985, and continues her earlier discussion of the intersectoral factor allocation problem, this time with reference to the crop production-TVE rather than the crop production-sidelines comparison. While the results obtained are of some interest—the TVE production function estimates will be discussed in Chapter 10 of this book—there are problems of comparability with the results for the 1970s, foremost among which is that township and village (then called brigade and team) enterprises already existed alongside team-run crop production and sidelines in the collective era, and cannot properly be viewed as a successor to collective era sideline activities. Rather, household factor allocation between crop production and sidelines in the 1980s is the direct successor to team factor allocation between the same two sectors in the 1970s. This allocation problem can be studied at the household level itself using household survey data, as is done in Chapter 8. However, it remains of interest to investigate whether, data problems notwithstanding, any further progress can be made in extending Wiemer's work to the 1980–1985 period using the team level data and following her own methodology as closely as proves feasible. The exercise is of interest not only in terms of the factor allocation theme, but also by way of continuing the analysis of growth sources and of changes in overall factor productivity.[20]

Changes in the available data necessitate several modifications of Wiemer's 1970s model. First, information on the number of work days is incomplete for the

---

[19]A different conjecture about the gap, offered by Wiemer, is that workers may have actively preferred noncrop production work, and that they intentionally sacrificed some income by pouring extra current inputs and capital into crop production to permit their own transfer out.

[20]The fact that team-level production functions represented an aggregation over household production units after completion of decollectivization was mentioned above as a limitation of this type of analysis. Insofar as this particular aggregation problem is concerned, it may be noted that a quasi-homothetic technology satisfies the necessary conditions for the existence of an aggregate production function, and that the Cobb-Douglas form which we use throughout this chapter is quasi-homothetic. The form is adopted here without testing against alternatives. Such tests for a modified version of the crop production function, reported in Chapter 9, are supportive of the choice of the Cobb-Douglas form.

1980s, since by 1983 teams neither allocated workpoints nor assigned workers to tasks, and they did not have estimates of members' work time. Therefore, information on the number of workers reported to be working in crop production and noncrop sectors must substitute for that on work days. Second, and as mentioned above, the series on gross value of assets deteriorates for most teams during the 1980s, with the indicated values declining even though the total amounts of individual capital goods such as tractors and horses reported to be in either the teams' or their member households' hands appear to have risen. A reasonable inference is that the gross value of asset series covers items still owned by the teams as such. An estimate of the capital stock of teams plus their member households can be obtained, however, by regressing individual capital goods on the gross value of assets series for years in which it appears to be more complete, then using the resulting coefficients to project the aggregate asset value series into later years.[21]

A somewhat more important change is necessitated by the fact that the series on several inputs are woefully incomplete for the sideline sector. The only feasible alternative is to substitute the category "team- and household-level nonagricultural (i.e., noncrop production) activities" for "sidelines," on both the input and output sides of the production function. The requisite information is then obtained simply by subtracting the reported crop sector output value, labor force, and expenditures, from the reported total output value, labor force, and expenditures. The resulting series should be largely the same as the missing series for sidelines alone, since the latter accounted for an average of 79% of total noncrop income in the 44 teams studied by Wiemer in 1970–1979, for which this statistic can be calculated.[22] As for the larger issue of the apparent decline in the quality of team level data in the 1980s as compared with the 1970s, which is due to the reduced role of the teams as accounting units, our own resource constraints dictated that no effort could be made to trouble-shoot for errors in variables in the exercise to be reported here. The data are simply taken at face value, with the hope that quality problems constitute a source of noise but not of significant bias. Note, however, that a substantial difference in our growth estimates for the post-1979 period from those obtained by Kim (1990), who attempts to deal with the quality issue by means of selected data deletions and adjustments, will be recorded in this chapter's conclusions, with Kim's own work to be explained in Chapter 7.

As in the crop production-sidelines analysis for the 1970s, there is no information available on allocation of capital stock between sectors for the crop production-noncrop production analysis of the full 1970–1985 period. Wiemer's method of endogenous estimation continues to be a possibility. However, repeated attempts to

---

[21]The projection used in what follows was first implemented by Si Joong Kim. Further details will be given in Chapter 7, in which his work is discussed. The same projection is also used in the analysis reported in Chapter 9. Wiemer used a similar projection in her estimate of the crop production function for 1983–1985.

[22]Our series for noncrop output is v18–v8, that for noncrop expenditures is v35–v28, and that for noncrop labor force is v144–v145, as listed in Putterman (1989c).

estimate values of the ϕ_i's for the same 44 teams included in Wiemer's analysis, by the simultaneous nonlinear method, proved unsuccessful, with the values of these capital allocation parameters failing to converge after numerous iterations.[23] Convergence was also elusive when we imposed the assumption of a single ϕ_i for all teams in a given brigade (village), and, too, when we tried the alternative assumption of a single ϕ for the entire sample, even though the latter approaches involved far fewer endogenous parameters. It was accordingly necessary to fall back upon some arbitrary assumption about the allocation of capital among sectors. The assumption adopted was that the 44 values of ϕ_i estimated by Wiemer for the 1970s allocation between crop production and sidelines also hold for capital allocation between crop production and noncrop production more generally for each team and for the longer period, 1970–1985.[24] In other words, we assumed that each team allocated $K_i\phi_i$ units of capital to crop production and $K_i(1 - \phi_i)$ units of capital to noncrop production, where K_i is the gross value of assets (or for the 1980s, its projection based on individual capital goods), varying by team and year, and ϕ_i is the capital allocation parameter estimated by Wiemer for 1970s data using endogenous methods, which varies among teams but is assumed to hold constant for a given team over time. The estimation then proceeds by ordinary least squares, and separately for each of the two sectors (crop production, noncrop production).

Three estimates for each sector, following this method, are shown in Table 4.5. These estimates were computed for the full period 1970–1985, and for the two subperiods 1970–1979 and 1980–1985. The 1970–1979 estimates were carried out for purposes of comparability with Wiemer's results for the same period, as well as for a fully consistent comparison with the new results for 1980–1985 using common variables and assumptions. The three estimates also allow us to implement tests for continuity of parameters across subperiods. The test for uniformity of all coefficients, including intercepts and elasticities, led to rejection of the homogeneity assumption at the 1% level for both crop production and noncrop production.[25] Table 4.6 presents

[23]The effort was repeated to test whether nonconvergence may have been due to a few "outlier" data points, but removal of increasing numbers of "outliers" failed to solve the problem.

[24]The same ϕ_i's cannot actually have held in both cases if some capital was used outside of crop production and sidelines—that is, in noncrop production activities other than those treated as "sidelines" by the team accounts. In that case, Wiemer's estimates may be biased, since they are based on the assumption that all team capital must be used in either one or the other of the sectors. However, if activities outside of crop production and sidelines are quantitatively inconsequential, this identity could hold as an approximation. Stability of these parameters across periods is an hypothesis maintained here in the absence of a more attractive alternative; this hypothesis could only have been tested *if* it had proven possible to estimate the ϕ's endogenously for each subperiod.

[25]The test is as given in Johnston (1984, p. 219). Using Johnston's notation, the test statistic for crop production is $[(RSS1 - RSS3)/k] \div [RSS3/(n - 2k)]$, where RSS1 is the residual sum of squares for the regression on the combined sample and RSS3 is the sum of the residual sums of squares for the regressions on the two subsamples, k is the number of independent variables, and n is the number of observations. This is distributed as F with 5, 594 degrees of freedom. In the regression results corresponding to Table 4.5, RSS1 = 41.02, RSS3 = 15.63 + 14.75 = 30.38, n = 604, k = 5, so F = 41.76, which is far in excess of the 3.04 value indicating a significant difference at the 1% level. For noncrop production, we have RSS1 = 219.67, RSS3 = 117.42 + 88.77 = 206.19, n = 580, and k = 4, so F = 9.36, which also far exceeds the critical value at the 1% level in this case.

Table 4.5. Dahe Team-Level Production Function Estimates (Author)

Variable	Crop Sector Coefficient (t statistic)		Noncrop Sector Coefficient (t statistic)	
1970–1985				
Constant	5.165	(16.043)	3.197	(9.978)
Labor	0.057	(1.749)	0.254	(4.601)
Land*	0.661	(13.446)	—	
Capital**	0.010	(0.399)	0.399	(9.538)
Current inputs	0.062	(1.662)	0.198	(10.356)
Time trend	0.086	(21.759)	0.085	(10.475)
	n = 604	R^2 : 0.719	n = 580	R^2 : 0.661
1970–1979				
Constant	4.649	(14.499)	3.422	(10.636)
Labor	0.102	(2.612)	0.139	(2.179)
Land^a	0.610	(10.609)	—	
Capital^b	0.015	(0.702)	0.404	(9.346)
Current inputs	0.150	(3.633)	0.232	(10.306)
Time trend	0.027	(4.489)	0.053	(3.760)
	n = 353	R^2 : 0.640	n = 341	R^2 : 0.670
1980–1985				
Constant	4.120	(6.928)	2.118	(3.034)
Labor	0.009	(0.211)	0.260	(2.682)
Land^a	0.467	(6.805)	—	
Capital^b	−.002	(0.047)	0.370	(4.380)
Current inputs	0.259	(4.486)	0.153	(3.773)
Time trend	0.133	(11.841)	0.219	(6.368)
	n = 250	R^2 : 0.550	n = 238	R^2 : .484

^{a}Cultivated area in *mu*. 1 *mu* = .0667 ha.
^{b}Capital allocation across sectors is based on the values obtained by Wiemer for 1970–1979.
Estimates are by ordinary least squares.
R^2 is adjusted in all cases.

the marginal products of the factors at average input levels as implied by the estimates shown in Table 4.5.

We begin discussion of the results by comparing the estimated elasticities with those obtained by Wiemer. For the 1970s, the estimates for crop production should differ only as a result of the change from labor estimated by days to labor estimated by number of workers.[26] Entry of the ϕ_i parameters in the present case as constants also permits calculations of the previously missing standard error on current inputs, with the result that the estimated coefficient turns to be significant at the 1% level. The other coefficients are also statistically significant at that level, with the exception of the one on capital, which was also not significant in Wiemer's estimate. With respect

[26]A change in units only would alter only the intercept of the equation. However, since the reported average days per worker used by Wiemer varies among teams, the effect of changing to the simpler measure is not the same across teams, so changes in other coefficients are also possible.

Table 4.6. Value of Marginal Product Estimates from Dahe Team-Level Data (Author)

	Labor (Y/worker)		Land (Y/hectare)	Capital (Y/Y1)		Current Inputs (Y/Y1)	
	Crop	Noncrop		Crop	Noncrop	Crop	Noncrop
1970	33.976	18.892	770.232	0.056	0.552	0.673	0.159
1971	33.929	24.969	753.939	0.051	0.626	0.636	0.268
1972	34.836	49.184	773.826	0.034	0.923	0.473	0.498
1973	34.580	81.381	722.144	0.036	1.852	0.398	0.605
1974	40.876	73.099	877.720	0.040	1.455	0.351	0.612
1975	38.910	61.548	837.502	0.031	1.163	0.303	0.541
1976	34.126	79.190	782.895	0.025	1.412	0.266	0.638
1977	40.999	92.637	927.345	0.027	1.597	0.305	0.594
1978	43.594	95.014	967.415	0.028	1.575	0.275	0.744
1979	52.492	71.572	1119.256	0.031	1.209	0.354	0.523
1980	5.456	170.462	1080.343	−0.0005	1.197	0.661	0.883
1981	5.820	167.435	1207.858	−0.005	1.080	0.693	0.866
1982	4.560	251.733	1015.231	−0.004	1.484	0.613	1.466
1983	7.966	278.588	1587.271	−0.004	1.769	0.979	1.066
1984	9.973	366.890	1787.841	−0.004	2.477	1.138	1.733
1985	11.703	513.695	2065.697	−0.005	3.421	1.109	0.572

to magnitudes, the elasticities on land and on the time trend are quite similar in the two estimates, while those on labor and capital are smaller and that on current inputs is larger in the current estimate.

The 1970s estimates for noncrop production can differ from Wiemer's for sidelines both because the same capital stock is now assumed to be employed in a somewhat broader range of activities, and because the number of outputs covered and the amounts of the other inputs employed are potentially larger. The change in the measure of labor also applies here, as does the fact that entry of the ϕ_i's as constants allows calculation of the standard error on the coefficient for current inputs. As with Wiemer's estimate, all of the coefficients turn out to be statistically significant at the 1% level. The coefficients on capital and current inputs are quite similar in the two estimates, while the coefficient on the time trend is somewhat larger and that on labor considerably smaller in the current case.

The last set of estimates permitting direct comparison is that for crop production in the 1980s. Wiemer's results for this period, not discussed earlier, also appear in Table 4.2. In this case, the sources of variation between those estimates and our own include the fact that Wiemer uses only the 1983–1985 data, while we use that for the full period 1980–1985. Second, while Wiemer assumed all capital to have been used in crop production, our estimate assigns to that sector only the portion of capital found by her to have been used in crop production in the 1970s.[27] As before, Wiemer

[27]There are also minor differences in the method of computing the projected capital stock based on individual capital goods.

imposes an assumption of constant returns to scale, while we leave the relevant coefficients unconstrained.[28] The estimates share the same measure of labor. The results show a significant deterioration in the fit of the data to the production function, both in comparison with the 1970s estimate for crop production, and in comparison with Wiemer's result for 1983–1985. When comparing the two periods, the adjusted R^2 declines from .64 to .55, and the coefficients on both labor and capital are without statistical significance in the 1980s estimate. There is a substantial decline in the coefficient on land and significant increases in the coefficients on current inputs and on the time trend, all of which are statistically significant at the 1% level for both subperiod estimates. The poor performance of the capital and labor measures both as compared with the 1970s and as compared with the shorter period 1983–1985 is probably due to the deterioration in data reliability, and Wiemer's decision to ignore the 1980–1982 observations is supported in this respect.

The last subsector estimate is the one not covered by Wiemer's analysis, that for noncrop production in the 1980s. The result here is encouraging. Although the adjusted R^2 for the equation declines from .67 for the 1970s to .48 for 1980–1985, the F value of the equation remains significant at the .01% level, and all coefficients are individually significant at the 1% level or better. Comparing the elasticities across subperiods, that for capital is fairly similar in the two subperiods, while the estimated elasticity of current inputs is somewhat smaller and that of labor is markedly higher in the later period. The estimated coefficient of the time trend is sharply higher.[29]

Average values of the marginal products of the factor inputs corresponding to the new estimates are shown in Table 4.6. The estimated marginal product of land averaged roughly Y 869.6 per hectare in the 1970s, consistent with the range estimated by Wiemer. It had risen to Y 1,889.1 per hectare in 1980–1985, a rather greater increase than indicated by her estimates. Our estimates of the marginal product of labor in crop production are smaller for both the 1970s and the 1980s. In the latter subperiod, our estimate is based on a statistically insignificant coefficient, so Wiemer's must be considered more reliable. The estimates of the marginal product of labor in sidelines and in noncrop production for the 1970s are more similar, but ours (for noncrop production) are still somewhat smaller. The two sets of estimates agree in showing labor's marginal product to have been much lower in crop production. For the 1970s, our estimated marginal product of capital is smaller in crop production and larger in noncrop production than are Wiemer's estimates for crop production and sidelines, respectively. Again, the estimates agree in showing capital's marginal product to be much lower in crop production. With regard to

[28]In contrast to the nonlinear simultaneous estimates for the 1970s, Wiemer's OLS estimates for 1983–1985 yield standard errors and thus t statistics on all of the estimated parameters.

[29]The reader may have noticed that the sums of the coefficients on the included factor inputs are below 1 in each estimate in Table 4.5, suggesting decreasing returns to scale. Given the indications of problems of data quality, we do not want to read too much into this result. Errors in variables, which tend to bias the estimates of positive coefficients toward zero, could suffice to explain it. We do not formally test a restriction of constant returns to scale.

current inputs, the estimates are rather similar, showing a lower marginal product in crop production and an increase in marginal product in that sector in the later subperiod.

Focusing on findings with respect to factor allocation, our own exercise for the 1970s shows an "overallocation" of factors to crop production, with the ratio of the average marginal product in noncrop production to that in crop production being 2.3 : 1 for labor, 2.0 : 1 for current inputs, and 43.0 : 1 for capital. Wiemer's finding that the marginal product gap is larger for capital than for labor is here confirmed and indeed greatly magnified, while the gaps for current inputs and for labor are no longer very different. Our hopes of obtaining evidence on whether the same type and degree of factor "misallocation" continued into the 1980s are dampened by the poor fit of the 1980–1985 production function for crop production. Insofar as can be surmised from the estimates, the marginal product gaps remained large, with the higher VMPs again in noncrop production. The VMP ratio rises sharply for labor, but it becomes meaningless (or, arguably, infinite) for capital, the VMP of which rises as compared with the 1970s for noncrop production, but becomes essentially zero for crop production. Given the insignificance of the elasticity estimates in the latter sector, little confidence can be placed in these magnitudes. Independent evidence obtained from household level data, to be presented in Chapter 9, is qualitatively quite consistent with these results, nonetheless.

Growth accounting exercises can also be performed on the basis of these estimates. To reduce the influence of changes in sample composition, input and output growth rates are estimated, as before, by regressing the log of each input or output on a time trend variable and a set of team dummies. According to Table 4.7.a, which shows the decomposition analysis for crop production in the 1970s, output value in the represented teams grew at a rate of 4.86% pcr year, while the time trend estimate of factor productivity growth is 2.67%. Average labor force in crop production declined by 0.23% per year, cultivated area declined by 0.02% per year, capital stock rose by 13.24% per year, and purchased inputs rose by 9.42% per year. Multiplying the growth rates in column 1 by the elasticities from Table 4.5, which also appear in column 2 of the present table, gives the growth contributions of each factor. Dividing these by total output growth indicates that growth of capital stock accounts for 4% of overall growth, and growth of current inputs for 29%; after subtracting the small output decline due to loss of labor and land, factor input change accounts for only 32.5% of output growth. The estimated trend rate accounts for another 55%, leaving 13% of crop output growth unexplained.[30]

---

[30]This is the only case in which the use of input and output growth rates computed from the averages of the input and output series in the base and terminal years gives a better fit than does use of the regression-based growth rate estimates. When the exercise is recomputed using the former method, the unexplained residual is only 4%. This may, however, be purely coincidental, and since estimates by the aggression method perform more satisfactorily in all other cases examined in this chapter, they are retained here as well for the sake of consistency.

Table 4.7. Growth Accounting with Author's Production Function Estimates for Dahe Teams

Factor or Variable	Growth Rate, %[a]	Elasticity	Contributed Growth Rate, %	Share of Total Growth Rate
a. Crop Sector, 1970–1979				
Labor	−0.23	.102	−0.02	.00
Land	−0.02	.610	−0.01	.00
Capital	13.24	.015	0.20	.04
Current Inputs	9.42	.150	1.41	.29
Trend	2.67		2.67	.55
Output	4.86			
Unexplained				.13
b. Noncrop Sector, 1970–1979				
Labor	7.51	.139	1.04	.05
Capital	13.24	.404	5.35	.27
Current Inputs	36.49	.232	8.47	.43
Trend	5.25		5.25	.26
Output	19.85			
Unexplained				−.01
c. Crop Sector, 1980–1985				
Labor	−5.12	.009	−0.05	.00
Land	−1.57	.467	−0.73	−.06
Capital	13.46	−.002	−0.03	.00
Current inputs	−1.08	.259	0.28	−.02
Trend	13.34		13.34	1.08
Output	12.40			
Unexplained				.01
d. Noncrop Sector, 1980–1985				
Labor	16.38	.260	4.26	.12
Capital	13.46	.370	4.98	.14
Current inputs	28.73	.153	4.40	.12
Trend	21.91		21.91	.61
Output	31.11			
Unexplained				.02

[a]From regression estimate. See text.

The corresponding analysis for the noncrop sector in the 1970s is shown in part b of Table 4.7. The table shows output value to grow at an annual rate of 19.85% while labor input grew at a 7.51% rate, capital stock at a 13.24% rate, and current inputs at a 36.49% rate. Multiplying by the estimated elasticities, this implies that labor force growth accounts for 5% of output growth, capital stock growth for 27%, and current input growth for 43%, for a total of 75% of growth explained by factor inputs. Since the time trend explains 26% of growth, the sum of technical and input growth "overexplains" output growth, but by 1% only.

For the 1980–1985 period, Table 4.7.c shows the growth decomposition for crop production. Here, the trend rate of 13.34% accounts for more than 100% of overall growth, which is estimated to have occurred at an average rate of 12.40% per year. All inputs except capital stock are estimated to have declined. (The reported growth in capital stock reflects that for both sectors combined, and may mask a decline in crop sector capital.) Combined input shrinkage (and the small negative impact of capital growth implied by the negative elasticity estimate for that factor) accounts for a 1.09% rate of output decline. The sum of input and trend growth rates thus leave less than 1% of output growth unexplained.

Part d of the table shows the corresponding analysis for the noncrop sector in 1980–1985. Here, all three inputs are estimated to have grown rapidly, each contributing between 4% and 5% rates of output growth. However, combined input growth explains only 38% of output growth, while the trend rate accounts for another 61%, leaving less than 2% of output growth unexplained.

The same crude corrections for price changes as applied to Wiemer's results can also be carried out here. These corrections are shown alongside those for Wiemer's results in Table 4.8. The general index of purchasing prices of farm and sideline products, used to deflate crop output, rose at a rate of 5.00% per year during 1980–1985, while the general index of retail prices of industrial products in rural areas, used to deflate the current inputs series, rose at a rate of 1.98% per year. The unweighted average of the two indices, used to deflate the noncrop output series, rose at a rate of 4.18% per year. Subtracting the second index weighted by the estimated output elasticity of current inputs from the appropriate output value index gives the price index for adjusting TFP, which is a 3.51% rate for crop production and a 1.82% rate for the noncrop sector in the 1970s, and a 4.49% rate for crop production and a 3.88% rate for the noncrop sector in 1980-85. The adjusted or "real" TFP growth rates are -0.84% for crops and 3.43% for noncrops in 1970-79, and 8.85% for crops and

Table 4.8. Inflation Adjustments of Output and TFP[a] Growth Rates

Estimate:	Author, 1970–1979		Author, 1980–1985		Wiemer, 1970–1979	
	Crop	Noncrop	Crop	Noncrop	Crop	Sideline
Output growth rate, %	4.86	19.85	12.40	36.11	4.5	14.2
TFP growth rate, %	2.67	5.25	13.34	21.91	2.4	3.9
Output price inflation rate, %	3.48	1.77	5.00	4.18	3.48	1.77
Input price inflation rate, %	−0.20	−0.20	1.98	1.98	−0.20	−0.20
Weight on inputs[b]	.15	.23	.26	.15	.09	.21
Inflation rate for TFP, %	3.51	1.82	4.49	3.88	3.50	1.81
Adjusted output growth rate, %	1.38	18.08	7.40	31.93	1.02	12.43
Adjusted TFP growth rate, %	−0.84	3.43	8.85	18.03	−1.10	2.09
Adjusted TFP share of output growth	−.609	.190	1.196	.565	−1.078	.168

[a]Total factor productivity.

[b]Estimated elasticity of output with respect to current inputs.

18.03% for noncrops in 1980-85. The output growth rates are deflated by the respective output value indices only, giving 1.38% for crops and 18.08% for noncrops in 1970-79, and 7.40% for crops and 31.93% for noncrops in 1980–1985. With these adjustments, TFP growth explains about 19% of output growth in the noncrop sector in the 1970s, and 57% of output growth in the crop sector in 1980-85. TFP growth is negative in the crop sector in the 1970s, and explains 122% of output growth in the crop sector in 1980–1985, when crop sector inputs were being reduced rapidly.

Inspecting the table, notice that Wiemer's and our own results for the 1970s are qualitatively similar for the crop sector, and attribute nearly the same share of output growth to TFP growth in the noncrop sector. Both sectors clearly grew more rapidly in the second period than in the first, even after the price correction. Noncrop production grew more rapidly than crop production in both periods, but the relative difference in growth rates narrowed in the second period. Crop sector growth in the 1970s is attributed to input growth alone, which must in fact compensate for declining factor productivity. Noncrop sector growth shows modest productivity growth in the 1970s, but substantially stronger productivity growth in the 1980s. Although productivity growth is only half as great in crop production as in the noncrop sector, it accounts for a larger share of output growth in crop production than in noncrop production during 1980–1985. This is in keeping with the belief that the change from collective to household-based farming, which directly affected the crop sector only, was the most important single cause of rural economic growth in that period. More direct analysis of the effects of that change will be the subject of Chapter 7.

Conclusions

Production function estimates based on the Dahe commune/township team data show that economic growth took place mostly outside of the crop production sector. The crop sector shifted from making a negligible contribution to growth in the 1970s to making a respectable contribution in the early 1980s, but the growth rate of noncrop output increased by an even larger absolute margin. Growth was overwhelmingly due to increased application of inputs, in the 1970s. Even in the noncrop sector, in which total factor productivity was rising at over 3% a year during that decade, TFP improvement accounted for less than 20% of output growth. During 1980–1985, the picture seemed to change to one in which productivity growth accounted for the better part of output growth in both sectors. These figures are only rough indicators, since the price deflators used are based on general indices rather than on data specific to Dahe.

Another warning regarding the interpretation of these findings is that they may substantially overstate the acceleration of output and productivity growth in 1980–1985 versus the 1970s at Dahe due to changes in the statistical reporting system. In particular, the transition to household-level farming in the early 1980s led both to greater inaccuracy of the team accounts and to inclusion of output generated by household activities that were ignored in the 1970s accounts since those accounts did not attempt to measure households' private production. This problem was considered by Kim (1990) in his analysis of the productivity effects of decollectivization at Dahe, and his solution, which is further discussed in Chapter 7, entails both a downward revision of crop output figures beginning in 1983, and also the conclusion that figures for the 1970s and 1980s may embody so many inconsistencies as to be basically incomparable.

Both in the collective 1970s and in the post-collective 1980s, there appeared to be large gaps between the productivity of each potentially reallocable input (labor, capital, and purchased current inputs) in the crop sector and its productivity in noncrop production. This could indicate that non-profit-maximizing resource allocation was imposed on teams and later on households by higher levels, for example by way of obligations to sell staple crops to the state (which persisted into the 1980s). It could also result from any of a number of factors leading to subsistence-oriented behavior, such as uncertainty regarding the availability and price of grain combined with farmer risk-aversion, or imposition of subsistence targets by higher levels. Finally, it could result from rationing of scarce inputs in favor of crop production, resulting in input prices that understate true scarcity values. These possibilities will be discussed further in Chapter 8, where the present chapter's findings with respect to intersectoral factor allocation will be supported by an analysis of household-level data for 1985. Although it will prove impossible to determine the relative contribution of each of the three factors listed here to the outcome, all will be shown to be part of the pattern of underdeveloped free markets, administered state purchases, and other interventions in the crop sector which emerges as a major continuity in the Chinese rural economy, transcending the boundary-line of economic reform.

5

Incentives in the
Collective Era[1]

As Chapter 1 noted, the presumed incentive deficiencies of the collective form of farm organization lie at the center of many analyses of the performance of China's agriculture in the 1960s and 1970s, and of the growth spurt that occurred in the early 1980s when China's agriculture was reorganized with individual households as basic production units. The data from Dahe township provide one of the only available resources for testing theories of incentives in collective farms against Chinese experience. This chapter begins with a discussion of those theories, then proceeds to hypothesis testing using the Dahe team-level data. Chapter 6 then investigates some related labor supply issues at the individual level, while Chapter 7 looks at the effects of decollectivization on farm productivity.

Theories of Incentives in Collective Farms

Much has been written about the disincentive to farm effort caused by collectivization, and the rise in farm productivity which followed the adoption of household-based farming systems in China in the early 1980s is consistent with the idea that such disincentives exist. Yet the source of the disincentive in question is often left imprecise. Some problems with motivating effort in collective farms almost certainly result from the nature of the planning and marketing institutions in which they are embedded—mandatory procurement systems, high implicit taxation of agriculture, and imposition of unprofitable production plans are examples. Other problems result from internal organization factors, such as the method of distributing collectively generated incomes. Even internal organization problems are not all of internal origin, nor are they always endemic to collective institutions as such. In the first place, internal organization problems can be of external origin—e.g., when egalitarian distribution policies are imposed by supervisory bodies or high level political leaders. Second, while problems of internal origin can be intrinsic to group production as such—including endemic dimensions of the problem of tying reward to effort—they

---

[1]Portions of the empirical exercise reported in this chapter were earlier published in Putterman (1990b), while the theoretical discussion borrows from Putterman (1986b, 1988b, 1989b).

can also be consequences of the cultural or technological milieu in which collective production is to be practiced—for example, labor intensive agriculture may pose problems for collective organization that do not exist in manufacturing industry. Discussions of the incentive problem that attribute it to the collective nature of production seem to imply that the problem is overwhelmingly intrinsic or endemic in nature, but this leaves open the question of the relative importance of external influences such as price and marketing policies, of external interventions in the internal management system, and of the role of cultural and technical factors, in leading to unsatisfactory incentive outcomes.

The case of the incentive problem in collective production is one in which economic analysis does not necessarily support economic "thought" in the sense of "opinions concerning economic subjects . . . especially concerning public policy . . . that . . . float in the public mind."[2] Formal microanalytic models of effort determination in collective production settings go back about a quarter of a century and may be grouped in two categories: those that assume individual effort to be an observable variable, which includes most of those developed before the late 1970s, and those that assume effort to be unobservable or observable with cost, which have been developed mostly in the past dozen years. The former find no basis for predicting an undersupply of effort in collectives, so long as the payment system is not overly restrictive. The latter reach conflicting conclusions and thus far have resisted formation of a scholarly consensus.

The observable effort branch has its earliest and simplest statement in Sen (1966a), which anticipates several of the themes of the later literature. Assume a technology which maps inputs of homogeneous labor and of nonlabor inputs into units of a homogeneous farm product,

$$Q = f(L, A, E, K, \theta) \tag{5.1}$$

where Q is output in physical units; L is the sum of labor units ℓ^i contributed by various workers indexed by i; A, E, and K are land, current inputs (expenditures), and capital; and θ represents the state of nature. Now, suppressing the nonlabor inputs and ignoring state uncertainty, write net value product

$$R = p\{g(L)\} - C = pQ - C_N = R(L) \tag{5.2}$$

where p is product price and C_N is the sum of nonlabor costs, both of which are fixed in the short run.[3] Note that, if some of the nonlabor inputs are contributed by the members in return for compensation, the latter is subsumed within C_N. The remainder R is distributed to the members $i = 1,2, \ldots, n$ who receive shares s^i such that

---

[2]Schumpeter (1954, p. 38).
[3]For greater generally, p itself may be viewed as a random variable from the standpoint of the collective. This possibility is in general suppressed in what follows.

$$\sum_{i=1}^{n} s^i R = R. \tag{5.3}$$

$s^i R$, which we shall hereafter denote by y^i, will be thought of as i's income from cooperative labor since, although it may not be tied specifically to the level of i's labor contribution, its payment depends on i's status as a working member of the cooperative.

Beginning with Sen (1966), shares s^i have been assumed in most formal analyses either to be equal,

$$s^i = \frac{1}{N} \tag{5.4a}$$

to be proportionate to labor input,

$$s^i = \frac{\ell^i}{L} \tag{5.4b}$$

or to be an average of (4a) and (4b) with weight $\alpha \in (0,1)$; that is,

$$s^i = \frac{\alpha}{N} + (1 - \alpha)\frac{\ell^i}{L} = A^i \tag{5.4c}$$

Shares (5.4a) correspond to the principle, "to each according to his needs" assuming equal "needs"; shares (5.4b) to the principle, "to each according to his work"; and (5.4c) may be dubbed a mixed distribution system. In (5.4b) and (5.4c), ℓ^i are assumed to be known or measured perfectly.

The incentive implications of the choice of (5.4a) or (5.4b), or, more generally, of the weight α in (5.4c), are found to depend upon the nature of interactions between labor inputs ℓ^i, ℓ^j, etc., or of the members' conjectures regarding these, and on where resources, technology, and members' preferences place the cooperative on the curves relating marginal and net average products of labor. Focusing first on the latter factor, assume that, with given levels of the nonlabor inputs, the marginal product of labor is first increasing, then declining, passing through the average net product curve R/L at its maximum, as illustrated by Figure 5.1. Now, differentiating member i's return $y^i = s^i R$ with respect to ℓ^i, assuming the general form (5.4c), we have

$$\frac{\partial}{\partial \ell^i}\left[\left\{\frac{\alpha}{N} + (1 - \alpha)\frac{\ell^i}{L}\right\}R\right] = A^i p Q_L \frac{\partial L}{\partial \ell^i} + (1 - \alpha)\left(1 - \frac{\ell^i}{L}\frac{\partial L}{\partial \ell^i}\right)\frac{R}{L} \tag{5.5}$$

as the marginal return to labor (where A^i stands for s^i of (4c)). (5.5) appears in Figure 5.1 as a family of dashed lines labeled $\partial y^i/\partial \ell^i$, which, assuming $0 < \partial L/$

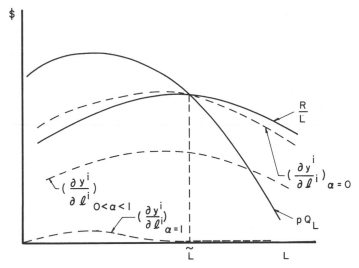

Figure 5.1. Marginal product, average net product, and marginal return to labor for varying values of aggregate labor input and of the degree of "distribution according to needs."

$\partial \ell^i < L/\ell^i$, are a weighted average of the curves pQ_L and R/L when $\alpha = 0$, a scalar multiple of the pQ_L curve, with the latter curve deflated by $N/(\partial L/\partial \ell^i)$, when $\alpha = 1$, and a weighted average of the first two curves when $0 < \alpha < 1$.

Consider, first, the case of strict distribution according to work ($\alpha = 0$). In this case, (5) may be rewritten as

$$\frac{\partial y^i}{\partial \ell^i} = \eta^i pQ_L + (1 - \eta^i) \frac{R}{L} \qquad (5.5a)$$

where $\eta^i = (\ell^i/L)(\partial L/\partial \ell^i)$ is the elasticity of aggregate labor supply with respect to the supply of labor to the cooperative by member i. For all $0 < \eta^i < 1$, (5a) is a weighted average of the marginal product of labor, pQ_L, and the average (net) product, R/L, and thus lies above the latter curve to the left of $\tilde{L}$ where $pQ_L = R/L$ and below it to the right of $\tilde{L}$, as illustrated by the dashed curve labeled $(\partial y^i/\partial \ell^i)_{\alpha=0}$ in the figure. The rational utility-maximizing member will set his marginal rate of substitution (MRS) between leisure and income equal to $\partial y^i/\partial \ell^i$, but Pareto optimality requires that he choose ℓ^i at which his MRS equals the value marginal product of labor, pQ_L. Therefore, work incentives are excessive if perceived aggregated labor input exceeds $\tilde{L}$ and inadequate if perceived aggregated labor input is less than $\tilde{L}$. Unless the perceived aggregate labor input is $\tilde{L}$ itself, the individual's private marginal return to labor fully coincides with her marginal labor product ($\partial y^i/\partial \ell^i = pQ_L$) only if the marginal effect of her labor supply on aggregate labor is equal to the inverse of her labor share ($\partial L/\partial \ell^i = L/\ell^i$).

At the opposite extreme, let distribution be strictly according to needs ($\alpha = 1$). Then (5) can be written as

$$\frac{\partial y^i}{\partial \ell^i} = \frac{1}{N} Q_L \frac{\partial L}{\partial \ell^i} \qquad (5.5b)$$

and, assuming that the reaction $\partial L/\partial \ell^i$ is less than N but greater than zero, $\partial y^i/\partial \ell^i$ appears as a scalar multiple of the marginal product curve, as illustrated by the dashed curve labeled $(\partial y^i/\partial \ell^i)_{\alpha=1}$ in the figure (which is drawn assuming that $\partial L/\partial \ell^i$ is in the neighborhood of 1, its Cournot-Nash value). In this case, labor incentives are suboptimal regardless of perceived L, since the right-hand side of (5b) is less than pQ_L for all $0 < \partial L/\partial \ell^i < N$.

Since the value of L relative to $\bar{L}$ will depend on the relationship between the cooperative's resources and its labor force, absent information on this relationship, it may be said that distributing all of the cooperative's net revenue according to labor contributions could as easily generate excessive as sub-optimal work incentives. For example, if the correctly anticipated L lies substantially to the right of $\bar{L}$, $\partial y^i/\partial \ell^i > pQ_L$ when $\alpha = 0$. However, it is clear that for identical members, whose equilibrium ℓ must be equal, there will exist an α such that $\partial y^i/\partial \ell^i = pQ_L$ for all i; labeling that value α^*, it can be defined by

$$\alpha^* = 1 - \frac{pQ_L}{R/L} \qquad (5.6)$$

(Sen, 1966a). α^* is the proportion of distribution according to needs, or simple sharing, that would be selected by a planner or cooperative leader whose objective is to maximize the utility of the members, or by the members themselves through majority voting (see below). If members differ in their preferences regarding leisure and income, equilibrium values ℓ^i and ℓ^j may differ. The value α^* given by (5.6) will then make $\partial y^i/\partial \ell^i = pQ_L$ for the member contributing the average labor input $\ell^{av} = L/N$, and will leave $\partial y^i/\partial \ell^i \gtrless pQ_L$ for others. Although the magnitude of the divergences may be small, Browning (1982) shows that it may be impossible to find a set of individualized "needs" payments capable of making $\partial y^i/\partial \ell^i = pQ_L$ for all i while also assuring a balanced budget.[4]

If perceived $L < \bar{L}$, (5.6) implies that $\alpha^* < 0$, which means that incentive optimality can be achieved by assessing taxes unrelated to labor input so that more than the value of the average net product can be paid out per contributed labor unit. The intuitive interpretation of both the $L > \bar{L}$ and $L < \bar{L}$ results is that, under Cournot-Nash and similar values of conjectures $\partial L/\partial \ell^i$, marginal payout is approximately equal to average net product, which is the value of the labor-day or other labor

---

[4]See, however, Cremer (1982), who discusses an alternative two-step process which can achieve optimality.

unit. Since this labor unit value can either exceed or fall short of labor's value of marginal product (VMP), incentive efficiency requires that the cooperative depart from pure "distribution according to work" by distributing some of the revenue without regard to labor input when L is large or by assessing taxes unrelated to labor input when L is small.

Cooperative managers or leaders aiming to maximize returns per labor unit would try to find a membership size N at which equilibrium $L = \bar{L}$ (Ward, 1958), as a byproduct of which this problem would not arise. But N is not even a medium-term choice variable in collectivized agricultures, wherein each rural dweller is attached to a local cooperative. Where population is large relative to resources, as for example in most parts of China, unless alternative employments are found, it will be impossible to move individual cooperatives back toward $\bar{L}$ without causing unemployment in the economy as a whole. The "super-optimal" incentives under "distribution according to work" are a "tragedy of the commons," wherein members seek to earn additional work-points bearing average net product returns although their incremental contributions to output are low. By distributing some revenue "according to needs," the cooperative can simultaneously increase equality of income distribution, achieve optimal work incentives, and permit full employment in a rural sector that may be overpopulated in the sense that marginal product is below subsistence wages (under which circumstances commercial farms facing a subsistence minimum wage would not offer employment to the full available labor force [Georgescu-Roegen, 1960]). On the other hand, political leaders who are concerned more with farm deliveries than with farmers' welfare, or who do not view the peasants' leisure as a good, could in principle use the excessive incentives of the system of strict distribution according to work to extract maximum labor from cooperative members (Israelsen, 1980).

"Cohesion" and "Matching"

So far, our discussion has focused on cases in which the expected reaction $\partial L/\partial \ell$ is a small positive number, implicitly assumed to be in the neighborhood of the Cournot-Nash value of unity, and in any case restricted to be no less than zero and no greater than the ratio of aggregate to individual labor L/ℓ^i (which equals the number of cooperative members N when members are identical). Some of the literature has explored the implications of permitting the expected reaction to take its upper-bound value, or of modeling the interdependence of labor supplies in other ways.

Bradley (1971), Bonin (1977), and Chinn (1979) consider the possibility that the individual perceives or expects $\partial L/\partial \ell$ to equal N, or in the case of non-identical workers, L/ℓ^i. Different reasons are given,[5] with Chinn considering the size of the

---

[5]Some of these are critiqued in Putterman, 1985b. More fundamentally, questions about the meaningfulness of a conjectural variations approach in a static model of oligopoly also apply to the present setting. These considerations would lead many theorists to adopt the Cournot-Nash assumption at the outset, and to dismiss the scenarios of this subsection. Below, we provide some suggestions for resolving this issue empirically.

response to be a function of workers' "emulation" of their peers and calling the case in which $\partial L/\partial \ell = L/\ell^i$ one of "perfect cohesion." Plugging this value into (5.5), we find that the expected marginal return to effort, which is the RHS of this equation, becomes a function of the marginal product of labor only, because the term containing R/L vanishes (i.e., R/L is multiplied by zero). Recalling the definition of A in (5.4c), we find that in the term containing it in (5.5), the value of marginal product is multiplied by exactly unity when $\alpha = 0$ or when ℓ is identical for all individuals i and α takes any value, and that VMP in (5.5) is multiplied by a number greater (less) than unity for values of ℓ^i greater (less) than the average value when the ℓ's differ and α is greater than zero. If individual preferences do not differ too sharply and the ℓ's tend to be similar, then the marginal return to effort is close to the value of the marginal product of effort whatever the value of α.

The conclusion to be drawn from the analysis of the "perfect cohesion" variant of the general cooperative effort model is that individual effort incentives would be optimal in the cooperative if income were distributed in proportion to effort (regardless of where aggregate effort puts the VMP/ANRP ratio), that incentives would also be optimal regardless of the distribution rule if the members have identical preferences regarding effort and leisure, and that even in the case of nonidentical workers and some distribution unrelated to effort, the departure from optimal incentives may not be pronounced. Further, the effect of shifting to "needs" distribution upon the aggregate effort supply of the cooperative's members is unclear, since some members may raise while others lower their effort levels. There is, then, no reason to expect the shift to "needs" distribution to produce a strong change in aggregate effort in either direction, under "perfect cohesion."

An alternative model, developed by Guttman and Schnytzer (1989), allows members to precommit themselves to matching one another's autonomous effort contributions at any constant rate. An effort contribution ℓ^i is here viewed as being the sum of an autonomous effort level and of a set of contributions that match the autonomous levels of each other member at whatever rate worker i has precommitted to. An equilibrium of this model is a set of matching rates that is a Nash equilibrium given knowledge of the matching rates and propensities to work (utility functions) of all other members; that is, an equilibrium exists when no member can make him or herself better off by selecting a different set of matching rates, given the matching rates and preferences of all of the other members. Within this set-up, Guttman and Schnytzer demonstrate the unexpected results that the effort supplied by individuals is socially optimal in a cooperative in which the level of "needs" distribution equals or exceeds the optimal α of Sen's analysis, including a cooperative practicing pure "needs" distribution ($\alpha = 1$), but that effort supplies fall below what is socially optimal when the share of "needs" distribution is below Sen's optimum, including the case of pure distribution according to work.[6] Guttman and Schnytzer point out that

---

[6]Optimality is achieved here with pure distribution according to work only when that is also the optimal distribution setting in Sen's mode—i.e., when labor's average net revenue product and its value of

unlike other models of incentives in cooperatives, their model has the virtue of correctly predicting that a Soviet *kolkhoz,* which distributes (or historically distributed) income according to work days, would generate inadequate incentives, while an Israeli *kibbutz,* which supports its members without regard to what job each performs, is thought to display relatively good effort outcomes. Whether the model's implications are consistent with other experiences, including that of China, remains to be investigated.

Since the predictions of the "perfect emulation" and "matching" variants of the incentive model differ from those of the version discussed in the previous section under a variety of conditions, their relative validity is in principle ascertainable on the basis of empirical observation. For example, suppose that the resource balance puts aggregate labor input to the right of $\bar{L}$ for a wide range of incentive schemes. Then the Sen model with $0 < \partial L / \partial \ell^i < L / \ell^i$ (and with limited "sympathy") predicts that aggregate cooperative effort will vary positively with the degree to which distribution is based upon labor rather than "needs,"[7] while the "matching" model predicts the opposite relationship between the distribution system and effort, at least for degrees of "needs" distribution below the optimal value in Sen's model. The "perfect cohesion" variant, on the other hand, predicts that aggregate effort will be more or less insensitive to changes in the distribution system.

A Flat Rations Model

A possible problem, for our purposes, with models of the sort just described is that they may misrepresent the nature of the actual system of "distribution according to needs" that operated in Chinese production teams. In particular, these models assume that any income to be distributed on an equal, "according to needs," or "work-disregarding" fashion, would be specified *as a proportion* of the team's total distributed income. How applicable would such models be if teams provided only a fixed income floor to each household, without reference to labor input, and then paid additional amounts for greater labor to those households whose labor earnings more than sufficed to cover this minimum ration?

To answer this question, consider Figure 5.2, in which the vertical axis measures the income distributed by the team to a household, and the horizontal axis measures the household's labor contribution to the team. Suppose that the team guarantees the household a basic income of at least $c = OC$, and an amount based on the household's work-points if the work-point value exceeds c. If R/L is the value of a work-point in the absence of the ration system and AB is the line indicating payments based on

---

marginal product are identical at equilibrium. The result that equilibrium effort is optimal when $\alpha = 0$ is less surprising than the result that effort is not only suboptimal but also is less than what is optimal (the opposite of Sen's result when $L > \bar{L}$ [Figure 5.1]). The first result fits within the genre of cooperative-like outcomes in a prisoners' dilemma that Guttman's "matching" model had already been shown to achieve in a number of parallel settings. (See the references given by Guttman and Schnytzer.)

[7]An additional requirement to assure that $\partial \ell^* / \partial \alpha > 0$ for all i is that VMP/ANRP not be too large. For further discussion, see Putterman (1986b, pp. 289–90).

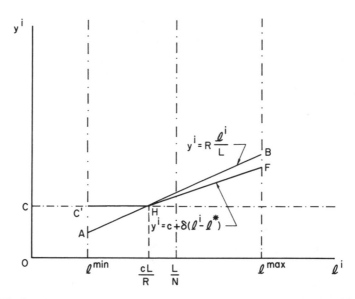

Figure 5.2. Distributed collective income as a function of labor input for given aggregate labor.

work-points for households with work-point totals in the range ($\varrho^{\min}$, $\varrho^{\max}$), then households whose work-point earnings are less than or equal to cL/R would need to be subsidized by the team to raise their incomes to c. But without an external source of subsidies, the team would no longer be able to pay households for which $\varrho > cL/R$ according to the schedule AB (HB). In order for remaining payments to rise proportionately with work-points, the payment line would have to be rotated downward to HF, chosen so that the area of triangle HBF equals that of the subsidy triangle AC'H.[8]

What is the impact of egalitarianism in the form depicted by the fixed rations model? First, households whose optimization in the absence of rations would lead them to contribute between $\varrho^{\min}$ and cL/R units of labor face a flat payment schedule, giving them no incentive to provide more than $\varrho^{\min}$ units of labor—or for that matter, any units of labor at all.[9] Second, households whose choice in the no-ration situation would have placed them to the right of cL/R labor units now face lowered marginal returns to effort, as shown by the less steeply rising slope of HF compared with HB. Further, the higher is the subsistence floor c, the longer will be the flat portion CH and

[8]On schedule HF, incomes are given by $y^i = c + \delta[\varrho^i - (cL/Q)]$, and are thus no longer strictly proportionate to labor input. A variant that retains such proportionality requires that y^i begin increasing with ϱ^i a discrete distance to the right of H. The results are qualitatively similar.

[9]Perhaps coercion or social pressures not explicitly modeled here could assure that labor input did not fall below $\varrho^{\min}$. Evidence for such coercion will be presented in Chapter 6. If workers in the $\varrho^{\min}$, cL/R range simply shift to working $\varrho^{\min}$, this in itself will reduce R, requiring a complete redrawing of the figure. Thus, this static diagram is only useful as a first approximation.

the less steep will be the rising portion HF, assuming a given L and R.[10] At least in the absence of cohesion and matching, then, the effect of egalitarianism in the form of fixed rations is (like that of proportionate "needs distribution") to reduce effort by self-interested workers, by totally eliminating material incentives for those at the bottom of the work-points scale, and by reducing those incentives less drastically for those whose work-points earn them more than the stipulated ration.[11]

Models with Imperfectly Observed Effort

The analysis of the first part of the previous section led to the result that, since marginal returns to labor would tend to reflect net average more than marginal product of labor in a system of distribution in proportion to work, incentives would be excessive when aggregate labor supply was expected to lead to marginal product being less than average net product. This result is perplexing in view of the frequent observation that collective farms suffer from weak work incentives.

One possible explanation lies in the fact that the models assume that the cooperative member, in selecting his labor input, knows with certainty the production function, the labor inputs of others, and the distribution rule; that there are no exogenous, stochastic factors affecting output; and that the member's labor input is accurately measured in homogeneous efficiency units. If any of these assumptions do not hold, effort must be rendered under conditions of uncertainty regarding its returns. Uncertainty regarding other members' labor and the distribution rule, added to production uncertainty which affects both group and household-level farm labor, would make cooperative production relatively less attractive to risk-averse farmers. However, in planned economies, where cooperative output is sold to the state at fixed prices while private output is sold in free markets at variable prices, price uncertainty could have an offsetting effect in favor of cooperative production (Bonin, 1977).

Imperfect information by the cooperative regarding individual members' labor contributions merits special consideration as a source of incentive failure. In the worst case, L can be inferred from output but the individual ℓ^i cannot be ascertained at all, forcing the cooperative to pay all workers equally or to otherwise arbitrarily divide net income without respect to actual labor contributions. This case is equivalent to pure "needs" distribution (4a), and also to what Holmström (1982) labels "simple sharing," in a paper in which he proves that it will not support a first-best effort equilibrium in a static setting. An analysis of Nash equilibrium effort allocation in a

---

[10]Of course, R/L is the maximum value of c supportable by labor input L, and its adoption implies that the payment schedule is completely flat. Even this would be viable only if the assumption of unchanged L were true despite the essential absence of individual work incentives. (Note that the rations model does not capture the "one Nth of marginal product" that the Sen-type model shows going to the worker even under complete egalitarianism, since it assumes the rations to be independent of R and L.)

[11]For further analysis, see Putterman (1988b), which shows that the reduction in marginal pay for those working more than cL/R units is in fact less under the fixed rations scheme than under the system in which a fixed proportion of income is distributed "according to work."

cooperative under this depiction of imperfect information, giving explicit consideration of the interdependence of individual workers' decisions through the effect of aggregate L, is provided by Carter (1987).

Somewhat more ambiguity attaches to the modeling of intermediate situations in which information on ℓ^i is potentially obtainable, but at positive cost. One possible approach, paralleling the literature on supervision in conventional firms (Calvo and Wellisz 1978; Shapiro and Stiglitz 1984; Bowles 1985), is to assume that the worker is observed in a given period with probability $0 < \rho < 1$, where ρ increases with supervision or monitoring. When she is observed, the cooperative knows ℓ^i and can pay the worker by (5.4b);[12] when not observed, the worker is paid her per capita share of net output.[13] Her expected income is

$$E(y^i) = \rho \, \frac{\ell^i}{L} R + (1 - \rho) \frac{1}{N} R \qquad (5.7)$$

if the probability of being monitored is uncorrelated with ℓ^i. Clearly, ρ in (5.7) functions precisely like $(1 - \alpha)$ in (5.4c). As a result, a worker's effort will in general decline as monitoring and ρ decline, with the limiting case of $\rho = 0$ being the no-information case already discussed. In view of the problems mentioned earlier, if monitoring were obtainable in continuously variable quantities at low but positive cost, the efficient cooperative might want to use enough units of monitoring to cause $(1 - \rho)$ to assume the value of α^* in (5.6), but never more than this; in other words, imperfect monitoring could be a functional substitute for "needs distribution." If monitoring is quite costly, however, values of ρ lower than $(1 - \alpha^*)$ might be optimal, adversely affecting the viability of the cooperative compared with independent peasant production.

That imperfect knowledge of effective labor input is not alone sufficient to render incentives inadequate is demonstrated by Putterman (1986a), Bonin and Putterman (1987a), and Putterman and Skillman (1988), who consider an alternative depiction of information. Suppose that

$$\hat{\ell}^i = \ell^i + k\epsilon \qquad (5.8)$$

where $\hat{\ell}^i$ is an imperfect estimate of ℓ^i, ϵ is a stochastic term, $\mu(\epsilon) = 0$, $\sigma_\epsilon^2 > 0$, and k is a shift factor varying inversely with the level of monitoring. If we substitute $\hat{\ell}^i$ for ℓ^i in (5.4c), it is clear that the risk-neutral worker is indifferent to, and will not adjust his effort in response to, changes in the level of monitoring. Risk-averse workers will be influenced by changes in k, which change the variance of ℓ^i, but the conjecture that their equilibrium effort will increase as the accuracy of measurement rises ($k\downarrow$) is not

---

[12]Aggregate L is presumably known from Q.
[13]Note that this scheme guarantees an expected but not an ex post balanced budget for the cooperative.

in general correct. For example, for the entire class of utility functions characterized by nonincreasing absolute risk aversion, as well as for the increasing absolute risk aversion case of utility quadratic in income ($U^i = ay^i - b\,(y^i)^2 - u(\ell^i)$, $a > 0$, $b > 0$, $a - 2by^i > 0$), workers may work more the more accurately $\hat{\ell}^i$ is measured if $L < \bar{L}$, but will work less the more accurately $\hat{\ell}^i$ is measured if $L > \bar{L}$. On the other hand, reasonable conditions support positive effort responses to monitoring when $\hat{\ell}^i$ is multiplicative rather than additive in the error term (that is, the addition sign is replaced by a multiplication sign in (5.8); see Putterman and Skillman, 1988) for values of L on both sides of $\bar{L}$.

A final possibility which has been explored is to assume that the worker-member is paid according to a proxy for effort, call it work-points, and to characterize the functional relationship between that proxy, true effort, and the level of monitoring in a manner than is both intuitively plausible and potentially consistent with the idea that poor monitoring is associated with low work effort. An example is provided by Lin (1988b, 1991), who posits that

$$\frac{\partial \hat{\ell}^i}{\partial \ell^i} \geq 0 \qquad (5.9a)$$

$$\frac{\partial \hat{\ell}^i}{\partial \theta} \leq 0 \qquad (5.9b)$$

$$\frac{\partial^2 \ell^i}{\partial \theta \partial \ell^i} > 0 \qquad (5.9c)$$

where $\hat{\ell}^i$ is the effort proxy and θ is the level of monitoring, and where (5.9a) holds with equality for $\theta = 0$. These assumptions suffice to guarantee that $\partial \ell^{i*}/\partial \theta > 0$ provided that workers share a common utility function so that $\ell^i = \ell = L/N$, all i. When the latter assumption is abandoned, $\partial \ell^{i*}/\partial \theta$ cannot be signed in the absence of further restrictions. Moreover, the signing of $\partial \ell^{i*}/\partial \theta$ in the identical-workers case also depends on the assumed nonstochastic nature of the $\hat{\ell}$ function ($\hat{\ell}^i = \hat{\ell}^j$ whenever $\ell^i = \ell^j$); but if each $\hat{\ell}$ is a non-stochastic function of an unobserved ℓ and a collective choice variable, θ, it may be wondered why the cooperative is unable to invert the function to discover true ℓ.

Incentives and Repetition

The models discussed thus far all assume that the worker determines effort in a given period without regard to future consequences. On the other hand, China's collective farms existed for many years with substantial continuity of membership. Game theorists have pointed out that repetition of a given choice situation ("repeated play of a game") can significantly alter predicted outcomes. This idea may be especially relevant in the case in which paying team members according to observed effort is thwarted by imperfection and costliness of effort monitoring.

Suppose that individual effort levels are completely unobservable. Then from a static, one period standpoint, the cooperative incentive problem is that of pure distribution according to "needs," as modeled in (5.4a). Cohesion and matching responses are not applicable if workers cannot observe one anothers' effort levels.[14] Therefore, the static theory predicts undersupply of effort. However, suppose that output itself is observable, and the relationship between aggregate effort and output is known. Then members of the cooperative can commit themselves in advance to supplying certain levels of effort, and their commitments can be checked in the aggregate, although not individually, by observing the level of output achieved.

MacLeod (1988) has shown that efficient effort levels can be sustained in a cooperative by a scheme of the type just mentioned, provided that the probability of termination of the game, and members' preferences for present over future utility, are not too high. Each member adopts the strategy of providing a Pareto-optimal effort level in each period so long as output in the previous period is consistent with all members having provided such effort. If output falls below the level corresponding to universal optimal effort by the cooperative's members, then members work at their static privately optimal effort levels, leading to a sharp decline in output. This set of strategies is a Nash equilibrium for all members. Once in effect, the strategies make it individually rational for each member to provide Pareto-optimal effort, for the threat that the cooperative will revert to the lower utility static effort equilibrium deters each one from reducing his or her effort, even though it would not be known who in particular had "shirked." The high probability of repetition and the low rate of present time preference are required so that members will not value the utility gained from shirking in one period more highly than the utility loss due to the collapse of the high-effort equilibrium in future periods.

It should be pointed out that while a high effort equilibrium is a possibility under the situation described above, the set of strategies that might sustain it is not the only possible Nash equilibrium strategy set. Therefore, selection of the optimal equilibrium, if not merely random, requires that members act according to a particularly stringent standard of individual and perhaps collective rationality. Note also that the optimal equilibrium may be unobtainable if output is a stochastic function of the effort levels—a realistic assumption in agricultural production. In that case, it will be impossible for members to distinguish between output shortfalls due to bad states of nature and those due to "shirking." This last factor may help to explain why attempts

---

[14]Another possibility is that members can privately observe one another's effort levels, but that the cooperative as a collectively cannot make such observations—e.g., the individual observations may be disputed by those who are observed, and may not be verifiable by outside parties. In this case effort interaction may still apply, as in the section above, although it might be pointed out that the ideas sketched there require some sense of dynamics to be fully plausible. The "matching behavior" idea also requires an unstated (probably also dynamic) "meta-model" to explain why precommitments, which are not transparently self-enforcing, are assumed to be adhered to.

to monitor and pay according to effort were in fact part of the incentive approach taken by China's agricultural production teams from the 1950s until decollectivization.[15]

Testing the Observable Effort Theory: Setting and Hypotheses

It is impossible to examine directly the accuracy of effort observation in a team production setting. We also lack data on variation in the level of monitoring among teams and over time. Indirect evidence on the degree to which monitoring was a problem can be obtained by testing theories that presume effort to be measurable. These more easily tested theories predict changes in team effort levels depending upon variation in team payment formulas. For example, the Sen theory predicts no effort variation if team members have high levels of altruism ("perfect sympathy"), and effort usually increasing with the degree of payment according to effort input otherwise, a prediction it makes in common with the flat rations variant. Chinn's and similar approaches allow effort again to be unaffected by changes in the payment system, in this case if there is a high degree of "cohesion" or positive interactions in effort supply, while Guttman and Schnytzer's model predicts higher effort under "needs" than "work" distribution assuming ability to precommit to, and to choose strategically, effort "matching rates." If effort is in fact positively correlated with the degree to which payment is based on a report of effort input, this supports the Sen theory and variants with imperfect sympathy and limited effort interactions, including the flat rations model, and it provides no support for the "matching" theory.[16] Positive variation of effort with "work payment" also contradicts extreme claims of labor unobservability which imply that payment in teams is in fact independent of effort, whatever the claim or intention of the rules adopted. (Further evidence on the quality of monitoring during the collective period will be discussed in an appendix to Chapter 7.)

What distribution systems were actually applied by rural production teams at Dahe and elsewhere in China, and how can we frame hypotheses based on the theories

---

[15]Lin, who holds (1986, 1988b) that the difficulty of monitoring individual effort led to low effort outcomes in China's collective farms, makes the novel argument (1990) that high effort levels were sustained by Chinese agricultural cooperatives in the late 1950s by a method akin to that of MacLeod, except that members used the threat of quitting the cooperatives, rather than that of reverting to low effort levels, to sustain high effort equilibria. In addition to the historical question of whether farmers in fact had the right to revert to private farming during that period, Lin's approach suffers from its failure to recognize the alternative incentive device which operates in the MacLeod model, and to discuss the issue of when the threat to quit will be more and when less effective than the threat to provide only static optimal effort. The latter issues are discussed in Dong and Dow (forthcoming) and in Putterman and Skillman (forthcoming). For a model that combines both MacLeod's "trigger strategy" incentive mechanism and a monitoring and penalty scheme, see Dong (1991).

[16]An important qualification is that the implications of matching have been assessed for proportionate needs distribution but not for a flat rations system. If all needs distribution were of the latter type, evidence that the level of needs distribution was negatively correlated with effort would not directly contradict the theory of matching.

above which can be operationalized using the available data? To begin with, in the period in question, aside from private plots limited to around 5% of the cultivated land, land was farmed collectively under the direction of team leaders. Able-bodied adult team members were expected to participate in collective labor, and received work-points according to the number of days worked or tasks completed.[17] Some incomes in cash and kind were distributed as advances, but final distribution was settled at the end of the year after deducting welfare, accumulation, and reserve funds from a team's after-tax net revenue and thereby determining net distributable income. Dividing the latter by the total number of work-points earned by team members gave the value of one work-point and, accordingly, the total value of payment owed to each member.

The income to be distributed, however, took the form of both cash, and of staple foodstuffs produced and retained by the team and valued in internal accounts at the base procurement prices set by the state. These staples were distributed only partly according to work-points; to guarantee basic food needs, the greater part was generally given to households according to number of members.[18] In Dahe, the proportion of distributed grain allocated on the basis of household population ranged from 60% to 80%, and grain accounted for an average of 74% of the income distributed to households in the 1970s at internal accounting values. While the latter practice has sometimes been thought of as a form of "distribution according to needs," its actual nature is somewhat more complicated, for households with greater "needs" were in principle supposed to pay for the grain that they received by taking a smaller portion of their compensation in the form of cash. In other words, the overall distribution of income from the team was to be proportionate to work-points earned, and only the composition of payments, in terms of grain versus cash, was to vary according to household demographics.

In practice, however, the system generated an egalitarian dilution of "distribution according to work" for two reasons. First, the accounting values of the foodstuffs involved, which were determined by base procurement prices, severely understated their economic value to the recipients, because peasants could usually obtain additional grain only at the far higher prices of private and black markets. The vector of payments which was proportionate to work-points at the nominal prices is thus seen to have been biased toward per capita equality when grain is valued at opportunity cost. Second, households having high ratios of dependents to workers, whose grain entitlements exceeded the value of their work-points (even at the low nominal grain price), were permitted to go into debt to their teams at zero interest, often over

---

[17]Task-based work-points were usually replaced by time-based points during the late 1960s and the 1970s under the influence of "Cultural Revolution" era ideology. Typically, each individual earned a fixed number of points per standard day, mostly determined by sex and perceived strength.

[18]Fixed equivalences between the rations of adults and children of various ages were set by higher-level authorities. Village residents who worked for a state entity such as a school or cooperative store were entitled to the privilege of purchasing state grain, and did not receive team rations.

indefinite periods of time. Thus, grain would in effect be lent to households on terms involving a substantial grant component.

Whether these two sources of egalitarianism affected work incentives in the manner of the mixed distribution system model of equation (5.4c) or after the fashion of the flat rations model depicted in Figure 5.2 cannot be established without knowing how the amount of grain allocated on the basis of household population was determined. Insofar as the per capita ration was fixed and unrelated to the level of the team's output, egalitarianism should have affected incentives as depicted in the flat rations model, in which there is an absolute floor on income from the collective sector, and those whose work-point earnings entitled them to more have incomes rising with work-points along a line with a positive income axis intercept.[19] If the level of the per capita ration was a function of the team's output level, on the other hand, then the model of (5.4c) applies for households earning more than the floor level, although the floor element of the rations model would still apply to households with insufficient work-points. While we do not know what formula was used to determine the level of per capita grain rations, there is evidence from the Dahe team level data that a team's output and the level of the rations that it distributed were significantly correlated,[20] suggesting that both models applied to some extent. In both models, an increase in the egalitarianism of distribution—in the first model via a rise in the share distributed equally, and in the second, by way of an increase in the guaranteed consumption standard and a reduced marginal payout to effort for households with work-point earnings bringing them above that floor—leads to a

[19]The argument in Putterman (1990b), p. 92 text and footnote 8, is in error in this regard. If the amount of subsidized grain to be distributed was fixed, then the subsidy was fixed, rather than being proportionate to net revenue as in Sen's "proportion distributed according to needs."

[20]When team accountants were asked to indicate retrospectively what proportion of distributed grain was distributed according to needs, for years in the 1970s, they generally gave round percentages such as 70% or 80%. This suggests either that the distribution formula was fixed in percentage terms, or that subsequent recollection is approximate only. Checks of the correlation, across teams in given years, between team net income (gross revenue minus production costs and taxes) per capita and per capita distributed grain show significant positive correlations in three of four years looked at (1973, 1976, and 1979 but not 1978). When per capita grain distributed according to needs (the product of distributed grain and the proportion mentioned above) is substituted for per capita distributed grain, the correlations retain the same pattern although with some weakening of significance levels (the 1979 correlation is significant at the 15% level, only). Due to missing data, there are not enough observations to compute correlations over time for given teams. Nonetheless, the cross-sectional correlations provide some evidence that, especially before 1978, the amount of income distributed in the form of grain rations was larger, in per capita terms, for teams with higher per capita earnings.
Cross-sectional correlations between per capita grain distributed as rations and the remainder of per capita collective distribution are significantly negative, which may reflect a tendency for higher-income teams to reduce the fraction of distribution on a ration basis. Rations may have increased with income, but at a declining rate, as teams adjusted their remaining grain and cash distributions upward more rapidly than they did their grain rations. In this case, there is sufficient complete data to compute correlations for the two variables over the 1970–1979 period for each of 19 teams. The results are positive and significant at the 10% level for eight teams, negative and significant for one team, and not significant for the remaining ones, so the evidence suggests that, despite the negative cross-sectional correlations, grain rations at least sometimes increased along with nonration disbursements, in line with the proportionate depiction of "needs distribution."

reduction in work incentives. Without specifying the relative roles played by each of the two elements, we can appeal to both models to hypothesize that self-interested peasants would have had a greater incentive to work in collective production, and that more work effort would have been supplied the more income was distributed in the form of cash and the less in the form of grain rations.[21]

The incentive implications of the decision on whether to retain net income in the team or to distribute it to individual members has not been addressed explicitly in the theoretical literature, but the theory is easily extended to predict its effects. This decision was taken by production team leaders with substantial influence from higher level authorities, and hence from political winds blowing through the rural economy. At Dahe, the average accumulation funds of the production teams varied from a low of 7.2% of net, after-tax team income in 1971 to a high of 23.5% in 1977. The average percentage of net income actually distributed varied from a low of 72.5% in 1977 to a high of 85.9% in 1979.

For private individuals, the savings/consumption decision has no direct effect on work incentives, for the individual allocates income between alternative uses until its contribution to utility is equalized on the margin. Members of Chinese agricultural production teams, however, had little or no control over their teams' decisions to distribute or retain income. Thus, although retention for such purposes as capital accumulation and production reserve funds could raise labor's productivity and earnings in future periods, and could accordingly have been desired by some households, its direct effect on incentives must be assumed to have been negative.[22] That is, the more of their team's income they expected to be withheld from distribution, the less would team members have been motivated to work in the collective sector. In terms of the models discussed above (see equations (5.2) and (5.5)), retained earnings could be considered part of C_N, and the higher its value, the lower would be R for given Q. This implies that team members responded to an expected marginal payment based on their individual workpoint ratings and on the expected value of the work-point as opposed to expected average team income including nondistributed funds.

Assuming that individual labor supply responded positively to increased mar-

---

[21]Although it might be desirable to write down a model combining the proportionate and fixed rations models formally, this would help us little here, since the extent to which egalitarianism was of the proportionate or of the fixed type cannot be determined from the Dahe data. See the previous note.

[22]It should be acknowledged that increased collective accumulation could raise members' work incentives if they had low rates of time preference, if the collective had attractive investment opportunities unavailable to individual households, and if there were no problems posed by the nature of property rights in the acquired assets. In this case, a *yuan* generated by a worker's effort could be valued more highly if directed to collective investment than if paid out as income. It seems probable, however, that for a substantial majority of households, collective accumulation rates exceeded the savings rates that would have prevailed in a household farm economy, and that households would accordingly have voted for more distribution if free to do so. Collective property rights may also have posed a problem, although not so much because of the familiar horizon problem (Furubotn and Pejovich, 1970)—which is less likely to arise when members expect to remain in the cooperative for life—and more because of collective choice problems compounded by lack of control over assets by team members as a collectivity.

ginal payments—either because cooperative labor was being compared with an alternative source of income such as work in the private plot and sidelines, or because income effects did not dominate in the comparison with leisure—the more of their team's income they expected to be withheld from distribution, the less would team members have been motivated to work in the collective sector. We therefore hypothesize that more labor flowed into the collective sector the lower was the share of team income that members expected to be withheld from distribution.

As discussed above, other sources of incentive effects have also been conceptualized in the theoretical literature. Examples include "team cohesion"—i.e., the degree to which a member expects to be emulated by coworkers if he increases his effort—and interhousehold "sympathy." However, we have no way of gauging the magnitudes of these factors based on the data from Dahe. Our two hypotheses on incentives, on the other hand, refer to variables for which measures at team level are available in that data set. To restate them:

First, the greater the proportion of net revenue that team members expected to be allocated to distribution, the greater the forthcoming work effort in the collective sector.

Second, the greater the proportion of distributed cash and grain that team members expected to take the form of grain, the smaller the forthcoming work effort in the collective sector.

Before the hypotheses can be made operational we must address two issues. The first concerns the modeling of expectations. Team members cannot be assumed to have known what would be distributed when making their work decisions. Consistent with intuition and to make use of the available data, we will therefore assume that the practice of recent past years was taken by members as an indicator of what to expect at the end of the current year. Using lagged values of the incentive variables will also aid in avoiding a potential problem of reverse causality when we turn to estimation. So the hypotheses will be operationalized in terms of the values of the relevant proportions in the one or two agricultural seasons previous to that of the labor input in question.

Second, how are we to measure forthcoming work effort? Two strategies are made possible by the available data. First, we have the variable, "work days," which was used as the measure of labor input in the analysis of Wiemer, reported in the previous chapter. According to statistical analysis and subsequent interviews at Dahe, this variable can be assumed to represent the aggregate number of work-points awarded to all team members in a year, in multiples of ten (the standard work day, for accounting purposes). If work points were the teams' own operational proxies for effort, and thus the effective labor units through which the incentive system of either equation (1) or (2) operated, we should find their number to be directly correlated with the incentive variables in the fashion predicted.

Examination of a second possibility is motivated by the fact that work-points are an imperfect proxy for effort. For a given team applying a fixed work-point scale, the imperfection results from the problems of measurement discussed earlier. When considering data generated from many teams over a number of years, there are further questions of variation in the work-point scale both across production units and over time. This consideration leads us to consider an alternative strategy in which the incentive effects of changes in the payment ratios are examined by way of their impacts upon total output as a function of a given size of workforce and levels of other input usage. In this approach, the "work days" variable is bypassed in favor of a cruder measure of labor, number of workers, and the variation in real effort is measured indirectly but perhaps more accurately in the form of variations in the "total factor productivity" of imperfectly measured factors.

The production function approach is open to the additional interpretation that some changes in productivity caused by altering the incentive variables may work through factors other than effort. One possibility is that more productive use is made of the nonlabor factors, due to the effects of incentives on what may be called the "allocative services of labor." Another is that qualitative improvements in labor may take place in dimensions that are not reflected in individualized rewards (work-points). In particular, there may be morale effects beyond those explicable by the neoclassical calculus of utility maximization, or physiological effects of higher consumption upon effort, each of which has been hypothesized to result from higher wages in some efficiency wage models.[23] Such disembodied effects of the incentive variables would be reflected in the production function model, but would be indistinguishable there from the hypothesized effects on measurable effort. However, by adding a production function equation to the model estimating the direct effect of incentives on work-points, any impact of the hypothesized incentives over and above their effects on measured effort can in principle be identified.

The Estimating Framework

The discussion above leads us to estimate two alternative models of the incentive effects of variation in the degree of revenue retention and in the form of payment. Model I tests the hypothesis that collective revenue allocation and payment parameters had incentive effects on members' effort supplies as measured by awarded work-points. Thus, we may write:

$$WP_{j,t} = f_1(I_{1,j,t-1}, I_{2,j,t-1}, \ldots) \tag{5.10}$$

where $WP_{j,t}$ is the number of work-points per worker in team j in period t, and where the I's are values of the two incentive variables for team j in period $t-1$. Specifically, letting R_g be team revenue, net of nonlabor costs and taxes, but gross of (i.e., including) accumulation and other retained funds, R be net distributed revenue

---

[23]See Akerlof (1982); Strauss (1986).

(as in (1)), and C and G be revenue distributed in cash and grain, respectively, so that $C + G = R$. Then we have

$$I_1 = R/R_g = (C + G)/R_g$$
$$I_2 = G/R = G/(C + G)$$

I_1 is expected to positively affect effort (WP) while I_2 is expected to negatively affect it. The ellipsis in equation (5.10) indicates that there may be other, as yet unspecified, variables, that influence WP, including some that available data will permit us to control for.

In addition to the direct effect of the hypothesized incentives on effort as measured by work-points and captured in (5.10), our estimating framework also attempts to capture any effects of the incentives, on output, that are uncorrelated with work-points. The relevant equation is

$$Q_{j,t} = f_2(W_{j,t}, WP_{j,t}, A_{j,t}, E_{j,t}, K_{j,t}, I_{1,j,t-1}, I_{2,j,t-1}, \theta) \qquad (5.11)$$

where Q is gross output in value terms, W is the number of workers in the team, A is the area farmed, E is current inputs (expenditures), K is capital stock, and θ is a stochastic element incorporating weather, prices, production targets, and other exogenous factors influencing Q.

Model II focuses on the direct effect of the incentive variables on output, when labor is measured by number of workers rather than work-points. The single equation to be estimated is identical to equation (5.11), except that it excludes $WP_{j,t}$.

Our choice of functional forms will be taken with a view to simplicity as well as the avoidance of obvious statistical problems. Thus, noting that the parameters of that function are not our chief concern in their own right, function (5.11) and its Model II variant will be basically of the log-log or Cobb-Douglas form, although these equations are now *behavioral* rather than ordinary production functions.[24] A possible difficulty arising in both (5.10) and (5.11) is that the two incentive variables, I_1 and I_2, are likely to be highly colinear, since the numerator of the first is the denominator of the second. Although such multicolinearity affects only the efficiency, not the unbiasedness, of the estimates, it seems desirable to limit its effects if possible, and this will be done by entering the first variable in logged form, the second linearly. An economic and mathematical justification for this follows from noting that while the hypothesized effect of grain distribution on incentives is negative *relative* to distribution of cash, even the rationed good should have a positive although smaller

---

[24]A production funtion may be considered "behaviorial" in nature when institutional or other nonfactor input variables appear in it as influences on the behavior of economic agents. Consequently, it can be viewed as a reduced form, and the parameters of the technology of production are not necessarily recoverable from it. See Gaynor and Pauly (1990), and McMillan et al. (1989), for expositions of this point.

effect on effort. (Egalitarian distribution causes the cooperative member to receive one Nth of his or her value of marginal product for additional effort, which is a positive although suboptimal inducement to such effort.) Thus, suppressing team and time subscripts, let the production function be rewritten as

$$Q = aW^{\alpha_1} WP^{\alpha_2} A^{\beta} E^{\gamma} K^{\delta} e^{\lambda ln\left(\frac{C+(1-\phi)G}{R_g}\right)} \epsilon(\theta)$$

where a, α_1, α_2, β, γ, δ, λ and ϕ are constants, and where ϵ (θ) is a stochastic term reflecting the influence of θ. The hypothesis predicts that λ and ϕ are positive, but ϕ is presumably less than 1.

Taking logarithms of both sides:

$$lnQ = lna + \alpha_1 lnW\ ed + \alpha_2 lnWP + \beta lnA + \gamma/nE + \delta lnK$$
$$+ \lambda ln\left(\frac{C + (1 - \phi)G}{R_g}\right) + \epsilon'$$

(where the last term stands for $ln(\epsilon(\theta))$). Then, *simplifying and making use of an approximation:*

$$\lambda ln\left(\frac{C + (1 - \phi)G}{R_g}\right) = \lambda ln\left(\frac{C + G - \phi G}{R_g}\right)$$
$$= \lambda ln\left(\left(\frac{C + G}{R_g}\right) \cdot \left[1 - \phi\left(\frac{G}{C + G}\right)\right]\right)$$
$$\approx \lambda ln\left(\frac{C + G}{R_g}\right) - \lambda\phi\left(\frac{G}{C + G}\right)$$

with the approximation holding more precisely for small values of $\phi\left(\dfrac{G}{C + G}\right)$. This leads to the following estimating equation, in which we restore time subscripts t and $t - 1$:

$$\ln Q_t = lna + \alpha_1 lnW_t + \alpha_2 lnW\ P_t + \beta lnA_t + \gamma lnE_t$$
$$+ \delta lnK_t + \lambda ln\left(\left(\frac{C + G}{R_g}\right)_{t-1}\right) - \lambda\phi\left(\left(\frac{G}{C + G}\right)_{t-1}\right) + \epsilon' \qquad (5.11')$$

Entry of I_1 and I_2 in log and linear form, respectively, will also be adopted for the Model II variant of (5.11), and for (5.10). There being no reason to prefer some other functional form, we also enter WP itself in log form in the latter equation. Note now that (the estimating versions of) (5.10) and (5.11) may be related as a recursive system in which ln(WP) is endogenous, appearing as the dependent variable in (5.10) and as an independent variable in (5.11). Simultaneous estimation requires, however, that there be at least one variable in (5.10) that is not also included in (5.11). Such variables may be found among characteristics of the team and its labor force that might be expected to affect the value of WP, although neither the magnitude nor the direction of that influence need be predictable on theoretical grounds. From the data set, we find two suitable series: the proportion of the team labor force classified as substandard or "half labor powers,"[25] and the proportion of the labor force said to be employed in agriculture. Entering these variables also in log form, we get as the estimating version of (5.10)

$$ln(W\,P_t) = b_0 + b_1 ln\left(\frac{C+G}{R_g}\right)_{t-1}) + b_2\left(\frac{G}{C+G}\right)_{t-1}) + b_3 ln\ ((W_h/W)_t)$$
$$+\ b_4 ln((W_a\,/W)_t) + u_t \hspace{4cm} (5.10')$$

where W_h and W_a are the number of "half labor powers" and of agricultural workers, respectively, and where u is an independent and identically distributed error term. Equations (5.10′) and (5.11′) are estimated simultaneously using two-stage least squares (2SLS).

The operationalization of variables in the model, in brief, is as follows. Q = total gross income of the team in the year in question, W = number of workers ("half labor power" counts as .5 "full labor power"), A = sown area in mu,[26] E = total current expenditures, K = value of capital assets, G = total distributed grain at internal accounting value, C = total distributed cash, R_g = total team revenue net of costs E and taxes, WP = total awarded work-points, W_h = number of "half labor powers," and W_a = number of agricultural workers.

Causality

The benefit of entering lagged values of the incentive variables from the point of view of testing strategy has been mentioned but should be stated more explicitly. This benefit derives from the danger of reverse causality in the relationship between the incentive variables and Q. In good years, in which a team experienced high values of Q for given factor inputs, it might have been possible to distribute a larger share of net income while meeting fixed targets for the accumulation and other retained funds.[27] Also, so long as the amount distributed was higher on a per capita basis, the proportion of distribution taking the form of grain would have tended to fall, by

[25]Team accounts list the total number of workers with subclassifications as "full" and "half" "labor powers," where the latter category might be an indicator of advanced age or disability. Call the number of the former W_f and that of the latter W_h. Our variable W is defined by $W = W_f + 0.5\,(W_h)$. To the extent that these weights are not fully appropriate, the ratio W_h/W may be independently reflected in WP.

[26]1 mu = .0667 ha. Sown area is used rather than cultivated area in the present analysis because it shows slightly more variation and thus permits inclusion of team dummies in the fixed-effects estimates (see below).

[27]We do not know for certain whether such targets existed.

Engel's law. In the current period, then, each incentive variable might be correlated with total factor productivity in the direction predicted, for reasons having nothing to do with incentives. Use of past values of the incentive variables ameliorates this problem.

It remains possible that some teams both consistently registered higher (or lower) output for given inputs and consistently distributed a larger share of net income and a smaller proportion of that share in the form of grain, over *several* years and for the nonincentive reasons just alluded to. This would mean that reverse causality would affect the estimates of (5.11) even with lagged incentive variables. One way to eliminate this problem is to include team dummy variables in the regression along with dummies for year which help control for weather and price variations. However, inclusion of such dummies poses a problem of its own: by transforming the remaining variable measures into deviations from their within-team (and year) means, the dummies may leave a high ratio of noise (e.g., measurement error) to meaningful signal (Griliches and Hausman, 1984) in those variables, leading to downward bias in estimated coefficients. This might not alter qualitative results, but is likely to produce implausible estimates of the standard production function parameters. We address the latter problem by alternately estimating each model under the assumption of random rather than fixed cross-section and time-series effects.[28] In our results, both FE (fixed effects) and RE (random effects) estimates provide qualitatively similar findings with respect to the incentive variables that are the focus of our hypotheses.

Estimation and Results

The number of production teams at Dahe varied during the 1970s, from which our data for the collective production era derive, from a low of 94 in 1978–1979 to a high of 100 in 1970–1975. Ideally, we should include in our sample all teams existing continuously during the 10 years for which we have data. Unfortunately, data on some of the required variables are missing for some years, especially for the early part of the decade. Looking for a subset of the data consisting of production teams for which all required variables are available for a continuous series of years, we find a set of 41 teams complete for the years 1974–1979. We perform our estimates on this subsample,[29] for which means and standard deviations are shown in Table 5.1.

Table 5.2 reports the results of the fixed and random effects estimates of equation (5.10), Table 5.3 reports the corresponding estimates of equation (5.11)

---

[28]The random effects approach is equivalent to performing OLS on data transformed by replacing each value with a weighted average of the original value, its deviation from the average value of that variable within the year of observation, and its deviation from the average value within the team under observation. It is thus a compromise between fixed effects and ordinary OLS. For a discussion, see Johnston (1984, pp. 396–407). The procedure employed in the estimates reported below is that of Fuller and Battesse (1974).

[29]Since 1974 lagged values of the incentive variables appear in observations for 1975, the resulting panel is only five observations deep, for a total of 205 observations.

Table 5.1. Means of Variables in the Sample

Variable	Mean	Standard Deviation
Gross value of output[a,b]	43,081.45	13,961.92
Number of workpoints	511.83	119.00
Number of workers[c]	92.24	36.69
Current inputs[a]	22,266.00	7,337.66
Sown area[d]	39.60	12.96
Capital[a]	26,120.34	7,638.14
$(C + G)/R_g$	0.797	0.085
$G/(C + G)$	0.741	0.105
W_a/W	0.853	0.150
W_h/W	0.332	0.179

[a]In *yuan*.
[b]Deflated to 1975 equivalent using general index of purchasing prices of farm and sideline products.
[c]Sum of "full labor powers" plus 0.5 times "half labor powers."
[d]Sum of cotton, wheat corn, gaoliang, millet, paddy rice, and miscellaneous grain sown areas in hectares.

(note that the two equations were estimated simultaneously in each case), and Table 5.4 shows the fixed and random effects results for the single equation of Model II. In addition to coefficients and t statistics, Tables 5.3 and 5.4 show the implied marginal products of the factor inputs, averaged across the included teams,[30] as well as the average implied marginal impacts on output of unit changes in the two incentive variables.

According to Table 5.2, the hypothesis of a positive effect of distribution from revenue is supported at the 5% level under both fixed and random effects estimations. The hypothesis of a negative effect of the share of grain in total distribution is supported at the 10% level in the random effects estimate, and the result in the fixed effects estimate is of the predicted sign but not significant. Table 5.3 shows no significant "excess" effects of the incentive variables on gross output value, after controlling for average work-points per worker and (via 2SLS) for the effects captured by equation (5.10'). The standard production function components of equation (5.11) also perform poorly: only current expenditures has a significant coefficient in both fixed and random effects variants, while two additional factors, number of workers and sown area, are significant in the latter variant. The sums of the factor coefficients are unreasonably high, and the (insignificant) coefficients for capital are negative. Recall that in the fixed-effects estimates we have a "noise-to-signal" problem, which in principle is only partially mitigated by the alternative random-effects estimates. Interpretation of the coefficients on standard inputs is also complicated by the behavioral nature of the production function. Some of the implied marginal products, i.e., those of workers and current inputs, are within the range of

[30]Note the difference from Chapter 4, where marginal products are evaluated at the averages of the input and output variables.

Table 5.2. Estimates of Equation (5.10′); Dependent Variable: Work-points per Worker

Variable	Fixed Effects Coefficient (t statistic)	Random Effects Coefficient (t statistic)
Constant	9.662 (74.923)[a]	9.415 (75.484)[a]
$(C + G)/R_g$	0.157 (2.372)[a]	0.151 (2.273)[a]
$G/(C + G)$	−0.406 (−1.595)	−0.164 (−1.845)[b]
W_a/W	−0.267 (−2.119)[a]	−0.128 (−1.086)
W_h/W	0.089 (2.023)[a]	0.097 (2.207)[a]
n	205	205
Adjusted R^{2c}	0.940	0.0149
Variance Components Analysis for Random Effects Estimate		
for cross-section		0.0477
for time-series		0.0034
for error		0.0049

[a]Significant at 5% level.
[b]Significant at 10% level.
[c]For RE estimate, R^2 not adjusted.
Source: Putterman (1990b, Table 1).

Wiemer's estimates as shown in Table 4.3, but those of land (represented here as sown area but by Wiemer as cultivated area) and capital are not within that range and appear far less plausible.[31] Finally, the variance components analyses for the RE variables indicate that time-series and cross-section variation is responsible for the better part of the variance not directly explained by the regression.

Model II looks for direct effects of the incentive variables on output, when labor input is measured by labor force only. Exclusion of the work-points per worker variable brings this specification closer to that of a standard production function, and the results for the factor inputs are sensible in this context, with the coefficients

---

[31]As stated in footnote 26 above, sown area was used in the present case because cultivated area showed too little variation over time, for given teams, to permit its use together with team dummy variables. However, sown area itself did not vary much over time for most teams. Thus, much of the difference in land inputs is probably "absorbed" in the coefficient on the dummy variables, resulting in an implausibly low estimated coefficient on sown area itself. Another reason why the coefficients on land in the behavioral production function estimates of Tables 5.2 and 5.3 are lower than those in other estimates in this book is that the estimates here are for the combined crop and noncrop sectors, whereas all other production function estimates in which land appears as an input are for the crop sector or a subset of that sector, only. Note that the coefficients on land are both larger and more significant in the random effects estimates in these tables, consistent with the reasoning above.

Table 5.3. Estimates of Equation (5.11); Dependent Variable: Gross Value of Output

Variable	Fixed Effects		Random Effects	
	Coefficient (t statistic)	Marginal Product[a]	Coefficient (t statistic)	Marginal Product[a]
Constant[b]	0.012 (0.001)		−1.979 (−0.578)	
Workers	0.289 (1.252)	142.873	0.188 (4.597)[c]	93.035
Work-points/workers	0.513 (0.539)	2.207	0.513 (1.407)	2.207
Sown area	0.042 (0.215)	56.130	0.227 (3.418)[c]	301.680
Current inputs	0.538 (9.635)[c]	1.057	0.582 (14.313)[c]	1.143
Capital	−0.088 (−1.241)	−0.152	−0.006 (−0.162)	−0.010
$(C+G)/R_g$	0.083 (0.594)	4,690.730	−0.069 (−0.809)	−3,893.597
$G(C+G)$	−0.137 (−0.742)	−5,897.817	−0.138 (−1.226)	−5,949.427
n	205		205	
Adjusted R^{2d}	0.940		0.8313	
Variance Components Analysis for RE Estimate				
for cross-section			0.0029	
for time-series			0.0063	
for error			0.0059	

[a]Average over marginal products of individual observations assuming coefficient estimates as shown. Marginal product of sown land is converted from per *mu* to per hectare basis.
[b]Reflects change of units for sown area.
[c]Significant at 5% level.
[d]For RE estimates, R^2 not adjusted.
Source: Putterman (1990b, Table 2).

summing to nearly 1 in the random effects estimates.[32] Table 5.4 shows that the hypothesized negative effect of distribution in the form of grain is confirmed at the 5% level in both estimating forms, while the hypothesized positive effect of distribution as opposed to retention of funds also appears in both the fixed and random effects runs, but approaches significance, at the 5% level, in the fixed effects run only.

With regard to the economic significance of the two incentive variables, the fixed effects estimate of Table 5.2 implies that a 1% increase in the share of team revenue that is distributed would produce a 0.16% increase in effort as measured by

[32]The comparatively smaller coefficients in the fixed effects version are again consistent with the "noise-to-signal" problem interpretation.

Table 5.4. Estimates of Model II[a]; Dependent Variable: Gross Value of Output

Variable	Fixed Effects		Random Effects	
	Coefficient (t statistic)	Marginal Product[b]	Coefficient (t statistic)	Marginal Product[b]
Constant	6.328 (3.971)[c]		7.177 (7.194)[c]	
Workers	0.170 (2.847)[c]	83.947	0.165 (4.348)[c]	81.569
Current inputs	0.535 (10.599)[c]	1.051	0.586 (14.423)[c]	1.151
Sown area	0.106 (0.742)	140.705	0.234 (3.445)[c]	310.725
Capital	−0.061 (−1.349)	−0.105	−0.007 (−0.202)	−0.012
$(C + G)/R_g$	0.145 (1.948)[d]	8,150.308	0.017 (0.259)	98.940
$G/(C + G)$	−0.218 (−2.216)[c]	−9,370.688	−0.244 (−2.396)[c]	−9,667.199
n	205		205	
Adjusted R^{2e}	0.933		0.8258	
Variance Components Analysis for RE Estimate				
for cross-section			0.0034	
for time-series			0.0062	
for error			0.0059	

[a]The estimating equation is identical to (5.11) except for the omission of *lnWP* as an independent variable.
[b]Average over marginal products of individual observations assuming coefficient estimates as shown.
[c]Significant at 5% level.
[d]Significant at 10% level.
[e]For RE estimate, R^2 not adjusted.
Source: Putterman (1987b, Tables III and IV).

work-points, while a 1% increase in the share of distribution taking the form of grain would lead to a 0.26% decline in effort. The more significant random effects estimate implies only a 0.11% decline. For Model II, the fixed effects estimates imply that a 1% increase in the share of revenue that is distributed would produce a 0.15% increase in gross value of output, while a 1% increase in the share of distribution taking the form of grain would produce a 0.15% decline in GVO.[33]

Both the two and one equation models were estimated in both fixed and random effects versions including an additional second lagged value of the incentive

[33]By 1% increase we mean a change from, say, .741 to .748. The change in (G/(C+G)) is evaluated at the mean of its distribution. Note that evaluation formulas differ because the first incentive variable is entered in log form, the second linearly. For coefficients on linear variables, we make the Kennedy adjustment (Goldberger, 1968; Derrick, 1984) according to which $\hat{b}_1 = exp[\hat{b}_1 - .5 \, var \, (b_1)] - 1$, where $\hat{b}_1$ is the initial coefficient estimate, $var(b_1)$ is the variance of the estimate, and $\hat{b}_1$ is the adjusted estimate.

variables. This has little effect on the other estimated coefficients, and only one of the new coefficients is significant; it is of predicted sign. Additional runs were also done with a larger number of teams for which data are complete for 5 years only, and a smaller set of teams for which data are complete for 10 consecutive years. Finally, both models were estimated substituting retrospectively created estimates of grain distributed by rationing in place of total grain distributed, in I_2. All of the results are qualitatively similar (although not identical) in the number of significant coefficients for the incentive variables, and the support of the signs of those coefficients for the hypotheses.

Conclusion

In this chapter, theoretical models of incentives in collective production teams have been surveyed, and hypotheses derived from two such models have been tested on the team level data from Dahe commune in the collective production era. The results provide modest support for the view that production team members responded positively to the expectation of greater remuneration for their work, and to that of a greater link between work and payment by virtue of less egalitarianism in the pay formula (less distribution in the form of food rations). Accordingly, the notion that the payment system did not matter, because of high interdependence between effort supplied by different individuals, or due to a high degree of altruism, is not supported by these exercises. Guttman and Schnytzer's model, which predicts a higher effort outcome under "needs" than under work-proportionate payment, is also not corroborated. Nor is there support for the notion that work-point-based payments provided no incentive, because the correlation between effort and work-points was negligible, or for the idea that there was no marginal response to material rewards in the teams, either because peasants in Mao's China had transcended material self-interest, or because the labor supply decision was effectively removed from team members' hands, determined by commune authorities, and implemented coercively.

Support for the hypothesis regarding grain distribution in both these and related estimates may be viewed as particularly remarkable. Earlier, it was mentioned that the nominal valuation of grain distributed to the member households in kind seriously understates the value of such income when measured in terms of opportunity cost, because peasants were ordinarily not entitled to purchase grain from the government at controlled prices and therefore would have had to pay higher prices for local free or black market purchases. One keen observer, Jean Oi (1989), goes so far as to argue that during much of the period in question, cash was of very little value to Chinese peasants, because of the lack of goods to purchase with it, while grain was of such high scarcity value as to have become a medium of exchange in many villages in preference to money. If this was true, there might appear to be grounds for arguing that cash distribution by the teams would have little if any incentive effects, and that only grain distribution would be valued. The argument behind our hypothesis regarding the effects of grain distribution depends upon the way in which grain was distributed, not on the relative value of grain versus cash.[34] That we obtained evidence of a negative incentive impact of distributing grain rather than cash is all the more striking in view of Oi's analysis.

In concluding, it would be tempting to use our findings to argue that commune leaders had at their disposal the tools to make the team production system more effective even without decomposing the teams into their constituent household units. That is, since more differentiated distribution and more moderate levels of savings and other withholdings of revenue appear to have had positive effects on work incentives, the teams observed in the 1970s may have been working within their frontiers of potential efficiency as the result of political-ideological pressures toward high rates of accumulation and egalitarian distribution of grain. However, it would be inappropriate to press this argument too far on the basis of the limited evidence at hand. It is probable that the narrow range of incentives on which this chapter has focused were by themselves incapable of achieving results of the kind brought about by decollectivization. More incentive-favoring values of the variables looked at here would only have been a first step in the direction of pushing the teams to their efficiency frontiers. To approach those frontiers more closely, a more serious effort to link pay with work, not merely with work days, and a more democractic and participatory process of team decision-making and implementation, would likely have been necessary. These internal changes would also have had to be complemented by external steps such as the price increases, market liberalization, and greater freedom to determine the mix of economic activities that were observed after 1978. Whether even such a broad array of changes would have sufficed to bring about an increase in team productivity on the order of what was demanded by the leaders of China's post-Mao modernization drive is an open question that cannot be answered definitively in view of the more radical path actually taken by China's reforms.

---

[34]In our tests, the value of income distributed in grain is the nominal one used in the team accounts, unadjusted for considerations of opportunity cost.

6

Labor Supply by Individuals*

Introduction

Whereas the empirical analysis of the previous chapter considered the effects of incentives upon labor supply to collectives by the aggregated labor forces of Dahe's production teams, the present chapter studies labor supply at the level of individual team members, using the survey data collected in 1980 with reference to the production year 1979. In that survey, individual household heads reported the total number of work-points and the total amount of payment received for labor contributions to their teams by each household member who provided such labor. In 1986, interviewees were asked to state retrospectively the number of work-points each member had earned for a typical day in 1979, information that was lacking in the 1980 survey and that, together with the data provided in the earlier survey, gives an indication of the number of calendar days worked in the collective sector by each household member. When combined with other information on individual and household characteristics, these data make possible an analysis of labor supply behavior by individuals complementary to the the analysis at team level in the previous chapter.

In this chapter, we again address the question of whether Dahe's workers responded to material incentives in determining their labor input to team production, but the models applied in the last chapter are used this time in a somewhat simpler fashion. With only one observation per individual, there is little that can be inferred from our data about interactions between the decisions of different team members, or the impact of varying distribution policies. However, with teams at Dahe large enough to render a one Nth share of marginal product small, a reasonable approximation based on equation (5.5) is that the individual worker expected to receive another unit of the *average net value per labor unit* for each additional unit of labor supplied—that is, he or she would receive the value of *one work-point* (denoted $\frac{R}{L}$ in equation (5.5)) for the corresponding input of work time or effort. With variation among individuals in work-point ratings (the number of work-points awarded for a

*This chapter is jointly authored by John P. Burkett, University of Rhode Island, and Louis Putterman.

day's labor), and variation among teams in the value of work-points, individuals faced differing "expected wages" for a standard day's labor, these being equal to the product of individual work-point rating and team work-point value. The impact of material incentives at this level of approximation comes down to the question of how differences in the "expected wage" influenced choices of labor contribution.[1]

As noted in Chapter 5, the equation of the individual's marginal rate of substitution of income for leisure with a higher marginal return to labor can lead to either larger or smaller labor supply, since while the substitution effect predicts a shift toward labor as its reward (and the relative price of leisure) rises, the income effect of higher earnings per labor unit can lead to the decision to enjoy more leisure. While in Chapter 5 we were forced to hypothesize the dominance of substitution effects at the aggregate level, the possibility of distinguishing between labor supplied in peak versus slack season permits us to remain more agnostic about the slope of individual labor supply curves for purposes of the present analysis. Specifically, even as it fails to provide an a priori prediction about the choice between labor and *leisure*, standard microeconomic theory unambiguously predicts that individuals will shift labor toward a more remunerative activity from a less remunerative competing activity. An application of this principle to the case of Chinese farm households in the collective production era is that when household members faced a choice on the margin between work for the team and work on their private plot or sidelines, an increase in the returns from collective work should have unambiguously increased collective labor supply—unless the latter was determined entirely by coercion or noneconomic factors. When private income earning opportunties were not a relevant alternative, on the other hand, the impact on individual labor supply of higher payment from the collective could have been either positive or negative.

Although the general theory of incentives in a collective farm was developed and discussed in the previous chapter without reference to heterogeneity of productive activities among workers or over time, interviews with former team leaders at Dahe township, conducted in 1986, suggested that such an approach might be inadequate for studying the labor supply behavior of different team members. In particular, these interviews suggested that team production activities should be divided into at least two analytically distinct seasons. During the slackest part of the agricultural season, between November and March (and especially December through February), these

---

[1]Looking at equation (5.5), it will be recognized that our approximation involves not only the assumption that $\frac{1}{N}$, $\frac{\varrho^i}{L}$, and η^i were of negligible size. For the expected incremental return to a unit of labor to be net revenue per work unit $\left(\frac{R}{L}\right)$, α, or the proportion of income distributed according to needs, would also have to be zero. This assumption would be consistent with the observed distribution of grain rations at below scarcity value internal accounting values provided that the expected quantity of rations was independent of the level of output. Our approach also remains defensible provided that any linkage between the latter variables was approximately the same across teams, since $(1 - \alpha)\frac{R}{L}$ and $\frac{R}{L}$ are then perfectly correlated, permitting the latter to proxy for the former.

leaders reported that there was often not enough productive work available to keep all members fully occupied, and that the available work was rationed out to team members according to leaders' sense of each household's need for additional work-points.[2] It can be surmised that in the same season, there was little productive work to be done in private plots and other household sidelines, and therefore, absent work rationing, the theory of individual labor supply based on the pure choice between labor and leisure should be applicable for this season. (That is, the relationship between the expected wage and the amount of labor supplied is theoretically indeterminate in the slack season.) During busy periods, on the other hand, there was more than enough work to do, and the teams competed with household activities for the available labor supply. If the opportunity cost of providing more collective labor was foregone private plot income, in the busy season, theory provides an unambiguous prediction about the impact of a change in the return to collective labor. In addition, whereas team members appear to have faced a ceiling for labor contributions in the slack season, perhaps predicated on household per capita earnings from other sources during the rest of the year, they may have faced mandatory minimum requirements for labor contribution during the busy season. For each individual, then, labor supply to the collective can be conceptualized as an unrestricted function of their collective "expected wage," with a maximum at the work-rationing ceiling, during the slack season, and a minimum work requirement in the busy season, with labor supply rising with "expected wage" above that requirement for those individuals for whom it was not binding.

An advantage of studying labor supply at the individual level is that it becomes possible to study the impact not only of the rate of return to each person's labor, but also of a variety of other demographic and economic factors such as individual age and sex, the demographic structure of the household (e.g., the ratio of dependents to income earners), and total household earnings. Such factors might not only have been taken into account in determining minimum labor requirements in the busy season and maximum requirements in the slack season, for different individuals; they may also have influenced the discretionary part of labor allocation (if any) in each season.

---

[2]Liu (1991), which appeared as this book was going to press, features an upper limit on labor contributions to the collective in his "temporal priority" analysis. While Liu's formal model does not address the possibility that available work might be limited in one part of the year but not another, and while most of his discussion assumes "first come, first served" rather than rationed job assignment, both seasonality and job sharing are mentioned elsewhere in his paper (pp. 619–20). We note that the duration of the slack season will have differed in southern China, where the climate is semi-tropical; however, Liu reports that a substantial slack season existed in Wuxi, in the Central Coast subregion considerably to the south of Huailu County. The necessity of work rationing if an efficient outcome is to obtain in the absence of sufficient incentive dilution by "needs distribution" is inherent in the Sen model, as discussed in Chapter 5, and is explicitly predicted by Sertel (1982), whose "internal wages" distribution concept bears a close relationship to "distribution according to work" in that model. As noted by Bonin and Putterman (1987b, p. 45), the chapters by Dirickx and Sertel and by Sertel, Basar, and Selbuz, in that book "show that enterprises using 'internal wage' schemes perform optimally only when internal wages are supplemented by quotas specifying maximum rewardable effort inputs."

This possible role in the voluntary choice of labor supply means that these variables will help us to obtain further evidence about whether individuals' participation in team labor was fixed by the authority of team and higher-level leaders, or was also a matter of discretion for individual team members.

A Formal Model

In the remainder of this chapter, we construct and estimate an econometric model to treat the issues just discussed. Specifically, we set out to answer the following questions: 1) What proportion of team collective workers supplied more than their minimum required labor input to the collective sector during the busy season? 2) By how much did such voluntary labor supply exceed the mandatory amount? 3) How did mandatory labor supply vary by age, sex, and household dependency ratio? 4) How did individuals' voluntary (busy season) labor supplies vary with the same variables, with implicit collective wage, and with household income? 5) What proportion of workers supplied less than their maximum allowed labor input during the slack season? 6) By how much did such labor supply fall short of the permissible amount? 7) How did permitted slack season labor supply vary by age, sex, dependency ratio, and income of other household members? 8) How did voluntary slack season collective labor supply vary with the same variables and with the collective wage? And finally, 9) What proportion of total collective labor fell within the busy and slack seasons (defined as seasons in which the constraint faced by team members was of a required minimum input and of a maximum allowable input, respectively)?

To answer these questions, we employ the following econometric model. In the busy season, individual j was required to work, say, ℓ_j^{min} days and would voluntarily work, say, $\ell_j^{b,vol}$ days.[3] For simplicity, we specify ℓ_j^{min} and $\ell_j^{b,vol}$ as linear functions; thus for some individuals ℓ_j^{min} could take negative values. However, labor time must be non-negative; hence, we specify busy season work days as max $(0, \ell_j^{min}, \ell_j^{b,vol.})$.

In the slack season we shall initially suppose that individual j was allowed to work, say, ℓ_j^{max} days and would voluntarily work, say, $\ell_j^{s,vol}$ days. Specifying ℓ_j^{max} and $\ell_j^{s,vol}$ as linear functions and taking into account the non-negativity of work days, we can represent slack season work days as min $[\max (0, \ell_j^{max}), \max (0, \ell_j^{s,vol.})]$. A simplification of this specification will be discussed below.

In view of the emphasis thus far placed on the distinction between busy and slack season labor, the reader may be surprised to learn that the Dahe household

---

[3]Note that the notations ℓ_j^{min} and ℓ_j^{max} as used in this chapter are unrelated to the ℓ^{min} and ℓ^{max} notations briefly introduced in Chapter 5, which denoted the minimum and maximum values of the distribution of labor times among members of a team.

survey data *do not* explicitly indicate how much labor was supplied in each season. Our analysis therefore hinges on the possibility of sorting out labor supply, information on which is provided only for the production season as a whole, by means of an estimation strategy that accomplishes the assignment of days to seasons by endogenous methods. The plausibility of our findings accordingly depends, among other things, on whether the strategy adopted is one in which we can place sufficient confidence.

Given data restrictions, the dependent variable in the model is total individual labor units in the collective sector, ℓ_j. We specify this as the sum of busy and slack season labor and a random error μ_j:

$$\ell_j = \max (0, \ell_j^{min}, \ell_j^{b,vol}) + \min [\max (0, \ell_j^{max}), \max (0, \ell_j^{s,vol})] + \mu_j. \quad (6.1)$$

In the exposition that follows, subscript *j* is dropped.

The error term μ is the only stochastic element of the specification. ℓ^{min}, $\ell^{b,vol}$, ℓ^{max}, and $\ell^{s,vol}$ are assumed to be deterministic. This stochastic specification—known as *GTZ* (after its originators, Ginsburgh, Tishler, and Zang, 1980)—has both advantages and disadvantages compared to a specification in which the variables within the max and min operators are stochastic but μ is absent—a specification known as *MN* (after Maddala and Nelson, 1974). On the plus side, the *GTZ* specification allows maximum likelihood estimation of the equation by any nonlinear least squares algorithm that does not require continuous first derivatives. Further, the *GTZ* estimator appears to have better small sample properties than the *MN* estimator (Sneessens, 1985)). On the minus side, the *GTZ* likelihood function possesses numerous local maxima, a problem that we address by trying numerous starting values for the parameters.

The components of total labor time are initially specified as follows:

$$\ell^{min} = \alpha_0 + \alpha_1 \, SEX + \alpha_2 \, [(m - n)/m] + \alpha_3 \, AGE + \alpha_4 \, AGE^2 + \alpha_5 \, BD1 \\ + \alpha_6 \, BD2 + \alpha_7 \, BD3 + \alpha_8 \, BD4 \quad (6.2)$$

$$\ell^{b,vol} = \beta_0 + \beta_1 \, W + \beta_2 \, W^2 + \beta_3 \, AGE + \beta_4 \, AGE^2 \\ + \beta_5 \, \lambda + \beta_6 \, [(m - n)/m] + \beta_7 \, SEX \quad (6.3)$$

$$\ell^{max} = \Gamma_0 + \Gamma_1 \, SEX + \Gamma_2 \, [(m - n)/m] + \Gamma_3 \, AGE + \Gamma_4 \, AGE^2 \\ + \Gamma_5 \bar{y} + \Gamma_6 \omega + \Gamma_7 \, BD1 \\ + \Gamma_8 \, BD2 + \Gamma_9 \, BD3 + \Gamma_{10} \, BD4 \quad (6.4)$$

$$\ell^{s,vol} = \delta_0 + \delta_1 \, W + \delta_2 \, W^2 + \delta_3 \, AGE + \delta_4 \, AGE^2 + \delta_5 \, \lambda + \delta_6 \, [(m - n)/m] \\ + \delta_7 \, SEX \quad (6.5)$$

where

SEX = 0 males, 1 for females,
m = number of household members,
n = number of working members in household,
(so $[(m - n)/m]$ = ratio of number of dependents to number of household members,)
AGE = age in years,
$BD1$, $BD2$, etc. = team or brigade dummies,[4]
ω = number of work-points earned in a full day's labor by the individual,
W = wage—*i.e.*, $\omega \times$ (value of work-point),
λ = size of private plot, in *mu*
$\bar{y}$ = household income per capita other than that earned by the individual

Although the placement of nonwage variables in the equations for ϱ^{min}, $\varrho^{b,vol}$, ϱ^{max}, and $\varrho^{s,vol}$ followed somewhat casual reasoning and was partly driven by statistical identification requirements, a few remarks about the equations are warranted. First, ϱ^{min} is specified so that minimum labor required in the busy season could vary by team, and might reflect leaders' discretion over whether young persons should work more than old, women should work more than men, and members of households with more dependents should work more or less than other workers. For example, older workers might have been permitted to work fewer days than those of prime age, and those with more small children or aged parents at home might have been permitted to work fewer days in the collective, to give them greater flexibility in caring for them, and women might have been permitted to work fewer days than men because of their responsibilities for cooking and other household tasks. In addition to the posited effect of the expected wage, the equation for $\varrho^{b,vol}$ allows for nonlinear effects of age, and for effects of private plot size, dependent ratio, and sex. Reasonable conjectures are that work would first increase and then decline with age, that those with larger private plots would work less for the team, and that those with more dependents would work more, in view of their more pressing need for income.[5]

The equation for ϱ^{max} allows the rationed ceiling on labor input in the slack season to vary among teams (which might have different capacities to absorb labor productively). This ceiling is also influenced by three considerations related to fairness: 1) members of households with more dependents to support are expected to be given more opportunities to earn work-points; 2) those in households already

---

[4]Since the five teams in which household survey data was collected were located in five different brigades, brigade and team dummy variables are equivalent.

[5]The second conjecture can be demonstrated to hold in a formal model of a two-sector collective farm, such as Putterman (1980), while the third will be postulated in the model of Chapter 9.

having relatively high per capita incomes based on the earnings of other members are expected to receive fewer such opportunities; and 3) those who require more work days to earn a given number of work-points are expected to receive more such opportunities. Age and sex variables are also permitted to influence ϱ^{max} on the conjecture that after taking fairness considerations into account, team leaders may still have favored prime age males in the allotment of available winter work because they were able to do the heavy rock clearing, field leveling, and similar work that predominated in that season. The equation for $\varrho^{s,vol}$ permits the same influences on voluntary labor supply in the slack as in the busy season.

After initial attempts proved unable to achieve convergence of the estimation algorithm for the model as just specified we were forced to make some changes. Conjecturing that few if any individuals in the sample voluntarily worked less than ϱ^{max} in the slack season, we respecified slack season labor as max $(0, \varrho^{max})$. On estimating the model thus respecified, we found that $BD1$ and $BD3$ had no significant effects. These variables were therefore dropped from the model, leaving the resulting specification as follows:

$$\varrho = \max (0, \varrho^{min}, \varrho^{b,vol}) + \max (0, \varrho^{max}) + \mu, \qquad (6.1')$$

where

$$\varrho^{min} = \alpha_0 + \alpha_1 \, Sex + \alpha_2 \, [(m - n)/m] + \alpha_3 \, Age + \alpha_4 \, Age^2$$
$$+ \alpha_6 \, BD2 + \alpha_8 \, BD4, \qquad (6.2')$$

$$\varrho^{max} = \Gamma_0 + \Gamma_1 \, Sex + \Gamma_2 \, [(m - n)/m] + \Gamma_3 \, Age + \Gamma_4 \, Age^2$$
$$+ \Gamma_5 \, \bar{y} + \Gamma_6 \omega + \Gamma_8 \, BD2 + \Gamma_{10} \, BD4, \qquad (6.4')$$

and $\varrho^{b,vol}$ remains as defined above.

Data and Estimation

In 1979, about 80% of the working members of the surveyed households listed their occupation as workers in their teams, while the remainder held a variety of jobs in brigade and commune enterprises, county and state enterprises, and elsewhere. Only the former were treated as observations in the analysis, although information on other household members entered the dependency ratio and household income variables. Information required for estimation of the model was found to be available for a total of 336 individuals belonging to 187 households. Means and standard deviations of the variables for this sample are reported in Table 6.1.[6] Initial estimates of (6.1') were

---

[6] ϱ is labor in "standard days," calculated as total work-points reported for 1979 divided by WKPTSDAY. The result may exceed 365 even when actual working days were substantially fewer. This is consistent with the idea that the standard work day *(laodongri)* was a concept applying to a number of

Table 6.1. Sample Means of the Variables

Variable Name	Mean	Standard Deviation
ℓ	352.88	105.91
Sex	0.48	0.50
$[(m - n)/m]$	0.56	0.27
Age	35.83	10.81
W	0.68	0.23
λ	0.26	0.05
$\bar{y}$	231.72	91.64
ω	9.93	1.40

Source: Burkett and Putterman (1991).

obtained using unweighted nonlinear least squares. On the basis of the residuals from these estimates, we rejected the hypothesis of homoskedastic disturbances, using a Lagrange multiplier test.[7] To correct for heteroskedasticity, we looked for a set of exogenous variables which might help to explain variation in the error terms, and posited the following model for the variance of the error:

$$
\begin{aligned}
v(\mu) = exp \, (\pi_0 &+ \pi_1 \, [(m - n)/m] + \pi_2 \, Age + \pi_3 \, W + \pi_4 \, \omega \\
&+ \pi_5 \, BD1 + \pi_6 \, BD_2 + \pi_7 \, BD3 + \pi_8 \, BD4 + \pi_9 \, CD2 + \pi_{10} \, CD3 \\
&+ \pi_{11} \, CD4 + \pi_{12} \, CD5 + \pi_{13} \, CD6 + \pi_{14} \, CD7 + \pi_{15} \, CD8) + \in ,
\end{aligned} \tag{6.6}
$$

where $CD2, \ldots, CD8$ are dummy variables for socioeconomic class[8] and $\in$ is a disturbance assumed to be independent and identically distributed.

Re-estimating the model by weighted nonlinear least squares, we obtain the results shown in the columns labeled WNLS in Table 6.2. The Lagrange multiplier statistic for homoskedasticity (LMH)—constructed by multiplying the number of observations (336) by the R^2 statistic for a regression of squared weighted residuals of the variables in our model of error variance (equation (6.6))—is below its critical value ($\chi^2_{.05} \, 15 = 25.00$), indicating that the WNLS estimator successfully corrects for heteroskedasticity. As is common in cross-sectional studies of individuals, the R^2

---

hours or set of tasks in such a manner that more than one of these could be recorded for an individual in a single calendar day. When the total labor days *(fenpei laodongri)* variable of our team level data is divided by the number of workers in a team, for years in the 1970s, the average number of days exceeds 400. Thus, those answering the question on the typical number of work-points earned per day in 1979 can be presumed to have done so in terms of their own rating per *laodongri,* and not per arithmetically average day of calendar time. Other variables in Table 6.1 are as defined above. Note that information on the size of private plots is taken from the team level data set and accordingly does not vary among individuals and households within a given team. Note also that the implied value of a work-point varied slightly among individuals within the same production team, an institutional impossibility which must be judged a case of "measurement error." To handle this problem, we treat the modal value of the work-point within each team as the uniform value for that team.

[7]The test statistic is TR^2, as defined by Judge et al. (1985, p. 447).

[8]As reported by the households, following the categories in use during the Mao era. These are discussed again in Chapter 11.

Table 6.2. Estimates of Equation (6.1′)

Segment	Variable	Statistic or Coefficient	Estimates WNLS		IV-WNLS	
		LMH	19.59		24.66	
		R^2	.2707		.2000	
ϱ^{min}	Intercept	α_0	374.2	(3.146)	371.9	(3.109)
	Sex	α_1	−17.11	(−0.801)	−33.39	(−1.391)
	[(m-n)/m]	α_2	70.84	(3.855)	49.77	(1.872)
	Age	α_3	−4.926	(−0.736)	−2.103	(−0.276)
	Age^2	α_4	.0200	(0.216)	−.0296	(−0.266)
	BD2	α_6	17.88	(0.622)	−22.84	(−0.670)
	BD4	α_8	63.35	(2.862)	46.26	(2.003)
$\varrho^{b,vol.}$	Intercept	β_0	65.38	(0.222)	−176.6	(−0.438)
	W (PW)	β_1	−152.3	(−0.325)	274.5	(0.355)
	W^2 (PW^2)	β_2	−2.21	(−0.007)	−197.5	(−0.394)
	Age	β_3	24.64	(2.234)	20.47	(2.139)
	Age^2	β_4	−.3139	(−2.271)	−.2806	(−2.177)
	λ	β_5	−471.4	(−1.238)	111.4	(0.202)
	[(m-n)/m]	β_6	−124.2	(−2.237)	−126.2)	(−2.251)
	Sex	β_7	85.35	(2.633)	87.26	(2.537)
ϱ^{max}	Intercept	Γ_0	166.3	(1.210)	149.3	(1.009)
	Sex	Γ_1	−158.9	(−2.656)	−134.6	(−3.312)
	[(m-n)/m]	Γ_2	−38.51	(−1.384)	−8.943	(−0.236)
	Age	Γ_3	3.096	(0.436)	2.745	(0.318)
	Age^2	Γ_4	−.0031	(−0.032)	.0135	(0.112)
	$\bar{y}$	Γ_5	−.0783	(−1.324)	−.0549	(−0.776)
	ω	Γ_6	−13.50	(−2.586)	−17.05	(−2.676)
	BD2	Γ_8	8.481	(0.303)	69.18	(2.001)
	BD4	Γ_{10}	−103.8	(−2.964)	−81.72	(−1.953)

The estimates, based on 336 individuals, are implemented in SAS. On the left are shown weighted nonlinear least squares (WNLS) estimates; on the right, instrumental variable weighted nonlinear least squares (IV-WNLS) estimates, where the wage W is replaced by an instrument PW. LMH is a Lagrange multiplier statistic for homoskedasticity (TR^2 as defined by Judge et al. (1985, p. 447)), the critical value of which at the .05 level is 25.0 Asymptotic t statistics are shown in parentheses. In large samples the critical value of t at the .05 level is 1.96.

Source: Burkett and Putterman (1991).

statistic is rather low. However, several of the estimated coefficients are significantly different from zero, as indicated by the asymptotic t statistics shown in parentheses.

The theoretical considerations discussed earlier in this chapter imply that the influence of the expected wage on labor supply should be unambiguously positive during the busy season, when the alternative to collective labor was not only leisure but also remunerative private work. However, the WNLS results for the relevant coefficients are not statistically significant, and they imply a negative sign for the effect of an increase of W on $\varrho^{b,vol.}$—i.e., the estimate of $\beta_1 + 2\beta_2 W$. How might this be explained? Suppose that an unobserved variable, say ability or tendency to be more hard-working on the job, is positively correlated with productivity in private-sector work as well as with W. However, both egalitarian influences on work-point differentiation and difficulties in measuring effort by individual workers in teams are likely to have caused the collective-sector "wage" to vary less than proportionately with individual ability and productivity in private-sector work. As a result, it would have been rational for individuals of lesser ability or effort preferences to accept low wages in collective work rather than still lower potential earnings in private work, whereas harder working or more capable individuals may have declined high wages in collective work in favor of still higher earnings in private work in otherwise similar circumstances.

In statistical terms, the problem is that the disturbance μ may be affected by ability or "drive" and hence may be correlated with W—resulting in a biased estimate of the effect of W on L. A solution is to replace W by an instrument—i.e., a variable correlated with W but not with μ. For this purpose, we use a predicted wage (PW) obtained from a regression of W on a constant and brigade dummies ($BD1, \ldots, BD4$). The R^2 statistic for this regression is .8106.[9]

Having replaced W by PW and W^2 by PW^2, we again carry out unweighted nonlinear least squares estimation and conduct a Lagrange multiplier test. This again rejects the hypothesis of homoskedasticity, and we therefore proceed to weighted estimation as described above. The resulting instrumental variable nonlinear least squares estimates (IV–$WNLS$) are shown on the right-hand side of Table 6.2. The Lagrange multiplier and R^2 statistics deteriorate compared to their values in the $WNLS$ estimates, but not alarmingly so. For most of the coefficients, the $WNLS$ and IV–$WNLS$ estimates and t statistics are similar. The remarks that follow are based on the IV–WNL results, although most of them would apply to the $WLNS$ results as well.

Apart from the constant term, all but one of the estimated coefficients affecting ϱ^{min} are insignificant at the .05 level. The exception is the estimate of α_8, which is significantly greater than zero, indicating that the corresponding brigade demanded more busy-season work than did the other brigades. The implication is that the minimum labor requirement of individual team members was essentially uniform across individuals within each team, and uniform also across four out of the five teams covered by the survey.[10]

Neither the estimate of β_1 nor that of β_2 is statistically significant at any meaningful level, but evaluated at the mean value of the expected wage (and of its instrument, PW), the sign of the estimated effect of that variable on voluntary labor supply is positive.[11] The fact that replacing W with PW reverses the sign of the estimated effect of the expected "wage" on $\varrho^{b,vol}$ lends credibility to our conjecture about the correlation of W, ability, and productivity in private-sector work, but there

---

[9]A problem with both W and PW is that the relationship between work-points and work time might vary across teams, contaminating the labor measure ϱ. Insofar as variation in PW is more restricted to inter-team differences than is that in W—indeed, PW is nothing other than the intra-team average of W—this problem is clearly more acute for the new measure (PW).

[10]The estimated coefficient on α_2 is positive and significant at the 10% level, suggesting that members of households with more dependents per worker were obligated to supply a higher number of work days per worker, a result that is somewhat counter-intuitive but that perhaps ought not to detain us given its borderline statistical significance.

[11]The esimated effect of PW on $\varrho^{b, vol}$ is equal to $\beta_1 + 2\beta_2 PW$. At the mean of W (PW), 0.68, the (insignificant) estimate for this expression becomes $274.5 + 2 * 0.68 * (-197.5) = 5.9$.

is still no indication of a significant positive impact of the "wage," which would be predicted by economic theory for the case of voluntary labor supply in the face of an alternative opportunity promising a known return to labor. The estimates of β_3 and β_4 are statistically significant and imply that labor supply to the team rose with age to age 36.5 years and declined with age thereafter.[12] The estimate of β_5 is counter-intuitively positive, since one would have expected voluntary collective labor to have been smaller for households having more land to farm privately, *ceteris paribus*. But the estimate is quite insignificant, perhaps reflecting the fact that we know only the average size of the private plot in each team. The estimate of β_6 is significant and negative, indicating that households with more dependents per working member supplied less voluntary labor to their teams, perhaps because more labor was needed at home for care of dependents, an activity that might also have been carried out jointly with some private production. The estimate of β_7 is significant and positive, implying that women provided significantly more voluntary labor in the busy season than did men. A possible explanation of this result is that the collective sector "wage" differential between men and women may have been smaller than their productivity difference in private-sector work, at least on average.[13] Note that the (insignificant) estimate of α_1 implies that the obligatory work input of men *exceeded* that of women.

The estimate of Γ_1 is significant and negative, indicating that women were not permitted to work as many days as men during the slack season, as hypothesized. Except for Γ_8 and Γ_{10}, which indicate that two of the teams had significantly higher and significantly (in this case at just short of the 5% level) lower slack period labor ceilings than the average,[14] the only other significant coefficient estimate is that of Γ_6, which is negative, indicating that individuals who earned fewer work-points in a day were permitted to work more days, a result that is consistent with the fairness reasoning discussed earlier.[15]

Before summarizing what answers to our original questions are implied by these estimates of the two season switching regressions model, it is interesting to compare them with estimates of a simpler, one equation OLS model, shown in Table 6.3. As in the first model, the dependent variable is labor days, l. All independent variables appearing in that model are also entered as independent variables here, with the exception of ω, which has been excluded because of its collinearity with W and the brigade dummies. One of the four brigade (team) dummies is also excluded, because it is redundant (collinear) given the other included information.[16] Two variants are

---

[12]The positive, negative sign pattern implies that LBVOL is concave in age, reaching a maximum at $-\beta_3/(2\beta_4)$, the estimate of which is $-20.47/[2(-.2806)] = 36.5$.

[13]There have been some contrasting although not inconsistent reports of hard-working and capable individual women who welcomed the transition from team to household-based farming because social norms prevented them from receiving more work-points than men under the team system.

[14]The general intercept Γ_0 is not itself significant.

[15]The estimated coefficients on per capita income from other sources is also negative, consistent with that reasoning, but that on number of dependents is negative, contrary to it. Both are quite insignificant.

[16]Since the available information on PLOT does not vary within each of the five brigades (teams), only three dummies can be used when it is included.

Table 6.3. Estimates of Naive OLS Model of Labor Supply

Variable	Coefficient	(t statistic)	Coefficient	(t statistic)
Intercept	367.489	(2.855)	1,230.799	(4.714)
W			−1020.73	(−3.111)
W^2			460.4	(2.452)
Sex	−32.920	(−2.753)	−73.670	(−4.558)
Age	4.486	(1.368)	9.852	(2.797)
Age^2	−0.061	(−1.489)	−0.139	(−3.062)
$[(m-n)/m]$	−23.174	(−1.050)	−20.811	(−0.961)
λ	−308.664	(−0.732)	−2,021.571	(−3.182)
$\bar{y}$	0.035	(0.451)	0.020	(0.264)
BD1	−37.801	(−1.830)	−37.350	(−1.830)
BD2	51.284	(2.641)	−49.911	(−1.474)
BD3	29.387	(0.774)	33.340	(0.844)
F value	3.104		3.939	
Prob > F	0.001		0.000	
R^2	0.081		0.121	
Adj. R^2	0.055		0.090	

shown: on the left, a version that excludes the two wage variables (W and W^2), and on the right, a version that includes them.

First, notice the importance of including the wage variables in the equation: there is a noticeable if not quite dramatic rise in the R^2 and F statistics when they are included, and three coefficients that are not statistically significant in the first version (those on AGE, AGE^2, and λ) become so in the second. The coefficients on these three variables and on W and W^2 are significant at (for W^2, near) the 1% level, although those on $[(m - n)/m]$ and $\bar{y}$ are far below conventional significance levels. The estimated coefficients on W and W^2 imply that labor days are declining in the expected wage at its mean value of 0.68, beginning to rise only after the expected wage exceeds 1.11. On the naive assumption of a uniform relationship between the dependent and independent variables, unmediated by consideration of seasonal distinctions and of a labor floor operating in one and ceiling operating in the other season, a statistically significant relationship between labor supply and expected wage is thus apparent. The sign is consistent with economic theory only if the effective alternative to collective labor was leisure. Such a situation might be viewed as having held true as a first approximation if there were strong political constraints against private economic activity, but as Chapter 3 has explained, this view is less plausible for 1979 than for earlier years. Our conjecture, above, about the correlation of W with unobserved ability, may better explain the result, instead.

Compare, now, the other estimated coefficients in the right hand variants of Tables 6.2 and 6.3. The naive Table 6.3 equation implies that women worked significantly fewer days than men, all else being equal; but the switching regression of Table 6.2 seems to pick up a richer structure, suggesting that while women were *permitted* to work significantly fewer days in the slack season (estimate of Γ_1 in ϱ^{max}

equation), they chose to work significantly more days during the busy season (estimate of β_7 in $\ell^{b,vol}$ equation), *ceteris paribus*. With respect to age, the naive equation shows a statistically significantly concave relationship, with rising until age 35.4 years and falling thereafter. This relationship is nearly identical with that implied by coefficients β_3 and β_4 in the $\ell^{b,vol}$ equation of the switching regression model, which describes voluntary peak season labor. Note, though, that no significant relationship was found between work days and age in either the busy season labor floor or the slack season labor ceiling equations of that model. The switching model is much more successful at discerning a significant relationship between labor supply and the dependency ratio: that relationship is positive in the busy season floor and negative in busy season voluntary labor supply, whereas these associations "wash out" of the simpler model of Table 6.3. The reverse is true of the size of the private plot, the effect of which is statistically insignificant in the one segment in which it appears in the switching regression, but significantly negative, consistent with theory, in the simpler model. Finally, the earnings of other household members display no significant effects on labor supply in either model.

Overall, comparison of the two tables suggests that there are both gains and losses from moving to the sophisticated switching from the naive single equation model. Significant correlations on W, W^2, and λ disappear in this transition, while they surface for $[(m - n)/m]$, and a more complex structure appears with respect to the effects of the SEX variable. The R^2 statistic is distinctly higher for the switching regressions, suggesting greater explanatory power on the whole. Since there are strong institutional and theoretical reasons to prefer the switching regression model, it is comforting to see that at the very least, it does not perform in a distinctly inferior fashion. The model demands a great deal from a relatively small data set of rather modest quality. The most important reason for preferring it is that, unlike the naive model, it is capable of providing at least tentative answers to most of the questions posed above. Some of those answers have already been mentioned. Answers to the remaining questions are as follows.

Both sets of estimates shown in Table 6.2 imply that 86.6% of labor supplied to the teams occurred in the busy season—that is, under conditions of a minimum labor requirement but no labor ceiling—while the remaining 13.4% occurred in the slack season—that is, under conditions in which labor supply was constrained by rationing of available work. The IV-WNLS (WNLS) estimates imply that 46.4% (46.7%) of included individuals supplied more than their minimum labor requirement during the busy season, that the average required labor input was 267 standard days, and that those individuals who supplied more than the requirement supplied an average of 64.1 (71.3) days more than their individual requirements.[17]

---

[17]Note that in dropping equation (6.5) of our original specification, we moved to the assumption that all individuals supplied their maximum permitted days in the slack season. This means we assume zero as the answer to the fifth question posed at the beginning of this section, and that the sixth and eighth questions are rendered irrelevant.

Conclusions

Our study of individual labor supply to teams using the Dahe household survey data complements the findings at the team level reported in the previous chapter. Although we did not find a significant effect of differential expected payments from teams on individuals' labor supply choices, demographic variables do appear to have affected the choice of labor supply, and a significant share of labor supplied appears to have been discretionary. This finding should be treated cautiously, since it derives from a relatively small local data set and from a model specification that demands a great deal of that limited data. If generalizable, however, it has the important implication that collective farms in China did not operate through coercion only, and that even if differential material incentives were not deployed effectively at Dahe, this is not because there was no scope for their use (i.e., no individual discretion in labor supply). By the same token, the finding that a little over half of labor supplied in the slack season, or about 40% of total collective labor, was supplied to meet binding minimum slack season requirements, supports the belief that minima existed and were enforced when necessary.[18]

While the finding that members exercised discretion in busy season labor supply may reassure us that theories of effort supply in teams that assume such discretion are not entirely off the mark, there is in fact much stronger evidence of the applicability of the theoretical models of Sen and others coming from this analysis of individual labor supply. As seen in Chapter 5, the Sen theory predicts that distribution based on work-points will cause the marginal return to labor to more closely reflect labor's (net) average than its marginal product, and that this might lead to an oversupply of labor. While that does not appear to have been a problem at Dahe during the busy season, when households had remunerative alternatives in the private sector,[19] our inability to estimate a version of our model containing a voluntary slack season labor supply curve, and the reports of team leaders in interviews, suggest that team members took advantage of all collective work opportunities offered them in the slack season, and that work rationing proved necessary. There is every reason to think that

---

[18]A matter of possible concern here is whether the presence of binding labor floors might invalidate the models discussed in Chapter 5, which did not consider them (except somewhat informally, when discussing the flat food rations variant). The significant scale of voluntary labor supply found in this chapter's analysis suggests that in any given team, effort supply varied on the margin based on the modeled factors. Chapter 5's team level analysis should remain valid, then, even if some individuals' effort levels were determined by binding minima.

[19]To be sure, we have not actually ruled out the possibility that Sen's theory was evidenced during the busy season too, in the sense that the marginal product of labor in the collective sector could have fallen below that in the private sector as workers compared their average product in the first with their marginal product in the second. Note that the noncollective sector alternatives just referred to had to be attractive compared to collective work to have played the role posited for them. Thus, the findings of this chapter are not inconsistent with the view that the private sector was more efficient than the collective sector, that it had better incentive features because of the absence of monitoring and free-rider problems, or that it operated in a more favorable environment in terms of the total or relative absence of production targets, price controls, and imposed accumulation and other charges. For a further discussion of conditions favoring the private sector, see Putterman (1985c).

this rationing was serving as a means of thwarting precisely the oversupply predicted by the model—that is, the willingness to supply labor even in the face of very low marginal social returns to that factor, in view of the ability to capture shares of labor's *average* returns under the terms of the collective payment system.

7

The Impact of Household Responsibility Systems on Farm Productivity

As we noted in Chapter 1, the problem of disentangling the contributions of different elements of the reform package to the overall effects of China's post-1978 rural economic reforms has been one of the most intriguing questions facing scholars since the end of the first stage of reform in 1984. While numerous changes in crop planning, the level of marketing restrictions, and pricing were clearly important, the policy element receiving pride of place in most discussions has been the most significant change from the political and ideological as well as the micro-organizational standpoint: the abandonment of team production and the restoration of the farm household to its status as China's basic crop production unit. The most commonly proffered analytical foundation for the belief that scrapping the team system accounted for most of the post-1978 gains—the notion that work incentives are inadequate in teams in which labor is imperfectly observable—was considered in Chapter 5. There, it was found that the validity of the incentive failure argument at the theoretical level depends upon the precise nature of the unobservability problem and of the available monitoring technology, on the type and degree of worker risk aversion, and on what payment schemes are considered admissible. The role of policy-induced egalitarianism was also suggested as an alternative explanation for incentive failure.

Empirically, casual support for the incentive failure view has come from widespread perceptions that collective farms have performed in a lackluster fashion in most countries that have based their agricultures on them, and from numerous anecdotal accounts of poor work incentives in collectives and of preferential effort supply to private plots. But because of its introduction in different localities at different dates, China's decollectivization holds out the possibility of providing more than just casual evidence on which to judge this issue. In this chapter, we examine statistical evidence on the effects of agricultural decollectivization, and of other economic reforms, on farm productivity in China. The first part of the chapter discusses studies in which institutional and other reforms are measured at national, provincial, or county levels. The second part examines a set of exercises based on the team level data from Dahe Township, considering in turn the impacts of the transitional form of household contracting adopted there during 1980–1982, and of the more radical *baogan daohu* system adopted there in 1983. An appendix uses models studied in Chapter 5 to draw further inferences from one of the studies.

Studies Using National or Regional Data

The problem of disentangling the effects of different reform elements and of estimating the separate impact of decollectivization in China has thus far been addressed using modern statistical methods by a small number of scholars, most of whom have used data compiled at relatively high levels of aggregation. In this section, we discuss five studies that use provincial level data, one study using national data, and one study using township level data in which the date of adopting household contracting varies across three counties.

The five studies using province-level data include four undertaken by Justin Yifu Lin (1986, 1987b, 1989a, 1992) and one undertaken by Si Joong Kim (1990). Lin's various efforts to tackle this problem all entail estimating modified Cobb-Douglas production functions in which the percentage of teams in each province practicing household responsibility systems has been added to the list of explanatory variables. But the studies differ from one another with respect to data coverage and specification. In the earliest of the studies, the dependent variable is combined crop and animal husbandry output value; in the second study, it is crop output value alone; and in the last two studies, it is output of seven grain and twelve cash crops aggregated with official 1980 price weights.[1] The first study covers the years 1980–1983; the second, the years 1981–1983 only; the third, the expanded period 1965 and 1970–1987;[2] and the last the same expanded period minus the year 1980.[3] Each set of estimates includes conventional factor inputs—land, labor, chemical fertilizer, and machine horsepower and draft animals (which the last two studies aggregate into a single capital measure).[4] They also include a measure of the percentage of teams implementing a form of household responsibility system, which rises nationally from 0 in 1978 and earlier years to 1% in 1979, 14% in 1980, 45% in 1981, 80% in 1982, 98%

---

[1]The author reports that these nineteen crops accounted for 92% of total acreage and for 72.5% of GVCO in 1980. In Lin (1989a), he argues that the less complete output series assembled from the physical output data is preferable to the published GVCO series because data on physical magnitudes are believed to be more reliable than those on values in the Chinese statistical system.

[2]This was the longest period, and 1965 the only year in the 1960s, for which province level data were then obtainable by Lin for the requisite variables.

[3]See Note 5 below.

[4]The 1986 study uses a more comprehensive livestock variable rather than draft animals only, while the 1989 and 1992 studies combine machine and draft animal power into a single capital variable, measured in horsepower. Land is measured as cultivated area in all of the studies except Lin (1987), which uses sown area. The 1986 paper uses combined labor force in crop production, animal husbandry, forestry, and fisheries, while the 1989 and 1992 papers attempt to separate out the crop sector labor force by multiplying the combined agricultural labor force series by a moving average of the ratio of crop output value to combined (crop, husbandry, forestry, and fishery) agricultural output value.

in 1983, and 99% in all subsequent years.[5] The 1981–1983 study includes estimates with and without dummy variables for years, the 1980–1983 study presents estimates with year dummies only, the 1965/70–1987 study presents estimates with and without a time trend but not with annual dummies, and the final study includes both estimates with a time trend variable and an estimate with year dummies. Estimates both with and without province fixed effects are presented in the first two papers, while the third includes only fixed-effects estimates, and the last both fixed-effects and generalized least squares estimates in which the values of all variables are replaced by the difference between the observed value and the provincial mean value. Each of the last two studies also estimates a stochastic frontier (Aigner et al., 1977) version of the regression including a time trend and province dummies. To avoid unwanted consequences of differences in the size of provinces, the 1989 and 1992 studies divide input and output measures by the number of production teams in each province in 1980.

Apart from Lin (1986), each study includes some explanatory variables in addition to the factor inputs mentioned above. In Lin (1987b), terms are added for the percentage of cultivated land that is irrigated and for interactions between that variable and each factor input. In the 1965/70–1987 estimates, each factor input is interacted, in most runs, with the share of teams practicing the household responsibility system, and four more variables are added: the multiple cropping index, the percentage of area sown to nongrain crops, a lagged rural fair consumer good market price index, and a state above-quota price index. Instead of the price indices just mentioned, Lin (1992) substitutes ratios of those indices to an input price index. This study retains the multiple cropping index and nongrain sown area variables, and it drops the interacted terms in favor of the simpler specification of the earlier studies, in which the proportion of teams practicing household farming enters as a free-standing explanatory variable. The estimated production functions are log-log in inputs and output, like the ones discussed in Chapters 4 and 5, with the institutional and other auxilliary variables entering linearly.

The first two columns of Table 7.1 present a pair of results obtained by Lin (1992) with and without dummy variables for years. With respect to the conventional factor inputs, the estimates in columns (1) and (2) (from Lin, 1992) appear far more satisfactory than those in Lin (1986) both with respect to levels and to statistical significance.[6] Despite marked difference in the factor coefficients, however, the

---

[5]Due to the absence of province level data on the latter variable for the first two years of the reform, Lin assumes it to be equal to 0 in each province in 1979 and 1980, except in Lin (1992), in which he instead drops the 1980 observations entirely.

[6]Estimates from that paper had been included in an earlier version of Table 7.1, but doubts raised by unusually high values of the output elasticity of labor led to the discovery that the results could not be replicated. Some references to the paper have been retained in view of the consistency of its estimates of the effects of the household responsibility system with those of other studies, and the simplicity and comparability to other studies of the functional form employed. (Still another set of estimates by Lin [1989] which came to the author's attention as this book was going to press show unusually high coefficients on

estimated coefficients on the percentage of teams adopting household responsibility systems (HRS) are statistically significant and of similar magnitude in runs spanning several of the studies: i.e., .16 for the 1980–1983 estimate (Lin, 1986), .18 for the 1981–1983 estimates (Lin, 1987b), .22 (.23) for the 1965/70–1987 estimate (Lin, 1989a) in OLS (stochastic frontier) variant, and .15 to .22 in the estimates of the final study (Lin, 1992 and column 2 of Table 7.1). These estimates are based on fixed-effects specifications[7] in which the HRS variable is not interacted with other measures. However, while the estimate just mentioned for 1981–1983 occurs in a regression including year dummies, the estimate for 1980–1983 appears in the absence of year dummies, and the value drops to .08 and loses its statistical significance when they are added. A qualitatively similar but less dramatic result occurs when Lin (1992) performs OLS estimates with both province and year dummies instead of first-differenced GLS estimates (with no control for years) for the 1965/70–79/81–85 period: in this case, the coefficient on household farming drops from .20 to .15 (compare columns (1) and (2) of Table 7.1).[8] When the responsibility system measure is interacted with the input variables in the estimates for 1965/70–1987 (Lin, 1989a), the coefficient on the measure by itself drops sharply and becomes statistically insignificant. However, the coefficients of the terms interacting the responsibility system measure with capital and with fertilizer are positive and significant, the coefficient of the land interaction term is negative and significant, and that of the labor interaction term is positive but insignificant. Added together, the significant interacting terms imply an impact of HRS on output of similar magnitude to the non-interacted coefficient estimates shown in Table 7.1.

Lin (1986, 1987b, 1992) concludes that the coefficients on the responsibility system variable in these equations provide an appropriate basis for measuring effects of the HRS reform, or agricultural decollectivization, on farm output and productivity. For example, arguing for acceptance of the estimate with province but without year dummies, Lin (1986) suggests that since 83.5% of teams in China adopted the responsibility system during this period, the implied productivity increase due to this change was roughly 13%, accounting for about 50% of the 26% growth in farm output

---

labor. In this case, the coefficients on land (sown area) and tractor horsepower, while smaller than those for labor, are also large, and the sums of the three coefficients exceed 1.5. The estimates are for 1980–1983, have crop output as dependent variable, include province dummies, and show the typical pattern wherein (a) the coefficient on HRS is larger when year dummies are excluded, and (b) that coefficient's value is .15 in the latter case.)

[7]Province fixed effects are clearly warranted since, with lower income provinces tending to drop team production earlier, endogeneity of decollectivization can otherwise be expected to lead to spurious estimates. Indeed, the estimates without fixed effects have small or negative and relatively insignificant coefficients on the institutional reform measure, consistent with this expectation. Two exceptions are (a) the 1980–1983 estimate without year dummies, in which the measure appears to capture much of the effect of the time trend, but is still insignificant, and (b) the GLS estimates in Lin (1992), which are for variables differenced from their province means, and would thus be expected to perform similarly to the province fixed-effects estimates, as indeed they do.

[8]In an estimate otherwise identical with that shown in column (1) to which a time trend variable is added, the coefficient on HRS is .19, but the coefficient on the trend is not statistically significant.

Table 7.1. Province-Level Production Function Estimates by Lin and Kim

Explanatory Variable	Dependent Variable[a]			
	Output of 19 Crops[b]			GVCO[b]
	(1)	(2)	(3)	(4)
Labor[a,c]	.13	.15		.081
	(.01)	(.03)		(.097)
Land[a,d]	.67	.58		.660
	(.04)	(.09)		(.291)
Capital[a,e]	.07	.10		.226
	(.02)	(.04)		(.107)
Fertilizer[a,f]	.19	.17		−.009
	(.01)	(.02)		(.039)
HRS[g]	.20	.15	.18	.176
	(.01)	(.05)	(.01)	(.037)
Government price ratio[h]			.002	.488
			(.000)	(.240)
Market price ratio[i]			.003	
			(.001)	
Nongrain crop area share[j]	.008	.008		.158
	(.001)	(.002)		(.062)
Multiple croping index	.002	.002		
	(.001)	(.001)		
Time trend			.021	.041
			(.003)	(.015)
Province dummies	No[k]	Yes	No	Yes
Year dummies	No	Yes	No[k]	(No)
Number of provinces	28	28	28	29
Years Included	1965, 1970–1979, 1981–1987			1981–1987
Adjusted R^2	.966			.9427
Source:	Lin (1992)			Kim (1990)

Numbers in parentheses are standard errors or asymptotic standard errors.

[a]Natural logarithm.

[b]Constant 1980 prices.

[c]Agricultural workers times crop production share of GVAO (moving average) in (1)–(3); agricultural workers minus rural industrial workers in (4).

[d]Cultivated area in (1)–(3), sown area in (4).

[e]Total horsepower of tractors and draft animals, in (1)–(3); horsepower of tractors, irrigation machines, mechanical harvesters, and draft animals, in (4).

[f]Chemical only, by weight. See studies for further details.

[g]Percentage of teams practicing household responsibility systems.

[h]Index of above-quota and contract prices divided by index of prices of industrial products in rural areas. Natural logarithm in (4).

[i]Index of rural fair market prices divided by index of prices of industrial products in rural areas.

[j]Nongrain sown area divided by total sown area. Natural logarithm in (4).

[k]Generalized least squares estimates using differences from group (province) means.

in that period. He revises this conclusion based on the 1981–1983 estimate that the output per unit of combined factor inputs rose an average of 19.7% on adoption of household farming, and states (1987b) that about 62% of output growth during 1980–1983 can be attributed to adoption of the responsibility system.[9] In Lin (1992), he performs a growth accounting exercise for the period 1978–1984, during which output of the nineteen included crops grew by 42.2% using 1980 prices. Basing this exercise on the GLS estimate without a time trend or year dummies, shown in column (1) of Table 7.1, he finds that 45.8% of this output growth is attributable to increases in inputs, with the lion's share (70%) due to growth in fertilizer application, while 48.6% is attributable to reforms including the household responsibility system, more favorable producer prices, and relaxed grain acreage constraints (see column (4) of Table 7.2). Ninety-six percent of the productivity growth attributable to reforms as a whole is assigned to household farming in particular, in this exercise.[10]

An interesting exercise that appears in Lin (1992), the results of which are displayed in column (3) of Table 7.1, is the estimation of a "supply-response function" in which only the proportion of teams practicing household farming, the two price ratios, and a time trend variable enter as explanatory variables. The idea here is that growth in inputs and changes in the multiple cropping index and in the percentage of land used for nongrain crops may reflect some combination of a trend in the availability of inputs, and in responses to the institutional and price changes.[11] Upon exclusion of the input variables, Lin finds that the estimated coefficients on time trend and price ratios become more significant and increase by an order of magnitude as compared with estimates in which the input variables appear, while the coefficient on the percentage of teams farming at the household level is virtually unaffected (compare columns (3) and (5) in Table 5 of Lin, 1992). Lin persuasively interprets this as evidence that while price changes influenced output primarily by affecting the demand for inputs, the effect of adoption of the HRS occurred as farmers

[9]The new conclusion results not only from the higher estimated coefficient, which is .18, but also from the adoption of a more precise method for computing the growth rate from the log-linear coefficient estimate, which gives the higher value .197. The same type of adjustment raises the estimated contribution of the HRS reform to growth in 1980–1983 based on the estimates of Lin (1986) from 51.5% to 55.4%.

[10]We show a lower estimate of the contribution of HRS to productivity growth in column (4) of Table 7.2 because it treats productivity growth as all growth not explained by changes in the level of factor inputs, whereas Lin defines it as growth specifically explained by his nonfactor variables. However, application of the so-called Kennedy adjustment for interpreting the coefficients on linear dummy variables in semilog specifications (see Chapter 5, note 33) raises the estimated contribution back to 96% even with our more standard definition of productivity growth, as shown by the numbers in parentheses in that column.

Lin (1989a) also performs a growth accounting exercise for the same period using the estimates in which the responsibility system measure is interacted with labor, land, capital, and fertilizer inputs, with no year dummies or time trend variable. The results are similar to those in Lin (1992), with the combined effect of the coefficients on interacted terms implying that the HRS raised output by 17.5%, thus accounting for 41% of output growth and for 94% of that portion of output growth due to increased total factor productivity.

[11]One could question Lin's failure to include the nongrain sown area variable, arguably a policy parameter in its own right, among the explanatory variables, however.

achieved higher output from given inputs.[12] It may also be taken as further confirmation of the direction and magnitude of the effect of adoption of household farming.

Kim (1990), whose work with the team-level data for Dahe Township will be discussed in the next part of this chapter, also undertakes work with province-level data similar to Lin's. Because some of the data used by Lin for years prior to 1981 were not available to him, Kim limits his analysis to data for the years 1981–1987. He uses the crop output value series in constant 1980 prices as dependent variable, and estimates a Cobb-Douglas behavioral production function including the same factor inputs as Lin (1989a, 1992), except that he uses sown rather than cultivated area and uses a different method to calculate the labor variable, and he normalizes by the number of households rather than the number of teams in each province. Kim's nonfactor input variables are (a) the proportion of teams adopting the HRS, (b) the ratio of the index of above-quota and contract prices of crops to the official index of prices of industrial products in rural areas, and (c) the share of sown area planted to nongrain crops. (a) and (b) are entered linearly, while (c) is entered in log form. Kim does not include a multiple cropping index, and he includes the size of the rural *nonfarm* labor force as one of the factor inputs in some estimates, to capture the impact of any labor contributed to crop production by these workers during peak-season breaks in nonagricultural employment, and in other hours after their nonagricultural work. He also makes minor adjustments in some series, such as an adjustment for the change of coverage of the series for agricultural labor force. He includes a time-trend variable and dummy variables to control for province fixed effects. His specification involves no interactive terms.

Despite his efforts to assemble more consistent data series, Kim's estimate of the behavioral production function (shown in column (4) of Table 7.1),[13] is not very

---

[12]In the papers discussed here and elsewhere, Lin repeatedly argues that introduction of the HRS raised measured total factor productivity by increasing the incentives of workers to supply effort and to use nonlabor inputs as effectively as possible. The results of the regressions in Lin (1989a) including interaction terms between the HRS measure and the levels of the conventional factor inputs are of interest in this regard. Whereas one might have expected the strongest effect to appear in the labor interaction term, the coefficient on that term is in fact insignificant, while the coefficients on the capital and fertilizer interaction terms are significantly positive, and that on the land interaction term significantly negative, as reported above. Lin suggests (1989a, footnote 41, p. 34) that this outcome is consistent with a "property rights" proposition: that increasing the security of ownership of a factor increases incentives to improve that factor's quality. In particular, he says, the shift to household contracting raised the security of farmer's rights to capital and current inputs, reduced the security of their rights to land (presumably because all team members had equal access to land in the collective era but contracts could be altered unilaterally by village officials, under the household farming system), and left unaltered their ownership right to their own labor. There is some tension between this explanation and Lin's incentive theory, according to which effort supply should have increased following the shift to household farming. Although Lin might argue that the increased effort shows up in the capital and fertilizer interaction coefficients, because that effort was applied (as predicted by property rights theory) to increasing the quality of those factors, it is nevertheless odd that an increase in effort per worker has no measured effect on the full coefficient of labor in these estimates.

[13]We show only the estimate with time trend, the full complement of reform measures, and the more standard specification for labor, the alternative specifications of the latter having produced insignificant and/or implausible results.

Table 7.2 Growth Accounting in the Lin, McMillan et al., and Kim Studies

Years Covered: Variable or Ratio	(1) 1978–1984	(2) 1981–1984	(3) 1984–1987	(4) 1978–1984	(5) 1984–1987
Output	61.8	31.8	4.4	42.23	4.21
Inputs	20.8	3.23	4.44	19.34	−0.42
Labor	[5.77][b]	0.19	0.20	1.91	−2.95
Land	[−0.98][b]	−0.04	0.04	−0.74	−1.61
Capital	[5.67][b]	3.71	4.33	4.57	1.88
Fertilizer	[6.65][b]	−0.27	−0.13	13.60	2.26
Multiple Cropping				−0.82	0.88[c]
Nongrain area share		2.14	1.98	1.56[c]	1.17[c]
Government Price ratio		−3.38	−8.98		
HRS		10.35	0.0	19.80 (21.91)[d]	0.0
Time trend		12.81	12.81		
Productivity growth ÷ output growth[a]	66.3 (86.2)	89.8	−0.9	54.20	109.98
Growth from HRS ÷ output growth	51.8 (70.5)	32.5	0.0	46.89 (51.88)[d]	0.0
Growth from HRS ÷ productivity growth	78 (81.9)	36.2	0.0	86.50 (95.72)[d]	0.0

Study on which based: (1): McMillan et al. (1989); (2): Kim (1990); (3): Kim (1990); (4): Lin (1992); (5): Lin (1992).

[a]Productivity growth is defined in this table as output growth minus growth attributable to changes in inputs. This differs from the definition in Lin (1992), which is the sum of all output growth explicitly attributed to noninput variables.

[b]Total percentage change of the factor input multiplied by factor weight, as given in McMillan et al. (1989), Table 1. The sum does not equal the implied total input change reported by those authors and in the input row of our table, suggesting that an alternative method of computation was employed.

[c]As in Lin (1992), no adjustment is made here for the fact that the independent variable is in level form while the dependent variable is a logarithm. If the Kennedy approach is used in this case, the adjustment has no effect on the resulting growth rate at the second decimal place.

[d]Applies the Kennedy adjustment method for interpreting the estimate of the coefficient on a dummy variable in semilog specification (Derrick, 1984). Lin's own estimates which are exclusive of such as adjustment are also shown (not in parentheses) in column (4).

Except for the last three rows, which are percentages, entries are overall percentage change in output or output percentage change attributable to the variable listed in the row heading.

Calculations based on the estimates of Kim (1990) use Model 1 of his Table 4 (shown in column (4) of Table 7.1, this book). These estimates do not match Kim's own growth accounting exercise, in his Table 9, which is based on his Model 3.

Calculations based on the estimates of Lin (1992) use the estimate shown in column (3) of Table 7.1. They match Lin's Table 6 except for the semilog adjustments, shown in parentheses, and for a difference in the definition of productivity growth (see note a).

Note: To calculate the predicted percentage change in output, the coefficient on a logged independent variable is multiplied by the percentage change in that variable, while the (transformed) coefficient on a linear independent variable is multiplied by the absolute change in that variable.

satisfactory. Only land and capital stock have statistically significant coefficients in the resulting estimates; the coefficient on fertilizer is negative and insignificant, while the coefficient on agricultural labor when entered alone, and those on both agricultural and nonagricultural labor when entered together, are positive and insignificant. Nonetheless, the estimate of the coefficient on land is similar to those obtained by Lin (1992), and is of broadly the same relative magnitude when compared with the estimated coefficients on capital and labor. The inferior quality of Kim's estimates is probably attributable in the main to the shallower time-dimension of the data panel.

Turning to the other variables in Kim's specification, the coefficients on institutional reform (household farming), (the log of) the price ratio, (the log of) the crop mix variable, and the time trend are all positive and statistically significant at the 10% level or better.[14] The coefficients on the institutional reform variable are .176 and .183 in the two runs, respectively, implying 18.9% and 20.0% effects on output when a team changed from collective to household farming. These estimates fall in the upper end of the range of estimates obtained by Lin. However, since 45% of teams had already adopted household farming in 1981, leaving only a 54% increase in the percentage of teams using household farming to occur between 1981 and 1984, adoption of household farming led to only about a 10% increase in total output, based on the estimated coefficients on the reform variable. As column (2) of Table 7.2 shows, for the 1981–1984 period, the coefficient on the time trend, .041, translates into a 12.8% increase in output. The increase in the nongrain share of sown area produces about a 2% increase in output, while slightly deteriorating terms of trade are estimated to be associated with a 3% decline. The total output growth is 31.8%, of which four-fifths (25.4%) is attributed to productivity growth. Thus, roughly equal amounts (in both cases, about 40%) of the productivity growth are attributed to the consolidation of household farming and to the time trend (technological change), with the remainder being an unexplained residual. Despite these differences in growth accounting results, Kim's estimates appear basically to confirm those of Lin, since the difference in the share of growth attributable to the shift to household farming is largely explicable by the choice of period, which 1) excludes the year in which the shift occurred in almost half of China, and 2) displays productivity growth much higher than the average for Lin's longer period, leading to a larger time trend coefficient. Lin's growth accounting also gives a higher estimate for the share of growth due to decollectivization because he bases that exercise on an estimate of the production function lacking both a time trend and year dummies. Although we can expect to have a lower estimate of the effects of the institutional reform on output when we include a trend rate or year dummies, allowing some of the observed output growth to be attributed to technological change or idiosyncratic factors, there is no way to be sure that some of that attribution is not spurious; that is, one can rule out neither an underestimate of the reform's effects when years or trend are controlled for nor an overestimate when they are not. Thus, an impartial position would appear to be that the best estimate of the effects of the reform might lie somewhere in between.

---

[14]The first two are significant at the 5% level in the runs with both one and two labor variables, and the last two are significant at the 5% level in the estimate with agricultural labor only, and at the 10% level in the estimate with both labor variables.

An even more aggregated level of data is used by McMillan et al. (1989) in their study of the impact of decollectivization on work incentives and output in Chinese agriculture. Looking only at the gross value of output and at the volumes of inputs to agriculture (including crops, animal husbandry, forestry, and fisheries) at the all-China level in two years, 1978 and 1984, these authors try to identify both the contribution of total factor productivity growth to output growth and the contribution of the shift to household farming to the growth in productivity for this 6-year period. Their strategy is to separate factor productivity change from input-based growth in output by a conventional growth accounting technique using factor elasticities imported from other studies, and to use the results together with a model of effort choice which, after accounting for the influence of the change in output price, attributes the residual productivity growth to change in the ratio of marginal incentives in the collective to that in the post-collective production regime. As summarized in column (1) of Table 7.2, they conclude that two-thirds of the 61.8% increase in GVAO over this period[15] was attributable to growth of factor productivity (here and above, including of course increases in effort per worker), that 78% (versus the 96% found by Lin [1992]) of the productivity increase was due to the change to household farming and the rest to price increases, and accordingly that the adoption of household farming accounted for 51.8% (versus Lin's 46.9%) of the period's output growth, or a 32% increase in output.[16] (The theoretical framework proposed by McMillan et al. causes their findings to have interesting and unanticipated implications regarding the extent of monitoring problems in China's pre-reform production teams, a discussion of which will be found in an appendix to this chapter.)

Lin (1987b) also attempted to identify the productivity effect of decollectivization by estimating production functions for grain output in three adjacent Anhui province counties in the first of which (Jiashan) most teams adopted a household responsibility system in 1980, and in the second (Fengyang) and third (Chuxian) of which this occurred in 1981. Input data on farm labor, draft animals, machine horsepower, and chemical fertilizer cannot be disaggregated to specific crops and are thus assumed used for grain, which accounted for 78% of sown area. Grain sown area is also entered in log-log (Cobb-Douglas) format, the share of cultivated land that is irrigated and that of sown area affected by natural disaster are entered linearly, and the irrigated share variable is interacted with the five factor input variables. While the data are at the level of townships, 102 of which existed in the three counties, no

---

[15]Note that the growth figure for the same period differs from that of Lin (1989) due to the difference in output concept.

[16]Factors accounting for the differences with Lin's findings include McMillan, Whalley, and Zhu's use of GVAO as opposed to crop data, different input variables, their national versus Lin's province level data, their imported versus Lin's endogenous elasticity estimates, and the fact that while they assume all residual growth after that accounted for by input growth and price change to be due to the change to household farming, Lin directly estimates the productivity effects not only of prices and decollectivization but also of the change in crop mix, and attributes the substantial residual in his growth accounting exercise to unknown factors such as weather. Note too that McMillan et al., like Kim but unlike Lin, use the index of above-quota prices rather than a market price index to account for the effects of price changes.

information on the number of teams adopting the responsibility system is available by township. The strategy is to estimate a separate production function for the townships of each county with data for 1979–1983, and to look for the impact of the main year of adopting HRS in the form of the coefficients on year dummy variables. Consistent with Lin's expectation, these show the largest jump in productivity (15.2%) to have occurred in Jiashan County in 1980, but in Fengyang (16.9%) and Chuxian (22.1%) counties in 1981. Since pricing and other policy variables are assumed to hold constant in any given year for the three counties, the fact that the largest productivity increases occurred in different years, corresponding to the different years of adoption of HRS, supports the view that the change to household farming was the main source of this productivity growth.

Each of the studies reviewed suffers from weaknesses or limitations of one kind or another. Although McMillan et al. test extensively for sensitivity to several parameter assumptions, they work with data aggregated to the national level, they borrow elasticity measures from other studies, and their results may be sensitive to their model specification, including the assumed utility function. In addition, they estimate the impact of decollectivization as the residual effect of reform after controlling only for price changes, which means that the estimate could be misleadingly absorbing the effects of market liberalization, changes in cropping policies and output mix, and any number of other factors, including differences in weather between the initial and terminal years.

The Lin and Kim studies using province level data also operate at levels of aggregation at which estimates of technological parameters are in principle unreliable, although the actual results, at least for the Lin studies using the deepest data panel, appear to be plausible.[17] This casts some doubt on estimates for the focal institutional variable.[18] The production function estimates on township level data

---

[17]It stretches credulity to assume that a common crop production function holds for Xinjiang, Sichuan, and Shandong, or that the aggregated data for, say, the province of Hebei, properly reflect technical relationships in both agriculturally advanced counties like Huailu and agriculturally backward counties in poor mountainous regions of the province. There is also the ubiquitous problem posed by the need to use factor input data rather than instruments, in view of the theoretical endogeneity of these inputs. Finally, there are numerous inputs excluded for simplicity or due to lack of reliable data, such as land quality, some current and capital inputs, and (in most of the studies) weather, and there are serious imperfections of fit between variable concepts and measures and between input and output series—the failure of Lin (1989a, 1992) to account for crops providing over a quarter of output value is a prime example. Nonetheless, the factor elasticities estimated in, e.g., Lin (1992), seem plausible insofar as they go, since (for the most part) they are statistically significant, they imply roughly constant returns to scale, and they give the largest weight to land, followed by fertilizer and labor, in which respects they resemble the team level estimates from Dahe Township and other estimates of Chinese agricultural production functions surveyed by Chiacu (1992). This is not true of the set of factor elasticities assumed in the main part of the analysis of McMillan et al. (1989), which are .5 for labor, .25 for land, .1 for capital, and .15 for current inputs.

[18]To test the sensitivity of McMillan et al.'s results to the choice of factor elasticities, we can adopt an extreme alternative to the weights used in their main case and sensitivity analysis, letting the coefficients of labor, land, capital, and current inputs be .1, .7, .1, and .1, respectively. (This puts a weight on land similar to that obtained by Lin in the estimate shown in column (1) of Table 7.1, and in the upper part of the range of estimates reported in this book. As noted by Chiacu, 1992, however, such a high output elasticity for land is less plausible when output is measured as broadly defined GVAO, as in McMillan et al.'s study.

from Anhui are preferable in this respect, but the effects of adoption of household farming can only be distinguished at county level, and in the nondiscriminating form of year dummies, in that study. Failure to distinguish between more and less radical forms of household responsibility systems might also be viewed as a drawback (see the next section). In the earlier studies, there are no controls for changes in prices or other reform policies, so that conjunction of measures such as market liberalization with adoption of the household responsibility system could cause spurious attribution of growth to the latter change. There are also problems with the price indices ultimately used by both Lin and Kim. The argument of Lin (1986) for exclusion of year dummies in 1980–1983 is weak,[19] and that author's preference for estimates that exclude both such dummies and a time trend variable, and accordingly obtain higher coefficients on the household farming measure, can be suspected of reflecting his prior beliefs about the effects of that reform. (Compare our argument in favor of an intermediate estimate, above.) Some details of his later exercise, such as the construction of the crop labor series, are also subject to criticism.[20]

Despite such concerns, failure to substantially reverse Lin's conclusions, and consistency of his results across a substantial number of specifications, provide strong support for the qualitative conclusion that the change from team to household farming was associated with a major increase in China's farm productivity.[21] The main doubts

---

See Chiacu's second essay for some related exercises.) Since sown area declined slightly between 1978 and 1984, while rapid current input growth receives less weight due to the lower elasticity assumption, the new values lead to a downward revision of the estimate of weighted input growth, to 8.51%, and a corresponding upward revision in the estimate of total factor productivity growth, to 53.25%. Thus, the proportion of growth explained by factor productivity growth rises from the 66.3% to 86.2%. The apportionment of productivity growth due to rising prices is affected only slightly by the new elasticities, and the share of overall growth attributed to institutional reform (HRS) thus rises sharply to 70.5%. (See the figures in parentheses in column (1) of Table 7.2.) There is also an implication for the estimate of the key collective incentive parameter, to which we will return in the appendix.

[19]The F test of the null hypothesis that the year dummies are jointly zero is rejected at the 5% but not at the 1% level, in that study. Lin argues that similarly of the estimated dummy variables with the productivity growth estimates derived from multiplying the share of teams newly adopting the responsibility system by .16 implies that each year's growth was essentially due to the adoption of the system. However, lacking further evidence (such as the higher values of the HRS coefficient for the deeper data panel of Lin, 1992, even when year dummies are included), the opposite conclusion would have been equally justified: the apparent effect of HRS could be due to spurious correlation with change over time due to technological or other factors.

[20]Lin does not mention an adjustment of the agricultural labor force series to reflect the change in the statistical system, which began to exclude workers in rural industry in 1984. This adjustment is made in Kim's estimates. Lin's estimates of the crop labor force using the crop share of output may import information from the dependent variable, although Lin does limit this effect by using a 3-year moving average.

[21]In addition to Kim's, another attempt to challenge Lin's results is that of Carolus (1992), completed too late for detailed discussion in this chapter. Carolus has some success in pressing the case that Lin's and Kim's studies underestimate the contribution of the change in crop mix to combined crop value growth: she shows that a much higher estimate of this effect (15% of 1978–1984 output growth versus Lin's 3.7% for that period and Kim's 6.7% for 1981–1984) is obtained by direct decomposition of the variation in output value into productivity, resource reallocation, and price effects, in place of multiple regression analysis. While she argues that as little as 11% of 1981–1984 output growth may have been due to decollectivization, her upper bound estimate that 43% of that period's crop growth could be due to decollectivization exceeds Kim's 32.5% share (Table 7.2), and her own estimates of the effect of household farming on output from province-level regressions are in the same range as those of Lin and Kim of which examples are given in Table 7.1.

that can be raised regarding the interpretations of Lin and McMillan et al., in this author's view, are those pertaining to the effectiveness of control for aspects of the reform other than the change in the form of the production unit and, relatedly, the question of exactly what the percentage of teams using household responsibility systems proxies for. Nongrain cultivated area and price indices may provide insufficient representations of broad changes in the types of administrative controls faced by localities, and of the changes in farmers' opportunity sets brought about by the opening up of markets. Most importantly, decollectivization appears to have been closely linked to the freeing of rural households to allocate labor and capital to noncrop sectors, a "liberation" that should in principle have induced them to economize on the use of time, effort, and other inputs in farming. The incentive effect, then, may have come not so much from the change in the link between effort and return in farming, as posited by Lin, as from the change in the opportunity cost of using resources in farming. Whether the latter could have been changed to an equal extent and with equal impact without altering the locus of crop production may be as much a political as an economic question, in China's case. We shall return to that question briefly in Chapter 11.

A Note on the "Second-Stage" Reform

Both Lin's (1989a, 1992) and Kim's (1990) province-level regression analyses permit estimates of the impact of pricing and other changes during the second half of the 1980s, when the so-called "second stage" of the agricultural reforms was initiated by the change from a quota to a contract system of state grain purchases (Chapter 1). Lin finds that the output of the nineteen crops covered by his study rose by 42.2%, or at a rate of 6.0% per year, during 1978–1984, but by only 4.2%, or at a rate of 1.4% per year, during 1984–1987. Kim finds that crop output in constant 1980 prices rose by 31.8%, or at a rate of 9.6% per year, during 1981–1984, and by 4.4%, or at a rate of 1.4% per year, during 1984–1987. Since the household responsibility system was assumed to be used by a constant 99% of teams in each province throughout 1984–1987, it had no further impact on output or productivity change.

Lin's 1989 estimate implies that 34% of explained 1984–1987 output growth was due to increases in inputs, while, due to the higher weights on shrinking labor and land inputs, his 1992 estimate implies that changes in inputs impacted negatively on output during that period (see column (5) of Table 7.2). Lin (1989a) eliminates the state above-quota price from his analysis, due to statistical insignificance. He finds that the effects of improving market prices account for 61% of 1984–1987 productivity growth, while a rising multiple-cropping index explains 23% of that growth and the increase in the nongrain share of cultivated area explains the remaining 16%. Lin (1992) eliminates both of the initially included price ratios from his production function analysis, due to their statistical insignificance, and he attributes 1984–1987 productivity growth to increased multiple cropping and nongrain area alone. However, he also undertakes a growth accounting exercise based on the "supply response function" estimate, mentioned above, in which both price ratios have significant coefficients. The result suggests that a deteriorating ratio of state procurement prices to input prices had a negative effect on output almost precisely offsetting the positive effect of an improving market price to input price ratio. Thus, explained productivity growth during 1984–1987 is attributed to the time trend, only.

Kim's slightly different input data series (e.g., he uses sown rather than cultivated area and does not include a multiple cropping index) imply that all inputs increased during 1984–1987. Together with his coefficient estimates, this implies that more than 100% of the 4.4% output growth of 1984–1987 was due to input growth, and that total factor productivity declined by a total of 1.1% during that period (see column (3) of Table 7.2). All of the explained decline in factor productivity is attributed by Kim's model to deteriorating farm prices: the value of the coefficient on the ratio of above-quota output to industrial products prices (which proxy for input prices) implies that the decline of that ratio from a value of .931 in 1984 to one of .760 in 1987 reduced combined crop output growth by about 2.7% per year. Indeed, Kim's estimates imply that the change from the above-quota price on marginal sales to the state in 1984 to the lower contract price in 1985, magnified by a jump in the index of industrial prices in rural areas from 105.8 in 1984 to 109.2 in 1985, would have translated into a 5.2% output drop in that one year alone. That amount exceeds the actual 1.7% drop in constant price crop output, with the difference largely explained by trend productivity growth, increased nongrain sown area, and increases in inputs. Assumed productivity growth (at the estimated trend rate of 1981–1987) and the increase in nongrain sown area have similar offsetting effects for the 1984–1987 period as a whole, although there remains a large unexplained negative residual.

Both Lin's supply response estimate and Kim's estimate support the idea that the lowering of the marginal state purchase price from the above-quota price of 1984 to the contract price of 1985 played a significant role in the downturn of overall crop output growth after 1984. The exact results are clearly senstive to model specification, as shown by the fact that Lin finds an offsetting effect due to market prices when he includes that variable,[22] and by statistical exclusion of both price ratios in Lin's production function runs. Also, since correlation does not prove causation, it cannot be inferred from these results that the above-quota and contract prices were necessarily viewed by farmers as the relevant marginal prices when making production and effort choices before and after commencement of the 1985 reform. Nonetheless, these statistical findings do provide useful corroboration to the judg-

---

[22]Kim (1990, pp. 80–81), criticizes use of the market price series in Lin (1989) on the grounds that market prices were of trivial importance to farmers during the earlier period covered by Lin's study, and that the price index for consumer goods in rural free markets, which Lin uses to proxy market prices for crops, is too inclusive to be reliable for the purpose intended.

ment of informed observers based on simple observation of policy changes and performance trends.

A Dahe Study

A study of the effects of decollectivization using the very local data gathered at Dahe commune/township can remedy some of the weaknesses of the more aggregate-level analyses just discussed, but is also subject to serious weaknesses of its own. Although aggregation problems are not entirely avoided when the output concept includes a number of different crops or other farm products, production technology and resources can be expected to have been far more homogeneous across Dahe's teams than across China's provinces (recall Chapter 2). With marketing and cropping policies largely invariant within a single locality, with data on crop mix and other factors being available to control for interteam differences, and with multiple observations permitting control for reverse causality between productivity and reform adoption, differences in factor productivity due to different dates of adoption of household responsibility systems may be reliably isolated in such data. The main general drawback is that it is unsafe to infer much for China as a whole from any one local case. In this respect, we should perhaps be especially wary about Dahe, since we have found that per hectare yields for major crops failed to rise there between 1980 and 1984, contrary to the pattern for China as a whole. Nonetheless, the impact of a change in the incentive regime upon effort supply may be qualitatively similar across environments despite differences in levels of development and in factor intensities.[23]

Other weaknesses in studying the reform's effects using the Dahe data stem not from general drawbacks of working at the team or household level, but rather from idiosyncratic factors related to the sequence of the reforms at Dahe and to the quality of specific variable series. With respect to sequence, the most ideal experiment encapsulated in the experience of Dahe was the adoption of the semi-decollectivized *lianchan jichou* system (see Chapter 3 and below) by some teams and not others in 1980 and 1981. But the results of that reform will be shown to have been far from dramatic, and the transitional nature of the system and its ultimate replacement by the more radical *baogan daohu* mean that more general conclusions about decollectivization cannot be drawn from these findings. With respect to *baogan daohu*, the value of the Dahe data is unfortunately undermined by two factors. First, adoption occurred on an across-the-board basis in a single year, causing inseparability of the effects of institutional change from those of weather and annual price changes. Second, there

---

[23]Note that we have *not* established, for Dahe, that *total* productivity did not rise for grain crops, as it could have if less labor or other inputs were used to obtain given levels of output. And our discussion in Chapter 3 dealt with per hectare yields of grain crops only, rather than of *crops* in the aggregate. The incentive effect of the reforms might have been qualitatively different at Dahe if something about the social cohesion or outlooks of its members, or its internal political dynamics, were distinctive, but the evidence for such distinctions in the observations either of the author or of Butler (1983, 1985) is limited.

are important inconsistencies of coverage in the output series, mentioned in Chapter 4 and discussed further in what follows. General data reliability for the 1980s, partly weakened by the dismantling of the teams, is also problematic.

The discussion of this section is based upon research conducted by Si Joong Kim (1990). In this research project, Kim studied the effects of both *lianchan jichou* and *baogan daohu* on agricultural productivity at Dahe, using the team level data for 1980–1984. In Chapter 3, we saw that roughly one-third of Dahe's teams adopted the first reform, which assigned plots to households and provided material rewards for output exceeding prespecified targets, in 1980; another third followed in 1981, and the remaining third in 1982. In 1983–1985, all Dahe teams practiced *baogan daohu*, under which households could retain or freely dispose of all output from their responsibility fields except that required for fulfillment of grain and cotton quotas, and for payment of state agricultural tax and (in some teams) team or village administrative, investment, and welfare levies.

Kim anticipated possible problems of shifting coverage between the 1970s data (collected in 1980) and the 1980s data (collected in 1986), as well as inconsistencies within the data for 1980–1985, due to the change from team to household production and accounting. He therefore began his work by thoroughly scrutinizing the team-level series for farm inputs and outputs. His first conclusion was that the apparent discontinuities between the 1970s data and that for 1980–1985 rendered any longitudinal analysis that included both series unreliable.[24] He also found numerous suspicious discontinuities of key series within the period 1980–1985, and an especially large number of such problems in the comparison of 1985 and 1984 data convinced him to delete the 1985 observations from his analysis.[25] His investigation of the values of three variables[26] intended to permit adjustment for inclusion of private plot and sideline output in the team series after adoption of *baogan daohu* also led to the pessimistic conclusion that the information given was irreparably undermined by inconsistent interpretations (see below). Finally, he found numerous implausible jumps in the series for output and labor input. After making some adjustments to smooth erratic behavior in the agricultural labor series, where information on team population and total and sideline labor could be used as supporting evidence, and after excluding cases in which team identities changed over time or in which systematic adjustments to erratic labor series were impossible, he was left with 55 teams for an analysis of the 1980–1982 period (focusing on the *lianchan jichou* reform), and with 54 teams for analysis of the 1980–1984 period (which also covers adoption of *baogan daohu*).

---

[24]Recall that we undertook such analysis in Chapter 4 despite Kim's warning, with results that were less than satisfactory, as he would have predicted.

[25]The deterioration of data quality due to decollectivization in the 1980s was also reflected in the poorer fit of production functions for that sub-period as compared with the 1970s which was seen in Chapter 4.

[26]These are data set 1, v156, v157, and v158.

Kim's Estimates of the Effects of Lianchan Jichou

The analysis for *lianchan jichou* involved estimating production functions for four different dependent variables: gross value of crop output (GVCO), and total wheat, corn, and cotton output in physical units.[27] The advantage of estimates for single products is that they are homogeneous, the technology can be assumed to be essentially the same across teams, and information is available on whether *lianchan jichou* (LJ) was practiced for each of three crops on an individual basis.[28] Gross crop output value, on the other hand, may be affected by price weights and changes in crop mix, involves an aggregation of several production technologies (for different crops), and the corresponding estimates must use a dummy variable indicating only whether *lianchan jichou* was adopted for *any* crop.[29] On the minus side, sown area is the only input variable for which the data support disaggregation by crop, so single-crop estimates are weakened by the need to make somewhat arbitrary assumptions about the allocation of labor, current inputs, and capital among crops, which may bias the estimated output elasticities of the inputs if those inputs were not used in the manner assumed, and could also bias estimates of the LJ coefficient if there are unknown systematic correlations between reform adoption and the shares of inputs going to particular crops. This problem exists with respect to the capital series even in combined crop output value estimates, since that variable is not disaggregated among crop and noncrop sectors; in this case, the full capital stock variable is simply entered in the farm production function without attempting to estimate or provide more refined assumptions about how capital was in fact allocated across sectors.[30]

The factor inputs entered are the same as in the studies reported in Chapters 4 and 5. Land is sown area in *mu*, current inputs are total value of agricultural expenditures in current *yuan*, labor is number of reported workers in agriculture (with some adjustments as mentioned above), and capital is total value of capital assets as projected from individual components based on a regression for 212 observations for 1980–1982.[31] In the GVCO runs, the four factor inputs and output are entered in log

---

[27]The units are catties (Chinese: *jin*). 1 catty = 0.5 kg.

[28]As noted in Chapter 3, a team could adopt *lianchan jichou* for corn but not wheat, and so forth.

[29]Entering separate variables for adoption with respect to each of the major crops was found to introduce multicollinearity problems, since most teams adopted *lianchan jichou* for at least two crops and many adopted it for all three crops. More detailed information about target levels and rewards are also given in the data set but repeated tests by Kim found no significant correlations with productivity, and results of these experiments are not explicitly reported by him.

[30]The alternative of using Wiemer's imputations from simultaneous two-sector estimates, which are discussed in Chapter 4, was not considered since those estimates were not available at the time of Kim's work.

[31]Gross value of capital assets (v128 of data set 1) was regressed on values of the following team-owned assets: total tractor horsepower (v104), total diesel engine horsepower (v106), total electric motor kilowatts (v108), the number of mechanical sowers (v109), the number of mechanical harvesters (v110), the number of mechanical threshers (v111), the number of winnowers (V112), the number of grinders (v113), the number of sprayers (v114), the number of pumps (v116), the number of mechanical wells (v118), the number of mules (v120), the number of horses (v121), and the number of horse carts (v126). Seventy-one teams were selected, the others either having too much missing data or "peculiar

Table 7.3. Means of Variables in Kim's Analysis of Dahe Teams[a]

	GVCO[b]	Sown Area[c]	Labor[d]	Current Inputs[e]	Capital[f]
1980	50,468	31.3	70.9	18,082	26,452
1981	48,375	30.9	71.8	18,376	27,149
1982	42,633	31.0	70.6	18,158	29,287
1983	52,643	31.6	69.3	17,305	33,647
1984	56,812	30.7	67.8	19,243	35,808
1980–1982	47,159	31.1	71.1	18,205	27,630
1980–1984	50,186	31.1	70.1	18,233	30,469

[a]Entries are averaged for the 55 teams used in the analysis shown in Tables 7.4–7.7, for 1980–1982, and for the 54 teams used in the analysis of Tables 7.8–7.10, for 1983 and 1984.

[b]Gross value of crop output in *yuan*, deflated to 1980 prices using general index of purchasing price of farm and sideline products. Figures for 1983–1985 are further deflated by the lower bound procedure described in the text, and therefore differ from the series used in the estimates shown in Table 7.8, which are those of Kim's upper bound adjustment.

[c]In hectares. Note that estimated constants in Tables 7.4–7.9 hold for land in *mu*, as in Kim's original tables.

[d]Numbers of workers in the crop sector. Details of adjustments to original data are given by Kim.

[e]In *yuan*, deflated to 1980 terms using general index of retail prices of industrial products in rural areas.

[f]Value of productive assets in *yuan*. Method of projection from component series is discussed in the text. No attempt is made to separate farm from nonfarm assets.

Source: Kim (1990, Part I, Table 15).

form, and the grain share of crop output value and a dummy variable indicating adoption of *lianchan jichou* for at least one crop, denoted LJ, are entered linearly. GVCO is deflated by the official general index of purchasing prices of farm and sideline products. The production function is estimated under three differing assumptions about the error term: first, that it was uncorrelated with years and teams (hence, OLS estimates without cross-sectional or time-series dummy variables); second, that it was correlated with both years and teams (hence, fixed-effects estimates, i.e., OLS estimates with year and team dummies); and third, that there are randomly distributed error components associated with years and teams, requiring use of an appropriate GLS estimator (i.e., a random effects model estimated with the Fuller-Battesse approach, as in Chapter 5). Means of the input and output series as reported by Kim are shown in Table 7.3. Results obtained with each of the three estimating methods are shown in Table 7.4, for the case in which the combined gross value of crop output (GVCO) is the dependent variable.

As with the 1970s estimates reported in Chapter 5, Table 7.4 shows that more of the conventional input variables attract statistically significant coefficients, and that

---

movements in their value of productive assets" in 1980 versus 1979. The regression result, which becomes the projection formula used by Kim, is: assetval = 4,233.69 + 60.72 (tractor hp) + 131.62* (diesel hp) − 26.45 (motor kw) + 1,035.89 (mech. sow.) + 4,807.9* (mech. harv.) − 60.21 (mech. thresh.) + 4,779.33* (winnow.) + 1,035.89 (grind.) − 358.17 (spray.) + 1,128.04* (pumps) − 552.35 (wells) + 1,335.18* (mules) + 464.4* (horses) + 558.68 (horse carts), where * denotes statistical significance at the 5% level. R^2 is .732, and the number of observations is 212.

Table 7.4. Estimates of Behavioral Production Function for Dahe Teams, 1980–1982

	Dependent Variable: GVCO		
Variable	OLS Coefficient (t statistic)	Fixed-Effects Coefficient (t statistic)	Random-Effects Coefficient (t statistic)
Constant	4.62 (9.68)[a]		5.76 (10.85)[a]
Labor	.023 (0.58)	.004 (.04)	.061 (1.24)
Land	.510 (7.58)[a]	.522 (3.32)[a]	.541 (7.34)[a]
Capital	.246 (4.67)[a]	.061 (.76)	.175 (2.97)[a]
Current inputs	.125 (2.84)[a]	.003 (0.85)	.048 (1.30)
LJ[b]	−.006 (−2.95)[a]	.057 (2.39)[a]	.0225 (1.11)
GR[c]	−.929 (−10.0)[a]	−1.01 (−16.7)[a]	−.99 (−18.2)[a]
R^2	.860	.947	
Number of teams	55	55	55
Number of years	3	3	3

[a]Significant at 5% level.
[b]Dummy for *lianchan jichou*.
[c]Grain share of gross value of crop output.
Source: Kim (1990, Part I, Table 1).

the sum of the estimated elasticities (0.90) is a more plausible value (closer to although still below one), for the OLS run, while all coefficients except that on land (which is quite stable here across runs) drop in value and lose significance in the fixed effects run. As before, the random effects outcome lies between these extremes. This pattern may accordingly be explained by the same noise-to-signal reasoning discussed in that chapter. The pattern of the estimated coefficient values follows the others seen thus far in that the coefficient on land is by far the largest, its absolute magnitude in the OLS and random effects runs lying between the 1970s and early 1980s estimates of both Wiemer and the author, in Chapter 4, and being almost identical with those reported in Table 5.3 of Chapter 5. The esimated coefficient on the capital stock variable is positive, more significant, and larger in magnitude than in the crop sector estimates other than Wiemer's for 1983–1985 (Table 4.1), providing some confirmation of the virtue of the data selection and capital series projection procedures of both Kim and that author. The estimated values of marginal products, based on OLS elasticities and calculated at average input values for 1980–1982, are

0.42 for capital, 15.26 for labor, 0.32 for expenditures, and 774.28 for land. While within the ranges of the 1970s and early 1980s estimates in Chapters 4 and 5, these fall substantially below Wiemer's estimates for 1983–1985, which are the most appropriate ones with which to compare them because of the comparable periods and input and output coverage, and the relatively good fit of Wiemer's equation.[32]

Kim included the grain share variable in the GVCO regression model in order to avoid confusing increases in value of output due to shifts in output composition and value, associated with the liberalization of crop planning and marketing, with increases in the physical productivity of inputs that were due to incentive effects of the production system reform. Its performance as the single most statistically significant variable in the regression confirms the expectation of the importance of crop mix as an element of change at Dahe.[33] That teams with higher grain shares suffered significantly lower output values per unit of combined inputs also adds to the evidence discussed in Chapter 3 that cropping decisions had not been fully left to the teams, or that the subjective value of grain differed sharply from both state and market prices reported for the period.[34]

The coefficient of LJ is statistically significant at the 5% level but of opposite sign in the OLS and fixed-effects estimates. A plausible explanation for this is that less productive teams were the first to adopt *lianchan jichou,* causing a spurious negative correlation between LJ and output in the OLS estimate. Such a correlation would be eliminated by controlling for team characteristics by use of a fixed-effects model. To test this explanation directly, Kim estimated a similar production function for 1977–1979, years preceding the adoption of *lianchan jichou* by any Dahe team, and found that dummy variable coefficients for 6 of the 7 brigades that were first to

---

[32]Note, however, that the difference in results for land can be explained by the fact that Wiemer uses cultivated area, while Kim uses sown area. Thus, land stands out as the input obtaining the most consistent elasticity and especially marginal product estimates across our studies, a finding which is not surprising in view of the consistently higher significance of the estimated coefficients on this variable. Possible economic explanations include the fact that land inputs are relatively accurately measured in our data, that there is little variation in effective input per unit of measured input, and that the technology of farm production is such that output is indeed more sensitive to variations in land than to changes in the level of any other input, at least within observed ranges of input usage.

[33]Note that the grain share variable in this study is a value share, rather than a share of cultivated or sown area, as in the province-level studies by Lin (1989a, 1992) and Kim (1990). It was constructed by multiplying gross grain output in physical terms by national average grain price data, then dividing by GVCO. This is only a rough indicator, since we lack detailed data on what portions of grain were sold by Dahe's teams at what prices. It is also not clear from a conceptual standpoint whether grain's share of crop output should be evaluated at the prices of actual sales or at market prices. Finally, while some differences in the magnitude and rate of change of the value share and area share measures of nongrain production are predictable—in particular, the value share will rise far more rapidly than the area share as nongrain production expands from low levels—there is no obvious basis for choosing between the two for purposes of this type of study.

[34]The crop output value series reportedly values grain sold to the state at quota and above-quota prices according to the quantities sold at each price, and remaining grain at the above-quota price. According to reports summarized by Sicular (1988b, p. 692), the market price of wheat averaged 20–30% above the above-quota price during 1980–1982, while that of corn averaged 15–25% below the above-quota price. This suggests that market and above-quota prices for Dahe's grain crops (in which wheat and corn were dominant) were roughly the same on average.

adopt *lianchan jichou* in 1980 were among the 8 coefficients of lowest value out of the coefficients estimated for 15 included brigades, supporting the conjecture that they had been less productive.

If the reform was conditioned on past team specific productivity, inclusion of team dummy variables in the regression for 1980–1982 should correct the resulting bias. Therefore, the coefficient on LJ in the fixed-effects (FE) estimate can be considered substantially more reliable than that in the OLS model with dummies. The random-effects (RE) model, on the other hand, was estimated primarily as a compromise intended to counter the loss of significance and downward biases on coefficients introduced by the noise-to-signal problem.[35] The standard procedure for testing the FE versus RE specifications, the Hausman (1978) test, picks the FE model as the better specification at 1% confidence level. However, Kim notes that this test may not be appropriate in the presence of measurement error, the very concern leading to consideration of the RE form. No firm conclusions can be reached, therefore. What must be noted, however, is that the improvement in significance obtained for some coefficients by moving from the FE to the RE specification does *not* hold for LJ. Using, as before, the Kennedy adjustment method, the .057 coefficient estimate on that variable in the FE run implies that implementation of *lianchan jichou* caused an average productivity increase of 5.8% for Dahe production teams, while no significant effect of *lianchan jichou* is indicated by the RE specification.

Kim's crop specific estimates for wheat, corn, and cotton are reproduced in Tables 7.5–7.8. Series of capital, labor, and current inputs were derived by assuming that each input was distributed across crops according to each crop's proportion of total sown area.[36] The resulting estimates follow a pattern similar to that of the GVCO runs in that the coefficients on the standard factor inputs have their largest sums, near .9 for wheat and corn, in the OLS models, and tend to suffer losses in value and significance in moving to the FE estimates, with the RE model lying somewhere in between. Looking at the OLS estimates, which are perhaps most reliable for this purpose, there are hints of differences in production technology among crops. Although the factor disaggregation problems discussed earlier make it impossible to judge with confidence, it would appear that corn production hinges more on land and labor than does wheat, while wheat production hinges more on capital and current inputs than does corn. This is plausible in that, as Chapter 3 indicated, field preparation, seeding, and sometimes threshing of wheat were done by machine, whereas most operations involving the corn crop were carried out by hand labor, at Dahe. Machine plowing and draft animal expenses (partly for brigade- or village service station-provided services) are elements of the current inputs variable. The

---

[35]I.e., the fact that the large amount of variation explained by team-specific factors may mean that much of the remaining variation in other variables is noise only. See again Chapter 5.

[36]Capital continues to be based on the projection, with no effort to subtract off the portion of the capital stock devoted to noncrop activities.

Table 7.5. Estimates of Behavioral Production Function for Dahe Teams, 1980–1982

Variable	Dependent Variable: Wheat Output		
	OLS Coefficient (t statistic)	Fixed-Effects Coefficient (t statistic)	Random-Effects Coefficient (t statistic)
Constant	4.38 (6.26)[a]		5.11 (7.39)[a]
Labor	.069 (1.00)	.174 (−.98)	.054 (.75)
Land	.312 (3.00)[a]	.273 (1.23)	.419 (4.00)[a]
Capital	.323 (3.39)[a]	.063 (.43)	.236 (2.49)[a]
Current inputs	.270 (3.63)[a]	.171 (2.15)[a]	.221 (3.41)
LJ[b]	−.050 (−1.25)	.031 (.66)	−.058 (−1.53)
$\bar{R}^2$	.678	.842	
Number of teams	55	55	55
Number of years	3	3	3

[a]Significant at 5% level.
[b]Dummy for *lianchan jichou*.
Source: Kim (1990, Part I, Table 3).

robust significance of the labor measure in the corn equation contrasts with its insignificance in the wheat and combined crop value estimates. Cotton shows a land elasticity like that for corn, a current input elasticity like that for wheat, and a low and insignificant elasticity for capital. The significant negative elasticity for labor might be the result of a spurious correlation, because teams with larger labor forces may cultivate less cotton, *ceteris paribus,* and we enter the value of agricultural labor force as a whole, not the labor devoted to cotton (which is unknown).[37] Note that these apparent differences in technology should strengthen the aggregation concerns raised earlier in connection with the estimation of combined crop production functions. (Related evidence of technological heterogeneity is found with respect to grain and nongrain crops in Chapter 9.)

Turning again to the estimates for LJ, which are the focus of Kim's analysis, we first note that in this case, the variable refers to practice of *lianchan jichou* for the specific crop, without implying its practice for the other two. Thus, these equations

[37]The simple correlation between the percentage of land sown to cotton and the number of workers per unit of land averages -0.475 in 1980, 1981, and 1982, significant at the .01% level in all 3 years. Such a correlation is to be expected since teams were self-sufficient in grain, so that those with less land per capita had less land left to devote to cotton and other nongrain crops.

Table 7.6. Estimates of Behavioral Production Function for Dahe Teams, 1980–1982

| Variable | Dependent Variable: Corn Output | | |
	OLS Coefficient (t statistic)	Fixed-Effects Coefficient (t statistic)	Random-Effects Coefficient (t statistic)
Constant	6.25 (13.01)^a		7.82 (14.03)^a
Labor	.112 (2.31)^a	−.289 (2.12)^a	.253 (3.88)^a
Land	.630 (8.07)^a	.178 (1.38)	.431 (4.84)^a
Capital	.021 (.31)	−.113 (−.110)	−.064 (−.80)
Current inputs	.180 (31.9)^a	.058 (1.08)	.141 (2.78)^a
LJ^a	−.028 (−.115)	.145 (4.64)^a	.116 (4.21)^a
$\bar{R}^2$	.786	.915	
Number of teams	55	55	55
Number of years	3	3	3

^{a}Significant at 5% level.
^{b}Dummy for *lianchan jichou*..
Source: Kim (1990, Part I, Table 4).

promise to give more specific estimates of the effects of the change in organization and incentive system upon productivity in the case of a specific production technology. That the system's effects could differ among products is suggested by Butler's account of the first trials as he observed them in 1980. After describing the responsibility system used in corn production by Jiacun Brigade, he writes:

> In the case of wheat . . . technical problems made it difficult to use the responsibility system because of the difficulty of determining exact yields from small parcels of land. To obtain an accurate measurement, wheat must be weighed dry, because wheat from different fields may lose different amounts of water in the drying process. With the shortage of labor, threshers, and drying grounds during the critical few days when wheat must be cut, threshed, and dried, teams could not afford to keep the harvest from individual plots separate.

Remarkably consistent with this discussion, Table 7.5 shows no significant effect of *lianchan jichou* on factor productivity with respect to wheat. On the other hand, Table 7.6 shows that the corn crop, which required far less collective coordination than wheat[38] and had more predictable yields, appears to have benefited from productivity

---

[38]E.g., no brigade-provided plowing, mechanical cultivation, or threshing.

Table 7.7. Estimates of Behavioral Production Function for Dahe Teams, 1980–1982

	Dependent Variable: Cotton Output		
Variable	OLS Coefficient (t statistic)	Fixed-Effects Coefficient (t statistic)	Random-Effects Coefficient (t statistic)
Constant	3.83 (5.14)[a]		3.86 (4.93)[a]
Labor	−.183 (−2.01)[a]	.380 (1.04)	−.161 (1.65)
Land	.628 (4.22)[a]	.172 (.40)	.604 (3.86)[a]
Capital	.108 (.85)	−.098 (−.32)	.122 (.91)
Current inputs	.245 (2.24)[a]	.044 (.29)	.229 (2.07)[a]
LJ[b]	−.230 (−4.94)[a]	.027 (.29)	−.156 (−2.58)[a]
$\bar{R}^2$	.546	.595	
Number of teams	55	55	55
Number of years	3	3	3

[a]Significant at 5% level.
[b]Dummy for *lianchan jichou*.
Source: Kim (1990, Part I, Table 5).

gains of as much as 15% due to introduction of *lianchan jichou*. Finally, Table 7.7 shows that cotton, with the greatest unpredictability among these crops, experienced insigificant or even negative productivity gains from introduction of the new system.[39]

How consistent are these findings that two of the three most important crops at Dahe experienced no productivity gains from introduction of *lianchan jichou* with the finding for the combined crop value variable (GVCO) of a 5.8% productivity increase based on the fixed-effect estimate? Since corn accounted for an average of just over one-quarter of the gross value of crop output among the sample teams,[40] a 15% productivity increase for that one crop could raise productivity for combined

[39]Computing the coefficient of variation (standard deviation divided by mean) of output per unit of land over the years 1970–1985 and averaging over teams, we obtain a value of .231 for corn, .309 for wheat, and .618 for cotton, confirming that cotton had the most variable and corn the least variable yields among the three crops at Dahe (52 teams provided sufficient data for this analysis). The corresponding numbers calculated for the 1970–1979 subperiod alone are .270 for corn, .372 for wheat, and .497 for cotton, which confirms the same ordering of variability while suggesting that both corn and wheat experienced more stable yields in the early 1980s than in the 1970s, whereas cotton's yields became less stable.

[40]This figure is computed using the national weighted average of quota and above-quota prices for corn, multiplied by the quantity of corn harvested. More specific data on how corn was valued in the Dahe internal accounts are not available.

crop output by $(.15)(.252) = 3.8\%$, accounting for about two-thirds of the 5.8% estimated growth. The remainder may be due to the transfer of resources saved in corn production to the production of higher value, nongrain crops.

In summary, Kim's findings suggest that while the semi-collectivized form of household responsibility system known as *lianchan jichou* may have had different degrees of efficacy for different crops, on balance it appears to have had a small positive effect on overall productivity in the crop production sector at Dahe once we have controlled for the fact that less productive teams introduced the system before more productive ones.

Extension to the Introduction of Baogan Daohu

The next step in Kim's analysis is to add the data for 1983 and 1984 to that for 1980, 1981, and 1982, in order to consider simultaneously the effects of both the *lianchan jichou* and the *baogan daohu* reforms.[41] The latter reform affected all crops in all Dahe teams beginning 1983, so the analysis here is for combined crop output value (GVCO) only. In the absence of variation among teams, the dummy variable for practice of *baogan daohu,* denoted BAO, equals one for all 1983 and 1984 observations, and zero otherwise. This means that it is impossible to distinguish between the effects of other factors that may have differed in those years, such as weather, and the effects of the reform.[42] As with the output value estimates for 1980–1982, Kim also uses the grain-share-of-output measure. He also provides explicit comparisons with estimates not including that measure, thereby demonstrating its impact on the estimates for the reform variables.

A serious and to some degree intractable problem facing Kim was the fact that upon adoption of full household contracting, team production accounts changed from being records of *collective* activity and of income payments to member households, to being estimates of *household* activity, reportedly based upon surveys of those households. With this change, an ambiguity arose regarding inclusion in these accounts of household earnings from the private plots and small sideline activities that had previously been ignored because they occurred outside of the collective economy. To accurately estimate the productivity impact of the shift to household farming, it is necessary to eliminate any inflation of the output series due to expanded coverage. (As before, ordinary price inflation is controlled for by deflating the GVCO data by the general index of purchasing prices of farm and sideline products.) As mentioned in Chapter 3, however, a survey form item that asked team accountants to

---

[41]As noted above, Kim excluded the data for 1985 due to evidence of reliability problems.

[42]Kim does report exercises in which indices are constructed by regressing data on monthly rainfall and average temperature, generated in the Huailu County weather station, on residuals from the crop production function for years in the 1970s, then including such an index in the 1980s regression discussed here. Inclusion of these indices make little difference to the result, and although some of them pick up statistically significant coefficients, the signs are not always positive, raising doubts about their ability to proxy for agriculturally beneficial weather.

distinguish between (a) "income produced under unified and contracted management," which was to include output on contracted plots (i.e., most Dahe land beginning 1983), and (b) "income produced under management by individual members," which was to include activities previously considered "private," failed to generate meaningful data. As an alternative, Kim tried to use our household survey data set to form an estimate of the percentage of 1983 and 1984 crop income that would have been excluded as private under the previous team accounting system. He added up the gross weight of vegetables grown on private plots in 1985 according to that data and estimated its share in combined crop income for those teams. He obtained alternative estimates of 15.2% and 24.6% respectively, the first using the vegetable price reported by township officials, the second using the average sale price of vegetables according to households' own reports. He adopts these two figures as low and high estimates of the proportion by which 1983 and 1984 crop data are inflated by broadened coverage. The smaller adjustments is used in Kim's "upper bound" estimate of the impact of *baogan daohu* on farm productivity, the larger adjustment in his "lower bound" estimate. For the upper bound estimate, the adjustment is made in the data for the 41 out of 54 included teams that show a more than 50% 1-year increase in current price GVCO in 1983 or 1984; in the lower bound estimate, it is made for the 47 of 54 teams showing a more than 35% increase in either year.

Tables 7.8 and 7.9 reproduce Kim's upper bound estimates of the effects of *baogan daohu* with and without inclusion of the grain share of crop output value as a crop mix indicator. Adjusted crop output value and the four conventional factor input variables[43] are entered in log form, the reform-reflecting variables linearly. The data for the 54 includable teams cover the years 1980–1984, and the LJ dummy variable is included both for consistency with Kim's earlier runs and for additional estimates of its effects in the expanded setting. As before, OLS estimates without dummy variables, fixed-effects estimates (OLS with team dummy variables), and random-effects estimates are shown. Note, however, that the fixed-effects estimates in this case do not include dummy variables for years, in part because year dummies for 1983 and 1984 would be perfectly collinear with the BAO dummy.

With respect to the estimated elasticities on the conventional factor inputs, these results are similar to those for the subperiod 1980–1982, except that the current inputs variable performs less satisfactorily, especially in the OLS equations. The sum of the estimated elasticities of conventional factors in Table 7.8 is .844 in the OLS estimate and smaller for the other estimates. Unlike the earlier run, some of the RE estimates pick up more significant coefficients on the input variables than either FE or OLS equations. Again, the Hausman test for specification favors the FE over the RE estimates, but interpretation remains open. Values of marginal products at average

---

[43]The current inputs variable is deflated in this case using the general index of retail prices of industrial products in rural areas.

Table 7.8. Estimates of Behavioral Production Function for Dahe Teams, 1980–1984

Variable	Dependent Variable: Adjusted GVCO Variant: Upper Bound Estimation with Grain Share		
	OLS Coefficient (t statistic)	Fixed-Effects Coefficient (t statistic)	Random-Effects Coefficient (t statistic)
Constant	5.41 $(17.3)^a$		6.73 $(18.2)^a$
Labor	.029 (1.09)	−.011 (−.18)	.093 $(2.65)^a$
Land	.540 $(12.0)^a$	.243 $(2.49)^a$	.523 $(9.85)^a$
Capital	.229 $(5.78)^a$	.015 (.34)	.080 $(2.15)^a$
Current inputs	.046 (1.58)	.067 $(2.68)^a$	.048 $(2.17)^a$
LJ^b	−.053 $(-2.87)^a$	−.005 (−.35)	.031 (1.81)
Bao^c	.008 (0.37)	.078 $(3.97)^a$	.085 (1.86)
GR^d	−1.00 $(-20.3)^a$	−1.03 $(-24.9)^a$	−1.04 $(-27.7)^a$
$\bar{R}^2$	.879	.939	
Number of teams	54	54	54
Number of years	5	5	5

^{a}Significant at 5% level.
^{b}Dummy for *lianchan jichou*.
^{c}Dummy for *baogan daohu*. Equals one for 1983 and 1984, zero otherwise.
^{d}Grain share of gross value of crop output.
Source: Kim (1990, Part I, Table 6).

input values for 1980–1984, based on OLS elasticities, are 20.77 for labor, 871.86 for land, 0.38 for capital, and 0.13 for current inputs (all figures in *yuan*), all of which are again in the range of the Chapter 4 and 5 estimates as a whole but below those of Wiemer for 1983–1985 in particular. The VMP estimates are not too different from those obtained by Kim for the shorter 1980–1982 period, with the exception of the substantially lower VMP for current inputs.

The most striking result shown by the tables is the very strong statistical significance of the crop mix measure, and the critical impact that its inclusion has on the estimated coefficient of BAO. This impact bears noting even if we cannot place much confidence in the specific estimates of the BAO coefficient derived under Kim's upper and lower bound assumptions, for it would also hold for any uniform

Table 7.9. Estimates of Behavioral Production Function for Dahe Teams, 1980–1984

Variable	Dependent Variable: Adjusted GVCO Variant: Upper Bound Estimation with Grain Share		
	OLS Coefficient (t statistic)	Fixed-Effects Coefficient (t statistic)	Random-Effects Coefficient (t statistic)
Constant	4.07 $(8.31)^a$		5.09 $(8.62)^a$
Labor	−.007 (−.15)	−.034 (−.28)	.079 (1.44)
Land	.611 $(8.53)^a$	−.110 (−.57)	.535 $(6.24)^a$
Capital	.215 $(3.40)^a$	−.046 (−.52)	.109 (1.56)
Current inputs	.084 (1.80)	.130 $(2.62)^a$	.096 $(2.15)^a$
LJ^b	−.138 $(-4.80)^a$	−.106 $(-3.63)^a$	−.036 (−1.06)
Bao^c	.147 $(4.40)^a$	.227 $(6.15)^a$	.234 $(3.66)^a$
$\bar{R}^2$	.691	.759	
Number of teams	54	54	54
Number of years	5	5	5

[a]Significant at 5% level.
[b]Dummy for *lianchan jichou.*.
[c]Dummy for *baogan daohu*. Equals one for 1983, 1984, zero otherwise.
Source: Kim (1990, Part I, Table 7).

correction to the output series required by the change in coverage.[44] Those aspects of reform policy that allowed Dahe's teams to increase the share of nongrain crops in their crop output had a strong positive effect on the returns to agricultural inputs which, if not controlled for, would permit a serious overestimate of the effect of the change in farm level organization (adoption of *baogan daohu*). For example, the productivity effect of the organizational reform as estimated under the fixed-effects specification falls from 25.3% to 8.1% in the upper bound estimates of Tables 7.7 and 7.8, and from 10.8% to 5.4% in the lower bound estimates (not shown). Although the correctness of all of these estimates hinges on the accuracy of the data and of the adjustments applied, it seems reasonable to conclude that the estimates of the equations which include the variable GR are more reliable than those which exclude that variable.[45]

[44]That is, for any correction that shaves (adds) the same proportion of output off of (to) each figure. It would also be expected to follow for any random set of corrections, although its disappearance under some nonuniform adjustments cannot be ruled out, so that the data coverage problem still precludes absolute confidence in this result.
[45]The fact that BAO and GR (grain share) are correlated because GR was still rising when BAO was

Table 7.10. Growth Accounting with Behavioral Production Function for Dahe Teams, 1980–1984

Factor or Variable	Growth Rate or Change[a]	Elasticity or Adjusted Coefficient[b]	Contributed Growth Rate	Share of Total Growth Rate
Labor	−1.11%	.093	−0.10%	−.02
Capital	7.86%	.080	0.63	.13
Land	−0.55%	.523	−0.29%	−.06
Current inputs	1.57%	.048	0.07%	.01
LJ	−0.241	.031	−0.19%	−.04
BAO	1.000	.088	2.13%	.42
GR	(−0.180)[c]	−.647	(2.79%)	(.55)[c]
GVCO	5.04%	—	—	—

[a]Based on Kim (1990, Part I, Table 15), and Dahe team accounts.
[b]Based on random-effects estimate, upper bound variant, in Kim (1990) as shown in Table 7.8.
[c]Imputations needed to explain total output growth, in lieu of data not provided by Kim. See discussion in text and footnote 48.

Finally, inclusion of the observations for 1983 and 1984, as compared to the estimates reported in Table 7.4, unexpectedly turns the coefficient on LJ negative in the FE runs, significant in those excluding GR, insignificant in those including GR. However, this coefficient is positive and significant at the 10% level for the upper bound RE estimate when GR is included. The most likely explanation is that Kim did not include dummy variables for time series variation (years) in these FE estimates. If 1982 was a poor year for crop production due to natural factors, then the fact that more teams practiced *lianchan jichou* in that year than in 1980 or 1981 could lead to the negative coefficient on LJ in Table 7.8. In fact, the fixed-effect model estimate reported in Table 7.4, in which the coefficient on LJ is positive, includes dummy variables for 1981 and 1982. The statistically significant values of those coefficients, not shown in that table, are 0.053 and −0.059, respectively, consistent with our conjecture that 1982 was a bad year. The positive coefficient on LJ for the random-effects model in Table 7.8, opposite to the signs on the coefficient in the OLS and FE models, may be explained by the fact that the RE model is the only one of the three providing some control for the year-specific error component, although it treats that error as a random variable.

Table 7.10 presents a growth decomposition analysis similar to those of Chapter 4. The analysis is based on the random effects estimates of Table 7.8, which are for Kim's upper bound on the effects of *baogan daohu* and include the crop mix variable GR. The first column gives the growth rates of crop output and inputs calculated

instituted means that it is difficult to accurately disentangle the separate effects of these two reform variables. Nonetheless, the resulting estimates are unbiased and efficient. Here and in the analysis for the shorter 1980–1982 period, Kim also performs a test, following Hausman (1978) and Nakamura and Nakamura (1981), for the possible endogeneity of GR, and rejects this possibility at conventional significance levels. See Kim (1990, pp. 29–30 and 39).

directly from the averages over teams as provided by Kim. Notice that crop output grew by 5.0% a year during 1980–1984 according to the table,[46] compared with a rate of 7.4% a year from 1980 to 1985, according to Table 4.8. The difference may be attributed in part to differences in sample size and period, but most of it is due to Kim's downscaling of many of the 1983 and 1984 output figures by 15.2% as a correction for coverage changes. Without this adjustment, his data imply an 8.8% annual growth rate for 1980–1984. The same column lists the total change in the two organizational variables and in crop mix. Since 13 of the 54 teams in Kim's sample practiced *lianchan jichou* in 1980 and none did in 1984, LJ is said to have declined by 0.241 (24.1%). BAO rose by 1.0, since no teams practiced it in 1980 and all did in 1984. Data on the average value of GR has not been supplied by Kim, and the approach taken in the table is described further, below.

The second column of the table lists the coefficients or elasticities estimated in the regression, with the coefficients for LJ, BAO, and GR being adjusted by the Kennedy method, as above, to give the predicted impacts on output (rather than the log of output) of a 1% change in each variable. The third column gives the contribution to the annualized growth rate of output due to each input or variable. These growth rate contributions are simply the product of the numbers in columns 1 and 2, for the input variables. For LJ, BAO, and GR, the products of those columns represent the total predicted change in output between 1980 and 1984, and therefore they must be adjusted to derive annualized growth rates.[47]

The last column of Table 7.10 shows the share of the overall output growth rate accounted for by the change in each input or variable. For Kim's subsample, only labor and land inputs contracted, while current inputs and capital stock rose during 1980–1984, for a small positive net contribution to output growth due to input changes. Abandonment of *lianchan jichou* by roughly one-quarter of the teams is expected to translate into an output decline of similar magnitude, so that these two effects partly cancel one another out. Adoption of *baogan daohu* appears to give rise to an 8.8% increase in total factor productivity, equivalent to a 2.13% annual growth rate, which would account for 42% of overall growth in the adjusted gross value of crop output (GVCO). Since Kim does not report figures for grain's share of GVCO, the table includes in parentheses the change in that variable which would explain the remaining portion of output growth. Unfortunately, we were unable to confirm such a change in our own attempt to replicate Kim's data.[48]

[46]Kim's Table 15 (1990) reports output growth based on the lower bound adjustment; the figures are accordingly modified to obtain the rate shown in Table 7.10. The method is to multiply the average 1984 output figure for the lower bound estimate by the ratio of the two adjustment factors, 1.246/1.152, then calculate the growth rate from the reported average 1980 output. Since the number of teams subject to Kim's adjustment differed in the lower and upper bound versions, this is only an approximation to the actual growth rate in the upper bound series.

[47]The procedure is to add 1 to each product, raise the resulting number to the (0.25) power, then subtract off 1 again.

[48]Kim reports that he used average state grain purchasing prices to evaluate each team's total grain output, and divided the resulting numbers by his adjusted GVCO series. While we find that average grain share of *unadjusted* GVCO declines for the teams in Kim's sample by about 14% (from .722 to .581) during

Focusing on the impact of the two stages of decollectivization, the fixed and random effects estimates of the effects of *baogan daohu* in Tables 7.8, and their counterpart lower bound estimates, not shown, remain our best available indicators of the range within which the true effects fell.[49] The estimates shown in Table 7.4, on the other hand, may be viewed as more reliable for *lianchan jichou,* because they control for year-specific effects. Insofar as these separate estimates can be brought together, a consistent interpretation is that adoption of *lianchan jichou* increased a

---

1980–1984, our computation shows GR more or less unchanged between 1980 and 1984 (although falling from 1982 to 1984) when the average of *adjusted* GVCO as reported by Kim is used. We are unable to explain the discrepancy.

[49]One may challenge Kim's adjustments as being excessively unfavorable to *baogan daohu* on a number of grounds. First, only four of roughly 250 households explicitly reported vegetable sales, so the vegetable price upon which Kim's lower bound estimate (his larger "trimming" of the GVCO series) rests is based on a painfully small sample. Second, a calculation by Kim combining household and team data for 1979 suggests that only 14.7% of total crop income, less than Kim's *upper* bound adjustment based on 1985 data, was from the private plots in that year. Third, it is possible that some "fattening" of GVCO figures began before 1983, since all teams were already practicing a form of household contracting *(lianchan jichou)* by 1982. Finally, we have no way of knowing just how much privately generated income made its way into the team accounts for 1983 and 1984. One can also list a number of factors favoring a large downward adjustment of reported 1983 and 1984 GVCO, however. First, it is possible that the small quantities of vegetables reported as produced and sold by the households in the household survey involved underreporting, perhaps with the aim of understating cash earnings that would be otherwise invisible to local officials. This would lead to an understatement of private plots earnings, even if vegetable prices were not as high as supposed in the lower bound adjustment. Second, with regard to the low estimated share of private plot earnings in 1979, Kim correctly points out that although this share is slightly below the low estimate for 1985, use of the latter estimate to calculate an upper bound estimate of the effects of *baogan daohu* on farm productivity is not unreasonable, since the importance of private plots probably grew after 1979 as liberalizing reforms occurred. We lack reliable data on private plot size at Dahe in 1979, but the fact that a portion of the "private plots" were still used for collective grain cultivation at that time suggests that remaining vegetable plots were likely to have been small. As noted in Chapter 1, the limit on the private plot share of cultivated area is reported to have risen in China as a whole from about 5% to 7% in 1978 to 15% in the second half of 1980 (Kojima, 1988, p. 711). The average private plot share stood at 11% in 1985 in the five Dahe household survey teams, possibly indicating an expansion of the private plots consistent with Kim's conjecture. Third, inflation of GVCO figures by inclusion of private plot output before 1983 is made less likely by the fact that under the *lianchan jichou* system, unlike *baogan daohu,* teams remained the units of accounting and distribution, and would have had no reason to check output on noncontracted fields. Also, downward adjustments of 1983 and 1984 GVCO were made only for those teams showing discrete jumps in GVCO in one or both years. The fact that no adjustment was made in the output series of 24% of the teams, in the upper bound estimate, and of 13% of the teams, in the lower bound estimate, also reduces the overall degree of adjustment in Kim's estimates. Finally, absence of controls for time in the regressions reported in Tables 7.8 and 7.9 means that the effects of *baogan daohu* and of the change in crop mix could be overestimated, because their coefficients could be biased upward by the presence of technological change. This is clear from a comparison of the relevant columns of Table 7.1 for the national (provincial) studies. Agricultural productivity growth at Dahe in the early 1980s may have lagged behind national trends, but the positive coefficients on BAO make it nearly certain that a growth trend variable would, if added to Kim's regressions, pick up a positive coefficient and reduce the coefficient on BAO itself. Although there is no way to separate productivity improvements due to institutional reforms from those due to technological changes of other origin, especially given the short time period analyzed here, the possibility of improvements in factor productivity due to improved seeds, fertilizer quality, etc., is a real one and serves to offset any tendency of Kim's adjustments to understate the effects of *baogan daohu* at Dahe. In the end, there is indeed no way to know how much private sector income made its way into the GVCO reports for 1983 and 1984, and Kim's implicit assumption that all of it did might be viewed as somewhat biased against *baogan daohu*. However, the author would conclude that Kim's estimates are still the best feasible and that the arguments raised in this note justify no greater revision than the treatment of his upper bound estimate as a central case, at the very most.

typical team's total factor productivity in crop production by 5.8%, while adoption of *baogan daohu* increased such a team's productivity by between 5.4% and 8.8%. The net productivity change due to replacing *lianchan jichou* with *baogan daohu* at Dahe Township would accordingly have averaged between −.4% and +3.0%, according to Kim's estimates.[50]

If these findings are not simply to be dismissed as the result of bad data or unreliable estimating techniques, a question to be addressed is why the magnitude of the productivity effect of adopting household contracting at Dahe (5–9%), as estimated by Kim, is so much smaller than those found by Lin and Kim himself for national (provincial) data (15–22%). Three possible answers will be considered. First, the difference could be due to the fact that other estimates have failed to control satisfactorily for crop mix changes. Second, the productivity gains from decollectivization of farming may have been more modest at Dahe than in the rest of China, on average, because the incentives for farm production remained weak in localities like Dahe in which there existed above-average opportunities in the noncrop sectors of the rural economy. Finally, productivity gains from decollectivization may have been smaller at Dahe simply because the collective system was operated there with a higher degree of efficiency than in more average Chinese communes.

Looking at these three explanations, the first one is not supported by the two more recent studies by Lin (1989a, 1992), which include a control for the change in crop mix but obtain results similar to those of this earlier studies. Nor is it supported by Kim's estimate using province-level data, in which only 2% out of an estimated 25.4% productivity increase during 1981–1984 is attributed to the increase of the nongrain share of sown area. However, while Lin's and Kim's national (provincial) studies control for crop mix by an area share measure, Kim's Dahe study uses a value share measure. Also, the grain share variable is entered in log form in Kim's national study but linearly in his Dahe study. Without more directly comparable estimates, we cannot know how the choice of proxy and of functional form for the grain share variable has affected the differing results for both that variable and the decollectivization measures.

The second explanation runs into difficulties because agricultural productivity increases are in no way ruled out in localities where market opportunities dictated that the proximate effect of liberalization should be the shifting of resources to nonagricultural pursuits. The reason, of course, is that input *reduction* is as potent a source of productivity gains as is output expansion, and localities with profitable alternative uses for their resources should if anything have been even more assiduous in

---

[50]Note that it would be a misinterpretation of Kim's results to suggest that the impacts of *lianchan jichou* and of *baogan daohu* must be added together to obtain the full impact of the reform process at Dahe. Since *baogan daohu* succeeded and replaced *lianchan jichou*, the results are in no sense additive. Readers who are uncomfortable with combining estimates based on separate regressions could, as an alternative, use the random-effects estimates for both reforms from Table 7.8 and its lower bound counterpart. This procedure leads to the conclusion that adoption of *lianchan jichou* raised productivity by 2.5 to 3.1%, and that the change to *baogan daohu* raised productivity by a further 2.9 to 5.7%.

economizing on resources applied to agriculture (insofar as they were free to make these choices). There is, to be sure, the possibility that imprecise measurement of inputs, especially labor, could help to explain the modest productivity gains at Dahe. In particular, if the labor input is measured by number of workers, unadjusted for quality, and if the workers remaining in agriculture tended on average to be the less productive ones, as accords with numerous reports, then the productivity increase implicit in a reduction in the labor force employed in agriculture will be understated by Kim's estimates. However, it is hard to see why this should not also be the case for the China-wide estimates using province-level data, so this line of reasoning seems unable to account for the *difference* in the results for Dahe. This leaves the possibility that productivity failed to grow because resources were *unable* to leave crop production as rapidly as they might otherwise have done on account of administrative constraints. Without effective production incentives, the productivity of resources that may have simply been trapped in the crop sector due to administrative interventions may have grown more slowly where the incentives to raise that productivity were lower due to the relatively low rewards to be attained.[51]

The third possibility, that the collective system was less detrimental to factor productivity in some localities than in others, is consistent at a general level with the variability of commune and production team performance across localities in the collective era, and there is every reason to suspect that Dahe People's Commune, along with similar units in other parts of China, had a relatively well managed collective farming system when compared with communes having less successful records of growth and structural change in the collective farming era. This third hypothesis may therefore be a reasonable explanation of the more modest productivity growth due to the reforms at Dahe. The only *caveat* here is that we can provide no independent test of this explanation, since we are unable to measure the comparative degree of inefficiency induced by collective farming except by reference to the differential gains from decollectivization, which are precisely what are to be explained here.

Summary and Conclusions

One of the most intriguing questions about China's agricultural reforms, from the standpoint of economic system analysis, has been what share of the growth in crop output and yields that occurred during the first half-decade of those reforms should be attributed to the restoration of households as basic farm units. In this chapter, we discussed some attempts to answer that question by econometric methods. These included one study using aggregated data for China as a whole (McMillan et al.,

---

[51]In other words, the incentive to raise the productivity of given agricultural resources could have been greater in less developed localities in which a relatively high value was placed on additional food, feed, or grain sales, than in more developed localities in which food was already abundant and the rewards from nonfarm activities were both large and accessible.

1989), five studies using province-level data for all or most of the country (Lin, 1986, 1987b, 1989a, 1992; and Kim, 1990), one study using township level data from three counties which returned to household farming in different years (Lin, 1987b), and a study of the effects of the two stages of institutional reform at Dahe Township which uses team-level data (Kim, 1990).

McMillan, Whalley, and Zhu use data for agriculture including animal husbandry, forestry, fishery, and sidelines at the national level for the initial year 1978 and the terminal year 1984. They apply the Solow-Denison type growth accounting method using factor elasticities borrowed from other studies, and they separate the effects of price changes and other reforms by means of a theoretical model of incentives including an assumed specification of farmers' utility functions. The studies by Lin and Kim estimate agricultural production functions using county level data, adding the percentage of households in each province practicing the household responsibility system to the set of explanatory variables which, in Lin (1989a, 1992) and Kim (1990), also includes controls for price changes and cultivation of nongrain crops. As Table 7.1 shows, most of these behavioral production function estimates produce similar estimates of the impact of adoption of household farming on total factor productivity: changing from team to household farming was associated with an increase of between 15% and 22% in the output generated by a given set of inputs. As Table 7.2 shows, the studies agree that more than one-half of the output growth of 1978–1984 or the early 1980s was due to increasing productivity (including unmeasurable increases in effort per worker), and they attribute between one-third and one-half of all output growth to the adoption of household farming. The later Lin and Kim studies also provide support for the proposition that the deterioration of the administered terms of trade facing staple crop producers played a major part in explaining the slowdown of agricultural growth after 1984. Lin's study of township-level data from three counties also leads him to the conclusion that most of the growth in grain output occurring there between 1979 and 1983 was attributable to the same reform.

Kim's study based on the team level data from Dahe Township also entails estimation of a behavioral production function in which indicators of adoption of household farming and the share of output due to grain are included, along with the conventional factor inputs, as independent variables. Separate estimates for the effects of the partially decollectivized system known as *lianchan jichou* show a 5.8% increase in the productivity of combined crop production, including a 15.5% increase in productivity with respect to the production of corn alone, and no significant effects of the system on factor productivity in the cases of wheat and cotton production. The higher productivity in producing corn can directly account for about two-thirds of the productivity increase for crops as a whole, with the remainder being due, perhaps, to the shifting of some of the resources saved into the production of crops of higher value. The estimates of the effect of the radical form of decollectivization called *baogan daohu* are rendered imprecise by the probable occurrence of accounting changes that cannot be corrected for with confidence due to the absence of appropriate data. Kim attempts to establish upper and lower bounds for the effects of the institutional change by forming low and high estimates of the degree to which later crop output data are inflated by inclusion of formerly uncounted private plot output. He concludes that the adoption of household farming raised output per unit of combined inputs by between 5.4% and 8.8%, as compared with the original collective production system. When combined with his estimates for the effects of *lianchan jichou* alone during the 1980–1982 period, these estimates imply that the net gain from the change from *lianchan jichou* to *baogan daohu* was no more than a 3.0% increase in output, and could even have been slightly negative. A result of at least equal interest and one in which greater confidence is warranted is the finding that the estimate of the impact of *baogan daohu* is far higher than just indicated if the crop mix variable is excluded from the regression.

The greater impact of the crop mix variable and the smaller impact of decollectivization in the Dahe analysis seems attributable to at least two but possibly three main factors. First, the freedom to vary the crop mix probably had a larger than average impact on crop value at Dahe, given the township's high concentration on grain and cotton in the collective era and the above-average opportunities to grow melons, vegetables, and other high-value crops for the nearby urban market in the reform era. Second, the impact of decollectivization on agricultural efficiency may have been smaller than average, because collective farming may have functioned with greater efficiency at Dahe than in more typical localities which recorded more mediocre agricultural performance in the 1970s. Finally, measurement of crop mix by a value ratio in the Dahe study but by a sown area ratio in the province-level studies of Lin and Kim make their respective results somewhat incomparable, and without more information we cannot tell what impact this difference of operative measure might have had.

The economists whose work has been surveyed in this chapter appear to have made some progress in attacking the problem of quantifying the impact of decollectivization and measuring its contribution to China's agricultural growth during the early reform period. There is little room for doubt, based on these studies, that the transition to household farming was associated with an increase in farm productivity large enough to explain a good deal of the crop output growth in China as a whole during 1978–1984. The magnitude of the effect of this change may well have varied among localities, ranging from rates approximating those based on the national regressions (15–22% in the year of introduction) in poor Anhui counties (Lin, 1987b) to 8% or less in a high grain-yield township such as Hebei's Dahe (Kim, 1990). There is evidence that the effects of reform might even have varied among crops (Kim's results on *lianchan jichou*). Nevertheless, the estimated effect on crop production as a whole is clearly positive in each case. What these empirical results do not allow us to do is to verify any particular explanation of this effect. Whether an improved link between effort and reward at the level of the producer, or some other factor such as the freeing of farmers to make decisions on the allocation of their labor time and of many other resources, accounts for the shift, cannot be determined from them. Supposing that the problem lay with the internal incentive system, there is also still the question of whether that problem was due to unsolvable difficulties with monitoring, or with constrained and incentive-dampening choices of distribution method. This final question is addressed in the Appendix.

Appendix to Chapter 7
Monitoring in the Collective Team:
Implications of McMillan, Whalley, and
Zhu's Study[1]

A central problem with the organization of team production is that if individual effort contributions are difficult to observe, feasible schemes for distributing the net product among participants may suffer from poor work incentives. Thus, Alchian and Demsetz (1972) argue that efficiency commonly requires that there be an agent who monitors and disciplines other team members in exchange for the right to retain team residual earnings, Holmström (1982) shows that monitoring may in some cases be disposed with, provided that there is a central agent who can perform a disciplinary and residual claiming function analogous to that of Alchian and Demsetz's monitor. These arguments imply that production in residual-sharing cooperative teams will be beset by free-rider problems occasioned by the inadequate reward discrimination which results from the absence of proper incentives to monitor and/or discipline other workers. Such disadvantages are thought to be multiplied in agricultural cooperatives, because farm production is considered especially difficult to monitor (Bradley and Clark, 1972; Stiglitz, 1974; Binswanger and Rosenzweig, 1986) and because scale economies, especially in labor-intensive systems, appear to be negligible (Putterman, 1989b).

The fact that restoration of household-based farming in early 1980s China led to a pronounced increase in output and productivity, has been viewed by some (e.g., Lin, 1988b; see also Nolan, 1988) as evidence in support of this thesis. Despite the studies discussed in Chapter 7, the degree to which the gains recorded during 1978–1984 reflected changes in farm level organization as opposed to being a result of policy changes in such areas as crop specialization, pricing, and opening of free markets, remains, as Perkins (1988) put it, a matter of some uncertainty. A more subtle question, however, is that of the extent to which any gains due to micro-

---

[1]This appendix incorporates the discussion in Putterman (1991), with minor amendments and additions.

organizational change should be attributed specifically to supervision problems of the type just mentioned. The contribution by McMillan, Whalley, and Zhu (1989; hereafter MWZ), which attempts to establish what share of the productivity gains from the reforms are due to the shift to household farming, has interesting and unstated implications regarding the question of monitoring and the observability of effort in China's collective era production teams.

As we have mentioned, MWZ combine a simple model of incentives and utility maximization with standard growth-accounting techniques and national-level data for the years 1978–1984 to reach the conclusion that 78% of the increase in agricultural productivity in China during the period in question can be attributed to non-price factors—principally "the incentive effects of the new responsibility system" (p. 782). But their model also provides a way to estimate the share of his or her marginal product which the individual farmer expected to receive under the collective system. Their results lead them to conclude that peasants expected to receive only about 30% of the value of output generated by incremental effort, and that each individual engaging in full-time farm work consequently supplied only a little over one-half (56%) as much effort under the communal system as under the household-based farming system that succeeded it. As mentioned in the chapter, MWZ's estimates depend on extremely aggregated data, specify the forms of production and utility functions by assumption, borrow estimates of the output elasticities from other studies, and attribute all productivity changes not due to the change in marginal output price to decollectivization, thus failing to allow for the effects of the change in product mix, of weather, or of technological change in the conventional sense. Although their extensive sensitivity testing shows that their results are fairly robust to changes in a number of the parameters included in their study, they may overestimate the impact of the change to household farming, and correspondingly underestimate the marginal incentives under collective farming, by lumping all productivity change other than the price response under the institutional reform heading.[2] In this appendix, it will be pointed out that if the conclusions of MWZ are correct, then although China's collective farms did indeed suffer from inadequate incentives, it may be wrong to attribute much of this to deficiencies in supervision. The essence of the argument is that even though earning 30% of one's marginal product is considerably less than receiving all of it, the marginal return to truly unobservable effort in a team of some sixty workers would be far smaller than 30%. Combined with the fact that a large part of team income was deliberately distributed on an equal basis, the 30% estimate may actually imply that observability conditions in the teams were rather good.

---

[2] On the other hand, as mentioned in footnote 18 of the chapter, alternative estimates based on a higher output elasticity of land raise the contribution to growth due to nonprice (i.e., institutional) factors as a whole. (See also footnote 4, below.) A second countervailing factor, the confounding of private and collective production, will be discussed toward the end of this appendix. MWZ undertake no sensitivity testing with respect to the form of their utility function, which may affect their estimate of marginal incentives in unknown ways.

The highly simplified equation used by MWZ to capture the change in the incentive system due to decollectivization is

$$y = \beta pq + c \tag{7A.1}$$

where y is individual income, p is the price on marginal output, q is per capita output, and β and c are constants. More specifically, β is "the fraction of the additional revenue generated that the peasant is allowed to keep" (p. 786), and although the microanalytic underpinnings of the claim are unclear for the case of the collective system, it is stated that

$$dy/d\ell_i = \beta pQ' \tag{7A.2}$$

where ℓ_i is worker i's effort, and Q' is marginal output.[3] Under household farming with fixed rents, β is assumed to equal one and c is assumed to be negative, while under the collective system β is expected to have been less than one and c to have been positive. Marginal incentives under household farming are therefore given by pQ'. As stated in the chapter, MWZ's strategy is to separate factor productivity from input-based growth in output by a conventional growth accounting technique. The factor productivity growth is then attributed to an increase in effort, and the respective contributions of higher prices and of strengthened marginal incentives, to eliciting that effort, are imputed by use of the first-order conditions for utility maximization. With the values of prices, output, and input quantities available in published data, and assuming the post-collective β to be one, the remaining unknown, which is the β for the collective period, can be imputed once the factor elasticities to serve as aggregation weights have been chosen and the utility function parameterized. The main estimate is that β was .3 in the collective period, meaning that the typical team member expected his or her earnings to rise by 30% of the value of the incremental product generated by any increase in his or her effort.[4]

---

[3] A problem with equations (7A.1) and (7A.2) is that they ignore the team character of production by implicitly assuming that an individual peasant produced a recognizable product. Under collective production, the anticipated effect of added effort on a worker's income would be through *group* total output, rather than average output, q. If Q is group total output, and $q = Q/N$, with N the number of workers in the group, equation (7A.1) would imply that the peasant keeps *one Nth* times β times the value of his marginal output (contrary to MWZ), because $dq/d\ell = (dQ/d\ell)/N$. Nonetheless, since the authors refer to (7A.1) as "a reduced form of a more complex reward structure" (p. 787), (7A.2) might be viewed in the same spirit, with the question for purposes of further analysis being how to interpret their model in terms of a more microanalytic one. This question is addressed below.

[4] As mentioned in footnote 18 of this chapter, MWZ's empirical analysis assumes factor weights (elasticities) that differ significantly from those in most of the estimates reported in this book. If a higher weight is given to land, the estimate of β tends to fall. For example, following the illustration begun in that note, let the elasticities of output with respect to labor, land, capital, and current inputs be assumed to be .1, .7, .1, and .1, respectively. Although the elasticity of output with respect to labor (MWZ's γ_1) affects the estimate of the utility curvature parameter z according to their equation (10) and the procedure described on p. 793 of their paper, it does not alter the full estimate of the exponent $(z - 1)/\gamma_1$ in that equation. Hence, it alters the estimate of β (in the terminology of equation (10), β_i or β_{1978}) only through its effect

MWZ do not identify the cause of low marginal incentives in the collective period. Two possible dampeners of incentives under team production, discussed in Chapter 5, are excessive equality of payments, and poor observability of individual effort. The MWZ model is not sufficiently microanalytic to distinguish between these two factors, but if linked to a more microanalytic model, their results can be made to do so. In particular, we will see how incentive models of the type discussed in Chapter 5 can be related to MWZ's marginal incentive equation (7A.2) to allow us to interpret their result in terms of such models.

We begin with a model in which effort is assumed to be observable. In the model, following Sen (1966), the portion of group net income received by the individual team member i is given by

$$y_i = [(\alpha/N) + (1 - \alpha)(\ell_i/L)]pQ \qquad (7A.3)$$

where $\alpha \in (0,1)$ is the share of net output distributed equally or "according to needs," $(1 - \alpha)$ is the share distributed "according to work," N is the number of team members, L is group total effort

$$L = \sum_{i=1}^{N} \ell_i$$

and pQ is output value net of nonlabor costs of production. In this case, if we assume that workers have Cournot-Nash beliefs regarding the interdependence of effort supplies (i.e., $d\ell_j/d\ell_i t = 0$, all $j \neq i$) and that each supplies the same amount of effort ex post, the payout to individual effort on the margin is

$$dy_i/d\ell_i = (1 /N)pQ' + (1 - \alpha)[(N-1)/ N](pQ/L) \qquad (7A.4)$$

(7A.4) resembles (7A.2) in that the worker receives a share of his marginal value product, but this share would be very small when N is sixty or more workers, as was typical for Chinese rural production teams. As will be familiar from Chapter 5, however, there is an added term in (7A.4) which is positive when at least some income is distributed according to labor shares. Apart from the values of α and N, the size of this term is determined by labor's *average net (revenue) product* (ANRP), here pQ/L. Given the size of Chinese production teams, MWZ's finding of $\beta = 0.3$ suggests that workers anticipated receiving, on the margin, a not insignificant fraction of their average net product (i.e., the value of work-points) in return for

---

on the estimate of the change in total factor productivity. With a larger weight on land, the only input the supply of which declined over the period, the estimated increase in total factor productivity rises, so the estimate of β falls, to .208. This would lead to a somewhat more pessimistic assessment of the seriousness of the monitoring problem, following the approach taken in this appendix (below). Consequences for MWZ's sources of growth analysis were discussed in the chapter note.

incremental effort. The relationship between our model and that of MWZ can be neatly summarized if we assume a fixed relationship between marginal and average net product at equilibrium—say $(Q/L)/Q' = X$. Then, setting (7A.4) = (7A.2), we have

$$\beta = (1/N)[1 + (1 - \alpha)(N - 1) X] \tag{7A.5}$$

which implies that (a) β exceeds $1/N$ whenever $\alpha < 1$ and $N > 1$, (b) β approaches unity, for $X = 1$, as α goes to zero, and (c) since X may in fact exceed one, so also can β. On the other hand, (d) β falls as α becomes larger or X becomes smaller.[5]

Now the model just discussed assumes effort to be perfectly observed. To see how consistent MWZ's findings are with that assumption, we introduce potential observability problems into the model, considering first the "random sampling" type depiction of monitoring familiar from efficiency wage models such as Shapiro and Stiglitz (1984). The worker is observed perfectly with probability ρ, and is not observed at all with probability $(1 - \rho)$. Individual payment in a cooperative can accordingly be given by[6]

$$y_i = \begin{array}{ll} (1 - \alpha)(\ell_i/L)pQ + \alpha pQ/N & \text{with probability } \rho \\ pQ/N & \text{with probability } (1 - \rho) \end{array} \tag{7A.6}$$

If we maintain the Cournot-Nash assumption and that of identical ex post effort, the expected marginal return to individual effort is

$$dE(y_i)/d\ell_i = (pQ'/N) + (1 - \alpha)\rho[(N - 1)/N](pQ/L) \tag{7A.7}$$

where (Roman) E is the expectation operator. (7A.7) differs from (7A.4) solely by inclusion of ρ in the second RHS term. Setting (7A.7) equal to (7A.2) yields a new analogue of (7A.5),

$$\beta = (1/N)[1 + (1 - \alpha)\rho(N - 1)X] \tag{7A.8}$$

---

[5] If Q' first increases and then decreases with L, as in Figure 5.1, X will be an increasing function of L, and large X may be indicative of a high population to nonlabor resource ratio. Treating X as fixed in the incentive function holds only as an approximation, in this case. On the other hand, as pointed out by a referee of the note on which this appendix is based, for a Cobb-Douglas production function X is a constant, equal to the reciprocal of the exponent on labor. In this case, β is higher (by (7A.5)) the smaller is the elasticity of output with respect to labor.

[6] A referee suggested that a more realistic reward function would be asymmetrical, entailing penalties for observed "shirking" but no reward for working more than a prescribed amount. This could be captured by letting the prescribed effort level be ℓ^* and rewriting the top part of the RHS of (7A.6) as $\max[(1 - \alpha)(\ell_i/L)pQ + \alpha pQ/N, (1 - \alpha)(\ell^*/L)pQ + \alpha pQ/N]$. It can be demonstrated that such a model gives even stronger results than that considered in the text, since the average value of $dE(y_i)/d\ell_i$ declines in this case if optimal ℓ_i for the symmetrical model is greater than ℓ^* for some members of the cooperative.

which indicates that reduced probability of observation has the same effect as increased "distribution according to needs." We might say that while setting a high α makes payment egalitarian by design, having a low ρ makes it egalitarian "by default."[7] This depiction conforms to the intuition of the observability and monitoring explanation of incentive failure in group production, in that poor monitoring has an immediate incentive-dampening impact, and should lead to a reduction of voluntarily selected effort levels. Furthermore, as the probability of individual variations in effort being detected goes to zero, β in (7A.8) goes to $1/N$, consistent with the incentive failure view that a worker in a collective production team receives exactly $1/N$th of his or her marginal product.

The basic logic of our inquiry should now be clear. Although MWZs estimate that team members received "only" 30% of their marginal product suggests that incentives stood to be improved by a transition to household farming, in which family members were claimants to 100% of their marginal (or residual) product, it is also at odds with the notion that effort observability was extremely poor, because for $N = 60$, β approaches .017, roughly one-twentieth of 30%, as ρ approaches zero. Thus, the $\beta = .3$ result implies immediately that there was substantial, if perhaps still imperfect, observability of effort in the teams, assuming that the "random sampling" approach offers a reasonable depiction of the problem. The main difficulty is that once ρ is accepted as positive, equation (7A.8) shows that intentional egalitarianism in distribution (α) and the average/marginal product gap (X) cut in opposite directions in determining what value of ρ is implied by a given estimate of β. Since intentional egalitarianism undercuts monitoring from an incentive standpoint, it is clear that the higher was α, the better must monitoring have been for any given value of β to be obtained. But with positive ρ (and $\alpha < 1$), a higher than expected value of β can also partly result from the positive weight placed on the average net product of labor in the distribution formula. If the average net product of labor is many times larger than the value of the marginal product and intentional egalitarianism of distribution is not great, only a modest degree of observability would be required to make the marginal payout a substantial fraction of that marginal product, causing β to be relatively large.

These countervailing considerations can be illustrated and a rough quantitative sense of the implications of MWZs findings can be obtained by assigning values of α and X based on available data and accounts of the collective system. Based on material discussed in previous chapters or available in other sources, we can form a number of estimates of the ratio of the value of the average net product of labor to the value of the marginal product of labor in Chinese collective agriculture. Estimates of

---

[7]Of course, if ρ can be influenced by monitoring effort, this way of phrasing the matter is somewhat misleading, since ρ is then also a choice variable. Note also that α could have been high not only because of the design of officials, but also because of the operation of social dynamics internal to the teams, in which case egalitarianism could be viewed as endogenous to the institution of group farming, and not an exogenous policy choice. It is nonetheless conceptually important to distinguish between such egalitarianism and observability problems as such.

the VMP of Dahe Commune team members' labor in agricultural and nonagricultural sectors combined presented in Chapter 5 range from about Y 82 to Y 143 (Tables 5.2 and 5.3). Although the production function from which these estimates are derived is a "behavioral" one (i.e., it includes institutional variables) and may therefore fail to accurately reflect the production technology as such, and although these estimates for the combined crop and noncrop sectors show markedly lower coefficients on land as compared with others in this study, the estimates of labor's VMP overlap the broader range of separate estimates for the crop and sideline (noncrop) sectors reported in Tables 4.3 and 4.5 of Chapter 4, and can accordingly be viewed as plausible. Indeed, the estimates resemble a weighted average of the crop and sideline sector marginal products of labor reported by Wiemer (Table 4.3), with a greater weight on agriculture being appropriate given its larger share of the labor force. Applying the 1980 shares of Dahe teams' labor in agriculture and nonagricultural sectors (Table 3.3) to Wiemer's 1979 estimates of labor's marginal products in the crop and sideline sectors gives a high estimate of Y 199 for the average marginal product of labor at Dahe. For present purposes, ANRP is simply the per worker income in cash and kind paid out to team members.[8] Table 3.2 of Chapter 3 shows this distributed income to have varied during the 1970s at Dahe from about Y 74 to Y 129 per capita, with an average of Y 95 per capita during 1974–1979, the years included in the Chapter 5 estimates. Using the 1975 ratio of .379 workers per family member at Dahe, this converts to Y 251.[9] Combining the VMP and ANRP estimates gives a range from about 1.3 to about 3.0 for the ratio X.

Alternative estimates come from national and provincial data. Estimating a standard Cobb-Douglas production function for the years 1980–1983, using the province-level data used by Lin (1987a), we obtain an estimated average VMP of about Y 88.[10] Reported per capita peasant agricultural income ranged from Y 150 to Y 222 in that period, income per working member of peasant households would have been about 2.25 times as high, but 35–40% should be deducted to correspond to private plot and nondistributed collective income in the collective period.[11] The estimate of ratio X is thus between 2.3 and 3.7. Last, using the estimated elasticity of labor from column (3) of Table 7.1 (from Lin, 1992) and data in the *China Statistical Yearbook,* the VMP of crop sector labor in 1978 is roughly estimated at Y 63,[12] in

---

[8]In Chapter 5, the concept of ANRP was used in a *per effort unit* sense.

[9]The figure of Y 216 used for comparison with Wiemer's VMP estimates in Chapter 4 is based on the longer 1970–1979 period.

[10]All inputs and output are as in Lin (1987a). Computations used the data tabulated by that author.

[11]One-quarter to one-third of peasant agricultural income in the collective period was from private plots and household husbandry activities. Since some of the figures here are generated by units already practicing household farming, a further deduction is required to account for the fact that households in the post-collective era retained some of the income that would have been held by their teams during the collective era, for which X is to be computed.

[12]Lin (1992) does not present his data in natural units, and time constraints prevented a more precise calculation from his original sources. We use overall agricultural labor force (p. 142) multiplied by the crop sector share of GVAO (p. 180), convert gross value of crop output (p. 180) to 1980 prices using the general index of purchasing prices of farm and sideline products (p. 692), then multiply by the share of Lin's 19 crops in GVCO in 1980 (72.5%) (all page numbers from State Statistical Bureau, 1988).

1980 prices, while rural net income per capita for 1978 is given by the *China Statistical Yearbook* as Y 133.[13] Shaving 40% from this figure for income from sectors outside of Lin's 19 crops and for private plot income, and multiplying by 2.25 to translate to per worker terms and by 1.30 to convert to 1980 prices, gives an estimate of roughly 3.7 for the ratio X. We consider a range of values for X going from 1.5 to 3.7.[14]

The degree of egalitarian distribution not attributable to poor monitoring is less readily established. Formally, only a small fraction of team output was distributed to indigent households without regard to work contributed. In most teams, however, the bulk of distribution took the form of an in-kind rationing of grain and other basic goods, on an age- and sex-adjusted per capita basis. As we have seen, while the nominal value of these goods was debited against households' work-points, the procedure still generated an egalitarian bias because (a) the accounting value used was far below the scarcity value of the items distributed, and (b) in poor teams, many households' work-point earnings did not cover their distributions, but they were permitted to owe the unpaid amount to the team indefinitely, without interest. As Nolan (1988) concludes, "in poor areas where most collective income was absorbed by grain consumption, adherence to party guidelines led to the bulk of personal income being allocated "according to need" with all the incentive problems that this involved" (Nolan, 1988, p. 57).[15] In addition, a very narrow range of differentiation of work-points resulted from ideological pressures and the group decision process mandated by Maoist leaders (Parish and Whyte, 1978; Chan et al., 1984). To quote Nolan again, "the range of work-point differentials was so small as to constitute a serious barrier to effective work incentives in the collective sector" (Nolan, 1988, p. 58). If variations in effort were registered on a narrow scale not because they were not perceived or observable, but for political and ideological reasons of the types discussed by those authors, this would constitute another bias toward egalitarianism *of noninformational origin*.

Suppose that the share of net collective distribution permitted to reflect differences in work contributions was no more than 20–40%, on average.[16] Letting X

---

[13]Lin (1992, p. 732).

[14]The main reason why the high end of this range extends above that used in Putterman (1991), is that some of the computations there neglected to convert per capita income to per worker terms.

[15]The same point was made by Luo Xiaopeng, former leading member of the Research Center for Rural Development (Beijing), at the Fairbank Center Rural China Workshop, Harvard University, December 20, 1991.

[16]In Chapter 5, we reported that 60–80% of distributed grain was apportioned on the basis of household population, and that grain accounted for an average of 74% of distributed income at internal accounting values, in Dahe teams in the 1970s. This would put α between .44 and .59 using those values and assuming that this grain distribution was viewed as free, rather than as a deduction from work-points. A large gap between the internal and local market prices of grain would suffice to shift this band up to the .6 to .8 band assumed in the illustrations. Effective and clearly understood deduction of grain disbursements from work-point entitlements would work in the opposite direction, but egalitarianism in the assessment of work-points, of which further evidence is given in Chapter 10, could neutralize this factor. Finally, Nolan's and Luo's arguments imply that α tended to be lower for richer units, so assuming an average α for China somewhat higher than that implied by the data for Dahe may be justified.

Table 7A.1. Monitoring Efficiency (ρ) as a Function of Egalitarian Distribution (α) and the ANRP/VMP Ratio (X)

	ρ	
α	X = 1.5	X = 3.7
0.6	0.48	0.19
0.8	0.96	0.39

range from 1.5 to 3.7, letting α range from 0.6 to 0.8, and letting $N = 60$, means that ρ, by equation (7A.8), would have fallen in the range 0.19–0.96, as shown in Table 7A.1. This suggests that observability was not nearly so bad as to generate a situation of de facto intra-team equality, as strong statements of the observability thesis have argued.[17] Indeed, these numbers leave open the possibility that there was no observability problem to speak of, only a problem of egalitarianism generated by in-kind rationing and narrow work-point differentials of noninformational origin. If, on the other hand, the share of payment according to work is construed to have been higher, say 60% or 70%, then MWZ's results have less sanguine implications for the team monitoring problem, but they are still quite inconsistent with the assumption that individual effort was nearly unobservable.[18]

Chapter 5 noted that there are other ways of depicting an observability problem, and these may lead to different conclusions.[19] For example, it was shown there that if poor observability takes the form of work-points that are unbiased estimates of true effort levels but with a variance that increases with the degree of imperfection of monitoring, then the effort levels of risk-neutral workers are unaffected by the quality of monitoring. Under the same depiction of observability, risk-averse workers characterized by nonincreasing absolute risk aversion (NIARA) are found to work *harder* the poorer is the quality of monitoring. The MWZ result is difficult to interpret in this context, since the model of those authors assumes risk-neutrality. If workers were in fact significantly risk-averse (and NIARA) and monitoring functioned

---

[17]See, for example, the "worst case" treatment, along these lines, by Carter (1987), who assumes that informational problems cause the cooperative member to act as if the expected to receive exactly $1/N$ times his marginal product (and no more). See also Lin (1987a, 1988b.)

[18]In a similar vein, MWZ's calculations lump together the small share of output produced on private plots and sidelines with the larger share produced collectively. Since their estimate of β is accordingly to be understood as the "average" marginal incentive of both private and collective operations, the value of β in the collective sector itself, which is the one to which the present analysis applies, should be adjusted downward from 0.3. We can readily adapt our microanalytic model to allow for a private sector (see, e.g., Putterman, 1980; and Putterman and DiGiorgio, 1985); however, the modified model would lack a closed form solution for β, which makes it difficult to know how seriously this factor would affect matters.

[19]Whereas MWZ's and my analyses condense both time and effort into the variable ℓ, a possibility not explored in this note is to model these two dimensions as distinct variables, the first being easy and the second very difficult to observe. The incentive to over-exertion assuming high X and low α in Sen-type models might then apply to work hours, but not to effort. It is not clear what additional insight might be derived from unbundling the two variables.

according to the present depiction, poorer monitoring would presumably have led to the imputation of a *higher* value of β than under risk-neutrality or perfect observability. Thus, high β would not imply good monitoring, as it did under the "random sampling" depiction of monitoring technology, but poor monitoring would have increased, rather than reduced, effort.[20] In a word, this alternative depiction of the observability problem does not support the observability-based explanation of incentive weakness in the teams regardless of the imputation about the level of marginal incentives.

[20]Note that team members would have a demand for costly monitoring as a means of raising their utility if not their incomes, under this set-up.

8

Household Factor Allocation and
Administrative Intervention in the
Post-Collective Era:
A Simulation Analysis*

In Chapter 4, we reported Wiemer's finding, from an analysis of Dahe's team accounts, that the marginal productivities of factors of production were significantly higher in sidelines than in crop production activities in the 1970s. Our attempt to extend her analysis into the post-collective period met up with serious problems of data availability and quality, but the results appeared to point in a similar direction. If the decollectivization of China's agriculture, the reopening of rural markets, and the releasing of rural labor to pursue profitable nonfarm opportunities constituted a transition to a market-based economy, in line with the portrayal of the reforms by some journalists and casual observers, the second set of results would appear to be puzzling. Following the reforms, households should have allocated their resources to the activities promising the highest returns, and the value of the marginal product of each transferable factor should have been the same in all activities undertaken by a given set of households. In the present chapter, we revisit the question of intersectoral factor allocation using the data generated by surveys of households in five of Dahe's production teams. In the first instance, the analysis parallels that of Chapter 4 by undertaking direct estimation of crop and sideline production functions, this time at the household level. This direct evidence is consistent with that based on the team data, again showing a large gap between returns in crop and noncrop activities.

In addition to intersectoral allocation of the transferable factors of production, this chapter focuses on the interhousehold allocation of agricultural land. Many Chinese economists have argued that a source of inefficiency in the post-Mao system has been the relatively egalitarian distribution of land contracts to households, and the absence of a market to allocate land to its most productive user.[1] Some have also argued that land use is overly fragmented, and that increasing farm productivity

---

*This chapter is jointly authored by Woosung Park, Kyung-Hee University, and Louis Putterman.
[1]For a review of opinions on this subject, see Christiansen (1987). The issues are again discussed in the next chapter, where the impact of egalitarian allocation is analyzed using team-level data.

requires the concentration of farm land into substantially larger, and possibly more mechanized, farms. In the villages from which our data were obtained, however, use of large machinery in key farm operations survived despite decollectivization, and scattering was minimized, because households were allocated sections of larger, contiguous fields, and because variations in soil characteristics were small. Our production function estimates provide no evidence of scale economies in the farm operations performed by households, and, on the contrary, suggest some diseconomies of scale despite the fact that the average household, which had 4.2 working members, cultivated just under 1 acre (0.4 ha) in 1985.

The present chapter takes a methodological step beyond the analysis of Chapter 4. A model of optimal factor allocation by households is constructed, and the model is calibrated with the Dahe household data by assigning the estimated production functions to the households, each of which retains its reported population, labor force, land endowment, and capital stock. Preferences for leisure versus income are also imputed to each household from their observed behavior and using an assumed functional form for household utility. Households are then permitted to optimize with respect to the allocation of labor, capital, and purchased inputs, and the results are compared with observed allocations. The exercises generate evidence that households operated under a binding crop production constraint, for most households fail to produce at the observed levels of 1985 when unconstrained allocation is assumed. An iterative search is then used to identify a hypothetical price at which observed crop output would be elicited voluntarily, and the efficiency of production under the price-induced solution is compared with that under a binding production requirement.

The simulation model is likewise used to explore the question of inter-household allocation of land. We simulate operation of a land market in which households can sublet land to or from others at a competitively determined rent. The result fails to indicate land concentration, and, on the contrary, entails a somewhat more equal distribution of land among households.

When the simulated subrental market operates without a crop output requirement, we also find that crop output declines, rather than rising, when the market operates. This appears to provide a warning that a more efficient allocation of land will not address the government's concerns about raising farm output in the absence of an adequate price structure. Finally, the analysis shows that the scarcity rent on land was far higher than the sum of the obligations paid by households, on the margin, and that in the absence of a market in land use rights or of appropriately adjusted land charges, households had no incentive to divest themselves of land they were inclined to work with relatively low intensity, and they enjoyed an implicit subsidy from society in the form of access to land at a nominal charge even as they paid an implicit tax in the form of contracted grain and cotton deliveries. Although partly neutralizing each other from a distributive standpoint, the simultaneous subsidy and tax can be argued to have had a seriously negative impact on the efficiency of rural resource allocation.

One way to check the accuracy of the model of household behavior which we employ is to simulate optimization in the face of all known contraints and compare the results with actually observed household behavior. If the model performs well, there should be no major difference between them. In the event, however, the optimal solution of the model differs from observed behavior in at least one important way. When households are assumed to match observed agricultural output, but are allowed to freely allocate labor and capital and to purchase (composite) current inputs in unrestricted quantities at the observed price, optimal household production of nonfarm sideline products and services is over four times the actually observed level, thanks to a massive increase in purchases of the latter inputs. Use of purchased inputs to meet agricultural production requirements also expands dramatically, replacing most labor and capital inputs. This finding might be interpreted as confirming reports that some of the purchased inputs were not, in fact, freely available at the prices at which they were obtained by households. Alternatively, their purchase may have had to be financed at very high interest rates. Evidence bearing on the second explanation was also obtained in a related, dynamic simulation, and will be reported in connection with our discussion of this finding.

In the course of our analysis, a number of simplifying assumptions must be introduced. While these will be discussed in some detail as we proceed, some of the more serious ones should be mentioned at the outset. First, due to the lack of sufficiently disaggregated input data, farm production must be treated, unrealistically, as a homogeneous activity, which means lumping commercial crops together with grain and cotton, grown primarily on state contract and for self-consumption. Second, unreliability of our data on capital allocation between farm and nonfarm activities forces us to impute that allocation, for the initial situation, as part of the process of production function estimation. Finally, our simulation encompasses two but largely ignores a third important sector of economic activity at Dahe Township discussed in Chapter 3, namely the collective and publicly owned enterprises in which some household members earned incomes as wage-earners.

In the next section, we introduce our model of household and village economic behavior under China's agricultural production responsibility system. We then discuss data problems and the estimation of the household production and utility functions. Next, we compute optimal household behavior based on the household data, parameter estimates, and model, first taking the observed agricultural output as a binding minimum, and then without that constraint. This is followed by the exercise in which we find the price at which the grain contracts are fulfilled voluntarily, in the aggregate, and we illustrate the inefficiency of meeting the target by administrative rather than price means. Finally, we examine the operation of a market for land sub-rental, and we present our conclusions.

Household Model

In Chapter 5, we looked at some models focusing on individual or household choice of effort within the context of a *collective* farming system. While some partial models of the new *household* farming system in China have been formulated to assist inquiries into the income distribution and incentive features of that system, more complete models specifying linkages between households in a village setting and incorporating the role of contractual and other production constraints appear to be lacking.

The need for special models of China's new rural economy can be questioned, since as household farming with a fixed rent obligation to the state and collective, the system should be suited to analysis using either standard models of a private farm economy, or models of the peasant producer-consumer household in an incomplete market setting, of the type introduced in the economic development literature of recent years.[2] Nevertheless, in order to examine the effects of policy alternatives such as changes in agricultural prices or the opening of a market to sublet land use rights, it is useful to write down an explicit model of peasant household behavior, and of interactions among households in the same market area. Such a model is meant to be altered to account for changing institutional constraints, and to be studied not through theoretical general equilibrium analysis, but by the method of computer simulation.

As is common in models of this genre, the household itself is taken as the main decision-making unit. The usual qualms with respect to intra-household decison-making, distribution, etc., may be valid, but are not explicitly treated, for reasons of tractability. A given household, indexed i, begins with a labor force, n^i, and a total population, $m^i \geqslant n^i$, that are taken as given. It receives use rights to l_i^o hectares of land, this area being related to the land endowment of its former production team, and to its own working and dependent population. In exchange for these rights, it is obligated to pay state agricultural tax and a fee to the collective unit (in 1985, the former production brigade, now called village), the sum of these being r_c yuan per hectare, and to sell a certain amount of produce (in practice, specified as grain and/or cotton, but in our analysis treated as units of homogeneous output) to the state. It also has an endowment of k^i yuan worth of capital goods (derived in part from past partition of collective capital goods, in part from savings out of the earnings of enterprise workers and the profits of household enterprises in the early post-collective period) which it may use in either agricultural or nonagricultural production activities.

Two ways of using available labor time and capital to earn household income are modeled. In crop production, the household uses contracted land, plus labor, capital, and purchased current inputs, to produce output for self-consumption, for sale to the state, for sale in the free market, and for the feeding of livestock. We abstract from many of the complexities of the operation of this sector, and treat its inputs and product as homogeneous. Total crop production, in value terms, is given by the function

---

[2]On the latter, see papers in Singh et al. (1986), Bardhan (1989), Braverman et al. (forthcoming), and the literature survey in Ellis (1988).

$$g^i = g(h_c^i, l_o^i, k_c^i, z_c^i) \tag{8.1}$$

where subscript c indicates input units allocated to crop production, and where h stands for labor and z for current inputs. Net income from the sector is given by

$$y_c^i = g(h_c^i, l_o^i, k_c^i, z_c^i) - r_c l_c^i - p_z z_c^i \tag{8.2}$$

where p_z is the price of current inputs, including financing costs.

In the other sector, *sideline* activities, households combine labor, capital, and purchased current inputs, to produce noncrop products and services, including pigs, poultry, and eggs, transportation and building services, noodles, beancurd, handicraft products, and commercial services. These activities are essentially unregulated, and taxation of earnings was at a rudimentary stage of development in 1985.[3] Sideline sector output, also in value terms, is given by

$$f^i = f(h_s^i, k_s^i, z_s^i) \tag{8.3}$$

where subscript s indicates input units allocated to sideline production. Net sideline income is thus

$$y_s^i = f(h_s^i, k_s^i, z_s^i) - p_z z_s^i \tag{8.4}$$

Labor, capital, and current inputs, are each treated as homogeneous, across as well as within the two sectors, but initially there are no markets for labor, land, or capital linking behavior across households.[4]

A third sector of the rural economy brings income to many of the households from which our survey data are obtained, but is not explicitly modeled by us. This is employment in wage-paying jobs, primarily in enterprises owned by the county government, the state, or the township and villages, but also in private individual and partnership enterprises. Although the decision to seek and accept employment in this sector is voluntary on the part of the household or its members, the allocation of other factors to it is not under the control of the households studied, and as a first approximation, the distribution of jobs to household members, may be taken as given, from the standpoint of the household's internal resource allocation. We go further, in the present version of our model, and ignore the sector, those working in it, and their incomes, entirely.[5]

---

[3]In the empirical work that follows, we treat the actual payment of taxes by a small number of household enterprises as part of current inputs.

[4]On the relative inactivity of these markets in rural China, see Lin (1988a). As mentioned, we simulate operation of a land market in a later section.

[5]This may influence the calibration of household utility functions which are based on the observed behavior of those employed in the two modeled sectors only, and on household population minus wage employees. However, we would not expect significant changes in qualitative findings to flow from this factor. Note that there was no reported hiring of labor for either agricultural or sideline enterprises of the households in our survey.

Each household is viewed as maximizing its utility, which is an increasing function of its total income and of the average leisure time of its working members. The two arguments of the utility function are treated as additively separable, and the function is taken to be concave in each argument, with the log form being specified to simplify parameterization. To assure that households having more members to feed will supply more labor, *ceteris paribus*, the marginal utility of income is made to vary positively with m^i by entering the latter multiplicatively in the term for utility from income.[6] Households are assumed to vary in their relative preferences over income and leisure. Specifically, they are assumed to maximize

$$U^i = \frac{m^i}{a^i} \log y^i + \log \left(\frac{n^i T - h_c^i - h_s^i}{n^i} \right) \tag{8.5}$$

where a^i is the index of preference for leisure, $y^i = y_c^i + y_s^i$ is household total income, and T is time endowment per worker.

From the outset, we consider two variants of our model. The first is as already set out. In the second variant, households face a minimum production constraint in the crop sector

$$g^i \geqslant \hat{g}^i \tag{8.6}$$

Such a constraint may be thought of as reflecting state sales requirements and self-provision of subsistence needs, but since g subsumes *all* crop output and is assumed homogeneous, the correspondence is not precise (see below). These two variants lead to two sets of solutions to the maximization of (8.5). Consider first the case in which constraint (8.6) is imposed. The maximization problem may be rewritten as

$$\max_{h_s^i, k_c^i, z^i} = U^i + \lambda(g^i - \hat{g}^i) \tag{8.7}$$

subject to (8.1), (8.2), (8.3), and (8.4), where U^i is as given by (8.5) and λ is the Lagrange multiplier associated with constraint (8.6). The solution of (8.7) can be written as the Kuhn-Tucker conditions:

[6]The same result may follow for the household welfare function of Sen (1966b), which for the case of equal sharing of work among workers and of income among members is $W = \Sigma u(y/m) - \Sigma v(h_c + h_s)$, in the present notation, with the summations being over household members and with $u' > 0$, $u'' \geqslant 0$, $v' \leqslant 0$, and $v'' \leqslant 0$. The requirement is that the second inequality hold strictly. The opposite result would follow from the utility function $U = u(y/m, [nT - h_c - h_s]/n)$ discussed by Rosenzweig (1988): here, effort per worker declines as m rises, since the impact of incremental income on household utility is smaller for larger m. Although a reader of an earlier version of this chapter has suggested that it would be more symmetrical to substitute y/m for y in (8.5), the equation in its present form has the properties required by us, and imputation of the a^i parameter specific to each household in the simulation exercise should suffice to assure local correspondence between the resulting utility function and that lying behind actual behavior. Models of labor supply and demographic differentiation are reviewed by Ellis (1988).

$$\frac{\partial L^i}{\partial h_c^i} = \frac{m^i}{a^i} \cdot \frac{1}{y^i} \cdot \frac{\partial g^i}{\partial h_c^i} - \frac{1}{n^i T - h_c^i - h_s^i} + \lambda^i \frac{\partial g^i}{\partial h_c^i} = 0 \qquad (8.8)$$

$$\frac{\partial L^i}{\partial h_s^i} = \frac{m^i}{a^i} \cdot \frac{1}{y^i} \cdot \frac{\partial f^i}{\partial h_s^i} - \frac{1}{n^i T - h_c^i - h_s^i} = 0 \qquad (8.9)$$

$$\frac{\partial L^i}{\partial k_c^i} = \frac{m^i}{a^i} \cdot \frac{1}{y^i} \cdot \left(\frac{\partial g^i}{\partial k_c^i} - \frac{\partial f^i}{\partial k_s^i}\right) + \lambda^i \frac{\partial g^i}{\partial k_c^i} = 0 \qquad (8.10)$$

$$\frac{\partial L^i}{\partial z_c^i} = \frac{m^i}{a^i} \cdot \frac{1}{y^i} \cdot \left(\frac{\partial g^i}{\partial z_c^i} - p_z\right) + \lambda^i \frac{\partial g^i}{\partial z_c^i} = 0 \qquad (8.11)$$

$$\frac{\partial L^i}{\partial z_s^i} = \frac{m^i}{a^i} \cdot \frac{1}{y^i} \cdot \left(\frac{\partial f^i}{\partial z_s^i} - p_z\right) = 0 \qquad (8.12)$$

$$\frac{\partial L^i}{\partial \lambda^i} = g^i - \hat{g}^i \geq 0, \ \lambda \geq 0 \text{ and } \lambda^i \cdot \frac{\partial L^i}{\partial \lambda^i} = 0 \qquad (8.13)$$

If the optimized contract output is larger than the state quota, λ is equal to zero by (8.13) and we have an interior solution. In this case the first-order conditions are:

$$\frac{\partial g^i}{\partial h_c^i} = y^i \cdot \frac{a^i}{m^i} \cdot \frac{1}{(n^i T \ ed - h_c^i - h_s^i)} \qquad (8.14)$$

$$\frac{\partial f^i}{\partial h_s^i} = y^i \cdot \frac{a^i}{m^i} \cdot \frac{1}{(n^i T - h_c^i - h_s^i)} \qquad (8.15)$$

$$\frac{\partial g^i}{\partial k_c^i} = \frac{\partial f^i}{\partial k_s^i} \qquad (8.16)$$

$$\frac{\partial g^i}{\partial z_c^i} = p_z \qquad (8.17)$$

$$\frac{\partial f^i}{\partial z_s^i} = p_z \qquad (8.18)$$

This case is identical to that in which constraint (8.6) does not exist at all. If the optimized contract output is less than the state quota, λ is greater than zero by (8.13) and we have a boundary solution. In this case, the household produces only the amount of the state quota in the contract sector. The resulting first-order conditions are:

$$\frac{\partial g^i}{\partial h_c^i} = y^i \cdot \frac{a^i}{m^i} \cdot \frac{1}{(n^i T - h_c^i - h_s^i)} \cdot \frac{m^i}{m^i + a^i \ y^i \lambda^i} \qquad (8.19)$$

$$\frac{\partial f^i}{\partial h_s^i} = y^i \cdot \frac{a^i}{m^i} \cdot \frac{1}{(n^i T - h_c^i - h_s^i)} \tag{8.20}$$

$$\frac{\partial g^i}{\partial k_c^i} = \frac{\partial f^i}{\partial k_s^i} \cdot \frac{m^i}{m^i + a^i y^{\,i} \lambda^i} \tag{8.21}$$

$$\frac{\partial g^i}{\partial z_c^i} = p_z \cdot \frac{m^i}{m^i + a^i y^{\,i} \lambda^i} \tag{8.22}$$

$$\frac{\partial f^i}{\partial z_s^i} = p_z \tag{8.23}$$

$$g^i(h_c^i, k_c^i, l_o^i, z_c^i) = \hat{g}^i \tag{8.24}$$

First, note the first-order conditions of the interior solution. Equations (8.14) and (8.15) state that the household supplies labor up to the point at which the increase in utility caused by the additional labor input in each production sector is equal to the decrease in utility resulting from the reduced amount of leisure, and that labor is allocated between the two sectors so that the marginal productivity of labor is the same in both sectors. Thus the household's time is allocated in a globally optimal fashion. Equation (8.16) gives the condition for the optimal allocation of capital between the two sectors. The choice of current inputs is optimal when the marginal productivities are equal to the opportunity cost of a unit of current inputs, as shown by equations (8.17) and (8.18).

Now, consider the maximization conditions of the boundary solution. Here the household will produce only the assigned amount in the contract sector. The rule for allocating factor inputs between the two sectors can be obtained from equations (8.19)–(8.24).

$$\frac{\frac{\partial g}{\partial h_c^i}}{\frac{\partial f}{\partial h_s^i}} = \frac{\frac{\partial g}{\partial k_c^i}}{\frac{\partial f}{\partial k_s^i}} = \frac{\frac{\partial g}{\partial z_c^i}}{\frac{\partial f}{\partial z_s^i}} = \frac{m^i}{m^i + a^i y^i \lambda^i} \leq 1 \tag{8.25}$$

The rule requires that the ratio of marginal products between the two sectors be identical for all factor inputs. Note that we have an interior solution when the ratio is equal to one, and that in the boundary solution in which the crop output constraint is binding, the marginal product of each factor is smaller in crop production than in sidelines. Note also that even in that case, efficiency is attained only from the standpoint of the individual household. The immobility of factor inputs across households implies that resources are not allocated efficiently within the community as a whole.

Table 8.1. Characteristics of Sample Households in 1985

	Mean	**S.D.**
Area farmed	0.404 ha.	0.150 ha.
Total capital goods (value)	Y 1,297.1	Y 4,537.5
Number of hshold members	5.5	2.1
Number of working members	4.2	2.0
Current inputs, crop sector	Y 391.5	Y 156.7
Current inputs, sideline sector	Y 845.0	Y 3,341.8
Gross income, crop sector	Y 1,873.0	Y 793.1
Gross income, sideline sector	Y 1,780.4	Y 2,250.2

Household Survey Data and Calibration of the Model

In our simulation analysis, household behavior is examined using the Dahe township household survey of 1986. The survey data, which have reference to activity in 1985, were used to construct our portrait of Dahe in Chapter 3 and are used extensively again in Chapter 10 to study income distribution. (Data for the same households in 1979 were the basis for the analysis in Chapter 6.) Two hundred twenty-one households provided data sufficient for inclusion in this analysis. Basic characteristics of those households are summarized in Table 8.1.

In our simulations, each household is modeled using its actually reported values of household population, labor force, and total capital stock. Households are assumed to choose production plans from fully specified crop and sideline sector production functions common to the whole sample. For simplicity, these are assumed to take the Cobb-Douglas form:[7]

$$f^i = e^{\alpha_0}(h_s^i)^{\alpha_1}(k_s^i)^{\alpha_2}(z_s^i)^{\alpha_3} \qquad (8.26)$$

$$g^i = e^{\beta_0}(h_c^i)^{\beta_1}(l_o^i)^{\beta_2}(k_c^i)^{\beta_3}(z_c^i)^{\beta_4} \qquad (8.27)$$

Households are assumed to make this choice so as to maximize utility functions of the form (8.5). The strategy for calibrating the model is to estimate the production functions on the basis of the survey data, then to impute the unobserved leisure preference parameters a^i for (8.5) from the choices reported by each household for 1985.

---

[7]As elsewhere in this study, the assumptions of homogeneous inputs, products, and technologies in each sector are heroic, but necessary to keep the exercises simple and in view of data limitations. Note that crop output is valued at sale price, when marketed, and at market price, otherwise. Since a large proportion of sales were at below-market state prices, this means that *g* will value a single product at two different prices, raising concern that the *value* production function need not be well-behaved. However, the market price averaged only about 20% above the state price in 1985, so that the magnitude of this problem is relatively modest.

The production functions are estimated by direct methods. Profit or cost function approaches were rejected because constraints on household choice may have led to outcomes inconsistent with profit-maximization. While use of instrumental variables to correct for the possible simultaneity of input and output decisions is desirable, available instruments are of limited value. Results obtained from IV estimates using variables outside of the set included in (8.26) and (8.27) provided statistically insignificant coefficients for all factors but land, in the contract sector, and an R^2 for the sideline sector equation significantly lower than that obtained by non-IV estimation. Instead, quadratic terms of the included exogenous variables were generated, and the first twelve principle components of the resulting variable set were used to estimate the production functions.[8]

In using the survey data to estimate the production functions, two important adjustments were made. First, individual labor-time use appeared to seriously understate part-time work in both sectors, with a number of households even reporting contract and/or sideline sector output but no corresponding labor time.[9] For households reporting zero labor time and positive output in a sector, we substituted labor time proxies extrapolated from the data of those households which provided positive labor time reports.[10]

The second adjustment concerns the distinction between capital goods used in crop production, and those used in sideline production. Although the survey asked that these be distinguished, we found that most households, including those with large sideline incomes, considered nearly all of their capital goods to be agricultural. It seems likely that equipment such as carts and tractors, which casual observation and in-depth interviews indicated were used primarily to transport construction materials or in commerce, were improperly listed as agricultural, producing a serious under-statement of the capital input to sideline activities. We therefore judged the reported breakdown to be uninformative, and decided to impute the inter-sectoral capital allocation by indirect methods. In particular, the model of the previous section implies that the marginal products of capital (as well as those of labor and variable

[8]Each principal component is a linear combination of the original variables, with coefficients equal to the eigenvectors of the covariance matrix. There are 27 quadratic terms generated by the seven exogenous variables in (8.26) and (8.27), so there are 27 principal components, of which twelve are chosen by the method described by Rao (1964). This may also be considered an IV estimation method, but no data from outside the initial variable set are introduced. For details on the estimation, see Park (1989, pp. 29–30).

[9]As mentioned in a previous footnote, use of hired labor was not reported, and it seems unlikely that unreported hired labor provides a general explanation for this anomoly. We surmise that much sideline sector labor, such as feeding pigs and chickens, was performed by children or by women who reported school attendance or housework as their sole activities (although an opportunity to report time allocation to three different activities was provided in the survey). It is also possibile that household members employed in wage jobs under-reported part time work in one or the other sector, but we ignored this in our estimation strategy, since these workers are not explicitly considered in the model.

[10]Contract sector labor time was projected as a linear function of mean age of household labor force and size of household labor force excepting those in full-time wage employment. Sideline sector labor time was projected as a linear function of the second variable only. For the sideline sector, the labor proxy had to be used for 100 out of 221 households; for the contract sector, for 7 households only.

inputs) will be related across sectors for any given household by a term of proportionality, which we may call θ, which is less than or equal to one as the crop production constraint is or is not binding. If we assume that the proportionality term is the same for all households,[11] then, taking the expressions for the marginal products of capital in the two sectors and relating them by this factor, we can solve for k_c^i and k_s^i in terms of k^i and θ, and rewrite (8.26) and (8.27) as

$$f^i = e^{\alpha_0}(h_s^i)^{\alpha_1}(k_s^i)^{\alpha_2}(z_s^i)^{\alpha_3} = e^{\alpha_0} (h_s^i)^{\alpha_1} \left(\frac{\theta \cdot \alpha_2 \cdot f^i \cdot k^i}{\theta \cdot \alpha_2 \cdot f^i + \beta_3 \cdot g^i} \right)^{\alpha_2} (z_s^i)^{\alpha_3} \quad (8.28)$$

and

$$g^i = e^{\beta_0}(h_c^i)^{\beta_1}(l_o^i)^{\beta_2}(k_c^i)^{\beta_3}(z_c^i)^{\beta_4}$$
$$= e^{\beta_0} (h_c^i)^{\beta_1}(l_o^i)^{\beta_2} \left(\frac{\beta_3 \cdot g^i \cdot k^i}{\theta \cdot \alpha_2 \cdot f^i + \beta_3 \cdot g^i} \right)^{\beta_3} (z_c^i)^{\beta_4} \quad (8.29)$$

Taking logs of the equations, we have a simultaneous nonlinear model as follows:

$$\log f = \alpha_0 + \alpha_1 \log\, h_s + \alpha_2(\log \theta + \log \alpha_2 + \log f$$
$$+ \log k - \log(\theta\alpha_2 f + \beta_3 g)) + \alpha_3 \log z_s \quad (8.30)$$

$$\log g = \beta_0 + \beta_1 \log\, h_c + \beta_3(\log \beta_3 + \log\, g + \log k$$
$$- \log(\theta\alpha_2 f + \beta_3 g)) + \beta_2 \log l_o + \beta_4 \log z_c \quad (8.31)$$

Estimation using principal components of the quadratic terms generated by the RHS variables (see above) is by iterated nonlinear three-stage least squares. The results are shown in Table 8.2, which also shows the average values of the marginal products of each factor implied by the estimated elasticities and the production data. The t ratios for all factors except labor and capital in crop production denote statistical significance, although the estimates for the sideline sector are generally more significant than those for crop production.

[11]This assumption is *not* implied by the model of the previous section. A method of estimation which permits a different value of θ to hold for each household was employed experimentally, but the results were unsatisfactory in that they entailed extremely low factor elasticities and insignificant coefficient estimates for all factors except land, in the crop sector production function. This might be explained in part by the fact that the assumption of a common cross-sectoral marginal productivity ratio for capital and current inputs (equality with the ratio for labor was not imposed) is inconsistent with the data, as the estimates below appear to suggest. Probably more significant is the fact that endogenous estimation with a unique value of θ for each household puts excessive weight on measurement errors and other idiosyncracies of individual household reports. The assumption of a *common* value of θ among households implies that land was allocated in such a fashion as to minimize the efficiency cost of meeting sales quotas, in the aggregate. Although there is no reason to believe that this condition held with any precision—some evidence that it did not comes from our own model (see below)—it is true that the same village authorities handled the distribution of land and of sales contracts, and that even if their goal was a "fair" (as opposed to efficient) sharing of the contract burden, some correspondence between the actual distributions and those required for the equal θ outcome appears likely.

Table 8.2. Production Function Estimates

Variable	Coefficient	t Statistic	Average Marginal Product
1. Sideline Production			
Constant (α_0)	2.2085	2.17	—
Labor (α_1)	0.2295	3.87	427.30
Capital (α_2)	0.2093	4.39	5.94
Current input (α_3)	0.6461	9.88	1.58
$n = 221$		$R^2 = 0.6726$	
2. Crop Production			
Constant (β_0)	17.1366	6.33	—
Labor (β_1)	0.0375	1.13	73.26
Land (β_2)	0.4648	2.22	2152.92
Capital (β_3)	0.0031	0.18	0.03
Current input (β_4)	0.2994	1.62	1.48
$n = 221$		$R^2 = 0.6347$	

Some of the estimates in Table 8.2 bear a reassuring resemblance to those found in the team level estimates in Chapters 4, 5, or 7. In particular, the estimated marginal product of land, at Y 2,153 per hectare, is quite close to the author's estimate for 1985, Y 2,066, shown in Table 4.6, which is based on an almost identical estimated elasticity of .467 for the 1980–1985 period (Table 4.5). In qualitative terms, the relative size and significance of the land coefficient is consistent with Wiemer's estimates and with those reported in Chapters 5 and 7. The marginal product of purchased current inputs, being not far above one, is broadly consistent with profit-maximizing choice, assuming a financing cost of about 50%. Similar numbers were obtained by Wiemer (Table 4.4) for sidelines in the late 1970s, by the author (Table 4.6) for crop and noncrop production around 1984, and by the author in Chapter 5 (Table 5.3).[12]

The estimated elasticity of labor in the sideline sector is similar to that obtained by the author for the noncrop sector in 1980–1985 (Table 4.5), and the corresponding marginal product falls between our 1984 and 1985 estimates of the same marginal product, based on the team data (Table 4.6). The statistically insignificant estimate of the coefficient on labor in the crop sector, while disturbingly low, is actually higher than our likewise insignificant estimate of the coefficient on labor in Table 4.5, and gives a correspondingly higher marginal product (compare Table 4.6). It falls between our estimates and those of Wiemer (Tables 4.2 and 4.5). Note also the

---

[12]The elasticity of current inputs in the crop sector shown in Table 8.2 is larger than most of Kim's team-level estimates for 1980–1982 and 1980–1984, shown in the tables of Chapter 7. The estimated elasticity of current inputs in the sideline sector is far higher than that estimated by Wiemer for that sector in the 1970s (Table 4.2) and by the author for 1980–1985 (Table 4.5).

similarity of the estimated coefficient to those obtained by Kim, for example, in the OLS and random effects models shown in Table 7.4.

Turning to capital, while the estimated elasticity of output with respect to that factor in the sideline sector is somewhat smaller than the team level estimates obtained by Wiemer for the 1970s (Table 4.2) and the author for 1980–1985 (Table 4.5), the resulting estimate of capital's marginal product is larger than, but not too dissimilar to, the author's estimate for 1985 shown in Table 4.6. The statistically insignificant estimated elasticity and the resulting estimate of the marginal product of capital in the crop sector are far lower than those obtained by Wiemer or Kim, but preferable to the author's estimates based on 1980–1985 team-level data, which are negative (Tables 4.5 and 4.6). With respect to the contrast with Wiemer and Kim's estimates, it should be noted that what is measured by the capital stock variable is different in the team and household level data, because the latter excludes items still owned by the teams as of 1985. Further remarks on capital follow shortly.

The estimates in Table 8.2 suggest that there were increasing returns to scale in sideline production and decreasing returns to scale in agricultural production. Tests of the hypothesis of constant returns to scale in the sideline sector ($\Sigma \ \alpha = 1$), in the crop sector ($\Sigma \ \beta = 1$), and of the joint hypothesis of constant returns to scale in both sectors, using the method of Gallant and Jorgenson (1979), reject all but the first hypothesis at the .01 level. The suggestion of decreasing returns to scale in agriculture could be important, in light of Chinese policy debates regarding land concentration (which, along with land tenure issues, are discussed as well in Chapter 9). An attempt to examine the robustness of this result using alternative combinations of principal components, alternative assumptions about missing values and capital allocation, and alternative specifications and estimating methods, showed individual parameter estimates to be unstable, but confirmed decreasing returns to scale in most cases.[13] Nonetheless, the accuracy and completeness of the Dahe household data are far from ideal, and a spurious indication of decreasing returns to scale could result from the bias of estimated coefficients toward zero as a consequence of measurement error. Finally, Dahe is only one township, so studies using other data sources are needed to further resolve the issue.[14] Note that the production function has been

---

[13]See Chiacu (1992). Treating intersectoral capital allocation as a function of household characteristics, Chiacu also performed statistical tests of the goodness of fit of the Cobb-Douglas functional form against translog and CES specifications. The results show the Cobb-Douglas to be superior for most of the capital allocation assumptions examined.

[14]The only production function estimate based on post-collective era household data of which the author was aware as this book went to press was that by Fleisher and Liu (1992). It uses combined data on 1,188 households located in six different geographic regions of China, derived from a survey conducted jointly by the World Bank and the Ministry of Rural Development of the P.R.C. The production function is log-log in combined output of grain, cotton, soybeans, and peanuts and inputs of capital, labor, land, and fertilizer, with the number of plots farmed by the household also entering as a logged, and education, farming experience, and a disaster dummy entering as linear independent variables. The results resemble most in this study in that land has the highest estimated coefficient, .702; labor follows at .201. The sum of the four conventional coefficients is 1.05, but there is a significant negative coefficient of -.057 on number of plots.

estimated at the level of the household farm, so that there may be increasing returns to scale in the provision of irrigation, plowing services, and mechanical threshing (which were done by the village), but nothing to be gained by having households perform such operations as weeding (by hoe), spraying for pests (by hand-operated backpack pump), and harvesting (by hand-held sickles), on a larger scale.[15]

The low significance level of the coefficient on capital in the agricultural production function should not cause too much surprise. Such results are not unusual in agricultural production studies in which one must settle for stock rather than flow measures of the capital input, and insignificant coefficients on capital in agriculture were found in a number of instances in the author's team-level estimates reported in Chapters 4 and 5 (see Tables 4.5 and 5.3). As in Wiemer's case, we have here the additional problem of an endogenous intersectoral allocation of capital.[16] The estimate of θ, 0.0053, is statistically insignificant (t ratio 0.15), and disturbingly small.[17] However, the imputed value has the not altogether implausible implication that 62% of all capital goods by value, or Y 683.89 per household, were used in agricultural production, versus 38%, or Y 400.10 per household, in the sideline sector.[18] The implied capital inputs by sector vary with total capital stock in a fashion consistent with intuition: from an average of 45% of capital in the sideline sector, for households with $k_i > Y\ 3,000$, to an average of only 14% of capital in the sideline sector, for households with $k_i < Y\ 250$.

Although casual observation would have suggested somewhat more capital allocation to sidelines, especially among better endowed households, our joint estimate of the two Cobb-Douglas production functions, under the imposed assumption that households share the same ratio of marginal productivities of capital across sectors, is nonetheless consistent with the interpretation that under their second-best

[15]Farm services provided at village level appear in household input data as current inputs, valued at the fees paid. Estimation at *plot* level (households averaged three separate parcels each) could conceivably show scale economies, but sufficiently disaggregated data on inputs other than land are not available. It might also be noted that observed DRS could result from crop composition or state sales contract obligation differences; that is, if households having more land devote a larger fraction to meeting low price sales obligations, this could show up as DRS in our production function in which the dependent variable is gross value of crop output. Chiacu attempts to test this conjecture and finds the evidence inconclusive.

[16]Comparing Wiemer's method with that of the present analysis, note that she computes a team-specific capital allocation parameter for 44 teams, while we compute a single parameter θ for all 221 households. The share of capital devoted to each sector nonetheless differs among units in both cases: for Wiemer, because it is the parameter to be computed; for the present model, because θ is a ratio of marginal products, and its common value among households with differing resources and allocation patterns implies *differing* allocations of capital. Wiemer's ability to compute team-specific parameters depends on the availability of multiple observations for each team, whereas only a single observation is available for each household in the present case.

[17]Note that we did not impose the condition of identical marginal product gaps for labor and purchased inputs implied by equation (8.25). We prefer to let the data speak for themselves where possible, rather than impose additional structure based on purely theoretical considerations. The actual average marginal product ratios, according to Table 8.2, are 0.17 and 0.93, respectively. Possible reasons for the marked differences in these ratios, contradicting equation (8.25), will be given presently.

[18]That this is close to the 68%/32% ratio obtained by Wiemer may also be viewed as reassuring. It is plausible that a somewhat greater proportion of capital went to sidelines in 1985 than in the 1970s.

allocation of inputs, apparantly dictated by the need to satisfy a crop output constraint, households "overallocated" capital to agriculture to the point at which its marginal product was only a small fraction of that in the sideline sector. The divergence of the imputed *average products* of capital is less extreme than that of its marginal products: average product is Y 4.45 per yuan of capital in the sideline sector, versus Y 2.86 per yuan of capital in agriculture. Indeed, if we compute the per-capital-unit average value of output *net of current input cost*, the difference largely disappears: Y 2.34 for sidelines, versus Y 2.27 for agriculture. In any event, it should be borne in mind that the intersectoral allocation of capital is allowed to vary freely to meet the model's optimization conditions, in the exercises that follow, so that from the standpoint of those exercises the accuracy of the capital allocation imputed by our estimating procedure is relevant only to the reliability of the technological parameters with which that imputed allocation is associated.

Despite some problematic features of the estimated production function, such as the low and insignificant estimated elasticities of labor and capital in the crop sector, it is as good an estimate as can be obtained from the Dahe household survey data, and amendments would be arbitrary. Hence, the estimates shown in Table 8.2 are used in what follows. With these estimates in hand, our last major task is imputation of the leisure preference coefficients of the household utility functions. Equation (8.20) allows us to solve for the coefficients (a^i) in terms of household income, population, labor force, labor allocation, and the marginal product of sideline labor, calculated as $(\hat{\alpha}_1/h_s^i)f^i$, where $\hat{}$ denotes the estimate shown in Table 8.2 and f^i is reported gross sideline output value. Equation (8.19) should give the same result. However, in the absence of reliable estimates of the individual θ^i terms, we choose to impute the a's from (8.20) alone.

Simulations

Actual and Simulated Behavior, with Crop Constraint

Table 8.3-a shows the actual reported allocation of land, labor, and current inputs, to the crop and sideline sectors, in 1985, for the 221 Dahe Township households included in our analysis. It also shows net and gross income by sector, the allocation of actual household capital stocks between the two sectors as imputed in our production function estimates, applicable two-sector totals and contract sector shares, and the total leisure of sample workers.[19] Table 8.3-b shows Gini coefficients of inequality computed on per worker, per capita, and per household bases from the

---

[19]Each worker is assumed to have a total of 250 units of time available, and this value is assigned to T in the relevant equations. Leisure is then calculated as $n^iT - h_c^i - h_s^i$. The number 250 is arbitrary but reasonable since 100 units of work time (or 100% of normal full-time work, in the wording of the survey form) then accounts for 40% of the 8,760 hours in the year, the remainder (along with any unused portion of the 100 units) being available for sleep, household tasks, and leisure activities.

Table 8.3. The Actual Situation in 1985

	Crop Sector (c)	Sideline Sector (s)	Total (c + s)	c/(c + s)%
a. Sample Total				
Land	89.6		89.6	100
Capital	144,511[a]	88,429[a]	232,940	62[a]
Labor	27,657	20,997	48,654	57
Current input	86,660	138,618	225,218	38
Net income	310,422	254,847	565,269	55
Gross income	413,940	393,465	807,405	51
Leisure			182,096	
	Per Worker	**Per Capita**		**Household**
b. Gini coefficients				
Land	0.2716	0.2015		0.2074
Capital	0.7495	0.7272		0.7340
Net income	0.3861	0.3409		0.3723

[a]Capital allocation between sectors is by imputation based on our estimates of (8.30) and (8.31).

sample data.[20] Estimated factor marginal products are as indicated in Table 8.2, and are therefore omitted here.

In our first simulation, each household is assumed constrained to produce at least its observed level of agricultural output.[21] It uses its assigned land for crop production, allocates its endowment of capital between crop and sideline production, allocates its time endowment between those two activities and leisure, and purchases as much homogeneous current input as it desires at the parametric price of Y 1 per unit plus Y 0.5 financing cost,[22] so as to maximize its utility (8.5) subject to the minimum crop output constraint. The computed solutions to this maximization problem, and the changes from the actual reported behavior, are summarized in Table 8.4-a, while the average values of each factor's marginal product in these solutions, by sector, is shown in Table 8.4-b. Table 8.4-c reports the new Gini coefficient for net income.[23]

[20]That is, we compute farm size per worker for each household, then compute the Gini coefficient for this variable over the 221 households to obtain the Gini coefficient of land per worker. The per capita coefficients are obtained by first dividing the measure for each household by the number of household members. The per household coefficients are computed from the data for the households, as given.

[21]Ideally, we would want to test whether households were constrained to produce given levels of products for sale to the state, and/or to meet their own consumption requirements, leaving production for the market and production of feedstuffs as strictly discretionary. The need to treat crop production as homogeneous, due to data limitations, rules out this option. Evidence that the posited constraints are binding is not inconsistent with the persistence of such discretionary behavior, which can be thought of as being subsumed within "inframarginal" output. However, treatment of crop production as homogeneous prevents the model from illustrating how the relaxing of state sales or self-consumption constraints might lead to expanded production of higher-value crops. The average proportions of state sales, self-consumption, feed, and marketed output in the reported output value are given below.

[22]The finance charge is chosen to roughly correspond to the gap between the value of the marginal product, indicated by Table 8.2, and the price of current inputs.

[23]The procedure leaves interhousehold land and capital distribution unchanged.

Table 8.4. Simulation with Crop Output Constraint

	Crop Sector (c)	Sideline Sector (s)	Total (c + s)	c/(c + s) %
a. Sample Total[a]				
Capital	1,361	231,558	232,919	0.6
	(−99.1)	(+161.9)	(0)	(−99.2)
Labor	5,104	43,240	48,344	10.6
	(−96.5)	(+105.9)	(−0.6)	(−81.4)
Current input	156,305	706,073	862,378	18.1
	(+80.5)	(+409.4)	(+282.9)	(−52.4)
Net income	247,567	933,056	1,180,624	21.0
	(−20.2)	(+266.1)	(+108.9)	(−61.8)
Gross income	420,453	1,639,130	2,059,583	20.4
	(+1.6)	(+316.6)	(+155.1)	(−60.0)
Leisure			182,405	
			(+0.2)	

	Crop Sector	Sideline Sector
b. Average Value of Marginal Product[b]		
Capital	2.46 (1.79)	3.43 (2.15)
Labor	709.73 (909.11)	1,081.57 (1,333,85)
Current input	1.06 (0.33)	1.50 (0)
Land	2,241.68 (483.66)	

	Per Worker	Per Capita	Household
c. Gini Coefficients			
Net income	0.4644	0.4329	0.4713

[a]The percentage changes from the actual situation of 1985 are presented in parentheses.
[b]Standard deviations are presented in parentheses.

For 82% of the households, the postulated crop production constraint is binding in the optimal solution. While 18% thus produced more than the assumed requirement, the amounts involved are small, since the combined gross value of crop output for the sample exceeds the assumed requirement by only 1.6%. Gross sideline sector output, on the other hand, is more than four times as great in the simulation as in actuality. This change is made possible by an over 400% expansion in sideline sector purchases of current inputs, and by an 80% expansion of purchases of those inputs for crop production, which permits over 95% of the capital and labor originally applied to farming to be released to the sideline sector. The large increase in purchased input use but small increase in output, in the crop sector, leads to a 20% decline in the net earnings of that sector, but this is strongly offset by a 266% increase in net earnings from sidelines, leading to a 109% jump in total net earnings. On average, households choose a slight increase in leisure, as well.

These results suggest that at least some types of current input (the heterogeneity of which are obscured by our simplified treatment) were not in fact available in unrestricted quantities at the observed price, or that the financing cost of Y 0.5 per Y 1 purchased is unrealistically low. Rationing of agricultural inputs at state-controlled prices was in fact the norm in rural China in 1985, and many of these inputs were supplied to farmers at Dahe by village agricultural service stations, most likely in limited amounts, applied at some standard level per hectare of land. Purchases of many nonagricultural inputs may have been financed with inexpensive Rural Credit Cooperative loans, which were also available only in limited amounts. Additional credit from informal sources was reported to be far more expensive.[24] A dynamic simulation exercise by Park suggested that a local market for funds at Dahe might have settled at an annual interest rate of 127%, in 1985.[25] At such a rate, current input purchases would be close to those actually reported in 1985, and far below those obtained in the optimization exercise summarized in Table 8.4.

It is interesting to note that when the constraint of limited current inputs or high marginal finance costs is lifted, households are able to fulfill assumed agricultural output requirements at far less cost in terms of suboptimal (or second best) use of labor and capital. The marginal products of those inputs are far closer to equality in the two sectors, in the solutions of Table 8.4, than in the actual and (for capital) imputed use as shown in Tables 8.2 and 8.3. We also note that the distribution of income becomes significantly less equal, whether measured in per worker, per capita, or per household terms, in the simulation. The main reason for this is that the rather unequal distribution of capital endowments becomes a more significant determinant of incomes, and the rather equal distribution of land a less significant one, when the sideline share of income is allowed to rise dramatically. The results suggest, then, that rationing of current inputs and credit in 1985 had an equalizing effect on incomes, although the comparison involves a change in both the total level and the distribution of current inputs.

Relaxing the Crop Output Constraint

We now repeat the exercise reported in Table 8.4 but with no minimum output requirement in the crop production sector. According to our data, 1985 grain and cotton prices averaged about 20% more in the market than in sales to the state. The reported gross agricultural output value reflects a mixture of state purchase prices (for sales of grain and cotton to the state, accounting for an average of 27% of gross value) and of market prices (for market sales [1%], self-consumption [54%], and use in

---

[24]See Feder et al. (1989).

[25]Park (1989) modifies the model discussed in this chapter, approximating an infinite horizon model with a moving two-period optimizing procedure. In the model, households' capital stocks are endogenized by allowing for the allocation of income in each period to either consumption or savings. The aggregate savings of the 221 households are allocated in a local capital market which clears at the interest rate at which the total investment demand equals the total savings supplied. Savings propensities are determined by a regression on the 1985 data, while the demand for funds is a function of the expected value of the marginal product of funds in both capital formation and the financing of current input purchases.

Table 8.5. Simulation Without Crop Output Constraint

	Crop Sector (c)	Sideline Sector (s)	Total (c + s)	c/(c + s) %
a. Sample Total[a]				
Capital	608	232,311	232,919	0.3
	(−55.3)	(+0.3)	(0)	(−50.0)
Labor	2,495	43,796	46,291	5.4
	(−51.1)	(+1.3)	(−4.2)	(−49.1)
Current input	71,387	711,259	782,649	9.1
	(−54.3)	(+0.7)	(−9.2)	(−49.7)
Net income	269,690	939,901	1,209,591	22.3
	(+8.9)	(+0.7)	(+2.5)	(+6.2)
Gross income	357,648	1,651,161	2,008,809	17.8
	(−14.9)	(+0.7)	(−2.5)	(−12.7)
Leisure			184,459	
			(+1.1)	
Utility			2,439	
			(+3.5)	

	Crop Sector	Sideline Sector
b. Average Value of Marginal Product[b]		
Capital	3.45 (2.18)	3.45 (2.18)
Labor	1,083.7 (1,336.4)	1,083.7 (1,336.3)
Current input	1.50 (0)	1.50 (0)
Land	1,956.22 (308.10)	

	Per Worker	Per Capita	Household
c. Gini Coefficients			
Net income	0.4604	0.4281	0.4662

[a]The percentage changes from the simulation with crop output constraint are presented in parentheses.
[b]Standard deviations are presented in parentheses.

rearing livestock, etc. [18%], for both staple and nonstaple crops).[26] In the present exercise, we will assume that all output is valued at market prices; this is accomplished by multiplying the agricultural production function, already assumed to be in value terms, by a factor of 1.05, which eliminates the influence of the procurement/ market price gap on the original estimate.[27] As before, households are assumed to use the land contracted by the collective for farm production, to freely allocate their capital endowments among the two activities and their available labor time among those activities and leisure, and to freely purchase current inputs at the given unit price and Y 0.5 financing charge, so as to maximize utility (8.5). The results of this optimization are summarized in Table 8.5.

[26]Shares of gross output value are calculated at the prices indicated. Animal feed and other uses are computed as a residual.
[27]For the data and methodology leading to this adjustment, see Park (1989, pp. 68–75).

Compared to actual reported output, total crop production declines by 13.6% with the abolition of restrictions. This drop in crop output is associated with reductions of over 50% in each of the three variable (or reallocable) inputs, compared with the constrained optimum of Table 8.4. This indicates that targets were met in the previous exercise at sharply increasing marginal costs. While *net* agricultural income is still lower than that actually reported, it is nearly 9% higher than in the constrained optimum, indicating that output in the constrained simulation was produced at a loss, on the margin.[28] Sideline sector activity, as shown in Table 8.5, changes little from that in Table 8.4, continuing to reflect enormous expansion (relative to the actual situation) through purchased input use and reallocation of capital and labor from agriculture. Also to be noted is the fact that average marginal products of capital, labor, and current inputs are now essentially equal across activities,[29] reflecting the elimination of constraint (8.6), and that income inequality has declined slightly from the first simulation, by all three measures. This suggests that some households suffered a heavier burden than others from their crop production requirements, although the minor magnitude of the change and the numerous sources of imprecision built into the simulation process mean that this point deserves little weight.

While the decline in crop output when the constraint is lifted is small relative to the decline in input use, it is by no means insignificant in the context of China's farm economy. Only 25% of grain produced in China was marketed (and of this, 83%, or 20.7% of total output, to the state) in 1985, and the corresponding figures for the Dahe households are 29% (all sold to the state). Although most of the cotton produced is for sale (94% of reported output was sold to the state by the Dahe households), grain and cotton command relatively low prices, and as a proportion of the total value of crop output of the Dahe households, combined grain and cotton sales to the state at official prices averaged 26% for the 221 households. The decline due to eliminating crop constraints is thus equivalent to a substantial portion of the volume of state purchases. Although the necessity of treating crop production as homogeneous prohibits rigorous identification of which outputs would contract, the results of this exercise are at least consistent with the suggestion that while contracts to sell grain and cotton to the state were nominally voluntary in 1985, they strongly influenced farmer behavior and were quite possibly viewed by farmers and overseen by local officials as being compulsory.

On average, the amount by which crop output declines is less than the value of output marketed to the state; however, there are a large number of individual

---

[28]It is rational for the households in that simulation to incur losses in crop production in order to meet obligatory output requirements while freeing capital and labor to earn higher returns in sideline production. Notice that equation (8.25) implies that current inputs will be purchased for the crop sector in quantities such that the value of their marginal product is a fraction of their purchase price.

[29]"The marginal products of capital and labor should be the same across sectors for any given household, but without a market for those factors of production, they need not be identical across households.

households whose reduction of farm output appears substantial enough to cut into self-consumption needs as well. Even those Dahe households that earned the bulk of their incomes from nonagricultural activities were observed to produce the vast majority of their food needs in actuality. The simulation exercise implies that if these households could treat food as readily available at roughly the going sales price, it would be economically rational for some of them to switch out of self-provision. That they in fact self-provided in 1985 is therefore in need of explanation. Two possibilities that come to mind here are, first, the joint hypothesis that (a) households were under administrative pressure to grow food crops on the land expressly distributed for self-provision purposes (i.e., the "grain ration land") as a result of self-sufficiency norms communicated to local officials by party and state bureaucracies, and that (b) holding "grain ration land" was viewed as a risk-reducing strategy by households, given uncertainties of the evolving land tenure system and other aspects of the changing rural environment. Second, it is quite possible that households did not treat ex post market prices as given when reaching their cropping decisions. While local free market grain prices turned out to be only about 20% higher than state prices in 1985, we saw in Chapter 7 that the difference rose to 300% and more nationally, by 1988. Peasants might even have been concerned that grain would become totally unavailable on local markets, as occurred in some years in the past. The decision to grow for self-provision could thus again have had an insurance aspect, which our model does not capture formally.

In fact, it is necessary to restate that this exercise was carried out after adjusting prices to the reported market level. Insofar as the above inferences about state contracts are correct, this implies that raising prices to the 1985 market level would not have been sufficient to elicit the output sold to the state. The remarks just made regarding the difference between actual and *anticipated* market prices may offer a partial explanation. That is, the voluntary portion of the observed output may have been produced in anticipation of a significantly higher price than that which eventually prevailed, so that optimal production when the expectation is instead that of the observed price falls below this. Beyond this, however, the results are consistent with the view that the free market in staple crops was so thin, played so auxiliary a role, and was so subject to governmental interventions, that its prices offer little indication of equilibrium levels. Although possibly understated so as to avoid disclosing cash income, the household reports that only 1% of their crop output was sold in the market are also consistent with such a view. In a word, with the exception of production of a few high-value crops as a commercial proposition, households may have formed their production plans primarily with state contracts and self-consumption requirements in mind, and the market may have been viewed as a means for disposing of unplanned and unwanted surpluses. It will be argued in Chapter 11 that this condition is less the result of some "traditional subsistence mentality" of the Chinese peasant than a reflection of the role to which the market for staple crops has tended to be relegated given the tension between that market and the official objective of procuring at partially confiscatory prices.

Achieving Observed Crop Output by Adjusting the Producer Price

Our model allows for the calculation of the (expected) crop price level at which the observed crop output level would be achieved without compulsion. Changes in crop price mean a multiplicative scaling up of the agricultural production function (8.26) without effect on factor elasticities. When households are assumed to allocate their input endowments and to purchase current inputs so as to maximize household utility, without a crop output constraint, the two sector character of the model assures that the level of crop output will be a continuous positive function of the crop price. Finding the price at which the required output is achieved by the sample households, in the aggregate, is thus easy to accomplish computationally by means of an iterative search procedure. The required price turns out to be 49% higher than the average market price, or 79.5% higher than the average state price of agricultural produce, in 1985. Factor allocations, output, marginal products, and Gini coefficients of the new solution are shown in Table 8.6. Due to our treatment of crop output as homogeneous (among other reasons), this cannot be used as a precise measure of the tax implicit in state purchases. Nevertheless, it may be suggestive of the order of magnitude of the price change that would have been necessary to elicit voluntary fulfillment of production and sales objectives at Dahe in 1985.

Several aspects of the price-induced solution to the crop supply problem deserve comment. First, our exercise continued to allow unrestricted use of current inputs at the listed price and assumed finance charge, totaling Y 0.5 per Y 1 of input. In the solution, the required crop output is achieved by means of a 49% increase in current inputs, coupled with a 99% reduction of capital and an 86% reduction in labor use, compared with the actual situation in 1985. This suggests that if current inputs were in fact in limited supply or much more costly to finance on the margin, it might have taken a much larger price increase to elicit this crop output level in a noncompulsory manner.[30] Second, when we compare the new solution with that shown in Table 8.4, where individual households respect the agricultural output targets by administrative requirement rather than as a response to the output price, we find that roughly the same quantity of output is produced using rather different combinations of inputs, depending upon the method of eliciting supply. In particular, the price induced optimum involves, in the aggregate, the use of 16% more capital, 22% less labor, and 17% less current inputs to reach the aggregate output target.[31] Although on Paretian

---

[30]A parallel point about the exercise in Table 8.5 is that crop output might have declined more sharply, there, if not for the assumed availability of these inputs.

[31]Output in physical terms is 1.6% smaller under the price solution, because we allowed households to exceed their targets in the other exercise, whereas here we adjusted the price upwards only until the original total output is exactly achieved in the aggregate, rather than by each individual household.

Table 8.6. Simulation with Voluntary Production of Observed Crop Output

	Crop Sector (c)	Sideline Sector (s)	Total (c + s)	c/(c + s) %
a. Sample Total[a]				
Capital	1,605	231,314	232,919	0.7
	(+16, +160)	(−0.1, −0.4)	(0)	(+17, +133)
Labor	3,991	34,821	38,812	10.3
	(−22, +60)	(−19, −21)	(−20, −16)	(−3, +91)
Current input	129,504	643,183	772,687	16.8
	(−17, +81)	(−9, −10)	(−10, −1)	(−7, +85)
Net income	502,763	849,952	1,352,715	37.2
	(+103, +86)	(−9, −10)	(+15, +12)	(+77, +67)
Gross income	648,837	1,493,135	2,141,972	30.3
	(+54, +81)	(−9, −10)	(+4, +7)	(+49, +70)
Leisure			191,938	
			(+5.2, +4.1)	

	Crop Sector	Sideline Sector
b. Average Value of Marginal Product[b]		
Capital	2.82 (1.98)	2.82 (1.98)
Labor	1,198.0 (1,399.5)	1,185.1 (1,397.3)
Current input	1.50 (0)	1.49 (0.1)
Land	3,548.43 (558.92)	

	Per Worker	Per Capita	Household
c. Gini Coefficients			
Net income	0.4233	0.3850	0.4217

[a]The first number in each set of parentheses is the percentage change from the simulation with crop output constraint, and the second number is the percentage change from the simulation with no constraint.
[b]The standard deviations are shown in parentheses.

grounds it seems reasonable to assume that the factor allocation observed in the price induced optimum represents a more socially efficient use of resources, it is worth noting that the difference partly reflects a change in which households produce what share of the total, and the corresponding changes in the inter-sectoral allocation of resources by households having differing sets of factor endowments. Thus, the change here also has distributional consequences. According to the tables, income is distributed more equally regardless of the basis of calculation (per worker, per capita, or per household) in the price induced solution than in either of the earlier simulations, one reason being that with the higher crop price generating higher returns from farming, the relatively equal land distribution has greater weight in determining the income distribution, and the relatively unequal capital distribution has less.

Operation of a Land Sub-Rental Market

On a number of occasions since the full-fledged household production responsibility system began to be widely practiced in China in the early 1980s, official pronouncements have opened the door to inter-household sub-contracting of land use rights. Reports indicate that such sub-contracting remains rare,[32] a likely reason being the continuing ambiguities surrounding the legal status of land use rights, and house-holds' fears that sub-contracting might lead to permanent loss of the plots involved without long-term compensation. In the present section, a modified version of our optimization model and the Dahe household data are used to examine the operation of a subrental market under the assumption that such a market could operate perfectly, in the sense that households are sure of receiving the pre-agreed payment for sub-rental, that there are no long-term consequences for land-use rights, and that the market for sub-rented land is competitive and functions openly with a free flow of information. In such a situation, the local sub-rental market should clear at a rent level at which the aggregate area offered for sub-rental exactly equals the aggregate area demanded by those wishing to expand their farms.

Our model easily accommodates a sub-rental market by assuming that the land actually farmed by household i is

$$l^i = l^i_o + l^i_s \qquad (8.32)$$

where l^i_s is the amount of land sub-rented. Note that l^i_s is positive if land is rented in, negative if land is rented out. The renting household pays the household sub-letting the land out a rent r_s per hectare, which is assumed to be common to the whole sample in market-clearing equilibrium.[33] To select a subrental level which maximizes its utility, a household will look for the value of l^i_s such that

$$\frac{\partial g^i(h^i_c, l^i, k^i_c, z^i_c)}{\partial l^i} = r_s \theta^i \qquad (8.33)$$

when constraint (8.6) holds, and

$$\frac{\partial g^i(h^i_c, l^i, k^i_c, z^i_c)}{\partial l^i} = r_s \qquad (8.34)$$

when there is no crop output constraint. Note that in (8.33) and (8.34), r_s is taken as parametric to the household, and h_c, k_c, and z_c (as well as h_s, k_s, and z_s in the corresponding equations) have been permitted to adjust so as to achieve utility maximization in view of the new level of land used by the household. (8.33) and (8.34) imply that optimal l^i_s is a function of r_s for all $i = 1,2, ..., n$. The market clearing condition for sub-rented land is

---

[32] According to Kojima (1988), the incidence was around 1% of contracted plots in 1985.

[33] We assume land quality to be uniform across the sample. Although Chapters 9 and 10 will take note of possible variation in land quality at Dahe, casual observation of the township (as mentioned in Chapter 3) suggests that the assumption of uniformity may be acceptable as a first approximation.

$$\sum_{i=1}^{N} l_s^i = 0 \qquad (8.35)$$

gives equilibrium rent. The remaining equilibrium conditions are as before, but with l^i substituted for l_o^i of the original system, and net income adjusted to reflect sub-rental payments or earnings

$$y^i = g^i(h_c^i, k_c^i, l^i, z_c^i) + f^i(h_s^i, \hat{k}^i - k_c^i, z_s^i) - r_c l_o^i - r_s l_s^i - p_z(z_c^i + z_s^i) \qquad (8.36)$$

In the new equibrium, land use will be more efficient, since the marginal product of land will be equal across households (as it was not previously).

The land market exercise to be reported here was carried out under the assumption that allocation of inputs to the two sectors occurs in the absence of a crop output constraint; hence, (8.34) rather than (8.33) describes the demand for land by each household. The results of household optimization and inter-household land market equilibrium for the 221 household sample are summarized in Table 8.7.

In the new equilibrium, crop production declines by an additional 6% over Table 8.5, which shows the simulated equilibrium without a crop output constraint and without a sub-rental market. Thus, while crop output in the latter is 14% below the observed 1985 output, in the present exercise it is 20% below observed crop output. The further flow of resources from crop production following operation of the sub-rental market presumably results from the fact that transforming the social opportunity cost of land into a private cost to households raises the marginal cost of crop production. The result is a further increase in the share of resources going to the sideline sector, and a small decline in households' consumption of leisure.

In the simulation, every household leases in or out in the sub-rental market, and the total area transacted amounts to 16.4% of the available land. As shown in Table 8.7-c, the post-sub-rental (operational) distribution of farm sizes becomes slightly more unequal, when measured on either a per worker or a per capita basis, although more equal in per household terms. The fact that the distribution of land among households does not become sharply more unequal in the simulation merits comment, since one might have anticipated either that some households would specialize in crop production while others shift more exclusively into sidelines, or that inequality of capital endowments would lead to a corresponding concentration of control over land. That neither occurs is probably to be attributed primarily to the decreasing returns to scale which characterize the estimated agricultural production technology. These decreasing returns mean that as a household expands its farm, the output per unit of each agricultural input declines, for any given factor mix. A more equal distribution of farms among households therefore leads to higher average farm productivity. The process of equalization of farm sizes *per household* undoes some of the egalitarianism in *per capita* and *per worker* terms that was built into the actual administrative land distribution at Dahe Township in 1985 (Chapter 9), leading to the

Table 8.7 Simulation With Sub-Rental Market and Without Crop Output Constraint

	Crop Sector (c)	Sideline Sector (s)	Total (c + s)	c/(c + s) %
a. *Sample Total*[a]				
Capital	518	232,401	232,919	0.2
	(−14.8)	(+0.0)	(0)	(−33.3)
Labor	2,517	43,984	46,501	5.4
	(+0.9)	(+0.4)	(+0.5)	(0)
Current input	67,274	713,143	780,417	8.6
	(−5.8)	(+0.3)	(−0.3)	(−5.5)
Net income	253,191	942,404	1,195,595	21.2
	(−6.1)	(+0.3)	(−1.2)	(−4.9)
Gross income	337,046	1,656,644	1,992,690	16.9
	(−5.8)	(+0.3)	(−0.8)	(−5.1)
Leisure			184,249	
			(−0.1)	

	Crop Sector		Sideline Sector	
b. *Average Value of Marginal Product*[b]				
Capital	3.46 (2.18)		3.46 (2.18)	
Labor	1,080 (1,331)		1,080 (1,331)	
Current input	1.50 (0)		1.50 (0)	
Land	1749.18 (0)			

	Per Worker	Per Capita	Household
c. *Gini Coefficients*			
Land	0.2734	0.2202	0.0729
Net income	0.4617	0.4300	0.4678

[a]Percentage changes from simulation without crop output constraint (Table 8.5) are shown in parentheses.
[b]Standard deviations are presented in parentheses.

higher Gini coefficients for those bases of calculation. Income is distributed roughly the same way in the new equilibrium as in that of Table 8.5.

The most striking finding from the exercise is that the equilibrium rent in the simulated sub-rental market is Y 1,749 per hectare, whereas the sum of taxes and obligations to the collective paid by Dahe households in 1985 amounted to only Y 195 per hectare. Since the market-clearing rent equals the value of land's marginal product in equilibrium, this shows that there is a positive rent component in households' agricultural incomes due to failure of the collective owners of land to charge market-clearing rents to its users. This positive rent is offset to a small degree only by the implicit tax hidden in the state sales obligation, which works out to Y 246 per hectare when calculated as the volume of those sales times the difference between the reported contract and market prices. Moreover, were the sales obligation to be maintained, or (even more) were the observed crop output to be elicited by means of higher prices, the rent on land would be substantially higher, as indicated by the average marginal products of land in Tables 8.4 and 8.6. On the other hand, calculated at the price that elicits the observed crop output voluntarily, which is 79.5% above the average level of state prices, the implicit tax in state contract purchases amounts to Y 1,077 per hectare, suggesting that what society takes back from the farm household when wearing its pro-urban procurement hat represents a significant chunk of what society gives the household when wearing its revolutionary land-conferring hat.

Conclusions

Although restricted by the need to treat crop production as homogeneous, the exercises reported in this chapter constitute a significant step toward the rigorous demonstration of important features of the household farm contracting system and of the economic environment in which it was embedded in mid-1980s rural China. In the first place, they provide strong evidence that at prevailing prices, most farm production was relatively unattractive when compared with sideline opportunities (at least in well-situated localities), and they suggest that the volume of staple crop production would substantially contract were administrative enforcement of sales requirements to be abandoned in the absence of price increases.

Second, the exercises suggest that the distribution of land to the villages at Dahe was at least mildly inefficient, in that marginal products of land diverged across households. This parallels the demonstration that there was a large free rent component in land distributed to households by the villages, since total tax and collective obligations were found to be far less than the market-clearing rental rate (land's value of marginal product) even at low crop prices and in the absence of crop production constraints. The discoveries of evidence of uncollected scarcity rent on land and of partially confiscatory purchases of crop output by the state are among the most important in this chapter, and will be given prominence in the analysis with which the book concludes in Chapter 11.

Third, the exercises suggested that access to current inputs is in practice restricted, perhaps both because inputs were in limited supply and rationed at the prices paid by households, and because the financing of additional purchases would be far more expensive than implied by our value of marginal product estimates for the inputs. In line with this conjecture, Park's dynamic simulation exercise finds the local market for funds clearing at an annual interest rate of 127%, substantially higher than the already high 50% assumed in the static exercises.

Operation of a land market somewhat surprisingly tended to increase the equality of the distribution of land per household, while slightly reducing the equality of the distribution of land per capita and per worker and having little effect on the distribution of income. The role of decreasing returns to scale in the estimated crop production function is evidently important here. Our data and the resulting estimates could turn out to be only locally true, and the imputed decreasing returns could also result from measurement error. Nonetheless, these results put up a warning flag to those Chinese economists and policymakers whose goal in land tenure reform has been to achieve land *concentration* on the presumption of *increasing returns to scale*. In this context, what the simulation exercise suggests, most generally, is that land redistribution through a market process will reflect the scale characteristics of the farm technology, even if they are unknown to planners, whereas an administrative redistribution (e.g., concentration) program may commit serious errors based on erroneous beliefs about scale economies.

At the same time, we should treat the observation of an equalizing land market with great caution, due to the fact that our analysis is a static one, that it abstracts from production uncertainty, risk aversion, and differences in farmer abilities, and that it represents markets as perfectly competitive. Those who have warned that land privatization might lead to economic stratification in a poor and land-scarce agrarian economy like China's cannot be held to be wrong by virtue of our simulations, since the stratification argument is a dynamic one and draws upon a richer depiction of the economy.

Finally, the fact that crop output declined, rather than rising, in the simulation of a land rental market without crop output constraints, provides a warning that a more efficient allocation of land will not address the government's concerns about raising farm output in the absence of an adequate price structure. It is not surprising that when farmers are deprived of the gift of underpriced land but not relieved of the disincentive of underpriced farm output, the result is a further exodus of resources from agriculture.

9

Post-Collective Land Tenure: An Analysis of Assignment Rules and Farm Productivity*

Introduction

From Adam Smith to John Stuart Mill, the classical economists focused much of their attention on the dual concerns of economic growth and the distribution of income. While the early 20th century saw these issues recede in importance compared to questions of allocative efficiency and the nature of the price system, these twin concerns, and the question of the relationship between distribution and growth, re-emerged in the post-War study of economic development. In the 1970s, some economists argued that distributive and developmental goals could be harmonized by more equally distributing not post-production income but rather pre-production assets, including land and education.[1] At the same time, development economists were moving toward a consensus that there were few if any economies of scale in agricultural production using technologies appropriate to LDC factor endowments. This finding supported the view that in the realm of land distribution, at least, equity and efficiency may not have to be traded off one against the other.[2] A reason commonly adduced for the superiority of family farms is the lower supervision cost and superior incentives of family labor.[3] To date, however, the theory of household effort choice has not been closely linked to the analysis of land distribution.

The decollectivization of agriculture which took place in China between 1979 and 1983 can be viewed as a land reform resulting in an egalitarian distribution of land among households. As Chapter 1 stated, China went through a more conventional

---

*This chapter is jointly authored by Martin Gaynor, Johns Hopkins University, and Louis Putterman.

[1] See, for example, Chenery et al. (1974). Note that whereas revolutionary redistribution such as that carried out by the People's Republic of China was applauded by some Western observers, mainstream economists advocated putting assets in the hands of the poor by spreading access to education, reforming land tenure (without uncompensated expropriation of current holders), and progressively distributing the proceeds of growth.

[2] See, for example, Johnston and Kilby (1974), and Dorner (1972). For references to more recent literature on the relationship between farm size and productivity, see Ellis (1988).

[3] See, for example, Binswanger and Rosenzweig (1986).

land reform, in which parcels were redistributed from landlords to poor peasants, before moving to a collective form of farm organization and land ownership in the 1950s. That first land reform left substantial inequalities in place, for land was confiscated only from the top strata of landlords and so-called "rich" peasants, not from moderately prosperous "upper middle" and "middle" peasants. Land remained private property after redistribution, and the distribution of land among households was not permanent but began changing immediately due to the active operation of a land market. Under the decollectivization, on the other hand, land was generally parceled out to households on very equal terms, recipients were granted only use rights, as opposed to ownership, and a market for subrental of land between households was slow to develop. While there is reason to believe that the distribution of land within villages was more equal under the post-collective system than under China's earlier land reform, it is not clear whether the degree of egalitarianism of access to land should be judged to have become more equal with the change from collective to household farming after 1978. On the one hand, collective team members could previously be thought of as having enjoyed equal rights to the fruits of a team's land. On the other hand, collective farming without vigorous democratic control by team members could be thought of as having deprived most peasants of effective rights over anything other than their small private plots, while concentrating what power over land was left to the locality in the hands of brigade and team cadres.

Even if the distribution of land use rights is thought of as having become *no more equal* under the decollectivization, the egalitarianism of land distribution under China's economic reforms is striking, since a central theme of those reforms was to break with the egalitarian past so as to create incentives for individual effort and initiative. Indeed, the apparent contradiction between the rhetorical theme of "fighting egalitarianism" and the degree of egalitarianism that in fact characterized land distribution following decollectivization raised questions in the minds of many reformers. As mentioned, a significant sub-rental market in land failed to develop in most localities following the reforms, and similar remarks appear to hold for agricultural labor markets.[4] In the absence of such markets, the labor forces of recipient households could be expected to have been the main determinant of the amount of labor actually applied to each parcel of land under the post-collective system, and with this in mind, Chinese commentators frequently expressed concern that the land had been divided up in too egalitarian a fashion to promote maximum productivity. In particular, writers such as Lin (1984) assumed that distribution of land on an equal per capita basis would lead to more uneven usage, and lower average

---

[4]See, again, Lin (1988a). Initially, there were ambiguities regarding the legality of both land sub-contracting and labor hiring. Moreover, peasants could not but remember that many landlords had been executed following China's revolution, and that the families of former landlords and rich peasants had suffered political persecution in periodic political campaigns during the three decades that followed. Also, in view of the ideological reversal represented by the reforms and the frequent institutional changes of its early years, peasants avoided sub-contracting land to all but close relatives, for fear that the primacy of their own rights as immediate contractees might not be respected unless they continued to farm it themselves.

productivity, than would distribution according to household labor force. Distribution according to number of workers actually engaged in farming, better still weighted by demonstrated proficiency in crop production, would yield the best results from a productivity standpoint. Many Chinese commentators also expressed concern that household contracting had given rise to diseconomies of small scale, both because of China's high man-to-land ratio, and due to the degree of plot scattering resorted to for purposes of risk reduction.[5] Finally, many worried about the fact that household rights to land were merely usufructory, as opposed to being those of full ownership. The main concerns here were (a) that households would have insufficient incentives to invest in land improvements and maintenance, given insecurity of tenure and irrecupability of what would in a private property regime be the capitalized value of improvements, and (b) that without land titles, the main source of farm collateral in other countries would be absent, causing retardation of the development of the rural credit market and hence similarly retarding agricultural investment.

The analysis of the last chapter had some implications for the farm scale and investment issues which might be drawn out more explicitly here. First, our analysis of the household level data from Dahe Township was not supportive of the supposition that farm productivity could be increased simply by increasing the scale of farms. Indeed, the production function estimates for crop production showed significantly decreasing returns to scale, although the parameters of the production function were not robust to changes in estimating method. The Dahe villages may be more representative of advanced townships in eastern China than of rural China as a whole; in the former, there is a good deal of mechanized cultivation at village level and the amount of plot scattering is minimal. However, this also suggests that there is a possibility of combining individual household farm-management with larger-scale field preparation, permitting different tasks to be carried out each on its efficient scale, while maintaining the incentive advantages of household responsibility for the final result.

At a broader level, the issue of farm scale must be considered in the light of two other major and closely related policy issues for China, those of decentralization of decision-making and of the price system. Whether the productivity of agricultural resources is maximized under a small, large, or a mixed-scale (e.g., "bi-modal")[6] farming system could, according to basic economic theory, be most easily determined simply by allowing the farm sector to operate in a competitive and decentralized fashion, with prices set by market forces, and then observing what scale of farm emerges as predominant from the competitive process. (Chapter 8 played out such a scenario by way of simulation, with concentration failing to result there because the

---

[5]One frequently cited study found that households held an average of nine separate parcels, making the average parcel size only slightly over .05 ha.
[6]See Johnston and Kilby (1975).

estimated technology showed decreasing rather than increasing returns to scale.) As Bruce Johnston and Peter Kilby (1975) noted in their influential book, market-determined prices are a crucial element of this strategy, for price distortions—in particular, low crop prices, artificially cheapened farm machine imports, and subsidized credit to the large farmer—have shown a tendency to support the growth of a sector of large-scale, mechanized farms that do not make best use of the land and, especially, labor forces of many less-developed countries. In these countries, governments have relied upon large farmers, who benefit from artificially created profitability, to supply their urban populations with food, and in some cases to generate agricultural export earnings, while pursuing protectionist strategies with implicit anti-agriculture biases that leave the vast majority of rural dwellers in poverty and underemployment, farming marginal tracts of land without adequate access to modern inputs.

In the pre-reform era, the main similarity of China's policies to those of the countries discussed by Johnston and Kilby was the administrative depressing of farm prices. Farm scale bi-modalism did not emerge in the sense of those authors, due to the pursuit of a socialist organizational path, although a bi-modalism of sorts might be seen in the targeting of intensive grain-base areas such as Huailu County whether by stated policy or on a de facto basis.[7] In essence, China's Mao-era leaders pursued large-scale agriculture with *unimodalism* of farm structure, by combining small peasant farms into larger collective ones. When the collective farm era was brought to a close by reason of perceived incentive failure, beliefs in agricultural scale economies and the benefits of mechanization remained latent in Chinese policy circles. These beliefs were undoubtedly a major factor behind expressed concerns over the scale of household-based farming and calls for concentrating land into fewer, larger-scale farms.

Economic theory would suggest that large farms would outcompete small ones and acquire more and more of the available land if there indeed existed economies of scale, if land markets were permitted to operate unobstructed, and if undistorted prices translated the underlying productivity advantages of large scale into an advantage in terms of privately realized profits. Since both open land markets and undistorted prices remained absent in 1980s China, it is impossible to know whether there were in fact productivity advantages to larger-scale farming (although more studies such as that of the previous chapter might provide further clues). Concentrating land by administratively shifting it into the hands of "specialized farm households," as in the widely reported concentration program of Beijing municipality's Shunyi County, might have been viewed by supporters as a way to over-ride the political restrictions on land market operation so as to achieve a more efficient farm

---

[7]Johnston and Kilby (1975) cited another type of bi-modalism in Soviet-type collective farm systems: the duality between the larger and more capital-using collective fields, and the smaller and more labor-intensive private plots.

scale structure. To the present author, however, the programs smack of exactly the type of economically irrational bi-modalism described by Johnston and Kilby. Large-scale grain farming near Beijing might help solve that city's food supply problems, but at a real resource cost exceeding its benefits. At the depressed prices offered by the Chinese government, grain production was not attractive to typical farmers, especially those whose advantageous locations made it easier for them to market higher-value crops. By giving land and credit with which to purchase machinery to some larger-scale farmers at zero or very low private cost, the government could make high-volume grain production privately profitable, but would thereby be sanctioning a socially wasteful use of scarce resources. It would have been much more rational to let grain and other farmgate prices rise to market levels, to make farmers pay the real opportunity cost for land, machinery, and credit, to allow farmers to choose what they wished to grow according to profitability criteria, and to let farms of appropriate size emerge through a flexible allocation process, of which the type of land market modeled in the previous chapter provides one example.

This brings us to the question of land tenure. In the model of Chapter 8, we considered how land could be reallocated among households through a process of rental, rather than buying and selling. The assumption, then, was that land remained the property of the local government. The model was kept simple by assuming that the difference between the agricultural tax paid by the households to which land was assigned by that government, and the scarcity rent established in the sub-rental market, would accrue to the household renting out its land. Another possibility, though, is for the local government itself to rent out the land at a market-clearing charge established by auction, or alternatively, to raise its own land taxes or rents to a level as close as it might like to but no greater than the market-clearing rent, with the result in either case being that the government appropriates the rents on land's scarcity value for public purposes. Any of these methods could in principle lead to an efficient allocation of land among households, while the combination of a scarcity rent with market-determined prices for output should lead to an improved allocation of rural resources, not only among crops, but also between crop production and other activities. In addition, if land rents were captured by the public sector, this would provide a means of making up for the loss of the resource transfers implicit in the purchasing of crops at submarket prices. The policy ramifications here will be discussed again in Chapter 11.

A question that remains is whether these proposals for fostering a more efficient static allocation of land among households are also capable of addressing the dynamic issues of investment in land improvements or maintenance of existing improvements, and of the use of land as collateral. Socialists and egalitarians might wish to preserve public ownership of land, partly as a check on the concentration of wealth that tends to occur over time as a result of differences in farming ability and luck,[8] and partly for the normative reason that the returns to scarce land are seen as rightly belonging to the

---

[8]See Putterman (1983b).

society in common, rather than to individuals. The question, however, is whether a collective or public form of land ownership combined with individual usufruct and allocation at scarcity rents can support dynamic efficiency. With respect to land improvements, the answer depends upon whether the users have a secure horizon of continuing land-use that is long in duration relative to the time-frame of relevant investments, and whether a system of compensation for improvements and penalties for deteriorations in land quality can be instituted to take care of cases of land transfer. The time-frame factor already lay behind the Chinese government's decision to declare that villages could contract land to households for as long as 15 years. Such a time span may suffice for certain kinds of maintenance and for households that would have continued to farm this land under any circumstances, but it may not be long enough for some types of investment; moreover, its efficacy will dwindle if it is not extended as the 15 years come to an end in the late 1990s, and it does not offer an efficient transfer mechanism for households that might prefer to move from farming to some other occupation but for the difficulty of recouping the value of their investment in land they have now worked for several years.[9]

In the long run, a system for public valuation of land improvements will have to be devised if transfers with full capitalization are to take place through the public sector. Public assessment mechanisms are common in the property tax systems of mixed economies, but valuations are linked to those in private markets, the existence of which is thus not really dispensed with. An alternative would be for the purchase of *long-term* use rights to take place among individuals, with the local government continuing to collect only the scarcity rent on unimproved land, while the value of improvements accrues to the "seller" of the use rights. In this case, the publicness of the land becomes blurred, although transfers might be monitored and subject to public approval for the sake of specific policy goals (including preventing excessive land concentration if this is desired for reasons of socioeconomic equity).

This leaves the issue of collateral, with respect to which the theoretical arguments and empirical evidence remain rather murky.[10] The advocates of private titling argue that the ability of private land to serve as collateral is a sine qua non for the full development of a rural credit system. Those who advocate reserving ownership rights to the local public sector may counter that an ideal function of the

---

[9]Wen (1991) suggests that rather than being the norm, the 15 year limit approved by central leaders in 1984 is an upper limit. He cites a survey of 274 villages according to which as of 1990, only 66% of villages had signed written contracts with resident farmers. In this group, 59% of the contracts were for a period of 10 years or less, fully 50% being for 5 years or less. Citing reports of land readjustment within a few years of initial allocation, Wen argues that the land allocations are inherently unstable, because the principle of "fairness" according to which allocations were initially made is inevitably and increasingly violated as households undergo demographic change, with the result that pressure grows to readjust the allocations. (One case of readjustment within the first 3 years of allocation under *baogan daohu* was reported by a village at Dahe, with leaders citing the need to allocate more land to nonagricultural uses. Village leaders indicated that theirs was the only village in Huailu County that had carried out such a redivision of the land, and that they had promised county officials that no further redivision would occur for 15 years, a remark strongly suggesting disapproval of the practice at the county level.)

[10]For a set of opposing views, see Feder et al. (1988), and Carter et al. (1989).

local government or collective in the post-collective farming period is as a guarantor of loans and a source of credit to individual households. There is perhaps insufficient experience in this area to draw definite conclusions, but the record of Israel's *moshavim,* which in some respects resemble China's post-collective villages, is not entirely reassuring with respect to financial solvency.[11] Private credit markets seem to have developed with vigor in some parts of China in the 1980s despite absence of private titles in land, but perhaps primarily where nonagricultural activities were relatively prominent, and where privately owned nonfarm assets were thus a viable form of collateral. We lack detailed information on credit transactions at Dahe Township, and discussion of evidence from other parts of China is outside the scope of this book.

We can now turn to the main focus of the chapter, the question of the allocation of land among households under China's existing post-collective institutions. Although numerous accounts have documented the productivity impact of China's agricultural reforms, the manner in which land was divided among households has received less attention. In the pages that follow, we develop a loose theoretical framework within which the impact of egalitarianism in land division on farm productivity can be treated.[12] The framework will then be tested empirically using data from the production teams of Dahe Township. In brief, we examine econometrically how variations in the degree of egalitarianism of the distribution of land to households in the years following the adoption of *baogan daohu* were related to allocative choices with respect to labor and current inputs, and to differences in the total productivity of the factors of production applied to agriculture. After controlling for the endogeneity of the choice of land distribution method, for households' input responses to that choice, and for soil quality and state delivery obligation levels, we will find suggestive if not conclusive evidence that productivity was related to the proportion of team land distributed on a per worker basis in a concave fashion, with a positive slope over most or all of the observed range of the land distribution parameter.

In the remainder of this section, we discuss relevant institutional background, and in the next section, we present our theoretical framework for treating the effect of land distribution on output in the absence of labor and land subrental markets. We ultimately generalize this framework to a rural economy in which households allocate resources to both agricultural and nonagricultural activities, and we bring in the effects of state procurement policies and endogenize the choice of land distribution method. In the third section, empirical operationalization and specification of

---

[11]In the *moshavim,* land, owned by a national quasi-governmental entity, is controlled by the village-community on a 99-year lease, but used by individual households who pay sub-leasing fees. Traditionally, the community or *moshav* also acted as a guarantor of loans taken out by individual members. During the inflationary years of the late 1970s and early 1980s, many *moshavim* ran up large debts that they were unable to pay back as individual members failed to repay their debts to their groups. For a discussion, see Kislev et al. (forthcoming).

[12]This framework is developed more formally in Gaynor and Putterman (1990).

econometric tests are taken up, followed by a discussion of the estimation and results. A concluding section summarizes our findings.

While a broad range of topics have been touched upon in this introduction, the focus of the remainder of the chapter is relatively narrow. Our purpose is to examine by both theoretical and empirical methods the claim that land was distributed to households, following the break-up of China's collective farms, in too egalitarian a fashion to support maximum farm output. This proposition itself is examined in a constrained context, in which the alternative to an egalitarian distribution based on household size is the method of distributing equal amounts per member of the workforce, a formula that can be considered nearly as egalitarian as the first one. Although limited, the exercise is nonetheless appropriate as a first step in studying China's rural reforms, since these two methods of land distribution were the only ones formally admitted in most of China in its first post-collective decade.[13]

Institutional Background

In Chapter 5 we noted that during the decades in which China's rural households were organized into production teams, a household was compensated for its labor contributions to its team by a combination of two methods. First, most teams retained the greater part of the grain and edible oils that they produced, and distributed most of these to member households on the basis of person equivalents, adjusted for age and sex. Second, teams distributed cash earnings, after deducting funds for capital accumulation, administration, and welfare, in proportion to the number of work-points earned by each member, where these points were to reflect the amount of work contributed. Although the cash value of foodstuffs distributed in kind was debited against this second part of the household's distribution, households whose work-points were insufficient to cover the value of those goods could go into debt to their teams for the shortfall. And since the internal accounting value of the distributed foodstuffs was based on the state procurement price rather than local market prices, we have argued that distributed food rations imparted an egalitarian dimension to the payment system even when fully "covered" by work-points.

In the villages of Dahe Township and in a substantial number of villages elsewhere in China, the method by which income in cash and kind had been distributed to households during the collective period had its direct reflection in the method by which land was distributed to them in the period of the household responsibility system. As reported in Chapter 3, the rations distributed on a per capita basis under the earlier form of organization were called *kouliang;* a portion of the land distributed to households under the responsibility system was (derivatively) known as *kouliang di,* or "grain ration land." According to the explanation given to the author

---

[13]Exceptions include various forms of land concentration, including programs involving so-called "specialized households."

by village authorities, this land was distributed in proportion to the number of persons in the household, with adjustments for age and sex, and was meant to be sufficient to allow households to produce their self-consumption requirements of grain. Another part of the land distributed to households by each team was referred to as *chengbao di*, or "contract land" and was said to be intended primarily for production for sale, especially on contract to the state. Contract land was said to be distributed in proportion to the number of laborers in the household, although some village officers said that adjustments had been made to take into account the wishes of households themselves (presumably in relation to their willingness to undertake contractual production of grain and cotton for sale to the government). As in the collective production period, each household also had a "private plot" *(ziliu di)*, generally a small garden plot located just beyond village walls, in which vegetables were grown for self-consumption and sale.[14]

The Effect of Land Distribution on Output: A Theoretical Framework

The essential hypothesis of this chapter concerning the likely effects of land distribution on output in the presence of demographic variation but in the absence of land and labor markets flows from four postulates about the effects of resource availability and of household size on households' behaviors. First, when comparing two households having equal numbers of workers but unequal numbers of nonworking members, we expect the working members of the larger household to provide more effort than their small-household counterparts, all else being equal. Our reasoning is that even if the workers in both households experience the same marginal disutility from effort at any common effort level, the marginal utility of income at that effort level (which by the *ceteris paribus* assumption corresponds to a common level of household income) would be higher for the larger household, since the income must be shared by more members.[15] Second, we expect a given household to increase

---

[14]Wen (1991) reports that a survey of 253 villages carried out by the R.C.R.D. and World Bank in 1988 found that 25% of the villages contracted land to their households according to a combination of household population and household labor force, as did the villages at Dahe; 4% contracted their land solely according to labor force, 69% solely according to population, and 1% contracted to production groups or farmed collectively. Within the set of villages using the mixed distribution approach, 63% of villages were said to assign 40–60% of village land according to population. Land allotted according to population was referred to as at Dahe as grain ration or household food plots, and obligations to sell crops to the state were attached to contract or duty but not to grain ration or food plots. Wen states that distribution on the basis of household population only dominates in "the vast inland rural areas," whereas division into "food plots and duty plots," or by both population and labor force, "prevails in places with both higher population pressure and land productivity." Dahe's membership in the second group is broadly consistent with this characterization.

[15]The analysis of individual labor supply in Chapter 6 of this book provides no conclusive evidence regarding the validity of the assumption that labor supply is increasing in the ratio of dependents to household members. According to Table 6.2, the imputed voluntary portion of labor supply to the *collective* in 1979 was negatively correlated with the dependency ratio of the household to which the worker belonged. However, the imputed mandatory portion of labor supply was positively correlated with the dependency ratio, and the regression shown in Table 6.3, which does not attempt to sort labor supply

its supply of effort as it has more resources (e.g., land) to work with, but to do so at a decreasing rate. Effort should increase in the presence of more complementary inputs because these cause the marginal product of effort to be larger at any given effort level. Effort should rise at a decreasing rate because the marginal utility of income increases at a decreasing rate while the marginal disutility of effort can be presumed to increase at an increasing rate. Our third postulate is that the rate at which the workers in a household increase their effort as they are supplied with additional units of land can be expected to be a positive function of the ratio of nonworkers to workers in the household. In other words, if two households have the same number of workers and the same amount of land, an additional unit of land will lead to a bigger increase in effort on the part of the workers with more nonworkers to feed, the basic intuition being that the extra income which the new land puts within their reach has greater marginal utility for the members of the large than of the small household, for the same reason as given under the first postulate.[16] The fourth postulate parallels the first one, but deals with variations in the number of workers rather than members. It says that if two households have equal populations but unequal workforces, the household with the larger workforce will supply a larger total amount of effort, all else being equal. The reason is that the marginal disutility of effort at a given total effort level is smaller for the working members of the household with a larger workforce, since that total effort level can be achieved by that household with less labor per worker.[17]

Figure 9.1 illustrates the first three postulates. The vertical axis measures h_a, the total agricultural effort of the workers in a farm household. The horizontal axis measures λ, the amount of land farmed by the household. For ease of exposition, households in the figure are assumed to have equal numbers of workers, but may have differing total numbers of members, m. Households are assumed to optimize in their choices of h_a with respect to their size, m, and their land allotments, λ. The two curves in the figure show how optimal effort levels h_a^* vary with the size of the land allotment for households of two different sizes, m_1 and m_2, where $m_1 < m_2$. Postulate 1 is reflected in the fact that the curve for the larger household (indexed by 2) lies everywhere above that for the smaller household (indexed by 1). Postulate 2 is

---

by period or motivational basis, finds no significant correlation between labor supply and dependency ratio. Furthermore, the analysis of Chapter 6 does not treat total labor supply in the collective period, which included that to the household's private activities. There is evidence (see Chapter 10) that households earning less per capita in the collective sector earned more per capita in the private sector. As reasoned by Griffin (e.g., in Griffin ed., 1984), members of households with more dependents at home may have needed to do more work closer to home, and therefore worked more in private activities. A finding that individual labor supply to the collective sector was uncorrelated with household size while that to private activities was positively correlated with that variable would be fully consistent with the present assumption.

[16]The result does not follow as automatically because the larger household is already assumed to be supplying more effort and thus to have a higher income. The postulate is nonetheless easily established in the formal model of Gaynor and Putterman (1992).

[17]For a formal model consistent with these four postulates, see Gaynor and Putterman (1992).

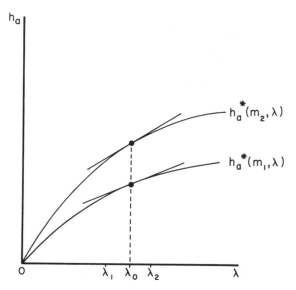

Figure 9.1. Effort supply as a function of land for households of differing sizes and identical workforces.

reflected in the fact that the h_a^* curves are increasing and concave in λ. Postulate 3 is reflected in the fact that the slope of the h_a^* curve is greater for the larger household at any common level of land allotment—e.g., λ_0 in the figure.

Consider, now, a village with a certain total population, labor force, and land endowment. Suppose that the village can allot its land among its constituent households either in proportion to their populations, in proportion to their work-forces, or according to a weighted average of the two. And suppose, finally, that the members of the village, or their leaders, wish to allot the land among households so as to maximize total output. (Following observed conditions at Dahe Township and reports from other localities in China, we continue to assume that households employ only their own labor and that land remains with those households to which it is allotted by the village.) As a first exercise, let m (as well as n) be identical across households—thus households share a common h_a^* curve in Figure 9.1—and consider the impact of land allocation upon total output. A first proposition to flow from our postulates is that with equal household sizes and labor forces, equal distribution of land uniquely maximizes output. Suppose that the equal division of land gives exactly λ_0 hectares to each household (see Fig. 9.1). Now, let the land endowment of some households be increased slightly, while that of other households is reduced. By concavity of the h_a^* curve, any redistribution of land must cause total effort to decrease, since those losing land decrease their effort more rapidly than those receiving land increase theirs. The reduction of total effort in the village, with a fixed total land endowment, implies a reduction of total output, F, unless counteracted by a better matching of effort to land parcels. But since households provided equal amounts of effort and had equal sized plots in the initial situation, marginal product of land and labor were equal across farms, so no such improvement is possible. Any move away from distributing λ_0 to each household thus reduces output, as claimed.

A second proposition to be demonstrated is that (a) when household size (but not the number of working members) varies, aggregate output is maximized at an unequal distribution of land among households, and (b) this allocation gives more land to households having more members. First, notice that when households differ in size, an equal allocation of land cannot maximize the output of the village, because households would be applying differing amounts of labor to common amounts of land, leading to differing marginal products of both land and labor across households (consider the position at common land allotment λ_0 when some households have m_1 and others m_2 members, in Fig. 9.1). Now, notice that a small increase in the amount of land given to larger households and a corresponding reduction in the amount of land given to smaller households leads to an unambiguous rise in output. For example, consider a move away from λ_0, in Figure 9.1, in which households of size m_2 get slightly more land and those of size m_1 lose an equal amount of land. As the larger households receive the additional land, they increase their effort at the rate shown by the tangent to the upper curve at λ_0, and as the smaller households lose this land, they reduce their effort at the rate shown by the tangent to the lower curve at λ_0. Since the rate of effort increase by the larger households exceeds the rate of effort reduction by the smaller households, total effort goes up at least for a small change in the distribution of land.

Concavity of the h_a^* curves means that the increased effort of the receiving household will eventually fail to exceed the reduced effort of the household losing land. For sufficiently large redistributions from small to large households, the slope of $h_a^*(m_1, \lambda)$ eventually exceeds that of $h_a^*(m_2, \lambda)$.[18] This observation leads us to our third proposition: that the output maximizing distribution of land gives some weight to both households' sizes and households' workforces. From the standpoint of the discussion thus far, the proposition amounts to saying that the redistribution of land from small to large households must stop before the allotment of land among households becomes strictly proportionate to household sizes. One way to see this is to reverse the assumptions and imagine, now, that households have the same number of members, but different numbers of workers. Then the fourth postulate implies that output would not be maximized by giving each household the same amount of land. This is because the households with larger workforces would apply more effort to that land, causing marginal products of labor and land to differ among households. Since both sets of marginal products would begin to converge as the two households moved from this equal allocation to one in which the households with more workers had more

---

[18]While this observation is meant to be helpful from an intuitive standpoint, it should be noted that equality of slopes is not a condition for maximization of overall output. For a more complete discussion, see again Gaynor and Putterman (1992).

and those with less workers less land, the output maximizing distribution of land is clearly one that gives some weight to the number of workers in the households.

Our fourth and final proposition is that if a village's land is distributed partly in proportion to the number of workers in each household and partly in proportion to the total size of each household, the village's total agricultural output can be expected to be a concave function of the land distribution parameter (i.e., the degree to which land is distributed according to workers versus household size). By the previous propositions, we know that the output-maximizing distribution of land is one that gives all weight neither to household sizes nor to household workforces. The only new content of this last proposition is the idea that there is a unique output-maximizing allocation, and that as one moves toward this allocation from either the purely size-reflecting or the purely workforce-reflecting allocation, output must steadily rise. The "well-behavedness" of total output as a function of the land allotment parameter is a reasonable expectation assuming concavity of households' utility functions in effort and income, and of the production function in effort and land.

Applying the Framework: Institutional and Policy Parameters

Application of the foregoing analysis to rural China in the 1980s requires that it be generalized to allow for the use of factors of production in addition to land and labor, and for the existence of other income sources. To allow for other factors of production, let each household have an endowment of capital, k, which it can devote to either agricultural or other uses. Let the household also be able to purchase current inputs, z, at a parametric price, normalized to unity. The household's income from crop production can be written

$$y_a = f(h_a, \lambda, k_a, z_a) - z_a \qquad (9.1)$$

where f is a production function in value terms, and where subscripts a indicate the portions of a given input devoted to crop production (agriculture).[19]

For purposes of the model to be estimated, it is not necessary to introduce explicit notation referring to the other activities in which the household may engage and invest resources, and from which it can draw income.[20] Rather, we will introduce

---

[19]Note that the same remarks regarding the dangers of aggregating heterogeneous inputs and outputs valued at heterogeneous prices into a function f, which will be assumed to be well-behaved, apply here as in previous chapters. We do attempt to treat grain and crops as a whole separately, to the extent that the data permit. The influence of separate state and market prices is addressed by controlling for variations in quota levels by econometric methods. Some effects of the quota system are discussed in the next section.

[20]While modeling resource allocation among sectors and explicitly incorporating nonagricultural variables into the estimation procedure might be desirable in principle, the analysis of the previous chapter suggests that intersectoral allocation at Dahe was constrained by forces that remain unclear in detail, and in Chapter 4 we found that the data on nonagricultural activities at the team level—at which the tests of this chapter are performed, for reasons explained below—was especially incomplete for the 1980s.

equations that model the resource flows into agriculture as functions of the available capital stock, number of workers, and other relevant economic variables, thus recognizing that the household may allocate only a portion of each resource to crop production. This approach is consistent with presuming that the choice made would be an optimizing one, influenced by factors including the way in which land is distributed, and subject to constraints of the type discussed in Chapters 4, 8, and again presently.

The model must also be expanded for estimation purposes in order to accommodate the effects of additional institutional factors, and to allow for potential endogeneity of some of the regressors. Let the behavioral agricultural production function[21] for a team of households be written as

$$F = F(N_a, Z_{a,}, K, \Lambda, S, \xi, Q) \tag{9.2}$$

where F is a village-level production function in value terms and where (suppressing the team index subscript) N_a represents the number of workers in agriculture (crop production) among team t households, Z_a represents agricultural expenditures (current inputs) of team t households, K represents the households' combined capital stocks, Λ is the total land available to be divided among them, S is a vector of soil quality indicators,[22] and Q is the quota or contract obligation for sale of grain to the state, per hectare of land. The variable ξ is the land distribution parameter which is the central focus of our analysis. Specifically, each household is assumed to receive a land allotment

$$\lambda_i = [\xi(n_i/N) + (1 - \xi)(m_i/M)]\Lambda \tag{9.3}$$

where n_i is the number of workers in the household, N is the number of workers in the village, and M is the number of persons in the village. Thus, ξ represents the proportion of village land that is divided based on household workforces assuming that the remainder must be divided in proportion to household size.

Function F thus includes the physical factors of production (including soil quality), and the institutional variables ξ and Q. The propositions presented above detail how ξ is expected to affect total effort supplied to agriculture by household workers. It must be noted that only part of this effect may be reflected in N_a, the allocation of *laborers* to agriculture, since some of it may take the form of variation in

---

[21]That (9.2) is a "behavioral" or "institutional" production function follows from the fact that the institutional factors ξ and Q appear in it as a result of behavior by economic agents. As elsewhere in this book, we note that the parameters of the technology of production are not necessarily recoverable from such a function.

[22]The innovation of including in this analysis proxies for soil quality, which were not used in the analysis of other chapters (especially 4 and 5, which also used team-level data) was the byproduct of a search for predictors of the land distribution and grain quota parameters (see equations (9.6) and (9.7) below). Having discovered potentially appropriate measures, we proceeded to use them also in other equations in which they appeared to be of possible relevance, such as the present one. As will be seen below, the indicators are available only at team level and are based on data for the early 1980s only.

unmeasured *effort*. Indeed, by virtue of that part of the effect of ξ upon effective labor input (H_a) which is not captured by changes in the number of workers, output can be expected to display a concave relationship with ξ, even after controlling for N_a.

For given levels and quality of inputs, we hypothesize that output measured in value terms will be negatively related to the quota level. The quota lowers the *value* of the gross value of agricultural (i.e., crop) output (GVCO) in two ways: it raises the proportion of grain sold at (low) state prices, and it shifts the composition of output toward grain, which tends to be a crop with lower return per unit inputs under China's distorted price structure. By reducing the expected returns to agriculture relative to other crops, especially if reinforced by local government interventions determining land allocation among crops, the quota may also have a disincentive effect that operates, unobservably, through the effort parameter. The effect on *grain output* per unit of inputs to *grain* is less clear. A binding grain quota will raise total grain production, but mostly by increasing inputs to the activity. Insofar as the use of grain for home consumption or for feed is preferred to its delivery to the government at low prices, there may again be a disincentive effect here which lowers output by way of lower effort.[23]

Our theoretical framework posited that the method of distributing land would affect output by its influence on the supply of agricultural work effort. Equation (9.2) captures the effects of ξ on F by way of variations in effort given a fixed number of workers in agriculture, but some effort adjustments may also take the form of changes in the number of workers who engage in agricultural activity as a principal occupation. In our expanded model, current inputs and capital used in agriculture may also be functions of ξ. Since input supplies will be affected also by other factors, such as input endowment levels, multivariate equations are needed if unbiased estimates of the effect of ξ on N_a and other input choices are to be obtained.

Because N_a and Z_a are chosen by member households in part in response to unobserved factor qualities (e.g., managerial ability or capital vintage), they may be correlated with the error term in a stochastic version of (9.2). In addition, the quota and the land distribution method may also be chosen by the team or village leadership based in part on such unobserved factors. Therefore, least squares estimates of the behavioral production function may suffer from simultaneous equations bias. The exogeneity test of Hausman (1978) and Wu (1973) is accordingly used to examine whether these variables can be treated as uncorrelated with the error term in the regression. The model is estimated by two-stage least squares, instrumenting for

---

[23] A theoretical analysis of the effects of the quotas on effort, output, and choice of land allocation rule might have to take into account that the tax implicit in quota obligations is attached to land allocated according to workforce ("contract land") but not to land allocated according to household population ("grain ration land"). However, we noted earlier the likelihood that the distinction between the two types of land exists only for accounting purposes, and does not take the form of a difference among plots. If this is so, then although the relationship between land allocations, household labor force, and household size should continue to adhere to the patterns predicted in our theoretical framework, it is unclear what force the differential tax on "contract land" would have.

those variables for which exogeneity is rejected. The full model, which is potentially recursive (in part, or in full), consists of (9.2) plus

$$N_a = g_1(S,N,K,\Lambda,LF,ZH,\xi,Q) \qquad (9.4)$$

$$Z_a = g_2(S,N,K,\Lambda,LF,ZH,\xi,Q) \qquad (9.5)$$

$$\xi = g_3(Q,S,(M/N)) \qquad (9.6)$$

$$Q = g_4(S,(M/\Lambda)) \qquad (9.7)$$

where LF and ZH are, respectively, a worker classification index and the share of current input costs borne by households as opposed to their teams or villages.[24]

In equation (9.7), soil quality is expected to be positively correlated with the grain sales quota assigned to the team, while population density is expected to be negatively correlated with the quota, due to the fact that teams having more fertile soil or less mouths to feed per hectare are expected to be asked to sell more to the state per hectare of land. In equation (9.6), we assume that ξ is negatively correlated with Q, since land intended for meeting quota obligations is reportedly distributed on the basis of household labor force. Teams with more fertile soil might have higher ξ if meeting quotas is the main reason for distributing land by labor force, since better soil makes it easier to meet the quota with less land. Teams with higher dependent ratios (M/N) are expected to choose higher ξ because a larger fraction of land will be needed to meet subsistence requirements.[25] Note that the hierarchical structure of equations (9.2) and (9.4)–(9.7) allows for the possibility that Q is determined by higher-level officials before ξ is selected by team or village leaders, as is likely to have occurred in practice.

Equations (9.4) and (9.5) model household allocation decisions, aggregated to the team level. Our theoretical discussion suggests that the number of agricultural workers in the team will be a concave function of ξ. If the latter is entered quadratically, for example, we expect a positive coefficient on ξ and a negative coefficient on its square. The influence of quotas on measured productivity has been discussed previously. The number of agricultural workers should be positively

---

[24]LF is the share of the workforce listed as "full labor powers"; total workforce consists of these plus "half labor powers," where the latter label may indicate immature or advanced age, or disabilities. ZH appears because teams or villages often paid part of the input costs to help offset the relative unattractiveness of crop production under conditions of partially controlled crop prices. The units of analysis are teams observed in specific years, although it is to be kept in mind that the farm production units are the households which compose the teams; a subscript index for the team and year should appear on most terms but is suppressed here.

[25]Rather than formally developing our model of the optimal land allocation rule to specify and predict the relationships in equation (9.6), we have relied on institutional knowledge and informal reasoning. Extending the model itself would be a desirable direction for future research as well as a test of its utility. Our discussion of the estimates for this equation will touch on a possible application of Wen's remarks regarding determinants of the land allocation rule in different regions of China.

related to soil quality, total capital stock, and total labor force. As each of the last two factors grow larger, their marginal products fall in all activities, so larger stocks of capital and numbers of workers should mean that at least a little more of each can be expected to find their way into crop production. If labor force classification is accurately based on physical status as suggested above, and if more able-bodied workers are less likely to be found in agriculture on a full-time basis, because of its low returns relative to construction and other trades, the labor force classification index could be negatively related to the number of agricultural workers. Although larger agricultural expenditure raises the marginal product of labor in agriculture so that for a larger amount of Z_a provided by the team or village we might expect larger N_a, labor and current input choices *by households* are simultaneous, and larger ZH implies larger total Z_a for any given amount provided by the team. Thus, no a priori hypothesis is offered on the effect of ZH. To the extent that Z is also determined by household choices and labor and current inputs are complements in production, the same signs can be expected in (9.5) as in (9.4).[26]

Econometric Analysis

Data and Specification

Our team level data indicate the proportions of land distributed to households on per capita and per worker bases in 1983–1985, as well as information on total input usage, land distribution by crop, and outputs achieved. The proportions of land distributed on the basis of household labor force versus household population in the sixty-one teams providing data on this and other included variables are given by Table 9.1. These proportions varied little for given teams during 1983–1985, so the variance shown by the table is primarily inter-team. Outputs and inputs, aggregated to team level, vary both across teams and among years; their average values are also shown in Table 9.1. In view of this variation and the availability of other needed data, it is possible to study the effects of differences in land distribution practices on agricultural factor productivity at the team level, keeping in mind that farm production was the responsibility of the individual households in each team.[27] While the issues addressed in this chapter could also be studied using the household survey

[26]Full symmetry would require that (9.4) and (9.5) be accompanied by a parallel equation for K_a, and that K_a rather than the full capital stock K appear in the agricultural production function (9.2). While this would be a more ideal approach, absence of data regarding the actual allocation of capital between sectors in our sample makes it impossible to implement.

[27]Aggregation of production over production units adds another concern to those of aggregation over products and price variation, discussed in a previous footnote. The same problem arises in all team level production function estimates for the post-collective period, including those of Chapters 4 and 7. As footnote 20 to Chapter 4 indicated, a quasi-homothetic technology satisfies the necessary conditions for the existence of an aggregate production function, and the Cobb-Douglas form is quasi-homothetic. In the present instance, we go beyond the exercises of the earlier chapters to explicitly compare the performance of the Cobb-Douglas with two other functional forms, and do not reject its use based on the appropriate specification tests.

Table 9.1. Means of Variables in the Sample[a]

Variable	Mean	Standard Deviation
Gross value of crop output[b]	76,626	23,030
Grain output[c]	125,165	33,944
Agr. labor force	68.69	25.21
Labor "quality" index[d]	0.88	0.07
Gross value of capital assets[b]	32,875	12,189
Cultivated area[e]	23.81	10.28
Grain cultivated area[e]	12.25	3.35
Total agricultural expenses[b]	18,832	7,008
Wheat target[f]	4,538.2	672.3
Corn target[f]	4,336.4	574.3
Cotton target[f]	737.7	260.5
Land index[f]	1.44	0.38
Percent land (ξ)	0.689	0.058
Grain quota per cultivated ha.[c]	1,823.0	808.5
Cost share ratio[g]	0.50	0.41
Population	221.2	69.9
Population per ha	10.06	2.72
Dependency ratio[h]	2.21	0.40

[a]Except for the land variables, entries are based on 183 observations containing all used in this chapter's analysis, which are from 61 teams for the years 1983–1985.

[b]In *yuan*.

[c]In kilograms.

[d]Number of "full labor powers" divided by working population.

[e]In hectares. Grain cultivated area is defined as the larger of autumn grain sown area and summer grain sown area.

[f]Land quality variables are as reported for 1982 only, and are for the same 61 teams. Targets were those set by the teams under *lianchan jichou* and are in kilograms per hectare. The land index is a weighted average of the fractions of land reported to be of high, medium, and low quality, with weights 2 = high, 1 = medium, 0 = low.

[g]Agricultural expenses borne by team divided by total agricultural expenses.

[h]Total population to working population.

data from Dahe, the small number of teams included in that survey (only 5) and the fact that the land division method was chosen at the team level means that the present strategy is to be preferred. Plans to study the impact of tenure status on productivity at the level of individual *plots* were abandoned when (as mentioned in Chapter 3) it was learned that the distinction between "grain ration" and "contract" land may have had significance only from the standpoint of village or team accounts, and that the plots may not have been distinguishable as to "tenure type" or basis of distribution from the standpoint of the households.

Turning to the choice of variables, we employ two measures of agricultural output: total grain output, measured by weight (in kilograms), and the gross value of crop output (GVCO), in *yuan*. Due to differences in institutional and technological factors relating to grain versus nongrain crop production, we estimate the entire equation system separately for grain and for GVCO. GVCO aggregates different crops, according to the accountants involved by using actual prices for both state and free market sales, in the case of marketed output, and using reported market prices, in the case of output consumed by team members.[28] Our estimates for grain employ the area cultivated to grain, rather than total cultivated area, to represent Λ in equations (9.4)–(9.6), except that they retain total cultivated area as denominator in the expression for population density in equation (9.7). The variable Q is represented by grain quota per hectare cultivated to grain, rather than per total hectare cultivated, in the grain variant of (9.7). With the exception of land, the data do not permit disaggregation of inputs by crop, so full input levels are entered in the grain variants of (9.2), (9.4), and (9.5) as if all crop production inputs were used for grain.

The GVCO and grain variants of our model each have strengths and weaknesses, the weakness of the former being the need to assume that crop production activity as a whole aggregates to a well-behaved production technology, and that of the latter being inability to disaggregate nonland inputs as between grain and nongrain crops. Rather than choose between these two imperfect approaches, we estimate our model in both variants. A third possibility, that of estimating a production function for nongrain crops, was pursued in preliminary estimates but was eliminated to reduce the number of permutations of the estimating process and because it suffers from the same limitation as the estimation for grain alone, that of inability to disaggregate inputs, while also having GVCO's limitation of aggregation across crops on the output side.[29]

The institutional reasons for distinguishing between grain and other crops have been discussed in other chapters, but may be summarized again here. As argued in Chapter 8, there is reason to believe that households operated as if under a constraint to provide their own subsistence requirements, primarily of grain, although there is more than one explanation of why they may have done so. On the one hand, local officials probably felt pressure from higher levels to do their part in solving China's grain production problem, an ever-present and focal political issue, and they may accordingly have taken steps to see that households produced their own requirements as well as meeting contractual obligations to the state. At Dahe in the early 1980s, as in 80% of the villages in eastern China and over 50% in the remainder of the country in 1987,[30] these steps probably included the constraining of planting choices through village planning of crop layout and rotations, and the implementation of these plans in conjunction with village-level plowing and planting of wheat and cotton.[31] On the other hand, prices in the free market for grain were unpredictable, and local officials occasionally closed that market or limited the quantities that could be transacted by each individual, as a way of protecting the supply to the state purchasing authorities. Under these conditions, households may have freely elected to produce their own grain needs, to avoid dependence on an unreliable source. When combined with the mandatory nature of contracts to produce grain for the state, these factors could have

---

[28]Since the accountants did not provide sufficiently disaggregated price and sales data to allow for a check on our parts, we cannot rule out the possibility of inconsistencies in the method of aggregation.

[29]In Gaynor and Putterman (1992) we circumvent the input disaggregation problem by estimating a structural model for grain output. See footnote 48, below.

[30]Sicular (1991, Table 2).

[31]Unified plowing was practiced in 76% of the eastern, 34% of the central, and 20% of the western villages, according to the source just cited.

led to household behavior consistent with the suggestion of many Chinese economists that the country's farmers first produced a targeted amount of grain for subsistence and contract sale purposes, then allocated their remaining resources according to profitability criteria.

The independent variables included in the model consist of physical factors of production and institutional factors hypothesized to affect behavior. The physical factors are labor, capital, land, and agricultural expenditures. As mentioned earlier, a worker classification index appears in (9.4) and (9.5). Capital is measured as the gross value of capital assets of the team. As in Chapters 4 and 7, we face the problem of there being no measure of the proportion of those assets dedicated to agriculture. The variables related to land input are the area of land cultivated, and a set of indicators of soil quality. Total cultivated area is utilized for estimating the GVCO production function: land area cultivated for grain for the grain production function. We employ four variables to proxy for soil quality: targets for wheat, corn, and cotton yields set by the teams during the *lianchan jichou* reform stage, and an index of land quality calculated from a classification scheme also used in that period.[32] The institutional factors are the percentage of land distributed on the basis of the number of workers (corresponding to the theoretical variable ξ),[33] the quota or contracted level of grain sales to the state denominated by total or grain cultivated area, and the share of agricultural expenses borne by the households as opposed to their teams or villages. The person/land ratio and the average dependency ratio in each team are used to predict the first two variables.

Estimation Procedure

We test three alternative forms for the behavioral production function. First, we consider an augmented Cobb-Douglas form of the type used also in the analysis of Chapter 5 and in that of Kim discussed in Chapter 7.[34] In estimating equation (9.2) by

---

[32]Under *lianchan jichou*, members were rewarded for exceeding the targets, and different targets were set for land ranked as of high, medium, and low quality. Assuming that higher targets were set for better quality land, and that targets reflected past yields, these targets should vary positively with underlying soil quality. Our target-based measures consist of the targets for each crop in each land grade weighted by the share of that grade in the team's cultivated area. The index is computed by adding together the shares of land of each quality, weighting high quality land by 2, medium quality land by 1, and low quality land by zero.

[33]In actuality, the data set provides a breakdown of land distributed under *baogan daohu* into the two categories "contract land" and "grain ration land," which were discussed in the Introduction of this chapter. For the reasons indicated there, we take the share distributed as "contract land" as opposed to that distributed as "grain ration land" to be our measure of the proportion of land distributed on the basis of household labor force, or ξ.

[34]In Gaynor and Putterman (1990) it is noted that this is a special case of the generalized power production function proposed by de Janvry (1972),

$$F_i = A\Pi(\beta_j q_{j\ i})\exp[\Sigma(\gamma_k x_{ki})] \exp(\epsilon\ f_i)$$

where F_i is output for observation i (team t in year y), the q_{ji} are physical factors of production, and the x_{ki} are institutional factors and quality measures.

this first form, output and conventional factor inputs are entered in log form, and institutional and quality variables are entered linearly. The two alternatives that we considered are a translog expansion of the augmented Cobb-Douglas in the physical factors, and an equation in which output is related to the inputs as well as the institutional variables linearly. Since the translog and augmented Cobb-Douglas forms are nested, a specification test to discriminate between the two is an F test on the additional terms included in the translog form. The linear and Cobb-Douglas forms are not nested; therefore a specification test for non-nested alternatives must be employed. We utilize the P_E test of Davidson, White, and MacKinnon (MacKinnon et al., 1983). Equations (9.4)–(9.7) are treated as linear.

The equation system is estimated recursively, as follows. First, equation (9.7) is estimated, and the predicted values of Q are entered in (9.6), where exogeneity of that variable is tested for by a Hausman test.[35] In (9.4) and (9.5), we test for exogeneity of ξ using the predicted values from (9.6), and for exogeneity of Q using the predicted values from (9.7).[36] In (9.2), we again test for exogeneity of ξ and Q as in (9.4) and (9.5), and we test for exogeneity of N_a and Z_a using predicted values from (9.4) and (9.5).

Although our data combined cross-section and time-series variation, because observed S (and in many cases ξ) does not vary across years for given teams, it is impossible to estimate (9.2)–(9.6) using a fixed-effects model. However, since there are potentially significant correlations over time in the data for each team, alternative estimates of (9.2) with a random-effects model were performed and will be compared with the OLS estimates.[37]

As indicated earlier, our measure of agricultural labor, the number of workers in agriculture, may not be a good measure of total effort applied to agriculture. Not only will effort per agricultural worker vary in ways that we cannot directly detect, but also nonagricultural workers may engage in part time agricultural work, especially during periods of peak labor demand (e.g., harvest time) when other activities are reported to be temporarily interrupted. In addition, there was a tendency for the most able workers to seek employment outside of agriculture, due to the low returns in that sector (related to government interventions). Finally, the reported information on agricultural workers is unreliable because in the period in question, labor was no longer allocated centrally by team leaders, whose estimates could therefore be

---

[35]We note again that ξ varies little if at all for a given team during the years 1983–1985, for which we estimate (9.2) through (9.5). We estimate (9.7) using only one observation per team, consisting of the values of the S indices for 1982 (the only year for which these data are available on a large majority of teams) and of M/N and Q for 1983. We then estimate (9.6) also using one observation per team, consisting of the 1983 value of ξ and the values just indicated for S, M/N, and Q, or predicted values from (9.7) for Q.

[36](9.4) and (9.5) are estimated for 1983–1985, using current data for all variables. Estimated Q is obtained from (9.7) in this case by entering current year values for Q and M/L in that equation.

[37]We considered the instrumental variable method of Hausman and Taylor (1981), but were concerned about achieving identification given the complexity of the model in (9.2)–(9.7), with its multiple sources of potential endogeneity.

inaccurate. To take advantage of the available information, we attempt to replace N_a in our estimating equation with

$$\tilde{N}_a = ([1 - c]N_a + cN) \tag{9.8}$$

where N is the total reported labor force, both agricultural and nonagricultural, and c is a constant of proportionality representing effective agricultural labor per nonagricultural worker as a share of that per agricultural worker. The latter constant can be estimated by nonlinear least squares, and the test for the effect of nonagricultural labor is a test of its statistical significance.

Results

As indicated previously, the number of agricultural workers (N_a), agricultural expenditures (Z_a), the state grain quota per hectare (Q), and the land distribution parameter (ξ) are all potentially endogenous independent variables in the production function (9.2). Upon estimation, the exogeneity of the number of workers in agriculture is rejected at the 1% level in both the grain and the GVCO production functions. Exogeneity of agricultural expenses is rejected at just under a 1% confidence level in the grain production function. It is not rejected for the GVCO production function. The exogeneity of the other variables cannot be rejected for either grain or GVCO. The exogeneity of the grain quota and the land distribution parameter cannot be rejected in the instrumenting equation for agricultural workers, but the exogeneity of these variables is rejected in the instrumenting equation for agricultural expenditures. Finally, the exogeneity of the grain quota as an independent variable explaining the land allocation method is rejected at the 1% level. The resulting system of equations is partially simultaneous (and partially recursive); therefore it is estimated using the method of instrumental variables.

The specification test for distinguishing between the augmented Cobb-Douglas form and the translog form is an F test for the joint significance of the variables added by a translog expansion of the augmented Cobb-Douglas. The variables are not jointly significant, nor are they individually significant. Therefore, the validity of the augmented Cobb-Douglas functional form cannot be rejected in favor of the translog form. The test of the augmented Cobb-Douglas versus the linear form is the P_E test for non-nested alternatives. The validity of the augmented Cobb-Douglas cannot be rejected, and the validity of the linear form is rejected at the 1% level. Based on these results we employ the augmented Cobb-Douglas functional form.

We also test for the explanatory power of the number of nonagricultural workers as a labor input. The test consists of a significance test on the coefficient c in equation (9.8). This parameter is not significantly different from zero; therefore, the number of nonagricultural workers is omitted from estimation, and we revert to estimating (9.2) unmodified by (9.8).

Last, we tested for the significance of within-team correlations over time by estimating a random-effects version of (9.2). However, the magnitudes of the coefficients and their significance levels are little altered from those obtained via standard least squares.

Table 9.2 contains the estimates of the parameters of the behavioral production functions for grain and gross value of crop output. The estimates were obtained using standard least squares and generalized least squares, for the random-effects model. Independent variables are instrumented as indicated by the exogeneity tests, with the

Table 9.2. Instrumental Variable Estimates of the Behavioral Production Function

Dependent Variable:	Ln (Grain)		Ln (GVCO)	
Independent Variable	**Least Squares**	**Random Effects**	**Least Squares**	**Random Effects**
Constant	4.43	4.64	8.18	9.29
	(1.47)	(1.50)	(3.51)	(3.66)
Ln (agricultural workers)[d]	0.13[a]	0.13[a]	0.25[a]	0.26[c]
	(0.025)	(0.025)	(0.08)	(0.08)
Ln (cultivated area)	0.79[a]	0.77[a]	0.36[a]	0.39[c]
	(0.04)	(0.043)	(0.11)	(0.108)
Ln (capital)	−0.003	−0.006	0.20[a]	0.20[c]
	(0.015)	(0.016)	(0.054)	(0.053)
Ln (agricultural expenses)[e]	0.17[a]	0.19[a]	0.098	0.02
	(0.046)	(0.05)	(0.061)	(0.06)
Wheat target	.0001	.0001	−.00002	−.00000
	(.00002)	(.00002)	(.00007)	(.00008)
Corn target	.00005	.00005	.00001	.00000
	(.00002)	(.00002)	(.00008)	(.00008)
Cotton target	.00005	.00005	.00017	.00107
	(.00005)	(.00005)	(.00015)	(.00147)
Ln (land index)	−0.15[a]	−0.12[a]	−0.10	−0.07
	(0.036)	(0.03)	(0.083)	(0.09)
Percent land	6.5[b]	5.84[a]	−10.99	−12.5
	(2.5)	(2.65)	(8.73)	(8.94)
Percent land, squared	−04.44	−3.95[b]	9.84	11.08
	(0.84)	(1.95)	(6.47)	(6.8)
Quota	.00000	.00000	.00004	.00001
	(.00000)	(.00000)	(.00003)	(.00003)
Cross-sectional var. component	—	0.0007	—	0.1
Time-series variance component	—	0.001	—	0.02
R^2	0.93	—	0.41	—
F	198.15[a]	—	10.96[a]	—
Number of observations	183	183	183	183

Standard errors are reported in parentheses below parameter estimates.
[a]Significant at 1% level.
[b]Significant at 5% level.
[c]Significant at 10% level.
[d]Instrumental variable for both grain and GVCO.
e Instrumental variable for grain only.

corresponding cases being noted in the table. Since neither the estimates of the coefficients nor their standard errors differ in any substantial way between the least squares and random-effects models, we simply discuss the least squares results contained in the first and third columns of the table. Results for the first-stage or instrumenting equations—i.e., the estimates of (9.4)–(9.7)—are displayed in Tables 9.3 and 9.4.

The major focus of the present analysis is the impact of the land distribution rule

Table 9.3. First Stage Regressions: Grain

Independent Variable	Dependent Variable			
	Agricultural Workers	Agricultural Expenses	Percent Land	Quota
Constant	177.28	−9,146,346.06[c]	1.18[a]	4,951.42
	(145.8)	(4,973,551.65)	(0.09)	(1,011.17)
Wheat target	.0015	−9.24	−.00000	0.0043
	(.0033)	(4.36)	(.00001)	(0.34)
Corn target	−.0173	17.12	−.00000	−0.19
	(.0035)	(7.11)	(.00001)	(0.35)
Cotton target	.0100	−53.00	−.00009	−0.31
	(.0061)	(20.72)	(.00002)	(0.67)
Land index	15.61[a]	−38,903.65	0.02	128.04
	(5.04)	(24,213.89)	(0.015)	(374.36)
Population per ha	—	—	−.00227	−78.8
			(.00173)	(46.1)
Quota[d]	−.0003	−172.15	−.00010	—
	(.0007)	(86.35)	(.00002)	
Dependency ratio	—	—	−0.034	—
			(0.026)	
Percent land[e]	−329.28	30,677,982.07[c]	—	—
	(416.93)	(16,509,302.22)		
Percent land, squared[c]	200.43	−23,853,448.87	—	—
	(303.84)	(12,790,348.08)		
Labor quality index	9.85	6064.07	—	—
	(10.16)	(5,438.32)		
Capital	−0.0002	0.084	—	—
	(0.0001)	(0.057)		
Cultivated area	−2.3988	548.88	—	—
	(0.5997)	(349.93)		
Total number of workers	0.843[a]	43.4	—	—
	(0.06)	(33.42)		
Cost share ratio	−12.06[a]	5,017.96[a]	—	—
	(3.62)	(1,972.63)		
R^2	0.793	0.345	0.27	0.03
F	59.264[a]	7.45[b]	10.83[a]	1.89[b]
Number of observations	183	183	183	183

Standard errors are reported in parentheses below parameter estimates.
[a,b,c]Denote significance levels as in Table 9.2.
[d]Instrumental variable in the percent land regression and agricultural expenses regression.
[e]Instrumental variable in the agricultural expenses equation.

Table 9.4. First Stage Regressions: GVCO

Independent Variable	Dependent Variables			
	Agricultural Workers	Agricultural Expenses	Percent Land	Quota
Constant	7,358.48[c]	−72,139.60	0.51[a]	1,822.79
	(3,940.71)	(69,824.88)	(0.08)	(575.11)
Wheat target	−.0005	.7137	−.00000	−0.097
	(.0053)	(1.618)	(.00001)	(0.19)
Corn target	−.0747	5.734	.00003	−0.15
	(.0227)	(2.080)	(.00002)	(0.20)
Cotton target	−.0400	−9.676	.00003	−0.33
	(.0293)	(3.506)	(.00003)	(0.38)
Land index	128.63	−2,891.04	−0.02	308.55
	(49.17)	(2713.34)	(0.016)	(212.89)
Population per ha	—	—	−.0022	87.89
			(.0017)	(26.24)
Quota[d]	−.1427	12.149	.00009	—
	(.0534)	(4.598)	(.00002)	
Dependency ratio	—	—	−0.034	—
			(0.026)	
Percent land[e]	−21,553.34[c]	30,946.45	—	—
	(11,658.35)	(194,837.01)		
Percent land, squared[e]	16,841.08[e]	6,744.00	—	—
	(8,988.03)	(142,055.17)		
Labor quality index	24.82[b]	8,589.83[c]	—	—
	(11.07)	(5,156.02)		
Capital	−0.00009	0.044	—	—
	(0.00013)	(0.053)		
Cultivated area	−.7496	720.69	—	—
	(.4498)	(161.47)		
Total number of workers	0.83[a]	−13.36	—	—
	(0.09)	(33.03)		
Cost share ratio	−10.83[a]	7,454.66[a]	—	—
	(3.83)	(1,865.19)		
R^2	0.79	0.39	0.27	0.15
F	53.98[a]	9.07[a]	10.83[a]	6.40[a]
Number of observations	183	183	183	183

Standard errors are reported in parentheses below parameter estimates.
[a,b,c]Denote significance levels as in Table 9.2.
[d]Instrumental variable in percent land, agricultural workers, and agricultural expenses regression.
[e]Insrumental variable in agricultural workers regression.

on production. We hypothesized a concave relationship between the proportion of land distributed on the basis of workforce rather than household size (ξ) and output. This relationship is supported by the estimates of the grain behavioral production function. The estimated relationship is quadratic, with the implied maximum at $\xi = 0.732$, or roughly the 67th percentile of the observed distribution of that parameter.[38] This result supports the fourth proposition put forth in our theoretical discussion: that there is an optimal value of the proportion of land distribution on the basis of workforce, and that that value is strictly less than one and strictly greater than zero. This is contrary to the Chinese claim that distributing land purely on the basis of number of workers would be optimal from the standpoint of maximizing output, although the intuition that output could be increased by distributing more land on the basis of workforce is supported in the neighborhood in which they are observed for the 67% of teams in which the observed land allocation parameter ξ is below the imputed optimum.[39]

The estimated parameters for the land distribution method are not significant at conventional levels in the GVCO production function, and the sign pattern is reversed from that in the grain production function. In order not to exaggerate the difference between the grain and GVCO estimates, it may be worth noting that while the (insignificant) coefficient estimates imply that GVCO declines as ξ rises from 0 to 0.56, the implied relationship of GVCO to ξ is positive in the range of most of the observations—i.e., those between 0.56 and 0.73, which account for 60% of the observations included in the regression estimates. GVCO is also positively related to ξ for values of ξ above 0.73, which account for another 33% of the sample. The slope of the output curve with respect to ξ is thus the same over most of the observed range of ξ using both output variables, although the second derivatives differ and statistical significance eludes the GVCO estimates. A possible reason for the stronger result for grain, and the greater consistency of that result with our theory, is that the number of dependents in the household may require more weight when trying to maximize grain output than crop output in the broad sense. This might be attributable to the fact that at Dahe, as elsewhere in China, most households strive for self-sufficiency in grain production in view of the uncertainties associated with reliance upon the free grain market in the current policy environment, as discussed earlier in the chapter and elsewhere in this book.[40]

The magnitude of the effect of the land distribution rule on output can be estimated by noting that the log-linear form of the estimating version of equation (9.2)

[38]Note that the implication that not all teams chose the optimal distribution rule could be misleading, because we are only able to infer what rule is optimal on average, not what rule is optimal given the circumstances of each individual team.

[39]But see again the previous footnote.

[40]Indeed, our results are consistent with the possibility that the theoretical framework presented in this chapter is only true for the special case of food, and not for income-producing activity in general. One reason might be that the need to spend more time caring for dependents cancels out the effect of the greater urgency of income in larger households, as a result of which there is no significant general relationship between work and the dependency ratio. According to this explanation, extra effort devoted to grain production by households with more dependents would be offset by reduced effort devoted to other activities. Were the distortions leading to self-sufficiency not present, the need for more food per worker in households with higher dependency ratios would result in a higher proportion of household expenditure being devoted to food, with no effect on productive activity, under this alternative hypothesis. More direct and general tests are required to determine whether the explanatory framework proposed in this chapter or the alternative hypothesis just mentioned has greater validity.

means that a 1% change in ξ is expected to change output by $(\hat{b}_1 + 2\,\hat{b}_2\,\xi)\%$, where $\hat{b}_1$ and $\hat{b}_2$ stand for the estimated coefficients on ξ and ξ^2, respectively. Thus, the least squares estimate for grain implies that grain output would rise by 0.42% for a 1% increase in ξ at the mean value of that variable, while a 1% increase in ξ implies a 1.15% rise in grain output when $\xi = .602$, one standard deviation below that variable's mean. The implied impact of ξ on grain output becomes still stronger as one moves further from the first variable's mean, although inference from the point estimate may become more hazardous also, in that case. The statistically insignificant least squares estimates for GVCO imply that that measure of output would rise by 2.49% for a 1% increase in ξ at its mean.[41]

The above conclusions stand to be modified if attention is also given to indirect effects through input choice, which are captured in equations (9.4) and (9.5). Before turning to these results, however, we briefly discuss the estimates of equations (9.6) and (9.7), and a few more aspects of the behavioral production function estimates.

The results of the first stage equations for the land distribution rule and quota per hectare are of potential interest because they may shed light upon factors affecting the choice of quota obligations and the land allocation rule. Aside from a curiously significant negative sign on the cotton target in the grain variant equation for ξ, and except for the intercept terms, the only significant explanatory variables are quota per hectare in the equation for ξ and population per hectare in the equation for the quota. In both cases, opposite signs are found in the grain and GVCO versions. Since the only difference between these versions, from the standpoint of these two equations, is that quota per hectare is denominated by total cultivated area in the GVCO version but by grain cultivated area in the grain version, this result appears to indicate that the quota per unit of cultivated land was increasing with population density, but that teams with higher population densities and quotas devoted a higher proportion of land to grain.[42] Correspondingly, while higher per hectare quotas are significantly associated with larger allocations of land according to workforce, as we had predicted (since more land would be required by such teams to meet contract obligations), the relationship between quotas and the land allocation rule is reversed when quotas are measured per hectare planted to grain, evidently because high quota teams used more land for grain. If Wen's observation that localities with greater population densities are more likely to have some distribution according to workforce is translated into a prediction that population density is positively correlated with the *degree* of distribution by workforce, that observation could be said to hold at the team level at Dahe, although it is only reflected indirectly, by way of the effect of population density on quota and of quota on ξ (see Table 9.4). On the other hand, no meaningful effects of soil quality or productivity are discernible in these equations.

---

[41]No adjustment of the coefficients to account for variance has been made in this case.

[42]Note also the greater statistical significance of the relationship between population density and the overall land/man ratio (i.e., that shown in the GVCO version).

The coefficients on the physical factors of production in Table 9.2 are reasonable. The coefficients for labor and land are positive and significant for both grain and GVCO. Capital has a negative insignificant effect on grain production, but a positive significant effect on GVCO. This could be due to the fact that capital is measured as the gross capital assets of the team, regardless of its use in production, and is thus a poor proxy for capital services in the production of crops in general, and more so for the production of any specific set of crops such as grain. Further, the nongrain crops included in GVCO may well have been more dependent upon capital input than was grain, which appears here to have a somewhat different pattern of responsiveness to the other factors, as well. In particular, the output elasticity of land is much higher for grain, while the elasticity of labor is higher for GVCO, and that of current inputs is statistically significant for grain but not GVCO. Consistent with the notion that land had a greater impact on grain than on other crops is the fact that most of the soil quality variables are significant for grain, but not for GVCO.[43]

Institutional as well as technological factors might play a role in explanation. In particular, the administrative interventions used to boost grain cultivated area and output, which were mentioned above, could have increased grain's dependence on land and purchased inputs while increasing that of nongrain crops on labor and household-held capital. Villages could more readily control the allocation, among crops, of land, fertilizer, and farm chemicals, than of household-owned implements and labor. Villages plowed and seeded the autumn wheat crop collectively, with the large tractors used being village rather than team owned, and thus failing to show up in team accounts. Such inputs as chemical fertilizer and pesticides were in some cases applied by the village, and in most cases their supply to the household was tied to the fulfillment of grain or cotton delivery contracts. The elasticity of output with respect to labor may be higher for GVCO than for grain since more capable workers focused their efforts on the higher value nongrain crops, on the margin.[44]

Finally, although data problems and the behavioral nature of the production function make these inferences less reliable, a brief look at the implied marginal products and indications regarding returns to scale is of interest. The estimated marginal products of the four factor inputs and their sums, which form estimates of the returns to scale, are shown in Table 9.5. The marginal product estimates can be compared with those of Wiemer, discussed in Chapter 4, for the same 3-year period (1983–1985) and also based on a subset of the Dahe team level data (see Table 4.3).

[43] An additional factor may be that our indicators emphasize suitability for grain production, rather than fertility in a more general sense. The significant negative signs on the "land index" are counterintuitive, since that index is constructed to vary positively with reported land grade. We nevertheless retain all four measures of soil quality to maximize the amount of information utilized.

[44] To see whether failure to control for crop mix might explain the weak relationship between the land distribution variables and output in the GVCO case, grain's share of GVCO by value, calculated as in the study by Kim discussed in Chapter 7, was added to equation (9.2). Although the added variable turned out to have a strongly significant negative coefficient, and while its addition led to some changes in the estimates of factor elasticities, it had no effect on the coefficients for ξ and its square.

Table 9.5. Estimates of Marginal Products and Returns to Scale[a]

	Output	
Marginal Product[b]	Grain[c]	GVCO
Number of agricultural workers	248.72	287.51
Cultivated area	7,419.19	1,178.71
Capital	−0.01	0.46
Agricultural expenses	1.16	0.40
Returns to scale[d]	1.09	0.91

[a]Calculated at the means of all variables, as given in Table 9.1.
[b]Based on least squares estimated of elasticities.
[c]In kilograms.
[d]Calculated as the sum of the coefficients on labor, capital, land, and agricultural expenses.

Looking at the GVCO estimates,[45] that for agricultural workers is only a little higher than Wiemer's estimate for 1985, that for land is near the center of her estimate range, and those for capital and current inputs are only a little below her estimates. The sum of the estimated elasticities of labor, capital, land, and current inputs or expenditures is 1.09 for grain, while it is 0.91 for GVCO if the statistically insignificant coefficient for current inputs is counted, 0.81 otherwise. Once again, we have no evidence of increasing returns to scale in agriculture.

Before concluding let us now return to the estimates of equations (9.4) and (9.5). In laying out our econometric model, we noted that while equation (9.2) captures the effect of the land allocation method on output by way of any variations in quantity and intensity of effort which are not reflected in the number of agricultural workers, N_a, our theoretical reasoning regarding the effect of land distribution on effort provides no justification for treating changes in observable labor input any differently from changes in effort. That is, if a change in ξ is predicted to raise output by leading to an increased supply of effort that is better distributed over the available land, effects that operate through observable effort (here, the number of agricultural workers) should have the same status as those that operate through unobservable effort. Extension to the multi-factor setting implies that effects via supply of other inputs need to be considered as well. The *total* impact of a change in ξ on output should thus be found by substituting equations (9.4) and (9.5) into (9.2) and totally differentiating, which gives us

$$dF/d\xi = \partial F/\partial\xi + (\partial F/\partial N_a)(\partial N_a/\partial\xi) + (\partial F/\partial Z_a)(\partial Z_a/\partial\xi) \qquad (9.9)$$

where the partial derivatives of F should be estimated by the coefficients in the estimating version of (9.2), and the derivatives of N_a and Z_a should be estimated by

[45]Those for grain are in physical units and thus not comparable with other estimates reported in this book.

the coefficients in the estimating versions of (9.4) and (9.5), respectively. Substituting the results in Tables 9.2, 9.3, and 9.4 without regard for statistical significance of the various estimates leads to the conclusion that F is a concave function of ξ for grain, with the maximum of output occurring when ξ takes the value .654, while F is a convex function of ξ for GVCO, with the minimum level of output occurring when ξ takes the value $0.556.$[46] These results are close to those obtained in thé output equation alone, with the main difference being that the maximum of F occurs at .654 rather than .732, for grain.[47] However, the huge coefficients on the land distribution variable in the agricultural expenditures equation (see Table 9.3) increase the implied quantitative sensitivity of grain output to that variable by one or two orders of magnitude, with implausible implications for inferences away from its mean.[48]

Conclusions

The first part of this chapter considered several broad issues of China's agricultural land tenure policy in the reform period. These issues were grouped under two headings: the desirability of land concentration (farming on a larger scale), and the desirability of making land saleable property. We have once again failed to find evidence of scale economies in agricultural production at Dahe Township. Our empirical results are not conclusive, however, and it is probably more important to stress the point that voluntary amalgamation or continued farming of smaller parcels by the farmers themselves is likely to allow the most appropriate response to whatever scale economies are in fact present, provided that decisions are made in an environment in which productivity can receive the weight that it deserves. No attempt

[46] As in our discussion, we use the least squares estimates of equation (9.2). For grain, we have:
$$dF/d\xi = [6.5 - 4.44(2\xi)](123,822) + (.13)[-329.28) + (200.43)(2\xi)]$$
$$+ (.17)[(30677982.07) - (23853448.87)(2\xi)]$$
while for grain GVCO, we have:
$$dF/d\xi = [-10.99 + 9.84(2\xi)](74,431) + (.25)[(-21553.34) + (16841.08)(2\xi)]$$
$$+ (.098)[(30946.45 + (6744)(2\xi)]$$
Hence, $dF/d\xi = 0$ when ξ equals .654 and .556, respectively.

[47] A different interpretation would follow from counting the statistically significant coefficients only. In the grain equations, the coefficient on agricultural expenses in Table 9.2 multiplied by the coefficient on ξ in the expenses equation of Table 9.3 would dominate the other significant terms, implying that F is increasing in ξ over its entire range. In the GVCO estimates, which had no statistically significant term in the output equation, the coefficients on agricultural workers in Table 9.2 and those on ξ in the agricultural workers equation in Table 9.4 are significant and together imply that F is a convex function of ξ with a minimum at .640. These interpretations are probably misleading, because the best unbiased estimates of the total effect include all of the relevant coefficients, significant or not.

[48] For example, a 1% increase in ξ from its mean implies a 16% decline in grain output, while a 1% increase in ξ beginning one standard deviation below its mean (i.e., at .602) implies a 23% increase in grain output. The difference in orders of magnitude between the estimate of ξ's effect via agricultural expenditures and the estimate of its direct effect (Table 9.2) is consistent with the possibility that that variable's main impact was on input choice. Nonetheless, the scale of this difference adds to concerns about the reliability of the total derivative estimates due to the implausibly high impact of ξ implied by them. In Gaynor and Putterman (1992), we develop an alternative model in which the analogues of equations (9.2), (9.4), and (9.5) in the present model are collapsed into a single reduced form equation. The results are qualitatively similar to those reported above.

was made to obtain direct evidence on the land tenure question in this chapter. These and other questions regarding land will be revisited in the final chapter of this book. The emphasis will once again be on the idea that policy debates in this area must pay close attention to the role of government interventions in pricing, marketing, and production planning, and that further tinkering with institutions is unlikely to lead to desirable changes of any fundamental magnitude until the underlying anti-agricultural bias of the Chinese economy is addressed in a direct manner.

Most of this chapter focused more narrowly on the productivity effect of the manner of distributing collective land to households under the Chinese economic reforms of the 1980s. A theoretical framework for predicting household behavior was developed for the observed case in which labor and land markets are largely nonexistent, and this framework led to the proposition that agricultural output would be a concave function of the proportion of land distributed according to workforce as opposed to household size. According to this proposition, output should increase initially as the workforce-based share of land distributed is increased, but it should then reach a maximum and decline, contrary to contentions that output increases monotonically as the share of land distributed on the basis of workforce rises.

In the reported empirical exercise, behavioral production functions were estimated for grain and for the gross value of crop output using the team-level data from Dahe Township in 1983–1985, the first 3 years under the *baogan daohu* system in that township. Under a quadratic specification, grain output displayed the expected concave relationship with the land distribution parameter. There was no statistically significant relationship that could be detected for the gross value of agricultural output, but the insignificant coefficient estimates implied a convex curve that rose over the range in which 93% of the observed values lie. Qualitatively similar conclusions hold after consideration is given to the indirect effects of land distribution on output through its effects on labor supply and the use of current inputs.

The analysis has suggested that the concern of Chinese commentators with the productivity consequences of the method of distributing land to households under the agricultural reforms was not entirely without grounding. Assuming the continued use of administrative rules, however, the results imply that productivity concerns require that land distribution give weight to both household workforces and household populations. The data from Dahe Township suggests that this was in fact done; moreover, most teams chose distribution rules that appear to have been fairly close to what would have maximized productivity, at least when measured by grain output, and their tendency to "err" on the side of equality of per capita incomes may be explicable on equity grounds. Collection or release by Chinese research units of sufficiently detailed data sets on other localities is necessary if tests are to be performed to determine the generality of these conclusions.

10

Income Distribution*

Introduction

As Chapter 9 suggested, absolute poverty, inequality, and the distribution of the benefits and costs of economic development have been important concerns of Western development economists in recent decades. Such concerns were also prominent in the political agenda of China's Communist Party, and were a major justification for the changes effected in the country's rural institutional and property rights structure during the first decade and a half of its rule, and for the rural organizational system that emerged and was maintained for the next 20 years. The reform leadership that came to power in 1978 adopted a strikingly different attitude toward inequality, arguing that economic progress necessitates that some "get rich" before others, much as an army moves forward in a column.

The preceding chapters of this book have focused on the production, incentive, and efficiency features of China's collective system, and the consequences, for those same dimensions, of its rural economic reforms. To a large extent, our interest centered on the implications of methods of distributing land, land use rights, and sales obligations, for productivity and efficiency outcomes. However, little attention was paid to *distributive outcomes* as a subject of interest in its own right. This chapter attempts to redress the imbalance of attention resulting from this focus by explicitly considering the distributive consequences of the commune system and of the reform process that replaced it. As in Chapters 3 through 9, most of the data considered are taken from Dahe Township. However, several additional sources of information on income distribution in rural China are also considered. For purposes of reference, comparisons with the results of micro level studies in other countries are given, as well.

A large literature exists dealing with the advantages, disadvantages, and implications of using one or another method of measuring income inequality. We employ some of the more common measures to examine the distribution not only of income but also of wealth, productivity, and other variables, but no attempt is made

*This chapter is jointly authored by Bingyuang Hsiung, National Taiwan University, and Louis Putterman. Earlier versions of the material presented here will be found in Hsiung and Putterman (1989) and in portions of Putterman (1989a).

in this chapter to contribute anything novel with respect to the issue of inequality measures as such. Rather, we use the most familiar measures, especially the Gini coefficient and the coefficient of variation, because these are well-known and facilitate comparability with other empirical studies.[1]

The Commune System and Income Distribution

As reviewed in Chapter 1, the first stage of China's rural transformation following the victory of the Communists in 1949 was the redistribution of land and the elimination of the landlord class. In the second phase, cooperatives were formed, ultimately coming to control nearly all farm land, and causing the great bulk of that land to be farmed collectively. In the third phase, coinciding with the Great Leap Forward, groups of 20 or more village-sized agricultural collectives were merged into people's communes. When that program was abandoned in the wake of famine and economic disaster, the commune system was restructured and stabilized in the framework of a three-tier system of ownership. Under that system, as we have seen, production teams averaging about twenty to thirty households became the basic units of farm production and income distribution; production brigades averaging eight teams and often corresponding to natural villages supervised the work of the teams and took on certain productive and service tasks to which their scale was deemed appropriate; and people's communes averaging nine brigades and often corresponding to a traditional market area, supervised the brigades and set up industries and services on their still larger scale. At the bottom of the structure, a fourth unit, the household, served as de facto unit of consumption and, to the extent permitted by restrictions that varied with the political climate, produced supplemental income from its private plot and household sidelines.

Under the system just described, inequalities of income among individuals were limited by a number of factors. First, intra-team income differences due to ownership of productive assets other than labor power were eliminated by collectivization of land, equipment, and draft animals. Inequalities could remain, however, in the form of inter-team, inter-brigade, inter-commune, and inter-regional variation due to differences in collectively owned factor endowments, and to possible favoritism in the provision of inputs and of more profitable (less unprofitable) production plans. Second, intra-team differences due to differing work abilities were reduced by a narrow range of differentiation of work-point payments, and inter-household differences due to differing ratios of workers to dependents were reduced by the

---

[1]As will be known to most readers, the Gini coefficient can be defined as the ratio of (a) the area between a 45° line of perfect equality and the Lorenz distribution curve to (b) the area of the right triangle below the 45° line, where the Lorenz curve plots cumulative shares of income or wealth against cumulative shares of population. The coefficient of variation is the standard deviation of the distribution divided by its mean. For a technical discussion dealing with the properties of these and other measures, see Champernowne (1974).

distribution of most grain according to household size,[2] and by the provision of basic needs to indigent members lacking the support of relatives. Inter-team and inter-brigade differences in incomes may in some cases have been reduced by the rationing of commune and brigade level jobs and investment funds to disadvantaged brigades and teams, and differences in distributed incomes among teams and brigades may have been moderated by policies requiring higher levels of income retention for collective uses in teams having higher incomes.[3] Interregional income differences in rural China could be quite substantial despite collectivization.[4] While Chapter 2 gave some indication of the extent of inter-regional inequalities in China during recent years, the analysis of the present chapter is almost exclusively concerned with inequalities within individual communes and their sub-units. Only some limited remarks regarding interregional inequality will be made, in the conclusions.

Many of the policies used to limit income inequality at local levels in China during the 1960s and 1970s came under attack from China's post-Mao leadership, especially after the third plenum of the 11th Central Committee of the C.C.P. in November, 1978. As we have seen, by the end of 1983, most farm production in China was undertaken by individual household units acting under contract to their production teams or villages.[5] Under this system households could market or keep for themselves all output above specified quota sales to the state, subject to the payment of fixed taxes and collective levies, thus becoming in effect fixed rent tenants to their local collective units. Households were also permitted to engage in a wider variety of private sideline activities which could account for an unrestricted share of their incomes. At the same time, commune (later township) and brigade (later village) enterprises grew rapidly, providing wage employment to numerous rural residents. These enterprises were joined by private enterprises and associations or partnerships as sources of local employment, while opportunities for contract work at county-center and urban factories (into which the individual peasant entered without the intermediation of his production team) provided other possible sources of income. Many of the checks on inter-household income inequality which existed in the commune system of the 1970s were thus eliminated in the 1980s. However, China's leaders regarded these changes in a positive light as necessary stimulae to individual initiative and exertion.

The remainder of this chapter is divided into four sections. In the first, we consider measures of and explanations for income inequality at the level of individuals and households under the collective system which existed until the late 1970s.

---

[2]See again the discussion in Chapter 5, and Putterman (1987a).

[3]See Griffin and Saith (1981).

[4]See Rawski (1982), Vermeer (1982), Lardy (1983), and Selden (1985).

[5]Differences of distributive implications between the more radical *baogan daohu* system and the intermediate *baochan* (output target) type reforms are discussed by Khan in Khan and Lee (1983). In the present chapter, "household responsibility system" can usually be taken to be synonymous with the more radical form, and no explicit attention is paid to the distinction between it and earlier versions of the reform system.

The principal resource used is the household survey data collected at Dahe in 1980 with reference to the year 1979, but results from other studies are also included. Toward the end of the section, we present concrete illustrations of differences in living standards at Dahe in 1979 by comparing a small number of relatively poor and an equal number of relatively rich households. In the second section, we consider inter-team and inter-brigade inequality under the collective system. Here, we use the team-level accounts which are available for Dahe on an annual basis from 1970 to 1979. The third and fourth sections again take up inter-household and inter-team inequality, respectively, but under the reformed system in which households are farm units and a greater variety of economic activities and organizational forms are present. At individual and household level, we rely on the household survey conducted in 1986 with reference to conditions in 1985, and at team and brigade level, we make use of annual data for the years 1980 through 1985. In these sections, comparisons of 1970s and 1980s results and conditions are featured prominently, since we are particularly interested in the impact of the *reforms* on inequality at each level. Section 3, like section 1, also provides illustrations of differing living standards by comparing "poor" and "rich" households, in this case based on the data for 1985.

Inequality Among Households and Individuals in the Collective Period

As we saw in Chapter 1, Dahe consists of 16 villages which vary in size from 847 households, in the market and commune headquarters village, to 111 households in the smallest one, with the average being about 250 households in the 15 nonhead-quarters villages.[6] Apart from variations in size, there is little to distinguish the villages with respect to natural resources. With the exception of some river-bed land lying a few meters lower than the adjacent plain, the land is more or less uniformly flat, a level plain transversed by tree-lined dirt roads and irrigation channels, here and there giving way to brick yards from which a layer of earth has been removed, or to an occasional patch of eroded waste land. With the exception again of the river bed, which is shared by five of the villages and accounts for no more than one-half of the plots cultivated by any of their teams, there are only slight variations in soil fertility, and all of the fields are irrigated. In the 1960s and 1970s, each village functioned as a production brigade,[7] and was subdivided into an average of six production teams, which contained an average of 54 households each in 1979.

As will be detailed below, the teams exhibit variation in cultivated area per capita, probably a survival from pre-collective days, also modified by subsequent population growth. Two paved roads, one running north from Shijiazhuang, the other connecting the commune with the county center to its west, cut through the

---

[6]Data for 1979.

[7]A partial exception are "East" and "West" brigades (Dongdui and Xidui) which were carved out of what was originally one village called Chengdongqiao. When brigades were renamed villages in the 1980s, the two entities were treated as separate villages.

commune, and a canal running alongside the first road bisects it and is spanned by several bridges. Since the distances are small, it is unlikely that proximity to roads alone explains a great deal of income variation, but influences of location upon relative development either in the recent or the more distant past cannot be ruled out—an example being that Jiacun Village, located at the intersection of the north-south and east-west paved roads, has shown signs of development into a small commercial center in recent years. Differences in leadership characteristics, village and sub-village social dynamics, connections to commune and higher-level officials and to urban factory personnel, etc., may have led to differences in the rates of growth of nonagricultural enterprises at both team and brigade levels, and to differences in the success of private sideline activities which became significant income sources in the years beginning 1978.

Income Distribution Among Individuals and Households

The Dahe household survey data, which was examined in a preliminary fashion in Chapter 3 and formed the basis for the analysis reported in Chapter 8, also makes possible an analysis of inequality among households and individuals at Dahe Commune. It will be recalled that the survey carried out in 1980 refers to the situation of each of the households in five of the ninety-four production teams existing at Dahe in 1979, and that these five teams were located in five different brigades (villages) and were meant to be representative of relatively rich, poor, and average teams, respectively. According to the team-level data for 1979, the five teams had the first, second, thirty-first, thirty-sixth, and eighty-fourth highest average distributed collective incomes per capita among the ninety-one teams providing data on that variable in that year. This suggests that the teams chosen would better represent the upper than the lower portion of inter-team variation in the commune, but that they do cover the greater part of the commune's income spectrum.

A difficulty with the use of data from 1979 as our only source of information on inter-household income variation *in the collective period* is that they may not be fully representative of income inequalities during that period given that the post-Mao reforms were already underway by the end of 1978. We have seen that Dahe's production teams continued to produce as collective units during 1979, and that the first of them to introduce a system of household contracting did so in 1980. Moreover, the system introduced then was of an intermediate nature, retaining unified distribution by work-points. On the other hand, 1979 saw more use of task-based (or "piece rate") work-points and allocation to households of responsibility for parts of the crop cycle on specific pieces of land in some Dahe teams. More important, from the standpoint of income distribution, is the fact that by 1979, peasants at Dahe probably had greater freedom to engage in household sideline production and to sell in free markets than had been the case earlier in the 1970s and during the late 1960s.

There is little that can be done about unrepresentativeness due to these factors. It should be pointed out that most of the micro level data available for comparison from other parts of China also comes from approximately the same period, i.e., at the end of the collective era, if not the beginning of the era of household farming.[8] Nevertheless, one basis for comparison with earlier conditions is available in the form of records of the distribution of collective income to households in one of Dahe's brigades, that of Dahe Village itself, for the years 1970, 1974, 1977, 1978, and 1979. Happily, one of the teams in the household survey also belongs to Dahe Village, so direct comparison is possible between 1979 and these earlier years.

We begin our discussion of inequality findings by looking at differences among the households of a given team. Many previous studies, based on small surveys conducted by visitors to China, obtained information, and hence computed indices of inequality, based upon distributed *collective* incomes only. However, several papers and two books by Keith Griffin, with collaborators (Griffin and Saith, 1981; Griffin and Griffin, 1984), report on inequality of both collective distributed incomes and of total household incomes, including sidelines, and we obtained the data of household surveys conducted by Griffin and Hay, and by Elisabeth Croll (1980), from which indices of income distribution can be computed directly. Griffin et al. hypothesize that the addition of household sideline income to distributed collective income tended to *reduce* rather than increase the inequality of income distribution, the reasoning being that households, some of whose members could not readily join in collective work either because of their own infirmities or the need to watch after young children or other dependents at home, could supplement their incomes by putting more energy into household sidelines like raising chickens and pigs, making organic fertilizer, and growing vegetables. To compare our results with those of Griffin and other studies, we report on both the inequality of distributed collective incomes, and that of total household income, in both cases on a per capita basis.

Turning first to inequality of household per capita incomes from all sources, data collected at team level show that the average per capita distributed *collective* income of households in 1979 was Y 128.64 over all teams in Dahe People's Commune. For the five teams surveyed at household and individual levels, the same team level statistic averages Y 156.33. The household data set shows average per capita income from *all* sources to be Y 301.52; owing to lack of data, the corresponding figure cannot be computed for the other eighty-nine teams. Looking now at the Gini coefficients for inequality of total per capita income among the households of given teams,[9] Table 10.1 shows that these range from a low value of .1457 to a high value

---

[8] Some evidence on income distribution among households in rural China between 1939 and 1974 is analyzed by Blecher (1976).

[9] We compute these coefficients over data for per capita rather than total income since the former concept comes closer to measuring the standard of living of each household's members. In principle, it would be still better to adjust the crude per capita income data to reflect differences in consumption requirements by age and sex, and to account for possible economies of scale in conversion of income into real consumption levels with growing household size (see, e.g., the use of the "adjusted adult equivalent unit" approach by Collier et al. 1986), since the computed coefficients may otherwise tend to overstate the

Table 10.1. Gini Coefficient of Per Capita Income of Households

Team	From Collective only, 1979		Total Income, 1979[a]	Total Income, 1985
Shuanghe brigade, team 2	.2262		.1831	.2689
(Dahe)		(68)		(66)
Zhifangtou brigade, team 2	.1555		.1457	.1953
(Dahe)		(37)		(35)
Dahe brigade, team 15	.1589		.1438	.3019
(Dahe)		(57)		(61)
Jiacun brigade, team 3	.1751		.1546	.2576
(Dahe)		(57)		(56)
Xiaohe brigade, team 3	.2027		.1899	.2456
(Dahe)		(24)		(24)
Dahe, combined household	.2480		.2092	.2717
survey		(243)		(242)
Zhang Qing, combined	.2097		.3141	—
household survey		(84)		
Beijing suburb (Croll)[b]	.1017		.1205	—
		(17)		
Shanghai suburb	.1441		.1352	—
(Croll)[b]		(23)		
Wugong brigade, team 2	.22		.19	—
(Selden)[c]		(232)		

Note: Figures in parentheses are number of households on which computation is based.

[a]Data for Dahe teams includes income from employment outside of the commune, while that for the other teams is limited to collective distributed income and household plot and sideline earnings.

[b]1980 data.

[c]1977 data. From Selden (1985, p. 199).

*Source:*Hsiung and Putterman (1989).

of .1899. The Gini coefficient of total per capita income by household over the full five-team sample is .2092. For purposes of comparison, we compute within-team Gini coefficients for 1979 total income per capita for eleven teams in Zhang Qing commune of Suzhou Municipality, Jiangsu Province, using data collected by Griffin and Hay (Ansell et al., 1982). As seen in Table 10.1, the coefficient for the combined household sample from Zhang Qing is .3141. Within individual teams, the computed Gini coefficients range from a low of .0690 to a high of .2281, with an average value of .1440. We also compute Gini coefficients for household per capita total income in teams in suburban Shanghai and Beijing communes studied by Croll (1980) in 1980. These coefficients turn out to be .1352 and .1205, respectively. Finally, we include

degree of inequality of living standards in the observed population. This more time-consuming exercise did not seem warranted, however, since little or no bias affecting our ability to identify *changes and variations in* inequality levels should result from failing to make such adjustments, and the rarity of this practice is such that comparability with other studies of rural China is better served by employing the simpler methodology adopted here. The life-cycle models examined in this and in a later section of the chapter provide an alternative method for assessing the degree to which variations in the demographic composition of households lie behind measured inequality levels.

the Gini coefficient for the same income concept for a team in Wugong Brigade, in southeastern Hebei Province, in 1977. As reported by Selden (1985), its value is .19. Thus, the coefficients for the Dahe teams fall in a common range with the Gini coefficients calculated for the other Chinese units.[10]

To assess whether inequality at Dahe and other Chinese villages and townships (communes) should be considered "high" or "low," it is useful to consider some international comparisons. Gini coefficients computed for an entire nation, or for its rural or urban sectors, are familiar; values of around .3 or less are usually considered low, .3 to .5 are moderate, and .5 and above are viewed as indicating high levels of inequality. Ginis (or other inequally measures) calculated for small local populations, such as a village, are less familiar, but some examples can nonetheless be found. A survey of research on agricultural development in Sub-Saharan Africa by Eicher and Baker (1982, p. 219) reports on studies which found intra-village Gini coefficients[11] of .34 in Sierra Leone and .28 in northern Nigeria. Village surveys in four regions of Tanzania allow computation of Gini coefficients of household total crop income for twenty-nine villages, which have an average value of .437.[12] A study of eighty-four villages in India finds that the average intra-village Gini coefficient for household total income is .46 (Gartrell, 1981; also cited by Selden, 1985). In their well-known study of an Indian village, Palanpur in Moradabad District of West Uttar Pradesh, Christopher Bliss and Nicholas Stern (1982) found that the Gini coefficient for distribution of income per capita across 111 households in 1974–1975 was .326. In another well-known study, Yujiro Hayami and Masao Kikuchi (1981, p. 178) report the Gini coefficient of household income among the 110 households of a "technologically stagnant village" in Java, Indonesia, to be 0.52. An intertemporal comparison with pre-Communist mainland China is also available. Based on Japanese survey data from three villages in northeast Hebei collected in 1936, Brandt and Sands (1988) compute Gini coefficients for household net income per capita of .391, .346, and .349. Inequality in villages at Dahe and in other Chinese communes during the collective production era was thus substantially less than that found in the other Asian and African studies, or in the pre-1949 Chinese survey, as knowledge of Chinese policy and ideology of the period would have led us to expect.[13]

---

[10]Two Guangdong Province teams for which Gini coefficients for 1974 household per capita incomes were computed by Blecher (1976), yielded values of .174 and .161, also within this range. Blecher's data were obtained from interviews conducted in Hong Kong, and cover collective earnings only.

[11]Whether over incomes of individuals, of households, or per capita incomes of households is not indicated.

[12]Self-consumed crops are valued at market price. These measures exaggerate inter-household inequality if noncrop earnings or distributions of collective income (the latter generally provided well under 10% of household incomes) had an equalizing effect. Failure to adjust for differences in household size most likely also increases the size of the coefficients. The data are those of the two surveys analyzed in detail in Putterman (1986b). Gini computations were performed by Michele Siegel.

[13]These comparisons could be biased by the absence of data from nonsocialist east Asian countries thought to have relatively equal distributions of income, such as Taiwan and South Korea. Unfortunately, we could not find published data on income distribution within villages for those countries.

If the hypothesis of Griffin et al. is correct, the Gini coefficients of per capita distributed collective income by household should be larger than those for income from all sources, indicating greater inequality. This is in fact the case for almost all of the data sets on which comparisons can be made, including those from Dahe. As Table 10.1 shows, the hypothesis is supported for all five teams there and for the combined sample. A retest of their hypothesis on the data analyzed by Ansell et al. (1982) is also supportive.[14] In eight of eleven teams for which household data are available, the Gini coefficient of total income per capita is lower than that of collective income per capita. However, when the data from all of these teams is combined, there is a substantially larger Gini coefficient for full income per capita than for collective income per capita, as also reported in Table 10.1, and the same relationship holds for the respective income concepts measured on an unweighted per household basis. Finally, Table 10.1 shows that Croll's data for the suburban Shanghai team, and Selden's finding from the Wugong team, are supportive of the hypothesis, while Croll's data for the suburban Beijing team are not.

As mentioned earlier, to see whether income inequality levels at Dahe Commune in 1979 may have changed substantially from those earlier in that decade, we can examine data on distribution of collective income to households in one of the brigades for five selected years beginning with 1970. All households in all fifteen teams of this, Dahe's largest brigade, including one of the five teams in the household survey, are covered. As Table 10.2 shows, for the brigade as a whole, the Gini coefficient for per capita distributed collective income by households ranged between .240 and .272, with no real trend. For the subsample consisting of the households in the one intensively surveyed team, the table shows the Gini coefficient for the same years to range between .221 and .244, with at most a slight rising trend. Although we cannot account for the difference of over .08 in the 1979 estimated Gini coefficient for this team based on data from the two different sources,[15] the inter-temporal data may

---

[14]A retest is required because the tests performed by Ansell et al. (1982) are unreliable due to a methodological error. Those authors state: "Private sector economic activities would increase inequality in the distribution of income only if the relative importance of private incomes rose with the level of per capita collective income." They therefore run a regression of the form:

$$PI/CI = a + bCI,$$

where PI is the household's private income, CI is its collective distributed income, and a and b are constants to be estimated. The authors assert that if b is significantly different from and less than zero, their hypothesis would be demonstrated. The equation and interpretation are used to analyze both inter-household and inter-team inequality and are restated by Griffin and Griffin (1984, p. 57) and by Marshall (1985, p. 140). The same hypothesis is put forward in Griffin and Saith (1982), although the evidence used there (and for one test, by Ansell et al., 1982) is direct inspection of inequality measures for each income concept, the method used in our own paper. The regression procedure does not constitute a legitimate test of their hypothesis, since it can be shown that a negative b is a necessary but not a sufficient condition for private income to reduce the inequality of the income distribution.

[15]Compare Table 10.1, row 3, and Table 10.2, column 2. The data introduced in this paragraph and reported on in Table 10.2 are those denoted "Data 2" in Putterman (1989c), and the household survey data from which results are reported in Table 10.1 is what is referred to as "Data 3." While the former were taken directly from brigade ledgers without household interviews, the latter were based on direct interviews of the household heads.

Table 10.2. Gini Coefficients of Distributed Collective Income Per Capita of Households, Dahe Brigade[a]

Year	Dahe Brigade	Team 15 of Dahe Brigade
1970	.2723	.2208
1974	.2402	.2207
1977	.2680	.2397
1978	.2407	.2400
1979	.2439	.2435

[a]Source differs from that of Table 10.1 as indicated in the text, footnote 15.
Source: Hsiung and Putterman (1989).

be viewed as providing weak evidence that there was no significant change in the intra-team and intra-brigade inequality of per capita distribution of collective incomes across households as the 1970s progressed. If the addition of other income sources tended to play an equalizing role, as Table 10.1 suggests that it did, and if the importance of those sources rose at the end of the decade, inequality of total income per capita at household level will if anything have been lower in 1979 than earlier in the decade.

Variation in Work-point Earnings

Within given production teams during the 1970s, the sources of inter-household income inequality can be classified under two headings: differences in incomes across workers with differing characteristics, and differences in worker-types and dependent-to-worker ratios across households. Production team workers received different incomes from their teams depending on the number of work-points they earned in the year. The latter depended on (a) the number of points each worker received for a typical day, itself a function of his or her abilities and the jobs s/he typically performed, and (b) the number of such days worked.[16] Regressing reported work-points per day on sex, age, and age squared using the household data for each of the five teams, we find significant negative effects of being female in all five teams, and significant positive coefficients on age and negative coefficients on age squared in four of the five teams. All things being equal, work-points per day rise until about 35 years of age and fall thereafter, in the majority of the teams. As Table 10.3 shows, the two age variables, the sex dummy, plus a constant explain an average of 49% of the

[16]As has been noted elsewhere in the book, not all income distributed was based on time pay. In 1979, many teams used task rates for certain jobs, including the awarding of a fixed number of points for the completion of several sequential jobs on a given piece of land. Points were also given for deliveries of household-produced organic fertilizer to the team. In the present analysis, as in that of Chapter 6, however, we treat work-points as fully convertible into work days using the work-points-per-day rating for each worker obtained in the Dahe surveys. The concept of "work day" is thus to be treated as a general measure of work input rather than a literal representation of calendar time.

Table 10.3. Determinants of Work-points per day, Dahe Township, 1979

Team	Constant	Age	Age^2	Sex[a]	Adj. R^2	Number of Cases
Shuanghe, team 2	6.9337 (6.022)	0.2190 (3.433)	−0.0023 (−3.924)	−1.6608 (−6.314)	.2857	123
Zhifangtou, team 2	3.0175 (3.937)	0.3700 (8.355)	−0.0048 (−8.215)	−0.8612 (−3.359)	.4762	87
Dahe, team 15	7.5356 (6.387)	0.1707 (2.674)	−0.0025 (−3.094)	−1.1345 (−4.665)	.2327	94
Jiacun, team 3	8.8237 (14.609)	0.1760 (5.432)	−0.0026 (−6.199)	−1.7647 (−11.505)	.5577	132
Xiaohe, team 3	12.3515 (10.753)	0.0138 (0.239)	−0.0008 (−1.129)	−2.6542 (−16.330)	.8808	50

Note: Numbers in parentheses are t-statistics.
[a]Male = 0, female = 1.
Source: Hsiung and Putterman (1989).

variance in work-points per day within these teams, and all of the coefficients are statistically significant in four of the five teams.

Variance Decomposition

In addition to factors (a) and (b), just noted, earnings from collective labor varied among individuals belonging to different production teams due to inter-team differences in work-point value. Following Chinn (1978), we can analyze the sources of variation in workers' incomes from collective work by taking logs of both sides of the equation (work-point income) = (number of days worked) × (number of work-points per day) × (value of each workpoint), and calculating the variance of each side. While Chinn performed this exercise at the team level using per capita averages for the eighteen production teams of a brigade in Fujian in 1962 (see below), we implement it at the level of individual workers in the five teams represented in our household survey. Table 10.4 gives the results for both our own and Chinn's data. The first column shows that at individual level in the pooled five team sample at Dahe, the largest part of the variance in earnings from the collective is attributable to differences in the number of days worked, while differences in points per day and in point value each played a smaller role. For the results using the pooled sample, all of the covariances are negative and one, that between the number of points per day and the number of work days, is quite large. However, the implied trade-off between days worked and points per day appears to result from the influence of the arbitrarily set points-per-day scale on indicated "work days," which need not correspond exactly to calendar time. Results for households *within* individual teams, where the value of the work-point is uniform and thus no longer a source of variance, still show variation in

Table 10.4. Decomposition of the Variance of the Logarithm of Per Capita Work-point Income

Team	Result for all Dahe Households (5 teams)	Result for Dahe Households, "Typical" Team[a]	Chinn's Result for Huli Teams
Var [log (income from work-points)]	.259	.271	.057
Var [log (number of work days)]	.254	.252	.021
Var [log (work-points per day)]	.122	.014	.016
Var [log (value of a work-point)]	.140	—	.060
2 cov [log (work days), log (points per day)]	2 (−.109)	2 (.003)	2 (−.011)
2 cov [log (work days), log (value)]	2 (−.006)	—	2 (−.003)
2 cov [log (points per day) log (value)]	2 (−.013)	—	2 (−.006)

[a]Representative team at Dahe is team 3 of Jiacun brigade.

Source: Hsiung and Putterman 1989). The final column is taken from Chinn (1978).

number of work days to be the major explanation of total variance, with the covariance of work days and points per day being small and of alternating signs in four out of five teams. The second column on the right-hand side of Table 10.4 gives illustrative results for one of the teams, team 3 of Jiacun Brigade. Comparing the final column, notice that Chinn found the value of workpoints to be the major source of variance. It seems likely that the difference in results is attributable to the fact that his data are not compiled at the level of individuals but are instead per capita averages over all individuals within separate teams. If so, we can conclude that earnings from collective work differed primarily because of differences in the amount of labor supplied, although average collective earnings differed among teams mostly because of differences in work-point values reflecting differences in the effective productivity of labor under prevailing institutions and prices.

Explanations of Individuals' Collective Earnings

As with variations in the number of work-points awarded per day, it is possible also to explain much of the variation in individuals' annual earnings from their production teams on the basis of sex and age. Annual earnings from the team are nothing but the product of work-points awarded per day and number of days worked, and the "naïve" OLS regression shown in Table 6.3 of Chapter 6, viewed beside Table 10.4, shows that both components are significantly correlated with these demographic fundamentals, so that we could expect their product also to be so correlated, unless the effects were mutually canceling in nature. Table 10.5 shows the results of an ordinary least squares regression, implemented by Woosung Park (1987), for the full Dahe household survey with individual collective earnings as dependent variable, and sex

Table 10.5. Determinants of Individual Income From the Collective Sector, Dahe Township, 1979[a]

Independent Variable	Estimated Coefficient	t Statistic
Constant	77.718	2.853
Team average colletive income	1.408	12.743
Dummy var 0 = male, 1 = female	−130.339	−10.966
Age dummy 0 = other, 1 = 13–22 years	−36.166	−2.038
Age dummy 0 = other, 1 = 41–60 years	−30.398	−2.044
Age dummy 0 = other, 1 = over 60 years	−78.034	−3.069
Occupation dummy, 1 = student	−140.754	−2.347
Occupation dummy, 1 = worker	125.231	7.894
Occupation dummy, 1 = team cadre	19.223	.761
Occupation dummy, 1 = brigade cadre	21.856	.493
Occupation dummy, 1 = teacher	27.367	.712
Occupation dummy, 1 = doctor	.451	.007
Occupation dummy, 1 = commune cadre	80.898	1.009
Education dummy, 1 = under 3 years	−51.691	−2.594
Education dummy, 1 = 4–5 years	−8.126	−.471
Education dummy, 1 = 9–10 years	−6.721	−.415
Education dummy, 1 = 12–13 years	−.983	−.052
Education dummy, 1 = over 13 years	217.440	2.650
R^2	0.465	
Number of cases	616	

[a]OLS regression.
Source: Hsiung and Putterman (1989), based on Park (1987).

and three age-bracket dummy variables as independent variables. In addition, five education-level dummy variables and seven occupation dummy variables were entered on the right-hand side of the equation, as was team average collective income, included to control for inter-team variation in the pooled sample. Variation with average team collective income and sex is as expected and significant. The age dummies, based on a reasonable if arbitrary set of brackets, are also significant and indicate a concave age-earnings profile, rising to the prime earning bracket of 23–40 years, and falling thereafter. Education shows no significant impact except at the extremes of high and low education, at each of which the direction of impact is as expected. Of the occupations, only student and worker status (the latter indicates an individual who worked in an enterprise outside of the team although s/he received his/her pay out of the team's overall distribution)[17] show effects significantly different from the base occupation, which is ordinary team member. Altogether, 46.5% of the variance appears to be explained by these factors.

[17]This was the conventional practice for workers in brigade and commune enterprises in China during the collective farming era. For a discussion of its implications, see Griffin and Saith 1981).

Table 10.6. Determinants of Household Per Capita Income, Dahe Township, 1979[a]

Independent Variable	Estimated Coefficient	t Statistic
Constant	−63.188	−0.605
Household population-to-workers ratio	−73.525	−6.000
Average work-points per days[b]	18.813	2.440
Average number of work days[b]	2.234	2.695
Value of work-points	313.749	9.983
Proportion of cadres among working members	−6.669	−0.143
Proportion of doctors, teachers, soldiers, and enterprise workers among working members	−17.307	−0.590

Number of valid cases: 195
Adjusted R^2: .447
F Statistic: 27.141

[a]OLS regression.
[b]Calculated over working members only.
Source: Hsiung and Putterman (1989).

Explaining Income Variation Among Households

Differences in per capita income among households should be determined by the same factors determining earnings variation among individuals, plus differences in household demographic composition. This is confirmed for one possible specification by the results of an OLS regression shown in Table 10.6. Household per capita income is entered as the dependent variable, and the independent variables are the ratio of the number of household members to the number of household income earners, the average number of collective work days worked by the latter, the average number of work-points earned in a day by the household's workers, the value of the work-point in the team to which the household belonged, the percentage of the household's income earners who were cadres at team, brigade, commune, or higher levels, and the percentage of the income earners who were (nonfarm) enterprise workers, soldiers, teachers, or doctors.[18] As implied by our estimate of Chinn's decomposition equation for the Dahe household data, household per capita income is positively and significantly related to average work days, average work-points per day, and value of work-points. Per capita income is significantly negatively correlated with the ratio of household size to workforce, although the drop of Y 73.5 attributable to a one unit increase in the ratio may be considered fairly mild. Finally, there is no correlation between per capita income and the occupational variables.[19]

[18]The two occupational variables are meant to capture all income earning occupations other than ordinary team farm workers.
[19]Since most of those in the second occupational category were enterprise workers, and the coefficient on that occupation (there labeled "worker") is positive and significant in the individual level regression of Table 10.5, this result is somewhat surprising. It is possible, however, that different occupations, including enterprise worker, influenced income primarily through effects on the number of days they worked and on

Approximately 45% of the variance in household per capita incomes is accounted for by the included variables.

Life-Cycle Model

It is sometimes pointed out that some inter-household income inequality can be attributed to household choice regarding family size and to changes in household composition as families proceed through the life cycle from family formation to child-rearing, to the maturity and departure of children, and to the gradual decline of activity by the original household members. From a normative standpoint, differences in living standards attributable to procreative choice and to differences in temporarily occupied positions in the life cycle may be more acceptable than those resulting from differences in factor endowments, abilities, and economic opportunities unrelated to life cycle.[20] China's commune system of the 1960s and 1970s may be hypothesized to have reduced the latter differences to relatively low levels, while having somewhat less effect on the former. It is therefore of interest to analyze the relative importance of these sources of income inequality. An exercise along these lines was carried out by John Gray in association with the Food Policy Study Group at Oxford University, using Griffin and Hay's data from Zhang Qing Commune.

Gray's analysis (1982) begins with computation of an equation giving individual collective earnings as a function of sex, two age dummies, and average distributed collective income of the team to which the individual belongs. Using the results of this equation, he estimates the implied average incomes for six types of workers (male and female workers falling into three different age groups) and adds a seventh category, children, who are assumed to earn no collective income. With these seven simple types, he then constructs a model of the household life cycle in which households evolve through sixteen stages, beginning as young married couples without children, and ending as old married couples whose children have left the home. Next, he postulates a frequency for each household type in the general population, and finally, he computes the coefficient of variation for the implied distribution of collective income across households, which turns out to be 0.347. Comparing this with the

---

the number of work-points they earned in a typical day. Also, the inclusion of private sector earnings in the income concept of the household but not the individual level regression could help to explain what otherwise appears to be an inconsistency between the two results.

[20]That is, if household A has a lower material living standard than household B because, say, A preferred children compared with income more than did B, the inequality between them might not be viewed as unjust. Similarly, while it might be desirable to create mechanisms for smoothing out consumption over the life cycle, if all households experience a common transition from relatively poor to relatively rich to relatively poor again, then differences between households A and B at time t would not reflect differences in their "life chances" or expected well-being over the life-cycle as a whole, and might not be viewed as unjust (although it is arguably *inefficient* if greater income smoothing is in fact feasible). The mathematical models of Gray and Park, discussed in this section, treat life-cycle (as opposed to fertility choice) differences only. For an argument in favor of using life-cycle adjusted measures of inequality, see Paglin (1975).

coefficient for the actual income distribution, 0.327, Gray concludes that variation within the life cycle accounts for by far the larger part of the overall income inequality at Zhang Qing in 1979.

A parallel analysis was carried out on the household survey data for Dahe by Park (1987). Park first estimates the OLS regression equation, reported above, explaining individual earnings from the collective sector as a function of within-team average collective income, sex, and dummy variables for age groupings, schooling, and job categories. Suppressing occupation, schooling, and team differences, he then uses the equation to predict average distributed collective income for the eight age and sex categories and assumes that children under 12 years earn zero collective income. Next, he posits a uniform life cycle, composed of eleven household composition stages, and assigns arbitrary but consistent frequencies to each composition type assuming a stationary distribution.[21] Like Gray, he then computes the coefficients of variation of household income (in this case, including noncollective sources) based on the simulated data and on the actual data. According to Park's computations, the first coefficient, .3269, is noticeably less than the second, .4451, suggesting, in contrast to Gray's findings for Zhang Qing, that a significant amount of inter-household income inequality at Dahe in 1979 was from sources other than life-cycle differences.

A Comparison of "Poor" and "Rich" Households in 1979

A more concrete sense of the degree of variation in household standards of living at Dahe in 1979 can be obtained by looking at some individual households at the low and high ends of the income spectrum. Several households, presumably supported by family members in other households, list no income at all in 1979.[22] We select two of these randomly and add the eight households with the lowest reported positive incomes per capita from the household survey. We also identify the ten households having the highest reported total income per capita in the survey, and compare these groups before describing one household from each in more detail. The ten "poor" households turn out to be drawn entirely from the two teams that show the lowest average per capita incomes on the basis of both the team and household surveys, while four of the five teams are represented among the ten "richest" households.

The average per capita income of the eight poorest households reporting positive incomes was Y 140.9 while that of the ten highest income households is Y 611.7. The "poor" households consumed an average of 225 kg of grain, of which 33.8% was coarse grain, whereas the "rich" households consumed an average of 319 kg of grain

---

[21]That is, a distribution such that each household can proceed through the life cycle without change over time in the proportion of the current population occupied by each household type.

[22]Any payments out of team or other collective welfare funds should have been reported in the survey. Although the survey also provided an opportunity to report transfers among households, very few were mentioned. We believe that this outcome reflects the insufficiently explicit survey design and respondents' reluctance to mention such transfers, rather than their actual frequency.

per capita, of which 27.4% was coarse grain.[23] Consumption figures for our sample households are high compared with the all China average per capita grain consumption in 1979 which is given by official sources as 207 kg.[24] There appears to be no special correspondence between membership in the "poor" or "rich" group, on the one hand, and factors such as age of the household head, or education and occupation of the family members, most of whom are simply team workers.[25] The two salient features that appear to distinguish high income from low in 1979 are the ratio of dependents to workers, and the average earnings of working members. The "poor" households have an average of 5.5 members, whereas the "rich" ones average only 2.6 members; yet the number of workers is similar: 2.9 for "poor" households, 2.2 for "rich." Working members of the "poor" households averaged Y 237 per year in earnings apart from household sidelines, while members of "rich" households averaged Y 445, despite the fact that the distribution of job classifications is quite similar in the two groups. Certainly, one-half of the workers in the poorer households suffered from working in poorer production teams, which were able to pay less (at year's end) for the same amount of work: team 3 of Jiacun village, to which these workers belonged, paid out an average of only Y 241 per worker, and its work-points were worth only Y .043, whereas the other four teams represented paid Y 357, Y 405, Y 430, and Y 435 per worker, and had work-points worth Y .091, Y .102, Y .060, and Y .058, respectively.[26] The other half of the "poorer" households' workers, from Dahe team 15, worked an average of 302 days per year while the average in their team was 376 days.[27] The workers in the "poorer" households probably also suffered from differences in work characteristics and abilities that are not identifiable from our data.[28]

For an example of a "poor" household in 1979, consider the Zhang family (here and below, we use pseudonyms), which has the third lowest per capita income among those reporting positive income in the household survey (Y 134). The Zhangs belonged to team 3 of Jiacun village, which had a distributed collective income per capita of Y 99 and a total income per capita of Y 227.[29] The household consisted of a

---

[23]Grain consumption figures for Dahe may include grain fed to livestock raised by the household.

[24]State Statistical Bureau (1988). The latter quantity of grain supplied 1,867 kilocalories or 79% of daily calorie requirements, according to the same source. The remainder of daily calorie requirements are likely to have been supplied by tubors, pulses, soya products, and other foods.

[25]There are in fact three team cadres among the members of the ten "poor" households, and none among "rich" household members. No brigade level cadres are represented among these households.

[26]The value of work-points are sometimes reported in terms of groups of ten work-points, which were viewed as equivalent to a standard work day. For comparison, the figures given here should be multiplied by ten.

[27]The number of days are calculated based on reported average work-points per day and total work-points earned.

[28]There is no systematic difference in the work-point per day rating of members of the "poor" and members of the "rich" households as compared with the average ratings in their teams.

[29]The fact that the share of income derived from collective distribution is much smaller than that typically derived from other studies is probably to be explained primarily by the number of residents working as employees of state and county-owned units both within and beyond the commune's boundaries, including the county town and Shijiazhuang. Incomes from such employment accrued directly to the household members concerned, and thus fall outside of collective income.

married couple, ages 35 and 34 years, their three daughters, ages 4, 8, and 10, Mr. Zhang's older brother, age 51, and Mr. Zhang's mother, age 66. The married Mr. Zhang was a worker in a county factory of another county, and earned Y 45 per month, while his wife and brother worked in the production team, where she earned Y 149 and he Y 128 for the year. Mr. Zhang's mother and three daughters earned no outside incomes, and the household reported sideline production worth Y 120. The seven Zhangs shared a house of five rooms and owned one bicycle, a clock, a watch, a radio, and Y 200 in savings. During 1979, they reported eating 250 kg of grain per capita, about half of which was coarse grain, and 6.4 kg of meat per capita.

An example of a "rich" household is provided by the Gao family of team 2 in Zhifangtou village, in the northeast part of the commune. The Gaos reported the second highest per capita income in the household survey (Y 707). The family consisted of three brothers, ages 23, 43, and 48 years, and their mother, age 65. Each of the brothers worked in the production team, where they earned Y 316, Y 334, and Y 362 plus special subsidies of Y 100, Y 120, and Y 400, respectively. There is no explanation of these relatively high earnings, except that one of the brothers reports being skilled in construction work. The household also reported Y 1,132 worth of sideline income, including Y 120 from the sale of a pig to the state and Y 300 from raising sheep. The four Gaos shared eight rooms but, like the Zhangs, owned only one bicycle, one clock, one watch, and one radio. Unlike the Zhangs, they reported having Y 1,000 worth of savings and owned a sewing machine. They ate 25 kg more grain per capita (275 kg per capita, in all) than the Zhangs, but in contrast, less than a quarter of it in the form of coarse grain, and they consumed an average of 25 kg of meat, including one of their home-fattened pigs.

Income Distribution Across Teams and Brigades in the Collective Period

Unlike differences of income among members of the same production team, income inequalities across production teams and brigades, even within a given commune, can be expected to have been influenced by differences in resource endowments above and beyond labor. Teams having better land, or more land per capita, could earn more income for their members provided that they worked with at least equal efficiency and that the advantage with respect to endowment was not entirely offset by higher compulsory sales quotas or inferior production plans (such as instructions to produce more low value crops). Inter-brigade differences in land endowments would have existed from the time of brigade formation out of extant natural villages, and differences in the population/resource balance would have evolved according to the demographic experience of each village, without moderation by redistribution of land. Inter-team differences within a given brigade would probably have been small at team formation in the late 1950s and early 1960s, but might also have grown due to different demographic histories since then, as there is unlikely to have been redistribution of land among teams in the interim.

At Dahe commune in 1970, the cultivated area ranged from a low of .074 ha per capita in Nanluoling brigade to a high of .137 ha per capita in Mengtong brigade, with an average of .105 ha per capita and a Gini coefficient of average per capita cultivated area by brigades (for the fifteen brigades providing data) of 0.0919. The range and Gini coefficient were approximately the same in 1979. Gini coefficients for cultivated area per capita by teams, calculated over all teams of the commune, are also quite close to those across brigades in both years, while Ginis for the distribution of cultivated land per capita by teams within individual brigades are even lower, averaging about .05 for three large brigades (Zhifangtou, Dahe, and Dutong) for which we computed them.

Differences in land endowments as measured by crude area cultivated may either under- or overstate the inequality of effective land resources, depending upon whether differences in land *quality* reinforce or (alternatively) offset those in area.[30] Our most direct measure of land quality is the breakdown of teams' lands into three grades that were used for setting output targets under the *lianchan jichou* system implemented by some teams in 1980, 1981, and 1982. Values can be reported for thirteen brigades. This information, which was used to construct the land quality index employed in the analysis of Chapter 9, is available for 13 of the 16 brigades. Once again, we assign a weight of 0 to land of "low quality," 1 to land of "middle quality," and 2 to land of "high quality," calculate an index for each team, and average it within brigades. This index varies from a low of 0.86 in Jiacun brigade to a high of 1.96 in Nanluoling brigade, with a Gini coefficient across brigades of .0936. Still at brigade level, there is a negative correlation of −.6024 between the land quality index and cultivated area per capita, significant at the .01% level,[31] suggesting that the two factors had mutually offsetting effects.[32]

Policy during the collective era could also have worked to offset the inequality based on land endowment, in the sense that teams having more land per capita were required to sell more grain in absolute terms, as well as a larger percentage of their total grain output, to the state. This idea is consistent with our data, in which we find that the correlation between cultivated area per capita and grain sales per capita at quota price is .3111, significant at the .1% level, when data are pooled over years.

[30]Recall the offsetting pattern implied by our analysis of inter-regional differences in Chapter 2, where farmers in provinces having high man-land ratios appeared to overcome this disadvantage by means of significantly higher agricultural productivity. Intensity of cultivation and fertilizer use are often inversely correlated with farm size in farm level data from Latin America and South Asia.

[31]This calculation relies on the quality index from data reported in 1982, the only year for which it is available for most teams, and data on area per capita from 1970. If we substitute area per capita in 1979, its correlation with the index is a somewhat smaller −.4572, significant at the still impressive .1% level.

[32]Given that the brigades were based on existing natural villages, it seems unlikely that the off-setting compensation was the result of policy during, or at the inception of, the collective era. More likely, village populations grew historically with appropriate reference to carrying capacity. A reverse relationship leading from population density and cultivation intensity to soil fertility, based on return of nutrients, etc., could also have been at work. (Note that our conclusions hold only subject to the assumption—on which some doubts are raised by the first stage regression results reported in Chapter 9—that the quality index is reliable for inter-brigade comparisons.)

The correlation between total per capita grain sales to the state (including those at above-quota prices) and cultivated area per capita is similarly positive and significant, as are the correlations between (a) cultivated area per capita and the proportion of total grain output sold at quota price and between (b) cultivated area per capita and the proportion of total grain output sold as opposed to retained by the teams (where the latter includes retentions for distribution to members). These factors may help to explain why although the correlation between distributed collective income per capita and cultivated area per capita, and that between distributed collective income per capita and the land quality index, are both positive, neither correlation is significant at the 10% level.

Aside from differences in land quality, in the quantity of cultivated land per capita, and in production plans and quota levels, teams and brigades will have differed in their levels of nonfarm activity, in their accumulation of capital for both agricultural and nonagricultural purposes, and in their leadership quality and overall organizational effectiveness. In 1970, a year for which teams in only eleven brigades provided data on the gross value of their capital assets, average team assets per capita varied from a low of Y 23.1 in Huozhai brigade to a high of Y 82.1 in Nanluoling brigade, with an inter-brigade Gini coefficient for assets of .1635. In 1979, when teams in fifteen brigades provided data, average team assets per capita ranged from Y 91.1 in Dongdui brigade to Y 204.8 in Shuanghe brigade, with a Gini coefficient of .1257. Productivity differences due to hidden differences such as those in management, profitability of production plans, and land quality (which may or may not be well proxied by the index previously referred to), can be imputed from estimated team or brigade dummy variables in production function estimates such as those discussed in Chapters 4, 5, and 7. One estimate undertaken specifically for this purpose used gross value of output as dependent variable, and gross value of assets, labor force, sown area, and the levels of capital stock, labor force, sown area, and current (variable) inputs as independent variables.[33] As elsewhere, inputs and outputs are entered in logs so that the production function is of the Cobb-Douglas form, with unrestricted returns to scale, and dummy variables are calculated for years and teams. The estimate is for the years 1970–1974, in which valid data for 28 teams could be included. The estimated variation in output for given inputs due to unobserved team effects ranges from 64% below to 296% above the productivity of the arbitrarily chosen base team.[34] Eighteen out of twenty-seven of the team dummies (including those associated with the low and high values just noted) are statistically significant at the 10% level, and the adjusted R^2 for the equation is .7460.

[33]Land is measured in sown area because lack of variation of cultivated area across years for given teams prevents use of team dummy variables, crucial to the present exercise. Note that the exercise involves estimating a production function for aggregate output, which includes both agricultural and nonagricultural production.

[34]As elsewhere in this book, the percentage productivity differential is estimated using the approximation discussed by Derrick (1984).

Table 10.7. Gini Coefficients of Distributed Colletive Income Per Capita Among Brigades

Commune	Province	No. of Brigades	Year	Coefficient	Source
Dahe	Hebei	16	1970	.0544	Authors' calculation
Dahe	Hebei	16	1979	.0813	Authors' calculation
Qie Ma	Hebei	9	1978	.0700	Griffin and Saith (1981)
Tang Tang	Guangdong	17	1978	.0927	Griffin and Saith (1981)
Wu Gong	Hebei	10	1978	.1825	Griffin and Saith (1981)
Evergreen	Beijing	12	1972	.1054	Marshall (1985)[a]
Evergreen	Beijing	12	1977	.0501	Marshall (1985)[a]
Mimu	Sichuan	12	1980	.08	Griffin and Griffin (1984)

[a]Calculation by Hsiung and Putterman based on the data provided.

Source: Hsiung and Putterman (1989).

Ultimately, interest in the distribution of assets such as land derives from concerns about the distribution of income. For analysis of inter-team and inter-brigade differences in per capita incomes at Dahe, we are forced to rely on the team-level accounts which lack data on household sideline earnings.[35] Taking average distributed collective income per capita in each of the 16 brigades at Dahe,[36] we find that the Gini coefficient of inequality among brigades is .0544 for 1970, .0813 for 1979. These figures are similar to those obtained in studies by other authors, as shown in Table 10.7; only one of the latter, for Wugong Commune in Hebei Province, is substantially above .10. That inequality of distributed collective incomes among brigades at Dahe was extremely low during the 1970s is also shown by the fact that the ratio of the income of the "richest" brigade, which distributed an average of Y 95.2 per capita, to that of the "poorest" brigade, which distributed Y 66.73, was 1.43 in 1970. The corresponding ratio in 1979 was 1.68 (with the brigades in question distributing Y 165 and Y 98.2, respectively).

The data provide interesting evidence about the mild increase in inequality among brigades at Dahe in 1979, compared with 1970. Rather than resulting from increasing differences among brigades with respect to productivity or asset bases, the change seems to reflect primarily the removal of controls on distribution which had themselves had a moderating effect on income differences earlier in the decade. This is shown by the computation of Gini coefficients among brigades using average per capita team income net of taxes and expenses. This income concept differs from per capita distributed collective income in that allocations to accumulation funds and other internal funds are not subtracted from it. The computed Gini coefficients are

[35]As discussed in the previous section, distribution of income, overall, may be either more or less equal than that of collective income; for example, if Griffin's hypothesis holds at team level, as his own results suggest that it does, our figures for distributed collective income exaggerate differences for total per capita income. Further independent evidence on the hypothesis is obtained below using data collected by David Zweig.

[36]We average over team-level data without weighting by size of team.

.0843 for 1970, .0897 for 1979. The higher 1970 inequality measure for per capita net income, as opposed to distributed income, suggests that relatively successful teams refrained from having their differential success fully reflected in their members' incomes, instead retaining higher shares of net earnings for collective uses. In view of the discussion of similar phenomena by observers such as Griffin, Blecher, and Zweig, it seems likely that this reflects policies and pressures from commune level leaders, who may in turn have been responding to similar pressures from still higher levels. In 1979, a year in which new incentive systems and market liberalization were beginning to come into play, this factor may have been operating to a lesser extent, or not at all.

Intra-commune inequality taking the production teams as units shows a similar pattern to that among brigades, although the increase of inequality of distributed income over time is not as pronounced. As reported in Table 10.8, the Gini coefficient for distributed income per capita across all reporting teams is .0808 in 1970 versus .1058 in 1979. For net income per capita (without deduction of the collective funds), the coefficient (not shown) is .1108 in 1970 and .1151 in 1979, a pattern consistent with the observation reported in the paragraph above. The ratio of distributed income per capita in the "richest" team to that of the "poorest" team rose from 1.72 in 1970 to 2.84 in 1979.[37]

The degree to which per capita incomes differed across teams within a given brigade can also be studied. Gini coefficients for average distributed collective income per capita for teams in five of the brigades at Dahe were computed for 1970 and 1979. The resulting values, shown in Table 10.8, fall in the .04 to .07 range in 1970[38] and in the .05 to .07 range in 1979. At Dahe, therefore, inequality among teams was lower within brigades than within the commune as a whole.[39] Intra-brigade Gini coefficients for collective distributed income at team level for a total of twenty-four brigades in five other communes, studied by various scholars, are also reported in Table 10.8. While several, like the brigades just reported upon at Dahe, have coefficients below .10, some of the reported values exceed .20, suggesting that inequality among teams within brigades at Dahe was low in comparison with other communes in China.

Because noncollective incomes are not reported in the team-level data set from Dahe, we are unable to test at either team or brigade levels the hypothesis of Griffin and co-authors that the addition of private income reduced inequality. However, three brigades studied by David Zweig (see Table 10.8) did provide data on average

[37] The incomes of the teams in question were Y 85.7 and Y 56.6 in 1970, and Y 213.5 and Y 75.1 in 1979.

[38] No data were reported for Zhifangtou village in 1970. Data on one of the twelve teams in Dutong village is missing for both years, so the Gini coefficient is for eleven teams only.

[39] As before, inter-team differences within brigades are generally higher for net collective income than for distributed collective income. The Gini coefficients for the former concept are .0594, .0374, 0.0793, and .0446 in 1970, and .0675, .0563, .0519, .0814, and .0742 in 1979, for Zhifangtou, Dahe, Dutong, Xuzhuang, and Xiaohe brigades, respectively.

Table 10.8. Gini Coefficients of Distributed Collective Income Per Capita Among Teams[a]

Brigade	Commune	Province	No. of Teams	Year	Coefficient	Source
All	Dahe	Hebei	81	1970	.0808	Authors' computation
All	Dahe	Hebei	92	1979	.1058	Authors' computation
Zhifangtou	Dahe	Hebei	10	1979	.0628	Authors' computation
Zhifangtou	Dahe	Hebei	10	1985	.0068	Authors' computation
Dahe	Dahe	Hebei	15	1970	.0499	Authors' computation
Dahe	Dahe	Hebei	15	1979	.0633	Authors' computation
Dahe	Dahe	Hebei	14	1985	.0625	Authors' computation
Dutong	Dahe	Hebei	11	1970	.0494	Authors' computation
Dutong	Dahe	Hebei	11	1979	.0533	Authors' computation
Dutong	Dahe	Hebei	13	1985	.0632	Authors' computation
Xuzhuang	Dahe	Hebei	3	1979	.0721	Authors' computation
Xuzhuang	Dahe	Hebei	3	1979	.0607	Authors' computation
Xuzhuang	Dahe	Hebei	3	1985	.0663	Authors' computation
Xiaohe	Dahe	Hebei	4	1979	.0381	Authors' computation
Xiaohe	Dahe	Hebei	4	1979	.0708	Authors' computation
Xiaohe	Dahe	Hebei	4	1985	.0426	Authors' computation
Qing Xiu	Jiang Ning	Jiangsu	26	1965	.0543	Zweig[b]
Qing Xiu	Jiang Ning	Jiangsu	26	1970	.0873	Zweig[b]
Qing Xiu	Jiang Ning	Jiangsu	26	1975	.0761	Zweig[b]
Qing Xiu	Jiang Ning	Jiangsu	26	1980	.0777	Zweig[b]
Wa Dian	Tang Quan	Jiangsu	11	1965	.0625	Zweig[b]
Wa Dian	Tang Quan	Jiangsu	11	1970	.0791	Zweig[b]
Wa Dian	Tang Quan	Jiangsu	11	1975	.0986	Zweig[b]
Wa Dian	Tang Quan	Jiangsu	11	1980	.1156	Zweig[b]
Chang Hong	Tang Quan	Jiangsu	7	1965	.1373	Zweig[b]
Chang Hong	Tang Quan	Jiangsu	6	1970	.1285	Zweig[b]
Chang Hong	Tang Quan	Jiangsu	6	1975	.2805	Zweig[b]
Chang Hong	Tang Quan	Jiangsu	7	1980	.2233	Zweig[b]
Heping	Dongnan	Sichuan	15	1981	.06	Griffin and Griffin (1984)
Chaotan	Yuanmenkou	Sichuan	5	1980	.05	Griffin and Griffin (1984)
Sunjin	Chunhe	Yunnan	8	1978–1981	.05–.06	Griffin and Griffin (1984)
Fubao	Lujia	Yunnan	4	1978	.12	Griffin and Griffin (1984)
Fubao	Lujia	Yunnan	4	1981	.08	Griffin and Griffin (1984)
Various	Zhang Qing	Jiangsu	Number varies	1979	.03–.21	Ansell et al. (1982)[c]
Huli	Pukou	Fujian	18	1963	.0744	Chinn (1978)[d]
Xintang	Tang Tang	Guangdong	19	1978	1947	Griffin and Saith (1981)

[a]Data for 1985 are for all reported income retained by households.

[b]Computation by Hsiung and Putterman based on an unpublished data set collected by David Zweig.

[c]A total of 15 intra-brigade inter-team Gini coefficients were computed by Hsiung and Putterman based on data reported for 163 teams in Table 1 of this source.

[d]Chinn computes the value of work-points based on an equation((1), p. 255) which assumes that the value of grain rations should be deducted from net team income before determining work-point value. As far as we are aware (based on a variety of secondary sources and on interviews with informants in China), this was never the practice in Chinese production teams. Rather, the value of rations was to be covered out of work-point income, with households unable to do this being permitted to incur debts to their teams (see, for example, Crook (1975) and Putterman (1988a)). Out computation of the inter-team Gini coefficient for Huli brigade is therefore based on an amended data series derived by adding columns two (WPY/N) and three (B) in Chinn's Table 4.

Source: Hsiung and Putterman (1989), except for 1985 Dahe data, which is calculated from the Dahe data sets.

Table 10.9. Gini Coefficient of Total Income Per Capita Among Teams, Three Jiangsu Brigades[a]

Brigade	Year			
	1965	1970	1975	1980
Qing Xiu	.0536	.0847	.0726	.0616
	(24)	(26)	(26)	(26)
Chang Hong	.1158	.1279	.2219	.1968
	(7)	(6)	(6)	(7)
Wa Dian	.1377	.1495	.1202	.0859
	(11)	(11)	(11)	(11)

[a]Computation by Hsiung and Putterman based on data provided by David Zweig.
Note: Figures in parentheses are number of teams on which computation is based.
Source: Hsiung and Putterman (1989).

household earnings from private plots and sidelines, which allow us to provide at least one additional test of that hypothesis considering inter-team differences within given brigades. The resulting Gini coefficients, with number of teams in parentheses, are shown in Table 10.9. Comparing these figures with those given in Table 10.8 for distributed collective income, we find that the hypothesis is consistently supported for two of the brigades, Qingxiu and Changhong, but rejected for one brigade, Wadian, except in 1980.

A final question for this section is whether such economic growth as took place at Dahe under the collective institutions of the 1970s had an equalizing or a disequalizing effect on inter-brigade and inter-team income distribution. Team net income per capita, in current *yuan,* grew at an average rate of 5.0% per annum during 1970–1979, with the rate varying among brigades from −0.5% per year in the slowest to 8.9% per year in the fastest developing brigades. Griffin and Saith argue that growth tended to have an equalizing effect across teams and brigades because of equalizing transfers or capital grants and due to the operation of diminishing returns to material inputs as the development process proceeded in each unit. On the other hand, Putterman (1988a) conjectures that poor teams might grow more slowly than richer teams if per capita distribution in kind took up a larger share of distributed collective income in the former and if such egalitarianism in distribution had the dampening effect on incentives which is predicted by some theories and partially confirmed by evidence presented in Chapter 5. A test of the proposition that more egalitarian distribution was associated with and hence perhaps responsible for slower rates of growth does find some support in the team data.[40] However, for the 74 teams for

[40]Growth rates for team net income per capita (i.e., net of production expenses and taxes but prior to deduction of accumulation and other nondistributed funds) were calculated by regressing that variable on a time trend, a set of team dummies, and a set of team dummies interacted with the time trend (paralleling the procedure used in Chapter 4). The average share of distributed income taking the form of cash as opposed to grain was then computed for each team, and a regression was estimated with growth rate as

which data are available for both 1970 and 1979, there is a negative correlation of .438, significant at the 1% level, between the percentage change in distributed collective income per capita over the decade[41] and distributed collective income per capita in 1970. This means that even though inequality was increasing gradually over the decade, there was no tendency for the originally "poor" to have grown less rapidly, in percentage terms, than the originally "rich."[42]

Inequality Among Households in 1985

Income differentiation among households at Dahe can be expected to have become greater in 1985 than in 1979. As reported in Chapter 3 and elsewhere, 1983 saw Dahe's households become basic production units in agriculture. Inequalities of earnings from agriculture were held in check by the fact that an average of 33% of the teams' lands were allocated to households on the basis of household population, to allow them to produce their grain consumption requirements. As noted in Chapter 9, the remainder of the lands, aside from the private plots (a small portion of the total cultivated area, the distribution of which did not change from the earlier era, when it was also allotted rather equally among households),[43] were divided according to household labor force, sometimes modified to reflect differences in labor allocation to farming (versus nonfarm activities) as well as households' own expressions regarding the amount of land they wished to farm. On the basis of land distribution alone, inequalities in 1985 need not have been much greater than those in 1979, when income generated collectively was shared partly according to work input and partly on the basis of household size. Some increase in inequality of household per capita incomes could have resulted from the fact that the proportion of distributed collective income taking the form of grain rations in the 1970s was typically above 50%, while the proportion of "collective" land contracted according to household population under *baogan daohu* averaged only 33%. More important, perhaps, was the fact that the household-based farming system may have caused incomes to be more sharply differentiated according to effective labor input than was the case under team production, because the teams had kept work-point differentials small and their assessments of differences in work intensity and quality were imprecise.

---

dependent variable and the cash share of distribution as explanatory variable. Complete data were available for only 17 teams when the distribution variable was averaged for the years 1970–1974 and growth rates were computed for 1970–1979. 26 teams had data with which to compute the average of the distribution variable for 1974–1976 and the growth rates for 1974–1979. The coefficient on the distribution variable was positive, as hypothesized, in the regressions for both periods and samples, and was significant at the 5% level for the 26 team sample.

[41]That is, (DCI79-DCI70)/DCI70, where DCI is distributed collective income per capita, and DCI79 is deflated to 1970 price terms.

[42]The seeming inconsistency of the negative association between base income and growth rate, on the one hand, and rising inequality, on the other, is addressed in the final section.

[43]In 1985, the only year for which the household data give private plots areas, these were highly but not perfectly correlated, within teams, with both household labor force and household size, although the latter was more likely the original basis for distribution.

Probably a more important source of income inequality, however, was the more pronounced occupational variation exhibited in 1985, the fact that many households derived the greater part of their incomes from nonagricultural activities, and the wide variety of wage levels and payment schemes operating in a larger number of enterprise types including private, partnership, village, township, county, and state-owned enterprises. As we have seen, agriculture's average share of gross value of output of households and production teams fell from 76% in 1980 to 55% in 1985. The proportion of the labor force employed in agriculture dropped from 75% in 1982 to 61% in 1985, according to team level data, but to as little as 46% in the households included in the household survey. Although village and township level nonfarm enterprises grew rapidly, their shares in all-level gross value of output remained roughly unchanged, while their wage payments to Dahe peasants as a share of total earnings[44] rose slightly from 11.5% to 13.2%. Meanwhile, peasants' combined incomes from all sources rose rapidly, to reach Y 590 in 1985, according to the team level data.

As anticipated, the Gini coefficients for per capita distribution of income from all sources, by household, rose in all five of the surveyed teams at Dahe, as shown in Table 10.1. The average of the five coefficients is .2727 in 1985, compared with .1715 in 1979. As also reported in the table, the Gini coefficient for the full sample of 246 households in 1985 is higher than the full sample Gini computed for 243 households in 1979. Figure 10.1 shows the Lorenz curves for the distributions of per capita income among survey households in the 2 survey years, and demonstrates that the curve corresponding to the observed distribution in 1985 is everywhere further from the reference line of perfect equality than is the curve for 1979. The post-reform Gini coefficients have thus moved substantially toward the levels of inter-household, intra-village inequality reported for pre-1949 Hebei villages by Brandt and Sands (1988; see above), although they still remained significantly below those levels.[45] An alternative and perhaps more graphic measure of inequality is the ratio of the average per capita income of the top decile of households to that of the bottom decile, as ranked by per capita income. The ratio for the household sample in 1985, using income data inflation-adjusted to 1979 basis (see below), is 6.52, whereas the ratio for 1979, using unaltered data, is 3.51.

We are aware of few studies that present household level income distribution data for the period following China's agricultural decollectivization or which permit an assessment of the changes in income distribution over time. Two recently published studies that do so are based on surveys that cover villages in different townships, and that are therefore not entirely comparable to ours. Nee (1991) reports

---

[44]Excluding state employment.

[45]This does not necessarily mean that local inequality was typically less in the mid-1980s than in pre-1949 Hebei. Although that may indeed have been the case, it should also be borne in mind that Dahe in 1985 had a stronger collective economy (and hence, perhaps, more pro-egalitarian administrative interventions) than did the average Hebei township.

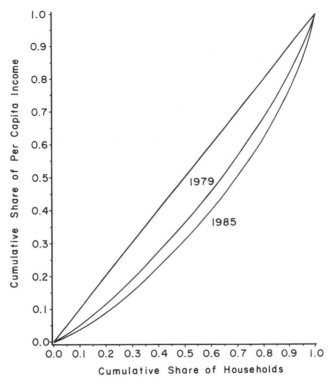

Figure 10.1. Lorenz curves of household per capita income, Dahe household survey, 1979 and 1985.

results from a survey of households in 30 villages in two counties located near the Xiamen Special Economic Zone in Fujian province. With the number of valid observations increasing from 492 in 1975 to 614 in 1985, he calculates Gini coefficients of household income (as opposed to per capita income) of .365 in 1975, .351 in 1980, and .371 in 1984, with the last year following completion of the reform.[46] He concludes that the various population quintiles benefited from the reforms in roughly proportionate fashion, causing income distribution to be little changed by the reform process. Zhu (1991) reports on a similar survey conducted in three counties in the Luoyang area of Henan province. The computed Gini coefficients of per capita income in this case *decline* between 1978 and 1985, from .1470 to .1350 in the first county and from .1722 to .1348 in the second county. Although the Gini coefficient rises from .1720 to .2352 in the third county, the combined coefficient for the sample of about 425 people (more or less equally distributed among

[46]The relatively high values for 1975 and 1980, as compared with studies reported earlier in the chapter, could be attributable both to inter-village variation, not present in those studies, and to the use of total rather than per capita household income. Evidence for the role of the second factor may be drawn from a comparison with the study by Zhu reported immediately below.

the three counties) declines from .2462 in 1978 to .2038 in 1985. While the scopes of the Nee and Zhu surveys are somewhat less local than that of the Dahe survey, they are nonetheless fairly local in character, and provide a contrasting picture of roughly constant or even declining income inequality during the early years of the reform.

Explaining Inequality and Rates of Income Growth

Following again the approach of Gray (1992), Park (1987) also constructed a life cycle model of income distributions based on the individual and household sample data for 1985. In this case, the computed coefficient of variation for the simulated population, in which only life-cycle differences affect incomes, is roughly the same as that for 1979; but the coefficient of variation of household total income as measured in the actual data is substantially higher: .5991 (compared to .3109 for the simulation). This implies that the growth in inequality of income distribution resulting from the reforms cannot be attributed to sharper variation of household earnings over a typical life cycle, and must instead be the result of newly introduced sources of inequality that may be less readily reconciled with equity concerns. That nearly one-half of inter-household inequality, as measured by the coefficient of variation, results from non-life-cycle sources in the decollectivized regime, while only about one-quarter did in the collective regime of 1979, also supports Gray's expectations regarding the influence of collective institutions on equality of distribution.

To analyze the sources of variation in per capita income across households, we estimated an OLS regression equation, the results of which are shown in Table 10.10. Per capita income of the household is as before the dependent variable, and the ratio of household population to number of income earners is again entered as an independent variable. This time, the variables pertaining to work-points, including

Table 10.10. Determinants of Household Per Capita Income, Dahe Township, 1985[a]

Independent Variable	Estimated Coefficient	t Statistic
Constant	1164.097	12.847
Household population-to-workers ratio	−194.812	−4.301
Porportion of workers in agriculture	−220.780	−3.059
Proportion of workers in transport, construction, commerce, and restaurants	535.511	4.740
Proportion of county contract workers	512.403	3.077

Number of valid cases: 237
Adjusted R^2 : 224
F statistic: 18.069

[a]OLS regression.
Source: Hsiung and Putterman (1989).

the number of work days for the collective, are no longer relevant or available. Three variables relating to occupation are entered: the proportion of income earners who are county contract workers; the proportion whose principal occupations are in the transportation, construction, commerce, and restaurant industries (the main private enterprise activities in 1985); and the proportion of income earners whose principal occupation is given as agriculture.[47] The results show a continued significant negative relationship between income per capita and the dependency ratio, strong positive effects of the proportion of contract workers and the proportion of workers in the various private nonfarm trades, and a strong negative relationship between per capita income and the share of household workers employed in agriculture. All variables and the F ratio for the regression are significant at the 1% level, but in this case only 22% of the variance is explained, compared with almost 45% in the parallel equation for 1979 (Table 10.6). To see whether this might be due to the absence of a variable capturing team-specific factors, which were captured to some degree by the value of work-points variable in the 1979 equation, we re-estimated the present equation adding team dummies. While two of these have significant coefficients, their inclusion adds only 4% to the explanatory power of the equation as measured by adjusted R^2. We also tested for the possibility that age and sex differences, which influenced work-points per day and number of work days in 1979 as indicated by the results in Tables 10.3 and 10.5, could account for a substantial part of the remaining variance. To the equation including team dummies, we therefore added variables for the share of household members over age 13 years who are (a) male, (b) aged 13–22, (c) aged 41–60, and (d) aged over 60. This caused the adjusted R^2 to rise by an additional 2% only (to 28%), and added only one significant coefficient (on (b), which is negative).

Since incomes at Dahe were generally higher in 1985 than in 1979, it is pertinent to ask whether the increase in inequality accompanied an improvement in living standard for all or nearly all households. The magnitude of the improvement is also of interest. As we saw in Chapter 3, the average per capita income of households providing complete data in the household surveys was Y 301.52 in 1979 (234 households) and Y 778.45 in 1985 (238 households). Deflating income in the form of self-consumed produce to terms commensurate with the prices of 1979 using the official general index of purchasing prices of farm and sideline products, and deflating cash income by the official general index of retail prices to its 1979 purchasing power equivalent, as in that chapter, the 1985 average becomes Y 583.03, which gives a 93% increase and an 11.6% annual growth rate. The inflation adjusted and unadjusted distributions of household earnings are shown in the third pair of

---

[47]These variables cover all occupations except workers in brigade, township, and partnership-run enterprises, plus a small number of teachers and specialists in orchard, animal husbandry, and fishery production. Separate variables to cover the last two categories were tested and produced insignificant coefficient estimates.

Table 10.11A. Household Per Capita Income by Y 200 Bands, 1979 and 1985, Dahe Township

	1979		1985 Unadjusted		1985 Adjusted	
	No. of hh's	% of hh's	No. of hh's	% of hh's	No. of hh's	% of hh's
Y 0–200	33	14.1	2	0.8	8	3.4
Y 200–400	159	67.9	31	12.8	58	24.4
Y 400–600	38	16.2	61	25.2	83	34.9
Y 600–800	3	1.3	59	24.4	50	21.0
Y 800–1000	1	0.4	39	16.1	18	7.6
Y 1000–1200	0	0.0	22	9.1	9	3.8
Y 1200–1400	0	0.0	8	3.3	5	2.1
Y 1400–1600	0	0.0	7	2.9	5	2.1
Y 1600–1800	0	0.0	6	2.5	0	0.0
Y 1800–2000	0	0.0	5	2.1	0	0.0
Above Y 2000Y	0	0.0	2	0.8	2	0.8

Table 10.11B. Change in Household Per Capita Income, 1979–1985

	Unadjusted Data		Adjusted Data	
	No. of households	% households	No. of households	% households
0–100% decline:	17	8.1	30	14.5
0–100% rise:	59	21.6	86	41.5
100–200% rise:	59	21.6	56	27.1
200–300% rise:	41	15.0	16	7.7
300–400% rise:	14	5.1	11	5.3
400–500% rise:	6	2.2	3	1.4
500–600% rise:	7	2.6	3	1.4
600–700% rise:	3	1.1	2	1.0
700–800% rise:	2	1.0	0	0
800–900% rise:	2	1.0	0	0
900–1000% rise:	1	0.5	0	0

Source: Hsiung and Putterman (1989).

columns of Table 10.11, which gives a breakdown of households by per capita income category in 1979 and 1985.

We can now ask the question, What percentage of households experienced an improvement in real incomes between 1979 and 1985, and how are the rates of improvement (or decline) distributed among households? Selecting all households in the sample that (a) existed as households in both years[48] and (b) provided full income

---

[48] As opposed to those that disappeared from the sample due to death or migration and those that were newly formed, e.g., following marriage.

data in both years, we find that 14.5% of the 207 households meeting these criteria experienced a decline in real income per capita,[49] 41.5% experienced increases of 0–100%, 27.1% experienced increases of 100–200%, 7.7% experienced increases of 200–300%, and 9.1% of households experienced increases in excess of 300%. Results for both the inflation adjusted and the nominal income data are reported in the lower portion of Table 10.11.

The discovery that some households in a rural township experiencing such vigorous growth as did Dahe suffered declines in real per capita income may surprise some readers and seem to confirm the suspicions of others who question the wisdom of the reforms from the standpoints of the protection of the economically weak, and of equity. Before strong conclusions are drawn, however, it is necessary to consider that life-cycle changes will tend to cause declines in per capita income for some households under normal economic circumstances, especially where there are few available methods of smoothing earnings streams over a lifetime.[50] Moreover, the impact of the addition of small children on household living standards is exaggerated by the change in income per capita, unless weights for consumption requirements by age, and adjustments for economies of scale in consumption, are employed. To investigate whether life-cycle changes can account for declining per capita incomes at Dahe, we computed, for each household, (a) the number of children born after 1979, (b) the percentage of persons aged 16 years or over who were older than 60 in 1985, and (c) the percentage change in the dependency ratio measured as total household population divided by number of working members. We then identified households in the upper quartile and in the upper decile of the distributions of values for each of these three variables.[51] Of the 30 households showing declining per capita incomes, we find that 13 were in the upper quartile and 6 in the upper decile of households by number of small children, 7 were in the upper quartile and 4 in the upper decile by percentage of old people, and 8 were in the upper quartile and 4 in the upper decile by percentage increase in dependency ratio. Nineteen of the 30 households were in the upper quartile and 11 were in the upper decile of at least one of the three distributions. The evidence thus suggests that well over one-half of the cases of declining real income are life-cycle related, and might have occurred with or without reform of the economic system.[52]

[49] Using unadjusted data, only 8.1% of households suffered declining per capita incomes. Four more households, which did not provide some of the data needed to perform the adjustment, are included in the unadjusted data series.

[50] As mentioned earlier, few inter-household transfers, such as those from children to aged parents, were reported by our survey households. We believe that this reflects reluctance to report such transfers, and we therefore consider the data to be incomplete in a way that could exaggerate inequalities. Nonreporting of some higher incomes could have had the opposite effect on measured inequality, but is not particularly relevant to the issues of the present paragraph.

[51] Due to repeating values, it was not possible to divide the sample at precisely the desired points, so the nearest break is employed. This causes the actual shares of households above our cut-offs to be 41% (one or more children) and 13.5% (two or more children) for variable (a), 27.1% and 10.8% for (b), and 27.6% and 13.3% for (c).

[52] We have not tried to provide a precise answer to the question of whether and by how much the sharpness of changes in per capita income due to life cycle may have been increased by the reforms.

Income and Class Background

One of the aims of China's 1949 revolution was to overturn the existing rural class structure, as perceived by the Chinese Communist Party; class labels assigned to individual peasants and their families during the land reform of the early 1950s played an important role in rural political struggles for almost three decades before being officially repudiated in 1979. It is therefore of some interest to ask (a) whether class background significantly affected income distributions at Dahe during the collective era, (b) if so, in what way (if at all) did this change by 1985, and (c) what bearing does this have on the distribution of relative benefits from the reforms. An inquiry along these lines is made possible by the fact that the household survey conducted in 1979 included information on the personal classification *(geren chengfen)* of each household head and the family background *(chushen)* of each household. The categories of the first variable are poor peasant, low-middle peasant, middle peasant, high-middle peasant, rich peasant, landlord, peasant, student, worker, and cadre. The second variable has the same categories except that worker and cadre do not appear, and a new category, "other," is included. Table 10.12 shows the average value of household per capita income in 1979 and 1985, and of the change over time for households identifiable in both years, with the data grouped by both household head classification and family background. The "student" and "other" categories are omitted, as are those categories for which no complete responses were obtained. Note that the household head classification and family background variables used in all of the correlations are those reported in 1979. There are no new data on these classifications, which in the interim had gone out of use, in the 1985 survey.

Six of the classifications and backgrounds (the six specific peasant types and landlord) lend themselves to unambiguous ordering. A seventh, "peasant," probably coincides with individuals who were not yet born or were children at the time of land reform. To increase the number of rankable cases, this category might be assumed equal to "middle peasant" as an approximation. Scanning the personal classification

---

Arguably, there was some increase, since a significant part of income was distributed on a per capita basis under the collective system. Comparison of Tables 10.6 and 10.10 suggests a significant increase in the absolute effect of dependency ratio on nominal income, but much of this is attributable to the increase in incomes overall. The fact that coefficients of variation based on simulated life-cycle variation (see above) were quite similar in 1985 and 1979 suggests that there was little change in the trade-off. A caution, however, is that Park's study considers how changes in earnings functions may have altered inequality assuming a given life cycle. He did not examine whether the typical life-cycle changed (with respect to age at marriage, family size, etc.) or whether observed life-cycles became more heterogeneous, and what the effects of the latter changes on income inequality may have been.

We also cannot rule out the possibility that some declines in per capita income are due to errors in the reports of income, or in their tabulation. One reason for concern is that twenty-four of the thirty households with declining incomes come from a single team, team 2 of Shuanghe Village. This raises the possibility that survey results were biased upward in 1979 or downward in 1985 (in which year the surveys were conducted by different individuals in different villages), or both. However, the number of cases of declining per capita income that appear to be explained by the three life-cycle factors is if anything greater for the twenty-four Shuanghe households than for the remaining six. This can be taken as evidence against the notion that the income decline in the Shuanghe survey households is purely imaginary.

Table 10.12. Average Household Per Capita Income by Household Head and Family
Classification, Dahe

	Average Income, 1979	Average Income, 1975	Income Ratio 1985/1979
Personal classification of household head (1979)			
Cadre	229.8 (7)	856.2 (33)	3.09 (6)
Worker	237.5 (6)	897.2 (6)	3.77 (6)
Peasant	285.9 (201)	779.7 (184)	2.95 (179)
Poor peasant	378.5 (15)	533.1 (13)	1.64 (13)
Middle peasant	315.2 (8)	694.8 (6)	2.27 (6)
High-middle peasant	267.9 (2)	— (0)	— (0)
Family background (1979)			
Peasant	— (0)	— (0)	— (0)
Poor peasant	313.0 (101)	728.2 (97)	2.706 (95)
Low-middle peasant	279.8 (25)	797.0 (23)	3.214 (21)
Middle peasant	296.9 (79)	782.2 (70)	2.959 (69)
High middle peasant	265.4 (17)	710.5 (15)	2.937 (15)
Rich peasant	274.7 (7)	558.9 (6)	2.139 (6)
Landlord	422.2 (4)	1318.2 (4)	3.081 (4)

Note: Figures in parentheses are the number of valid cases on which each average is based.
Source: Hsiung and Putterman (1989).

portion of the table, we see an apparent negative correlation between per capita
income in 1979 and class rank, under the convention that poor peasant rank is
considered low, and rich peasant rank high. If, further, we treat "peasant" as
equivalent to "middle peasant" and assign the numbers 0 to poor peasant, 1 to
low-middle peasant, etc., up to 6 for high-middle peasant, the resulting personal
classification variable (which excludes cadres and workers) has a negative correlation
of −.178 with 1979 per capita income, which is significant at the 1% level. The same
variable, on the other hand, has a positive correlation of .126 with per capita income
in 1985, which is significant at the 5% level. The switch in direction of correlation
suggests that households headed by persons of "higher" class background saw greater
relative improvements in income than did those of "lower" class background. This is
confirmed by the fact that the same personal classification variable has a positive
correlation of .152, which is significant at the 5% level, with the change in income per
capita as a percentage of its base year level. Note also that cadre-headed households,
which reported the lowest average per capita incomes of all groups in 1979, report one
of the highest levels in 1985, although the change could be influenced by the change
in the number of cases for which income data were given.

Almost the same pattern appears in the family background portion of the table,
but for this variable, there are no uncategorized "peasant" cases, and there are cases
of rich peasant and landlord backgrounds. Contrary to the pattern, the four households of landlord background have the highest average per capita incomes in 1979,

and raised their incomes at a faster than average rate in the years leading up to 1985, giving them extraordinarily high incomes in that year. Despite this partial exception, per capita income appears to be related to class background in both years. Persons of "good" class background (from the C.C.P.'s standpoint) and their families appear to have been benefiting from favoritism of one kind or another even at the tail end of the collective era, but families of "bad" class background, on average, seemed still to have either the connections or the entrepreneurial drive and abilities, or both, to prosper relative to their neighbors under the "liberal" policies of the 1980s. Households of landlord origin (contrary to the pattern for that year) were already relatively well off in 1979 but (in conformity with the pattern for the latter year) better off still in 1985. The families of the few reporting team level cadres had low per capita incomes in 1979; the larger number of reporting households headed by cadres in 1979 that reported incomes in 1985 were relatively well off in the latter year.[53] Given the small number of cases involved and the fact that an in-depth study of the issue was not conducted, it is clear that we should not generalize from these findings.[54]

A Comparison of "Poor" and "Rich" Households in 1985

A concrete sense of household living standards and of differences between "poor" and "rich" households in 1985 can once again be obtained by intensive examination of a subsample of the data. As before, we choose two households indicating no total income figure plus eight households having the lowest positive total incomes per capita as our "poor" sample, and the ten households with highest per capita incomes as our "rich" sample. As before, the "poor" households come (with one exception) from the two teams with the lowest average per capita incomes in 1985 (which are not, however, the same teams as in 1979), while four teams are represented among the ten "rich" households. The average per capita income of the eight "poor" households reporting positive incomes is Y 211.56, while that of the ten "rich" households is Y 2,391.68, both figures being in unadjusted current terms.[55] The "poor" households owned an average of Y 152 per capita worth of consumer goods such as bicycles, watches, tape recorders, and washing machines, and had an average housing area of 22.3 m^2 per capita, of which 47% had been built after 1980. The

[53]Since the classification variable is based on 1979 data, many of the individuals in question may have ceased to be cadres by 1985.

[54]With regard to the personal classification of household head variable, a particular danger is that if "peasant" status was assigned only to households formed after the early 1950s, there is a correlation of this status with age of household head. This means that the fact that neither poor nor middle peasants did as well as "peasant"-headed households in 1985 could simply reflect the advanced age of the first two groups. The same would not seem to apply, however, to the classification by family background, since the absence of households classified as "peasant" implies that households formed after land reform inherited the class background label of the household head's family of origin.

[55]Note that the ratio of the average incomes in the "richest" group to the average incomes in the "poorest" group rises from 4.34 in 1979 to 11.30 in 1985, providing another measure of increasing income differentiation.

"rich" households owned an average of Y 435 worth of consumer goods per capita, and had an average housing area of 31.56 m^2 per capita, of which 80% had been built after 1980. "Poor" households consumed an average of 199 kg of grain per capita, of which 6.4% was coarse grain, while "rich" households consumed an average of 214 kg of grain, of which 4.6% was coarse.[56] Members of "poor" households reported consuming an average of Y 23.4 per capita worth of meat and Y 69.5 per capita worth of other nonstaple foods, whereas members of "rich" households reported consuming Y 105.5 per capita of meat and Y 195.9 per capita of other nonstaples.

Judged by their possession of consumer goods and housing, the "poor" households in our sample do not appear to have been very poor by Chinese rural standards. Their average 1985 income of Y 212 per capita[57] was below the national average peasant income of Y 397.60 for the same year, and placed them in the poorest quintile of rural population according to a national household survey.[58] However, three of the ten "poor" households had black and white television sets, which was well above the national average of 1.2 in ten although below the level of the "rich" households of whom six in ten had sets, one of them color. Two of the ten households had washing machines, versus 12.6% of households nationally but compared with five in ten of the "rich" households. There was one bicycle for every three persons in the "poor" households, versus a bicycle per 5.5 persons nationally, and compared with over one for every two for the "rich" households.[59] Finally, the average floor space per capita in the "poor" households, at 22 m^2, was above the national rural average in 1985, 17.34 m^2. These factors suggest that by 1985, Dahe was quite prosperous by national standards, and that the reported income data for at least some poor households at Dahe could be misleading, due to outright understatement or as the result of unrepresentatively low income for the survey year only.

Household dependency ratios again play a role in explaining relative per capita income, but less so than in 1979. The "poor" households averaged 4.3 members and 2.1 workers, whereas the "rich" households averaged 3.1 members and 2.1 workers. This time, occupation plays an obvious role. Of 21 income earners in the ten "poor" households, fully 13 gave agriculture as their main occupation, 5 worked in village enterprises, and 1 listed "other" as occupation. Of 21 income earners in the ten "rich"

[56]Average reported per capita grain consumption is lower in 1985 than in 1979, according to the household survey. If this is not a statistical anomaly, it can perhaps be attributed to an increase in other foodstuffs in the diet. Grain "distributed to the households" (i.e., retained by them—an archaic accounting term was chosen by the township statistical officer for the survey form) in 1985 was 351.3 kg per capita versus 253.2 kg per capita in 1979, from team level data. This suggests that households had more grain available to them in 1985; hence, either consumption was under-reported in the household survey, or large amounts of grain were used to feed household livestock.

[57]Based on the eight households providing positive income data.

[58]*Statistical Yearbook of China 1986*, p. 582, indicates that only 12% of rural households in China had incomes of less than Y 200 in 1985.

[59]National data refer to rural households only, with the exception of those for washing machines, which refer to both urban and rural households. The national average ratios of persons to households are used to convert data from per person to per household form as necessary. Source: *Statistical Yearbook of China 1986* (State Statistical Bureau, 1986).

households, only 7 gave agriculture as main occupation, 3 gave a village enterprise, 1 a county enterprise, and 2 a township enterprise, while there were 3 transportation workers (probably tractor drivers), a construction worker, a commercial worker, a restaurant worker, and 2 "other." Moreover, all of the 7 agricultural workers among the 'rich' households were women, while 7 of the 13 agricultural workers among the "poor" households were men. This strongly suggests that higher incomes were linked to having at least the male income earners of the household work in nonagricultural activities. The proportion of income coming from agriculture was 97.7% in the "poor" households versus only 45.5% in the "rich" ones.

An example of a "poor" household is the Liu family of Zhifangtou village, whose per capita income of Y 217 in 1985 had fallen (even in nominal terms) from a level of Y 222 in 1979. The family consisted of a couple, ages 36 and 30 years, and their two young sons, ages 2 and 4. Both Mr. Liu and his wife were ordinary production team workers in 1979 and both worked only in agriculture in 1985. The Lius reported only Y 82.5 worth of consumer durables, including a sewing machine, two wrist watches and one bicycle. They owned no radio, television set, tape recorder, clock, washing machine, electric fan, or sofa. The four Lius shared a house consisting of only 42 m², evidently the same three rooms which they occupied in 1979.[60] In 1985, they consumed 192.5 kg of grain per capita, 97% of it fine grain, and 10 kg of meat plus Y 100 worth of other nonstaple foods per capita. It may be noted that the small decline in the Liu's per capita income between 1979 and 1985 was caused in large part by the addition of two young children; the nominal level of their total household income nearly doubled over the period. On the other hand, some of the latter increase is attributable to the higher valuation of self-consumed produce, which hardly affects their real living standard. That the Lius failed at least relatively to benefit under the reforms, and that this failure may be associated with their reliance on agriculture, is a conclusion that still stands despite the recognition that their change of fortunes is substantially based on life-cycle factors that would have had a similar effect with or without the change in institutional structure.

For an example of a "rich" family, we look at the Hu household of Jiacun village, whose per capita income rose from Y 276 in 1979 to Y 2,835 (the third highest in the household survey) in 1985. The household consisted of husband and wife, ages 47 and 40 years, a daughter, aged 19, sons ages 16 and 14, and a daughter-in-law, age not indicated. The source of the family's high income was a transportation enterprise (the family most likely owned a small tractor), in which the principal worker was the 16 year old son, and from which gross earnings were Y 10,400. The father worked in a restaurant where he earned Y 1,260 per year. The mother and daughter-in-law both worked on the family's farm, where the two sons reported working part time (about

---

[60]The household survey uses rooms in 1979 but square meters in 1985 as the unit of measure of housing area. In 1979, the Lius reported having three rooms, while in 1985 they reported that none of their housing area was built after 1979.

Table 10.13. Growth Rate of Income, Household Survey Teams, Dahe

Team	Average Per Capita Income, 1979	Average Per Capita Income, 1985[a]	Annual Growth Rate. %
Dahe, team 15	250.47	634.08	16.74
	(50)	(58)	
Jiacun, team 3	227.02	661.82	19.50
	(57)	(56)	
Xiaohe, team 3	281.67	637.57	14.15
	(24)	(23)	
Zhifangtou, team 2	373.12	521.23	5.73
	(37)	(35)	
Shuanghe, team 2	371.59	485.07	4.54
	(66)	(66)	

Note: Figures in parentheses are number of valid observations on households.
[a]Adjusted data. Growth rate is that of the team average, which is inclusive of data for some households not present in both survey years.
Source: Hsiung and Putterman (1989).

10% of the work year). The six Hus reported owning Y 767 of consumer durables per capita, including a black and white television set, a washing machine, a motor bike, three bicycles, a sewing machine, a sofa, a clock, and five wrist watches. They shared a house of 120 m², giving them 20 m² per capita as compared to the Lius' 10.5.[61] In 1985, they consumed 210 kg of grain per capita, 95% of it fine grain, and ate 16.7 kg of meat and Y 260 worth of other nonstaple foods per capita.

Inequality at Team and Brigade Level in the 1980s

The five teams examined in the household survey, for which data are available from the team survey also, provide an interesting starting point for examining the differential impact of the reforms at team and brigade levels. As Table 10.13 shows, the adjusted growth rates computed for these teams from the household survey data vary from 4.25% per year to 20.35% per year. Notably, it is the teams reporting higher incomes in 1979 that grew more slowly, and those reporting lower incomes that grew more rapidly: the table shows an almost perfect inverse correlation between initial income and income growth rate. As might be expected from this, the Gini coefficients at team level for average total income and average distributed/retained income[62] per capita among these five teams declined between 1979 and 1985, going

---

[61]Recall, though, that the four Lius included two small children, whereas the Hus are all adults. Since the Hus' house was also built before 1979, we can assume that it consisted of the eight rooms which they reported then (see the previous note), giving them 1.3 rooms per capita compared with the Lius' 0.75.

[62]For 1979, income distributed to households by the teams, plus household income from other sources. For 1985, income retained by the households, i.e., not turned over to the collective or the state.

Table 10.14. Gini Coefficient of Income per Capita of Teams, Dahe[a]

Year	Coefficient	Moving Average of Coefficient
1970	.081	—
1971	.089	.081
1972	.072	.079
1973	.075	.070
1974	.062	.075
1975	.087	.075
1976	.075	.078
1977	.071	.078
1978	.089	.089
1979	.106	.120
1980	.165	.132
1981	.124	.131
1982	.103	.136
1983	.181	.144
1984	.149	.178
1985	.203	—

[a]For 1970s, distributed collective income. For 1980s, income from all sources except state employment, as reported in team-level accounts.
Source: Hsiung and Putterman (1989).

from .136 to .086 based on the household survey and from .160 to .112 based on the team survey.

What appears to be evidence of equalizing income growth also comes from the full team survey. There, a significant negative correlation is found between the percentage change in distributed income per capita[63] and the initial level of income per capita, over the period 1979–1985, suggesting that relatively poor teams tended to grow more rapidly, and relatively rich teams to grow more slowly. Recall, however, that although we found a similar correlation between income growth and initial income level when studying the change in inter-team income distribution reported for the 1970–1979 period, incomes per capita became relatively less rather than more equal over that period. The same turns out to be the case for the full team sample during 1979–1985. As Table 10.14 shows, the Gini coefficient for distributed income per capita is erratic during the period, but in no case lower than the 1979 value, and significantly higher on average than in the 1970s.[64] The appearance of an overall rising trend is supported by examination of the series of 3-year moving averages of the coefficient, which can be computed for the years 1971–1984.

[63]That is, the difference between distributed income per capita in the terminal year and that in the initial year, divided by the value in the initial year. See also note 41, above.

[64]Income from household sidelines is included in the 1980s but not 1970s. If Griffin's hypothesis holds, this should mean that the 1970s coefficients *overstate* the degree of inequality relative to those for the 1980s.

The concurrence of a negative correlation of growth rates with initial incomes, on the one hand, and of an increase in the Gini coefficient, on the other, illustrates the phenomenon known as regression toward the mean. If each team drew its income level randomly from a given set of incomes generating the same overall income distribution in each of two periods, teams that drew low incomes the first time would on average experience a large increase of incomes in the second draw, while teams that drew high incomes would tend to experience a decline. The same principle may carry over even if (a) the distribution is changing somewhat over time, e.g., experiencing an increase in variance, (b) all or almost all incomes are increasing over time (in which case the likely decline for an above-average team would be a relative rather than absolute one), and (c) incomes are not drawn entirely randomly. In the present case, for example, per capita incomes of the members of different teams remain positively correlated across periods despite the negative correlation of their growth rates and their initial incomes.[65] In sum, there is no contradiction, in fact, between the finding that poor teams tended to experience more rapid growth than rich ones, and the finding that cross-sectional income variation increased over time.

Another measure of inequality considered earlier shows an even greater degree of widening over time. The ratio of distributed collective income of the "richest" to the "poorest" team was 1.72 in 1970 and 2.84 in 1979. The ratio of distributed incomes in 1985, now including household sideline income (and income from contracted household farming which has replaced team-level farm production), is 5.84. It is also interesting to look again at the net income concept, that is gross revenue minus production costs and taxes, but before deduction of funds retained by the teams. The "richest" to "poorest" ratio for this measure is essentially constant between 1970 (2.71) and 1979 (2.76), but it rises to 6.36 in 1985. We may conclude from this that whereas the increase in the inter-team income gap between 1970 and 1979 was the result of unleashing the latent inter-team differences that existed throughout the 1970s but were suppressed by differential accumulation decisions, the growth of inequality in the early 1980s was based directly on changes in the variances of per capita productivity of labor and other resources, and in available supplies of the latter, across teams.

Finally, it is also possible to carry out on team data the same type of exercise reported in the previous section at household level—that is, to look at the distribution of changes in income (in this case, per capita distributed income) between 1979 and 1985 across teams. Accepting the team-level data as given, Table 10.15 shows that per capita distributed income rises for all 90 teams for which we have the requisite data. The modal range of increases is 300–400%, with 24 teams falling in this category. Twenty-three teams saw per capita distributed income increase by 200–300%, 15 teams saw increases of 400–500%, 14 saw increases of less than 200%, and 14 saw increases of more than 500%. However, the indicated changes are misleading,

[65]The authors are indebted to Harl Ryder for a clarifying discussion on these points.

Table 10.15. Change in per Capita Distributed Income of Teams, 1979–1985

% Change	Unadjusted Data		Adjusted Data[a]	
	No. of Teams	% of Teams	No. of Teams	% of Teams[b]
0–100% decline	0	0.0	6	6.7
0–100% rise	6	6.7	37	41.1
100–200% rise	8	8.9	37	41.1
200–300% rise	23	25.6	9	10.0
300–400% rise	24	26.7	1	1.1
400–500% rise	15	16.7	0	0.0
500% + rise	14	15.6	0	0.0

[a]See text for assumptions used.
[b]Excluding teams for which the data are not available from both years.
Source: Hsuing and Putterman (1989).

because incomes from noncollective sources would be counted in the final but not the initial year, while a downward adjustment for inflation is also desirable in the final year. Assuming that in 1979 the same percentage of incomes (namely 62.7%) came from collective distribution in these 90 teams as in the five teams of the household survey, and assuming that the average adjustment factor for the household sample (1985 income in terms of 1979 prices is 74.7% of 1985 nominal income) holds for the full team sample, the results change: 37 teams experienced increases of 0–100% in real per capita income, thus measured, the same number experienced increases of 100–200%, 9 saw their incomes rise by 200–300%, and 1 team had its income rise by 300–400%. Six teams experienced *declines* in real per capita distributed income, on the basis of the adjusted data.

Turning to inequality among villages, we find a further increase in the Gini coefficient of distributed income among the sixteen former brigades. That coefficient, which went from .0544 in 1970 to .0813 in 1979 continued its rise to .1252 in 1985.[66] The ratio of the average income in the highest income village, Dahe, to that in the lowest income village, Xidui, is 3.7 : 1, although if we exclude Xidui on suspicion of noncomparable coverage and substitute the next poorest village, Nanluoling, we get a more modest 1.83 : 1 ratio.[67] Income differences among teams in given villages showed no tendency to widen, and in at least one case appeared to fall significantly (see Table 10.8).

Unfortunately, there is reason to treat the results reported in this section with extreme caution. There is a disparity between the 1985 per capita income of Dahe

[66]Note again that whereas the income concept used was distributed collective income, in 1970 and 1979, it is income retained by households, in 1985.

[67]Xidui's reported average income of Y 194.94 is much lower than that of the next poorest village, Nanluoling, which reported average income of Y 394.40. Also, the rate of increase in Xidui's reported income is much slower than other villages. There is accordingly reason to suspect that its accountants were less thorough in considering relevant income sources than were their counterparts in other villages. See the discussion on data reliability below.

Village's team 15 as reported in the team accounts (Y 430.1, one of the lowest in the township) and as calculated from the household survey (Y 811.80, among the three higher income teams out of the five). This raises the possibility that some teams that reported low incomes in 1985 were ignoring some member income sources that might more than offset the apparent poverty implied by the limited sources accounted for. A check of income sources against total income as reported in the household versus team level surveys for all five teams covered by both surveys fails to support the view that team 15 is exceptional. As noted in Chapter 4 and especially Chapter 7, the methodology of team income reporting in the mid-1980s may have lacked uniformity owing to the fact that teams had ceased to be the units at which level the reported incomes were generated, and because the cadres concerned failed to establish or communicate common standards for inclusion of incomes reported by constituent households.[68] Hence, some of the greater heterogeneity of incomes at team level in the mid-1980s may be due to heterogeneity of coverage, and the decline in per capita incomes for some teams could be more illusory than real. By the same token, some of the apparent homogeneity in the incomes of teams in the same village (Table 10.8) could also be illusory, a result of incomplete surveying of individual teams combined with application of a common set of methods and assumptions by those responsible for supplying the survey data in each village.

Conclusions

Although distributive and developmental goals were not deemed inconsistent by China's leadership under Mao Zedong, the policies of the Mao era suggest that a relatively great weight was placed on equality, with some willingness to sacrifice current output and even the rate of economic growth in order to further the attainment of a classless rural society at the local level. Except during the Great Leap Forward, a link continued to be maintained between household labor contributions and household earnings, so that equality was never absolute. Nonetheless, our study of income inequality at Dahe commune/township confirms the expectation of very low levels of differentiation during the collective period. Both inter-household and inter-team inequality were quite low at Dahe during the 1970s, the last decade of that period and the one to which our detailed data pertain.

That the linkage of income to work was based primarily upon simple ascriptive attributes as opposed to substantive work assessments is suggested by the fact that differences in work-points ratings, according to which collective incomes were divided among individual team members, could be substantially predicted by variation in age and sex. With these attributes having substantial impacts upon the amount of labor supplied, as seen in Chapter 6, they likewise go a long way toward predicting income distributed to individuals by the teams, which by formula is based

---

[68]This suggests that caution is advisable more generally when analyzing recent Chinese data based on reports passed up administrative hierarchies from team or village levels.

upon differences in number of days worked and number of work-points awarded per day. The resulting pattern of differentiation among individuals in turn implies a pattern of inequality of per capita incomes across households that is largely explained by differences in household composition related to varying positions in the life cycle.

At Dahe and other sites of research in China, inequality of total income per capita at the household level was lower than that of the portion of income distributed by teams, indicating an equalizing effect of earnings from other sources, including private plots. Inequality of distributed collective income across brigades and teams was also found to be less than that of the teams' potentially distributable earnings in the early 1970s at Dahe, due to a positive correlation between retained collective income and the latter variable. Also, differences in procurement levels and land quality appear to have reduced or eliminated the effect of differences in per capita land endowments on per capita incomes.

Inequality of distributed collective incomes per capita at team level in Dahe rose in 1979 to more closely approximate that of net collective revenue. Inequality of both measures rose thereafter; Gini coefficients roughly doubled between the 1970s and 1983–1985, although we cannot say how much of this change is due to a likely increase in the inconsistency of coverage in the team data. Gini coefficients of household per capita incomes within teams also came close to doubling between 1979 and 1985. Gains from the transition to the household contracting system and a more varied contractual and organizational environment were unevenly distributed among households. Some households even appeared to suffer absolute declines in real income, although the evidence suggests that many of these underwent life-cycle changes that might also have reduced incomes in the absence of reforms. In sum, it seems safe to conclude from the study of Dahe that intra-township inequality there increased following the move to household farming and the diversification of the local economy. By the same token, while the amount of change was appreciable, it can be concluded that the level of inequality that resulted remained fairly low by international standards.

This chapter has not concerned itself with inter-regional inequalities, but it may be appropriate to close with what limited information on the subject can be gleaned from the data discussed in Chapter 2. We found there that differences in the level of economic development between different regions and subregions of China are substantial. Those differences seem to be explained primarily by differences in resource endowments, including access to natural and manmade transportation routes, and in the historical process of industrialization, which got an earlier start in places such as Shenyang, Shanghai, and Tianjin. Whether to build on the advantages of the more industrialized and favorably located coastal cities or to emphasize the diffusion of industry into China's interior has been a subject of policy vacillation during the decades since 1949. While China under Mao Zedong tended to favor diffusion, post-Mao China's philosophy of "letting some get rich first" has had its regional corollary of relaxed constraints on coastal province industrialization. Those aspects of the liberalization of rural economic policy that allowed individuals with better access to capital, technology, or markets to achieve more rapid improvements in income than their less advantaged neighbors can also be expected to have had similar affects at the inter-regional level. Localities providing accessible outlets for the marketing of high-value farm produce, a strong demand for construction labor and materials, sub-contracting opportunities with nearby urban enterprises, and other sources of financial surpluses with which to invest in a variety of nontraditional enterprises, can be expected to have experienced more rapid economic growth than did more geographically isolated regions where most resources continued to be devoted to subsistence farm production.

One piece of evidence that is broadly consistent with this expectation is the series on per capita peasant income from the *Statistical Yearbook of China*. The Gini coefficient for the 27 province-level units for which data are available in 1980, giving equal weight to each unit, is .1377. The Gini for the same provinces in 1984 is .1612, while that for 1988 is .1916.[69] The gap between the average peasant income in the highest income province and that in the lowest income province widens from 2.79 : 1 in 1980 to 3.55 : 1 in 1984 and to 3.83 : 1 in 1988. The gap between the unweighted average of the average incomes in the top three provinces to the corresponding average for the bottom three provinces similarly widens from 2.17 : 1 in 1980 to 2.63 : 1 in 1984 and to 2.85 : 1 in 1988.[70] Comparing these rural income data by province with overall per capita incomes by state in the United States, Byrd and Gelb (1990, p. 360) find higher coefficients of variation in China than in the United States. A similar finding holds for inequality among counties within provinces and states (Byrd and Gelb, 1990, p. 361). Household-level studies provide a less consistent picture, however. Selden (1992) reports that rising inequality among Chinese rural households during 1978–1985 was followed by declining inequality thereafter.[71] Khan et al. (1991) cite a World Bank study according to which the Gini coefficient for rural China fell between 1978 and 1982, but rose thereafter through 1986. Despite the apparent differences between these findings, the report cited by Khan et al. (1991) suggests that the rural Gini coefficient for China was virtually the same in 1985 as in 1978, much as Selden finds the Gini for 1988 to be comparable to that for 1980. At a household level for China as a whole, then, there may not have been much long-term movement in inequality, suggesting that changes in the distribution of rural incomes within provinces may have acted to cancel out increasing inequality among provinces during the reform period.

---

[69]The missing provinces were Qinghai and Tibet. Data for these provinces, although available, is not included in our calculations for 1984 and 1988, to assure comparability. Data for Hainan, available for 1988, is also excluded.

[70]The highest average peasant income is consistently registered by Shanghai, followed by Beijing and Tianjin. If these three municipalities are removed from the sample, the ratios go from 1.83 : 1 in 1980 to 2.20 : 1 in 1984 to 2.65 : 1 in 1988, for the single province comparison, and from 1.76 : 1 in 1980 to 1.90 : 1 in 1984 to 2.20 : 1 in 1988, for the comparison of the top three and bottom three provinces. The latter comparisons are based on unweighted averages across provinces.

[71]Computation by Selden based on data reported in *Changes and Development in China 1949–1989*.

11

Conclusions

We began this book by summarizing the major changes and the equally significant continuities characterizing China's rural economy in the transition from the collectivist 1960s and 1970s to the post-collective 1980s. It was suggested, in the "Introduction," that the complexity of Chinese society can be compared to that of the elephant that is described in seemingly conflicting ways by members of a proverbial group of blind men. As we draw our study to a close, are we any closer to understanding this enormous beast, or even the narrower aspect of China which is its rural economy? We begin by surveying the findings of the previous chapters, starting with Chapter 2.[1]

Review of Major Findings

In some respects, our focus on data from a single locality has clearly placed us in danger of befalling the fate of the blind men. Every effort was made to put our local study into perspective, but most of the specific analysis of this book has nonetheless made use of data from that locality alone, and we need to be cautious about generalizing from our micro findings.

Just as we declare the need for caution in drawing macro conclusions from micro findings, so our survey of China's regional diversity, in Chapter 2, also supplied much reason for caution about statements based on Chinese averages. Of the six macro regions defined for purposes of that survey, two, the coastal provinces and the northeast, stood out as having distinctly higher average incomes than the remainder of China, with the central coastal subregion being even more exceptional in that regard. Typically, provinces with higher per capita incomes and outputs overall also showed higher rural incomes, which were explained in part by higher rates of rural industrialization and crop diversification. Although these provinces (with the exception of the northeast) would appear to be put at a disadvantage by their higher than average man-land ratios, their agricultures generally employ more irrigation, more fertilizer, and more machinery, and their per capita and per hectare crop outputs are high by national standards. In terms of economic structure, industry's share of gross

---

[1]Instead of trying to summarize our discussion of the broad sweep of China's recent rural development history in Chapter 1, we will pick up the thread of that discussion following the next section.

rural output value in the central coast subregion (65.3%) was more than twice that of any noncoastal region, and that subregion's two provinces and one municipality, although containing less than 11% of China's rural population, accounted for nearly 42% of the country's township and village enterprise output and for 37% of its rural industrial output in 1987. Likewise, only four provinces and the municipality of Shanghai, with under 30% of the country's agricultural population, produced over 55% of its rural industrial output in that year. Figures on the extent of rural industrialization in China based on all-China averages are thus dangerously misleading.

Among coastal provinces, Hebei stands out as relatively poor and underdeveloped. Arguably, it is not only more representative of China as a whole than is any other coastal province, but it can even be said to be as good a microcosm of China as any province one might choose. Our examination of inter-county variation within Hebei found a high degree of variation in per capita output, income, and economic structure, resembling the differences among provinces.

Unfortunately from the standpoint of representativeness, Huailu County belongs near the top rank of Hebei counties by per capita income and other measures; and Dahe Township is typical of the county in these respects. Dahe's per capita income and its industrial share of output in the mid-1980s resembled the averages for coastal China more than for China as a whole. All the same, Dahe's economic development level remained modest in comparison with the upper 10–20% of townships in Jiangsu, Zhejiang, Liaoning, or Guangdong, so while it was far above average for China as a whole, it remained safely below the still less representative "front rank" of townships. Dahe was also not atypical of Chinese rural areas in having a grain-dominated economy, especially in the 1970s, and it was similar to a great many townships in coastal China in the degree of collective coordination of irrigation, planting, and plowing.

Although Dahe may not be representative of poorer and more remote townships in terms of its level of economic development and agricultural intensity, the universe of moderately advanced Chinese localities with good access to urban areas and transport networks, of which Dahe can be considered relatively typical, is by no means a trivial one; it comprises a larger farm population than that of all but the largest developing nations. Also, at least some behavioral regularities, such as the impacts of policy changes and the effects of institutional variables on economic outcomes, may be generalizable in qualitative terms even where differences in absolute magnitudes due to differing developmental starting points and opportunities are large.

That there may be advantages as well as limitations of examining a unit such as Dahe was illustrated in Chapter 3 by our discussion of its response to the initial stage of agricultural reforms in the area of grain production. The fact that grain yields stagnated at Dahe after 1979 was argued to be at one and the same time a measure of its unrepresentativeness, and a predictor of general Chinese trends later in the decade. Per hectare fertilizer use and per sown hectare grain output at Dahe in 1979 probably placed the township among counterparts in the top 10% of Chinese counties in 1980. The unresponsiveness of grain production to the change in farm organization at Dahe reflected the fact that adjustment toward more economically optimal behavior was in its atypical case a matter of reducing rather than increasing the intensity of cultivation. Comparison with other high-yield counties throughout China confirmed that Dahe was not alone, at least insofar as the upper 10% of counties showed much smaller increases in fertilizer use and slower gains in yields than did more average counties. And the leveling off of grain yields in early 1980s Dahe could be viewed as a harbinger of the national trend in the post-1984 period, when more Chinese townships had approached Dahe's earlier levels of agricultural input usage, and when the pattern of relative returns to grain production versus other rural activities more widely resembled that which already prevailed in more favored localities such as Dahe a few years earlier.

Whatever its representativeness, the detail of data available from Dahe permitted econometric investigations of economic behavior of collective era production teams and team members of a type not attempted elsewhere. In Chapter 4, we saw evidence of a gradual total factor productivity decline in agriculture and moderate productivity growth in the nonagricultural team production sector at Dahe in the collective period (1970–1979), and of more substantial productivity growth in the early post-collective period (1980–1985). We also noted, with Wiemer, that factor marginal products appeared to be much higher in the sideline than in the agricultural sector. We interpreted this, provisionally, as evidence of the existence of binding self-provision and state quota constraints in agriculture. Of special interest was the fact that these constraints appeared to persist into the post-collective period, although weakness of the team-level data for that period make corroboration at the household level (in Chapter 8) important.

In Chapters 5 and 6, analyses of effort supply to team production pointed to the conclusions that (a) a significant fraction of work days were contributed in a discretionary as opposed to coerced fashion, and (b) increased use of cash disbursements based on individual work contributions appeared to have some efficacy as an incentive to effort. While the first result confirmed the potential applicability of theories of collective farm effort supply that have presumed such individual discretion, the second was in accord with a central proposition in a subset of those theories. The analysis at the individual level (in Chapter 6) failed to discern any direct effect of differential material incentives (expected "wages"); however, its consistency with verbally reported rationing of slack season work was very much in accord with another major proposition of the theoretical literature—that is, the "tragedy of the commons" implication of an average net product reward system which is implicit in the analysis of Sen (1966). In addition to supporting both Sen's model of the effects of "needs"- versus "work"-based distribution and a "flat rations" analogue to that model, the team level analysis of Chapter 5 provided some support for an extension of Sen's model in which we took explicit account of retention of some earnings by the teams. Few of these findings were entirely robust to specification and few occurred at very high levels of statistical significance, yet there were also no statistically significant contradictions of these results. At the broadest level, it is safe to say that rational choice analysis of behavior in collective era China received some corroboration from the Dahe studies. More specifically, the evidence was consistent with theories that assume at least some observability of effort, effort-avoiding and income-seeking preferences, a nondominant role for intra-group altruism, and low levels of conjectural variations or strategic effort matching.

Chapter 7 dealt with efforts to establish the precise effects of the decollectivization of farming upon farm growth and productivity. We began by discussing studies using province-level and national data for China as a whole. These studies consistently found that the transition to household farming raised the productivity of farm inputs (usually by some 15–20%), and that growth in factor productivity accounted for over one-half of agricultural growth between 1978 and 1984. While the share of factor productivity growth attributed to the shift to household farming was found to be sensitive to the choice of period and of inclusion of a trend variable or time dummies, none of the results challenged the contention that decollectivization bore a greater responsibility for the period's growth than did price changes or changes in cropping patterns. We argued that it still remained unclear whether it was the change in incentive system per se or the freeing of farmers to pursue a wider set of opportunities that explains the output growth. Insofar as incentive effects were of the essence, we also pointed out in the appendix to Chapter 7 that the findings of McMillan, Whalley, and Zhu, while supportive of the notion that marginal incentives were stronger in the post-collective period, are quite inconsistent with the view that it was impossible to differentiate rewards under collective farming because individual effort was so nearly unobservable. Combining the theoretical models discussed in Chapter 5 with those authors' results and other data led us to conclude that express egalitarianism, as opposed to the de facto egalitarianism that could result from observability problems, remains a plausible explanation of low marginal incentives in the collective era.

In the second part of Chapter 7, we discussed Kim's attempts to estimate the productivity impact of the two-step transition from collective to household farming at Dahe Township. After controlling for endogeneity of the adoption decision, his estimates for the 1980–1982 period indicated that the intermediate reform system known as *lianchan jichou* increased overall factor productivity in the cropping sector by about 6% during the 1980–1982 period, for those teams that practiced it. When Dahe's three most important crops were looked at individually using the earlier period's data, a significant positive impact was found only for corn, in the production of which total factor productivity rose by as much as 15%. In interpreting this result, we found that it may constitute an illustration of the economics of monitoring, for among the three crops, only corn had both relatively stable yields and low costs of yield measurement. Ex post yield measurement was necessary to the operation of *lianchan jichou,* while yield stability was beneficial, since the system required accurate projections of the yields to be expected on given plots with standard levels of labor and input application.

The transition to the more radical system of household farming, *baogan daohu,* was found by Kim to have been associated with a roughly 5–8% increase in total factor productivity (as compared with collective farming) at Dahe, when changes in the crop mix are controlled for by entering the grain share of gross crop output value as an independent variable. Without this control, the estimated impact of *baogan daohu* rises sharply to a new range of TFP increase lying between 10% and 23%. In evaluating Kim's findings, we discussed three possible explanations of the fact that the estimated productivity gain from decollectivization at Dahe is more modest than national estimates. First, the difference could be due to the fact that other estimates have failed to control satisfactorily for crop mix changes. Second, the productivity gains from decollectivization of farming may have been more modest at Dahe than in China, on average, because the incentives for farm production remained weak in localities like Dahe in which there existed above-average opportunities in the noncrop sectors of the rural economy. Finally, productivity gains from decollectivization may have been smaller at Dahe because the collective system had been operated there with a higher degree of efficiency than in more average Chinese communes. The first explanation was found to be partially undermined by those national studies, undertaken after Kim's work with the Dahe data, that included a control for grain sown area; differences in the control variable and in functional forms meant that the explanation could not be ruled out entirely, however. The second explanation turned out to be logically suspect, since even where agricultural returns were low, farmers would have strong incentives to economize on farm inputs so as to conserve resources for more profitable undertakings. The argument might nonetheless be salvaged by appealing to the existence of administered resource allocation and barriers to factor mobility. No objection was raised with respect to the third explanation, but it remains conjectural insofar as we could provide no independent corroboration of it.

Some aspects of economic behavior in the post-collective period that were examined in Chapters 8 and 9 may be generalizable to much of rural China, although their specific manifestations at Dahe may be influenced by its above-average opportunity-set. The explorations of Chapter 8 strongly suggested that the liberalization of decision-making implicit in decollectivization has been subject to important constraints. Despite the imprecision entailed by our inability to disaggregate agricultural production into staple and nonstaple crops, we could conclude with some confidence that household utility-maximization is irreconcilable with the choices households were observed to make in 1985 without the introduction of some type of crop output constraint or a much higher than observed shadow price for crops. Our estimate was that crop prices on average would have had to be 49% higher than those reported for the local market, and almost 80% higher than the average state price, in 1985, to have elicited the observed production and contract sales on a voluntary basis. This estimate is almost certainly biased downward with respect to staple crops owing to our inability to disaggregate and exclude nonstaples, as well as to the unrealistic assumption that variable inputs were readily available at low prices. We saw some evidence that the constraint affecting crop production went beyond sales contracts to the state to include some self-provision of foodstuffs, and we conjectured that households made their production decisions in expectation of a higher market price than prevailed ex post, and that those decisions were influenced by risk-averse responses to uncertainty about both the price and the availability of grain. Alternatively, or in addition, households may have experienced pressure from local administrative organs to produce their staples requirements. The exercise in any case provided further confirmation that the constraint implicit in Wiemer's findings from the team level data of the collective period persisted into the post-collective era, as our extension of her work using the team level data had already suggested in Chapter 4. The degree to which this constraint operates and the extent of sacrificed potential income entailed by it is likely to vary from region to region in China, being stronger and larger in townships like Dahe than in more remote townships in Hebei or in China's central region, but stronger still in more highly industrialized and commercialized townships such as those of southern Jiangsu. How widely self-provision clashes with income maximization, and why self-provision occurs, is a major question to be explored in the remainder of the present chapter.

The simulations reported in Chapter 8 also contained some clues regarding the operation of the markets or allocation systems for financial resources and purchased current inputs. While the estimated marginal productivity of the latter in household crop production and sideline activities had suggested the existence of a roughly 50% per annum opportunity cost for financing input purchases, simulated input demand assuming such finance rates and perfectly elastic supply led to massive substitution of the inputs for capital and labor in the crop sector, and to a vast expansion of their use in sidelines, leading to a quadrupling of that sector's output. While interpretation requires recognition of the actual heterogeneity of these inputs both within and between sectors, the result strongly suggests that either (a) real finance charges at least for marginal input purchases far exceeded the 50% level imputed from our production function estimates, or (b) there existed rationing of purchased inputs, credit, or both, so that the supply curve(s) facing farm households were not in fact horizontal at the reported/imputed average prices, or that both (a) and (b) held. Consistent with this, further experimentation with the simulation model, by Park, suggested that finance rates sufficient to explain actual input usage by the sample households in 1985 would have to have been in the neighborhood of 125% per year, the same level at which a simulated local capital market for those households equilibrated. There is reason to think that input rationing, rationing of low-cost official credit, and the high cost of informal credit all contributed to the observed output, although our data do not permit us to ascertain the relative contributions of each factor.

The model of Chapter 8 and the analysis of Chapter 9 provided insights into the character of the land tenure system of the post-collective period. Chapter 8 demonstrated conclusively that the explicit cost of land to farm households contracting it from their teams or villages was a small fraction (about 9% in the presence of an output quota, and 11% in its absence) of its value to those households as a productive asset, even when the latter value was depressed by artificially lowered producer prices. Also, as would be expected under a system in which land had been assigned to households under formal rules not fully reflecting the use that each would make of it, marginal products of land were found to vary among households, and either output could be increased or binding crop targets could be attained with less cost in other resources by redistributing land among households so as to equalize its marginal product across farms. On the other hand, the extent of land transactions predicted by our simulations was not particularly large, and operation of a sub-rental market or use of a bidding system to achieve a more efficient allocation of land at Dahe might not have produced very substantial efficiency gains there at least in 1985, the 3rd year following the contracting out of its villages' land. This was partly due to the fact that Park's production function estimate, like the others in this study, found no scale economies operating in Dahe agriculture, so that the relatively equal land division achieved by administrative methods was not a major source of efficiency losses. In fact, simulated land transactions led to a more rather than less equal distribution of farm sizes among households.

While its introduction took up a number of issues relating to land distribution and land tenure in China's rural reforms, the main analysis of Chapter 9 was prompted by the concern of some Chinese commentators that land was allocated to households in too egalitarian a manner, and that at the very least this allocation should put more weight on households' workforces and less on their populations. Analysis of this issue began with the development of a theoretical framework which suggested that complete movement to a labor-force based distribution of land would not maximize output within the constrained set of alternatives consisting only of distribution by workforce, by population, and by mixes of the two. That the (constrained) optimal distribution rule would stop short of distribution on an entirely per-worker basis followed from the plausible assumption that household effort tends to vary positively with household size for any given size of labor force. The empirical analysis in the chapter at least partially supported the theory's prediction. Specifically, the hypothesized concave relationship between the degree to which administrative allocations were proportionate to household labor forces (as opposed to populations) and the total factor productivity of resources applied to crop production was borne out by a team level study that controlled for the endogeneity of the choice of allocation rule, for the contract obligation level, and for differences in soil quality, when output was proxied by grain production. No statistically significant correlation was found for output measured by gross crop output value, although the insignificant coefficients implied a positive relationship between productivity and distribution by labor force.

The distributional effects both of the collective system and of decollectivization were examined in Chapter 10. Consistent with the limited extent of private income-generating activities, with the fact that intra-team income differences were attributable primarily to differences in household demographic structures, and with the homogeneity of resource endowments among Dahe brigades and teams, intra- and inter-team inequality was found to be quite modest in the 1970s. Low inequality is also consistent with the large role played by age and gender differences in explaining work-point rating differentials, with the modest scope of those differentials, and with the importance of population-based in-kind distribution in teams' disbursements to households. The limited differentiation of work-points and their linkage with conspicuous personal characteristics are in turn consistent either with the hypothesis of nondifferentiability of collective payments due to monitoring problems, or with the idea that politico-ideological forces (some of which might have been internal ones) pushed teams toward egalitarianism. Evidence on the superior efficacy of even mildly differentiated cash distribution over egalitarian distribution of foodstuffs (Chapter 5) and indirect evidence on the efficacy of monitoring itself (Chapter 7, appendix) are consistent with the second hypothesis, although the exact degree to which egalitarianism was of policy versus informational origin remains impossible to ascertain.

Indications of other equalizing forces were also found in the collective-era data. First, procurement levels appear to have varied positively with per capita land endowments, helping to mitigate the effects of demographically driven inequality of endowments among Dahe's teams. Second, Griffin's finding that households with smaller collective earnings were permitted to compensate for this by engaging in more private production activities was corroborated by the Dahe household sample, in which intra-team inequality of combined collective plus private earnings was less than that from collective distribution alone. Third, there was evidence that inter-team and inter-brigade income differentials were suppressed until the end of the 1970s by virtue of the higher collective revenue retention levels of the more prosperous teams and brigades, causing inequality of distributed incomes to be significantly less than that of total net collective earnings.

With regard to the distributional effects of the transition to a household-based farm organization and a more diversified rural economy under the economic reforms of the 1980s, the Dahe data first of all provided clear confirmation of the expected increase in inequality, with Gini coefficients roughly doubling both for inter-household and for inter-team samples—although we have less confidence in the latter finding due to possible measurement problems. A complementary modeling approach found that the share of inter-household inequality in per capita income (measured by the coefficient of variation) not predicted by life-cycle differences rose from about 26% at the beginning of the reforms, in 1979, to roughly 48% in 1985. Consistent with this, it was found that the increase in inter-household inequality was not primarily due to increased income changes over a given life cycle. Although the estimated impact of the population to workers ratio rose at a somewhat more rapid rate than did average income, regression analysis suggested that the increment in

Inter-household inequality was primarily due to increasing occupational differentiation, with those households in which a larger proportion of the workforce remained in agriculture being the main losers in the race toward higher living standards.

Variation among teams and households in the rate of income growth between 1979 and 1985, years in which average real income per capita at Dahe rose by an estimated 93% (or 11.6% annually), was also examined. At the household level, the distribution of gains was skewed, with about 42% of households experiencing up to 100% increases in per capita incomes, another 27% exhibiting increases of between 100% and 200%, and smaller numbers having increases of up to 700%. Interestingly, as many as 14.5% of households seemed to have experienced declines in per capita income, which, while substantially explicable on the basis of life-cycle factors, nonetheless suggests that not all boats rose with the rising tide of the more differentiated economy even at as rapidly growing a township as Dahe.

Some Implications of Our Findings

Extrinsic and Intrinsic Problems of Collective Farming

Having concluded a review of our findings at the micro level, what broader conclusions might we reach about China's agriculture as a whole? Before turning to a discussion of the reform period, some remarks about China's agriculture during the collective era are pertinent. Many conclusions about that era remain somewhat conjectural, for they depend partly on counterfactual scenarios on which history as it has unfolded has shed little light. Nonetheless, the pattern of findings in the micro-studies just summarized points in a general direction that might be spelled out more systematically here.

Because much of the focus will be on failures, it is appropriate to begin by acknowledging some successes. In the 1960s and 1970s, China's agriculture did not perform badly, overall, compared to the agricultures of other densely populated Asian countries. Yields were increased sharply through intensification of input application. Extension of irrigation, increasing use of chemical fertilizer, and dissemination of improved seeds, the hallmarks of what has been known elsewhere as the "green revolution," were successfully promoted, in part on the basis of indigenous technical innovation. The commune system safeguarded a minimal welfare standard for most residents where more conventional regimes generated vast numbers of landless and destitute. The comparison of achieved life expectancies with those of similarly poor countries is especially telling. Even the figures on farm production in the narrowest sense are not consistent with the belief that group farm institutions guaranteed universal and totally unchecked loafing. In a significant minority of cases, achievements went beyond bare "survival with equity": substantial local capital formation occurred and rural industry made a healthy start.

That the system did not achieve more can be attributed, in the author's view, to four factors or sets of factors. The first consists of the complex of macro- and mesoeconomic policies (using the terminology of Chapter 1) that has been modified but not overthrown in the post-collective era, and that is therefore among the main examples of continuity across regimes. These policies fit under the twin headings of state extraction and anti-trade bias. State extraction refers to forced procurement and the turning of the terms of trade against agricultural producers. Anti-trade bias refers to the minimization of production for exchange, and the maximization of self-sufficiency, from the nation down to the province, county, and team.

The second factor is the egalitarian and anti-incentivist character imposed upon the collective units, including the narrow range of workpoint differentials, the favoring of time rates, and the large share of output distributed on a per capita basis. These factors put a ceiling on the performance of the micro-organizational units (the production teams) by constraining their internal policies, and they can be argued to have been of largely external origin and not intrinsic to the collective nature of farm operation. Of course, the distinction between external and internal factors may be beside the point, because the entire institutional structure of rural collectivism was imposed on the villages from the outside and, it might be argued, could never have sprung up on the initiative of the rural people themselves. Nonetheless, we do have historical examples of changes in the internal practices of cooperative and collective farms in China attendant upon the winds of political change (as recorded by Parish and Whyte, 1978; Shue, 1980; Chan et al., 1984; and Zweig, 1989; among others), so conjectures about how teams would have performed under circumstances permitting more self-determination may not be entirely pointless. While we cannot rule out the possibility that the very form of the collective institution (and, to draw on a point of Lin's, its inescapability from the standpoint of the peasant) led to egalitarianism, perhaps in part because of the nature of rural social relations, there is at least a chance that more "economistic" practices, of just the sort vilified by Maoist leaders, would have arisen and persisted in the event of greater internal control.

The third factor, already hinted at in the last paragraph, is the coercive aspect of the institutional regime. This aspect has heretofore been touched upon mostly tangentially, as in the discovery of minimum collective work requirements in Chapter 6. More broadly, the extractive character of China's overall development strategy with respect to agriculture meant that acquiescence to state policies depended on the monopolization of the sources of economic and political power by Communist Party cadres, and on the ubiquitous threat of scapegoating by class label for any who openly opposed those policies. The Stalinist framework within which the rhetoric of mass participation played itself out meant that the potential of collective entities to emerge as participatory and democratic organizations was compromised from the start.[2] When combined with the anti-incentivist aspect of the Party's approach to team

[2]While there is evidence of internal democracy at the team level, teams were so constrained in their choices that this could not translate into democratic control over parameters that mattered, or enthusiasm for the decisions that were to be carried out.

production, this meant that a successful cooperative dynamic of pulling together for maximal productive effort, and of mutual monitoring to thwart free-riding, faced less than ideal conditions of nurturance.

Saved for last are the intrinsic diseconomies of the group form of farm organization. Given the sufficiency of the first three reasons why collective agriculture came up short as a development vehicle in the Mao era, it is unclear how large a role these played. Certainly, whereas the commune system's great strength has been said to have been its embracing of a multi-tiered structure in which activities having different scale requirements could each be assigned to an appropriate tier,[3] there is a very real question as to whether such appropriateness of assignment of activities can be said to have held for many of the crop production tasks that were assigned to teams rather than to the family units which predominate in the agricultures of both developed and developing countries. Despite the doubts raised in this book regarding some common explanations of incentive failure, there is little question that a problem of incentives in team production does need to be addressed if effort is to be elicited from group members in a manner comparable to that put forth on the family farm. The issue that remains, once the external checks on performance have been accounted for as detailed above, is whether the best that can be achieved even in the absence of such checks is good enough. There is every reason to believe that under the best of circumstances, there will be at least some incentive slippage in group production, so the form is unlikely to be beneficial from the standpoint of many members unless there exist scale economies or a unique capacity to insure members against personal disaster which offset that slippage. China's transition to the household responsibility system provides support for the view that even where a substantial degree of mechanization and of large-scale irrigation works figured importantly in the crop production process, labor-intensive tasks such as weeding, transplanting, and manual application of fertilizers and pesticides could be carried out in small family subplots with little or no loss of productivity. Actual incentive slippage in most of the teams of the collective era can be assumed to have been far more than the minimum conceivable, owing to the influence of the first three factors discussed above. Thus, net benefits of carrying out the entire production cycle at team level would have existed only under unusual circumstances, such as the presence of charismatic leadership and strong group cohesion.

The Success and Failure of Agricultural Reform

Turning now to the post-collective era, what can be said about the reasons for the comparative success of China's agricultural reforms in their first half-decade, and the reasons why reform seemed incomplete and results more mixed in the remainder of the 1980s? Even without undertaking the micro-studies that occupy most of this book,

[3] See Waterston (1974).

widely available knowledge of China's rural economic situation would make it possible to identify causes of the growth spurt that resulted from China's rural reforms. Elsewhere in China, as at Dahe Township, a substantial portion of the increase in farmers' incomes during the first stage of the reforms resulted from the higher prices received for given volumes of crop sales. Another portion of the increase in incomes was due to increased crop output resulting both from the incentive effects of the more favorable prices offered by state and broadened market, and from the parallel effects of the transition to the micro-organizational arrangements of the reform era. The transfer of resources from lower to higher value activities—e.g., from grain production to production of more lucrative crops, and from crop production to industry and services—also played a large part in peasant income gains. What made this transfer possible was the loosening of administrative controls over resource allocation and the greater efficiency in farming that resulted from better micro-organization and from the freedom to pursue other activities in the time saved by more intensive work. There was also a multiplier effect built into the reforms in that the higher incomes occasioned by the initial stages of reform created rural purchasing power that spurred growth by creating demand for additional consumer goods and services.

It is worth remembering, of course, that other sources of rural growth in the reform era had little if anything to do with reform, and instead reflected continuities with China's policies of the 1960s and 1970s. In particular, state investment in fertilizer and farm machinery production capacity, the proliferation of tubewell irrigation technology, and the development and diffusion of high-yielding seed varieties, along with some of the more labor-intensive farm capital construction work of the Mao era (such as field terracing and improvement of irrigation and drainage systems), either continued to develop (e.g., greater production and use of fertilizer), or showed continuing payoffs (fructification of collective-era farm capital by reform-enhanced labor effort), in the post-Mao period. In these respects, the mobilization capacity of the Chinese state continued to stand out. However, only changes of the types listed above, and not the continuities and spill-over effects of previous policies, are capable of explaining the *improvement* in the growth rate of the Chinese rural economy.[4]

To list the sources of gains is also to begin to identify the constraints on the progress of China's reform era rural economy, and of its national economy more generally. To some extent, improved crop prices and greater freedom for diversified activities represented untapped opportunities for positive sum gains to both peasants and other actors in the economy, and thus indicated areas in which value extraction and the suppression of peasant initiative had previously been carried to economically irrational extremes. The scope for improvements in the terms of trade between the

---

[4]The exception are decisions taken in the 1970s to undertake critical investments which came on line after the reforms. See our discussion of the case of chemical fertilizer in Chapter 1.

peasants and the state was hardly unlimited, however. On the contrary, from the outset of the reforms, the state felt the budgetary burden of subsidizing urban food rations while paying higher prices to farmers, and as higher prices for uncontrolled rural products eroded the relative attractiveness of staples production, the freedoms of choice that had been extended to peasants began to pose a threat to assured supplies of the latter products. While the spread of China's green revolution to more rural areas played a major and potentially sustainable role in the achievement of agricultural output growth in the 1980s, the gains from micro-organizational change had a one-shot character. Indeed, some aspects of that change may actually have undermined China's ability to sustain improvements in farmland quality, so that part of the early 1980s increases in crop production might properly be viewed as a spending down of farm capital accumulated in the heyday of collectivism but difficult to replace or expand upon in the new epoch. With limited state and local government willingness to invest in more manufactured farm inputs, weakening incentives for farmers to make such investments and a neglected farm infrastructure seemed to spell trouble for Chinese agriculture. Despite much rhetoric to the contrary, and over the protests of some bolder reform advocates, the response of the Chinese state in the second half of the 1980s was in key respects one of renewed if comparatively subtle coercion, rather than of a further push to marketize the rural sector.

The largely failed attempt to enter into a second stage of reform through elimination of two-tiered pricing for cotton, in 1984, and for grain, in 1985, epitomizes the predicament of China's rural development policy in the second half of the first reform decade. As was noted in Chapter 1, elimination of above-quota purchases, while reducing the budgetary burden upon the state, also noticeably dampened peasants' incentives to produce grain in the absence of a developed and reliable market for their surpluses. Neither mandatory procurements from peasant households at sub-market prices, nor subsidized sales to urban households through the state grain shops, were eliminated, so that the unified purchase and supply system was terminated only in name. With the returns on nonstaple farming, noncrop agricultural activities (such as animal husbandry), and rural service and industrial activities rising rapidly relative to state purchase prices for staples, fulfillment of state contracts became ever more onerous for peasants and a larger and larger administrative problem for officials.

This is a good place to return to the somewhat complex question of why most peasants continued to produce grain not only for the state but also for their own consumption even as the relative profitability of other crops appeared to be rising rapidly in many parts of China. In view of the anxiety about grain production felt by high-level leaders and reflected in many published pronouncements, there is reason to suspect that household contractees of village collective lands not only were required to fulfill the terms of state contracts for grain and other staples, but also in many cases were under administrative pressure to plant grain to meet their own consumption needs. While formal planning of the area to be planted to grain ceased to be practiced for China as a whole as of the early 1980s, planning by other names was widespread because officials from the province level down were under pressure from their superiors to contribute to the solution of China's "grain problem." In the more economically advanced rural areas, where the incentives to switch to other crops were strongest, implementation of these plans was facilitated by the practice of village-level cultivation and planting of grain and other staple crops (such as was observed in Dahe's villages in the mid-1980s). Thus, a Ministry of Agriculture report cited by Sicular (1991, Table 2) found that 76% of villages practiced unified plowing, and 80% had village planning of crop rotation and layout, in China's eastern third in 1987, while village level crop planning occurred in over 50% of villages in central and western China as well.[5]

However, it was probably unnecessary to coerce rural households into providing for their own subsistence needs in most townships. The reason is that government policy and the reenforcing effects of China's overstrained and underdeveloped transportation system saw to it that using land for more profitable crops and purchasing grain in the free market was not a reliable alternative for most households. Not only did free market prices fluctuate and rise to high levels in some years following 1985, but perhaps more importantly, the market could cease to exist altogether whenever the state chose to close it down to assure that its purchasing targets were met before "surpluses" went to the market.[6] In such circumstances, few households could afford to gamble with further specialization unless supported by official arrangements that guaranteed the availability of staples in exchange for their nonstaple produce.

In terms of causality, it appears that the underdevelopment of China's free grain markets was in large part a result of the continued involvement of the state in the purchase of grain at submarket prices and its distribution at subsidized prices in the cities. So long as these transactions were to take place at prices that made them economically unattractive to farmers, the state was forced to keep a tight reign on the competing movement of grain through private channels. As has been mentioned, the difficulty of meeting state purchasing targets also led to the erection of barriers against inter-regional movements of grain, and unwillingness to allow private grain traders to operate at large scales further reduced the scope of the market. The resulting underdevelopment of free grain markets can be expected to have had a significant dampening effect upon agricultural specialization, probably causing substantial losses to overall farm output.

[5]The three-region division is presumably the same as mentioned in Chapter 2, footnote 10. Based on data collected in forty villages in Central Jiangsu covering the period 1983–1988, Rozelle (1991) presents evidence that maintaining grain output levels was a central criterion on which village leaders were judged by their superiors. Rozelle's micro studies and conclusions, completed as this book was in preparation, appear to be strongly consistent with the arguments of this section.
[6]See again the survey result reported by Sicular (1991) (cited in footnote 85 of Chapter 1).

Can Reform be Completed? Replacing Hidden with Open Taxation

Why did China's leaders continue to block the possibility of further gains from agricultural specialization and trade in the late 1980s? We have earlier argued that the basic reason for the underpricing of staples purchased on contract (but in essence still administratively procured) from China's farmers was the state's determination to tax agriculture in order to support industrialization and the living standard of the urban population. Protection of urban workers was a constant source of political anxiety for the government because the initial gains of reform were enjoyed most by peasants, and to a disproportionate extent by precisely those peasants with whom urban dwellers were likely to come in contact, the residents of the rural areas nearest the cities. More broadly, the reforms tended to benefit those with access to private business opportunities or the ability to resell scarce resources diverted from state channels. For this reason, the possibility that inflation would overwhelm the more modest gains of ordinary state employees caused more resentment on their parts, and more concern on the part of the government, than might otherwise have been the case. We have also seen how strains had been placed on the state budget by the very price increases that fueled rural growth in the early part of the reform period, since those higher prices had not been passed on to urban consumers. These budgetary strains were exacerbated by the steep decline in revenues which resulted from the reduced appropriation of enterprise profits by the central government, a result not only of the fact that enterprises were permitted to retain much of their profits, but also of the fact that enterprise profits were simply dropping, perhaps because the economy was shifting to a more competitive mode.[7] Neither the state itself, nor, in its judgment of the political situation, the urban workforce could afford to absorb further farm prices increases.

But assuming that letting the urban population absorb the shock of transition to more equal terms of exchange between city and countryside was politically infeasible, and that state preferences or national imperatives ruled out a substantial slowing down of the industrialization program, might there not still exist some way to reduce the costs imposed on the development of the rural sector? A number of analysts have answered in the affirmative. Their suggestion[8] is to replace the taxation implicit in below-market staples purchases by the state with a tax based on the scarcity value of land, which would be lump-sum in nature for a farm of given size. Urban workers and state enterprises would purchase staple produce from the farm sector at market prices, but the state could compensate for higher costs of living and higher production costs

---

[7]Naughton (1992).

[8]Lardy (1983, pp. 218–9,) cites a recommendation to this effect by the late eminent Chinese economist Sun Yefang. A similar proposal had strong support in Zhao Ziyang's "rural think-tank," the Research Center for Rural Development (R.C.R.D.; see Song, 1987). The varying views of Chinese writers are discussed by Christiansen (1988). The proposal is also made by Wiens (1987). A discussion of experiments along the proposed lines as well as of methods of reducing subsidized grain supply to the urban population is found in Kung (1992).

of affected enterprises by a suitably chosen redistribution of land tax proceeds. Calculated correctly, the change from a hidden tax through pricing of administered purchases to an explicit tax on land might have no net static effect on either rural or urban incomes. However, by eliminating the single most important impediment to the complete decentralization of rural economic mangement, thus allowing farm households to allocate labor and other resources in a free and rational manner in response to market opportunities, the change could lead to major gains in allocative efficiency. Moreover, with the elimination of the motive for government interventions in agricultural markets, regional and national agricultural product markets could develop, permitting expanded local specialization to take place in a nonadministered manner. Finally, scarcity-linked taxation of land use could facilitate a more efficient distribution of land among rural households, by encouraging those who would farm less intensively in the absence of such a tax to cede their land to other households whose members find it advantageous to give more emphasis to farming. The gain in efficiency of resource allocation across both agricultural and nonagricultural activities throughout the rural economy could provide a major spur to its development, one that would perhaps be of roughly the same order of magnitude as the gains from the first stage of China's rural reforms.

The logic of this proposal, and its feasibility, are strongly supported by the analysis in Chapter 8, which found evidence that households at Dahe Township in 1985 engaged in crop production under a binding output constraint, that the prices received by them (including state payments for grain and cotton) were substantially below those that would have elicited the same production and sales on a voluntary basis, and that farm households nonetheless enjoyed scarcity rents from land utilization only a small fraction of which was taken from them in the form of agricultural tax and collective obligations. Our computations showed that the amount of tax implicit in crop sales to the state, as measured by the gap between the estimated price sustaining voluntary production at observed crop output levels and the price actually received, averaged about Y 1,077 per hectare of land cultivated[9] in 1985. A rough indication of the market-clearing (sub-)rent level under the output price of the voluntary solution is given by the average value of the marginal product of land in the simulated price-based solution (Table 8.6), which is Y 3,548 per hectare.[10] This is Y 3,353 more than the existing level of combined agricultural tax and collective obligations, Y 195 per hectare. Thus, the amount that could have been collected by way of a market-clearing tax on land use would have exceeded the amount implicitly

[9]Recall that the price at which observed crop output was elicited voluntarily in the simulation was 79.5% above the average observed state price. Park reports that the total volume of sales to the state by the sample households in 1975 was Y 120,997. The added sales value with a 79.5% mark-up would have been Y 96,193. From Table 8.1, we see that a total of 89.3 ha were cultivated by the 221 sample households. This yields the figure Y 1,077 = Y 96,193/89.3 as the average hidden tax per cultivated hectare.

[10]The VMP of land might differ somewhat were a sub-rental market to operate in conjunction with the hypothetical uncontrolled product market. Since no simulation of this situation was performed, we use the estimate from Table 8.6 as an approximation.

obtained through administered pricing and obligatory sales contracts (Y 3,353 > Y 1,077).[11] Although the degree of land reallocation among households following operation of a land market (or, equivalently, imposition of a land tax with the right of transfer to other households) was small in our simulation, more significant gains through better resource allocation when output is elicited by market prices were hinted at by the simulation shown in Table 8.6, and additional gains could accrue through greater intra-sectoral efficiency in agriculture, a possibility that cannot be captured by the simulation model because of its lumping of heterogeneous products into a uniform output category.

The political feasibility of such an approach is evidently another matter. Perhaps the Communist Party's claim to legitimacy with the rural population (if any such claim still existed) rested heavily on the fact that it had eliminated the landlord class and replaced the payment of rents that once averaged in the neighborhood of 50% of output value with relatively modest agricultural taxes. Party leaders might accordingly fear that the imposition of substantially higher taxes on land would pose an unacceptable threat to the rural population's tolerance of their rule. This factor should not have posed a problem if it could have been demonstrated that the elimination of obligatory sales and submarket purchasing prices would at least compensate for the increase in agricultural tax. However, the profound character of the policy change and the difficulty of predicting its exact consequences or, more specifically, the levels of tax and other quantitative parameters required for its successful implementation, undoubtedly caused considerable fear and trembling in any policy-makers who gave the idea serious thought.[12] In addition, early local experiments with variants of the proposal appeared to have been incomplete and of a piecemeal nature, and to have led

[11]Corroborating evidence at the national level is found in the previously cited report by the Development Institute (1987). The authors estimate that the total value of collectively owned land contracted to households in the mid-1980s was about 2 trillion *yuan*. Using the 1988 cultivated area of 95.7 million ha for a rough calculation (which will undervalue the contracted land by failing to subtract the area of private plots), this implies a value of Y 20,894 per hectare. Discounting future payments at 10% a year, that translates into an annual rental value of Y 1,899 per hectare, slightly over half the figure estimated from the Dahe data. (The difference may be partly attributable to the above-average productivity of Dahe's farmland, as well as to unknown differences in the Institute's methodology.) The average amount paid by contracting households to their collective units in China in 1985 was Y 10.79, according to the report. According to a World Bank background paper (1990b), the loss to farmers due to compulsory grain sales at submarket prices averaged Y 17.43 billion during 1985–1988. This works out to Y 182 per hectare, using the same cultivated area figure as above. The rank order of these estimates (rental value > implicit procurement tax > explicit payment to the collective) matches those from the Dahe data.

[12]An indication of timidity on the issue is that even some R.C.R.D. proponents of a transition from price-based (hidden) taxation to rent-based (open) taxation have suggested that the tax apply only to land used for commercial purposes and for the fulfillment of state contracts, and that private plots and "food ration land" continue to be allocated according to household population, without charge (see Wiemer, 1990b). The magnitudes estimated for Dahe Township in Chapter 8, and reviewed in the previous paragraph, also raise the possibility that if the land tax and output prices are both permitted to rise to market-clearing levels, the tax revenue could substantially exceed the level of the "hidden tax" implicit in the state purchasing system, whereupon the effect on farmers' incomes would *not* be neutral. The R.C.R.D. proposal would be one way of addressing this problem, if real. However, that proposal is also discouragingly suggestive of the entrenchment of the idea that peasants must continue to produce their own food requirements, and it might therefore be suggestive of limits on the extent to which the "rent for tax" reform would open the way to an invigoration of markets and to further agricultural specialization, as envisaged in our discussion.

to inconclusive and in some cases discouraging results.[13] Perhaps, the most important factor, finally, was simply conservative leaders' gut preference for administrative controls over the workings of market forces, especially when it came to a matter that had been so central to the concerns of the Communist state since its inception.

Other questions about the proposal can be raised from a more narrowly economic standpoint. First, the crux of the proposal, as has been stated, is to move from a system in which agricultural taxation is hidden in the pricing of involuntary crop sales, to one in which taxation is explicit and directly tied to land use. A possible objection, however, is that the change would be a superficial one, for the current method of distributing land use rights and state sales contracts causes the tax already to be tied to the amount of land farmed, in practice. Yet even if there is some merit in this claim, it would be incorrect to conclude from it that the change to collecting land rents and freeing product markets would not have fundamental allocative consequences. The reason is that the tax is currently assessed on deliveries of staple crops only. By discouraging the application of fertilizer and labor to production of those crops, and by thus making it necessary for village officials to set aside a larger fraction of their cultivable land to achieve any given production goal for grain, the tax distorts the whole pattern of resource allocation among crops. Replacing it with a noncrop-specific tax should eliminate this effect and permit gains from improved allocation of all resources among crops as well as to noncrop production activities. Moreover, the gains from improved allocative efficiency for a given crop mix at the local level are likely to be surpassed by another set of gains, those resulting from the increased specialization among localities that would occur in the wake of a freeing of crop markets. As has been argued above, a full-scale market liberalization has heretofore been blocked by the conflict between the state procurement system and private trade.

Some caution is required in assessing a third allocative benefit, the improved allocation of resources between crop production and other rural activities that can be expected to result from a shift to a more fully marketized rural economy. Although there is reason to believe that the hidden tax on staple crops has depressed crop production as a whole relative to other rural sectors, the replacement of the hidden tax by a land rent would not be a stimulus to agriculture, pure and simple, if combined with complete freedom of farmers in determining the amount of land they wished to farm each year. The reason is that if viewed as a variable cost, a land tax would raise the marginal cost of agricultural production relative to other activities. The benefit of making this cost explicit, as we have noted, would be that farmers would be induced to assess the effort they intended to put into farming before leasing in land, leading to better overall land utilization. The simulation reported in Table 8.7 of Chapter 8 demonstrated, however, that an increase in the marginal cost of crop production without a corresponding increase in marginal revenue (i.e., output price) could have the effect of leading some resources to be shifted from crop production to noncrop

---

[13]This, at least, is the impression given by discussion with R.C.R.D. researchers in 1989 and 1990. Kung's discussion of the most recent experience (1992) is more upbeat in this regard.

sectors. This effect should be offset by the increase in output prices that would indeed follow upon the end of the procurement system and the opening up of agricultural trade, but it is one more reason to keep a close eye on the relative magnitudes of the rent and price shifts.

A final objection raised by some Chinese analysts is that if agricultural prices were determined entirely by the market, China might become reliant upon imports of agricultural products to a degree that would undermine its national security. Although the author would venture the view that China can afford to import somewhat more of its food requirements provided that its internal agricultural policies are sound, this question need not be addressed further here, for the freeing of domestic markets and policies on international trade are in principal separable issues. Even if restraints on import dependence are desired for political reasons, that is, full marketization of the rural economy could still be implemented, since domestic grain prices could be raised to levels adequate to assure self-sufficiency simply by imposing duties or quantitative restrictions on the importation of grain products. No domestic price or market would need to be controlled, in this case.

Some Final Remarks on the Land Question

Having discussed the land tax proposal, some concluding remarks about the more general issues of land tenure are now in order. As mentioned in Chapter 9, some Chinese economists have expressed the view that fully efficient land use, including adequate investments in land improvements and maintenance, are inconsistent with China's current agricultural institutions due to the absence of private ownership rights in land. The thrust of the argument of this book has been that the main problems of Chinese agriculture in the post-collective period were those associated with bad allocation decisions due to distorted prices and administrative interventions, rather than maladapted property rights. To be sure, taking a broader view of property rights, one could say that the contingent nature of the Chinese farmer's access to land is all of one piece with the extent of administrative intervention in farming—that is, that the interventions of local and higher level officials in the affairs of the farmers are symptomatic of the absence of a regime of economic freedom and a corresponding restriction of the scope of state action. Here, however, we use the term property rights more narrowly, in connection with the comparison of a system in which land can only be rented by the farmer with one in which the farmer can hold private title to it. We proceed, though, on the general understanding that the broader form of economic freedom is to be presumed insofar as is practicable, in keeping with the overall spirit of China's economic reforms.

It was recognized in Chapter 9 that a system of public or local government land ownership, with allocation of individual use rights through a rental or bidding procedure, might suffer from deficiencies with respect to investment in land, unless the means exist by which to compensate users for improvements and penalize them for deterioration in the parcels rented by them. In the author's view, this question remains an open one, although it points to an area in which the response of China's policy-makers has shown clear deficiencies, thus far. The need for or usefulness of private titles as a support for the development of the rural credit market, in which it would serve the function of collateral, is also debatable, with both issues deserving additional research. Even if it can be shown that there are some unavoidable costs in these areas, the possibility that continued public or collective control of land would nonetheless be a useful tool for safeguarding equity in access to land, thus serving as a form of rural social insurance, might stand as an offsetting consideration. This point may be an important one so long as many rural Chinese remain extremely poor and the ratio of land to population dictates high competitive returns to agricultural land and low returns to labor.[14] Regardless of how one feels about these propositions, one central implication of the arguments just summarized should be emphasized: namely, that any move to privatize land *without* also addressing the pricing problems on which our discussion has focused would be likely to accomplish little good, and might well bring significant harm.

First, consider the question of agricultural investment. If land were given to farmers as private property without addressing the problems of the current farm price structure and the associated constraints on cropping choice, the tendency to underinvest in land improvements would remain. There would also, of course, be no real impact on production incentives. Second, there is the question of what price, if any, farmers are to be charged for the land that they obtain. If each farmer were to receive the land which he or she presently uses, and if this transfer were to be made at zero price and without any additional assessment of tax, the rents of land will have been transferred to the farmers in perpetuity. This would rule out the substitution of assessments based on the scarcity value of land for the present tax implicit in state purchases (i.e., the proposal discussed in the last subsection), possibly stalling price rectification indefinitely. Finally, suppose that the transfer to private hands were to take place at positive prices, which could be established through a competitive bidding process. So long as the farm price structure had not first been reformed, land prices would tend to be depressed below true social scarcity values, and the collective owner (be it the state or the local community) would have foregone a substantial source of income and assured that any future price reform will also amount to a granting of rents to the landowners.

Rural Reform, Structural Change, and China's Economy[15]

The proposal to replace the hidden tax implicit in China's current staple crop purchasing system with an explicit land use tax seems in principle capable of addressing many of the inefficiencies that remained pervasive in the rural economy

---

[14]The pattern of factor elasticities repeatedly discovered by our studies appears to be pertinent here.
[15]Much of this section parallels the discussion in Putterman (1992b). For other views on these themes, see the articles in the symposium on "Institutional Segmentation, Structural Change, and Economic Reform in China," *Modern China*, January and April 1992.

after the decollectivization of agriculture in the first part of the 1980s. Land would be allocated to those who would use it most productively; users would allocate land among crops according to market signals reflecting consumer willingness to pay the full production cost of each product; administrative intervention in cropping plans would be unnecessary; the state crop purchasing apparatus could be abolished, and the state could concentrate on improving the transport infrastructure which is the main public contribution required by the agricultural marketing sector; with output markets further freed, the subsistence character of Chinese farming could be reduced in favor of specialization; and with farming no longer subject to discriminatory pricing, resources could flow freely among rural uses, without the need for special subsidies, input award programs, or administrative pressures to assure that basic needs for staple crops are met. But what of the overall economic structure and policy environment in which this or any rural reform program having similar objectives would have to be carried out? Several basic questions arise here, and will be addressed in this final section. First, is continued taxation of agriculture by the urban sector desirable and/or necessary? Second, what is the relationship between further reform in the rural sector, and the reform of China's economy as a whole? Is the completion of agricultural reform possible without a more general price reform and a reform of the state industrial sector? And how can agricultural reform contribute to the rapid development of the Chinese economy as a whole?

With regard to the first question, this book has not attempted a comprehensive analysis of the terms of exchange between agriculture and the urban sector in contemporary China. To carry out such an analysis, we would have to account for the combination of explicit agricultural tax, the hidden state purchase tax, and profits from sales of industrial products to the rural sector, on the one hand, and for direct state investment in agriculture plus any subsidy element in sales of selected farm inputs to the countryside, on the other.[16] Such an accounting is fraught with problems, and turns, in the final analysis, on the reference prices used to measure the subsidy and tax elements of each flow (see Stone, 1988). Without attempting an accounting of this *net* (two-way) flow, however, it is clear enough that there does exist a flow of income *out* of agriculture in the form of taxes, monopoly profits on inputs sold to farmers, profits of state enterprises that are able to pay a given real wage and purchase agricultural raw materials at lower money cost owing to low staples prices, and living standards of the state workers themselves.[17] The question to be

---

[16]This list may not be exhaustive. For example, Scott Rozelle suggests that the state contributed to agriculture by paying the salaries of some rural cadres, who provided useful organizational capabilities (personal communication).

[17]For example, the World Bank (1991, p. 146) estimates that total consumer food subsidies ranged from Y 24.7 to Y 26.4 billion annually during 1985–1988. The implicit tax paid by producers is estimated at an additional Y 19 billion in 1986 (World Bank, 1991, p. 32) or Y 11 billion for rice, wheat, and corn alone (World Bank, 1990b, p. 17). Thus, consumer subsidies, paid by the state and farmers, totaled over Y 40 billion. While no accounting of subsidies to farmers is offered, the Bank states that "the economic value of the input subsidies is likely to be small . . . when compared with the hidden consumer subsidy and the indirect producer tax" so that "omission of this item would not alter orders of magnitude" (1991, p. 33, footnote 39).

addressed is whether the continuation of the flows in this direction at magnitudes comparable to those of the recent past are either desirable or necessary.

The *desirability* of these transfers is in the author's opinion a more difficult question to address than is that of their *necessity*. For the issue of how large a share of the burden of financing industrialization should be borne by agriculture and the rural population not only opens up questions of distributive equity which would transport us into a complex evaluative domain, but also demands an assessment of the tricky question of the optimal balance between agriculture and industry in the overall process of economic development. At a normative level, one may counterpose the universalistic principle of equality against the argument that the long history of the evolution of living standards in China's rural and urban areas would make a sudden equalization of living standards between them a "cruel and unusual punishment" to the urbanites. On a programatic level, one may note that while depressed agricultural growth due to extractive state-agriculture relations has been persuasively argued to be the weakest link in many development strategies, no country has heretofore achieved successful industrial development without some active policy bias in favor of industry, including a strategy to promote capital formation. The transfer of savings from agriculture to industry has been a normal part of such a strategy.

Whether desirable or not, however, continuation of unequal relations may well be unavoidable in view of the politico-economic realities of present-day China. One such reality is that the real incomes of most of China's permanent urban population have long depended upon the availability of foodstuffs and of goods such as cloth at prices made feasible only by the suppression of market forces in the movement of staples out of the rural sector. While per capita grain consumption rose by a modest 2.7% between 1952 and 1957, and while it stood slightly below the 1952 level in 1978, per capita consumption of cloth rose by 19.4% between 1952 and 1957, and by a further 17.7% to 1978, with a disproportionate share of the gains going to urban residents. At the same time, what would have been the supply curve of agricultural products under a free market regime suffered a downward shift with land reform and collectivization, because the more equal distribution of income in the rural sector translated into a greater aggregate demand for food consumption within that sector, so that even constant levels of supply of agricultural products could be maintained in the context of uncontrolled agricultural markets only with higher prices. The controlled price and mandatory procurement system which permitted the state to secure urban food supplies and living standards without increases in wage levels has continued in one form or another through four decades.

The other beneficiary of the transfer from agriculture is the state's industrialization program. The low wages made possible by low procurement prices have translated directly into higher state enterprise profits, as also have the low procurement prices of some farm products used directly as raw materials—e.g., fibers. State enterprise profits have traditionally been the main source of state revenue, and they continue to be the primary source of investment funds, whether in the form of profits retained by enterprises, or in that of funds collected by the state and disbursed to other projects.

It is one thing to argue that forcing rural areas to support urban living standards and industrial investment is not *justified,* another to suggest that these processes can be terminated in the near future. It is unclear why urban workers deserve to enjoy a nearly three-fold advantage over average rural residents with respect to standards of living. The underwriting of the state investment budget is questionable on efficiency grounds, since investment in state enterprises probably generates lower social returns than would investment in organizations more sensitive to the discipline of market forces. However, it is unlikely that a sharp reduction in urban living standards could be implemented without an extraordinarily high degree of political repression. Such a policy would appear to spell political suicide for China's Communist Party, which has managed to maintain power for over 40 years in part because of its fulfillment of certain guarantees in the area of income and services. And if Party rule were ended by a popular uprising involving significant urban participation, the resulting government would also be unlikely to permit sharp reductions in urban living standards. Abandonment of the state investment program is difficult to imagine while the Communist Party remains in power. These factors lead us to predict that taxation of agriculture to support urban workers will continue in China for an unknown period of time, while a tax to support industrial investment will survive at least as long as does the rule of the Chinese Communist Party.[18]

Letting the Rural Sector Lead the Way

Rural marketization and the greater economic efficiency that can be hoped to follow it can be achieved with or without an end to urban and state privileges if the inefficient method of transfer embodied in quantitative purchase plans and submarket purchase prices is replaced by a more efficient method of taxation, such as a land tax. As rural resource allocation becomes more efficient, the dynamism which in the late 1980s was most characteristic of rural nonfarm activities would diffuse throughout the rural sector, which could accordingly continue to experience high rates of economic

---

[18]After this conclusion was drafted, the Chinese government announced major increases in urban food prices, which were to be combined with measures to reduce the volume of subsidized supplies by reducing the monthly ration sales to individual residents and gradually eliminating low-price provision to breweries and other large consumers of grain (see U.S.D.A., 1991, and Kung, 1992). Producer prices were also further increased, the 1984 grain harvest was finally surpassed in a convincing manner, and grain trade was set to be invigorated by the expansion of regional wholesale markets (World Bank, 1991). While some observers have suggested that food subsidies had become insignificant relative to the incomes of urban Chinese, and could well be dispensed with (see the discussion by Kung and the analysis in World Bank, 1991), the 1991 consumer side price increases were once again accompanied by new subsidies to workers' pay. And higher producer prices were accompanied by a return to use of the term "quota sales," the most explicit acknowledgement to date of the failure of the mid-1990s effort to commercialize staple crop marketing. Note, too, that even if food subsidies and low price procurements could be eliminated without a replacement flow of new taxes on farmers, unequal relations between the urban and rural sectors would continue to exist so long as there exist restrictions on permanent migration, a state monopoly on credit which is made available to state projects at rates far below those that would prevail otherwise, and obstacles to wage-based competition by rural workers for state and urban collective industrial jobs.

growth. State industry, on the other hand, seems likely to remain comparatively inefficient. The mixed success of efforts to bring about its reform by gradual means will lead to increased calls to dismantle the entire state industrial structure as soon as possible, emulating the "shock therapy" approach advocated by Poland as the 1990s began. The burden of the above analysis is that this may be less feasible (and perhaps, too, less desirable) in China than in Eastern Europe, owing to the lower living standards at which the country begins the reform process, and what one might accordingly surmise would be the lower capacity to absorb the hard blow of institutional and structural change. The challenge for China may instead be that of finding the least inefficient way to preserve the standards of living of incumbent state employees, while adopting policies that permit the nonstate sectors—agriculture, rural industry and services, and private urban enterprise—to grow as rapidly as possible. When the marginal productivity of labor in the nonstate sector reaches equivalence with the full social wage of state workers, no special protection of those workers' living standards will be required, and the market can become the primary method of resource allocation throughout the economy.

Here, it is desirable to emphasize the powerful forces already working for rapid development, especially in rural industry. After unnecessarily hobbling its rural handicrafts sector and making a false start on rural industrialization in the Great Leap Forward, China's rural institutions ultimately proved a conducive framework for the growth of small-scale industries and workshops, and rural nonfarm activity was the most rapidly growing sector of the Chinese economy between 1978 and 1988. There was also a dynamic synergy between rural industry and another sector that played a leading role in both the reform process and China's 1980s economic growth: exports. Rural industry, with its relative flexibility, proved an ideal source for small-scale production of clothing, toys, and similar products under marketing and/or investment arrangements with foreign firms, including those operating in southeast China out of Hong Kong and Taiwan. Rural enterprises in the central coast were equally successful in finding their own export markets. The sector's share of China's exports grew rapidly from 4.5% in 1984 to 19.3% in 1989.[19] Rural industrial growth was temporarily slowed by the government's late 1980s contractionary policy, which discriminated against the sector, but it proved difficult to suppress. Apparently recognizing that the relative success of China's post-Mao reform program is in no small part due to the flexibility and entrepreneurship exhibited by the rural nonfarm sector, the post-"Beijing Spring" leadership has ultimately taken pains to embrace rural industry and to reject the notion that support for the sector should be especially associated with ousted reformist leaders.

By taking measures to eliminate the artificial biases against staple crop production, the forces of growth in China's rural areas can be further released,

[19]Based on Foreign Broadcast Information Service reports as related by David Zweig in a talk on "Internationalizing Rural China," Fairbank Center for East Asian Research Seminar, Harvard University, November 9, 1990.

accelerating the progress of the national economy and hastening the point at which special protection of urban industrial workers can be dispensed with. Perhaps the main reason for tempering this optimistic assessment—aside from the possibility that policy-makers will prove too conservative to grasp their opportunity—is that as Chapter 2 emphasized, rural industrial growth has been geographically concentrated, so that the "taking off" of the economy that has already begun and that would be sustained in the scenario just sketched, could leave much of China's hinterland behind. After 30 years of trying to redress this imbalance by administrative methods, the Chinese government has come to accept such inequalities in growth rates as a fact of life. It does indeed seem the better part of wisdom to let the forces of diffusion from the other high-growth centers of East Asia work their way through China's proximate coastal regions in a more or less natural fashion, for the rapid climb to middle-income status by provinces containing one-third to one-half of China's population probably augurs better for China as a whole than would measures that could slow down that process. The challenge for China is to foster the growth which can carry it from mere survival to at least modest prosperity, while negotiating the trade-offs between the well-being of future versus present, and of well-positioned versus disadvantaged citizens, in a manner that is both rational and humane.

References

Aigner, D., K. Lovell, and P. Schmidt, 1977, "Formulation and estimation of stochastic frontier production function models," *Journal of Econometrics,* 6: 21–38.

Akerlof, George, 1982, "Labor contracts as partial gift exchange," *Quarterly Journal of Economics,* 97: 543–69.

Alchian, Armen and Harold Demsetz, 1972, "Production, information costs, and economic organization," *American Economic Review,* 62: 777–95.

Ansell, Alison, Roger Hay, and Keith Griffin, 1982, "Private production and income distribution in a Chinese commune," Reprint Series 122E, Institute of Commonwealth Studies, Oxford University. (Reprinted from *Food Policy,* February 1982, pp. 3–12.)

Ash, Robert F., 1988, "The evolution of agricultural policy," *China Quarterly,* 126: 529–555.

Ashton, Basil, Kenneth Hill, Alan Piazza, and Robin Zeitz, 1984, "Famine in China, 1958–61," *Population and Development Review,* 10: 613–46.

Bardhan, Pranab K., ed., 1989, *The Economic Theory of Agrarian Institutions.* Oxford: Clarendon Press.

Barkai, Haim, 1977, *Growth Patterns of the Kibbutz Economy* (Contributions to Economic Analysis 108). New York: North-Holland.

Barkai, Haim, 1987, "Kibbutz efficiency and the incentive conundrum," in S. Hedlund, ed.: *Incentives and Economic Systems.* London: Croom Helm, pp. 228–63.

Bernstein, Thomas P., 1984, "Stalinism, Chinese peasants and famine: grain procurements during the great leap forward," *Theory and Society,* 13 (3): 339–78.

Binswanger, Hans and Mark Rosenzweig, 1986, "Behavioral and material determinants of production relations in agriculture," *Journal of Development Studies,* 22: 503–39.

Blecher, Marc, 1976, "Income distribution in small rural Chinese communities," *China Quarterly,* 68: 797–816.

Blinder, Alan S., ed., 1990, *Paying for Productivity: A Look at the Evidence.* Washington, DC: The Brookings Institution.

Bliss, Christopher J. and Nicholas H. Stern, 1982, *Palanpur: The Economy of an Indian Village.* New York: Oxford University Press.

Bonin, John P., 1977, "Work incentives and uncertainty on a collective farm," *Journal of Comparative Economics,* 1: 77–97.

Bonin, John P., and Louis Putterman, 1987a, "Incentives and monitoring in cooperatives under labor-proportionate sharing schemes," Working Paper No. 87-18, Department of Economics, Brown University.

Bonin, John P., and Louis Putterman, 1987b, *Economics of Cooperation and the Labor-Managed Economy.* (Fundamentals of Pure and Applied Economics, No. 14.) London: Harwood Academic Publishers.

Bowles, Samuel, 1985, "The production process in a competitive economy: Walrasian, Neo-Hobbesian, and Marxian models," *American Economic Review,* 75: 16–36.

Bradley, Michael E., 1971, "Incentives and labor supply on Soviet collective farms," *Canadian Journal of Economics*, 4: 342–52.

Bradley, Michael and M. Gardner Clark, 1972, "Supervision and efficiency in socialized agriculture," *Soviet Studies*, 23: 465–73.

Brandt, Loren and Barbara Sands, 1988, "Land concentration and income distribution," Paper prepared for an ACLS/SSRC Conference on Economic Methods for Historical Research.

Browning, Martin J., 1982, "Cooperation in a fixed-membership labor-managed enterprise," *Journal of Comparative Economics*, 6: 235–47.

Bruton, Henry, 1965, *Principles of Development Economics*. Englewood Cliffs: Prentice-Hall.

Burkett, John P. and Louis Putterman, 1991, "The supply of labor by individuals to a Chinese collective farm: the case of Dahe commune," Brown University Department of Economics Working Paper No. 91-1.

Butler, Steven B., 1983, "Field research in China's communes: view of a 'guest'," in A. Thurston and B. Pasternack, ed., *The Social Sciences and Fieldwork in China*, pp. 99–121. Boulder, CO: Westview.

Butler, Steven B., 1985, "Price scissors and commune administration in Post-Mao China," in William L. Parish, ed: *Chinese Rural Development: The Great Transformation* Armonk, NY: M. E. Sharpe,. pp. 95–114.

Byrd, William A. and Alan Gelb, 1990, "Why industrialize? The incentives for rural community governments," in W. Byrd and Lin Qingsong, eds: *China's Rural Industry: Structure, Development and Reform*, New York: Oxford University Press (for the World Bank), pp. 358–87.

Byrd, William A. and Lin Qingsong, eds., 1990, *China's Rural Industry: Structure, Development and Reform*. New York: Oxford University Press (for the World Bank).

Calvo, G. A. and S. Wellisz, 1978, "Supervision, loss of control, and the optimum size of the firm," *Journal of Political Economy*, 86: 945–52.

Carolus, Carol, 1992, "Sources of Chinese agricultural growth in the 1980s," unpublished Ph.D. dissertation, Boston University.

Carter, Michael R., 1987, "Risk sharing and incentives in the decollectivization of agriculture," *Oxford Economic Papers*, 39: 577–96.

Carter, Michael R., Keith D. Wiebe and Benoit Blarel, 1989, "Tenure security for whom? An econometric analysis of the differential impacts of land policy in Kenya," Land Tenure Center, University of Wisconsin-Madison, August.

Champernowne, D. G., 1974, "A comparison of measures of inequality of income distribution," *Economic Journal*, 84: 787–816.

Chan, Anita, Richard Madson, and Jonathan Unger, 1984, *Chen Village: The Recent History of a Peasant Community in Mao's China*. Berkeley: University of California Press.

Changes and Development in China 1949–1989, 1990. Beijing: Beijing Review Press.

Chao, Kang, 1970, *Agricultural Production in Communist China, 1949–65*. Madison: University of Wisconsin Press.

Chenery, Hollis, Montek Ahluwalia, C.L.G. Bell, John Duloy, and Richard Jolly, 1974, *Redistribution with Growth*. London: Oxford University Press.

Cheng, Chu-yuan, 1982, *China's Economic Development*. Boulder, CO: Westview Press.

Chiacu, Ana, 1992, "Essays in migration and development economics," Unpublished Brown University Ph.D. Dissertation.

Chinn, Dennis L., 1978, "Income distribution in a Chinese commune," *Journal of Comparative Economics*, 2: 246–65.

Chinn, Dennis L., 1979, "Team cohesion and collective-labor supply in Chinese agriculture," *Journal of Comparative Economics*, 3: 375–394.

Christiansen, Flemming, 1987, "Private land in China? some aspects of the development of socialist land ownership in post-Mao China," *Journal of Communist Studies*, 3: 55–70.

Christiansen, Flemming, 1988, "Labor transfer and the Chinese rural development model after Mao," in J. Hinderink *et al.*, eds: *Successful Development in Third World Countries*. Amsterdam: Koninklijk Nederlands Aardrijkskundig Genootschap.

Christiansen, Flemming, 1990, "Social division and peasant mobility in mainland China: The implication of the Hukuo system," *Issues and Studies*, 26 (4): 23–42.

Christiansen, Flemming, 1992, "'Market transition' in China: The case of the Jiangsu Labor Market, 1978–1990," *Modern China*, 18: 72-93.

Coady, Dave, Gang Qiao, and Athar Hussain, 1990, "The production, marketing and pricing of vegetables in China's cities," China Programme Paper No. 6, Development Economics Research Programme, London School of Economics, May.

Collier, Paul, Samir Radwan, and Samuel Wangwe, 1986, *Labor and Poverty in Rural Tanzania*. Oxford: Clarendon Press.

Communist Party Committee of Dahe Township and Dahe Township People's Government, 1990, "Connect with Dahe's practice, explore Dahe's way," *(Lianxi Dahe Shiji, Tansuo Dahe zhi Lu)*, (July 10; no publisher; Chinese; 23 pp.)

Cremer, Jacques, 1982, "On the efficiency of a Chinese-type work-point system," *Journal of Comparative Economics*, 6: 343–52.

Croll, Elisabeth J., 1980, "The Chinese household and its economy: urban and rural survey data," Queen Elizabeth House Contemporary China Centre Resource Paper, Oxford, England.

Crook, Frederick W., 1975, "The commune system in the people's republic of China, 1963–74," in U.S. Congress Joint Economic Committee: *China: A Reassessment of the Economy* Washington: U.S. Government Printing Office,.pp. 366–410.

Crook, Frederick W., 1990, "Land tenure in the people's republic of China," CPE Agriculture Report (Centrally Planned Economies Branch, Economic Research Service, U.S. Department of Agriculture) 3 (6): 35–49 (Nov./Dec., mimeo).

Davis, Deborah, 1989, "Chinese social welfare: policies and outcomes," *China Quarterly*, 119: 577–97.

de Janvry, Alain C., 1972, "The class of generalized power production functions," *American Journal of Agricultural Economics*, 54: 234–7.

Dernberger, Robert, 1989, "The drive for economic modernization and growth: performance and trends," Paper prepared for the International Conference on a Decade of Reform under Deng Xiaoping, Brown University, November 4–7, 1987. Revised.

Derrick, Frederick W., 1984, "Interpretation of dummy variables in semilogarithmic equations: sample implications," *Southern Economic Journal*, 50: 1185–1188.

Development Institute of the State Council's Research Center for Rural Development, Comprehensive Problems Group, 1987, "Peasants, the market, and innovation in the institution—on the deep structural reform in rural areas after 8 years of fixing farm output for each household," Chinese version in *Jingji Yanjiu*, 1 (January 20, 1987), pp. 3–16; translation in Foreign Broadcast Information Service, April.

Dong, Xiaoyuan, 1991, "Production and monitoring incentives in China's collective farming: theory and evidence," Unpublished Ph.D. dissertation, Department of Economics, University of Edmonton.

Dong, Xiaoyuan and Gregory Dow, forthcoming, "Does free exit reduce shirking in production teams?" *Journal of Comparative Economics*.

Dorner, Peter, 1972, *Land Reform and Economic Development*. Harmondsworth: Penguin.

Eicher, Carl K. and Doyle C. Baker, 1982, *Research on Agricultural Development in Sub-Saharan Africa: A Critical Survey*. Department of Agricultural Economics, Michigan State University. MSU International Development Paper No. 1.

Ellis, Frank, 1988, *Peasant Economics: Farm Households and Agrarian Development*. Cambridge: Cambridge University Press.

Estrin, Saul, Derek Jones and Jan Svejnar, 1987, "The productivity effects of worker participation: producer cooperatives in western economies," *Journal of Comparative Economics*, 11: 40–61.

Feder, Gershon, Tongroj Onchan, Yongyuth Chalamwong, and Chira Hongladarom, 1988, *Land Policies and Farm Productivity in Thailand*. Baltimore: Johns Hopkins University Press (for the World Bank).

Feder, Gershon, Lawrence Lau, Justin Lin, and Luo Xiaopeng, 1989, "Agricultural credit and farm performance in China," *Journal of Comparative Economics*, 13: 508–526.

Field, Robert M., 1988, "Trends in the value of agricultural output, 1978–86," *China Quarterly*, 116: 556–91.

Fleisher, Belton and Yunhua Liu, 1992, "Economies of scale, plot size, human capital, and productivity in Chinese agriculture," *Quarterly Review of Economics and Business* (in press).

Freyhold, Michaela von, 1979, *Ujamaa Villages in Tanzania: Analysis of a Social Experiment*. New York: Monthly Review Press.

Friedman, James, 1977, *Oligopoly and the Theory of Games*. Amsterdam: North-Holland.

Friedman, Milton, 1990, "Four steps to freedom," *National Review*, 42: 33–6 (May 14).

Fuller, Wayne and George Battesse, 1984, "Estimation of linear models with crossed-error structure," *Journal of Econometrics*, 2: 67–78.

Furubotn, Eirik and Svetozar Pejovich, 1970, "Property rights and the behavior of the firm in a socialist state: the example of Yugoslavia," *Zeitschrift für Nationalökonomie*, 30: 431–54.

Gartrell, John W., 1981, "Inequality within rural communities in India," *American Sociological Review*, 46: 768–782.

Gaynor, Martin and Mark V. Pauly, 1990, "Compensation and productive efficiency in partnerships: evidence from medical group practice," *Journal of Political Economy*, 98: 544–73.

Gaynor, Martin and Louis Putterman, 1990, "Productivity consequences of alternative land division methods in China's decollectivization: an econometric analysis," Paper presented at the December 1990 meetings of the Allied Social Sciences Association, Washington, D.C.

Gaynor, Martin and Louis Putterman, 1992, "Productivity consequences of alternative land division methods in China's decollectivization: an econometric analysis," Working Paper No. 91-20, Department of Economics, Brown University, and Working Paper No. 270, Department of Economics, Johns Hopkins University; revised.

Georgescu-Roegen, Nicholas, 1960, "Economic theory and agrarian economics," *Oxford Economic Papers*, 12: 1–40.

Ginsburgh, Victor, Asher Tishley, and Israel Zang, 1980, "Alternative estimation methods for two-regime models: a mathematical programming approach," *European Economic Review*, 13: 207–288.

Goldberger, A. S., 1968, "The interpretation and estimation of Cobb-Douglas functions," *Econometrica*, 35: 464–72.

Gray, John G., 1982, "Individual collective income, the household lifecycle and the distribution of household collective income in a Chinese commune," Queen Elizabeth House, Oxford, Unpublished.

Griffin, Keith, ed., 1984, *Institutional Reform and Economic Development in the Chinese Countryside*. London: Macmillan.

Griffin, Keith and Kimberly Griffin, 1984, "Institutional change and income distribution," in K. Griffin, ed: *Institutional Reform and Economic Development in the Chinese Countryside*. London: MacMillan, pp. 20–75.

Griffin, Keith and Ashwani Saith, 1981, *Growth and Equality in Rural China*. Tokyo: Maruzen.

Griliches, Zvi and Jerry A. Hausman, 1984, "Error-in-variables in Panel data," NBER Technical Paper No. 37.

Guttman, Joel and Adi Schnytzer, 1989, "Strategic work interactions and the Kibbutz-Kolkhoz paradox," *Economic Journal*, 99: 686–99.

Hartford, Kathleen, 1985, "Socialist agriculture is dead; long live socialist agriculture! Organizational transformations in rural China," in Elizabeth Perry and Christine Wong, eds: *The Political Economy of Reform in Post-Mao China*. Cambridge: Council of East Asian Studies, Harvard University, pp. 31–61.

Hausman, Jerry A., 1978, "Specification tests in econometrics," *Econometrica*, 46: 1251–77.

Hausman, Jerry A. and William E. Taylor, 1981, "Panel data and unobservable individual effects," *Econometrica*, 49: 1377–98.

Hayami, Yujiro and Masao Kikuchi, 1981, *Asian Village Economy at the Crossroads: An Economic Approach to Institutional Change*. Baltimore: Johns Hopkins University Press.

Hebei Province Statistical Bureau and Hebei Province Academy of Social Sciences Economic Research Institute, 1986, 1987, 1988, *Hebei Economic Statistical Yearbook 1986, 1987, 1988* [Chinese]. Beijing: China Statistics Publishing Company.

Hoff, Karla, Avi Braverman, and Joseph Stiglitz, eds., forthcoming, *The Economics of Rural Organization*. New York: Oxford University Press.

Holmström, Bengt, 1982, "Moral hazard in teams," *Bell Journal of Economics*, 13: 324–40.

Hsiung, Bingyuang and Louis Putterman, 1989, "Pre- and post-reform income distribution in a Chinese commune: the case of Dahe township in Hebei province," *Journal of Comparative Economics* 13: 406–45.

Huang, Philip C. C., 1990, *The Peasant Family and Rural Development in the Yangzi Delta, 1350-1988*. Stanford: Stanford University Press.

Hussain, Athar and Nicholas Stern, 1990, "On the recent increase in death rates in China," Paper No. 8, China Programme, Development Economics Research Programme, London School of Economics.

Israelsen, L. Dwight, 1980, "Collectives, communes, and incentives," *Journal of Comparative Economics*, 4: 99–124.

Johnston, J., 1984, *Econometric Methods*. 3rd ed. New York: McGraw-Hill.

Johnston, Bruce F. and Peter Kilby, 1975, *Agriculture and Structural Transformation: Economic Strategies in Late-Developing Countries*. New York: Oxford University Press.

Joint Publication Research Service [JPRS], 1986, China Report, Agriculture, July 24 (JPRS-CAG-86-028); selected translations from the 1983 China Agricultural Yearbook. Beijing: Nongye Chubanshe.

Judge, George G., W. E. Griffiths, R. Carter Hill, Helmut Lutkepohl, and Tsoung-Chao Lee, 1985, *Theory and Practice of Econometrics*. New York: Wiley.

Khan, Azizur Rahman, Keith Griffin, Carl Riskin, and Zhao Renwei, 1991, "Household income and its distribution in China," unpublished, draft, December.

Khan, Azizur Rahman and Eddy Lee, 1983, *Agrarian Policies and Institutions in China After Mao*. Bangkok: I. L. O. Asian Employment Programme.

Kim, Si Joong, 1990, "Productivity effects of economic reforms in China's agriculture," Unpublished Brown University doctoral dissertation, May.

Kislev, Yoav, Zvi Lerman and Pinhas Zusman, forthcoming, "Cooperative credit in agriculture—The Israeli experience," in Karla Hoff, Avi Braverman, and Joseph Stiglitz, eds: *The Economics of Rural Organization*. New York: Oxford University Press.

Kojima, Reeitsu, 1988, "Agricultural organization: new forms, new contradictions," *China Quarterly*, 127: 706–735.

Kung, James Kaising, 1992, "Food and agriculture in post-reform China: the marketed surplus problem revisited," *Modern China* 18: 138–70.

Lardy, Nicholas R., 1983, *Agriculture in China's Modern Economic Development*. New York: Cambridge University Press.

Lardy, Nicholas R., 1986, "Prospects and some policy problems of agricultural development in China," *American Journal of Agricultural Economics*, 68: 451–7.

Lazear, Edward P., 1991, "Labor economics and the psychology of organizations," *Journal of Economic Perspectives*, 5 (2): 89–110.

Leibenstein, Harvey, 1966, "Allocative efficiency vs. X-efficiency," *American Economic Review*, 56: 392–415.

Leibenstein, Harvey, 1978, *General X-Efficiency Theory and Economic Development*. New York: Oxford University Press.

Lin, Justin Yifu, 1986, "The impacts of the household responsibility system on China's agricultural production," Manuscript, Department of Economics, University of Chicago, May.

Lin, Justin Yifu, 1987, "Household farm, cooperative farm, and efficiency: evidence from rural decollectivization in China," Yale University Economic Growth Center Discussion Paper No. 533, March.

Lin, Justin Yifu, 1988a, "Rural factor markets in China after the household responsibility system reform," in Bruce Reynolds, ed: *Chinese Economic Policy: Economic Reform at Midstream*. New York: Paragon House, pp. 169–203.

Lin, Justin Yifu, 1988b, "The household responsibility system in China's agricultural reform: a theoretical and empirical study," *Economic Development and Cultural Change*, 36 (Supplement): 199–234.

Lin, Justin Yifu, 1989a, "Rural reforms and agricultural productivity growth in China," UCLA Working Paper No. 576, December.

Lin, Justin Yifu, 1989b, "The household responsibility system in China's rural reform," in A. Maunder and A. Valdes, eds: *Agriculture and Governments in an Interdependent World* (Proceedings of the 12th International Conference of Agricultural Economists). Hants, England: Dartmouth Publishing Co., pp. 453–62.

Lin, Justin Yifu, 1990, "Collectivization and China's agricultural crisis in 1959–1961," *Journal of Political Economy*, 98: 1228–52.

Lin, Justin Yifu, 1991, "Supervision, peer presure, and incentives in a labor-managed firm," *China Economic Review* 2: 215–29.

Lin, Justin Yifu, 1992, "Rural reforms and agricultural growth in China," *American Economic Review*, 82: 34–51.

Lin, Zili, 1984, "More on the distinctively Chinese path of developing socialist agriculture," *Social Science in China,* Translated from *Zhongguo Shehui Kexue,* Spring, 1983, no. 4, pp. 79–123.

Liu, Minquan, 1991, "Intersectoral labor allocation on China's communes: a temporal-priority analysis," *Journal of Comparative Economics,* 15: 602–26.

Liu, Zengyu, Liang Wenshu and Wu Weihan, 1990, *Dahe Township's Transformation.* Shijiazhuang: Hebei People's Publishing Company (June; Chinese).

Ma, Rong, 1987, "Migrant and ethnic integration in rural Chifeng, Inner Mongolia, China," Unpublished Brown University Department of Sociology Ph.D. dissertation.

MacKinnon, James G., Halbert White and Ralph Davidson, 1983, "Tests for model specification in the presence of alternative hypotheses: some further results," *Journal of Econometrics,* 21: 53–70.

MacLeod, Bentley, 1988, "Equity, efficiency, and incentives in cooperative teams," in D. Jones and J. Svejnar, eds: *Advances in the Economic Analysis of Participatory and Labor Managed Firms.* Vol. 3. Greenwich, CT: JAI Press, pp. 5–23.

Maddala, G. S., and Forrest D. Nelson, 1974, "Maximum likelihood methods for models of markets in disequilibrium," *Econometrica,* 42: 1013–1030.

Marshall, Marsh, 1985, *Organizations and Growth in Rural China.* London: Macmillan.

McMillan, John, John Whalley, and Lijing Zhu, 1989, "The impact of China's economic reforms on agricultural productivity growth," *Journal of Political Economy,* 97: 781–807.

Morawetz, David, 1983, "The kibbutz as a model for developing countries or on maintaining full economic equality in practice," in Frances Stewart, ed: *Work, Income, and Inequality: Payment Systems in the Third World.* New York: St. Martin's Press.

Nakamura, Alice and Masao Nakamura, 1981, "On the relationships among several specification error tests presented by Durbin, Wu, and Hausman," *Econometrica,* 49: 1583–8.

Nalbantian, Haig R., ed., 1987, *Incentives, Cooperation and Risk Sharing: Economic and Psychological Perspectives on Employment Contracts.* Totowa, NJ: Rowman and Littlefield.

Naughton, Barry, 1992, "Implications of the state monopoly on industry," *Modern China,* 18: 14–41.

Nee, Victor, 1991, "Social inequalities in reforming state socialism: between redistribution and markets in China," *American Sociological Review,* 56: 267–82.

Nee, Victor and Su Sijin, 1990, "Institutional change and economic growth in China: the view from the villages," *Journal of Asian Studies,* 49: 3–25.

Nolan, Peter, 1976, "Collectivization in China: some comparisons with the USSR," *Journal of Peasant Studies,* 3: 192–220.

Nolan, Peter, 1983, "Decollectivization of agriculture in China, 1979-82: a long-term perspective," *Cambridge Journal of Economics,* 7: 381–403.

Nolan, Peter, 1988, *The Political Economy of Collective Farms: An Analysis of China's Post-Mao Rural Reforms.* Boulder, Colorado: Westview Press.

Nurkse, Ragnar, 1957, *Problems of Capital Formation in Underdeveloped Countries,* Oxford: Basil Blackwell.

Oi, Jean C., 1986a, "Peasant households between plan and market: cadre control over agricultural inputs," *Modern China,* 12: 230–51.

Oi, Jean C., 1986b, "Peasant grain marketing and state procurement: China's grain contracting system," *China Quarterly,* 106: 272–90.

Oi, Jean C., 1989, *State and Peasant in Contemporary China: The Political Economy of Village Government.* Berkeley: University of California Press.

Oi, Jean C., 1990, "Economic management and rural government: bureaucratic entrepreneurship in local economies," Paper presented at the Association for Asian Studies Meetings, Chicago, April.

Paglin, Morton, 1975, "The measurement and trend of inequality: a basic revision," *American Economic Review*, 65: 598–609.

Parish, William L. and Martin K. Whyte, 1978, *Village and Family in Contemporary China*. Chicago: University of Chicago Press.

Park, Woosung, 1987, "The effects of the change of economic system on income distribution and application to China," Mimeo., Brown University, August; also revised as Part III of Park, 1989.

Park, Woosung, 1989, "Household production behavior and income distribution in a 1980s Chinese township: a simulation analysis," Unpublished Brown University Ph.D. dissertation, May.

Perkins, Dwight, 1988, "Reforming China's economic system," *Journal of Economic Literature*, June, 26: 601–45.

Perkins, Dwight, and Shahid Yusuf, 1984, *Rural Development in China*. Baltimore: Johns Hopkins University Press.

Piazza, Alan, 1983, "Trends in food and nutrition availability in China, 1950–81," World Bank Staff Working Papers No. 607. Washington, D.C.: World Bank.

Putterman, Louis, 1980, "Voluntary collectivization: a model of producers' institutional choice," *Journal of Comparative Economics*, 4: 125–157.

Putterman, Louis, 1983a, "Incentives and the kibbutz: toward an economics of communal work motivation," *Zeitschrift für Nationalökonomie*, 43: 157–188.

Putterman, Louis, 1983b, "A modified collective agriculture in rural growth-with-equity: reconsidering the private unimodal solution," *World Development*, 11: 77–100.

Putterman, Louis, 1985a, "The restoration of the peasant household as farm production unit in China: some incentive theoretic analysis," *The Political Economy of Reform in Post-Mao China*, in Elizabeth Perry and Christine Wong, eds: Cambridge, MA: Council on East Asian Studies, Harvard University Press, pp. 63–82.

Putterman, Louis, 1985b, "On the interdependence of labor supplies in producers' cooperatives of given membership," In Derek C. Jones and J. Svejnar, eds: *Advances in the Economic Analysis of Participatory and Labor-Managed Firms, Vol. I*, Greenwich, CT: JAI Press, pp. 87–105.

Putterman, Louis, 1985c, "Extrinsic versus intrinsic problems of agricultural cooperation: anti-incentivism in Tanzania and China," *Journal of Development Studies*, 21: 175–204.

Putterman, Louis, 1986a, "Work motivation and monitoring in a collective farm," Brown University Department of Economics Working Paper No. 84-28, October 1984. Revised, December 1986.

Putterman, Louis, 1986b, *Peasants, Collectives and Choice: Economic Theory and Tanzanian Villages*. Greenwich, CT: JAI Press.

Putterman, Louis, 1987a, "The incentive problem and the demise of team farming in China," *Journal of Development Economics*, 26: 103–127.

Putterman, Louis, 1987b, "Effort, productivity and incentives in a 1970s Chinese people's commune," Working Paper No. 87-13, Department of Economics, Brown University, Revised December.

Putterman, Louis, 1988a, "People's Republic of China: systemic and structural change in a North China township," *American Journal of Agricultural Economics*, 70: 423–430.

Putterman, Louis, 1988b, "Ration subsidies and incentives in the pre-reform Chinese production team," *Economica,* 218: 235–247.

Putterman, Louis, 1988c, "Group farming and work incentives in collective-era China," *Modern China,* 14: 419–50.

Putterman, Louis, 1989a, "Entering the post-collective era in North China: Dahe township," *Modern China,* 15: 275–320.

Putterman, Louis, 1989b, "Agricultural producers' cooperatives," in Pranab Bardhan, ed: *The Economic Theory of Agrarian Institutions* New York: Oxford University Press, Chapter 16, pp. 319–39.

Putterman, Louis, ed., 1989c, *Hebei Province, Dahe Commune/Township Data Sets and Codebook.* Ann Arbor: Center for Chinese Studies, University of Michigan.

Putterman, Louis, 1990a, *Division of Labor and Welfare: An Introduction to Economic Systems.* New York: Oxford University Press.

Putterman, Louis, 1990b, "Effort, productivity and incentives in a 1970s Chinese people's commune," *Journal of Comparative Economics,* 14: 88–104.

Putterman, Louis, 1991, "Does poor supervisability undermine teamwork? Evidence from an unexpected source," *American Economic Review,* 81: 996–1001.

Putterman, Louis, 1992a, "Industrial and agricultural investment coordination under 'plan' and 'market' in China," in Susan Barr and James Roumasset, eds: *The Economics of Cooperation: East Asian Development and the Case for Pro-Market Intervention.* Boulder, CO: Westview Press, pp. 121–43.

Putterman, Louis, 1992b, "Dualism and reform in China," *Economic Development and Cultural Change,* 40: 467–93.

Putterman, Louis and Marie DiGiorgio, 1985, "Choice and efficiency in a model of democratic semi-collective agriculture," *Oxford Economic Papers,* 37: 33–53.

Putterman, Louis and Gil Skillman, Jr., 1988, "The incentive effects of monitoring under alternative compensation schemes," *International Journal of Industrial Organization,* 6: 109–119.

Putterman, Louis and Gilbert L. Skillman, forthcoming, "The role of exit costs in the theory of cooperative teams," *Journal of Comparative Economics.*

Rao, C., 1964, "The use and interpretation of principal component analysis in applied research," *Sankya A,* 26: 329–58.

Rawski, Thomas G., 1982, "The simple arithmetic of Chinese income distribution," *Keizai Kenkyu,* 22: 12–33.

Riskin, Carl, 1987, *China's Political Economy: The Quest for Development Since 1949.* Oxford: Oxford University Press.

Riskin, Carl, 1990, "Food, poverty, and development strategy in the People's Republic of China," In Lucile F. Newman et al., eds: *Hunger in History: Food Shortage, Poverty, and Deprivation.* Cambridge, MA: Basil Blackwell, pp. 333–52.

Rosenzweig, Mark, 1988, "Labor markets in low-income countries," in H. Chenery and T. N. Srinivasan, eds: *Handbook of Development Economics, Vol. I.* Amsterdam: North-Holland, pp. 713–62.

Rozelle, Scott, 1991, "The economic behavior of village leaders in China's reform economy," Unpublished Ph.D. Dissertation, Cornell University.

Schumpeter, Joseph A., 1954, *History of Economic Analysis.* New York: Oxford University Press.

Selden, Mark, 1982, "Cooperation and conflict: cooperatives and collective formation in China's countryside," in Mark Selden and Victor Lippit, eds: *The Transition to Socialism in China.* Armonk, NY: M. E. Sharpe, pp. 32–97.

Selden, Mark, 1985, "Income Inequality and the State," in William L. Parish, ed: *Chinese Rural Development: The Great Transformation*, Armonk: NY: M. E. Sharpe, pp. 193–218.

Selden, Mark, 1992, "State, cooperative and market: reflections on Chinese developmental trajectories," in Louis Putterman and Dietrich Rueschemeyer, eds: *Markets and States in Development: Synergy or Rivalry?* Boulder, CO: Lynne Rienner.

Sen, Amartya K., 1966a, "Labor allocation in a cooperative enterprise," *Review of Economic Studies*, 33: 361–371.

Sen, Amartya K., 1966b, "Peasants and dualism with or without surplus labor," *Journal of Political Economy*, 74: 424–450.

Sen, Amartya, K., 1988, "The concept of development," in H. Chenery and T. N. Srinivasan, eds: *Handbook of Development Economics, Vol. I*. Amsterdam: North-Holland, pp. 9–26.

Sertel, Murat R., 1982, *Workers and Incentives*. Amsterdam: North-Holland.

Shapiro, Carl and Joseph Stiglitz, 1984, "Equilibrium unemployment as a worker discipline device," *American Economic Review*, 74: 433–44.

Shue, Vivienne, 1980, *Peasant China in Transition: The Dynamics of Development Toward Socialism, 1949-56*. Berkeley: University of California Press.

Sicular, Terry, 1986, "Using a farm-household model to analyze labor allocation on a Chinese collective farm," in Inderjit J. Singh, Lyn Squire, and John Strauss, eds: *Agricultural Household Models: Extensions, Applications, and Policy*. Baltimore: Johns Hopkins University, pp. 277–305.

Sicular, Terry, 1988a, "Grain pricing: a key link in Chinese economic policy," *Modern China*, 14: 451–86.

Sicular, Terry, 1988b, "Agricultural planning and pricing in the post-Mao period," *China Quarterly*, 116: 671–705.

Sicular, Terry, 1991, "China's agricultural policy during the reform period," in Joint Economic Committee, Congress of the United States, *China's Economic Dilemmas in the 1990s: The Problems of Reforms, Modernization, and Interdependence, Vol. I*. Washington: U. S. Government Printing Office, pp. 340–64.

Singh, Inderjit, Lyn Squire, and John Strauss, eds., 1986, *Agricultural Household Models: Extensions, Applications, and Policy*. Baltimore: Johns Hopkins University Press.

Sneessens, Henri R., 1985, "Two alternative stochastic specifications and estimation methods for quality rationing models," *European Economic Review*, 29: 111–136.

Song, Guoqing, 1987, *"Cong Tongguo Tongxiao dao Tudishui,"* (From the Compulsory Purchasing System to Land Tax) in Gao Xiaomeng and Song Guoqing, eds: *Zhongguo Liangshi Wenti Yanjiu* (Research on China's Grain Problem). Beijing: Zhongguo Guanli Chubanshe.

State Statistical Bureau, 1986, *Statistical Yearbook of China 1986*. Hongkong: Economic Information and Agency.

State Statistical Bureau, 1988, *China Statistical Yearbook 1988*. Beijing: China Statistical Information and Consultancy Service Center.

State Statistical Bureau, 1990a, *China Statistical Yearbook 1990*. Beijing: China Statistical Information and Consultancy Service Center.

State Statistical Bureau, 1990b, *China Urban Statistics 1988*. New York: Praeger.

State Statistical Bureau, 1990c, *China Statistical Yearbook 1989*. Beijing: China Statistical Information and Consultancy Service Center.

State Statistical Bureau Rural Social and Economic Statistics Department, 1989, *China County-Level Rural Economic Statistical Abstract (1980–1987) (Zhongguo Fenxian Nongcun Jingji Tongji Gaiyao)*. Beijing: China Statistics Publishing Company.

Stiglitz, Joseph, 1974, "Incentives and risk sharing in share-cropping," *Review of Economic Studies*, 41: 219–55.

Stone, Bruce, 1988, "Developments in agricultural technology," *China Quarterly*, 116: 767–822.

Stone, Bruce, 1990, "The next stage of agricultural development: implications for infrastructure, technology and institutional priorities," in T. C. Tso, ed., *Agricultural Reform and Development in China*. Beltsville, MD: IDEALS, Inc., pp. 47–93.

Strauss, John, 1986, "Does better nutrition raise farm productivity?" *Journal of Political Economy*, 94: 297–320.

Tang, Anthony, 1984, *An Analytical and Empirical Investigation of Agriculture in Mainland China, 1952–1980*. Taipei, Republic of China: Chung-Hua Institution for Economic Research.

Tang, Anthony, 1986, *A Theoretical and Empirical Analysis of Agriculture in China, 1952–1979*. Taipei: Chung-Hua Institute of Economic Research.

Taylor, Jeffrey R., 1988, "Rural employment trends and the legacy of surplus labor, 1978–86," *China Quarterly*, 116: 736–66.

Travers, Lee, 1984, "Post-1978 rural economic policy and peasant income in China," *China Quarterly*, 98: 251–259.

Tsou, Tang, Marc Blecher, and Mitch Meisner, 1982, "The responsibility system in agriculture; its implementation in Qiyang and Dazhai," *Modern China*, 8: 41–103.

Unger, Jonathan, 1985, "The decollectivization of the Chinese countryside: a survey of twenty-eight villages," *Pacific Affairs*, 58: 585–606.

United States Department of Agriculture, Economic Research Service, 1991, *China Agriculture and Trade Report* (RS-91-3), July.

Vermeer, E. B., 1982, "Income differentials in rural China," *China Quarterly*, 89: 1–33, March.

Vogel, Ezra F., 1989, *One Step Ahead in China: Guangdong under Reform*. Cambridge: Harvard University Press.

Walker, Kenneth R., 1966, "Collectivization in retrospect: the 'socialist high tide' of autumn 1955–Spring 1956," *China Quarterly*, 26: 1–43.

Walker, Kenneth R., 1984, *Food Grain Procurement and Consumption in China*. Cambridge: Cambridge University Press.

Walker, Kenneth R., 1988, "Trends in crop production, 1978–86," *China Quarterly*, 116: 592–63.

Walker, Kenneth R.. 1989, "40 years on: provincial contrasts in China's rural economic development," *China Quarterly*, 119: 448–80.

Ward, Benjamin, 1958, "The firm in Illyria: market syndicalism," *American Economic Review*, 68: 566–89.

Waterston, Albert, 1974, "A viable model for rural development," *Finance and Development*, 11 (4): 22–5.

Watson, Andrew, 1983, "Agriculture looks for 'shoes that fit': the production responsibility system and its implications," *World Development*, 11: 705–30.

Webb, Shwu-Eng, 1991, "China's agricultural commodity policies in the 1980s," pp. 38–45 in United States Department of Agriculture, Economic Research Service: *China Agriculture and Trade Report* (RS–91-3), July.

Wen, Guanzhong James, 1989, "The current land tenure system and its impact on long-term performance of farming sector: the case of modern China," Unpublished Ph.D. Dissertation, University of Chicago.

Wen, Guanzhong James, 1991, "Land tenure system, uncertainty in property rights and distortions in farmers' investment—the case of modern China," Unpublished manuscript.

Wiemer, Calla, 1990a, "Reform and the constraints on rural industrialization in China," University of Hawaii Working Paper No. 89-1, revised 6/4/90.

Wiemer, Calla, 1990b, "Grain prices, land rent, and food self-sufficiency in China," University of Hawaii Working Paper No. 90-28.

Wiemer, Calla and Liu Xiaoxuan, "Price reform in China: the transition to rationality," in M. Jan Dutta and Zhang Zhongli, eds: *China's Economic Reform, 1978–1988*. Greenwich, CT: JAI Press.

Wiens, Thomas B., 1985, "Poverty and progress in the Huang and Huai River Basins," in William L. Parish, ed: *Chinese Rural Development: The Great Transformation*. Armonk, NY: M. E. Sharpe, pp. 57–94.

Wiens, Thomas B., 1987, "Issues in the structural reform of Chinese agriculture," *Journal of Comparative Economics,* 11: 372–84.

Williamson, Oliver, Michael Wachter, and Jeffrey Harris, 1975, "Understanding the employment relation: the analysis of idiosyncratic exchange," *Bell Journal of Economics,* 6: 250–78.

World Bank, 1983a, *China: Socialist Economic Development. Volume II: The Economic Sectors*. Washington: The World Bank.

World Bank, 1983b, *China: Socialist Economic Development. Volume III: The Social Sectors*. Washington: The World Bank.

World Bank, 1983c, *World Tables, Third Edition*. Baltimore: Johns Hopkins University Press.

World Bank, 1990a, *China: Between Plan and Market. A World Bank Country Study*. Washington, DC: The World Bank.

World Bank, 1990b, "Consumer food subsidies," MAT-1 Working Paper No. 2.

World Bank, 1991, *China: Options for Reform in the Grain Sector. A World Bank Country Study*. Washington, July.

Zhu, Ling, 1991, *Rural Reform and Peasant Income in China*. New York: St. Martin's Press.

Zweig, David, 1985, "Strategies of policy implementation: policy 'winds' and brigade accounting in rural China, 1968–78," *World Politics,* 37: 267–93.

Zweig, David, 1989, *Agrarian Radicalism in China, 1968-81*. Cambridge: Harvard University Press.

Zweig, David, 1990, "Evaluating China's rural policies: 1949–1989," *The Fletcher Forum of World Affairs,* 14: 18–29.

Index

Aggregation problem, 37–38, 125–27, 137n, 208, 240, 278n, 282n, 284, 345

Allocative efficiency, 46–47, 122–25, 134–37, 142–43, 238, 245, 259–60, 264–65, 271, 346, 355, 357

Baogan daohu, 34, 97, 108–10, 120–21, 206–7, 216–24, 272, 344. *See also* Household responsibility system

Capital
  allocation among sectors, 128–31, 134–37, 143, 208, 247–48, 251–52
  elasticity of output with respect to, 129, 131, 140–42, 171–73, 209–12, 219, 250
  marginal product of, 135–36, 142–43, 171–72, 210–11, 219, 250, 251–52, 281, 293–94
  rural capital construction, 38, 351–52

Class, 9–10, 184, 267, 298, 328–30. *See also* Stratification, social

Coercion, 26, 349, 352
  in collectivization, 348
  in labor supply, 156n, 175, 190
  in output deliveries, 26, 43. *See also* Crop choice, administrative interventions in; minimum production constraint

Cohesion. *See* Labor, interdependence

Collectivization, 26
  end of, 47
  rationale for, 25–31

Credit
  cost of, 240, 249, 253, 254–55, 264
  rationing of, 345

Crop choice
  administrative interventions in, 4, 33, 44, 96–97, 101, 109, 115–16, 135–36, 197, 279, 292, 352–53
  effect of on agricultural productivity, 197, 200, 202, 203n, 204, 211, 219–21, 223, 293n, 344
  minimum production constraint, 239, 243, 253

Current inputs
  elasticity of output with respect to, 131, 141–42, 172–73, 210, 219, 249n

marginal product of, 135–36, 143, 171–72, 210–11, 219, 249, 254–55, 293–94
rationing of, 136, 239–40, 254–55, 345

Dahe Township
  collective period, 85–92
  compared to others in China, 95–96, 119–20, 341–42
  distribution systems, 161–64
  early history, 84
  growth accounting, 131–34, 143–46, 220–24
  late 1980s in, 114–19
  reform period, 92–114
  representativeness, 7, 52–53, 75, 83, 119, 341–42

Decision-making, democracy in, 164, 176, 349

Decollectivization. *See* Household responsibility system

Deng Xiaoping, 5, 29n, 31–32, 107

Dependency ratio, 179–80, 182, 187, 189, 243, 274, 281, 285, 331

Distribution. *See also* Income; Land; Payment systems
  according to needs, 150, 152, 153–55, 161–64, 165, 171–76, 231, 235–36, 342–43
  according to work, 150–51, 153–54, 161–64, 165, 171–76, 231, 235–36, 231, 342–43
  income, 255, 259–60, 263, 297–339
  by rations, 155–57, 235, 342–43
  versus retention of collective earnings, 164–65, 171–74

Economies of scale. *See* Returns to scale

Effort, observability of, 21, 23, 157–61, 228–37

Egalitarianism, 22–23, 42, 148, 156, 162–63, 267, 343, 347, 349

Errors in variables (measurement or data errors), 127, 136, 138, 170, 206–7

Extraction of farm output, 18–19, 26, 28–31, 49, 348–49

Fertilizer, 29, 36–37, 44–45, 95–96, 351. *See also* Current inputs